FOURTH EDITION

Introduction to
Business Law

Jeffrey F. Beatty
Boston University

Susan S. Samuelson
Boston University

Dean A. Bredeson
University of Texas

SOUTH-WESTERN
CENGAGE Learning·

Australia • Brazil • Japan • Korea • Mexico • Singapore • Spain • United Kingdom • United States

**Introduction to Business Law,
Fourth Edition**

Jeffrey F. Beatty, Susan S. Samuelson, and Dean
A. Bredeson

Vice President of Editorial, Business: Jack
  W. Calhoun

Editor-in-Chief: Rob Dewey

Senior Acquisitions Editor: Vicky True-Baker

Developmental Editor: Jennifer King

Editorial Assistant: Benjamin Genise

Marketing Director: Lisa Lyne

Marketing Manager: Laura-Aurora Stopa

Senior Marketing Communications Manager:
  Sarah Greber

Senior Content Project Manager: Holly Henjum

Senior Media Editor: Kristen Meere

Manufacturing Planner: Kevin Kluck

Production Service/Compositor: Integra Software
  Services Pvt. Ltd.

Senior Art Director: Michelle Kunkler

Cover and Internal Design: Lou Ann Thesing

Cover Image: © Glowimages/Getty Images, Inc.

Rights Acquisitions Specialist: Amber Hosea

For product information and technology assistance, contact us at
Cengage Learning Customer & Sales Support, 1-800-354-9706

For permission to use material from this text or product,
submit all requests online at **www.cengage.com/permissions**
Further permissions questions can be emailed to
permissionrequest@cengage.com

Exam*View*® is a registered trademark of eInstruction Corp.
Windows is a registered trademark of the Microsoft Corporation
used herein under license. Macintosh and Power Macintosh are
registered trademarks of Apple Computer, Inc. used herein
under license.

© 2008 Cengage Learning. All Rights Reserved.

Library of Congress Control Number: 2011940423

ISBN-13: 978-1-133-18815-5

ISBN-10: 1-133-18815-X

South-Western
5191 Natorp Boulevard
Mason, OH 45040
USA

Cengage Learning products are represented in Canada by
Nelson Education, Ltd.

For your course and learning solutions, visit **www.cengage.com**
Purchase any of our products at your local college store or at our
preferred online store **www.cengagebrain.com**

Printed in the United States of America
1 2 3 4 5 6 7 15 14 13 12 11

CONTENTS: OVERVIEW

CONTENTS

Looking for more examples for class? Find all the latest developments on our blog at **bizlawupdate.com**. To be notified when we post updates, just "like" our Facebook page at Beatty Business Law or follow us on Twitter @bizlawupdate.

NOTE FROM THE AUTHORS

New to This Edition

A NEW CHAPTER: PRACTICAL CONTRACTS

The contracts chapters in this and other business law texts focus on the *theory* of contract law. And that theory is important. But our students tell us that theory, by itself, is not enough. They need to know how these abstract rules operate in *practice*. They want to understand the structure and content of a standard agreement. Our students ask questions such as: Do I need a written agreement? What do these legal terms *really* mean? Are any important provisions missing? What happens if a provision is unclear? Do I need to hire a lawyer? How can I use a lawyer most effectively? These are the questions that we answer in this new chapter. As an illustration throughout the chapter, we use a real contract between a movie studio and an actor.

LANDMARK CASES

As a general rule, we want our cases to be as current as possible — reporting on the world as it is now. However, sometimes students can benefit from reading vintage cases that are still good law and also provide a deep understanding of how and why the law has developed as it has. Thus, for example, we have added *Miranda v. Arizona*. Reading this case provides students with a much better understanding of why the Supreme Court created Miranda rights. And this context helps students follow the recent Supreme Court rulings on *Miranda*. Other landmark cases include: *Palsgraf v. Long Island Railroad*, *Griggs v. Duke Power Co.* and *Chiarella v. United States*.

THE NEW PATENT LAW

This statute represents the most major change in patent law in our lifetime.

END OF CHAPTER MATERIAL

To facilitate student learning and class discussion, we have overhauled the study questions at the end of the chapters. They are now divided into five parts:

1. Matching Questions. These are designed to refresh the students' recollection of basic principles and terminology. Answers are available online.

2. True False Questions. Also a basic overview of important concepts, with answers available online.

3. Multiple Choice Questions. Many instructors use this format in their tests so it seemed appropriate to provide practice questions. Students find online answers helpful.

4. Essay Questions. Students can use these as study questions and professors can also assign them as written homework problems.

5. Discussion Questions. Instructors can use these questions to enhance class discussion. If assigned in advance, students will have a chance to think about the answers before class. This format is familiar to students because business cases often pose discussion questions in advance.

STAYING CURRENT: OUR BLOG, FACEBOOK AND TWITTER

Business law changes rapidly. To find out about new developments, visit our blog at bizlawupdate. com. If you "like" our Facebook page at Beatty Business Law or follow us on Twitter @bizlawupdate, you will automatically receive a notification whenever we post to the blog.

The Beatty/Samuelson Difference

Our goal in writing this book was to capture the passion and excitement, the sheer enjoyment, of the law. Business law is notoriously complex, and as authors, we are obsessed with accuracy. Yet this intriguing subject also abounds with human conflict and hard-earned wisdom, forces that can make a law book sparkle. We are grateful to the faculty who tell us that this introductory business law text is like no other—a book that is precise and authoritative *yet a pleasure to read*.

A BOOK FOR STUDENTS

We have written this book as if we were speaking directly to our students. We provide black letter law, but we also explain concepts in terms that hook students. Over the years, we have learned how much more successfully we can teach when our students are intrigued. No matter what kind of a show we put on in class, they are only learning when they want to learn.

Every chapter begins with a story, either fictional or real, to illustrate the issues in the chapter and provide context. Chapter 27, on cyberlaw, begins with the true story of a college student who discovers nude pictures of himself online. These photos had been taken in the locker room without his knowledge. What privacy rights do any of us have? Does the Internet jeopardize them? Students want to know—right away.

Most of today's undergraduates were not yet born when George H. W. Bush was elected president. They come to college with varying levels of preparation; many now arrive from other countries. We have found that to teach business law most effectively we must provide its context. Chapter 24, on accountants, explains how a changing culture within Arthur Andersen led to the firm's downfall during the Enron scandal.

At the same time, we enjoy offering "nuts and bolts" information that grabs students. In Chapter 25, on consumer law, we bring home the issue of credit history by providing phone numbers and websites that students can use to check their own credit reports.

Students respond enthusiastically to this approach. One professor asked a student to compare our book with the one that the class was then using. This was the student's reaction: "I really enjoy reading the [Beatty & Samuelson] textbook and I have decided that I will give you this memo ASAP, but I am keeping the book until Wednesday so that I may continue reading. Thanks! :-)"

We are touched by unsolicited comments from students, such as this one posted on Amazon:

> This text is well written and easy to understand. The interactive case examples given in the text were very helpful for me to understand and put into immediate practice critical reasoning skills of the terms as well as the various [sic] processes. Because of my very busy schedule, I found the way the text is laid out to be user friendly…. The interactive student website for the text is helpful and user friendly for testing your understanding and retention.

Strong Narrative

The law is full of great stories, and we use them. Your students and ours should come to class excited. In Chapter 3, on dispute resolution, we explain litigation by tracking a double indemnity lawsuit. An executive is dead. Did he drown accidentally, obligating the insurance company to pay? Or did the businessman commit suicide, voiding the policy? The student follows the action from the discovery of the body, through each step of the lawsuit, to the final appeal. The chapter offers a detailed discussion of dispute resolution, but it does so by exploiting the human drama that underlies litigation.

Students read stories and remember them. Strong narratives provide a rich context for the remarkable quantity of legal material presented. When students care about the material they are reading, they persevere. We have been delighted to find that they also arrive in class eager to question, discuss, and learn.

Authoritative

We insist, as you do, on a law book that is indisputably accurate. A professor must teach with assurance, confident that every paragraph is the result of exhaustive research and meticulous presentation. Dozens of tough-minded people spent thousands of hours reviewing this book, and we are delighted with the stamp of approval we have received from trial and appellate judges, working attorneys, scholars, and teachers.

We reject the cloudy definitions and fuzzy explanations that can invade judicial opinions and legal scholarship. To highlight the most important rules, we use bold print, and then follow with vivacious examples written in clear, forceful English. (See, for example, the description of an automatic stay in Chapter 16, on bankruptcy, p. 284.)

Comprehensive

Staying comprehensive means staying current. Look, for example, at the important field of corporate governance. We present a clear path through the thicket of new issues, such as proxy access and executive compensation. We want tomorrow's business leaders to anticipate the challenges that await them and then use their knowledge to avert problems.

Humor

Throughout the text, we use humor—judiciously—to lighten and enlighten. Not surprisingly, students have applauded this—but is wit appropriate? How dare we employ levity in this venerable discipline! We offer humor because we take law seriously. We revere the law for its ancient traditions, its dazzling intricacy, its relentless though imperfect attempt to give order and decency to our world. Because we are confident of our respect for the law, we are not afraid to employ some levity. Leaden prose masquerading as legal scholarship does no honor to the field.

Humor also helps retention. Research shows that the funnier or more bizarre the example is, the longer students will remember it. Students are more likely to remember a contract problem described in a fanciful setting, and from that setting recall the underlying principle. By contrast, one widget is hard to distinguish from another.

Features

We chose the features for our book with great care. Each feature responds to an essential pedagogical goal. Here are some of those goals and the matching feature.

Exam Strategy

GOAL: To help students learn more effectively and to prepare for exams. In preparing this feature, we asked ourselves: What do students want? The short answer is—a good grade in the course. How many times a semester does a student ask you, "What can I do to study for the exam?" We are happy to help them study and earn a good grade because that means that they will also be learning. Several times per chapter, we stop the action and give students a two-minute quiz. In the body of the text, again in the end-of-chapter review, and also in the Instructor's Manual, we present a typical exam question.

Here lies the innovation: We guide the student in analyzing the issue. We teach the reader—over and over—how to approach a question: to start with the overarching principle, examine the fine point raised in the question, apply the analysis that courts use, and deduce the right answer. This skill is second nature to lawyers but not to students. Without practice, too many students panic, jumping at a convenient answer and leaving aside the tools they have spent the course acquiring. Let's change that. Students love the Exam Strategy feature.

Here is an example of Exam Strategy, from Chapter 6, on negligence:

EXAM Strategy

Question: Jenny asked a neighbor, Tom, to water her flowers while she was on vacation. For three days, Tom did this without incident, but on the fourth day, when he touched the outside faucet, he received a violent electric shock that shot him through the air, melted his sneakers and glasses, set his clothes on fire, and seriously scalded him. Tom sued, claiming that Jenny had caused the damage when she negligently repaired a second-floor toilet. Water from the steady leak had flooded through the walls, soaking wires and eventually causing the faucet to become electrified. You are Jenny's lawyer. Use one (and only one) element of negligence law to move for summary judgment.

Strategy: The four elements of negligence we have examined thus far are duty to this plaintiff, breach, factual cause, and foreseeable type of injury. Which element seems to be most helpful to Jenny's defense? Why?

Result: Jenny is entitled to summary judgment because this was not a foreseeable type of injury. Even if she did a bad job of fixing the toilet, she could not possibly have anticipated that her poor workmanship could cause *electrical* injuries—and violent ones—to anybody.[1]

YOU BE THE JUDGE

GOAL: Get them thinking independently. When reading case opinions, students tend to accept the court's "answer." Judges, of course, try to reach decisions that appear indisputable, when in reality they may be controversial—or wrong. From time to time, we want students to think through the problem and reach their own answer. Most chapters contain a "You Be the Judge" feature, providing the facts of the case and conflicting appellate arguments. The court's decision, however, appears only in the Instructor's Manual. Since students do not know the result, discussions are more complex and lively. Students disagree with the court at least half the time. They are thinking.

ETHICS

GOAL: Make ethics real. We ask ethical questions about cases, legal issues, and commercial practices. Is it fair for one party to void a contract by arguing, months after the fact, that there was no consideration? What is wrong with bribery? We believe that asking the questions and encouraging discussion reminds students that ethics is an essential element of justice and of a satisfying life.

---

[1]Based on *Hebert v. Enos*, 60 Mass. App. Ct. 817, 806 N.E.2d 452 (Massachusetts Court of Appeals, 2004).

CASES

GOAL: Bring case law alive. Each case begins with a summary of the facts followed by a statement of both the issue and the decision. Next comes a summary of the court's opinion. We have written this ourselves, to make the judges' reasoning accessible to all readers, while retaining the court's focus and the decision's impact. We cite cases using a modified blue-book form. In the principal cases in each chapter, we provide the state or federal citation, the regional citation, and an appropriate electronic citation. We also give students a brief description of the court.

EXAM REVIEW AND QUESTIONS

GOAL: Encourage students to practice! At the end of the chapters, we provide a list of review points and several additional "Exam Strategy" exercises. To support students' different learning styles, we provide five types of questions in the Practice Exam: Matching, True/False, Multiple Choice, Essay Questions and Discussion Questions. We also include these types of questions:

- Ethics. This question highlights the ethical issues of a dispute and calls upon the student to formulate a specific, reasoned response.

- CPA Questions. For topics covered by the CPA exam, administered by the American Institute of Certified Public Accountants, the practice tests include questions from previous CPA exams.

Answers to all the Matching, True/False, and Multiple Choice questions are available to the students online. on the Beatty *Introduction to Business Law* Web site at **www.cengagebrain.com**.

Author Transition

Jeffrey Beatty fought an unremitting ten-year battle against a particularly aggressive form of leukemia which, despite his great courage and determination, he ultimately lost. Jeffrey, a gentleman to the core, was an immensely kind, funny and thoughtful human being, someone who sang and danced, and who earned the respect and affection of colleagues and students alike. In writing these books he wanted students to see and understand the impact of law in their everyday lives as well as its role in supporting human dignity, and what's more, he wanted students to laugh.

Because of the length of Jeffrey's illness, we had ample time to develop a transition plan. Through a combination of new and old methods (social media and personal connections), we were able to identify a wonderfully talented group of applicants – graduates of top law schools who had earned myriad teaching and writing prizes. We read two rounds of blind submissions and met with finalists. In the end, we are thrilled to report that Dean Bredeson has joined the Beatty/Samuelson author team. A member of the faculty at the University of Texas McCombs School of Business, Dean is a devoted teacher who has received the School's highest teaching award for the last four years. He is also the author of the text, *Applied Business Ethics*. Dean has a number of qualities that are essential to a textbook writer—a keen insight into explaining complex material in an engaging manner, meticulous attention to detail, an ability to meet deadlines, and a wry sense of humor.

Teaching Materials

For more information about any of these ancillaries, contact your Cengage/South-Western Legal Studies in Business Sales Representative for more details, or visit the Beatty *Introduction to Business Law* Web site at **www.cengagebrain.com**.

INSTRUCTOR'S MANUAL

The Instructor's Manual, available on both the IRCD and the Instructor's Support Site at www.cengagebrain.com, includes special features to enhance class discussion and student progress:

- Dialogues. These are a series of questions and answers on pivotal cases and topics. The questions provide enough material to teach a full session. In a pinch, you could walk into class with nothing but the manual and use the Dialogues to conduct an exciting class.

- Action learning ideas. These are interviews, quick research projects, drafting exercises, classroom activities, commercial analyses, and other suggested assignments that get students out of their chairs and into the diverse settings of business law.

- A chapter theme and a quote of the day.

- Updates of text material.

- Additional cases and examples.

- Answers to You Be the Judge cases from the text and to the Exam Review questions found at the end of each chapter.

Test Bank

The test bank offers hundreds of essay, short answer and multiple choice problems, and may be obtained online at **www.cengagebrain.com**, or on the Instructor's Resource CD.

ExamView Testing Software—Computerized Testing Software

This testing software contains all of the questions in the printed test bank. This easy-to-use test creation software program is compatible with Microsoft Windows. Instructors can add or edit questions, instructions, and answers; they can also select questions by previewing them on the screen, selecting them randomly, or selecting them by number. ExamView gives instructors the ability to create and administer quizzes online, whether over the Internet, a local area network (LAN), or a wide area network (WAN). The ExamView testing software is available on the Instructor's Resource CD.

Instructor's Resource CD (IRCD)

The IRCD contains the ExamView testing software files, the test bank in Microsoft Word files, the Instructor's Manual in Microsoft Word files, and the Microsoft PowerPoint Lecture Review Slides.

Microsoft PowerPoint Lecture Review Slides

PowerPoint slides are available for use by instructors for enhancing their lectures. Download these slides at **www.cengagebrain.com**. The PowerPoint slides are also available on the IRCD.

Business Law CourseMate

Cengage Learning's Business Law CourseMate brings course concepts to life with interactive learning, study, and exam preparation tools—including an e-book—that supports the printed textbook. Designed to address a variety of learning styles, students will have access to flashcards, Learning Objectives, and the Key Terms for quick reviews. A set of autogradable, interactive quizzes will allow students to instantly gauge their comprehension of the material. On the instructor's side, all quiz scores and student activity are mapped within a set of intuitive student performance analytical tools called Engagement Tracker, which helps the instructor identify at-risk students. An interactive blog helps connect book concepts to real-world situations happening now.

BUSINESS LAW DIGITAL VIDEO LIBRARY

This dynamic online video library features over 60 video clips that spark class discussion and clarify core legal principles. The library is organized into four series:

- *Legal Conflicts in Business* includes specific modern business and e-commerce scenarios.

- *Ask the Instructor* contains straightforward explanations of concepts for student review.

- *Drama of the Law* features classic business scenarios that spark classroom participation.

- *LawFlix* contains clips from many popular films and television shows, including *Mary Tyler Moore*, *Midnight Run*, and *Notting Hill*.

- *Real World Legal* takes students out of the classroom and into real life situations, encouraging them to consider the legal aspects of decision-making in the business world.

- *Business Ethics in Action* challenges students to examine ethical dilemmas.

Access to the Business Law Digital Video Library is available as an optional package with each new student text at no additional charge. Students with used books can purchase access to the video clips online. For more information about the Business Law Digital Video Library, visit **www.cengage.com/blaw/dvl**.

A HANDBOOK OF BASIC LAW TERMS, BLACK'S LAW DICTIONARY SERIES

This paperback dictionary, prepared by the editor of the popular *Black's Law Dictionary*, can be packaged for a small additional cost with any new South-Western Legal Studies in Business text.

STUDENT GUIDE TO THE SARBANES-OXLEY ACT

This brief overview for business students explains the Sarbanes-Oxley Act, what is required of whom, and how it might affect students in their business life. Available as an optional package with the text.

Interaction with the Authors

This is our standard: Every professor who adopts this book must have a superior experience. We are available to help in any way we can. Adopters of this text often call us or e-mail us to ask questions, obtain a syllabus, offer suggestions, share pedagogical concerns, or inquire about ancillaries. One of the pleasures of working on this project has been our discovery that the text provides a link to so many colleagues around the country. We value those connections, are eager to respond, and would be happy to hear from you.

Jeffrey F. Beatty

Susan S. Samuelson
Phone: (617) 353-2033
Email: ssamuels@bu.edu

Dean A. Bredeson
Phone: (512) 471-5248
Email: bredeson@mail.utexas.edu

ACKNOWLEDGMENTS

We are grateful to the following reviewers who gave such helpful comments for the third edition revisions:

Joseph F Adamo
Cazenovia College

Joan P. Alexander
Nassau College

Victor Alicea
Normandale College

Basil N. Apostle
Purchase College, SUNY

Lee Ash
Skagit Valley College

Loretta Beavers
Southwest Virginia Community
College

Theodore R. Bolema
Anderson Economic
Group, LLC

Joseph T. Bork
University of St. Thomas

Karen E. Bork
Northwood University

Beverly Woodall Broman
Everest Institute—Pittsburgh, PA

Jeff W. Bruns
Bacone College

E. Katy Burnett
Kentucky Community & Technical
College Systems Online

Bruce W. Byars
University of North Dakota

Dianne L. Caron
The Art Institute of Seattle

Amy F. Chataginer
Mississippi Gulf Coast Community
College

Tim Collins
Kaplan Career Institute—ICM Campus

Michael Combe
Eagle Gate College

Mark DeAngelis
University of Connecticut

Laura C. Denton
Maysville Community and Technical
College

Julia G. Derrick
Brevard Community College

Dr. Joe D. Dillsaver
Northeastern State University

Ted Dinges
Metropolitan Community
College—Longview

Nicki M. Dodd
Guilford Technical Community
College

Bradley L. Drell
Louisiana College, Pineville

Donna N. Dunn
Beaufort County Community College

Jameka Ellison
Everest University—Lakeland

Traci C. Etheridge
Richmond Community College

Gail S.M. Evans
University of Houston—Downtown

Alfred E. Fabian
Ivy Tech Community College

Jerrold M. Fleisher
Dominican College—Orangeburg, New
York

Andrea Foster
John Tyler Community College—Chester
Campus

Daniel F. Gant
Savannah River College

Jolena M. Grande
Cypress College, CA

Marina Grau
Houston Community College

Wade T. Graves
Grayson County College

John P. Gray
Faulkner University

Scott R. Gunderson
Dakota County Technical
College, MN

Diane A. Hagan
Ohio Business College—Sandusky

Ruth Ann Hall
The University of Alabama

Robert L. Hamilton
Columbia College—Orlando Campus

Jason M. Harris
Augustana College, SD

Toni R. Hartley
Laurel Business Institute

Tony Hunnicutt
Ouachita Technical College

Robert F. Huyck
Mohawk Valley Community College

Christopher R. Inama
Golden Gate University

Joseph V. Ippolito
Brevard College

David I. Kapelner
Merrimack College

Jack E. Karns
East Carolina University

Mark King
Indiana Business College

Hal P. Kingsley
Trocaire College

Kailani Knutson
Porterville College

Samuel Kohn
New York Institute of Technology

Carl Korman
Community College of Vermont

Douglas Kulper
University of California, Santa Barbara

Kimberly S. Lamb
Stautzenberger College

Greg Lauer
North Iowa Area Community College

Dennis G. Lee
Southwest Georgia Technical College

Paul Leiman
Johns Hopkins University

Paulette S. León
Northwestern Technical College—Rock Spring, GA

Leslie S. Lukasik
Skagit Valley College, Whidbey Island Campus

David MacCulloch
Westmont College

Jerome P. McCluskey
Manhattanville College

MarySheila McDonald
Philadelphia University

Arin S. Miller
Keiser University

Ronald K. Minnehan
California Lutheran University

Tonia Hap Murphy
University of Notre Dame

John J. Nader
Davenport University

Terri J. Nix
Howard College

Cliff Olson
Southern Adventist University

Steven C. Palmer
Eastern New Mexico University

Denielle Pemberton
Johns Hopkins University

Nicole Pierone
Yakima Valley Community College

Linda E. Plowman
The Art Institute of Pittsburgh

Matthew B. Probst
Ivy Tech Community College of Indiana
—Lawrenceburg

Anne Montgomery Ricketts
University of Findlay

Sandra Robertson
Thomas Nelson Community College

Bruce L. Rockwood
Bloomsburg University of Pennsylvania

R. J. Ruppenthal
Evergreen Valley College

Mark R. Solomon
Walsh College—Troy, MI

Harilaos I. Sorovigas
Michigan State University

Kim D. Steinmetz
Everest College—Phoenix, AZ

Kenneth R. Taurman, Jr., JD
Indiana University Southeast

Natalie L. Turner
Middle Georgia Technical College—
Warner Robins

Marion R. Tuttle
New Jersey Institute of
Technology

Janet M. Velazquez
Kansas City Kansas Community
College

William V. Vetter
Prairie View A&M University

Jamie S. Waldo
Chadron State College

Deborah B. Walsh
Middlesex Community College, MA

David B. Washington
Augsburg College

Albert B. West
Providence College School of Continuing
Ed.—Providence, R.I.

Mathew C. Williams
Clover Park Technical College

Ira Wilsker
Lamar Institute of Technology

Kelly Collins Woodford
University of South Alabama

Gilbert Ybarra
International Business College

John W. Yeargain
Southeastern Louisiana University

Eric D. Yordy
Northern Arizona University

Bruce Yuille
Mid Michigan Community College

ABOUT THE AUTHORS

Jeffrey F. Beatty was an Associate Professor of Business Law at the Boston University School of Management. After receiving his B.A. from Sarah Lawrence and his J.D. from Boston University, he practiced with the Greater Boston Legal Services representing indigent clients. At Boston University, he won the Metcalf Cup and Prize, the university's highest teaching award. Professor Beatty also wrote plays and television scripts that were performed in Boston, London, and Amsterdam.

Susan S. Samuelson is a Professor of Business Law at Boston University's School of Management. After earning her A.B. at Harvard University and her J.D. at Harvard Law School, Professor Samuelson practiced with the firm of Choate, Hall and Stewart. She has written many articles on legal issues for scholarly and popular journals, including the *American Business Law Journal, Ohio State Law Journal, Boston University Law Review, Harvard Journal on Legislation, National Law Journal, Sloan Management Review, Inc. Magazine, Better Homes and Gardens* and *Boston Magazine*. At Boston University, she won the Broderick Prize for excellence in teaching. Professor Samuelson is the Faculty Director of the Boston University Executive MBA program.

Dean A. Bredeson is a Senior Lecturer at the University of Texas' McCombs School of Business, where he has been on the faculty for 16 years. He also holds a J.D. from the University of Texas. He has previously published *Student Guide to the Sarbanes-Oxley Act* and two textbooks which explore the intersection of law and ethics: *Applied Business Ethics* and *Ethics in the Workplace*. He is a four-time winner of the Lockheed-Martin Award, which is awarded each year to the one member of the faculty at McCombs with the highest student course evaluations in undergraduate courses. He is also among the youngest-ever recipients of the Board of Regents Teaching Award, the UT System's highest teaching honor.

The Legal Environment

CHAPTER 1

INTRODUCTION TO LAW

© r.nagy/Shutterstock.com

Near Campus

Alan Dawson dumped his Calculus II textbook into his backpack. Outside, a light snow began to fall. With a sigh, he left his apartment and headed out into the early December evening.

Halfway to the library, he encountered a group of his friends. "Alan!" one of them said.

"Oh, hey, Gary," Alan replied. "Are you guys studying, too?"

"Nope. We," Gary said with a flourish, "are all done with finals. We're going out. You should come with us."

"I can't. I have my Calculus final at noon tomorrow."

"And that gives you plenty of time to go to Thirsty's with us. And …" Gary raised his eyebrows up and down, "Carrie's going to be there."

"Come on, Dawson! Be a man! Come on!" the others encouraged him. Without a word, Alan reversed direction and headed away from the library. His friends cheered loudly.

> When he opened the door, he saw Alan rolling around on the floor, groaning.

At Thirsty's Bar

Anna stood behind the bar and watched four bikers enter. They wore jackets with gang insignia, and each had on a purple headscarf. One of them approached the bar. "Four Budweisers," he said to Anna.

Gathering her courage, Anna said, "Look, you guys know you can't wear your colors in here."

"What are you gonna do about it, missy?" the biker asked. He leaned closer to her and insisted. "Four. Beers."

Anna thought about it for a moment, then gathered four Budweiser longnecks and placed them on the bar. The biker tossed down a $10 bill, took the beers, and joined his three associates at a table.

Anna eyed the telephone on the counter behind her. The owner of Thirsty's had told her, "You see any gang colors in here, you call the cops immediately." But the bikers were watching her, and she decided not to make a call right away.

At a back table

"I'm not going home for a few more days," Alan said to Carrie.

"I'm not either. We should do something."

"Yeah," Alan said, trying hard to not seem too excited. "Have you, ah, seen the new DiCaprio movie? We could go see it."

"That would be great."

Alan made small talk, blissfully unaware of the bikers or anyone else in the bar.

Eventually, he excused himself and made his way to the restroom.

As he washed his hands, he saw two bikers in the mirror. "Howdy, college boy," one of them said.

Twenty minutes later

"Hey, where the hell is Alan?" Gary asked. Several people shrugged. Carrie said, "He got up a while ago. I think he went to the restroom."

Gary frowned and headed back to the men's room. When he opened the door, he saw Alan rolling around on the floor, groaning. His shirt was torn, and his face was bloody. "Oh, man, what happened? Are you OK?" Gary asked.

"No," Alan replied.

Gary thumbed 911 on his cell phone.

"Wait a moment," you may be thinking. "Are we reading a chapter on business law or one about biker crimes in a roadside tavern?" Both. Later in the chapter, we examine a real case that mirrors the opening scenario. The crime committed against Alan will enable us to explore one of the law's basic principles, negligence. Should a pub owner pay money damages to the victim of gang violence? The owner herself did nothing aggressive. Should she have prevented the harm? Does her failure to stop the assault make her responsible? What begins as a gang incident ends up an issue of commercial liability.

Law is powerful, essential, and fascinating. We hope this book will persuade you of all three ideas. We place great demands on our courts, asking them to make our large, complex, and sometimes violent society into a safer, fairer, more orderly place. Judges must reason their way through countless complex issues.

THREE IMPORTANT IDEAS ABOUT LAW

Power

A driver is seriously injured in an automobile accident and the jury concludes that the car had a design defect. The jurors award her *$29 million*. A senior vice-president congratulates himself on a cagey stock purchase but is horrified to receive, not profits, but a prison sentence. A homeless person, ordered by local police to stop panhandling, ambles into court and walks out with an order permitting him to beg on the city's streets. The strong hand of the law touches us all. To understand something that powerful is itself power.

Suppose, some years after graduation, you are a mid-level manager at Sublime Corp., which manufactures and distributes video games. You are delighted with this important position in an excellent company—and especially glad that you bring legal knowledge to the job. Sarah, an expert at computer-generated imagery, complains that Rob, her boss, is constantly touching her and making lewd comments. That is sexual harassment, and your knowledge of *employment law* helps you respond promptly and carefully. You have dinner with Jake, who has his own software company. Jake wants to manufacture an exciting new video game in cooperation with Sublime, but you are careful not to create a binding deal (*Contract law*). Jake mentions that a similar game is already on the market. Do you have the right to market one like it? That answer you already know (*Intellectual property law*).

LuYu, your personnel manager, reports that a silicon chip worker often seems drowsy; she suspects drug use. Does she have the right to test him (*Constitutional law* and *employment law*)? On the other hand, if she fails to test him, could Sublime Corp. be liable for any harm the worker does (*Tort law and agency law*)?

In a mere week, you might use your legal training a dozen times, helping Sublime to steer clear of countless dangers. During the coming year, you encounter many other legal issues, and you and your corporation benefit from your skills.

It is not only as a corporate manager that you will confront the law. As a voter, investor, juror, entrepreneur, and community member, you will influence and be affected by the law. Whenever you take a stance about a legal issue, whether in the corporate office, the voting booth, or as part of local community groups, you help to create the social fabric of our nation. Your views are vital. This book will offer you knowledge and ideas from which to form and continually reassess your legal opinions and values.

Importance

We depend upon laws for safe communities, functioning economies, and personal liberties. An easy way to gauge the importance of law is to glance through any newspaper and read about nations that lack a strong system of justice. Notice that these countries cannot ensure physical safety and personal liberties. They also fail to offer economic opportunity for most citizens. We may not always like the way our legal system works, but we depend on it to keep our society functioning.

Fascination

Law is intriguing. When the jury awarded $29 million against an auto manufacturer for a defective car design, it certainly demonstrated the law's power. But was the jury's decision right? Should a company have to pay that much for one car accident? Maybe the jury was reacting emotionally. Or perhaps the anger caused by terrible trauma *should* be part of a court case. These are not abstract speculations for philosophers. Verdicts such as this may cause each of us to pay more for our next automobile. Then again, we may be driving safer cars.

SOURCES OF CONTEMPORARY LAW

It would be nice if we could look up "the law" in one book, memorize it, and then apply it. But the law is not that simple. Principles and rules of law come from many different sources. Why is this so?

We inherited a complex structure of laws from England. Additionally, ours is a nation born in revolution and created, in large part, to protect the rights of its people from the government. The Founding Fathers created a national government but insisted that the individual states maintain control in many areas. As a result, each state has its own government with exclusive power over many important areas of our lives. What the Founding

Fathers created was **federalism**: a double-layered system of government, with the national government and state governments each exercising important but limited powers. To top it off, the Founders guaranteed many rights to the people alone, ordering national and state governments to keep clear. They achieved all of this in one remarkable document: the United States Constitution.

Federalism
A double-layered system of government, with the national and state governments each exercising important but limited powers.

United States Constitution

America's greatest legal achievement was the writing of the **United States Constitution** in 1787. It is the supreme law of the land, and any law that conflicts with it is void. This federal Constitution does three basic things. First, it establishes the national government of the United States, with its three branches. Second, it creates a system of checks and balances among the branches. And third, the Constitution guarantees many basic rights to the American people.

United States Constitution
The supreme law of the land.

BRANCHES OF GOVERNMENT

The Founding Fathers sought a division of government power. They did not want all power centralized in a monarch or anyone else. And so, the Constitution divides legal authority into three pieces: legislative, executive, and judicial power.

Legislative power gives the ability to create new laws. In Article I, the Constitution gives this power to the Congress, which is comprised of two chambers—a Senate and a House of Representatives.

The House of Representatives has 435 voting members. A state's voting power is based on its population. Large states (Texas, California, Florida) send dozens of representatives to the House. Some small states (Wyoming, North Dakota, Delaware) send only one. The Senate has 100 voting members—two from each state.

Executive power is the authority to enforce laws. Article II of the Constitution establishes the President as commander-in-chief of the armed forces and the head of the executive branch of the federal government.

Judicial power gives the right to interpret laws and determine their validity. Article III places the Supreme Court at the head of the judicial branch of the federal government. Interpretive power is often underrated, but it is often as important at the ability to create laws in the first place. For instance, the Supreme Court ruled that privacy provisions of the Constitution protect a woman's right to abortion, although neither the word "privacy" nor "abortion" appears in the text of the Constitution.[1] And at times, courts void laws altogether. For example, in 1995, the Supreme Court ruled that the Gun-Free School Zones Act of 1990 was unconstitutional because it exceeded Congressional power over interstate commerce.[2]

CHECKS AND BALANCES

Sidney Crosby might score 300 goals per season if checking were not allowed in the National Hockey League. But because opponents are allowed to hit Crosby and the rest of the Penguins, he is held to a much more reasonable 50 goals per year.

Political checks work in much the same way. They allow one branch of the government to trip up another.

The authors of the Constitution were not content to divide government power three ways. They also wanted to give each part of the government the power over the other two branches. Many people complain about "gridlock" in Washington, but the government is sluggish by design. The Founding Fathers wanted to create a system that, without broad

---

[1] *Roe v. Wade*, 410 U.S. 113 (1973).
[2] *United States v. Alfonso Lopez, Jr.*, 514 U.S. 549 (1995).

agreement, would tend towards inaction. The President can veto Congressional legislation. Congress can impeach the President. The Supreme Court can void laws passed by Congress. The President appoints judges to the federal courts, but these nominees do not serve unless approved by the Senate.

Many of these checks and balances will be examined in more detail later in the text.

FUNDAMENTAL RIGHTS

The Constitution also grants many of our most basic liberties. For the most part, they are found in the amendments to the Constitution. The First Amendment guarantees the rights of free speech, free press, and the free exercise of religion. The Fourth, Fifth, and Sixth Amendments protect the rights of any person accused of a crime. Other amendments ensure that the government treats all people equally and that it pays for any property it takes from a citizen.

By creating a limited government of three branches and guaranteeing basic liberties to all citizens, the Constitution has become one of the most important documents ever written.

Statutes

The second important source of law is statutory law. The Constitution gave to the United States Congress the power to pass laws on various subjects. These laws are called **statutes,** and they can cover absolutely any topic at all, so long as they do not violate the Constitution.

Almost all statutes are created by the same method. An idea for a new law—on taxes, health care, texting while driving, or anything else—is first proposed in the Congress. This idea is called a *bill*. The House and Senate then independently vote on the bill. To pass Congress, the bill must get approval from a simple majority of each of these chambers.

If Congress passes a bill, it goes to the White House. If the President signs it, a new statute is created. It is no longer a mere idea; it is the law of the land. If a President *vetoes* a bill, it does not become a statute unless Congress overrides the veto. To do that, both the House and the Senate must approve the bill by a 2/3 majority. At this point, it becomes a statute without the President's signature.

Statute
A law passed by Congress or by a state legislature.

Common Law

Binding legal ideas often come from the courts. Judges generally follow *precedent*. When courts decide a case, they tend to apply the same legal rules that other courts have used in similar cases. **The principle that precedent is binding on later cases is *stare decisis*, which means "let the decision stand."** *Stare decisis* makes the law predictable, and this in turn enables businesses and private citizens to plan intelligently.

It is important to note that precedent is only binding on *lower* courts. If the Supreme Court, for example, decided a case in one way in 1965, it is under no obligation to follow precedent if the same issue arises in 2015.

Sometimes, this is quite beneficial. In 1896, the Supreme Court decided (unbelievably) that segregation—separating people by race in schools, hotels, public transportation, and so on—was legal. In 1954, on the exact same issue, the Court changed its mind.

In other circumstances, it is more difficult to see the value in breaking with an established rule.

Stare decisis
The principle that precedent is binding on later cases.

Court Orders

Judges have the authority to issue court orders that place binding obligations on specific people or companies. An injunction, for example, is a court order to stop doing something. A judge might order a stalker to stay more than 500 yards away from an ex-boyfriend or girlfriend. Courts have the authority to imprison or fine those who violate their orders.

Administrative Law

In a society as large and complex as ours, the executive and legislative branches of government cannot oversee all aspects of commerce. Congress passes statutes about air safety, but United States senators do not stand around air traffic towers, serving coffee to keep everyone awake. The executive branch establishes rules concerning how foreign nationals enter the United States, but presidents are reluctant to sit on the dock of the bay, watching the ships come in. Administrative agencies do this day-to-day work.

Most government agencies are created by Congress. Familiar examples include the Environmental Protection Agency (EPA), the Securities and Exchange Commission (SEC), and the Internal Revenue Service (IRS), whose feelings are hurt if it does not hear from you every April 15. Agencies have the power to create laws called *regulations.*

> Presidents are reluctant to sit on the dock of the bay, watching the ships come in.

CLASSIFICATIONS OF LAW

We have seen where laws come from. Now we need to classify them. First, we will distinguish between criminal and civil law. Then we will take a look at the intersection between law and morality.

Criminal and Civil Law

It is a crime to embezzle money from an employer, to steal a car, and to sell cocaine. **Criminal law** concerns behavior so threatening that society outlaws it altogether. Most criminal laws are statutes, passed by Congress or a state legislature. The government itself prosecutes the wrongdoer, regardless of what the bank president or car owner wants. A district attorney, paid by the government, brings the case to court. The injured party, for example the owner of the stolen car, is not in charge of the case, although she may appear as a witness. The government will seek to punish the defendant with a prison sentence, a fine, or both. If there is a fine, the money goes to the state, not to the injured party.

Civil law is different, and most of this book is about civil law. **Civil law** regulates the rights and duties between parties. Tracy agrees in writing to lease you a 30,000-square-foot store in her shopping mall. She now has a legal duty to make the space available. But then another tenant offers her more money, and she refuses to let you move in. Tracy has violated her duty, but she has not committed a crime. The government will not prosecute the case. It is up to you to file a civil lawsuit. Your case will be based on the common law of contracts. You will also seek equitable relief—namely, an injunction ordering Tracy not to lease to anyone else. You should win the suit, and you will get your injunction and some money damages. But Tracy will not go to jail.

Some conduct involves both civil and criminal law. Suppose Tracy is so upset over losing the court case that she becomes drunk and causes a serious car accident. She has committed the crime of driving while intoxicated, and the state will prosecute. Tracy may be fined or imprisoned. She has also committed negligence, and the injured party will file a lawsuit against her, seeking money.

Law and Morality

Law is different from morality, yet the two are obviously linked. There are many instances when the law duplicates what all of us would regard as a moral position. It is negligence to drive too fast in a school district, and few would dispute the moral value of that law. And

Criminal law
Concerns behavior so threatening that society outlaws it altogether.

Civil law
Regulates the rights and duties between parties.

similarly with contract law: if the owner of land agrees in writing to sell property to a buyer at a stated price, the seller must go through with the deal, and the legal outcome matches our moral expectations.

On the other hand, we have had laws that we now clearly regard as immoral. Seventy-five years ago, a factory owner could legally fire a worker for any reason at all—including, for example, her religion. It is immoral to fire a worker because she is Jewish—and today, the law prohibits it. Finally, there are legal issues where the morality is not so clear. Suppose you serve alcohol to a guest who becomes intoxicated and then causes an automobile accident, seriously injuring a pedestrian. Should you, the social host, be liable? This is an issue of tort liability, which we examine in Chapter 5. As with many topics in this book, the problem has no easy answer. As you learn the law, you will have an opportunity to re-examine your own moral beliefs. One of the goals of Chapter 2, on ethics, is to offer you new tools for that task.

WORKING WITH THE BOOK'S FEATURES

In this section, we introduce a few of the book's features and discuss how you can use them effectively. We will start with cases.

Analyzing a Case

A law case is the decision a court has made in a civil lawsuit or criminal prosecution. Cases are the heart of the law and an important part of this book. Reading them effectively takes practice. This chapter's opening scenario is fictional, but the following real case involves a similar situation. Who can be held liable for the assault? Let's see.

KUEHN V. PUB ZONE

364 N.J. Super. 301, 835 A.2d 692,
Superior Court of New Jersey, Appellate Division, 2003

CASE SUMMARY

Facts: Maria Kerkoulas owned the Pub Zone bar. She knew that several motorcycle gangs frequented the tavern. From her own experience tending bar, and conversations with city police, she knew that some of the gangs, including the Pagans, were dangerous and prone to attack customers for no reason. Kerkoulas posted a sign prohibiting any motorcycle gangs from entering the bar while wearing "colors"; that is, insignia of their gangs. She believed that gangs without their colors were less prone to violence, and experience proved her right.

Rhino, Backdraft, and several other Pagans, all wearing colors, pushed their way past the tavern's bouncer and approached the bar. Although Kerkoulas saw their colors, she allowed them to stay for one drink. They later moved towards the back of the pub, and Kerkoulas believed they were departing. In fact, they followed a customer named Karl Kuehn to the men's room, where, without any provocation,

they savagely beat him. Kuehn was knocked unconscious and suffered brain hemorrhaging, disc herniation, and numerous fractures of facial bones. He was forced to undergo various surgeries, including eye reconstruction.

Although the government prosecuted Rhino and Backdraft for their vicious assault, our case does not concern that prosecution. Kuehn sued the Pub Zone, and that is the case we will read. The jury awarded him $300,000 in damages. However, the trial court judge overruled the jury's verdict. He granted a judgment for the Pub Zone, meaning that the tavern owed nothing. The judge ruled that the pub's owner could not have foreseen the attack on Kuehn and had no duty to protect him from an outlaw motorcycle gang. Kuehn appealed, and the appeals court's decision follows.

Issue: *Did the Pub Zone have a duty to protect Kuehn from the Pagans' attack?*

Decision: Yes, the Pub Zone had a duty to protect Kuehn. The decision is reversed, and the jury's verdict is reinstated.

Reasoning: Whether a duty exists depends on the foreseeability of the harm, its potential severity, and the defendant's ability to prevent the injury. A court should also evaluate society's interest in the dispute.

A business owner generally has no duty to protect a customer from acts of a third party unless experience suggests that there is danger. However, if the owner could in fact foresee injury, she is obligated to take reasonable safety precautions.

Kerkoulas knew that the Pagans engaged in random violence. She realized that when gang members entered the pub, they endangered her customers. That is why she prohibited bikers from wearing their colors—a reasonable rule. Regrettably, the pub failed to enforce the rule. Pagans were allowed to enter wearing their colors, and the pub did not call the police. The pub's behavior was unreasonable and it is liable to Kuehn.

ANALYSIS

Let's take it from the top. The case is called *Kuehn v. Pub Zone*. Karl Kuehn is the **plaintiff**, the person who is suing. The Pub Zone is being sued, and is called the **defendant**. In this example, the plaintiff's name happens to appear first, but that is not always true. When a defendant loses a trial and files an appeal, *some* courts reverse the names of the parties for the appeal case.

The next lines give the legal citation, which indicates where to find the case in a law library or online.

The *Facts* section provides a background to the lawsuit, written by the authors of this text. The court's own explanation of the facts is often many pages long and may involve complex matters irrelevant to the subject covered in this book, so we relate only what is necessary. This section will usually include some mention of what happened at the trial court. Lawsuits always begin in a trial court. The losing party often appeals to a court of appeals, and it is usually an appeals court decision that we are reading. The trial judge ruled in favor of Pub Zone, but in the appellate decision we are reading, Kuehn won.

The *Issue* section is very important. It tells you what the court had to decide—and why you are reading the case.

The *Decision* section describes the court's answer to the issue posed. A court's decision is often referred to as its **holding**. The court rules that the Pub Zone did have a duty to Kuehn. The court **reverses** the trial court's decision, meaning it declares the lower court's ruling wrong and void. The judges reinstate the jury's verdict. In other cases, an appellate court may **remand** the case; that is, send it back down to the lower court for a new trial or some other action. If this court had agreed with the trial court's decision, the judges would have **affirmed** the lower court's ruling, meaning to uphold it.

The *Reasoning* section explains why the court reached its decision. The actual written decision may be three paragraphs or 75 pages. Some judges offer us lucid prose, while others seem intent on torturing the reader. Judges frequently digress and often discuss matters that are irrelevant to the issue on which this text is focusing. For those reasons, we have taken the court's explanation and cast it in our own words. If you are curious about the full opinion, you can always look it up.

Let us examine the reasoning. The court points out that a defendant is liable only if he has a duty to the plaintiff. Whether there is such a duty depends on the foreseeability of the injury and other factors. The judges are emphasizing that courts do not reach decisions arbitrarily. They attempt to make thoughtful choices, consistent with earlier rulings, which make good sense for the general public.

The court also points out what it is *not* deciding. The court is *not* declaring that all businesses must guarantee the safety of their patrons against acts by third parties. If an owner had no reason to foresee injury from a third party, the owner is probably not be liable for such harm. However, if experience indicated that the third party presented serious

Plaintiff
The person who is suing.

Defendant
The person being sued.

Holding
A court's decision.

Reverse
To declare the lower court's ruling wrong and void.

Remand
To send a case back down to a lower court.

Affirm
To uphold a lower court's ruling.

danger, the owner was obligated to act reasonably. The judges note that Kerkoulas knew the Pagans could be violent and had taken reasonable precautions by prohibiting gang colors. However, the pub failed to enforce its sensible rule and failed even to telephone the police. By the very standard the pub had created, its conduct was unreasonable. The court therefore concludes that the Pub Zone was liable for the Pagans' injury to Kuehn, and the judges reinstate the jury's verdict for the injured man.

EXAM Strategy

This feature gives you practice analyzing cases the way lawyers do—and the way *you* must, on tests. Law exams are different from most others because you must determine the issue from the facts provided. Too frequently, students faced with a law exam forget that the questions relate to the issues in the text, and those discussed in class. Understandably, students new to law may focus on the wrong information in the problem, or rely on material learned elsewhere. The *Exam Strategy* feature teaches you to figure out exactly what issue is at stake and then analyze it in a logical, consistent manner. Here is an example, relating to the element of "duty," which the court discussed in the *Pub Zone* case.

Question: The Big Red Traveling (BRT) Carnival is in town. Tony arrives at 8:00 p.m., parks in the lot, and is robbed at gunpoint by a man who beats him and escapes with his money. There are several police officers on the carnival grounds, but no officer is in the parking lot at the time of the robbery. Tony sues, claiming that brighter lighting and more police in the lot would have prevented the robbery. There has never before been any violent crime—robbery, beating, or other incident—at any BRT carnival. BRT claims it had no duty to protect Tony from this harm. Who is likely to win?

Strategy: Begin by isolating the legal issue. What are the parties disputing? They are debating whether BRT had a duty to protect Tony from an armed robbery committed by a stranger. Now ask yourself: How do courts decide whether a business has a duty to prevent this kind of harm? The Pub Zone case provides our answer. A business owner is not an insurer of the visitor's safety. The owner generally has no duty to protect a customer from the criminal act of a third party unless the owner could foresee it is about to happen. (In the *Pub Zone* case, the business owner *knew* of the gang's violent history and could have foreseen the assault.) Now apply that rule to the facts of this case.

Result: There has never been a violent attack of any kind at a BRT carnival. BRT cannot foresee this robbery, and has no duty to protect against it. The carnival wins.

"You Be the Judge"

Many cases involve difficult decisions for juries and judges. Often both parties have legitimate, opposing arguments. Most chapters in this book will have a feature called "You Be the Judge," in which we present the facts of a case but not the court's holding. We offer you two opposing arguments based on the kinds of claims the lawyers made in court. We leave it up to you to debate and decide which position is stronger or to add your own arguments to those given.

The following case is another negligence lawsuit, with issues that overlap those of the *Pub Zone* case. This time the court confronts a fight that resulted in death. The victim's distraught family sued the owner of a bar, claiming that an employee was partly responsible for the death. Once again, the defendant asked the court to dismiss the case, claiming he owed no duty to protect the victim—the same argument made by the Pub Zone.

But there is a difference—this time, the defendant owned the bar across the street, not the one where the fight took place. Could this neighbor be held legally responsible for the death? You be the judge.

You be the Judge

Facts: In the days before cell phones, a fight broke out at Happy Jack's Saloon. A good Samaritan ran across the street to the Circle Inn, where he asked the bartender to let him use the telephone to call the police. The bartender refused.

Soldano v. O'Daniels

141 Cal. App. 3d 443
Court of Appeal of California, 5th Appellate District, 1983

Back at Happy Jack's Saloon, the fight escalated, and a man shot and killed Soldano's father. Soldano sued the owner of the Circle Inn for negligence. He argued the bartender violated a legal duty when he refused to hand over the inn's telephone, and that, as the employer of the bartender, O'Daniels was partially liable for his father's death.

The lower court dismissed the case, citing the principle that generally, a person does not have a legal responsibility to help another unless he created the dangerous situation in the first place. Soldano appealed.

You Be The Judge: *Did the bartender have a duty to allow the use of the Circle Inn's telephone?*

Argument for the Defendant: Your honors, my client did not act wrongfully. He did nothing to create the danger. The fight was not even on his property. We sympathize with the plaintiff, but it is the shooter, and perhaps the bar where the fight took place, who are responsible for the his father's death. Our client was not involved. Liability can be stretched only so far.

The court would place a great burden on the citizens of California by going against precedent. The Circle Inn is Mr. O'Daniel's private property. If the court imposes potential liability on him in this case, would citizens be forced to open the doors of their homes whenever a stranger claims an emergency? Criminals would delight in their newfound ability to gain access to businesses and residences by simply demanding to use a phone to "call the police."

The law has developed sensibly. People are left to decide for themselves whether to help in a dangerous situation. They are not legally required to place themselves in harm's way.

Argument for the Plaintiff: Your honors, the Circle Inn's bartender had both a moral and a legal duty to allow the use of his establishment's telephone. The Circle Inn may be privately owned, but it is a business open to the public. Anyone in the world is invited to stop by and order a drink or a meal. The good Samaritan had every right to be there.

We do not argue that the bartender had an obligation to break up the fight or endanger himself in any way. We simply argue he had a responsibility to stand aside and allow a free call on his restaurant's telephone. Any "burden" on him or on the Circle Inn was incredibly slight. The potential benefits were enormous. The trial court made a mistake in concluding that a person *never* has a duty to help another. Such an interpretation makes for poor public policy.

There is no need to radically change the common law. Residences can be excluded from this ruling. People need not be required to allow strangers into their homes. This court can simply determine that businesses have a legal duty to allow the placement of emergency calls during normal business hours.

Chapter Conclusion

We depend upon the law to give us a stable nation and economy, a fair society, a safe place to live and work. But while law is a vital tool for crafting the society we want, there are no easy answers about how to create it. In a democracy, we all participate in the crafting. Legal rules control us, yet we create them. A working knowledge of the law can help build a successful career—and a solid democracy.

EXAM REVIEW

1. **FEDERALISM**   Our federal system of government means that law comes from a national government in Washington, D.C., and from 50 state governments. (p. 5)

2. **SOURCES OF LAW**   The primary sources of contemporary law are:

   - United States Constitution

   - Statutes, which are drafted by legislatures

   - Common law, which is the body of cases decided by judges, as they follow earlier cases, known as *precedent*

   - Court orders, in which a judge which place binding obligations on specific people or companies; and

   - Administrative law, the rules and decisions made by federal and state administrative agencies. (pp. 4–7)

3. **CRIMINAL AND CIVIL LAW**   Criminal law concerns behavior so threatening to society that it is outlawed altogether. Civil law deals with duties and disputes between parties, not outlawed behavior. (p. 7)

EXAM Strategy

Question: Bill and Diane are hiking in the woods. Diane walks down a hill to fetch fresh water. Bill meets a stranger, who introduces herself as Katrina. Bill sells a kilo of cocaine to Katrina, who then flashes a badge and mentions how much she enjoys her job at the Drug Enforcement Agency. Diane, heading back to camp with the water, meets Freddy, a motorist whose car has overheated. Freddy is late for a meeting where he expects to make a $30 million profit; he's desperate for water for his car. He promises to pay Diane $500 tomorrow if she will give him the pail of water, which she does. The next day, Bill is in jail and Freddy refuses to pay for Diane's water. Explain the criminal law/civil law distinction and what it means to Bill and Diane. Who will do what to whom, with what results?

Strategy: You are asked to distinguish between criminal and civil law. What is the difference? Criminal law concerns behavior that threatens society and is therefore outlawed. The government prosecutes the defendant. Civil law deals with the rights and duties between parties. One party files a suit against the other. Apply those different standards to these facts. (See the "Result" at the end of this section.)

3. Result: The government will prosecute Bill for dealing in drugs. If convicted, he will go to prison. The government will take no interest in Diane's dispute. However, if she chooses, she may sue Freddy for $500, the amount he promised her for the water. In that civil lawsuit, a court will decide whether Freddy must pay what he promised; however, even if Freddy loses, he will not go to jail.

MATCHING QUESTIONS

Match the following terms with their definitions.

___A. Statute	1. Law created by judges
___B. Administrative agencies	2. Let the decision stand
___C. Common law	3. A law passed by Congress or a state legislature
___D. *Stare decisis*	4. The supreme law of the land
___E. United States Constitution	5. The IRS; the EPA; the FCC; the SEC

TRUE/FALSE QUESTIONS

1. T F The idea that current cases must be decided based on earlier cases is called legal positivism.
2. T F Civil lawsuits are brought to court by the injured party, but criminal cases must be prosecuted by the government.
3. T F Congress established the federal government by passing a series of statutes.
4. T F The federal government has three branches: executive, legislative, and administrative.
5. T F Law is different from morality, but the two are closely linked.

MULTIPLE-CHOICE QUESTIONS

1. More American law comes from one country than from any other. Which country?
   (a) France
   (b) England
   (c) Germany
   (d) Spain
   (e) Canada

2. Under the United States Constitution, power that is not expressly given to the federal government is retained by
   (a) The courts
   (b) The Congress
   (c) The Founding Fathers
   (d) The states and the people
   (e) International treaty

3. Judges use precedent to create what kind of law?

   (a) Common law

   (b) Statutes

   (c) National law

   (d) Local law

   (e) Empirical law

4. If the Congress creates a new statute with the President's support, it must pass the idea by a _____ majority vote in the House and the Senate. If the President vetoes a proposed statute and the Congress wishes to pass it without his support, the idea must pass by a _____ majority vote in the House and Senate.

   (a) simple; simple

   (b) simple; 2/3

   (c) simple; 3/4

   (d) 2/3; 3/4

5. What part of the Constitution addresses most basic liberties?

   (a) Article I

   (b) Article II

   (c) Article III

   (d) The Amendments

ESSAY QUESTIONS

1. Union organizers at a hospital wanted to distribute leaflets to potential union members, but hospital rules prohibited leafletting in areas of patient care, hallways, cafeterias, and any areas open to the public. The National Labor Relations Board (NLRB) ruled that these restrictions violated the law and ordered the hospital to permit the activities in the cafeteria and coffee shop. The NLRB cannot create common law or statutory law. What kind of law was it creating?

2. The stock market crash of 1929 and the Great Depression that followed were caused in part because so many investors blindly put their money into stocks they knew nothing about. During the 1920s, it was often impossible for an investor to find out what a corporation was planning to do with its money, who was running the corporation, and many other vital facts. Congress responded by passing the Securities Act of 1933, which required a corporation to divulge more information about itself before it could seek money for a new stock issue. What kind of law did Congress create? Explain the relationship between voters, Congress, and the law.

3. **ETHICS** The greatest of all Chinese lawgivers, Confucius, did not esteem written laws. He believed that good rulers were the best guarantee of justice. Does our legal system rely primarily on the rule of law or the rule of people? Which do you instinctively trust more?

4. Burglar Bob breaks into Vince Victim's house. Bob steals a flat-screen TV and laptop and does a significant amount of damage to the property before he leaves.

Fortunately, Vince has a state-of-the-art security system. It captures excellent images of Bob, who is soon caught by police.

Assume that two legal actions follow, one civil and one criminal. Who will be responsible for bringing the civil case? What will be the outcome if the jury believes that Bob did in fact burgle Vince's house? Who will be responsible for bringing the criminal case? What will the outcome be this time if the jury believes that Bob did in fact burgle Vince's house?

5. *Kuehn v. Pub Zone* and *Soldano v. O'Daniels* both involve attacks in a bar. Should they come out in the same way? If so, which way—in favor of the injured plaintiffs or owner-defendants? Or, should they have different outcomes? What are the key facts that lead you to believe as you do?

DISCUSSION QUESTIONS

1. Do you believe that there are too many lawsuits in the United States? If so, do you place more blame for the problem on lawyers or on individuals who go to court? Is there anything that would help the problem, or will we always have large numbers of lawsuits?

2. In the 1980s, the Supreme Court ruled that it is legal for protesters to burn the American flag. This activity counts as free speech under the Constitution. If the Court hears a new flag-burning case in this decade, should it consider changing its ruling, or should it follow precedent? Is following past precedent something that seems sensible to you: always, usually, sometimes, rarely, or never?

3. When should a business be held legally responsible for customer safety? Consider the following statements, and circle the appropriate answer.

    a. A business should keep customers safe from its own employees.

    strongly agree   agree   neutral
    disagree   strongly disagree

    b. A business should keep customers safe from other customers.

    strongly agree   agree   neutral
    disagree   strongly disagree

    c. A business should keep customers safe from themselves. (Example: an intoxicated customer who can no longer walk straight.)

    strongly agree   agree   neutral
    disagree   strongly disagree

    d. A business should keep people outside its own establishment safe if it is reasonable to do so.

    strongly agree   agree   neutral
    disagree   strongly disagree

4. In his most famous novel, *The Red and the Black*, the French author Stendhal (1783–1842) wrote: "Prior to laws, what is natural is only the strength of the lion, or the need of the creature suffering from hunger or cold, in short, need." Do you agree with Stendhal? Without laws, would society quickly crumble?

5. At the time of this writing, voters are particularly disgruntled. A good many seem to be disgusted with government. For this question, we intentionally avoid distinguishing between Democrats and Republicans, and we intentionally do not name any particular President. Consider the following statements, and circle the appropriate answer.

    a. I believe that members of Congress usually try to do the right thing for America.

    strongly agree   agree   neutral
    disagree   strongly disagree

    b. I believe that Presidents usually try to do the right thing for America.

    strongly agree   agree   neutral
    disagree   strongly disagree

    c. I believe that Supreme Court Justices usually try to do the right thing for America.

    strongly agree   agree   neutral
    disagree   strongly disagree

CHAPTER 2

BUSINESS ETHICS AND SOCIAL RESPONSIBILITY

© r.nagy/Shutterstock.com

Three people talk about their temptation to lie:

1. During college, I used drugs—some cocaine, but mostly prescription painkillers. Things got pretty bad. At one point, I would wait outside emergency rooms hoping to buy drugs from people who were leaving. But that was three years ago. I went into rehab and have been clean ever since. I don't even drink. I've applied for a job but the application asks if I have ever used drugs illegally. I am afraid that if I tell the truth, I will never get a job. What should I say on the application?

2. I process payroll at my company, so I know how much everyone earns, including the top executives. This could make for some good gossip, but I have never told anyone about the salaries. Then yesterday the CEO went to my boss to confirm that *she* does the processing for top management. It turns out that it is against company policy for me to be doing it, but my boss handed it off to me anyway. She lied to the CEO and said she was doing it. Then she begged me not to tell the truth if the CEO checked with me. Now he has called me to go see him. What do I say if he asks about the payroll?

3. I am in charge of a project to redesign software that is one of our company's top products. Most of our engineers are French, and I studied the language in college. I enjoy going out with the team in the evenings. We have become pretty good friends. Recently, my boss told me that once the project is finished, all the engineers will be laid off. He joked about how "the French will be fried when they find out." Since they are not U.S. citizens, they will have to leave the country unless they get jobs right away. If I tell them the boss's

> I've applied for a job, but the application asks if I have ever used drugs illegally. I am afraid that if I tell the truth, I will never get a job. What should I say?

plan, they will start looking for other jobs and my project could be in the tank. That would be really bad for the company, not to mention a disaster for me. One of the engineers wants to make an offer on a house so asked me about his future at the company. What do I say?

INTRODUCTION

This text, for the most part, covers legal ideas. The law dictates how a person *must* behave. This chapter examines **ethics,** or how people *should* behave. It will examine ethical dilemmas that commonly arise in workplaces, and present tools for making decisions when the law does not require or prohibit any particular choice.

Ethics
The study of how people ought to act.

If a person is intent on lying, cheating, and stealing his way through a career, then he is unlikely to be dissuaded by anything in this or any other course. But for the large majority of people who want to do the right thing, it will be useful to study new ways of approaching difficult problems.

Ethics lies largely beyond the realm of law, and so we present a unique feature in this chapter. You will notice that it contains "Ethics Cases" and discussion questions in place of law cases. It is our hope that these scenarios will generate lively classroom debates on right and wrong. It is important for future leaders to hear a variety of points of view. In your career, you will work with diverse groups of people. If you have insight into how different people perceive ethical issues, you will be better off.

We also hope that hearing these different points of view will help you develop your own Life Principles. These principles are the rules by which you live your life. For example, the opening scenario dealt with lying. It is easy to say, "I will always tell the truth," but many people believe that it is ethically acceptable to lie in certain situations. For example, a large man holding a big knife demands, "Where's Jamie?" You know where Jamie is, but you might be tempted to send the murderer off in the opposite direction and then call the police. At the other end of the spectrum, you could decide that you will lie whenever it seems to be in your best interest. The problem with this approach is that you will soon find that no one trusts you. Where in between these two extremes do your Life Principles fit? Something to think about throughout this chapter (and throughout your life). If you develop these Life Principles now, you will be prepared when facing ethical dilemmas in the future.

In this chapter, we will present five basic issues:[1]

1. Why bother to act ethically at all?

2. What is the most important consideration when making an ethical decision? To do the right thing for the right reason? Or to do what produces the most favorable results?

3. Should you apply your personal ethics in the workplace? Or should you have different ethical values at home and at work?

4. Is the primary role of corporations to make money? Or do they have responsibilities to workers, communities, customers, and other "stakeholders"?

5. When, if ever, is lying acceptable?

---

[1]Some of the ethics cases and discussion questions featured in this chapter are adapted from *Applied Business Ethics* by Dean A. Bredeson, Cengage Learning, 2011.

Why Bother to Act Ethically at All?

Ethical decision making generates a range of benefits for employees, companies, and society. Although ethical business practices are not required, the remainder of this chapter makes the case that they are sound.

Society as a Whole Benefits from Ethical Behavior

John Akers, the former chairman of IBM, argues that without ethical behavior, a society cannot be economically competitive. He puts it this way:

> Ethics and competitiveness are inseparable. We compete as a society. No society anywhere will compete very long or successfully with people stabbing each other in the back; with people trying to steal from each other; with everything requiring notarized confirmation because you can't trust the other fellow; with every little squabble ending in litigation; and with government writing reams of regulatory legislation, tying business hand and foot to keep it honest. That is a recipe not only for headaches in running a company, it is a recipe for a nation to become wasteful, inefficient, and noncompetitive. There is no escaping this fact: the greater the measure of mutual trust and confidence in the ethics of a society, the greater its economic strength.[2]

People Feel Better When they Behave Ethically

Researchers who study happiness find that people expect material goods to make them happier than they actually do. Sure, you enjoy driving that snappy new car home from the dealership, but afterward your happiness quickly returns to its natural base level. People find themselves on the so-called hedonic treadmill—struggling to buy more and more things so they can get that buyer's high, only to discover that they can never buy enough to maintain the thrill. Almost no matter how much people earn, they feel they would be happier if their income were just a little bit higher. So what does make people happy in the long run? Good relationships, satisfying work, ties to the community—all available at no additional cost.

Every businessperson has many opportunities to be dishonest. Consider how one person felt when he resisted temptation:

> Occasionally a customer forgot to send a bill for materials shipped to us for processing.... It would have been so easy to rationalize remaining silent. After all, didn't they deserve to lose because of their inefficiency? However, upon instructing our staff to inform the parties of their errors, I found them eager to do so. They were actually bursting with pride.... Our honesty was beneficial in subtle ways. The "inefficient" customer remained loyal for years.... [O]ur highly moral policy had a marvelously beneficial effect on our employees. Through the years, many an employee visited my office to let me know that they liked working for a "straight" company.[3]

Profitability is generally not what motivates managers to care about ethics. Managers want to feel good about themselves and the decisions they have made; they want to sleep at night. Their decisions—whether to lay off employees, install safety devices in cars, burn a cleaner fuel—affect peoples' lives. When two researchers asked businesspeople why they cared about ethics, the answers had little to do with profitability:

---

[2]David Grier, "Confronting Ethical Dilemmas," unpublished manuscript of remarks at the Royal Bank of Canada, September 19, 1989.

[3]Hugh Aaron, "Doing the Right Thing in Business," *Wall Street Journal,* June 21, 1993, p. A10.

The businesspeople we interviewed set great store on the regard of their family, friends, and the community at large. They valued their reputations, not for some nebulous financial gain but because they took pride in their good names.[4]

Unethical Behavior Can Be Very Costly

Unethical behavior is a risky business strategy—it may lead to disaster. An engaged couple made a reservation, and put down a $1,500 deposit, to hold their wedding reception at a New Hampshire restaurant. Tragically, the bride died four months before the wedding. Invoking the terms of the contract, the restaurant owner refused to return the couple's deposit. In a letter to the groom, he admitted, "Morally, I would of course agree that the deposit should be returned." When newspapers reported this story, customers deserted the restaurant and it was forced into bankruptcy—over a $1,500 disagreement.[5] Unethical behavior does not *always* damage a business, but it certainly has the potential of destroying a company overnight. So why take the risk?

Even if unethical behavior does not devastate a business, it can cause other, subtler damage. In one survey, a majority of those questioned said that they had witnessed unethical behavior in their workplace and that this behavior had reduced productivity, job stability, and profits. Unethical behavior in an organization creates a cynical, resentful, and unproductive workforce.

Although there is no *guarantee* that ethical behavior pays in the short or long run, there is evidence that the ethical company is more *likely* to win financially. Ethical companies tend to have a better reputation, more creative employees, and higher returns than those that engage in wrongdoing.[6]

But if we decide that we want to behave ethically, how do we know what ethical behavior is?

UTILITARIAN VERSUS DEONTOLOGICAL ETHICS

When making ethical decisions, people sometimes focus on the reason for the decision—they want to do what is right. Thus, if they think it is wrong to lie, then they will tell the truth no matter what the consequence. Other times, people think about the outcome of their actions. They will do whatever it takes to achieve the right result, no matter what they have to do to obtain it. This choice—between doing right and getting the right result—has been the subject of much philosophical debate.

Utilitarian Ethics

In 1863, Englishman John Stuart Mill wrote *Utilitarianism*. He was not the first person to write on utilitarian ethics, but his book has best stood the test of time. To Mill, a correct decision was one that tended to maximize overall happiness and minimize overall pain. Risk management and cost-benefit analyses are examples of utilitarian business practices.

---

[4]Amar Bhide and Howard H. Stevenson, "Why Be Honest If Honesty Doesn't Pay?" *Harvard Business Review*, Sept.-Oct. 1990, pp. 121–29, at 127.

[5]John Milne, "N.H. Restaurant Goes Bankrupt in Wake of Wedding Refund Flap," *Boston Globe*, Sept. 9, 1994, p. 25.

[6]For sources, see "Ethics: A Basic Framework," Harvard Business School case 9-307-059.

Utilitarianism is, in some ways, an almost mathematical approach to ethics. Consider this classic example. If you have two extra baseball tickets and two friends, and if you decide to share the tickets, you might be naturally inclined to give one to each friend. But what if one of your friends likes baseball and the other does not? The transaction might look something like this:

Friend 1: (1 ticket) x (1 unit of happiness per ticket) = 1 unit of happiness produced

Friend 2: (1 ticket) x (0 unit of happiness per ticket) = 0 units of happiness produced

Overall happiness generated by the gifts = 1 unit of happiness.

A utilitarian might suggest giving both tickets to the friend who would appreciate them. The transaction might then look like this:

Friend 1: (2 tickets) x (1 unit of happiness per ticket) = 2 units of happiness produced

Friend 2: (0 tickets) x (0 unit of happiness per ticket) = 0 units of happiness produced

Overall happiness generated by the gifts = 2 units of happiness.

The best Hollywood line that reflects utilitarian thinking comes from *Star Trek II: The Wrath of Khan*. Toward the end, Mr. Spock saves the *Enterprise* but in so doing takes a lethal dose of radiation. Captain Kirk cradles the dying Spock and says, "Spock! WHY?" Spock replies, "Because Captain, the needs of the many outweigh the needs of the few (cough) or one."

The critics of utilitarian thought are many. Some argue that it is simply not possible to "measure" happiness in the way that one would measure distance or the passage of time. Others say that utilitarians simply let the ends justify the means, and that they allow for bad behavior so long as the it generates good in the end. A third group argues that utilitarian and other hedonistic philosophies err in equating pleasure with ethical behavior and pain with wrongful behavior. Caring for an elderly relative with Alzheimer's disease, for example, might generate little pleasure and much pain, but is it still a worthwhile and good endeavor.

Deontological Ethics

Many ethicists believe that utilitarians have it all wrong, and that the *results* are not as important as the *reason* for which the decision is made. To a deontological thinker, the ends do not justify the means.

The best-known proponent of the deontological model was 18th-century German philosopher Immanuel Kant. He thought that human beings possessed a unique dignity and that no decision that treated people as commodities could be considered just, even if the decision tended to maximize overall happiness, or profit, or any other quantifiable measure. In his view, a sense of duty or obligation was the best justification for any action. Although not all followers of deontological ethics agree with Kant's specific ideas, most agree that utilitarianism is lacking, and that winning in the end does not automatically make a decision right. Ethical decisions, they argue, are those made for good and moral reasons in the first place, regardless of the outcome.

In the following example, both sides end up better off, but is the operation ethically sound?

◆ Ethics Case: HIV Treatment ◆

Alpha Company has developed a new drug that is an effective treatment for HIV. It is not a cure, but it postpones the onset of AIDS indefinitely.

Before this breakthrough, HIV-positive patients were treated with a "cocktail" of medications. Although effective, the combination of drugs required patients to take several pills at a time several times per day. Alpha Company's drug is a single pill that must be taken only twice per day. Because it is more convenient, patients are less likely to miss doses.

Alpha spent tens of millions of dollars developing the drug, but now that is has been developed, each pill only costs a few dollars to manufacture. Alpha charges $4,150 for a 30-day supply, or about $50,000 per year. The pills are generally not covered by insurance plans. The older "cocktail" of drugs is still available from other drug companies at a much lower cost.

Alpha has a program that makes its drug available at no cost in extreme circumstances, and about 1 percent of the patients taking the drug receive it directly from Alpha at no charge. Alpha has several successful drugs and had earnings of nearly three billion dollars last year.

Some activists have called on Alpha to do the following:

- Reduce the price of its drugs for all patients to $35,000 per year. This would be $10,000 above the cost of the older treatment.

- Expand its free drug program to cover 10 percent of the drug's current users.

QUESTIONS

1. Should Alpha meet the first demand and reduce its prices across the board? What is a fair price?

2. Should Alpha meet the second demand and expand its free drug program? What guidelines should it use?

3. Justify your answers to Questions 1 and 2 using the ideas presented in this section. Utilitarians might respond to this scenario by saying, "A profitable drug company will stay in business longer, develop more useful medications, and benefit more people in the long run. Alpha is under no ethical obligation to make either policy shift." A Kantian thinker might opine, "Alpha has a duty to help people when it is able to do so. It should reduce the price to all patients and provide free drugs to those who need it. Which line of reasoning makes more sense to you?

APPLYING PERSONAL ETHICS IN THE WORKPLACE

Should you behave in the workplace the way you do at home, or do you have a separate set of ethics for each part of your life? What if your employees behave badly outside of work—should that affect their employment? Consider the following case.

◆ Ethics Case: No sheen on Sheen ◆

Charlie Sheen, the star of the hit CBS TV show, "Two and a Half Men," has admitted to using large quantities of cocaine. He has been hospitalized with drug overdoses and has been charged with both misdemeanor and felony drug offenses which have led to probation several times. When asked about entering rehab, he said that only losers go to recovery programs and he could cure himself with his mind. He openly spent tens of thousands of dollars on prostitutes. His second wife filed a restraining order against him, alleging that he had pushed her down the stairs and threatened to kill her. He was also charged with a felony for threatening his third wife. She alleges that he held a knife to her throat and said, "You better be in fear. If you tell anybody, I'll kill you." Then there was the widely reported incident in the Plaza Hotel in New York City in which the police escorted him to the hospital after he trashed his room and threatened the prostitute he had hired—all while his ex-wife and children slept in a room across the hall. Five months later, the police removed his twin sons from his house after their mother obtained a restraining order. On a radio show, Sheen made anti-Semitic comments about his boss, called him a clown and a charlatan, and said that he "violently hated him." This boss was the most successful producer of comedy shows in the business.

QUESTIONS:

1. If CBS fired Sheen from his TV show, the network would lose tens of millions of dollars. At what point, if any, should CBS have fired him? If not for this, then for what?

2. Would you fire a warehouse worker who behaved this way? How much revenue does an employee have to bring in to be able to buy his way out of bad behavior?

3. What would you say to someone who argues that the goal at work is to make as much money as possible, but at home it is to be a kind and honorable human being?

STAKEHOLDER ETHICS

A fundamental question in business ethics is: *What is the purpose of a corporation?* The answer to this question has changed over time. To begin at the beginning …

In a famous 1919 lawsuit, Henry Ford was sued by the Dodge brothers and other major shareholders of Ford Motor Company.[7] The shareholders were upset because Ford paid essentially no dividends, despite fabulous profits. The shareholders complained, especially about Ford's use of corporate profits to support humanitarian and charitable works. The Michigan Supreme Court found in favor of the shareholders because corporation laws at the time required corporate boards to put shareholders first. The Dodge brothers won enough money to start their own car company, which still exists as part of Chrysler.

Companies were legally required to follow the "shareholder model" until the decade after the close of World War II. In the late 1940s and early 1950s, the attitude of many powerful politicians toward corporations changed. Many believed that American companies had contributed mightily to stopping the Nazis, and that without the massive volume of armaments and supplies that American corporations produced, Hitler might well have been victorious. There was a feeling that corporations were an essential part of society.

Many politicians wanted corporations to be able to participate more fully in American life. They softened restrictive language in corporation laws, so that companies could "do good deeds." Such action was not and is still not required, but it is allowed.

Definitions

THE SHAREHOLDER MODEL

Noted economist Milton Friedman argued that corporations have two primary responsibilities. First, they must comply with the law. Second, they must make as much money as possible for shareholders. In his view, if shareholder and stakeholder interests conflict, the company should act in the best interests of the shareholders. After all, only shareholders

---

[7]*Dodge v. Ford* 170 N.W. 668 (Mich. 1919).

have put their own money on the line. To do otherwise is, according to Friedman, "imposing a tax" on the shareholders.

THE STAKEHOLDER MODEL

The alternative point of view is that corporations should take care of more than shareholders alone. It is not that the owners of a corporation should be ignored—shareholders are included as one of several groups of stakeholders in a firm. But, a company must also look out for (among others) its employees, its customers, and the communities in which it operates. It may even be that companies have an obligation to broader interests such as "society" or "the environment."

The basic notion of stakeholder ethics is that even if a company will make less profit for shareholders, it should nonetheless pay decent wages, support charitable causes, and so forth. A great many Fortune 500 companies put the stakeholder model into practice.

The Debate

Every executive will treat employees well if she believes that doing so will lead to increased profits. Every executive is in favor of donating money to charity if the donation improves the company's image and thereby pays for itself. But such win-win cases are not ethical dilemmas.

In a true dilemma, a company considers an action that would not increase the shareholders' return in any certain or measureable way. In such cases, the shareholder model advises, "Don't spend the shareholders' money." The stakeholder model counsels, "It is often reasonable to consider the interests of stakeholders other than the owners."

As with most ethics questions, neither side is "right" in the sense that everyone agrees or that the law requires following either set of ideas. Countless companies follow each of the models.

The remainder of this section examines a company's ethical obligation to three specific stakeholders: employees, customers, and international contractors.

The Organization's Responsibility to Its Employees

Organizations cannot be successful without good workers. In many circumstances the shareholder and stakeholder models agree that employees should be treated well. Disgruntled workers are likely to be unmotivated and unproductive. But sometimes looking out for employees may not lead to higher profits. In these cases, does an organization have a duty to "take care" of its workers? The shareholder model says no; the stakeholder model takes the opposite view.

Corporate leaders are often faced with difficult decisions when the issue of layoffs arises. Choices can be particularly difficult to navigate when outsourcing is an option. *Outsourcing* refers to cutting jobs at home and relocating operations to another country.

Read the following scenario and critique the CEO's decision making.

◆ Ethics Case: The Storm after the Storm ◆

Yanni is the CEO of Cloud Farm, a company that provides online data centers for Internet companies. Because these data centers are enormous, they are located in rural areas where they are often the main employer. A series of tornados has just destroyed a data center near Farmfield, Arkansas, a town with a population of roughly 5,000 people. Farmfield is a two-hour drive from the nearest city, Little Rock.

Here is the good news: the insurance payout will cover the full cost of rebuilding. Indeed, the payout will be so generous that Cloud Farm could build a bigger and better facility than the one destroyed. The bad news? Data centers are much more expensive to build and operate in the United States than in Africa, Asia, or Latin America. Yanni could take the money from the insurance company and build three data centers overseas. He has asked Adam and Zoe to present the pros and cons of relocating.

Adam says: "If we rebuild overseas, our employees will never find equivalent jobs. We pay $20 an hour, and the other jobs in town are mostly minimum-wage. And remember how some of the guys worked right through Christmas to set up for that new client. They have been loyal to us—we owe them something in return. And it's not just bad for Farmfield or Arkansas, it's bad for the country. We can't continue to ship jobs overseas."

Zoe responds: "That is the government's problem, not ours. We'll pay to retrain the workers, which, frankly, is a generous offer. Our investors get a return of 4 percent; the industry average is closer to 8 percent. If we act like a charity to support Farmfield, we could all lose our jobs. It is our obligation to do what's best for our shareholders—which, in this case, happens to be what's right for us, too."

QUESTIONS

1. If you were in Yanni's position, would you rebuild the plant in Arkansas or relocate overseas?

2. Do you agree with Zoe's argument that it is the government's responsibility to create and protect American jobs, and that it is a CEO's job to increase shareholder wealth?

3. Imagine that you personally own $10,000 worth of shares in Cloud Farm. Would you be upset with a decision to rebuild the data center in the United States?

4. If Cloud Farm decides to rebuild in Arkansas, should it pay the workers while the center is being rebuilt? If yes, should it apply to all the workers, or just the high-level ones who might leave if they were not paid?

5. What is your Life Principle on this issue? Would you be willing to risk your job to protect your employees?

An Organization's Responsibility to Its Customers

Customers are another group of essential stakeholders. A corporation must gain and retain loyal buyers if it is to stay in business for long. Treating customers well usually increases profits and helps shareholders.

But when, if ever, does an organization go too far? If a leader "puts customers first" in a way that significantly diminishes the bottom line, has she acted inappropriately? The shareholder model says yes.

After reading the following scenario, assess which option is best.

◆ Ethics Case: Fanning Customer Wrath ◆

Mark is the plant manager at Cooper Fan Company. For six months, he has been angling to ink a deal with Rooms-to-Go, a housewares company. With this contract, company profits would soar and he could hire 75 new workers. It would not hurt his bonus or job security, either. But now the shift foreman at the factory is reporting bad news—an engineer says there may be a problem with the 300 model, one of Cooper's most popular offerings. With a sinking heart, Mark goes to investigate.

Ann, the engineer, shows Mark the standard remote control. "Notice," she says, "four buttons—Lo, Hi, Off, and Reverse." Mark hits the Lo button, and a ceiling fan just above his head starts to rotate lazily. He pushes Off, and the blades slow to a stop.

"So what's the problem?" Mark asks.

"It's the Reverse button. Most of our models have a switch on top of the fan itself that allows for the fan to spin clockwise or counterclockwise. This way, fans can blow air downward in the summer to cool the room and then draw air upward in the winter to make the same room feel warmer. But that means twice a year, homeowners have to drag out a ladder to change the switch."

"The 300 solves this problem by putting the Reverse button on the remote control. No ladders, no changing of switches. The problem is that the remote allows the reverse feature to be engaged while the fan is running. Watch. "

Ann presses Hi on the remote and waits for the blades to cycle up to speed. When the blades are a blur, she pushes Reverse. There are several rapid clicks and a soft grinding sound as the blades lose speed. The noises stop after a few seconds, the blades slow, come to a stop, change direction, and begin to speed up again.

"If someone does that once or twice, no problem," Ann says. "But eventually, the fans all fail. We tested 50 of them—switching back and forth between Hi and Reverse over and over. At somewhere between 75 and 150 reversals they break. For most of them, it isn't a big problem—they just stop working. Three of them emitted sparks but did nothing else. One of them started a fire. And the last one threw out a half-inch piece of metal from the inner casing. Probably wouldn't kill someone, but it could certainly have put out an eye."

"So who's going to switch back and forth like that 75 times?" Mark asks.

"A kid might want to make a game of it. And, although there have been no reports of any problems, it may be that we are just lucky. So far. The engineers have designed a new fan that solves this problem. But what do we do in the meantime about the 50,000 300s that have already been sold?"

Here are Mark's options:

- Recall all the 300s. Fixing or replacing the fans would probably cost several million dollars. A recall would also jeopardize the Rooms-To-Go contract.

- Never issue a recall. If a fan fails and someone sues, it would probably cost $20,000 to $200,000 per incident. But if someone dies in a fire or is disabled by flying debris, then all bets are off. There is no upper limit on a worst-case scenario like that.

- Delay the recall until for a month or two, until the Rooms-to-Go contract is resolved one way or the other.

QUESTIONS

1. If you were in Mark's position, would you recommend a recall today? How about in two months, after the Rooms-to-Go deal has been completed?

2. Ann's testing showed 6 percent "bad" results (sparks) and 4 percent "really bad" results (fire and thrown metal). Would your answers to Question 1 change if Ann's testing had shown 18 percent "bad" and 12 percent "really bad" results? What if it had shown the same number of "bad" results but zero "really bad" results?

3. What Life Principle are you applying in this situation?

4. Assume that no recall is made, that a fan started a fire and burned a home in your town to the ground, and that a local newspaper identified the ceiling fan as the cause. The newspaper later reports that the Cooper Fan Company knew about the potential problem and did nothing about it. As a consumer, would you consider buying Cooper fans, or would you pass them by even if they were competitive in pricing, appearance, and features?

Organization's Responsibility to Overseas Contract Workers

Do an American company's ethical obligations end at the border? What ethical duties does an American manager owe to stakeholders in countries where the culture and economic circumstances are very different? Should American companies (and consumers) buy goods that are produced in sweatshop factories?

> **Industrialization has always been the first stepping stone out of dire poverty.**

Industrialization has always been the first stepping stone out of dire poverty—it was in England in centuries past, and it is now in the developing world. Eventually, higher productivity leads to higher wages. In China, factory managers have complained that their employees want to work even longer hours to earn more money. The results in China have been nothing short of remarkable: during the Industrial Revolution in England, per-capita output doubled in 58 years; in China, it took only 10 years.

During the past 50 years, Taiwan and South Korea welcomed sweatshops. During the same period, India resisted what it perceived to be foreign exploitation. Although all three countries started at the same economic level, Taiwan and South Korea today have much lower levels of infant mortality and much higher levels of education than India.[8]

When governments or customers try to force factories in the developing world to pay higher wages, the factory owners typically either relocate to lower-wage countries or mechanize, thereby reducing the need for workers. In either case, the local economy suffers. Companies argue that higher wages lead to increased prices, which in turn drive away customers.

◆ Ethics Case: The Dragon's Den ◆

Ellen is the CEO of a large electronics manufacturer that makes cell phones, among other items. She is reviewing a consultant's report on Quality Dragon Limited, which operates the factory in China where the cell phones are made. She is considering whether to renew the firm's contract for a new three-year term.

The consultant "infiltrated" the Quality Dragon factory by getting a job and working there for a month. Portions of the consultant's report follow.

> We were awakened at 5 a.m. every day. They always shouted at us and ordered us to hurry. We were fed a poor meal, and were always at our stations by 5:30, although work did not begin until 6. We worked from 6 until 1 p.m. with one 10-minute restroom break at 9 a.m. We were not permitted to talk to coworkers. If we did, even quietly, we were docked pay and the supervisors screamed at us. If we made an assembly error, we lost pay and the supervisors screamed at us. If we yawned, we lost pay and the supervisors screamed at us. If we failed to meet an hourly quota, we lost pay and the supervisors screamed at us.
>
> I drilled holes into the outer casing of your phones at the place where a charger can be plugged in. My quota was to process 120 per hour. The holes had to be perfectly located and perfectly straight. Every 30 seconds, a new one. It was difficult to keep focus. I tried to make fewer than 10 errors per day. One day I made only 4 errors. Another day I made 18. On that day, my supervisor slapped me and docked me my entire day's pay.
>
> We had 30 minutes for lunch. The company provides a poor meal. We were permitted to pay for better food at the cafeteria, but it was very expensive. We could speak quietly at lunch.
>
> At 1:30, we went back to work until 8:30. We had another 10 minute break at 4:30. Work was more difficult in the afternoon. The sun warmed the factory. Water was not allowed on the assembly floor. Sometimes, water was available at the restroom break. The supervisors were angrier and less patient after lunch. They called us names that no one should be called. If we missed our quota, we had to work late. This happened several times over the month.
>
> Eventually, we were fed and returned to our dorm. We had 12 men to a room, and we slept in bunk beds that were three bunks high. The room smelled bad, and there were ants.

---

[8]The data in this and the preceding paragraph are from Nicholas D. Kristof and Sheryl Wu Dunn, "Two Cheers for Sweatshops," *New York Times Magazine*, Sept. 24, 2000, p. 70.

We worked six days per week. On Sundays, most workers spent much of their day sleeping. The company did provide televisions and chess sets in the recreation building.

I was supposed to earn $150 for the month. But the supervisors always looked for reasons to dock my pay. No one gets full pay. I ended up with $110 at the end of the month. For long-term workers, "take-home pay" is actually lower because there are things they must buy from the factory store. Workers are required to shave, but they have to buy their own razor blades. They also have to buy soap. The company provides a jumpsuit once a year, but workers have to buy socks and underwear.

Life in the factory could be worse, but it is very difficult.

QUESTIONS

1. Is the CEO morally required to use her negotiating power to insist upon better treatment of the people who make her company's products? What is your Life Principle?

2. In your opinion, does the treatment described seem reasonable? If not, what parts of the consultant's story indicate to you that workers are being treated wrongfully?

3. Assume that correcting the problems listed below would each result in a 1 percent cost increase for this company. Assume that you are in Ellen's position as CEO. Place a checkmark by the items that you would insist upon, keeping in mind that each one increases your labor costs.

   - Reducing employees' workdays to a maximum of 12 hours

   - Improving the quality of food served to employees

   - Eliminating the practice of reducing pay for employees who exceed their quota for errors

   - Building additional dorms so that workers sleep with no more than four to a room

   - Prohibiting unpaid or forced overtime

4. As a consumer, are you keenly aware of how much things cost? Would you notice if food prices rose by 5 percent? What about smart phones, computers, and televisions—would a 5 percent increase in the price of these items be noticeable? What if the increase was 2 percent? How much extra would you be willing to pay for your cell phone so that workers could be treated better than the ones in this factory?

WHEN, IF EVER, IS LYING ACCEPTABLE?

We are taught from an early age that we must tell the truth. And usually, honesty is the best policy. The consequences of lying can be severe: students are suspended, employees are fired, and witnesses are convicted of perjury. Sometimes the problems are more subtle but still significant: a loss of trust, a loss of opportunities.

But in some specific circumstances, intentional deception is tolerated, and even admired. In sports, for example, athletes spend countless hours perfecting techniques designed to trick opponents. If Peyton Manning looks one way and throws the other, no one is upset, even though his intention is to deceive the defensive backs. In other settings, lying is equally acceptable. When poker players bluff their way through lousy hands, we call them "skilled."

But what about in business? Does the presence of *competition* make a difference? Can the ends ever justify the means when it is not a life-and death situation? Consider the following scenario.

◆ Ethics Case: Truth [?] in Borrowing ◆

"Yes," Harold insisted indignantly. "I *am* going to walk in there and give them a file of fake documents. And hope to heaven that I can walk out of there with a $100,000 loan, even if it is fraudulent. What of it? Ethics are all very well when business is good, but now I'm desperate. Without that loan, no payroll and then no business."

"And what happens when you get caught?" his brother demanded. "Don't expect me to come visit you in jail every Sunday."

"Don't worry, they'll never figure it out. I'm only exaggerating the numbers a little, and I've never fudged a single thing in 20 years of banking with them. They won't look too closely. And it's not like the bank is going to lose its money. Orders are already picking up, and they'll come all the way back, just like they did in the last two recessions. I'll pay the bank every penny back—with interest—this time next year. Who gets hurt?"

QUESTIONS

1. Rate Harold's plan to lie to his bank to secure the $100,000 loan so that he is able to pay his employees. Is it completely wrongful? Completely justified? Somewhere in between? How does it fit with your Life Principle?

2. Now assume that a year passes, and that business does in fact pick up for Harold's company. He is able to repay the loan in full, with interest. No one is laid off from his company, no one misses a paycheck, and his lie is never caught. Is your assessment of his actions the same? Do the ends at least partially justify the means?

3. What is your Life Principle about telling lies? When is making a misrepresentation acceptable? To protect someone's life or physical safety? To protect a job? To protect another person's feelings? To gain an advantage? When others expect it and may do the same? (Would poker be different from cheating on an exam or on your taxes?)

4. What would you say about the three examples in the opening scenario? Do you have the same rule when lying to protect yourself, as opposed to others?

Chapter Conclusion

Even employees who are ethical in their personal lives may find it difficult to uphold their standards at work if those around them behave differently. Managers wonder what they can do to create an ethical environment in their companies. In the end, the surest way to infuse ethics throughout an organization is for top executives to behave ethically themselves. When leaders assess the impact that their decisions will have on stakeholders, they go a long way towards behaving ethically.

Few employees will bother to "do the right thing" unless they observe that their bosses value and support such behavior. To ensure a more ethical world, managers must be an example for others, both within and outside their organizations.

EXAM REVIEW

1. **ETHICS** The law dictates how a person *must* behave. Ethics governs how people *should* behave. (p. 17)

2. **LIFE PRINCIPLES** Life Principles are the rules by which you live your life. If you develop these Life Principles now, you will be prepared when facing ethical dilemmas in the future. (p. 17)

3. **WHY BOTHER TO ACT ETHICALLY AT ALL?**
   - Society as a whole benefits from ethical behavior.
   - People feel better when they behave ethically.
   - Unethical behavior can be very costly.
   - Ethical behavior is more likely to pay off . (pp. 18–19)

4. **UTILITARIANSIM V. DEONTOLICAL ETHICS** Utilitarian thinkers believe that moral actions produce the greatest good for the greatest number. Deontological thinkers such as Immanuel Kant argue that, when assessing whether a decision is the most ethical choice, the end result is immaterial. Kantian thinkers believe that moral choices must be made for sound reasons, and that decisions motivated by a sense of duty or a respect for human dignity are particularly ethical. (pp. 19–21)

5. **PERSONAL V. WORK ETHICS** Should you apply your personal ethics in the workplace, or should you have different ethical values at home and at work? (pp. 21–22)

6. **GOAL OF CORPORATIONS** Is the primary role of corporations to make money, or do companies have responsibilities to workers, communities, customers, and other stakeholders? (pp. 22–27)

7. **ETHICS OVERSEAS** What ethical duties does an American manager owe to stakeholders in countries where the culture and economic circumstances are very different? Should American companies (and consumers) buy goods that are produced in sweatshop factories? (pp. 25–27)

8. **LYING** When, if ever, is lying acceptable? (pp. 27–28)

MATCHING QUESTIONS

___A. shareholder model

___B. stakeholder model

___C. utilitarianism

___D. deontological ethics

1. requires doing "the greatest good for the greatest number"

2. requires business decisions that maximize the owners' return on investment

3. focuses on the reasons for which decisions are made

4. requires business leaders to consider employees, customers, communities, and other groups when making decisions

TRUE/FALSE QUESTIONS

1. T F Immanuel Kant was a noted utilitarian thinker.

2. T F The shareholder model requires that business leaders consider the needs of employees when making decisions.

3. T F Modern China has experienced slower economic growth than did England during the Industrial Revolution.

4. T F John Stuart Mill's ideas are consistent with business use of risk management and cost-benefit analyses.

5. T F Society as a whole benefits from ethical behavior.

MULTIPLE-CHOICE QUESTIONS

1. Milton Friedman was a strong believer in the _____ model. He _____argue that a corporate leader's sole obligation is to make money for the company's owners.

   (a) shareholder; did

   (b) shareholder; did not

   (c) stakeholder; did

   (d) stakeholder; did not

2. In the 1919 lawsuit *Dodge v. Ford*, the Dodge brothers and other major shareholders sued Henry Ford and his board of directors over nonpayment of dividends. The Michigan Supreme Court sided with _____. Incorporation laws at the time _____ companies to follow the shareholder model.

   (a) Ford; required

   (b) Ford; permitted

   (c) the Dodge brothers; required

   (d) the Dodge brothers; permitted

3. Which of the following historic events led to a significant change in corporation laws and permitted companies to follow the stakeholder model?

   (a) The Great Depression

   (b) World War II

   (c) The election of John F. Kennedy

   (d) The moon landing

   (e) The Supreme Court's decision in *Brown v. Board of Education*

4. Which of the following wrote *Utilitarianism*, and believed that moral actions should "generate the greatest good for the greatest number"?

   (a) Milton Friedman

   (b) John Stuart Mill

   (c) Immanuel Kant

   (d) None of the above

5. Which of the following believed that the dignity of human beings must be respected, and that the most ethical decisions are made out of a sense of duty or obligation?

    (a) Milton Friedman

    (b) John Stuart Mill

    (c) Immanuel Kant

    (d) None of the above

ESSAY QUESTIONS

1. Executives were considering the possibility of moving their company to a different state. They wanted to determine if employees would be willing to relocate, but they did not want the employees to know the company was contemplating a move because the final decision had not yet been made. Instead of asking the employees directly, the company hired a firm to carry out a telephone survey. When calling the employees, these "pollsters" pretended to be conducting a public opinion poll and identified themselves as working for the new state's Chamber of Commerce. Has this company behaved in an ethical manner? Would there have been a better way to obtain this information?

2. When a fire destroyed the Malden Mills factory in Lawrence, Massachusetts, its 70-year-old owner, Aaron Feuerstein, could have shut down the business, collected the insurance money, and sailed off into retirement. But a layoff of the factory's 3,000 employees would have been a major economic blow to the region. So instead, Feuerstein kept the workers on the payroll while he rebuilt the factory. These actions gained him a national reputation as a business hero. Many consumers promised to buy more of the company's patented Polartec fabric. In the end, however, the story did not have a fairy-tale ending: five years after the fire, Malden Mills filed bankruptcy papers. The company was not able to pay off the loans it had incurred to keep the business going.

    Did Feuerstein do the right thing?

3. Many socially responsible funds are now available to the investor who wants to make ethical choices. The Amana Fund buys stocks that comply with Islamic laws. For example, it will not invest in holdings that earn interest, which is prohibited under Islamic law. The Ava Maria Fund is designed for Catholic investors, the Timothy Funds for evangelicals. The Sierra Fund focuses on environmentally friendly investments, while the Women's Equity Fund chooses companies that promote women's interests in the workplace. On average, however, these socially responsible investments earn a lower return than standard index funds that mirror the performance of a stock index, such as the Standard & Poor's 500.

    Are socially responsible funds attractive to you? Do you now, or will you in the future, use them in saving for your own retirement?

4. When James Kilts became CEO of Gillette Co., the consumer products giant had been a mainstay of the Boston community for a hundred years. But the organization was going through hard times: its stock was trading at less than half its peak price, and some of its storied brands of razors were wilting under intense competitive pressure. In four short years, Kilts turned Gillette around—strengthening its core brands,

cutting jobs, and paying off debt. With the company's stock up 61 percent, Kilts had added $20 billion in shareholder value.

Then Kilts suddenly sold Gillette to Procter & Gamble Co. (P&G) for $57 billion. So short was Kilts's stay in Boston that he never moved his family from their home in Rye, New York. The deal was sweet for Gillette shareholders—the company's stock price went up 13 percent in one day. And tasty also for Kilts—his payoff was $153 million, including a $23.9 million reward from P&G for having made the deal and for a "change in control" clause in his employment contract that was worth $12.6 million. In addition, P&G agreed to pay him $8 million a year to serve as vice chairman after the merger. When he retires, his pension will be $1.2 million per year. Moreover, two of his top lieutenants were offered payments totaling $57 million.

Any downside to this deal? Four percent of the Gillette workforce—6,000 employees—were fired. If the payouts to the top three Gillette executives were divided among these 6,000, each unemployed worker would receive $35,000. The loss of this many employees (4,000 of whom lived in New England) had a ripple effect throughout the area's economy. Although Gillette shareholders certainly benefited in the short run from the sale, their profit would have been even greater without this $210 million payout to the executives. Moreover, about half the increase in Gillette revenues during the time that Kilts was running the show were attributable to currency fluctuations. A cheaper dollar increased revenue overseas. If the dollar had moved in the opposite direction, there might not have been any increase in revenue. Indeed, for the first two years after Kilts joined Gillette, the stock price declined. It wasn't until the dollar turned down that the stock price improved.

Do CEOs who receive sweeteners have too strong an incentive to sell their companies? Is it unseemly for them to be paid so much when many employees will lose their jobs?

5. Many of America's largest consumer product companies, such as Wal-Mart, Nike, and Land's End, buy fabric produced in China by Fountain Set Holdings Ltd. Chinese government investigators recently discovered that Fountain Set has contaminated a local river by dumping dye waste into it. What responsibility do U.S. companies have to ensure safe environmental practices by overseas suppliers?

DISCUSSION QUESTIONS

1. Darby has been working for 14 months at Holden Associates, a large management consulting firm. She is earning $75,000 a year, which *sounds* good, but does not go very far in New York City. It turns out that her peers at competing firms are typically paid 20 percent more and receive larger annual bonuses. Darby works about 60 hours a week, more if she is traveling. A number of times, she has had to reschedule her vacation or cancel personal plans to meet client deadlines. She hopes to go to business school in a year and has already begun the application process.

Holden has a policy that permits any employee who works as late as 8:00 P.M. to eat dinner at company expense. The employee can also take a taxi home. Darby is in the habit of staying until 8 P.M. every night, whether or not her workload requires it. Then she orders enough food for dinner, with leftovers for lunch the next day. She has managed to cut her grocery bill to virtually nothing. Sometimes she invites her boyfriend to join her for dinner. As a student, he is always hungry and broke. Darby often uses the Holden taxi to take them back to his apartment, although the cab fare is twice as high as to her own place.

Sometimes Darby stays late to work on her business school applications. Naturally, she uses Holden equipment to print out and photocopy the finished applications. Darby has also been known to return catalog purchases through the Holden mailroom on the company dime. Many employees do this and the mailroom workers do not seem to mind.

Is Darby doing anything wrong? How would you behave in these circumstances?

2. H. B. Fuller Co. of St. Paul is a leading manufacturer of industrial glues. Its mission statement says the company "will conduct business legally and ethically." It has endowed a university chair in business ethics and donates 5 percent of its profits to charity. But now it is under attack for selling its shoemakers' glue, Resistol, in Central America. Many homeless children in these countries have become addicted to Resistol's fumes. So widespread is the problem that glue-sniffers in Central America are called "resistoleros." Glue manufacturers in Europe have added a foul-smelling oil to their glue that discourages abusers. Fuller fears that the smell may also discourage legitimate users. What should H.B. Fuller do?

3. According to the Electronic Industries Association, questionable returns have become the toughest problem plaguing the consumer electronics industry. Some consumers purchase electronic equipment to use once or twice for a special occasion and then return it—a radar detector for a weekend getaway or a camcorder to record a wedding. Or a customer might return a cordless telephone because he cannot figure out how it works. The retailer's staff lacks the expertise to help, so they refund the customer's money and ship the phone back to the manufacturer labeled as defective. Excessive and unwarranted returns force manufacturers to repackage and reship perfectly good products, imposing extra costs that squeeze their profits and raise prices to consumers. One retailer returned a cordless telephone that was two years old and had been chewed up by a dog. What ethical obligations do consumers and retailers have in these circumstances?

4. Genentech, Inc., manufactured Protropin, a genetically engineered version of the human growth hormone. This drug's purpose was to enhance the growth of short children. Protropin was an important product for Genentech, accounting for more than one-third of the company's total revenue of $217 million. Although the drug was approved for the treatment of children whose bodies made inadequate quantities of growth hormone, many doctors prescribed it for children with normal amounts of growth hormone who simply happened to be short. There was no firm evidence that the drug actually increased growth for short children with normal growth hormone. Moreover, many people questioned whether it is appropriate to prescribe such a powerful drug for cosmetic reasons, especially when the drug might not work. Nor was there proof that Protropin was safe over the long term. Was Genentech behaving ethically? Should it have discouraged doctors from prescribing the drug to normal, short children?

5. Rapper Ice-T's song "Cop Killer" generated significant controversy when it was released. Among other things, its lyrics anticipate slitting a policeman's throat. Such lyrics have become reasonably common today, but they were much less common 20 years ago.

When "Cop Killer" was recorded, Time Warner, Inc., was struggling with a $15 billion debt and a depressed stock price. Had Time Warner renounced rap albums with harsh themes, its reputation in the music business—and future profits—might have suffered. This damage might even have spilled over into the multimedia market, which was crucial to Time Warner's future.

Did Time Warner do anything wrong when it decided to release "Cop Killer"?

COURTS, LITIGATION, AND ALTERNATIVE DISPUTE RESOLUTION

© r.nagy/Shutterstock.com

Tony Caruso had not returned for dinner, and his wife, Karen, was nervous. She put on some sandals and hurried across the dunes to the ocean shore a half mile away. She soon came upon Tony's dog, Blue, tied to an old picket fence. Tony's shoes and clothing were piled neatly nearby. Karen and friends searched frantically throughout the evening. A little past midnight, Tony's body washed ashore, his lungs filled with water. A local doctor concluded he had accidentally drowned.

> **A little past midnight, Tony's body washed ashore, his lungs filled with water.**

Karen and her friends were not the only ones distraught. Tony had been partners with Beth Smiles in an environmental consulting business, Enviro-Vision. They were good friends, and Beth was emotionally devastated. When she was able to focus on business issues, Beth filed an insurance claim with the Coastal Insurance Group. Beth hated to think about Tony's death in financial terms, but she was relieved that the struggling business would receive $2 million on the life insurance policy.

Several months after filing the claim, Beth received this reply from Coastal: "Under the policy issued to Enviro-Vision, we are liable in the amount of $1 million in the event of Mr. Caruso's death. If his death is accidental, we are liable to pay double indemnity of $2 million. But pursuant to section H(5), death by suicide is not covered. After a thorough investigation, we have concluded that Anthony Caruso's death was an act of suicide. Your claim is denied in its entirety." Beth was furious. She was convinced Tony was incapable of suicide. And her company could not afford the $2 million loss. She decided to consult her lawyer, Chris Pruitt.

THREE FUNDAMENTAL AREAS OF LAW

This case is a fictionalized version of several real cases based on double indemnity insurance policies. In this chapter, we follow Beth's dispute with Coastal from initial interview through appeal, using it to examine three fundamental areas of law: the structure of our court systems, litigation, and alternative dispute resolution (ADR).

When Beth Smiles meets with her lawyer, Chris Pruitt brings a second attorney from his firm, Janet Booker, who is an experienced **litigator;** that is, a lawyer who handles court cases. If they file a lawsuit, Janet will be in charge, so Chris wants her there for the first meeting. Janet probes about Tony's home life, the status of the business, his personal finances, everything. Beth becomes upset that Janet doesn't seem sympathetic, but Chris explains that Janet is doing her job: she needs all the information, good and bad.

Litigation versus Alternative Dispute Resolution

Janet starts thinking about the two methods of dispute resolution: litigation and alternative dispute resolution. **Litigation** refers to lawsuits, the process of filing claims in court, trying the case, and living with the court's ruling. **Alternative dispute resolution** is any other formal or informal process used to settle disputes without resorting to a trial. It is increasingly popular with corporations and individuals alike because it is generally cheaper and faster than litigation.

Litigation
The process of resolving disputes in court.

Alternative dispute resolution
Resolving disputes out of court, through formal or informal processes.

ALTERNATIVE DISPUTE RESOLUTION

Janet Booker knows that even after expert legal help, vast expense, and years of work, litigation may leave clients unsatisfied. If she can use alternative dispute resolution (ADR) to create a mutually satisfactory solution in a few months, for a fraction of the cost, she is glad to do it. In most cases the parties **negotiate,** whether personally or through lawyers. Fortunately, the great majority of disputes are resolved this way. Negotiation often begins as soon as a dispute arises and may last a few days or several years.

Mediation

Mediation is the fastest growing method of dispute resolution in the United States. Here, a neutral person, called a mediator, attempts to guide the two disputing parties toward a voluntary settlement.

A mediator does not render a decision in the dispute but uses a variety of skills to move the parties toward agreement. Mediators must earn the trust of both parties, listen closely, defuse anger and fear, explore common ground, cajole the parties into different perspectives, and build the will to settle. Good mediators do not need a law degree, but they must have a sense of humor and low blood pressure.

Of all forms of dispute resolution, mediation probably offers the strongest "win-win" potential. Because the goal is voluntary settlement, neither party needs to fear that it will end up the loser. This is in sharp contrast to litigation, where one party is very likely to lose. Removing the fear of defeat often encourages thinking and talking that are more open and realistic than negotiations held in the midst of a lawsuit. Studies show that more than 75 percent of mediated cases do reach a voluntary settlement.

Mediation
A form of ADR in which a neutral third party guides the disputing parties toward a voluntary settlement.

Arbitration

In this form of ADR, the parties agree to bring in a neutral third party, but with a major difference: the arbitrator has the power to impose an award.

Arbitration
A form of ADR in which a neutral third party has the power to impose a binding decision.

The arbitrator allows each side equal time to present its case and, after deliberation, issues a binding decision, generally without giving reasons. Unlike mediation, arbitration ensures that there will be a final result, although the parties lose control of the outcome. Arbitration is generally faster and cheaper than litigation.

Judge Judy and similar TV shows are examples of arbitration. Before the shows, people involved in a real dispute sign a contract in which they give up the right to go to court over the incident and agree to be bound by the host's decision. Parties in arbitration give up many rights that litigants retain, including discovery. *Discovery*, as we see below, allows the two sides in a lawsuit to obtain documentary and other evidence from the opponent before trial. Arbitration permits both sides to keep secret many files that would have to be divulged in a court case, potentially depriving the opposing side of valuable evidence. A party may have a stronger case than it realizes, and the absence of discovery may permanently deny it that knowledge.

Janet Booker proposes to Coastal Insurance that they use ADR to expedite a decision in their dispute. Coastal rejects the offer. Coastal's lawyer, Rich Stewart, insists that suicide is apparent.

It is a long way to go before trial, but Janet has to prepare her case. The first thing she thinks about is where to file the lawsuit.

COURT SYSTEMS

The United States has over 50 systems of courts. One nationwide system of *federal* courts serves the entire country. In addition, each individual *state*—such as Texas, California, and Florida—has its own court system. The state and federal courts are in different buildings, have different judges, and hear different kinds of cases. Each has special powers and certain limitations.

State Courts

The typical state court system forms a pyramid, as Exhibit 3.1 shows.

TRIAL COURTS

Trial courts
Determine the facts and apply to them the law given by appellate courts.

Almost all cases start in trial courts, the ones endlessly portrayed on television and in film. There is one judge and there will often (but not always) be a jury. This is the only court to hear testimony from witnesses and receive evidence. **Trial courts** determine the facts of a particular dispute and apply to those facts the law given by earlier appellate court decisions.

In the Enviro-Vision dispute, the trial court will decide all important facts that are in dispute. How did Tony Caruso die? Did he drown? Assuming he drowned, was his death an accident or a suicide? Once the jury has decided the facts, it will apply the law to those facts. If Tony Caruso died accidentally, contract law provides that Beth Smiles is entitled to double indemnity benefits. If the jury decides he killed himself, Beth gets nothing.

Jurisdiction
A court's power to hear a case.

Jurisdiction refers to a court's power to hear a case. A plaintiff may start a lawsuit only in a court that has jurisdiction over that kind of case. Some state trial courts have very limited jurisdiction, while others have the power to hear almost any case. In Exhibit 3.1, notice that some courts have power only to hear cases of small claims, domestic relations, and so forth. Courts must have two types of jurisdiction.

Subject matter jurisdiction means that a court has the authority to hear a particular type of case. In addition to subject matter jurisdiction, courts must also have **personal jurisdiction** over the defendant. Personal jurisdiction is the legal authority to require the defendant to stand trial, pay judgments, and the like. Personal jurisdiction generally exists if:

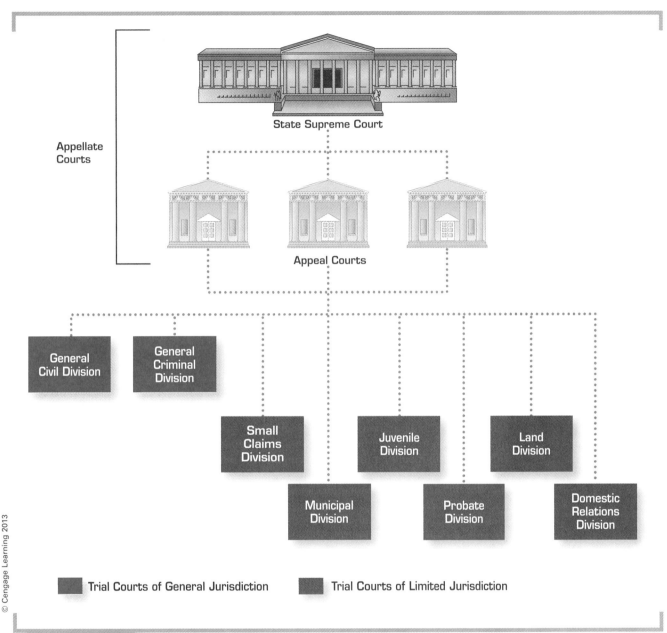

Appellate Courts

State Supreme Court

Appeal Courts

General Civil Division

General Criminal Division

Small Claims Division

Juvenile Division

Land Division

Municipal Division

Probate Division

Domestic Relations Division

■ Trial Courts of General Jurisdiction   ■ Trial Courts of Limited Jurisdiction

EXHIBIT 3.1   A trial court determines facts, while an appeals court ensures that the lower court correctly applied the law to those facts.

- The defendant is a resident of the state in which a lawsuit is filed; or

- The defendant files documents in court, such as an answer to the complaint; or

- A **summons** is *served* on a defendant. A summons is the court's written notice that a lawsuit has been filed against the defendant. The summons must be delivered to the defendant when she is physically within the state in which the lawsuit is filed; or

- A **long-arm statute** applies. These statutes typically claim jurisdiction over someone who does not live in a state but commits a tort, signs a contract, causes foreseeable harm, or conducts "regular business activities" there. Under the Due Process Clause of the Constitution, courts can use long-arm statutes only if a defendant has had minimum contacts with a state. In other words, it is unfair to require a defendant to stand trial in another state if he has had no meaningful interaction with that state.

In the following Landmark Case, the Supreme Court explains its views on this important constitutional issue.

Landmark Case

INTERNATIONAL SHOE CO. v. STATE OF WASHINGTON

326 U.S. 310
Supreme Court of the United States, 1945

Facts: Although International Shoe manufactured footwear only in St. Louis, Missouri, it sold its products nationwide. It did not have offices or warehouses in the state of Washington, but it did send about a dozen salespeople there. The salespeople rented space in hotels and businesses, displayed sample products, and took orders. They were not authorized to collect payment from customers.

When the State of Washington sought contributions to the state's unemployment fund, International Shoe refused to pay. Washington sued. The company argued that it was not engaged in business in the state and, therefore, that Washington courts had no jurisdiction over it.

The Supreme Court of Washington ruled that International Shoe did have sufficient contacts with the state to justify a lawsuit there. International Shoe appealed to the United States Supreme Court.

CASE SUMMARY

operated continuously in Washington for many years. Their presence has been more than occasional or casual. And the agents' activities have generated a significant number of sales for the company. Washington's collection action is directly related to commercially valuable activities that took place within the state's borders.

Due Process merely requires reasonable fairness. International Shoe has benefitted greatly from activities in Washington, and it faces no injustice if this suit proceeds. The minimum contacts doctrine is satisfied.

Affirmed.

Issue: *Did International Shoe have sufficient minimum contacts in the state of Washington to permit jurisdiction there?*

Decision: Yes, the company had minimum contacts with the state.

Reasoning: Agents for International Shoe have

APPELLATE COURTS

Appellate courts

Higher courts which generally accept the facts provided by trial courts and review the record for legal errors.

Appellant

The party filing an appeal of a trial verdict.

Appellate courts are entirely different from trial courts. Three or more judges hear the case. There are no juries, ever. These courts do not hear witnesses or take new evidence. They hear appeals of cases already tried below. **Appellate courts** generally accept the facts given to them by trial courts and review the trial record to see if the court made errors of law.

An appellate court reviews the trial record to make sure that the lower court correctly applied the law to the facts. If the trial court made an error of law, the appeal court may require a new trial. Suppose the jury concludes that Tony Caruso committed suicide but votes to award Enviro-Vision $1 million because it feels sorry for Beth Smiles. That is an error of law; if Tony committed suicide, Beth is entitled to nothing. An appellate court will reverse the decision, declaring Coastal the victor.

The party that loses at the trial court generally is entitled to be heard at the intermediate court of appeals. The party filing the appeal is the **appellant**. The party opposing the appeal (because it won at trial) is the **appellee**. A party that loses at the court of appeals may *ask* the state supreme court to hear an appeal, but the state's highest court may choose not to accept the case.

Appellee
The party opposing an appeal.

Federal Courts

As discussed in Chapter 1, federal courts are established by the United States Constitution, which limits what kinds of cases can be brought in any federal court. For our purposes, two kinds of civil lawsuits are permitted in federal court: federal question cases and diversity cases.

FEDERAL QUESTION CASES

A claim based on the United States Constitution, a federal statute, or a federal treaty is called a **federal question case**.[1] Federal courts have jurisdiction over these cases. If the Environmental Protection Agency (EPA), a part of the federal government, orders Logging Company not to cut in a particular forest, and Logging Company claims that the agency has wrongly deprived it of its property, that suit is based on a federal statute (a law passed by Congress) and is thus a federal question. Enviro-Vision's potential suit merely concerns an insurance contract. The federal district court has no federal question jurisdiction over the case.

Federal question case
A claim based on the United States Constitution, a federal statute, or a federal treaty.

DIVERSITY CASES

Even if no federal law is at issue, federal courts have jurisdiction when (1) the plaintiff and defendant are citizens of different states and (2) the amount in dispute exceeds $75,000. The theory behind diversity jurisdiction is that courts of one state might be biased against citizens of another state. To ensure fairness, the parties have the option to use a federal court as a neutral playing field.

Enviro-Vision is located in Oregon and Coastal Insurance is incorporated in Georgia.[2] They are citizens of different states and the amount in dispute far exceeds $75,000. Janet could file this case in United States District Court based on diversity jurisdiction.

Diversity case
A lawsuit in which the plaintiff and defendant are citizens of different states *and* the amount in dispute exceeds $75,000.

TRIAL COURTS

United States District Courts are the primary trial courts in the federal system. The nation is divided into about 94 districts, and each has a district court. States with smaller populations have one district, while those with larger populations have several. There are also specialized trial courts such as Bankruptcy Court, Tax Court, and others, which are, you will be happy to know, beyond the scope of this book.

APPELLATE COURTS

United States Courts of Appeals These are the intermediate courts of appeals. As the map below shows, they are divided into "circuits," most of which are geographical areas. For example, an appeal from the Northern District of Illinois would go to the Court of Appeals for the Seventh Circuit.

United States Supreme Court This is the highest court in the country. There are nine justices on the Court. One justice is the chief justice and the other eight are associate justices. When they decide a case, each justice casts an equal vote.

---

[1] 28 U.S.C. §1331 governs federal question jurisdiction and 28 U.S.C. §1332 covers diversity jurisdiction.
[2] For diversity purposes, a corporation is a citizen of the state in which it is incorporated and the state in which it has its principal place of business.

EXAM *Strategy*

Question: Mark has sued Janelle based on the state common law of negligence. He is testifying in court, explaining how Janelle backed a rented truck out of her driveway and slammed into his Lamborghini, doing $82,000 in damages. Where would this take place?

A   State appeals court

B   United States Court of Appeals

C   State trial court

D   Federal District Court

E   Either state trial court or Federal District Court

Strategy: The question asks about trial and appellate courts, and also about state versus federal courts. One issue at a time, please. What are the different functions of trial and appellate courts? *Trial* courts use witnesses, and often juries, to resolve factual disputes. *Appellate* courts never hear witnesses and never have juries. Applying that distinction to these facts tells us whether we are in a trial or appeals court.

   State trial courts may hear lawsuits on virtually any issue. *Federal District Courts* may only hear two kinds of cases: federal question (those involving a statute or constitutional provision); or diversity (where the parties are from different states *and* the amount at issue is $75,000 or higher). Apply what we know to the facts here.

Result: We are in a trial court because Mark is testifying. Could we be in Federal District Court? No. The suit is based on state common law. This is not a diversity case because the parties live in the same state, and this is not an appeal of a previous trial, so this is not an appeals court.

   Janet Booker decides to file the Enviro-Vision suit in the Oregon trial court. She thinks that a state court judge may take the issue more seriously than a Federal District Court judge.

LITIGATION

Pleadings

Pleadings

The documents that begin a lawsuit, consisting of a complaint, the answer, and sometimes a reply.

The documents that begin a lawsuit are called the **pleadings**. The most important are the complaint and the answer.

COMPLAINT

Complaint

The pleading that starts a lawsuit, this is a short statement of the facts alleged by the plaintiff, and his or her legal claims.

The plaintiff files in court a **complaint**, which is a short, plain statement of the facts she is alleging and the legal claims she is making. The purpose of the complaint is to inform the defendant of the general nature of the claims and the need to come into court and protect his interests.

   Janet Booker files the complaint, as shown below. Because Enviro-Vision is a partnership, she files the suit on behalf of Beth, personally.

STATE OF OREGON
CIRCUIT COURT

Multnomah County

Civil Action No. _____

_____
Elizabeth Smiles,
Plaintiff

JURY TRIAL DEMANDED

v.
Coastal Insurance Company, Inc.,
Defendant

_____

COMPLAINT

Plaintiff Elizabeth Smiles states that:

1. She is a citizen of Multnomah County, Oregon.
2. Defendant Coastal Insurance Company, Inc., is incorporated under the laws of Georgia and has as its usual place of business 148 Thrift Street, Savannah, Georgia.
3. On or about July 5, 2012, plaintiff Smiles ("Smiles"), Defendant Coastal Insurance Co, Inc. ("Coastal") and Anthony Caruso entered into an insurance contract ("the contract"), a copy of which is annexed hereto as Exhibit "A." This contract was signed by all parties or their authorized agents, in Multnomah County, Oregon.
4. The contract obligates Coastal to pay to Smiles the sum of two million dollars ($2 million) if Anthony Caruso should die accidentally.
5. On or about September 15, 2012, Anthony Caruso accidentally drowned and died while swimming.
6. Coastal has refused to pay any sum pursuant to the contract.
7. Coastal has knowingly, willingly and unreasonably refused to honor its obligations under the contract.

WHEREFORE, plaintiff Elizabeth Smiles demands judgment against defendant Coastal for all monies due under the contract; demands triple damages for Coastal's knowing, willing, and unreasonable refusal to honor its obligations; and demands all costs and attorney's fees, with interest.
ELIZABETH SMILES,
By her attorney,
[Signed]
Janet Booker
Pruitt, Booker & Bother
983 Joy Avenue
Portland, OR
October 18, 2012

Answer

Coastal has 20 days in which to file an answer. Coastal's **answer** is a brief reply to each of the allegations in the complaint. The answer tells the court and the plaintiff exactly what issues are in dispute. Since Coastal admits that the parties entered into the contract that Beth claims they did, there is no need for her to prove that in court. The court can focus its attention on the issue that Coastal disputes: whether Tony Caruso died accidentally.

If the defendant fails to answer in time, the plaintiff will ask for a **default judgment**, meaning a decision that the plaintiff wins without a trial. Recently, two men sued Pepsi, claiming that the company stole the idea for Aquafina water from them. They argued that they should receive a portion of the profits for every bottle of Aquafina ever sold.

Pepsi failed to file a timely answer, and the judge entered a default judgment in the amount of $1.26 billion. On appeal, the default judgment was overturned and Pepsi was able to escape paying the massive sum, but other defendants are sometimes not so lucky.

It is important to respond to courts on time.

Answer
The defendant's response to the complaint.

Default judgment
A decision that the plaintiff in a case wins without going to trial.

CLASS ACTIONS

Class action
A suit filed by a group of plaintiffs with related claims.

Suppose Janet uncovers evidence that Coastal denies 80 percent of all life insurance claims, calling them suicide. She could ask the court to permit a **class action**. If the court granted her request, she would represent the entire group of plaintiffs, including those who are unaware of the lawsuit or even unaware they were harmed. Class actions can give the plaintiffs much greater leverage, since the defendant's potential liability is vastly increased. Because Janet has no such evidence, she decides not to pursue a class action.

DISCOVERY

Discovery
The pre-trial opportunity for both parties to gather information relevant to the case.

Discovery is the critical, pre-trial opportunity for both parties to learn the strengths and weaknesses of the opponent's case.

The theory behind civil litigation is that the best outcome is a negotiated settlement and that parties will move toward agreement if they understand the opponent's case. That is likeliest to occur if both sides have an opportunity to examine the evidence their opponent will bring to trial. Further, if a case does go all the way to trial, efficient and fair litigation cannot take place in a courtroom filled with surprises. On television dramas, witnesses say astonishing things that amaze the courtroom. In real trials, the lawyers know in advance the answers to practically all questions asked because discovery has allowed them to see the opponent's documents and question its witnesses. The following are the most important forms of discovery.

Interrogatories These are written questions that the opposing party must answer, in writing, under oath.

Depositions These provide a chance for one party's lawyer to question the other party, or a potential witness, under oath. The person being questioned is the **deponent**. Lawyers for both parties are present.

Deponent
The person being questioned in a deposition.

Production of Documents and Things Each side may ask the other side to produce relevant documents for inspection and copying; to produce physical objects, such as part of a car alleged to be defective; and for permission to enter on land to make an inspection, for example, at the scene of an accident.

Physical and Mental Examination A party may ask the court to order an examination of the other party, if his physical or mental condition is relevant, for example, in a case of medical malpractice.

Janet Booker begins her discovery with interrogatories. Her goal is to learn Coastal's basic position and factual evidence and then follow up with more detailed questioning during depositions. Her interrogatories ask for every fact Coastal relied on in denying the claim. She asks for the names of all witnesses, the identity of all documents, the description of all things or objects that they considered. She requests the names of all corporate officers who played any role in the decision and of any expert witnesses Coastal plans to call.

Coastal has 30 days to answer Janet's interrogatories. Before it responds, Coastal mails to Janet a notice of deposition, stating its intention to depose Beth Smiles. Beth and Janet will go to the office of Coastal's lawyer, and Beth will answer questions under oath. But at the same time Coastal sends this notice, it sends 25 other notices of deposition. It will depose Karen Caruso as soon as Beth's deposition is over. Coastal also plans to depose all seven employees of Enviro-Vision; three neighbors who lived near Tony and Karen's beach house; two policemen who participated in the search; the doctor and two nurses involved in the case; Tony's physician; Jerry Johnson, Tony's tennis partner; Craig Bergson, a college roommate; a couple who had dinner with Tony and Karen a week before his death; and several other people.

Rich, the Coastal lawyer, proceeds to take Beth's deposition. It takes two full days. He asks about Enviro-Vision's past and present. He learns that Tony appeared to have won their biggest contract ever from Rapid City, Oregon, but that he then lost it when he had a fight with Rapid City's mayor. He inquires into Tony's mood, learns that he was depressed, and probes in every direction he can to find evidence of suicidal motivation. Janet and Rich argue frequently over questions and whether Beth should have to answer them. At times, Janet is persuaded and permits Beth to answer; other times, she instructs Beth not to answer. For example, toward the end of the second day, Rich asks Beth whether she and Tony had been sexually involved. Janet instructs Beth not to answer. This fight necessitates a trip into court. As both lawyers know, **the parties are entitled to discover anything that could reasonably lead to valid evidence.** Rich wants his questions answered and files a motion to compel discovery. The judge will have to decide whether Rich's questions are reasonable.

A **motion** is a formal request to the court. Before, during and after trial, both parties will file many motions. A **motion to compel discovery** is a request to the court for an order requiring the other side to answer discovery. The judge rules that Beth must discuss Tony's romantic life only if Coastal has evidence that he was involved with someone outside his marriage. Because the company lacks any such evidence, the judge denies Coastal's motion.

At the same time, the judge hears one of Beth's **motions for a protective order.** Beth claims that Rich has scheduled too many depositions; the time and expense are a huge burden to a small company. The judge limits Rich to 10 depositions. Rich cancels several depositions, including that of Craig Bergson, Tony's old roommate. As we will see, Craig knows crucial facts about this case, and Rich's decision not to depose him will have major consequences.

E-Discovery The biggest change in litigation in the last decade is the explosive rise of electronic discovery (e-discovery). Companies send hundreds, thousands, or even millions of emails every day. Many have attachments that are sometimes hundreds of pages long. In addition, businesses large and small have vast amounts of data stored electronically. All this information is potentially subject to discovery.

It is enormously time-consuming and expensive for companies to locate all the relevant material, separate it from irrelevant or confidential matter, and furnish it. A firm may be obligated to furnish *millions* of emails to the opposing party. In one recent case, a defendant had to pay 31 lawyers full time for six months just to wade through an ocean of e-documents and figure out which had to be supplied and how to produce it. Not surprisingly, this data eruption has created a new industry: high-tech companies that assist law firms in finding, sorting, and delivering electronic data.

Who is to say what must be supplied? What if an email string contains individual emails that are clearly privileged (meaning a party need not divulge them), but others that are not privileged? May a company refuse to furnish the entire string? Many will try. However, some courts have ruled that companies seeking to protect email strings must create a log describing every individual email and allow the court to determine which are privileged.[3]

When the cost of furnishing the data becomes burdensome, who should pay, the party seeking the information or the one supplying it? In a recent $4 million corporate lawsuit, the defendant turned over 3,000 emails and 211,000 other documents. But the trial judge noted that many of the email attachments—sometimes 12 to an email—had gone missing, and it required the company to produce them. The defendant protested that finding the attachments would cost an additional $206,000. The judge ordered the company to do it and bear the full cost.

Both sides in litigation sometimes use gamesmanship during discovery. Thus, if an individual sues a large corporation, the company may deliberately make discovery so expensive that the plaintiff cannot afford the legal fees. And if a plaintiff has a poor case, he might intentionally try to make the discovery process more expensive than his settlement offer.

Motion
A formal request to the court.

---

[3]*Universal Service Fund Telephone Billing Practices Litigation,* 232 F.R.D. 669 (D. Kan. 2005).

Even if a defendant expects to win at trial, an offer to settle a case for $50,000 can look like a bargain if discovery alone will cost $100,000. Some defendants refuse, but others are more pragmatic.

The following case illustrates a common discovery problem: refusal by one side to appear for deposition. Did the defendant cynically believe that long delays would win the day, given that the plaintiff was 78 years old? What can a court do in such a case?

STINTON V. ROBIN'S WOOD, INC.

45 A.D. 3d 203, 842 NYS2d 477
New York App. Div., 2007

CASE SUMMARY

Facts: Ethel Flanzraich, 78 years old, slipped and fell on the steps of property owned by Robin's Wood. She broke her left leg and left arm. Flanzraich sued, claiming that Robin's Wood caused her fall by negligently painting the stairs. The defendant's employee, Anthony Monforte, had painted the steps. In its answer to the complaint, Robin's Wood denied all the significant allegations.

During a preliminary conference with the trial judge, the parties agreed to hold depositions of both parties on August 4. Flanzraich appeared for deposition, but Robin's Wood did not furnish its employee, Monforte, nor did it offer any other company representative. The court then ordered the deposition of the defendant to take place the following April 2. Again, Robin's Wood produced neither Monforte nor anyone else. On July 16, the court ordered the defendant to produce its representative within 30 days. Once more, no one showed up for deposition.

On August 18—over *one year* after the original deposition date—Flanzraich moved to strike the defendant's answer, meaning that the plaintiff would win by default. The company argued that it had made diligent efforts to locate Monforte and force him to appear. However, all the letters sent to Monforte were addressed care of Robin's Wood. Finally, the company stated that it no longer employed Monforte.

The trial judge granted the motion to strike the answer. That meant that Robin's Wood was liable for Flanzraich's fall. The only remaining issue was damages. The court determined that Robin's Wood owed $22,631

for medical expenses, $150,000 for past pain and suffering, and $300,000 for future pain and suffering. One day later, Flanzraich died of other causes. Robin's Wood appealed.

Issue: *Did the trial court abuse its discretion by striking the defendant's answer?*

Decision: No, the trial court did not abuse its discretion. Affirmed.

Reasoning: Normally, a lawsuit must be decided on the evidence and reasonable conclusions. However, if a defendant fails to respond to discovery requests, and its failure is willful, extreme, and disrespectful of the court, a trial judge may strike the defendant's answer altogether.

Robin's Wood failed to comply with three orders to appear for deposition. The company never produced Monforte while he worked there. It failed to notify the plaintiff when Monforte left, and it made no effort to produce another employee for deposition. The company did everything it could to ensure that Flanzraich would never speak with its worker. Had the company at least produced another representative, Flanzraich could have learned where Monforte had gone because the record indicates Robin's Wood knew his whereabouts.

These delays were particularly menacing to Flanzraich's case because she was elderly—a fact well known to the company. A trial judge may respond to such offensive conduct with appropriate orders.

SUMMARY JUDGMENT

Summary judgment
A ruling that no trial is necessary because essential facts are not in dispute.

When discovery is completed, both sides may consider seeking summary judgment. **Summary judgment** is a ruling by the court that no trial is necessary because some essential facts are not in dispute. The purpose of a trial is to determine the facts of the case; that is, to decide who did what to whom, why, when, and with what consequences. If relevant facts are not in dispute, then there is no need for a trial.

In the following case, the defendant won summary judgment, meaning that the case never went to trial. And yet, this was only the beginning of trouble for that defendant, Bill Clinton.

JONES V. CLINTON

990 F. Supp. 657, 1998 U.S. Dist. LEXIS 3902
United States District Court for the Eastern District of Arkansas, 1998

CASE SUMMARY

Facts: In 1991, Bill Clinton was governor of Arkansas. Paula Jones worked for a state agency, the Arkansas Industrial Development Commission (AIDC). When Clinton became president, Jones sued him, claiming that he had sexually harassed her. She alleged that in May 1991, the governor arranged for her to meet him in a hotel room in Little Rock, Arkansas. When they were alone, he put his hand on her leg and slid it toward her pelvis. She escaped from his grasp, exclaimed, "What are you doing?" and said she was "not that kind of girl." Upset and confused, she sat on a sofa near the door. She claimed that Clinton approached her, "lowered his trousers and underwear, exposed his penis, and told her to kiss it." Jones was horrified, jumped up, and said she had to leave. Clinton responded by saying, "Well, I don't want to make you do anything you don't want to do," and pulled his pants up. He added that if she got in trouble for leaving work, Jones should "have Dave call me immediately and I'll take care of it." He also said, "You are smart. Let's keep this between ourselves." Jones remained at AIDC until February 1993, when she moved to California because of her husband's job transfer.

President Clinton denied all the allegations. He also filed for summary judgment, claiming that Jones had not alleged facts that justified a trial. Jones opposed the motion for summary judgment.

Issue: *Was Clinton entitled to summary judgment, or was Jones entitled to a trial?*

Decision: Jones failed to make out a claim of sexual harassment. Summary judgment was granted for the president.

Reasoning: To establish this type of sexual harassment case, a plaintiff must show that her refusal to submit to unwelcome sexual advances resulted in specific harm to her job.

Jones received every merit increase and cost-of-living allowance for which she was eligible. Her only job transfer involved a minor change in working conditions, with no reduction in pay or benefits. Jones claims that she was obligated to sit in a less private area, often with no work to do, and was the only female employee not to receive flowers on Secretary's Day. However, even if these allegations are true, all are trivial and none is sufficient to create a sexual harassment suit. Jones has demonstrated no specific harm to her job.

In other words, the court acknowledged that there were factual disputes but concluded that even if Jones proved each of her allegations, she would still lose the case because her allegations fell short of a legitimate case of sexual harassment. Jones appealed the case. Later the same year, as the appeal was pending and the House of Representatives was considering whether to impeach President Clinton, the parties settled the dispute. Clinton, without acknowledging any of the allegations, agreed to pay Jones $850,000 to drop the suit.

Janet and Rich each consider moving for summary judgment, but both correctly decide that they would lose. There is one major fact in dispute: did Tony Caruso commit suicide? Only a jury may decide that issue. As long as there is some evidence supporting each side of a key factual dispute, the court may not grant summary judgment.

EXAM *Strategy*

Question: You are a judge. Mel has sued Kevin, claiming that while Kevin was drunk, he negligently drove his car down Mel's street and destroyed rare trees on a lot that Mel owns, next to his house. Mel's complaint stated that three witnesses, at a bar, saw Kevin take at least eight drinks less than an hour before the damage was done. In Kevin's answer, he denied causing the damage and denied being in the bar that night.

Kevin's lawyer has moved for summary judgment. He proves that three weeks before the alleged accident, Mel sold the lot to Tatiana.

Mel's lawyer opposes summary judgment. He produces a security camera tape proving that Kevin was in the bar, drinking beer, 34 minutes before the damage was done. He produces a signed statement from Sandy, a landscape gardener who lives across the street from the scene. Sandy states that she heard a crash, hurried to the windows, and saw Kevin's car weaving away from the damaged trees. She is a landscape gardener and estimates the tree damage at $30,000 to $40,000. How should you rule on the motion?

Strategy: Do not be fooled by red herrings about Kevin's drinking or the value of the trees. Stick to the question: should you grant summary judgment? Trials are necessary to resolve disputes about essential factual issues. Summary judgment is appropriate when some essential facts are not disputed. Is there an essential fact not in dispute? Find it. Apply the rule. Being a judge is easy!

Result: It makes no difference whether Kevin was drunk or sober, whether he caused the harm, or whether he was at home in bed. Mel did not own the property at the time of the accident. He cannot win. You should grant Kevin's summary judgment motion.

Well over 90 percent of all lawsuits are settled before trial. But the parties in the Enviro-Vision dispute are unable to compromise and are headed for trial.

> Well over 90 percent of all lawsuits are settled before trial.

Adversary system
A system based on the assumption that if two sides present their best case before a neutral party, the truth will be established.

TRIAL

Adversary System

Our system of justice assumes that the best way to bring out the truth is for the two contesting sides to present the strongest case possible to a neutral fact-finder. Each side presents its witnesses and then the opponent has a chance to cross-examine. The **adversary system** presumes that by putting a witness on the stand and letting both lawyers question her, the truth will emerge.

The judge runs the trial. Each lawyer sits at a large table near the front. Beth, looking tense and unhappy, sits with Janet. Rich Stewart sits with a Coastal executive. In the back of the courtroom are benches for the public. Today, there are only a few spectators. One is Tony's old roommate, Craig Bergson, who has a special interest in the trial.

Right to Jury Trial

Not all cases are tried to a jury. As a general rule, both plaintiff and defendant have a right to demand a jury trial when the lawsuit is for money damages. For example, in a typical contract lawsuit, such as Beth's insurance claim, both plaintiff and defendant have a jury trial right whether they are in state or federal court. Even in such a case, though, the parties may waive the jury right, meaning they agree to try the case to a judge. Also, if the plaintiff is seeking an equitable remedy, such as an injunction (an order not to do something), there is no jury right for either party.

Although jury selection for some cases takes many days, in the Enviro-Vision case the first day of the hearing ends with the jury selected. In the hallway outside the court, Rich offers Janet $200,000 to settle. Janet reports the offer to Beth and they agree to reject it. Craig Bergson drives home, emotionally confused. Only three weeks before his death, Tony had accidentally met his old roommate and they had had several drinks. Craig believes that what Tony told him answers the riddle of this case.

Opening Statements

The next day, each attorney makes an opening statement to the jury, summarizing the proof he or she expects to offer, with the plaintiff going first. Janet focuses on Tony's successful life, his business and strong marriage, and the tragedy of his accidental death.

Rich works hard to establish a friendly rapport with the jury. If members of the jury like him, they will tend to pay more attention to his presentation of evidence. He expresses regret about the death. Nonetheless, suicide is a clear exclusion from the policy. If insurance companies are forced to pay claims they did not bargain for, everyone's insurance rates will go up.

Burden of Proof

In civil cases, the plaintiff has the **burden of proof**. That means that the plaintiff must convince the jury that its version of the case is correct; the defendant is not obligated to disprove the allegations.

The plaintiff's burden in a civil lawsuit is to prove its case by a **preponderance of the evidence**. The plaintiff must convince the jury that his or her version of the facts is at least *slightly* more likely than the defendant's version. Some courts describe this as a "51–49" persuasion, that is, that plaintiff's proof must "just tip" credibility in its favor. By contrast, in a criminal case, the prosecution must demonstrate **beyond a reasonable doubt** that the defendant is guilty. The burden of proof in a criminal case is much tougher because the likely consequences are, too. See Exhibit 3.2.

Burden of proof
The obligation to convince the jury that a party's version of the case is correct.

Preponderance of the evidence
The standard of proof required for a civil case.

Beyond a reasonable doubt
The government's burden in a criminal prosecution.

Plaintiff's Case

Since the plaintiff has the burden of proof, Janet puts in her case first. She wants to prove two things. First, that Tony died. That is easy, since the death certificate clearly demonstrates it and since Coastal does not seriously contest it. Second, in order to win double indemnity damages, she must show that the death was accidental. She will do this with the testimony of the witnesses she calls, one after the other. Her first witness is Beth. When a lawyer asks questions of her own witness, it is **direct examination**. Janet brings out all the evidence she wants the jury to hear: that the business was basically sound, though temporarily troubled, that Tony was a hard worker, why the company took out life insurance policies, and so forth.

Direct examination
is when a lawyer asks questions of his or her own witness.

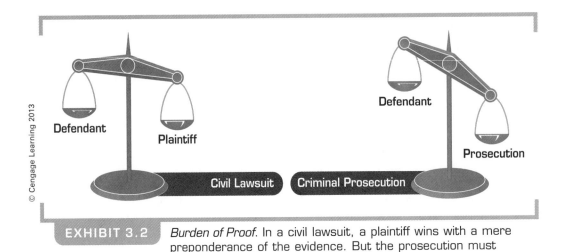

© Cengage Learning 2013

EXHIBIT 3.2	*Burden of Proof.* In a civil lawsuit, a plaintiff wins with a mere preponderance of the evidence. But the prosecution must persuade a jury beyond a reasonable doubt in order to win a criminal conviction.

Cross-examination

A lawyer asks questions of an opposing witness.

Then Rich has a chance to **cross-examine** Beth, which means to ask questions of an opposing witness. He will try to create doubt in the jury's mind. He asks Beth only questions for which he is certain of the answers, based on discovery. Rich gets Beth to admit that the firm was not doing well the year of Tony's death; that Tony had lost the best client the firm ever had; that Beth had reduced salaries; and that Tony had been depressed about business.

Janet uses her other witnesses, Tony's friends, family, and coworkers, to fortify the impression that his death was accidental.

Defendant's Case

Rich now puts in his case, exactly as Janet did, except that he happens to have fewer witnesses. He calls the examining doctor, who admits that Tony could have committed suicide by swimming out too far. On cross-examination, Janet gets the doctor to acknowledge that he has no idea whether Tony intentionally drowned. Rich also questions several neighbors as to how depressed Tony had seemed and how unusual it was that Blue was tied up. Some of the witnesses Rich deposed, such as the tennis partner Jerry Johnson, have nothing that will help Coastal's case, so he does not call them.

Craig Bergson, sitting in the back of the courtroom, thinks how different the trial would have been had he been called as a witness. When he and Tony had the fateful drink, Tony had been distraught: business was terrible, he was involved in an extramarital affair that he could not end, and he saw no way out of his problems. He had no one to talk to and had been hugely relieved to speak with Craig. Several times Tony had said, "I just can't go on like this. I don't want to, anymore." Craig thought Tony seemed suicidal and urged him to see a therapist Craig knew. Tony had said that it was good advice, but Craig is unsure whether Tony sought any help.

This evidence would have affected the case. Had Rich Stewart known of the conversation, he would have deposed Craig and the therapist. Coastal's case would have been far stronger, perhaps overwhelming. But Craig's evidence will never be heard. Facts are critical. Rich's decision to depose other witnesses and omit Craig may influence the verdict more than any rule of law.

Closing Argument

Both lawyers sum up their case to the jury, explaining how they hope the jury will interpret what they have heard. Judge Rowland instructs the jury as to its duty. He tells them that they are to evaluate the case based only on the evidence they heard at trial, relying on their own experience and common sense.

He explains the law and the burden of proof, telling the jury that it is Beth's obligation to prove her case. If Beth has proven that Tony died by means other than suicide but not by accident, she is entitled to $1 million; if she has proven that his death was accidental, she is entitled to $2 million. However, if Coastal has proven suicide, Beth receives nothing. Finally, he states that if they are unable to decide between accidental death and suicide, there is a legal presumption that it was accidental. Rich asks Judge Rowland to rephrase the "legal presumption" part, but the judge declines.

Verdict

The jury deliberates informally, with all jurors entitled to voice their opinion. Some deliberations take two hours; some take two weeks. Many states require a unanimous verdict; others require only, for example, a 10–2 vote in civil cases.

This case presents a close call. No one saw Tony die. Yet even though they cannot know with certainty, the jury's decision will probably be the final word on whether he took his own life. After a day and a half of deliberating, the jury notifies the judge that it has reached a verdict. Rich Stewart quickly makes a new offer: $350,000. The two sides have the right to settle up until the moment when the last appeal is decided. Beth hesitates but turns it down.

The judge summons the lawyers to court, and Beth goes as well. The judge asks the foreman if the jury has reached a decision. He states that it has: the jury finds that Tony Caruso drowned accidentally and awards Beth Smiles $2 million.

APPEALS

Two days later, Rich files an appeal to the court of appeal. The same day, he phones Janet and increases his settlement offer to $425,000. Beth is tempted but wants Janet's advice. Janet says the risks of an appeal are that the court will order a new trial, and they would start all over. But to accept this offer is to forfeit over $1.5 million. Beth is unsure what to do. The firm desperately needs cash now, and appeals may take years. Janet suggests they wait until oral argument, another eight months.

Rich files a brief arguing that there were two basic errors at the trial: first, that the jury's verdict is clearly contrary to the evidence; and second, that the judge gave the wrong instructions to the jury. Janet files a reply brief, opposing Rich on both issues. In her brief, Janet cites many cases that she claims are **precedent**: earlier decisions by the state supreme court on similar or identical issues.

Appeal Court Options

The court of appeal can **affirm** the trial court, allowing the decision to stand. The court may **modify** the decision, for example, by affirming that the plaintiff wins but decreasing the size of the award. (That is unlikely here; Beth is entitled to $2 million or nothing.) The court might **reverse and remand**, meaning it nullifies the lower court's decision and returns the case to the trial court for a new trial. Or it could simply **reverse**, turning the loser (Coastal) into the winner, with no new trial.

Precedent
Earlier decisions by a court on similar or identical issues, on which subsequent court decisions can be based.

Affirm
To allow a court decision to stand as is.

Modify
To let a court decision stand, but with changes.

Reverse and remand
To nullify a lower court's decision and return a case to trial.

Reverse
To rule that the loser in a previous case wins, with no new trial.

Janet and Beth talk. Beth is very anxious and wants to settle. She does not want to wait four or five months, only to learn that they must start all over. With Beth's approval, Janet phones Rich and offers to settle for $1.2 million. Rich snorts, "Yeah, right." Then he snaps, "$750,000. Take it or leave it. Final offer." After a short conversation with her client, Janet calls back and accepts the offer.

LITIGATION

1. PLEADINGS	**2. DISCOVERY**	**3. PRE-TRIAL MOTIONS**
Complaint	Interrogatories	Class action
Answer	Depositions	Summary judgment
	Production of documents and things	
	Physical and mental examinations	
4. TRIAL	**5. JURY'S ROLE**	**6. APPEALS**
Jury selection	Judge's instructions	Affirm
Opening statements	Deliberation	Modify
Plaintiff's case	Verdict	Reverse
Defendant's case		Remand
Closing argument		

Chapter Conclusion

No one will ever know for sure whether Tony took his own life. Craig Bergson's evidence might have tipped the scales in favor of Coastal. But even that is uncertain, since the jury could have found him unpersuasive. After two years, the case ends with a settlement and uncertainty—both typical lawsuit results. The vaguely unsatisfying feeling about it all is only too common and indicates why litigation is best avoided—by reasonable negotiation.

EXAM REVIEW

1. **ALTERNATIVE DISPUTE RESOLUTION**   Alternative dispute resolution (ADR) is any formal or informal process to settle disputes without a trial. Mediation and arbitration are the two most common forms. (pp. 35–36)

2. **COURT SYSTEMS**   There are many systems of courts, one federal and one in each state. A federal court will hear a case only if it involves a federal question or diversity jurisdiction. (pp. 36–40)

3. **TRIAL AND APPELLATE COURTS**   Trial courts determine facts and apply the law to the facts; appellate courts generally accept the facts found by the trial court and review the trial record for errors of law. (p. 39)

Question: Jade sued Kim, claiming that Kim promised to hire her as an in-store model for $1,000 per week for eight weeks. Kim denied making the promise, and the jury was persuaded: Kim won. Jade has appealed, and she now offers Steve as a witness. Steve will testify to the appeals court that he saw Kim hire Jade as a model, exactly as Jade claimed. Will Jade win on appeal?

Strategy: Before you answer, make sure you know the difference between trial and appellate courts. (See the "Result" at the end of this section.)

4. **PLEADINGS** A complaint and an answer are the two most important pleadings; that is, documents that start a lawsuit. (p. 40)

5. **DISCOVERY** Discovery is the critical pretrial opportunity for both parties to learn the strengths and weaknesses of the opponent's case. Important forms of discovery include interrogatories, depositions, production of documents and objects, physical and mental examinations, and requests for admission. (pp. 42–44)

6. **MOTIONS** A motion is a formal request to the court. (p. 43)

7. **SUMMARY JUDGMENT** Summary judgment is a ruling by the court that no trial is necessary because some essential facts are not in dispute. (pp. 44–45)

8. **RIGHT TO A JURY** Generally, both plaintiff and defendant may demand a jury in any lawsuit for money damages. (p. 47)

9. **BURDEN OF PROOF** The plaintiff's burden of proof in a civil lawsuit is preponderance of the evidence, meaning that its version of the facts must be at least slightly more persuasive than the defendant's. In a criminal prosecution, the government must offer proof beyond a reasonable doubt in order to win a conviction. (p. 47)

Question: In Courtroom 1, Asbury has sued Park, claiming that Park drove his motorcycle negligently and broke Asbury's leg. The jury is deliberating. The jurors have serious doubts about what happened, but they find Asbury's evidence slightly more convincing than Park's. In Courtroom 2, the state is prosecuting Patterson for drug possession. The jury in that case is also deliberating. The jurors have serious doubts about what happened, but they find the government's evidence slightly more convincing than Patterson's. Who will win in each case?

Strategy: A different burden of proof applies in the two cases. (See the "Result" at the end of this section.)

10. **VERDICT** The verdict is the jury's decision in a case. (p. 49)

11. **APPELLATE COURT RULINGS**   An appeal court has many options. The court may affirm, upholding the lower court's decision; modify, changing the verdict but leaving the same party victorious; reverse, transforming the loser into the winner; or reverse and remand, sending the case back to the lower court. (p. 49–50)

> **3. Result:**   Trial courts use witnesses to help resolve factual disputes. Appellate courts review the record to see if there have been errors of law. Appellate courts never hear witnesses, and they will not hear Steve. Jade will lose her appeal.
>
> **9.Result:**   In the civil lawsuit, Asbury must merely convince the jury by a preponderance of the evidence. He has done this, so he will win. In the prosecution, the government must demonstrate proof beyond a reasonable doubt. It has failed to do so, and Patterson will be acquitted.

MATCHING QUESTIONS

Match the following terms with their definitions.

_____ A. Arbitration
_____ B. Diversity jurisdiction
_____ C. Mediation
_____ D. Interrogatories
_____ E. Deposition

1. A pretrial procedure involving written questions to be signed under oath
2. A form of ADR in which the parties themselves craft the settlement
3. A pretrial procedure involving oral questions answered under oath
4. The power of a federal court to hear certain cases between citizens of different states
5. A form of ADR that leads to a binding decision

TRUE/FALSE QUESTIONS

1. T F One advantage of arbitration is that it provides the parties with greater opportunities for discovery than litigation does.
2. T F In the United States, there are many separate courts, but only one court *system*, organized as a pyramid.
3. T F If we are listening to witnesses testify, we must be in a trial court.
4. T F About one-half of all lawsuits settle before trial.
5. T F In a lawsuit for money damages, both the plaintiff and the defendant are generally entitled to a jury.

MULTIPLE-CHOICE QUESTIONS

1. A federal court has the power to hear
   (a) Any case.
   (b) Any case between citizens of different states.
   (c) Any criminal case.
   (d) Appeals of any cases from lower courts.
   (e) Any lawsuit based on a federal statute.

2. Before trial begins, a defendant in a civil lawsuit believes that even if the plaintiff proves everything he has alleged, the law requires the defendant to win. The defendant should
   (a) Request arbitration.
   (b) Request a mandatory verdict.
   (c) Move for recusal.
   (d) Move for summary judgment.
   (e) Demand mediation.

3. In a civil lawsuit,
   (a) The defendant is presumed innocent until proven guilty.
   (b) The defendant is presumed guilty until proven innocent.
   (c) The plaintiff must prove her case by a preponderance of the evidence.
   (d) The plaintiff must prove her case beyond a reasonable doubt.
   (e) The defendant must establish his defenses to the satisfaction of the court.

4. Mack sues Jasmine, claiming that she caused an automobile accident. At trial, Jasmine's lawyer is asking her questions about the accident. This is
   (a) An interrogatory.
   (b) A deposition.
   (c) Direct examination.
   (d) Cross-examination.
   (e) Opening statement.

5. Jurisdiction refers to
   (a) The jury's decision.
   (b) The judge's instructions to the jury.
   (c) Pre-trial questions posed by one attorney to the opposing party.
   (d) The power of a court to hear a particular case.
   (e) A decision by an appellate court to send the case back to the trial court.

ESSAY QUESTIONS

1. State which court(s) have jurisdiction as to each of these lawsuits:

    (a) Pat wants to sue his next-door neighbor Dorothy, claiming that Dorothy promised to sell him the house next door.

    (b) Paula, who lives in New York City, wants to sue Dizzy Movie Theatres, whose principal place of business is Dallas. She claims that while she was in Texas on holiday, she was injured by their negligent maintenance of a stairway. She claims damages of $30,000.

    (c) Phil lives in Tennessee. He wants to sue Dick, who lives in Ohio. Phil claims that Dick agreed to sell him 3,000 acres of farmland in Ohio, worth over $2 million.

    (d) Pete, incarcerated in a federal prison in Kansas, wants to sue the United States government. He claims that his treatment by prison authorities violates three federal statutes.

2. **ETHICS** Trial practice is dramatically different in Britain. The lawyers for the two sides, called *solicitors*, do not go into court. Courtroom work is done by different lawyers, called *barristers*. The barristers are not permitted to interview any witnesses before trial. They know the substance of what each witness intends to say but do not rehearse questions and answers, as in the United States. Which approach do you consider more effective? More ethical? What is the purpose of a trial? Of pretrial preparation?

3. Claus Scherer worked for Rockwell International and was paid over $300,000 per year. Rockwell fired Scherer for alleged sexual harassment of several workers, including his secretary, Terry Pendy. Scherer sued in United States District Court, alleging that Rockwell's real motive in firing him was his high salary.

    Rockwell moved for summary judgment, offering deposition transcripts of various employees. Pendy's deposition detailed instances of harassment, including comments about her body, instances of unwelcome touching, and discussions of extramarital affairs. Another deposition, from a Rockwell employee who investigated the allegations, included complaints by other employees as to Scherer's harassment. In his own deposition, which he offered to oppose summary judgment, Scherer testified that he could not recall the incidents alleged by Pendy and others. He denied generally that he had sexually harassed anyone. The district court granted summary judgment for Rockwell. Was its ruling correct?

4. Annie and Bart are coworkers. In fact, they share a cubicle wall. Recently, they were involved in a fender-bender in the company parking lot. Each blames the other for the accident, and the two have stopped speaking. Would you advise them to try to settle their dispute through arbitration, mediation, or with a traditional lawsuit? Why?

5. Raul lives in Georgia. He creates custom paintings and sells them at a weekly art fair near Atlanta. Sarah lives in Vermont. While on vacation in Georgia, she buys one of Raul's paintings for $500. Soon after she returns home, she decides the painting is ugly, calls Raul, and demands a refund. Raul refuses. Sarah wants to sue him in Vermont. Raul has never been to Vermont and has never sold a painting to anyone else from Vermont. Do Vermont courts have personal jurisdiction over Raul? Why or why not?

Discussion Questions

1. In the Tony Caruso case described throughout this chapter, the defendant offers to settle the case as several stages. Knowing what you do now about litigation, would you have accepted any of the offers? If so, which ones? If not, why not?

2. The burden of proof in civil cases is fairly low. A plaintiff wins a lawsuit if he is 51 percent convincing, and then he collects 100 percent of his damages Is this result reasonable? Should a plaintiff in a civil case be required to prove his case beyond a reasonable doubt? Or, if a plaintiff is only 51 percent convincing, should get only 51 percent of his damages?

3. Large numbers of employees have signed mandatory arbitration agreements in employment contracts. Courts usually uphold these clauses. Imagine that you signed a contract with an arbitration agreement, that the company later mistreated you, and that you could not sue in court. Would you be upset? Or would you be relieved to go through the faster and cheaper process of arbitration?

4. Imagine a state law that allows for residents to sue "spammers"—those who send uninvited commercial messages through email—for $30. One particularly prolific spammer sends messages to hundreds of thousands of people.

   John Smith, a lawyer, signs up 100,000 people to participate in a class action lawsuit against a spammer. According to the agreements with his many clients, Smith will keep 1/3 of any winnings. In the end, Smith wins a $3,000,000 verdict and pockets $1,000,000. Each individual plaintiff receives a check for $20.

   Is this a lawsuit reasonable use of the court's resources? Why or why not?

5. Usually, both a plaintiff and defendant can demand a jury trial in cases asking for cash damages. If you were involved in a trial with $50,000 at stake, would you *want* a jury trial? Would you trust a group of strangers to arrive at a fair verdict, or would you prefer a judge to decide the case? Would your answer depend upon whether you were the plaintiff or defendant?

CHAPTER 4

CONSTITUTIONAL, STATUTORY, ADMINISTRATIVE, AND COMMON LAW

© r.nagy/Shutterstock.com

The consultant started his presentation to the energy company's board of directors. "So I don't have to tell you that if the Smith-Jones bill ever passes Congress, it will be an utter disaster for your company. The House already passed it. The President wants it. The only thing that has kept it from becoming law this summer is that the Senate has been too chicken to bring it up for a vote in an election year. Here's the bottom line: to be comfortable, you need three candidates who see things your way to beat current Senators who support the bill."

> "Look, we're all against the Smith-Jones bill. But is this plan, ah … *legal*?"

The next slide showed a large map of the United States with three states highlighted in red. "These are your best bets. Attempting wins here would cost $60 million—not so much for a billion-dollar-a-year operation.

"The money would go to saturation advertising from Labor Day to Election Day. I want to buy TV ads during local news programs all day, and during most prime-time shows. I want every viewer to see your ads at least a dozen times before they go to the polls.

"In state #1, the challenger—your candidate—is a squeaky-clean state representative, but no one knows much about her outside her own district. She carries herself well, has a nice family. People will like her if they see her. Your money makes sure people will see her.

"In state #2, your guy hasn't really done much. But his grandfather was a hero at Normandy, and his dad was a coal miner. Great-grandparents were immigrants who came through New York with nothing in their pockets—I can see the ad with the Statue of Liberty already. A lot of voters will appreciate his family's story. This strategy will work if we have the funds to tell the story often enough."

"In state #3, we go negative. Really negative. Our opponent has been in the Senate a long time, and he's taken maybe 100,000 photos. We have three of them showing him with world leaders who have become unpopular of late. We're going to use them to tell a story about the senator putting foreign interests above American jobs and national security. People are angry, they think America is losing its place in the world. Our polling shows that this kind of campaign will be highly effective."

"You need to get into this election. All of your stakeholders benefit if the Smith-Jones bill dies—your workers stay on the job, your shareholders make more money, and your customers pay lower prices. Corporations are nothing more or less than the people who work for them, and they have the right to express their political opinions. These ads would simply be giving your workers the chance to exercise their right to free speech."

The CFO interupted, "Look, we're all against the Smith-Jones bill. But is this plan, ah … *legal*?"

CONSTITUTIONAL LAW

Government Power

The Constitution of the United States is the greatest legal document ever written. No other written constitution has lasted so long, governed so many, or withstood such challenge.

It sits above everything else in our legal system. No law can conflict with it. The chapter opener raises a constitutional issue: does Congress have the right to prohibit corporations from spending money to affect elections, or are these actions protected as free speech under the First Amendment? We will discuss this more later in the chapter when we look at the *Citizens United* case.

In 1783, seven years after declaring it, 13 American colonies *actually gained* surprising independence from Great Britain. Four years later, the colonies sent delegates to craft a new constitution, but they faced conflicts on a basic issue: how much power should the federal government be given? The Framers, as they have come to be called because they made or "framed" the original document, had to compromise. **The Constitution is a series of compromises about power.**

SEPARATION OF POWERS

One method of limiting power was to create a national government divided into three branches, each independent and equal. Each branch would act as a check on the power of the other two, avoiding the despotic rule that had come from London. Article I of the Constitution created a Congress, which was to have legislative, or lawmaking, power. Article II created the office of president, defining the scope of executive, or enforcement, power. Article III established judicial, or interpretive, power by creating the Supreme Court and permitting additional federal courts.

Consider how the three separate powers balance one another: Congress was given the power to pass statutes, a major grant of power. But the president was permitted to veto legislation, a nearly equal grant. Congress, in turn, had the right to override the veto, ensuring that the president would not become a dictator. The president was allowed to appoint federal judges and members of his cabinet, but only with a consenting vote from the Senate.

FEDERALISM

The national government was indeed to have considerable power, but it would still be *limited* power. Article I, section 8, describes those issues on which Congress may pass statutes. If an issue is not on the list, Congress has no power to legislate. Thus Congress may create and regulate a post office because postal service is on the list. But Congress may not pass statutes regulating child custody in a divorce: that issue is not on the list. Only the states may legislate child custody issues.

Power Granted

CONGRESSIONAL POWER

Article I of the Constitution creates the Congress, with its two houses. Representation in the House of Representatives is proportionate with a state's population, but each state elects two senators. Congress may perform any of the functions enumerated in Article I, section 8, such as imposing taxes, spending money, creating copyrights, supporting the military, declaring war, and so forth. None of these rights is more important than the authority to raise and spend money (the "power of the purse"), because every branch of government is dependent upon Congress for its money. One of the most important items on this list of congressional powers concerns trade.

Interstate Commerce. "The Congress shall have power to regulate commerce with foreign nations, and among the several states." This is the **Commerce Clause**: Congress is authorized to regulate trade between states. For example, if Congress passed a law imposing a new tax on all trucks engaged in interstate transportation, the law is valid. Congress can regulate television broadcasts because many of them cross state lines.

The Affordable Healthcare Act is a sweeping recent statute that may result in as many as 30 million uninsured Americans gaining health care coverage. Almost immediately after it passed, many states sued, arguing that the law violated the Constitution by exceeding Congress's power to regulate interstate commerce.

The challenge centers on a provision (which the press refers to as the "individual mandate") in the Act that requires many people to purchase health insurance or face fines. The states argue that requiring people to buy something is fundamentally different from regulating people who *voluntarily* decide to participate in commerce.

At the time of this writing, three panels of federal judges have agreed with the states, declaring the law void, while two others have ruled the statute constitutional. The Supreme Court will surely have the final word. In the end, the fate of this law hinges upon how the justices define "commerce."

The Commerce Clause
Gives Congress the power to regulate commerce with foreign nations and among states.

EXECUTIVE POWER

Article II of the Constitution defines the executive power. Once again, the Constitution gives powers in general terms. **The basic job of the president is to enforce the nation's laws.** Three of his key powers concern appointment, legislation, and foreign policy.

Appointment. As we see later in this chapter, administrative agencies play a powerful role in business regulation. The president nominates the heads of most of them. These choices dramatically influence what issues the agencies choose to pursue and how aggressively they do it. For example, a president who wishes to push for higher air quality standards may appoint a forceful environmentalist to run the Environmental Protection Agency (EPA), whereas a president who dislikes federal regulations will choose a more passive agency head.

Legislation. The president and his advisers propose bills to Congress and lobby hard for their passage. The executive also has veto power.

Foreign Policy. The president conducts the nation's foreign affairs, coordinating international efforts, negotiating treaties, and so forth. The president is also the commander in chief of the armed forces, meaning that he heads the military.

JUDICIAL POWER

Article III of the Constitution creates the Supreme Court and permits Congress to establish lower courts within the federal court system. Federal courts have two key functions: adjudication and judicial review.

Adjudicating Cases.   The federal court system hears criminal and civil cases. All prosecutions of federal crimes begin in a United States District Court. That same court has limited jurisdiction to hear civil lawsuits, a subject discussed in Chapter 3, on dispute resolution.

Judicial Review.   **Judicial review** refers to the power of federal courts to declare a statute or governmental action unconstitutional and void. The courts can examine acts from any branch of federal or state government. If Ohio passed a tax on milk produced in other states, a federal court would declare the law void, as a violation of the Commerce Clause. Exhibit 4.1 illustrates the balance among Congress, the president, and the Court.

Is judicial review good for the nation? Those who oppose it argue that federal court judges are all appointed, not elected, and that we should not permit judges to nullify a statute passed by elected officials because that diminishes the people's role in their government. Those who favor judicial review insist that there must be one cohesive interpretation of the Constitution and the judicial branch is the logical one to provide it. The following example of judicial review shows how immediate and emotional the issue can be. The case involves a prosecution for a brutal

Judicial review

Refers to the power of federal courts to declare a statute or governmental action unconstitutional and void.

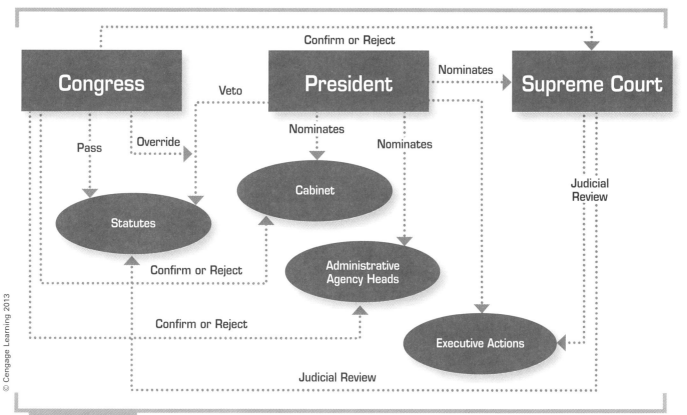

© Cengage Learning 2013

EXHIBIT 4.1   The Constitution established a federal government of checks and balances. Congress may pass statutes; the president may veto them; and Congress may override the veto. The president nominates cabinet officers, administrative heads, and Supreme Court justices, but the Senate must confirm the nominees. Finally, the Supreme Court (and lower federal courts) exercise judicial review over statutes and executive actions.

crime. Cases like this force us to examine two questions about judicial review. What is the proper punishment for such a horrible crime? Just as important, *who should make that decision*—appointed judges, or elected legislators?

You be the Judge

KENNEDY V. LOUISIANA

128 S.Ct. 2641
United States Supreme Court, 2008

Facts: Patrick Kennedy raped his 8-year-old step-daughter. A forensic expert testified that the girl's's physical injuries were the most severe he had ever witnessed. The jury also heard evidence that the defendant had raped another 8-year-old. Kennedy was convicted of aggravated rape because the victim was under 12 years of age.

The jury voted to sentence Kennedy to death, which was permitted by the Louisiana statute. The state supreme court affirmed the death sentence, and Kennedy appealed to the United States Supreme Court. He argued that the Louisiana statute was unconstitutional. The Eighth Amendment prohibits cruel and unusual punishment, which includes penalties that are out of proportion to the crime. Kennedy claimed that capital punishment was out of proportion to rape and violated the Eighth Amendment.

Six states had passed laws permitting capital punishment for child rape, though the remaining 44 states had not. Louisiana argued that the statute did not violate the amendment and that the voters must be allowed to express their abhorrence of so evil an act.

You Be the Judge: *Did the Louisiana statute violate the Constitution by permitting the death penalty in a case of child rape? Is it proper for the Supreme Court to decide this issue?*

Argument for Kennedy: The court's interpretation of the Constitution must evolve with society. The Eighth Amendment requires that punishment be proportionate to the crime. A national consensus opposes the death penalty for any crime other than murder. Capital punishment exists in 36 states, but only 6 of those states allow it for child rape. No state has executed a defendant for rape since 1964. As horrifying as child rape is, society merely brutalizes itself when it sinks to the level of capital punishment for a crime other than murder.

There are also policy reasons to prohibit this punishment. Children may be more reluctant to testify against perpetrators if they know that a prosecution could lead to execution. Also, a young child may be an unreliable witness for a case where the stakes are so high. It is the responsibility of this court to nullify such a harmful law.

Argument for Louisiana: Child rape is one of the most horrifying of crimes. The defendant damages a young person, destroys her childhood, and terrifies a community. Only the severest of penalties is sufficient.

Six states have recently passed statutes permitting capital punishment in these cases. It is possible that a consensus is developing *in favor* of the death penalty for these brutal assaults. If the court strikes down this law, it will effectively stifle a national debate and destroy any true consensus.

Kennedy argues that capital punishment might be bad policy—but that is a question for voters and legislatures, not for courts. Obviously, the citizens of Louisiana favor this law. If they are offended by the statute, they have the power to replace legislators who support it. The court should leave this issue to the citizens. That is how a democracy is intended to function.

Protected Rights

The original Constitution was silent about the rights of citizens. This alarmed many, who feared that the new federal government would have unlimited power over their lives. So in 1791, the first 10 amendments, known as the Bill of Rights, were added to the Constitution, guaranteeing many liberties directly to individual citizens.

The amendments to the Constitution protect the people of this nation from the power of state and federal government. The **First Amendment** guarantees rights of free speech, free press, and religion; the **Fourth Amendment** protects against illegal searches; the **Fifth Amendment** ensures due process; the **Sixth Amendment** demands fair treatment for defendants in criminal prosecutions; and the **Fourteenth Amendment** guarantees equal protection of the law.

The First Amendment
Protects freedom of speech.

We consider the First, Fifth, and Fourteenth Amendments in this chapter and the Fourth, Fifth, and Sixth Amendments in Chapter 7, on crime.

The "people" who are protected include citizens and, for most purposes, corporations. Corporations are considered persons and receive most of the same protections. The great majority of these rights also extend to citizens of other countries who are in the United States.

Constitutional rights generally protect only against governmental acts. The Constitution generally does not protect us from the conduct of private parties, such as corporations or other citizens. Constitutional protections apply to federal, state, and local governments.

FIRST AMENDMENT: FREE SPEECH

The First Amendment states that "Congress shall make no law ... abridging the freedom of speech...." In general, we expect our government to let people speak and hear whatever they choose. The Framers believed democracy would work only if the members of the electorate were free to talk, argue, listen, and exchange viewpoints in any way they wanted. If a city government prohibited an antiabortion group from demonstrating, its action would violate the First Amendment. Government officers may not impose their political beliefs on the citizens. The government may regulate the *time, place,* and *manner* of speech, for example, by prohibiting a midnight rally, or insisting that demonstrators remain within a specified area. But outright prohibitions are unconstitutional.

"Speech" includes symbolic conduct. Does that mean flag burning is permissible? The following case is about that issue.

TEXAS V. JOHNSON

491 U.S. 397, 109 S. Ct. 2533, 1989 U.S. LEXIS 3115
United States Supreme Court, 1989

CASE SUMMARY

Facts: Outside the Republican National Convention in Dallas, Gregory Johnson participated in a protest against policies of the Reagan administration. Participants gave speeches and handed out leaflets. Johnson burned an American flag. He was arrested and convicted under a Texas statute that prohibited desecrating the flag, but the Texas Court of Criminal Appeals reversed on the grounds that the conviction violated the First Amendment. Texas appealed to the United States Supreme Court.

Issue: *Does the First Amendment protect flag burning?*

Decision: Affirmed. The First Amendment protects flag burning.

Reasoning: The First Amendment literally applies only to "speech," but this Court has already ruled that the Amendment also protects written words and other conduct that will convey a specific message. For example, earlier decisions protected a student's right to wear a black armband in protest against American military actions. Judged by this standard, flag burning is symbolic speech.

Texas argues that its interest in honoring the flag justifies its prosecution of Johnson, since he knew that his action would be deeply offensive to many citizens. However, if there is a bedrock principle underlying the First Amendment, it is that the government may not prohibit the expression of an idea simply because society finds it offensive.

The best way to preserve the flag's special role in our lives is not to punish those who feel differently, but to persuade them that they are wrong. We do not honor our flag by punishing those who burn it, because in doing so we diminish the freedom that this cherished emblem represents.

One of the most important recent developments in constitutional law concerns the ability of *organizations* to engage in political speech. In the case that follows, a sharply divided Supreme Court weighed in on the issue raised in this chapter's opening scenario.

CITIZENS UNITED v. FEDERAL ELECTION COMMISSION

130 S. Ct. 876
Supreme Court of the United States, 2010

CASE SUMMARY

Facts: Citizens United, a nonprofit organization, produced a documentary on presidential candidate Hillary Clinton. The group wanted to run television ads promoting *Hillary: the Movie.* The Bipartisan Campaign Reform Act of 2002 banned "electioneering communication" by corporations and unions for the 30 days before a presidential primary. Citizens United challenged the Act, arguing that it violated the First Amendment.

Issue: *Did the Bipartisan Campaign Reform Act violate the First Amendment?*

Decision: Yes, the law violated the First Amendment.

Reasoning: Prohibiting organizations from "electioneering communications" amounts to censorship. Speech is vital to a democracy, and it must not be suppressed.

Corporations are protected by the First Amendment, and therefore, they have the right to express their political views. Yet, under this statute, any negative portrayal of a politician on television, radio, or YouTube, that takes place near an election could be a felony.

Corruption should be curbed, but not at the expense of free speech. Americans must be allowed to decide for themselves which ideas are worthy of discussion. The government cannot make the decision for them.

Fifth Amendment: Due Process and the Takings Clause

Ralph is a first-semester senior at State University, where he majors in finance. With a 3.6 grade point average and outstanding recommendations, he has an excellent chance of admission to an elite law school—until his life suddenly turns upside down. Professor Watson, who teaches Ralph in marketing, notifies the school's dean that the young man plagiarized material that he included in his recent paper. Dean Holmes reads Watson's report and sends Ralph a brief letter: "I find that you have committed plagiarism in violation of school rules. Your grade in Dr. Watson's marketing course is an 'F.' You are hereby suspended from the University for one full academic year."

Ralph is shocked. He is convinced he did nothing wrong, and wants to tell his side of the story, but Dean Holmes refuses to speak with him. What can he do? The first step is to read the Fifth Amendment.

Two related provisions of the Fifth Amendment, called the Due Process Clause and the Takings Clause, prohibit the government from arbitrarily depriving us of our most valuable assets. Together, they state: "No person shall be … deprived of life, liberty, or property without due process of law; nor shall private property be taken for public use, without just compensation." We will discuss the civil law aspects of these clauses, but due process also applies to criminal law. The reference to "life" refers to capital punishment. The criminal law issues of this subject are discussed in Chapter 7.

PROCEDURAL DUE PROCESS

Procedural due process
Ensures that before the government takes liberty or property, the affected person has a fair chance to oppose the action.

The government deprives citizens or corporations of their property in a variety of ways. The Internal Revenue Service (IRS) may fine a corporation for late payment of taxes. The Customs Service may seize goods at the border. As to liberty, the government may take it by confining someone in a mental institution or by taking a child out of the home because of parental neglect. The purpose of **procedural due process** is to ensure that before the government takes liberty or property, the affected person has a fair chance to oppose the action.[1]

The Due Process Clause protects Ralph because State University is part of the government. Ralph is entitled to due process. Does this mean that he gets a full court trial on the plagiarism charge? No. **The type of hearing the government must offer depends upon the importance of the property or liberty interest.** The more important the interest, the more formal the procedures must be. Regardless of how formal the hearing, one requirement is constant: the fact finder must be neutral.

In a criminal prosecution, the liberty interest is very great. A defendant can lose his freedom or even his life. The government must provide the defendant with a lawyer if he cannot afford one, adequate time to prepare, an unbiased jury, an opportunity to present his case and cross-examine all witnesses, and many other procedural rights.

A student faced with academic sanctions receives less due process but still has rights. State University has failed to provide Ralph with due process. The school has accused the young man of a serious infraction. The school must promptly provide details of the charge, give Ralph all physical evidence, and allow him time to plan his response. The university must then offer Ralph a hearing, before a neutral person or group, who will listen to Ralph (as well as Dr. Watson) and examine any evidence the student offers. Ralph is not, however, entitled to a lawyer or a jury.

THE TAKINGS CLAUSE

Kabrina owns a 10-acre parcel of undeveloped land on Lake Halcyon. She plans to build a 20-bedroom inn of about 35,000 square feet—until the state environmental agency abruptly halts the work. The agency informs Kabrina that, to protect the lake from further harm, it will allow no shoreline development except single-family houses of 2,000 square feet or less. Kabrina is furious. Does the state have the power to wreck Kabrina's plans? To learn the answer, we look to another section of the Fifth Amendment.

The **Takings Clause** prohibits a state from taking private property for public use without just compensation. A town wishing to build a new football field *does* have the right to boot you out of your house. But the town must compensate you. The government takes your land through the power of eminent domain. Officials must notify you of their intentions and give you an opportunity to oppose the project and to challenge the amount the town offers to pay. When the hearings are done, though, the town may write you a check and grind your house into goalposts, whether you like it or not.

The Takings Clause
Prohibits a state from taking private property for public use without just compensation.

If the state actually wanted to take Kabrina's land and turn it into a park, the Takings Clause would force it to pay the fair market value. However, the state is not trying to seize the land—it merely wants to prevent large development.

"My land is worthless," Kabrina replies. "You might just as well kick me off my own property!" **A regulation that denies** *all beneficial use* **of property is a taking and requires compensation.** Has the government denied Kabrina all beneficial use? No, it has not. Kabrina retains the right to build a private house; she just can't build the inn she wants. The environmental agency has decreased the value of the land, but it owes her nothing. Had the state forbidden *all* construction on her land, it would have been obligated to pay Kabrina.

Fourteenth Amendment: Equal Protection Clause

Shannon Faulkner wanted to attend The Citadel, a state-supported military college in South Carolina. She was a fine student who met every admission requirement that The Citadel set except one: she was not a man. The Citadel argued that its long and distinguished history

---

[1]In criminal cases, procedural due process also protects against the taking of life.

demanded that it remain all male. Faulkner responded that she was a citizen of the state and ought to receive the benefits that others got, including the right to a military education. Could the school exclude her on the basis of gender?

The Fourteenth Amendment provides that "No State shall ... deny to any person within its jurisdiction the equal protection of the laws." This is the **Equal Protection Clause**, and it means that, generally speaking, all levels of government must treat people equally. Unfair classifications among people or corporations will not be permitted. **Regulations based on gender, race, or fundamental rights are generally void.** Shannon Faulkner won her case and was admitted to The Citadel. The Court found no justification for discriminating against women. Any regulation based on race or ethnicity is *nearly certain* to be void; one based on gender is *likely* to be void. Similarly, all citizens enjoy the *fundamental right* to travel between states. If Kentucky limited government jobs to those who had lived in the state for two years, it would be discriminating against a fundamental right, and the restriction would be struck down.

The Equal Protection Clause
Requires that the government must treat people equally.

EXAM Strategy

Question: Megan is a freshman at her local public high school; her older sister, Jenna, attends a nearby private high school. Both girls are angry because their schools prohibit them from joining their respective wrestling teams, where only boys are allowed. The two girls sue based on the United States Constitution. Discuss the relevant law and predict the outcomes.

Strategy: One girl goes to private and one to public school. Why does that matter? Now ask what provision of the Constitution is involved and what legal standard it establishes.

Result: The Constitution offers protection from the *government*. A private high school is not part of the government, and Jenna has no constitutional case. Megan's suit is based on the Equal Protection Clause. Regulations based on gender are generally void. The school will probably argue that wrestling with stronger boys will be dangerous for girls. However, courts are increasingly suspicious of any sex discrimination and are unlikely to find the school's argument persuasive.

STATUTORY LAW

Statutes
Laws passed by Congress or state legislatures.

Most new law is statutory law. **Statutes** affect each of us every day, in our business, professional, and personal lives. When the system works correctly, this is the one part of the law over which we the people have control. We elect the local legislators who pass state statutes; we vote for the senators and representatives who create federal statutes. If we understand the system, we can affect the largest source of contemporary law. If we live in ignorance of its strengths and pitfalls, we delude ourselves that we participate in a democracy.

As we saw in Chapter 1, there are many systems of government operating in the United States: a national government and 50 state governments. Each level of government has a legislative body. In Washington, D.C., Congress is our national legislature. Congress passes the statutes that govern the nation. In addition, each state has a legislature, which passes statutes for that state only. In this section, we look at how Congress does its work creating statutes. State legislatures operate similarly, but the work of Congress is better documented and obviously of national importance.

Committee Work

Congress is organized into two houses, the House of Representatives and the Senate. Either house may originate a proposed statute, which is called a **bill**. After a bill has been proposed, it is sent to an appropriate committee.

Bill
A proposed statute.

If you visit either house of Congress, you will probably find half a dozen legislators on the floor, with one person talking and no one listening. This is because most of the work is done in committees. Both houses are organized into dozens of committees, each with special functions. The House currently has about 27 committees (further divided into about 150 subcommittees), and the Senate has approximately 20 committees (with about 86 subcommittees). For example, the Armed Services committee of each house oversees the huge defense budget and the workings of the armed forces. Labor committees handle legislation concerning organized labor and working conditions. Banking committees develop expertise on financial institutions. Judiciary committees review nominees to the federal courts. There are dozens of other committees, some very powerful, because they control vast amounts of money, and some relatively weak.

When a bill is proposed in either house, it is referred to the committee that specializes in that subject. Why are bills proposed in the first place? For any of several reasons:

- *New Issue, New Worry.* In recent years, voters have been increasingly irate about abuses in campaign financing, and, after years of hearings, Congress finally passed legislation designed to reduce excessive political donations.

- *Unpopular Judicial Ruling.* If Congress disagrees with a judicial interpretation of a statute, the legislators may pass a new statute to modify or "undo" the court decision. For example, if the Supreme Court misinterprets a statute about musical copyrights, Congress may pass a new law correcting the Court's error.

- *Criminal Law.* When legislators perceive that social changes have led to new criminal acts, they may respond with new statutes. The rise of Internet fraud has led to many new statutes outlawing such things as computer trespass and espionage, fraud in the use of cell phones, identity theft, and so on.

Congressional committees hold hearings to investigate the need for new legislation and consider the alternatives. Suppose a congressperson believes that a growing number of American corporations locate their headquarters offshore to escape taxes. She requests committee hearings on the subject, hoping to discover the extent of the problem, its causes, and possible remedies. After hearings, she proposes a bill she believes will remedy the problem. If the committee votes in favor of the bill, it goes to the full body, meaning either the House of Representatives or the Senate. If the full body approves the bill, it goes to the other house.

The bill must be voted on and approved by both branches of Congress. If both houses pass the bill, the legislation normally must go to a conference committee, made of members from each house, to resolve differences between the two versions. Assuming both houses then pass the same version of the bill, the bill goes to the president. If the president signs the bill, it becomes law. If the president opposes the bill, he will veto it, in which case it is not law. When the president vetoes a bill, Congress has one last chance to make it law: an override. Should both houses re-pass the bill, each by a two-thirds margin, it becomes law over the president's veto.

COMMON LAW

What, if anything, must you do if you see someone in danger? Are you required to help? We will examine this issue to see how the common law works.

Common law

Legal precedents created by appellate courts.

The **common law** is judge-made law. It is the sum total of all the cases decided by appellate courts. The common law of Pennsylvania consists of all cases decided by appellate courts in that state. The Illinois common law of bystander liability is all the cases on that subject decided by Illinois appellate courts. Two hundred years ago, almost all the law was common law. Today, most new law is statutory. But common law still predominates in tort, contract, and agency law, and it is very important in property, employment, and some other areas.

> ## What, if anything, must you do if you see someone in danger? Are you required to help?

We focus on appellate courts because they are the only ones to make rulings of law, as discussed in Chapter 3. In a bystander case, it is the job of the state's highest court to say what legal obligations, if any, a bystander has. The trial court, on the other hand, must decide facts: was this defendant able to see what was happening? Was the plaintiff really in trouble? Could the defendant have assisted without peril to himself?

Stare Decisis

Stare decisis

Means "let the decision stand," and describes a court's tendency to follow earlier cases.

Nothing perks up a course like Latin. *Stare decisis* means "let the decision stand." It is the essence of the common law. The phrase indicates that once a court has decided a particular issue, it will generally apply the same rule in future cases. Suppose the highest court of Arizona must decide whether a contract for a new car, signed by a 16-year-old, can be enforced against him. The court will look to see if there is precedent; that is, whether the high court of Arizona has already decided a similar case. The Arizona court looks and finds several earlier cases, all holding that such contracts may not be enforced against a minor. The court will apply that precedent and refuse to enforce the contract in this case. Courts do not always follow precedent but they generally do: *stare decisis*.

Two words explain why the common law is never as easy as we might like: *predictability* and *flexibility*. The law is trying to accommodate both goals. The need for predictability is apparent: people must know what the law is. If contract law changed daily, an entrepreneur who leased factory space and then started buying machinery would be uncertain if the factory would actually be available when she was ready to move in. Will the landlord slip out of the lease? Will the machinery be ready on time? The need for predictability created the doctrine of *stare decisis*.

Yet there must also be flexibility in the law, some means to respond to new problems and changing social mores. We cannot be encumbered by ironclad rules established before electricity was discovered. These two ideas may be obvious, but they also conflict: the more flexibility we permit, the less predictability we enjoy. We will watch the conflict play out in the bystander cases.

Bystander Cases

This country inherited from England a simple rule about a bystander's obligations: you have no duty to assist someone in peril unless you created the danger. In *Union Pacific Railway Co. v. Cappier*,[2] through no fault of the railroad, a train struck a man, severing an arm and a leg.

---

[2]66 Kan. 649, 72 P. 281 (1903).

Railroad employees saw the incident happen but did nothing to assist him. By the time help arrived, the victim had died. In this 1903 case, the court held that the railroad had no duty to help the injured man. The court declared that it was legally irrelevant whether the railroad's conduct was inhumane.

As harsh as this judgment might seem, it was an accurate statement of the law at that time in both England and the United States: bystanders need do nothing. With a rule this old and well established, no court was willing to scuttle it. What courts did do was seek openings for small changes.

Eighteen years after the Kansas case of *Cappier*, the court in nearby Iowa found the basis for one exception. Ed Carey was a farm laborer, working for Frank Davis. While in the fields, Carey fainted from sunstroke and remained unconscious. Davis simply hauled him to a nearby wagon and left him in the sun for an additional four hours, causing serious permanent injury. The judges said that was not good enough. Creating a modest exception to the bystander rule, the court ruled that when an employee suffers a serious injury *on the job*, the employer must take reasonable measures to help him. Leaving a stricken worker in the hot sun was not reasonable, and Davis was liable.[3]

Remember the *Soldano v. O'Daniels* case from Chapter 1, in which the bartender refused to call the police? As in the earlier cases we have seen, this case presented an emergency. But the exception created in *Carey v. Davis* applied only if the bystander was an employer. Should the law require the bartender to act—that is, should it carve a new exception? Here is what the California court decided:

> Many citizens simply "don't want to get involved." No rule should be adopted [requiring] a citizen to open up his or her house to a stranger so that the latter may use the telephone to call for emergency assistance. As Mrs. Alexander in Anthony Burgess's *A Clockwork Orange* learned to her horror, such an action may be fraught with danger. It does not follow, however, that use of a telephone in a public portion of a business should be refused for a legitimate emergency call.
>
> We conclude that the bartender owed a duty to [Soldano] to permit the patron from Happy Jack's to place a call to the police or to place the call himself. It bears emphasizing that the duty in this case does not require that one must go to the aid of another. That is not the issue here. The employee was not the good samaritan intent on aiding another. The patron was.

And so, courts have made several subtle changes to the common law rule.

EXAM Strategy

Question: When Rachel is walking her dog, Bozo, she watches a skydiver float to earth. He lands in an enormous tree, suspended 45 feet above ground. "Help!" the man shouts. Rachel hurries to the tree and sees the skydiver bleeding profusely. She takes out her cell phone to call 911 for help, but just then Bozo runs away. Rachel darts after the dog, afraid he will jump in a nearby pond and emerge smelling of mud. She forgets about the skydiver and takes Bozo home. Three hours later, the skydiver expires.

The victim's family sues Rachel. She defends by saying she feared that Bozo would have an allergic reaction to mud, and that in any case, she could not have climbed 45 feet up a tree to save the man. The family argues that the dog is not allergic to mud, that even if he is, a pet's inconvenience pales compared to human life, and that Rachel could have phoned for emergency help without climbing an inch. Please rule.

---

[4]*Carey v. Davis*, 190 Iowa 720, 180 N.W. 889 (1921).

> **Strategy:** The family's arguments might seem compelling, but are they relevant? Rachel is a bystander, someone who perceives another in danger. What is the rule concerning a bystander's obligation to act? Apply the rule to the facts of this case.
>
> **Result:** A bystander has no duty to assist someone in peril unless she created the danger. Rachel did not create the skydiver's predicament. She had no obligation to do anything. Rachel wins.

ADMINISTRATIVE LAW

Before beginning this section, please return your seat to its upright position. Stow the tray firmly in the seat back in front of you. Turn off any cell phones, laptops, or other electronic devices. Sound familiar? Administrative agencies affect each of us every day in hundreds of ways. They have become the fourth branch of government. Supporters believe that they provide unique expertise in complex areas; detractors regard them as unelected government run amok.

> Before beginning this section, please return your seat to its upright position. Stow the tray firmly in the seat back in front of you.

Many administrative agencies are familiar. The Federal Aviation Administration, which requires all airlines to ensure that your seats are upright before takeoff and landing, is an administrative agency. The IRS expects us to report in every April 15. The EPA regulates the water quality of the river in your town. The Federal Trade Commission (FCC) oversees the commercials that shout at you from your television set.

Other agencies are less familiar. You may never have heard of the Bureau of Land Management, but if you go into the oil and gas industry, you will learn that this powerful agency has more control over your land than you do. If you develop real estate in Palos Hills, Illinois, you will tremble every time the Appearance Commission of the City of Palos Hills speaks, since you cannot construct a new building without its approval. If your software corporation wants to hire an Argentine expert on databases, you will get to know the complex workings of Immigration and Customs Enforcement: no one lawfully enters this country without its nod of approval.

Administrative agencies use three kinds of power to do the work assigned to them: they make rules, investigate, and adjudicate.

Rule Making

One of the most important functions of an administrative agency is to make rules. In doing this, the agency attempts, prospectively, to establish fair and uniform behavior for all businesses in the affected area. To create a new rule is to promulgate it. Agencies promulgate two types of rules: legislative and interpretive.

LEGISLATIVE RULES

These are the most important agency rules, and they are much like statutes. Here, an agency is changing the law by requiring businesses or private citizens to act in a certain way. For example, the FCC promulgated a rule requiring all cable television systems with more than 3,500 subscribers to develop the capacity to carry at least 20 channels and to make some of those channels available to local community stations. This legislative rule has a heavy financial impact on many cable systems. As far as a cable company is concerned, it is more important than most statutes passed by Congress. Legislative rules have the full effect of a statute.

INTERPRETIVE RULES

These rules do not change the law. They are the agency's interpretation of what the law already requires. But they can still affect all of us.

In 1977, Congress amended the Clean Air Act in an attempt to reduce pollution from factories. The act required the EPA to impose emission standards on "stationary sources" of pollution. But what did "stationary source" mean? It was the EPA's job to define that term. Obscure work, to be sure, yet the results could be seen and even smelled, because the EPA's definition would determine the quality of air entering our lungs every time we breathe. Environmentalists wanted the term defined to include every smokestack in a factory so that the EPA could regulate each one. The EPA, however, developed the "bubble concept," ruling that "stationary source" meant an entire factory, but not the individual smokestacks. As a result, polluters could shift emission among smokestacks in a single factory to avoid EPA regulation. Environmentalists howled that this gutted the purpose of the statute, but to no avail. The agency had spoken, merely by interpreting a statute.

Investigation

Agencies do a wide variety of work, but they all need broad factual knowledge of the field they govern. Some companies cooperate with an agency, furnishing information and even voluntarily accepting agency recommendations. For example, the United States Product Safety Commission investigates hundreds of consumer products every year and frequently urges companies to recall goods that the agency considers defective. Many firms comply. Other companies, however, jealously guard information, often because corporate officers believe that disclosure would lead to adverse rules. To force disclosure, agencies use subpoenas and searches. A **subpoena** is an order to appear at a particular time and place to provide evidence. A **subpoena** *duces tecum* requires a person to produce certain documents or things.

Subpoena
An order to appear at a particular time and place. A **subpoena** *duces tecum* requires the person to produce certain documents or things.

Adjudication

To **adjudicate** a case is to hold a hearing about an issue and then decide it. Agencies adjudicate countless cases. The FCC adjudicates which applicant for a new television license is best qualified. The Occupational Safety and Health Administration (OSHA) holds adversarial hearings to determine whether a manufacturing plant is dangerous.

Most adjudications begin with a hearing before an **administrative law judge** (ALJ). There is no jury. After all evidence is taken, the ALJ makes a decision. The losing party has a right to appeal to an appellate board within the agency. A party unhappy with that decision may appeal to federal court.

Adjudicate
To hold a formal hearing about an issue and then decide it.

Administrative law judge
An agency employee who acts as an impartial decision maker.

Chapter Conclusion

The legal battle over power never stops. When may a state outlaw waterfront development? Prohibit symbolic speech? Other issues are just as thorny, such as when a bystander is liable to assist someone in peril, or whether a government agency may subpoena corporate documents. Some of the questions will be answered by that extraordinary document, the Constitution, while others require statutory, common law, or administrative responses. There are no easy answers to any of the questions because there has never been a democracy so large, so diverse, or so powerful.

EXAM REVIEW

1. **CONSTITUTION**   The Constitution is a series of compromises about power. (p. 57)

2. **CONSTITUTIONAL POWERS**   Article I of the Constitution creates the Congress and grants all legislative power to it. Article II establishes the office of president and defines executive powers. Article III creates the Supreme Court and permits lower federal courts; the article also outlines the powers of the federal judiciary. (pp. 57–59)

3. **COMMERCE CLAUSE**   Under the Commerce Clause, Congress may regulate interstate trade. A state law that interferes with interstate commerce is void. (p. 58)

EXAM Strategy

Question: Maine exempted many charitable institutions from real estate taxes but denied this benefit to a charity that primarily benefited out-of-state residents. Camp Newfound was a Christian Science organization, and 95 percent of its summer campers came from other states. Camp Newfound sued Maine. Discuss.

Strategy: The state was treating organizations differently depending on the states their campers come from. This raised Commerce Clause issues. What does that clause state? (See the "Result" at the end of this section.)

4. **PRESIDENTIAL POWERS**   The president's key powers include making agency appointments, proposing legislation, conducting foreign policy, and acting as commander in chief of the armed forces. (pp. 58–59)

5. **FEDERAL COURTS**   The federal courts adjudicate cases and also exercise judicial review, which is the right to declare a statute or governmental action unconstitutional and void. (pp. 59–60)

6. **FIRST AMENDMENT**   The First Amendment protects most freedom of speech, although the government may regulate the time, place, and manner of speech. In recent years, the Supreme Court has significantly expanded the free speech rights of organizations. (pp. 61–62)

7. **PROCEDURAL DUE PROCESS**   Procedural due process is required whenever the government attempts to take liberty or property. (pp. 62–63)

8. **TAKINGS CLAUSE**   The Takings Clause prohibits a state from taking private property for public use without just compensation. (p. 63)

9. **EQUAL PROTECTION CLAUSE**   The Equal Protection Clause generally requires the government to treat people equally. (pp. 63–64)

10. **LEGISLATION**   Bills originate in congressional committees and go from there to the full House of Representatives or Senate. If both houses pass the bill, the

legislation normally must go to a conference committee to resolve differences between the two versions. If the president signs the bill, it becomes a statute; if he vetoes it, Congress can pass it over his veto with a two-thirds majority in each house. (pp. 64–65)

11. **STARE DECISIS** *Stare decisis* means "let the decision stand," and it indicates that once a court has decided a particular issue, it will generally apply the same rule in future cases. (p. 66)

12. **COMMON LAW** The common law evolves in awkward fits and starts because courts attempt to achieve two contradictory purposes: predictability and flexibility. (pp. 66–68)

13. **BYSTANDER RULE** The common-law bystander rule holds that, generally, no one has a duty to assist someone in peril unless the bystander himself created the danger. Courts have carved some exceptions during the last 100 years, but the basic rule still stands. (pp. 66–68)

14. **ADMINISTRATIVE AGENCIES** Congress creates federal administrative agencies to supervise many industries. Agencies promulgate rules and investigate and adjudicate cases. (pp. 68–69)

EXAM Strategy

Question: Hiller Systems, Inc. was performing a safety inspection on board the M/V *Cape Diamond*, an oceangoing vessel, when an accident occurred involving the fire extinguishing equipment. Two men were killed. OSHA attempted to investigate, but Hiller refused to permit any of its employees to speak to OSHA investigators. What could OSHA do to pursue the investigation? What limits would there be on OSHA's work?

Strategy: Agencies makes rules, investigate, and adjudicate. Which is involved here? (Investigation.) During an investigation, what power has an agency to force a company to produce data? What are the limits on that power? (See the "Result" at the end of this section.)

3. Result: The Commerce Clause holds that a state statute that discriminates against interstate commerce is almost always invalid. Maine was subsidizing charities that served in-state residents and penalizing those that attracted campers from elsewhere. The tax rule violated the Commerce Clause and was void.

14. Result: OSHA can issue a subpoena *duces tecum*, demanding that those on board the ship, and their supervisors, appear for questioning and bring with them all relevant documents. OSHA may ask for anything that is (1) relevant to the investigation, (2) not unduly burdensome, and (3) not privileged. Conversations between one of the ship inspectors and his supervisor is clearly relevant; a discussion between the supervisor and the company's lawyer is privileged due to attorney-client privilege.

MATCHING QUESTIONS

Match the following terms with their definitions:

___ A. Statute

___ B. Equal Protection Clause

___ C. Judicial review

___ D. Takings Clause

___ E. *Stare decisis*

___ F. Promulgate

1. The power of federal courts to examine the constitutionality of statutes and acts of government.

2. The part of the Constitution that requires compensation in eminent domain cases.

3. The rule that requires lower courts to decide cases based on precedent.

4. The act of an administrative agency creating a new rule.

5. A law passed by a legislative body.

6. Generally prohibits regulations based on gender, race, or fundamental rights.

TRUE/FALSE QUESTIONS

Circle true or false:

1. T F The government may not prohibit a political rally, but it may restrict when and where the demonstrators meet.

2. T F The Due Process Clause requires that any citizen is entitled to a jury trial before any right or property interest is taken.

3. T F The government has the right to take a homeowner's property for a public purpose.

4. T F A subpoena is an order punishing a defendant who has violated a court ruling.

5. T F A bystander who sees someone in peril must come to that person's assistance, but only if he can do so without endangering himself or others.

6. T F Administrative agencies play an advisory role in the life of many industries but do not have the legal authority to enforce their opinions.

MULTIPLE-CHOICE QUESTIONS

1. Colorado passes a hotel tax of 8 percent for Colorado residents and 15 percent for out-of-state visitors. The new law

   (a) Is valid, based on the Supremacy Clause.

   (b) Is void, based on the Supremacy Clause.

   (c) Is valid, based on the Commerce Clause.

   (d) Is void, based on the Commerce Clause.

   (e) Is void, based on the Takings Clause.

2. Suppose a state legislature approves an education plan for the next year that budgets $35 million for boys' athletics and $25 million for girls' athletics. Legislators explain the difference by saying, "In our experience, boys simply care more about sports than girls do." The new plan is

   (a) Valid.

   (b) Void.

   (c) Permissible, based on the legislators' statutory research.

   (d) Permissible, but probably unwise.

   (e) Subject to the Takings Clause.

3. Congress has passed a new bill, but the president does not like the law. What could happen next?

   (a) The president must sign the bill whether he likes it or not.

   (b) The president may veto the bill, in which case it is dead.

   (c) The president may veto the bill, but Congress may attempt to override the veto.

   (d) The president may ask the citizens to vote directly on the proposed law.

   (e) The president may discharge the Congress and order new elections.

4. Which of these is an example of judicial review?

   (a) A trial court finds a criminal defendant guilty.

   (b) An appeals court reverses a lower court's ruling.

   (c) An appeals court affirms a lower court's ruling.

   (d) A federal court declares a statute unconstitutional.

   (e) A congressional committee interviews a potential Supreme Court justice.

5. What is an example of a subpoena?

   (a) A court order to a company to stop polluting the air.

   (b) A court order requiring a deponent to answer questions.

   (c) A federal agency demands various internal documents from a corporation.

   (d) The president orders troops called up in the national defense.

   (e) The president orders Congress to pass a bill on an expedited schedule.

Essay Questions

1. In the early 1970s, President Richard Nixon became embroiled in the Watergate dispute. He was accused of covering up a criminal break-in at the national headquarters of the Democratic Party. Nixon denied any wrongdoing. A United States District Court judge ordered the president to produce tapes of conversations held in his office. Nixon knew that complying with the order would produce damaging evidence, probably destroying his presidency. He refused, claiming executive privilege. The case went to the Supreme Court. Nixon strongly implied that even if the Supreme Court ordered him to produce the tapes, he would refuse. What major constitutional issue did this raise?

2. Gilleo opposed American participation in the war in the Persian Gulf. She displayed a large sign on her front lawn that read, "Say No to War in the Persian Gulf, Call Congress Now." The city of Ladue prohibited signs on front lawns, and Gilleo sued. The city claimed that it was regulating "time, place, and manner." Explain that statement, and decide who should win.

3. **YOU BE THE JUDGE WRITING PROBLEM:** An off-duty, out-of-uniform police officer and his son purchased some food from a 7-11 store and were still in the parking lot when a carload of teenagers became rowdy. The officer went to speak to them and the teenagers assaulted him. The officer shouted to his son to get the 7-11 clerk to call for help. The son entered the store, told the clerk that a police officer needed help, and instructed the clerk to call the police. He returned 30 seconds later and repeated the request, urging the clerk to say it was a Code 13. The son claimed that the clerk laughed at him and refused to do it. The policeman sued the store. **Argument for the Store:** We sympathize with the policeman and his family, but the store has no liability. A bystander is not obligated to come to the aid of anyone in distress unless the bystander created the peril, and obviously the store did not do so. The policeman should sue those who attacked him. **Argument for the Police Officer:** We agree that, in general, a bystander has no obligation to come to the aid of one in distress. However, when a business that is open to the public receives an urgent request to call the police, the business should either make the call or permit someone else to do it.

4. Until recently, every state had a statute outlawing the burning of American flags. But in *Texas v. Johnson*, the Supreme Court declared such statutes unconstitutional, saying that flag burning is symbolic speech, protected by the First Amendment. Does Congress have the power to overrule the Court's decision?

5. You begin work at Everhappy Corp. at the beginning of November. On your second day at work, you wear a political button on your overcoat, supporting your choice for governor in the upcoming election. Your boss glances at it and says, "Get that stupid thing out of this office or you're history, chump." You protest that his statement (a) violates your constitutional rights and (b) uses a boring cliche. Are you right?

DISCUSSION QUESTIONS

1. Consider the doctrine of *stare decisis*. Should courts follow past rulings, or should they decide cases anew each time, without regard to past decisions? For example, should *Texas v. Johnson* stand because it is precedent, or should the justices take a "fresh look" at the issue of flag burning?

2. Should administrative agencies be able to "tell business what to do"? Do you favor administrative regulations on the environment, safety, and discrimination, or do they amount to "big government"?

3. Return to the opening scenario and the *Citizens United* case. Is political advertising purchased by corporations appropriate? Do you agree with the five members of the Supreme Court who voted to allow it, or with the four who dissented and would have drawn distinctions between free speech by individuals and organizations? Why?

4. **ETHICS** Is political advertising by a nonprofit political organization like Citizens United any more or less appropriate than advertising by for-profit corporations like the one described in the opening scenario? If you were a board member in the opening scenario, which (if any) of the three ads would you vote to authorize?

5. All spending bills must originate in the House of Representatives. Is it fair for the House to refuse to fund government programs that its majority does not like? For example, the House made a recent attempt to cut off funding for public broadcasting. Is this reasonable in a time of a budget crunch, or should the House leave "Big Bird" alone?

CHAPTER 5

INTENTIONAL TORTS AND BUSINESS TORTS

In a small Louisiana town, Don Mashburn ran a restaurant called Maison de Mashburn. *The New Orleans States-Item* newspaper reviewed his eatery, and here is what the article said:

" 'Tain't Creole, 'tain't Cajun, 'tain't French, 'tain't country American, 'tain't good. I don't know how much real talent in cooking is hidden under the mélange of hideous sauces which make this food and the menu a travesty of pretentious amateurism, but I find it all quite depressing. Put a yellow flour sauce on top of the duck, flame it for drama, and serve it with some horrible multiflavored rice in hollowed-out fruit and what have you got? A well-cooked duck with an ugly sauce that tastes too sweet and thick and makes you want to scrape off the glop to eat the plain duck. [The stuffed eggplant was prepared by emptying] a shaker full (more or less) of paprika on top of it. [One sauce created] trout à la green plague [while another should have been called] yellow death on duck."

Mashburn sued, claiming that the newspaper had committed libel, damaging his reputation and hurting his business.[1] Trout à la green plague will be the first course on our menu of tort law. Mashburn learned, as you will, why filing such a lawsuit is easier than winning it.

> 'Tain't Creole, 'tain't Cajun, 'tain't French, 'tain't country American, 'tain't good.

---

[1] *Mashburn v. Collins*, 355 So.2d 879 (La. 1977).

This odd word "tort" is borrowed from the French, meaning "wrong." And that is what it means in law: a tort is a wrong. More precisely, a **tort** is a violation of a duty imposed by the *civil* law. When a person breaks one of those duties and injures another, it is a tort. The injury could be to a person or her property. Libel, which the restaurant owner in the opening scenario alleges, is one example of a tort. A surgeon who removes the wrong kidney from a patient commits a different kind of tort, called *negligence*. A business executive who deliberately steals a client away from a competitor, interfering with a valid contract, commits a tort called *interference with a contract*. A con artist who tricks you out of your money with a phony offer to sell you a boat commits fraud, yet another tort.

Because tort law is so broad, it takes a while to understand its boundaries. To start with, we must distinguish torts from criminal law.

It is a crime to steal a car, to embezzle money from a bank, to sell cocaine. As discussed in Chapter 1, society considers such behavior so threatening that the government itself will prosecute the wrongdoer, whether or not the car owner or bank president wants the case to go forward. A district attorney, who is paid by the government, will bring the case to court, seeking to send the defendant to prison, fine him, or both. If there is a fine, the money goes to the state, not to the victim.

In a tort case, it is up to the injured party to seek compensation. She must hire her own lawyer, who will file a lawsuit. Her lawyer must convince the court that the defendant breached some legal duty and ought to pay money damages to the plaintiff. The plaintiff has no power to send the defendant to jail. Bear in mind that a defendant's action might be both a crime *and* a tort. A man who punches you in the face for no reason commits the tort of battery. You may file a civil suit against him and will collect money damages if you can prove your case. He has also committed a crime, and the state may prosecute, seeking to imprison and fine him.

Tort
A violation of a duty imposed by the civil law.

EXAM **Strategy**

Question: Keith is driving while intoxicated. He swerves into the wrong lane and causes an accident, seriously injuring Marta. Who is more likely to file a tort lawsuit in this case, Marta or the state? Who is more likely to prosecute Keith for drunk driving? Could there be a lawsuit and a prosecution at the same time? In which case is Keith more likely to be found *guilty*, a civil suit or a criminal prosecution?

Strategy: Only one of these parties can prosecute a criminal case and in only one kind of case can a defendant be found guilty.

Result: Only the government prosecutes criminal cases. Marta may urgently request a prosecution, but the District Attorney will make the final decision. And only in a criminal case can a defendant be found guilty. However, Marta is free to sue Keith for the injuries he has caused, even if he is simultaneously prosecuted. She can recover money damages for her injuries, whether or not Keith is found guilty in the criminal case.

Tort law is divided into categories. In this chapter, we consider **intentional torts**, that is, harm caused by a deliberate action. The newspaper columnist who wrongly accuses someone of being a drunk has committed the intentional tort of libel. In the next chapter, we examine **negligence and strict liability,** which involve injuries and losses caused by neglect and oversight rather than by deliberate conduct.

Intentional torts
Involve harm caused by deliberate action.

INTENTIONAL TORTS

Defamation

The First Amendment guarantees the right to free speech, a vital freedom that enables us to protect other rights. But that freedom is not absolute.

The law of defamation concerns false statements that harm someone's reputation. Defamatory statements can be written or spoken. Written defamation is called **libel**. Suppose a newspaper accuses a local retail store of programming its cash registers to overcharge customers, when the store has never done so. That is libel. Oral defamation is **slander**. If Professor Wilson, in class, refers to Sally Student as a drug dealer when she has never sold drugs, he has slandered her.

There are four elements to a defamation case. An **element** is something that a plaintiff must prove to win a lawsuit. The plaintiff in any kind of lawsuit must prove all the elements to prevail. The elements in a defamation case are:

- **Defamatory statement.** This is a statement likely to harm another person's reputation. Professor Wisdom's accusation will clearly harm Sally's reputation.

- **Falseness.** The statement must be false. If Sally Student actually sold marijuana to a classmate, then Professor Wisdom has a defense to slander.

- **Communicated.** The statement must be communicated to at least one person *other than the plaintiff*. If Wisdom speaks privately to Sally and accuses her of dealing drugs, there is no slander.

- **Injury.** In many slander cases, the plaintiff generally must show some injury. Sally's injury would be poorer reputation in the school, embarrassment, and humiliation. But in slander cases that involve false statements about sexual behavior, crimes, contagious diseases, and professional abilities, the law is willing to assume injury without requiring the plaintiff to prove it. Lies in these four categories amount to **slander** *per se*.

Libel cases are treated like cases of slander per se, and courts award damages without proof of injury.[2]

OPINION

Remember that the plaintiff must demonstrate a "false" statement. Opinions, though, cannot be proven true or false. For that reason, **opinion is generally a valid defense in a defamation suit.**

Mr. Mashburn, who opened the chapter suing over his restaurant review, lost his case. The court held that a reasonable reader would have understood the statements to be opinion only. "A shaker full of paprika" and "yellow death on duck" were not to be taken literally but were merely the author's expression of his personal dislike.

PUBLIC PERSONALITIES

The rules of the game change for those who play in the open. Government officials and other types of public figures such as actors and athletes receive less protection from defamation. In the landmark case *New York Times Co. v. Sullivan*,[3] the Supreme Court

---

Libel
Written defamation.

Slander
Oral defamation.

Element
A fact that a plaintiff must prove to win a lawsuit.

---

[2]When defamation by radio and television became possible, the courts chose to consider it libel, analogizing it to newspapers because of the vast audience. This means that in broadcasting cases, a plaintiff generally does not have to prove damages.
[3]376 U.S. 254, 84 S. Ct. 710, 1964 U.S. LEXIS 1655 (1964).

ruled that the free exchange of information is vital in a democracy and is protected by the First Amendment to the Constitution. Therefore, to win a defamation case, a public official or public figure must prove actual malice by the defendant.

Actual malice means that the defendant knew the statement was false or acted with reckless disregard of the truth. If the plaintiff merely shows that the defendant newspaper printed incorrect statements, even very damaging ones, that will not suffice to win the suit. In the *New York Times v. Sullivan* case, the police chief of Birmingham, Alabama, claimed that the *Times* falsely accused him of racial violence in his job. He lost because he could not prove that the *Times* had acted with actual malice. If he had shown that the *Times* knew the accusation was false and published it anyway, he would have won.

Actual malice

Means that the defendant in a defamation suit knew his or her statement was false or acted with reckless disregard of the truth.

False Imprisonment

False imprisonment is the intentional restraint of another person without reasonable cause and without consent. False imprisonment cases most commonly arise in retail stores, which sometimes detain employees or customers for suspected theft. Most states now have statutes governing the detention of suspected shoplifters. **Generally, a store may detain a customer or worker for alleged shoplifting provided there is a reasonable basis for the suspicion and the detention is done reasonably.** To detain a customer in the manager's office for 20 minutes and question him about where he got an item is lawful. To chain that customer to a display counter for three hours and humiliate him in front of other customers is unreasonable and false imprisonment.

False imprisonment

The intentional restraint of another person without reasonable cause or consent.

Battery and Assault

Assault and battery are related but not identical. **Battery** is an intentional touching of another person in a way that is harmful or offensive. There need be no intention to hurt the plaintiff. If the defendant intended to do the physical act and a reasonable plaintiff would be offended by it, battery has occurred.

If an irate parent throws a chair at a referee during his daughter's basketball game, breaking the man's jaw, he has committed battery. But a parent who cheerfully slaps the winning coach on the back has not committed battery because a reasonable coach would not be offended.

Assault occurs when a defendant performs some action that makes a plaintiff fear an imminent battery. It is assault even if the battery never occurs. Suppose Ms. Wilson shouts "Think fast!" at her husband and hurls a toaster at him. He turns and sees it flying at him. His fear of being struck is enough to win a case of assault, even if the toaster misses. If the toaster happens to strike him, Ms. Wilson has also committed battery.

Battery

A harmful or offensive bodily contact.

Assault

An action that causes another person to fear an imminent battery.

EXAM Strategy

Question: Patrick owns a fast food restaurant that is repeatedly painted with graffiti. He is convinced that 15-year-old John, a frequent customer, is the culprit. The next time John comes to the restaurant, Patrick locks the men's room door while John is inside. Patrick calls the police, but because of a misunderstanding, the police are very slow to arrive. John shouts for help, banging on the door, but Patrick does not release him for two hours. John sues for assault, battery, and false imprisonment. A psychiatrist testifies that John has suffered serious psychological harm. Will John win?

> **Strategy:** The question focuses on the distinctions among three intentional torts. Battery: an offensive touching. Assault: causing an imminent fear of battery. False imprisonment: a store may detain someone if it does so reasonably.
>
> **Result:** Locking John up for two hours, based on an unproven suspicion, was clearly unreasonable. Patrick has committed false imprisonment, and John will win. However, Patrick did not touch John or create a reasonable fear of contact, so there has been no battery or assault.

Fraud

Fraud
Injuring someone by deliberate deception.

Fraud is injuring another person by deliberate deception. It is fraud to sell real estate knowing that there is a large toxic waste deposit underground of which the buyer is ignorant. Fraud is a tort, but it typically occurs during the negotiation or performance of a contract, and it is discussed in detail in Unit 2, on contracts.

Intentional Infliction of Emotional Distress

Intentional infliction of emotional distress
Extreme and outrageous conduct that causes serious emotional harm.

A credit officer was struggling in vain to locate Sheehan, who owed money on his car. The officer finally phoned Sheehan's mother, falsely identified herself as a hospital employee, and said she needed to find Sheehan because his children had been in a serious auto accident. The horrified mother provided Sheehan's whereabouts, which enabled the company to seize his car. But Sheehan himself spent seven hours frantically trying to locate his supposedly injured children, who in fact were fine. He was not injured physically, but he sued for his emotional distress—and won. The **intentional infliction of emotional distress** results from extreme and outrageous conduct that causes serious emotional harm. The credit company was liable for the intentional infliction of emotional distress.[4] The following case arose in a setting that guarantees controversy—an abortion clinic.

JANE DOE AND NANCY ROE v. LYNN MILLS

212 Mich. App. 73, 536 N.W.2d 824, 1995 Mich. App. LEXIS 313
Michigan Court of Appeals, 1995

CASE SUMMARY

Facts: Late one night, an anti-abortion protestor named Robert Thomas climbed into a dumpster located behind the Women's Advisory Center, an abortion clinic. He found documents indicating that the plaintiffs were soon to have abortions at the clinic. Thomas gave the information to Lynn Mills. The next day, Mills and Sister Lois Mitoraj created signs, using the women's names, indicating that they were about to undergo abortions and urging them not to "kill their babies."

Doe and Roe (not their real names) sued, claiming intentional infliction of emotional distress (as well as breach of privacy, discussed later in this chapter). The trial court dismissed the lawsuit, ruling that the defendants' conduct was not extreme and outrageous. The plaintiffs appealed.

---

[4]*Ford Motor Credit Co. v. Sheehan*, 373 So.2d 956, 1979 Fla. App. LEXIS 15416 (Fla. Dist. Ct. App. 1979).

Issue: *Have the plaintiffs made a valid claim of intentional infliction of emotional distress?*

Decision: The plaintiffs have made a valid claim of intentional infliction of emotional distress.

Reasoning: A defendant is liable for the intentional infliction of emotional distress only when his conduct is outrageous in character, extreme in degree, and utterly intolerable in a civilized community. A good test is whether the average member of the community would respond to the defendant's conduct by exclaiming, "Outrageous!"

These defendants have a constitutional right to protest against abortions, but they have no such right to publicize private matters. Their behavior here might well cause the average person to say, "Outrageous!" The plaintiffs are entitled to a trial, so that a jury can decide whether the defendants have inflicted emotional distress.

DAMAGES

Compensatory Damages

Mitchel Bien, a deaf mute, enters the George Grubbs Nissan dealership, where folks sell cars aggressively. Very aggressively. Maturelli, a salesman, and Bien communicate by writing messages back and forth. Maturelli takes Bien's own car keys, and the two then test drive a 300ZX. Bien indicates he does not want the car, but Maturelli escorts him back inside and fills out a sales sheet. Bien repeatedly asks for his keys, but Maturelli only laughs, pressuring him to buy the new car. Minutes pass. Hours pass. Bien becomes frantic, writing a dozen notes, begging to leave, threatening to call the police. Maturelli mocks Bien and his physical disabilities. Finally, after four hours, the customer escapes.

Bien sues for the intentional infliction of emotional distress. Two former salesmen from Grubbs testify that they have witnessed customers cry, yell, and curse as a result of the aggressive tactics. Doctors state that the incident has traumatized Bien, dramatically reducing his confidence and self-esteem and preventing his return to work even three years later.

The jury awards Bien damages. But how does a jury calculate the money? For that matter, why should a jury even try? money can never erase pain or undo a permanent injury. The answer is simple: money, however inexact and ineffective, is the only thing a court has to give. A successful plaintiff generally receives **compensatory damages**, meaning an amount of money that the court believes will restore him to the position he was in before the defendant's conduct caused an injury. Here is how damages are calculated.

First, a plaintiff receives money for medical expenses that he has proven by producing bills from doctors, hospitals, physical therapists, and psychotherapists. If a doctor testifies that he needs future treatment, Bien will offer evidence of how much that will cost. The **single recovery principle** requires a court to settle the matter once and for all, by awarding a lump sum for past and future expenses.

Second, the defendants are liable for lost wages, past and future. The court takes the number of days or months that Bien has missed (and will miss) work and multiplies that times his salary.

> Bien becomes frantic, writing a dozen notes, begging to leave, threatening to call the police.

Compensatory damages
Are intended to restore the plaintiff to the position he was in before the defendant's conduct caused injury.

Single recovery principle
Requires a court to settle a legal case once and for all, by awarding a lump sum for past and future expenses.

Third, a plaintiff is paid for pain and suffering. Bien testifies about how traumatic the four hours were and how the experience has affected his life. He may state that he now fears shopping, suffers nightmares, and seldom socializes. To bolster the case, a plaintiff uses expert testimony, such as the psychiatrists who testified for Bien. In this case, the jury awarded Bien $573,815, calculated as in the following table:[5]

Past medical	$ 70.00
Future medical	6,000.00
Past rehabilitation	3,205.00
Past lost earning capacity	112,910.00
Future lost earning capacity	34,650.00
Past physical symptoms and discomfort	50,000.00
Future physical symptoms and discomfort	50,000.00
Past emotional injury and mental anguish	101,980.00
Future emotional injury and mental anguish	200,000.00
Past loss of society and reduced ability to interact socially with family, former fiancee, and friends, and hearing (i.e., nondeaf) people in general	10,000.00
Future loss of society and reduced ability to socially interact with family, former fiancee, and friends, and hearing people	5,000.00
TOTAL	$573,815.00

Punitive Damages

Punitive damages

Punish the defendant for conduct that is extreme and outrageous.

Here we look at a different kind of award, one that is more controversial and potentially more powerful: punitive damages. Punitive damages are not designed to compensate the plaintiff for harm because compensatory damages will have done that. **Punitive damages** are intended to punish the defendant for conduct that is extreme and outrageous. Courts award these damages in relatively few cases. When an award of punitive damages is made, it is generally in a case of intentional tort. The idea behind punitive damages is that certain behavior is so unacceptable that society must make an example of it. A large award of money should deter the defendant from repeating the mistake and others from ever making it.

Although a jury has wide discretion in awarding punitive damages, the U.S. Supreme Court has ruled that a verdict must be reasonable. In awarding punitive damages, a court must consider three "guideposts":

- The reprehensibility of the defendant's conduct.

- The ratio between the harm suffered and the award. Generally, the punitive award should not be more than 9 times the compensatory award. The Supreme Court, it is important to stress, does not completely prohibit punitive damages that exceed the

---

[5]The compensatory damages are described in *George Grubbs Enterprises v. Bien*, 881 S.W.2d 843, 1994 Tex. App. LEXIS 1870 (Tex. Ct. App. 1994). In addition to the compensatory damages described, the jury awarded $5 million in punitive damages. The Texas Supreme Court reversed the award of punitive damages, but not the compensatory. Id., 900 S.W.2d 337, 1995 Tex. LEXIS 91 (Tex. 1995). The high court did not dispute the appropriateness of punitive damages, but it reversed because the trial court failed to instruct the jury properly as to how it should determine the assets actually under the defendants' control, an issue essential to punitive damages, but not to compensatory damages.

9-to-1 ratio. The justices merely state that such awards should be reserved for rare cases of unusually reprehensible conduct.

- The difference between the punitive award and any civil penalties used in similar cases.[6]

A California Court of Appeals decided the following case after the establishment of the three guideposts. How should it implement the Supreme Court's guidelines? You be the judge.

You be the Judge

BOEKEN V. PHILIP MORRIS, INCORPORATED

127 Cal. App.4th 1640, 26 CalRptr.3d 638
California Court of Appeals, 2005

Facts: In the mid-1950s, Richard Boeken began smoking Marlboro cigarettes at the age of 10. Countless advertisements, targeted at boys aged 10 to 18, convinced him and his friends that the "Marlboro Man" was powerful, healthy, and manly. At the time, scientists uniformly believed that cigarette smoking caused lung cancer, but Philip Morris and other tobacco companies waged a long-term campaign to convince the public otherwise. Philip Morris also added ingredients to its cigarettes to increase their addictive power.

Boeken saw the Surgeon General's warnings about the risk of smoking but he trusted the company's statements that cigarettes were safe. Beginning in the 1970s, he tried many times to stop but always failed. Finally, in the 1990s, he quit after he was diagnosed with lung cancer but resumed smoking again once he had recovered from the surgery.

Boeken filed suit against Philip Morris for fraud and other torts. He died of cancer before the case was concluded.

The jury found Philip Morris liable for fraudulently concealing that cigarettes were addictive and carcinogenic. It awarded Boeken $5.5 million in compensatory damages and also assessed punitive damages—of $3 *billion*. The trial judge reduced the punitive award to $100 million. Philip Morris appealed.

You Be the Judge: *Was the punitive damage award too high, too low, or just right?*

Argument for Philip Morris: The court should substantially reduce the $100 million punitive award because it is totally arbitrary. The Supreme Court has indicated that punitive awards should not exceed compensatory damages by more than a factor of 9. The jury awarded Mr. Boeken $5.5 million in compensatory damages, which means that punitive damages should absolutely not exceed $49.5 million. We argue that they should be even lower.

Cigarettes are a legal product, and our packages have displayed the Surgeon General's health warnings for decades. Mr. Boeken's death is tragic, but his cancer was not necessarily caused by Marlboro cigarettes. And even if cigarettes did contribute to his failing health, Mr. Boeken chose to smoke throughout his life, even after major surgery on one of his lungs.

Argument for Boeken: The Supreme Court says that cases may exceed the 9-to-1 ratio if the defendant's behavior is particularly bad. Phillip Morris created ads that targeted children, challenged clear scientific data that its products caused cancer, and added substances to its cigarettes to make them more addictive. Does it get worse than that?

The behavior of Phillip Morris has caused terrible harm. The plaintiff died a terrible death from cancer. The company's cigarettes kill 200,000 American customers each year, while its *weekly* profit is roughly $100 million. At a minimum, the court should keep the punitive award at that figure. But we ask that the court reinstate the jury's original $3 billion award.

---

[6]The U.S. Supreme Court applied the guideposts in *State Farm v. Campbell.* In the case, the Campbells suffered emotional distress but no physical injuries. The Utah Supreme Court awarded them $1 million in compensatory damages and $145 million in punitive damages. The U.S. Supreme Court found the punitive award excessive and remanded the case, ordering the Utah Supreme Court to hold to a single-digit ratio between compensatory and punitive damages.

Tort Reform and the *Exxon Valdez*

Some people believe that jury awards are excessive and need statutory reform, while others argue that the evidence demonstrates excessive awards are rare and modest in size. About one-half of the states have passed limits. The laws vary, but many distinguish between **economic damages** and **non-economic damages**. In such a state, a jury is permitted to award any amount for economic damages, meaning lost wages, medical expenses, and other measureable losses. However, non-economic damages—pain and suffering and other losses that are difficult to measure—are capped at some level, such as $500,000. In some states, punitive awards have similar caps. These restrictions can drastically lower the total verdict.

In the famous *Exxon Valdez* case, the U.S. Supreme Court placed a severe limit on a certain type of punitive award. The ship's captain had been drunk, and when the *Exxon Valdez* ran aground, it caused massive, permanent environmental damage. The jury awarded $5 billion in punitive damages, which the Supreme Court reduced to $507 million, equivalent to the compensatory damages awarded. However, it is unclear how influential the decision will be. The case arose in the isolated area of maritime law, which governs ships at sea. Courts may decide not to apply the *Exxon Valdez* reasoning in other cases.

BUSINESS TORTS

Tortious Interference with a Contract

Competition is the essence of business. Successful corporations compete aggressively, and the law permits and expects them to. But there are times when healthy competition becomes illegal interference. This is called **tortious interference with a contract**. To win such a case, a plaintiff must establish four elements:

- There was a contract between the plaintiff and a third party;

- The defendant knew of the contract;

- The defendant improperly induced the third party to breach the contract or made performance of the contract impossible; and

- There was injury to the plaintiff.

Tortious interference with a contract
Occurs when a defendant deliberately harms a contractual relationship between two other parties.

Because businesses routinely compete for customers, employees, and market share, it is not always easy to identify tortious interference. There is nothing wrong with two companies bidding against each other to buy a parcel of land, and nothing wrong with one corporation doing everything possible to convince the seller to ignore all competitors. But once a company has signed a contract to buy the land, it is improper to induce the seller to break the deal. The most commonly disputed issues in these cases concern elements 1 and 3: was there a contract between the plaintiff and another party? Did the defendant improperly induce a party to breach it? Defendants will try to show that the plaintiff had no contract.

Intrusion

Intrusion
A tort if a reasonable person would find it offensive.

Intrusion into someone's private life is a tort if a reasonable person would find it offensive. Peeping through someone's windows or wiretapping his telephone are obvious examples of intrusion. In a famous case involving a "paparazzo" photographer and Jacqueline Kennedy Onassis, the court found that the photographer had invaded her privacy by making a career out of photographing her. He had bribed doormen to gain access to hotels and restaurants she visited, had jumped out of bushes to photograph her young children, and had driven powerboats dangerously close to her. The court ordered him to stop.[7] Nine years later, the paparazzo was found in contempt of court for again taking photographs too close to Ms. Onassis. He agreed to stop once and for all—in exchange for a suspended contempt sentence.

Commercial Exploitation

Commercial exploitation prohibits the unauthorized use of another person's likeness or voice for commercial purposes. For example, it would be illegal to run a magazine ad showing actress Keira Knightley holding a can of soda, without her permission. The ad would imply that she endorsed the product. Someone's identity is her own, and it cannot be used for commercial gain unless she permits it. Ford Motor Company hired a singer to imitate Bette Midler's version of a popular song. The imitation was so good that most listeners were fooled into believing that Ms. Midler was endorsing the product. That, ruled a court, violated her right to be free from commercial exploitation.

Commercial exploitation
Prohibits the unauthorized use of another person's likeness or voice for business purposes.

Chapter Conclusion

This chapter has been a potpourri of misdeeds, a bubbling cauldron of conduct best avoided. Although tortious acts and their consequences are diverse, two generalities apply. First, the boundaries of intentional torts are imprecise, the outcome of a particular case depending to a considerable extent upon the fact finder who analyzes it. Second, the thoughtful executive and the careful citizen, aware of the shifting standards and potentially vast liability, will strive to ensure that his or her conduct never provides that fact finder an opportunity to give judgment.

EXAM REVIEW

1. **TORT**   A tort is a violation of a duty imposed by the civil law. (pp. 77–78)

2. **DEFAMATION**   Defamation involves a defamatory statement that is false, uttered to a third person, and causes an injury. (p. 78)

EXAM Strategy

Question: Benzaquin had a radio talk show. On the program, he complained about an incident in which state trooper Fleming had stopped his car, apparently for lack of a proper license plate and safety sticker. Benzaquin explained that the license plate had been stolen and the sticker had fallen onto the dashboard, but Fleming refused to let him drive away. Benzaquin and two young grandsons had

---

[7]*Galella v. Onassis*, 487 F.2d 986, 1973 U.S.App.LEXIS 7901 (2d Cir. 1973).

to find other transportation. On the show, Benzaquin angrily recounted the incident, then described Fleming and troopers generally: "arrogants wearing trooper's uniforms like tights"; "we're not paying them to be dictators and Nazis"; "this man is an absolute barbarian, a lunkhead, a meathead." Fleming sued Benzaquin for defamation. Comment.

Strategy: Review the elements of defamation. Can these statements be proven true or false? If not, what is the result? Look at the defenses. Does any of them apply? (See the "Result" at the end of this section.)

3. **FALSE IMPRISONMENT** False imprisonment is the intentional restraint of another person without reasonable cause and without consent. (p. 79)

4. **BATTERY AND ASSAULT** Battery is an intentional touching of another person in a way that is unwanted or offensive. Assault involves an act that makes the plaintiff fear an imminent battery. (p. 79)

EXAM Strategy

Question: Caudle worked at Betts Lincoln-Mercury, a car dealer. During an office party, many of the employees, including the president, Betts, were playing with an electric auto condenser, which gave a slight shock when touched. Some employees played catch with it. Betts shocked Caudle on the back of his neck and chased him around. The shock later caused Caudle to suffer headaches, to pass out, to experience numbness, and eventually to require nerve surgery. He sued Betts for battery. Betts defended by saying that it was all horseplay and that he had intended no harm. Please rule.

Strategy: Betts argues that he intended no harm. Is intent to harm an element of Caudle's case? (See the "Result" at the end of this section.)

5. **INTENTIONAL INFLICTION OF EMOTIONAL DISTRESS** The intentional infliction of emotional distress involves extreme and outrageous conduct that causes serious emotional harm. (pp. 80–81)

6. **DAMAGES** Compensatory damages are the normal remedy in a tort case. In unusual cases, the court may award punitive damages, not to compensate the plaintiff but to punish the defendant. (pp. 81–83)

7. **TORTIOUS INTERFERENCE WITH A CONTRACT** Tortious interference with a contract involves the defendant unfairly harming an existing contract. (p. 84)

8. **COMMERCIAL EXPLOITATION** Protects the exclusive right to use one's own name, likeness, or voice. (p. 85)

2. Result: The court ruled in favor of Benzaquin, because a reasonable person would understand the words to be opinion and ridicule. They are not statements of fact because most of them could not be proven true or false. A statement like "dictators and Nazis" is not taken literally by anyone.[8]

4. Result: The court held that it was irrelevant that Betts had shown no malice toward Caudle nor intended to hurt him. Betts intended the *physical contact* with Caudle, and even though he could not foresee everything that would happen, he is liable for all consequences of his intended physical action.

MATCHING QUESTIONS

Match the following terms with their definitions:

___A. Interference with a contract

___B. Fraud

___C. Defamation

___D. False imprisonment

___E. Punitive damages

___F. Intentional infliction of emotional distress

___G. Commercial exploitation

1. Money awarded to punish a wrongdoer

2. Intentionally restraining another person without reasonable cause

3. Intentional deception, frequently used to obtain a contract with another party

4. Deliberately stealing a client who has a contract with another

5. Violation of the exclusive right to use one's own name, likeness, or voice

6. Using a false statement to damage someone's reputation

7. An act so extreme that an average person would say, "Outrageous!"

TRUE/FALSE QUESTIONS

Circle true or false:

1. T F A store manager who believes a customer has stolen something may question him but not restrain him.

2. T F Becky punches Kelly in the nose. Becky has committed the tort of assault.

3. T F A defendant cannot be liable for defamation if the statement, no matter how harmful, is true.

4. T F In most cases, a winning plaintiff receives compensatory and punitive damages.

5. T F A beer company that wishes to include a celebrity's picture in its magazine ads must first obtain the celebrity's permission.

---

[8]*Fleming v. Benzaquin*, 390 Mass. 175, 454 N.E.2d 95 (1983).

MULTIPLE-CHOICE QUESTIONS

1. A valid defense in a defamation suit is
    (a) Falseness
    (b) Honest error
    (c) Improbability
    (d) Opinion
    (e) Third-party reliance

2. Joe Student, irate that he received a B– on an exam rather than a B, stands up in class and throws his laptop at the professor. The professor sees it coming and ducks just in time; the laptop smashes against the chalkboard. Joe has committed
    (a) Assault
    (b) Battery
    (c) Negligence
    (d) Slander
    (e) No tort, because the laptop missed the professor

3. Marsha, a supervisor, furiously berates Ted in front of 14 other employees, calling him "a loser, an incompetent, a failure as an employee and as a person." She hands around copies of Ted's work and mocks his efforts for 20 minutes. If Ted sues Marsha, his best claim will be
    (a) Assault
    (b) Battery
    (c) Intentional infliction of emotional distress
    (d) Negligence
    (e) Interference with a contract

4. Rodney is a star player on the Los Angeles Lakers basketball team. He has two years remaining on his four-year contract. The Wildcats, a new team in the league, try to lure Rodney away from the Lakers by offering him more money, and Rodney agrees to leave Los Angeles. The Lakers sue. The Lakers will
    (a) Win a case of defamation
    (b) Win a case of commercial exploitation
    (c) Win a case of intentional interference with a contract
    (d) Win a case of negligence
    (e) Lose

5. Hank and Antonio, drinking in a bar, get into an argument that turns nasty. Hank punches Antonio several times, knocking him down and breaking his nose and collarbone. Which statement is true?
    (a) Antonio could sue Hank, who might be found guilty.
    (b) Antonio and the state could start separate criminal cases against Hank.
    (c) Antonio could sue Hank, and the state could prosecute Hank.
    (d) The state could prosecute Hank, but only with Antonio's permission.
    (e) If the state prosecutes Hank, he will be found liable or not liable, depending on the evidence.

ESSAY QUESTIONS

1. Caldwell was shopping in a K-Mart store, carrying a large purse. A security guard observed her looking at various small items such as stain, hinges, and antenna wire. On occasion, she bent down out of sight of the guard. The guard thought he saw Caldwell put something in her purse. Caldwell removed her glasses from her purse and returned them a few times. After she left, the guard approached her in the parking lot and said that he believed she had store merchandise in her pocketbook, but he was unable to say precisely what he thought was put there. Caldwell opened the purse, and the guard testified that he saw no K-Mart merchandise in it. The guard then told Caldwell to return to the store with him. They walked around the store for approximately 15 minutes, while the guard said six or seven times that he saw her put something in her purse. Caldwell left the store after another store employee indicated she could go. Caldwell sued. What kind of suit did she file, and what should the outcome be?

2. Tata Consultancy of Bombay, India, is an international computer consulting firm. It spends considerable time and effort recruiting the best personnel from India's leading technical schools. Tata employees sign an initial three-year employment commitment, often work overseas, and agree to work for a specified additional time when they return to India. Desai worked for Tata, but then he quit and formed a competing company, which he called Syntel. His new company contacted Tata employees by phone, offering more money to come work for Syntel, bonuses, and assistance in obtaining permanent resident visas in the United States. At least 16 former Tata employees left their work without completing their contractual obligations and went to work for Syntel. Tata sued. What did it claim, and what should be the result?

3. For many years, Johnny Carson was the star of a well-known television show, *The Tonight Show.* For about 20 years, he was introduced nightly on the show with the phrase, "Here's Johnny!" A large segment of the television-watching public associated the phrase with Carson. A Michigan corporation was in the business of renting and selling portable toilets. The company chose the name "Here's Johnny Portable Toilets," and coupled the company name with the marketing phrase, "The World's Foremost Commodian." Carson sued. What claim is he making? Who should win, and why?

4. You are a vice-president in charge of personnel at a large manufacturing company. In-house detectives inform you that Gates, an employee, was seen stealing valuable computer equipment. Gates denies the theft, but you fire him nonetheless. The detectives suggest that you post notices around the company, informing all employees what happened to Gates and why. This will discourage others from stealing. While you think that over, the personnel officer from another company calls, asking for a recommendation for Gates. Should you post the notices? What should you say to the other officer?

5. Pacific Express began operating as an airline in 1982. It had routes connecting western cities with Los Angeles and San Francisco, and by the summer of 1983, it was beginning to show a profit. In 1983, United Airlines tried to enter into a cooperative arrangement with Pacific in which United would provide Pacific with passengers for some routes so that United could concentrate on its longer routes. Negotiations failed. Later that year, United expanded its routes to include cities that only Pacific had served. United also increased its service to cities in which the two airlines were

already competing. By early 1984, Pacific Express was unable to compete and sought protection under bankruptcy laws. It also sued United, claiming interference with a prospective advantage. United moved for summary judgment. Comment.

DISCUSSION QUESTIONS

1. In the *Exxon Valdez* case, the Supreme Court limited punitive damages in maritime cases to no more than the compensatory damages awarded in the same case. In cases that do not involve maritime law, the ratio is usually limited to 9-to-1. Which is the better guideline? Why?

2. You have most likely heard of the *Liebeck v. McDonalds* case. Liebeck spilled hot McDonald's coffee in her lap, suffering third degree burns. At trial, evidence showed that her cup of coffee was brewed at 190 degrees, and that, more typically, a restaurant's "hot coffee" is in the range of 140-160 degrees.

   A jury awarded Liebeck $160,000 in compensatory damages and $2.7 million in punitive damages. The judge reduced the punitive award to $480,000, or three times the compensatory award.

   Comment on the case, and whether the result was reasonable.

3. Celebrities often have problems with tabloids and the paparazzi. It is difficult for public figures to win libel lawsuits because they must show actual malice. Intrusion lawsuits are also tricky, and flocks of photographers often stalk celebrities at all hours.

   Is this right? Should the law change to offer more privacy to famous people? Or is a loss of privacy just the price of success?

4. This chapter described two lawsuits in which juries initially gave awards of $100 million or more. Is there any point at which the raw number of dollars is just too large? Was the original jury award excessive in *Boeken v. Philip Morris* or the *Exxon Valdez* case?

5. Many retailers have policies that instruct employees *not* to attempt to stop shoplifters. Some store owners fear false imprisonment lawsuits and possible injuries to workers more than losses related to stolen merchandise. Are these "don't be a hero" policies reasonable? Would you put one in place if you owned a retail store?

CHAPTER 6

NEGLIGENCE AND STRICT LIABILITY

Submitted for your consideration: a timeline.

3:25 p.m.—Jake, an 18-year-old freshman, sits in his Calculus I class, bored to tears. He receives a text: "Beta Zeta rush party TONIGHT!!!" He perks up.

9:15 p.m.—Jake drives with his roommate over to the Beta Zeta rush party.

9:32 p.m.—Jake and his roommate arrive at the Beta Zeta house. No one checks for ID.

9:36 p.m.—Jake gets a beer from a keg and drinks it.

9:37 p.m.—Jake pours himself another beer and heads outside.

9:58 p.m.—After listening to the band for awhile, Jake returns to the keg and gets a third beer.

10:24 p.m.—Jake faces off with his roommate. He chugs a beer slightly faster than the roommate, and his skills are praised by the Beta Zetas.

10:48 p.m.—Jake bongs a beer.

10:51 p.m.—Jake bongs another beer.

11:53 p.m.—Jake gets a seventh and eighth beer and "double fists."

12:26 a.m.—Jake poses with both beers for his roommate, who takes an iPhone photo.

12:27 a.m.—Jake's roommate sends the picture to everyone on his contact list.

12:28 a.m.—Jake receives the first of many texts making fun of him.

12:35 a.m.—Jake finds his roommate, shoves him, and threatens to kick his ***.

12:38 a.m.—Jake tells his roommate, "I love you man," and heads off to find another beer.

1:14 a.m.—Jake drinks a tenth and final beer.

1:48 a.m.—Jake and his roommate leave the Beta Zeta house. Jake drives his car.

1:49 a.m.—Jake's roommate suggests getting some tacos.

1:54 a.m.—Jake tries to park his car at Taco Bell, but he misses the brake pedal. He drives his car through a large plate glass window and does $50,000 damage to the restaurant.

> If you give a party, should *you* be responsible for any damage caused by intoxicated guests?

Who should pay for this damage? Jake is clearly at fault, but should the Beta Zetas share legal responsibility for the property damage? The question leads to other, similar issues: should a *restaurant* that serves alcohol to a minor be liable for harm that the youth might cause? Should the restaurant be responsible for serving an intoxicated *adult* who causes damage? If you give a party, should *you* be responsible for any damage caused by intoxicated guests?

These are all practical questions—worth considering before you entertain—and moral ones as well. They are also typical issues of negligence law. In this contentious area, courts continually face one question: *when someone is injured, how far should responsibility extend?*

NEGLIGENCE

We might call negligence the "unintentional" tort because it concerns harm that arises by accident. Should a court impose liability? The fraternity members who gave the party were not trying to damage the Taco Bell, but the damage occurred. Is it in society's interest to hold the fraternity responsible?

Things go wrong all the time, and people are hurt in large ways and small. Society needs a means of analyzing negligence cases consistently and fairly. We cannot have each court that hears such a lawsuit extend or limit liability based on an emotional response to the facts. One of America's greatest judges, Benjamin Cardozo, offered an analysis more than 80 years ago. In a case called *Palsgraf v. Long Island Railroad*, he made a decision that still influences negligence thinking today.

Landmark Case

PALSGRAF V. LONG ISLAND RAILROAD

248 N.Y. 339; 162 N.E. 99
Court of Appeals of New York, 1928

CASE SUMMARY

Facts: Helen Palsgraf was waiting on a railroad platform. As a train began to leave the station, a man carrying a plain package ran to catch it. He jumped aboard but looked unsteady, so a guard on the car reached out to help him as another guard, on the platform, pushed from behind. The man dropped the package, which struck the tracks and exploded—since it was packed with fireworks. The shock knocked over some heavy scales at the far end of the platform, and one of them struck Palsgraf. She sued the railroad.

Issue: *Was the railroad liable for Palsgraf's injuries?*

Holding: No, the railroad was not liable.

Reasoning: No one could foresee that what the guards did would harm someone standing at the far end of the platform. Therefore, it does not matter whether or not the guards were careless. For the railroad to be liable, Palsgraf had to show not just that a wrong took place, but that the wrong was to *her*. Negligence in the air is not enough. For example, if a driver speeds through city streets, it is easy to see that someone may be hurt. But, in this case, even the most cautious mind would not imagine that a package wrapped in a newspaper would spread wreckage throughout the station.

The railroad employees owed Palsgraf a duty to be reasonably cautious and vigilant. They did not owe a duty to prevent all harm, no matter how unlikely.

This case was important in establishing the rules of negligence. Courts are still guided by Judge Cardozo's decision.

To win a negligence case, a plaintiff must prove five elements. Much of the remainder of the chapter will examine them in detail. They are:

- **Duty of Due Care.** The defendant had a legal responsibility *to the plaintiff.* This is the point from the *Palsgraf* case.

- **Breach.** The defendant breached her duty of care or failed to meet her legal obligations.

- **Factual Cause.** The defendant's conduct actually caused the injury.

- **Proximate Cause.** It was *foreseeable* that conduct like the defendant's might cause *this type of harm.*

- **Damages.** The plaintiff has actually been hurt or has actually suffered a measureable loss.

To win a case, a plaintiff must prove all of the elements listed above. If a defendant eliminates only one item on the list, there is no liability.

Duty of Due Care

Each of us has a duty to behave as a reasonable person would under the circumstances. If you are driving a car, you have a duty to all the other people near you to drive like a reasonable person. If you drive while drunk or send text messages while behind the wheel, then you fail to live up to your duty of care.

But how *far* does your duty extend? Most courts accept Cardozo's viewpoint in the *Palsgraf* case. Judges draw an imaginary line around the defendant and say that she owes a duty to the people within the circle, but not to those outside it. The test is generally "foreseeability." If the defendant could have foreseen injury to a particular person, she has a duty to him. Suppose that one of your friends posts a YouTube video of you texting behind the wheel and her father is so upset from watching it that he falls down the stairs. You would not be liable for the father's downfall because it was not foreseeable that he would be harmed by your texting.

Let us apply these principles to a case that, like the opening scenario, involves a fraternity party.

HERNANDEZ V. ARIZONA BOARD OF REGENTS

177 Ariz. 244, 866 P.2d 1330, 1994 Ariz. LEXIS 6
Arizona Supreme Court, 1994

CASE SUMMARY

Facts: At the University of Arizona, the Epsilon Epsilon chapter of Delta Tau Delta fraternity gave a welcoming party for new members. The fraternity's officers knew that the majority of its members were under the legal drinking age, but they permitted everyone to consume alcohol. John Rayner, who was under 21 years of age, left the party. He drove negligently and caused a collision with an auto driven by Ruben Hernandez. At the time of the accident, Rayner's blood alcohol level was 0.15, exceeding the legal limit. The crash left Hernandez blind and paralyzed.

Hernandez sued Rayner, who settled the case based on the amount of his insurance coverage. The victim also sued the fraternity, its officers and national organization, all the fraternity members who contributed money to buy the alcohol, the university, and others. The trial court granted summary judgment for all defendants, and the court of appeals affirmed. Hernandez appealed to the Arizona Supreme Court.

Issue: *Did the fraternity and the other defendants have a duty of due care to Hernandez?*

Decision: Yes, the defendants did have a duty of due care to Hernandez. Reversed and remanded.

Reasoning: Historically, Arizona and most states have considered that *consuming* alcohol led to liability, but not *furnishing* it. However, the common law also has had a longstanding rule that a defendant could be liable for supplying some object to a person who is likely to endanger others. Giving a car to an intoxicated youth is an example of such behavior. The youth might easily use the object (the car) to injure other people.

There is no difference between giving a car to an intoxicated youth and giving alcohol to a young person with a car. Both acts involve minors who, because of their age and inexperience, are likely to endanger third parties. Furthermore, furnishing alcohol to a minor violates several state statutes. The defendants did have a duty of due care to Hernandez and to the public in general.

SPECIAL DUTY: LANDOWNER'S LIABILITY

The common law applies special rules to a landowner for injuries occurring on her property. In most states, the owner's duty depends on the type of person injured.

Trespasser
A person on someone else's property without consent.

- **Lowest Liability: Trespassing Adults.** A **trespasser** is anyone on the property without consent. A landowner is liable to a trespasser only for intentionally injuring him or for some other gross misconduct. The landowner has no liability to a trespasser for mere negligence. Jake is not liable if a vagrant wanders onto his land and is burned by defective electrical wires.

- **Mid level Liability: Trespassing Children.** The law makes exceptions when the trespassers are **children**. If there is some manmade thing on the land *that may be reasonably expected to attract children*, the landowner is probably liable for any harm. Daphne lives next door to a day-care center and builds a treehouse on her property. Unless she has fenced off the dangerous area, she is probably liable if a small child wanders onto her property and injures himself when he falls from the rope ladder to the treehouse.

Licensee
A person on property for her own purposes, but with the owner's permission.

- **Higher Liability: Licensee.** A **licensee** is anyone on the land for her own purposes but with the owner's permission. A social guest is a typical licensee. A licensee is entitled to a warning of hidden dangers that the owner knows about. If Juliet invites Romeo for a late supper on the balcony and fails to mention that the wooden railing is rotted, she is liable when her hero plunges to the courtyard.

  But Juliet is liable only for injuries caused by *hidden* dangers—she has no duty to warn guests of obvious dangers. She need not say, "Romeo, oh Romeo, don't place thy hand in the toaster, Romeo."

Invitee
A person who has a right to be on property because it is a public place or a business open to the public.

- **Highest Liability: Invitee.** An **invitee** is someone who has a right to be on the property because it is a public place or a business open to the public. The owner has a duty of reasonable care to an invitee. Perry is an invitee when he goes to the town beach. If riptides have existed for years and the town fails to post a warning, it is liable if Perry drowns. Perry is also an invitee when he goes to Dana's coffee shop. Dana is liable if she ignores spilled coffee that causes Perry to slip.

With social guests, you must have *actual knowledge* of some specific hidden danger to be liable. Not so with invitees. You are liable even if you had *no idea* that something on your property posed a hidden danger. Therefore, if you own a business, you must conduct inspections of your property on a regular basis to make sure that nothing is becoming dangerous.

The courts of some states have modified these distinctions, and a few have eliminated them altogether. California, for example, requires "reasonable care" as to all people on the owner's property, regardless of how or why they got there. But most states still use the classifications outlined above.

SPECIAL DUTY: PROFESSIONALS

A person at work has a heightened duty of care. While on the job, she must act as a reasonable person *in her profession*. A taxi driver must drive as a reasonable taxi driver would. A heart surgeon must perform bypass surgery with the care of a trained specialist in that field.

Two medical cases illustrate the reasonable person standard. A doctor prescribes a powerful drug without asking his patient about other medicines she is currently taking. The patient suffers a serious drug reaction from the combined medications. The physician is liable for the harm. A reasonable doctor *always* checks current medicines before prescribing new ones.

On the other hand, assume that a patient dies on the operating table in an emergency room. The physician followed normal medical procedures at every step of the procedure and acted with reasonable speed. In fact, the man had a fatal stroke. The surgeon is not liable. A doctor must do a reasonable professional job, but she cannot guarantee a happy outcome.

SPECIAL DUTY: HIRING AND RETENTION

Employers also have special responsibilities.

In a recent one-year period, more than 1,000 homicides and 2 million attacks occurred in the workplace. Companies must beware because they can be liable for hiring or retaining violent employees. A mailroom clerk with a previous rape and robbery conviction followed a secretary home after work and killed her. Even though the murder took place off the company premises, the court held that the defendant would be liable if it knew or should have known of the mail clerk's criminal history.[1] In other cases, companies have been found liable for failing to check an applicant's driving record, contact personal references, or search criminal records.

Courts have also found companies negligent for *retaining* dangerous workers. If an employee threatens a coworker, the organization is not free to ignore the menacing conduct. If the employee acts on his threats, the company may be liable.[2]

Breach of Duty

The second element of a plaintiff's negligence case is **breach of duty**. Courts apply the *reasonable person* standard: a defendant breaches his duty of due care by failing to behave the way a reasonable person would under similar circumstances. "Reasonable person" means someone of the defendant's occupation. A taxi driver must drive as a reasonable taxi driver would. An architect who designs a skyscraper's safety features must bring to the task far greater knowledge than the average person possesses.

Breach of duty
A defendant breaches his duty of due care by failing to behave the way a reasonable person would under similar circumstances.

Causation

We have seen that a plaintiff must show that the defendant owed him a duty of care, and that the defendant breached the duty. To win, the plaintiff must also show that the defendant's breach of duty *caused* the plaintiff's harm. Courts look at two separate causation issues: was the defendant's behavior the *factual cause* of the harm? Was *it the proximate cause?*[3]

---

[1] *Gaines v. Monsanto*, 655 S.W.2d 568, 1983 Mo. LEXIS 3439 (Mo. Ct. App. 1983).
[2] *Yunker v. Honeywell*, 496 N.W.2d 419, 1993 Minn. App. LEXIS 230 (Minn. Ct. App. 1993).
[3] Courts often refer to these two elements, grouped together, as *proximate cause* or *legal cause*. But, as many courts acknowledge, those terms have created legal confusion, so we use *factual cause* and *foreseeable types of harm*, the issues on which most decisions ultimately focus.

FACTUAL CAUSE

Factual cause
The defendant's breach led to the ultimate harm.

If the defendant's breach led to the ultimate harm, it is a factual cause. Suppose that Dom's Brake Shop tells a customer his brakes are now working fine, even though Dom knows that is false. The customer drives out of the shop, cannot stop at a red light, and hits a bicyclist crossing the intersection. Dom is liable to the cyclist. Dom's unreasonable behavior was the factual cause of the harm. Think of it as a row of dominoes. The first domino (Dom's behavior) knocked over the next one (failing brakes), which toppled the last one (the cyclist's injury).

Suppose, alternatively, that just as the customer is exiting the repair shop, the bicyclist hits a pothole and tumbles off her cycle. Dom has breached his duty to his customer, but he is not liable to the cyclist—she would have been hurt anyway. This is a row of dominoes that veers off to the side, leaving the last domino (the cyclist's injury) untouched. No factual causation.

PROXIMATE CAUSE

Proximate cause
Refers to a party who contributes to a loss in a way that a reasonable person could anticipate.

For the defendant to be liable, the *type of harm* must have been reasonably *foreseeable* . In the first example just discussed, Dom could easily foresee that bad brakes would cause an automobile accident. He need not have foreseen *exactly* what happened. He did not know there would be a cyclist nearby. What he could foresee was this *general type* of harm involving defective brakes. Because the accident that occurred was of the type he could foresee, he is liable.

By contrast, assume the collision of car and bicycle produces a loud crash. Two blocks away, a pet pig, asleep on the window ledge of a twelfth-story apartment, is startled by the noise, awakens with a start, and plunges to the sidewalk, killing a veterinarian who was making a house call. If the vet's family sues Dom, should it win? Dom's negligence was the factual cause: it led to the collision, which startled the pig, which flattened the vet. Most courts would rule, though, that Dom is not liable. The type of harm is too bizarre. Dom could not reasonably foresee such an extraordinary chain of events, and it would be unfair to make him pay for it. See Exhibit 6.1. Another way of stating that Dom is not liable to the vet's family is by calling the falling pig a *superseding cause*. When one of the "dominoes" in the row is entirely unforeseeable, courts will call that event a superseding cause, letting the defendant off the hook.

EXAM Strategy

Question: Jenny asked a neighbor, Tom, to water her flowers while she was on vacation. For three days, Tom did this without incident, but on the fourth day, when he touched the outside faucet, he received a violent electric shock that shot him through the air, melted his sneakers and glasses, set his clothes on fire, and seriously scalded him. Tom sued, claiming that Jenny had caused the damage when she negligently repaired a second-floor toilet. Water from the steady leak had flooded through the walls, soaking wires and eventually causing the faucet to become electrified. You are Jenny's lawyer. Use one (and only one) element of negligence law to move for summary judgment.

Strategy: The four elements of negligence we have examined thus far are duty to this plaintiff, breach, factual cause, and foreseeable type of injury. Which element seems to be most helpful to Jenny's defense? Why?

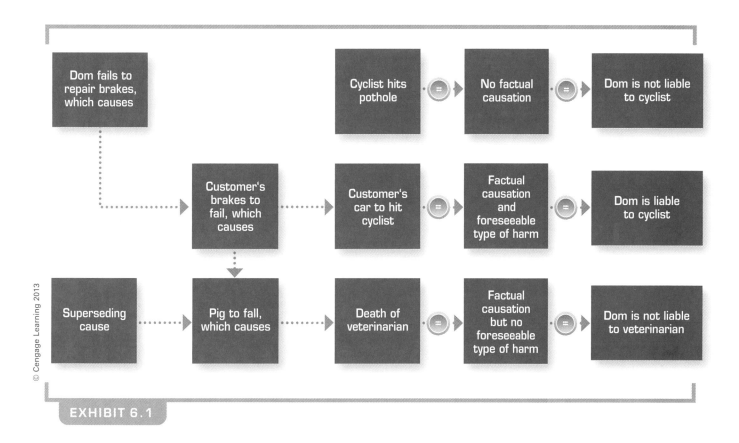

EXHIBIT 6.1

Result: Jenny is entitled to summary judgment because this was not a foreseeable type of injury. Even if she did a bad job of fixing the toilet, she could not possibly have anticipated that her poor workmanship could cause *electrical* injuries—and violent ones, at that—to anybody.[4]

Res Ipsa Loquitur.   Normally, a plaintiff must prove factual cause and foreseeable type of harm to establish negligence. But in a few cases, a court may be willing to infer that the defendant caused the harm, under the doctrine of ***res ipsa loquitur*** ("the thing speaks for itself"). Suppose a pedestrian is walking along a sidewalk when an air conditioning unit falls on his head from a third-story window. The defendant, who owns the third-story apartment, denies any wrongdoing, and it may be difficult or impossible for the plaintiff to prove why the air conditioner fell. In such cases, many courts will apply *res ipsa loquitur* and declare that the facts imply that the defendant's negligence caused the accident. If a court uses this doctrine, then the defendant must come forward with evidence establishing that it did not cause the harm.

Because *res ipsa loquitur* dramatically shifts the burden of proof from plaintiff to defendant, it applies only when (1) the defendant had exclusive control of the thing that caused the harm; (2) the harm normally would not have occurred without negligence; and (3) the plaintiff had no role in causing the harm. In the air conditioner example, most states would apply the doctrine and force the defendant to prove she did nothing wrong.

Res ipsa loquitur
Means "the thing speaks for itself" and refers to cases where the facts *imply* that the defendant's negligence caused the harm.

---

[4]Based on *Hebert v. Enos*, 60 Mass. App. Ct. 817, 806 N.E.2d 452 (Mass. Ct. App. 2004).

Damages

Finally, a plaintiff must prove that he has been injured or that he has had some kind of measureable losses. In some cases, injury is obvious. For example, Ruben Hernandez suffered grievous harm when struck by the drunk driver. But in other cases, injury is unclear. **The plaintiff must persuade the court that he has suffered harm that is genuine, not speculative.**

Some cases raise tough questions. Among the most vexing are suits involving *future* harm. Exposure to toxins or trauma may lead to serious medical problems down the road—or it may not. A woman's knee is damaged in an auto accident, causing severe pain for two years. She is clearly entitled to compensation for her suffering. After two years, all pain may cease for a decade—or forever. Yet there is also a chance that in 15 or 20 years, the trauma will lead to painful arthritis. A court must decide today the full extent of present *and future* damages; the single recovery principle, discussed in Chapter 5, prevents a plaintiff from returning to court years later and demanding compensation for newly arisen ailments. The challenge to our courts is to weigh the possibilities and percentages of future suffering and decide whether to compensate a plaintiff for something that might never happen.

The following case examines a different issue: may a plaintiff recover damages because of the emotional injury suffered when a relative is harmed *if she does not see the accident that led to the harm?*

RA V. SUPERIOR COURT

154 Cal. App. 4th 142, 64 Ca. Rptr. 3d 539
California Court of Appeals, 2007

CASE SUMMARY

Facts: Michelle Ra and her husband, Phil, were shopping in an Armani Exchange in Old Town, Pasadena. Michelle was looking at merchandise in the women's section while Phil examined men's sweaters, about 10 or 15 feet away. Michelle was not facing her husband when she heard a loud bang. A large, overhead store sign had fallen, striking Phil and seriously injuring him. Michelle turned, saw her husband bent over in pain, and hurried to him. Ten days later, Michelle suffered a miscarriage, which she attributed to the accident.

The Ras sued Armani for negligence in permitting the sign to fall and also for the emotional distress suffered by Michelle. This case concerns only Michelle's claim. The trial court granted summary judgment to the store, declaring that Michelle had not made a valid claim of bystander recovery because she had not seen the accident occur. She appealed.

Issue: *May a bystander recover for emotional distress caused by an accident that she did not see?*

Decision: A bystander may not recover for emotional distress caused by an accident unless she witnessed it. Summary judgment affirmed.

Reasoning: Michelle testified that when she heard the crash, "I was not sure if he was involved, but I knew the sound came from the direction—the part of the store he was in."

To recover for negligent infliction of emotional distress as a bystander, a plaintiff must prove she (1) is closely related to the injury victim; (2) is present at the scene of the event and is aware it is injuring the victim; and (3) suffers serious emotional distress as a result. Someone who hears an accident but does not then know it is causing injury to a relative does not have a viable bystander claim for emotional distress, even if she learns the truth moments later.

It is the trauma caused by *witnessing* the injury to a close relative that gives rise to a lawsuit. Michelle did not witness the accident and cannot prevail.

DEFENSES

Assumption of the Risk

Good Guys, a restaurant, holds an ice-fishing contest on a frozen lake to raise money for accident victims. Margie grabs a can full of worms and strolls to the middle of the lake to try her luck, but she slips on the ice and suffers a concussion. If she sues Good Guys, how will she fare? She will fall a second time. Wherever there is an obvious hazard, a special rule applies. **Assumption of the risk: a person who voluntarily enters a situation that has an obvious danger cannot complain if she is injured.** Ice is slippery, and we all know it. If you venture onto a frozen lake, any falls are your own tough luck.

NFL players assume substantial risks each time they take the field, but some injuries fall outside the rule. In a game between the Jets and the Dolphins, Jets assistant coach Sal Alosi, standing on the sideline, tripped Dolphins player Nolan Carroll during a punt return. The trip was not a "normal" part of a football game, and the "assumption of the risk" doctrine would not prevent Carroll from recovering damages.

Assumption of the risk
A person who voluntarily enters a situation of obvious danger cannot complain if she is injured.

Contributory and Comparative Negligence

Sixteen-year-old Michelle Wightman was out driving at night, with her friend Karrie Wieber in the passenger seat. They came to a railroad crossing, where the mechanical arm had descended and warning bells were sounding, in fact, had been sounding for a long time. A Conrail train, SEEL-7, had suffered mechanical problems and was stopped 200 feet from the crossing, where it had stalled for roughly an hour. Michelle and Karrie saw several cars ahead of them go around the barrier and cross the tracks. Michelle had to decide whether she would do the same.

> ... the mechanical arm had descended and warning bells were sounding, in fact, had been sounding for a long time.

Long before Michelle made her decision, the train's engineer had seen the heavy Saturday night traffic crossing the tracks and realized the danger. A second train had passed the crossing at 70 miles per hour without incident. SEEL-7's conductor and brakeman also understood the peril, but rather than posting a flagman, who could have stopped traffic when a train approached, they walked to the far end of their train to repair the mechanical problem. A police officer had come upon the scene, told his dispatcher to notify Conrail of the danger, and left.

Michelle decided to cross the tracks. She slowly followed the cars ahead of her. TV-9, a freight train traveling at 60 miles per hour, struck the car broadside, killing both girls instantly.

Michelle's mother sued Conrail for negligence. The company claimed that it was Michelle's foolish risk that led to her death. Who wins when both parties are partly responsible? It depends on whether the state uses a legal theory called *contributory negligence*. Under **contributory negligence**, if the plaintiff is even *slightly* negligent, she recovers nothing. If Michelle's death occurred in a contributory negligence state, and the jury considered her even minimally responsible, her estate would receive no money.

Critics attacked this rule as unreasonable. Under those terms, a plaintiff who was 1 percent negligent could not recover from a defendant who was 99 percent responsible. So most states threw out the contributory negligence rule, replacing it with comparative negligence. In a **comparative negligence** state, a plaintiff may generally recover even if she is partially responsible. The jury will be asked to assess the relative negligence of the two parties.

Contributory negligence
A plaintiff who is even *slightly* negligent recovers nothing.

Comparative negligence
A plaintiff may generally recover even if she is partially responsible.

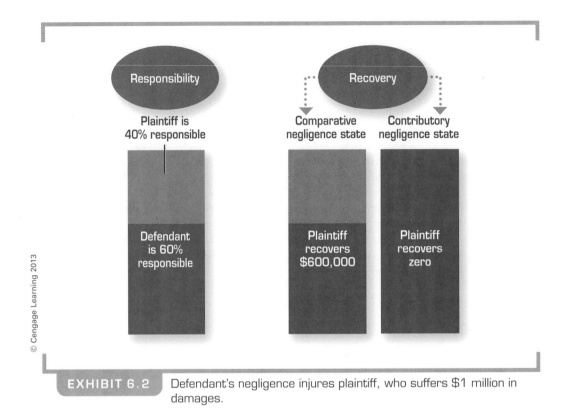

© Cengage Learning 2013

EXHIBIT 6.2 Defendant's negligence injures plaintiff, who suffers $1 million in damages.

Michelle died in Ohio, which is a comparative negligence state. The jury concluded that reasonable compensatory damages were $1 million. It also concluded that Conrail was 60 percent responsible for the tragedy and Michelle 40 percent. See Exhibit 6.2. The girl's mother received $600,000 in compensatory damages.[5]

STRICT LIABILITY

Strict liability

A high level of liability assumed by people or corporations who engage in activities that are very dangerous.

Some activities are so naturally dangerous that the law places an especially high burden on anyone who engages in them. A corporation that produces toxic waste can foresee dire consequences from its business that a stationery store cannot. This higher burden is **strict liability**. There are two main areas of business that incur strict liability: ultrahazardous activity and defective products. We discuss **defective products** in Chapter 13, on product liability.

Ultrahazardous Activity

Defective products

Generally lead to strict liability. See Chapter 13.

Ultrahazardous activities

A defendant engaging in such acts is virtually always liable for resulting harm.

Ultrahazardous activities include using harmful chemicals, operating explosives, keeping wild animals, bringing dangerous substances onto property, and a few similar activities where the danger to the general public is especially great. A defendant engaging in an **ultrahazardous activity** is virtually always liable for any harm that results. Plaintiffs do not have to prove duty, breach, or foreseeable harm. Recall the deliberately bizarre

---

[5]*Wightman v. Consolidated Rail Corporation*, 86 Ohio St.3d 431, 715 N.E.2d 546 (Ohio 1999).

case we posed earlier of the pig falling from a window ledge and killing a veterinarian. Dom, the mechanic whose negligence caused the car crash, could not be liable for the veterinarian's death because the plunging pig was not foreseeable. But if the pig had been jolted off the window ledge by Sam's Blasting Company, doing perfectly lawful blasting for a new building down the street, Sam would be liable. Even if Sam had taken extraordinary care, he would lose. The "reasonable person" rule is irrelevant in a strict liability case.

You be the Judge

NEW JERSEY DEPARTMENT OF ENVIRONMENTAL PROTECTION V. ALDEN LEEDS, INC.

153 N.J. 272; 708 A.2d 1161; 1998 N.J. LEXIS 212; Supreme Court of New Jersey, 1998

Facts: The Alden Leeds company packages, stores, and ships swimming pool chemicals. The firm does most of its work at its facility in Kearns, New Jersey. At any given time, about 21 different hazardous chemicals are present.

The day before Easter, a fire of unknown origin broke out in "Building One" of the company's site, releasing chlorine gas and other potentially dangerous byproducts into the air. There were no guards or other personnel on duty. The fire caused $9 million in damage to company property. Because of the danger, the Department of Environmental Protection (DEP) closed the New Jersey Turnpike and half a dozen other major highways, halted all commuter rail and train service in the area, and urged residents to stay indoors with windows closed. An unspecified number of residents went to local hospitals with respiratory problems.

Based on New Jersey's air pollution laws, the DEP fined Alden Leeds for releasing the toxic chemicals. The appellate court reversed, declaring that there was no evidence the company had caused the fire or the harm. The case reached the state's high court.

You Be the Judge: *Is the company responsible for the harm?*

Argument for Alden Leeds: Alden Leeds did nothing wrong. Why should the company pay a fine? The firm was licensed to use these chemicals and did so in a safe manner. There is no evidence the company caused the fire. Sometimes accidents just happen. Do not penalize a responsible business simply to make somebody pay. The state should go after careless firms that knowingly injure the public. Leave good companies alone so they can get on with business and provide jobs.

Argument for the Department of Environmental Protection: This accident made innocent people sick and caused massive difficulties for tens of thousands. It makes no difference why the accident happened. That is the whole point of strict liability. When a company chooses to participate in an ultrahazardous activity, it accepts full liability for anything that goes wrong, regardless of the cause. If you want the profits, you accept the responsibility. Alden Leeds must pay.

Chapter Conclusion

Negligence issues necessarily remain in flux, based on changing social values and concerns. A working knowledge of these issues and pitfalls can help everyone—business executive and ordinary citizen alike.

EXAM REVIEW

1. **ELEMENTS OF NEGLIGENCE**   The five elements of negligence are duty of due care, breach, factual causation, proximate causation, and damages. (pp. 92–93)

2. **DUTY**   If the defendant could foresee that misconduct would injure a particular person, he probably has a duty to her. (pp. 93–94)

3. **LANDOWNER'S LIABILITY**   In most states, a landowner's duty of due care is lowest to trespassers; higher to a licensee (anyone on the land for her own purposes but with the owner's permission); and highest of all to an invitee (someone on the property by right). (pp. 94–95)

4. **BREACH**   A defendant breaches by failing to meet his duty of care. (p. 95)

5. **FACTUAL CAUSE**   If an event physically led to the ultimate harm, it is the factual cause. (p. 96)

6. **PROXIMATE CAUSE**   For the defendant to be liable, the type of harm must have been reasonably foreseeable. (p. 96)

7. **DAMAGES**   The plaintiff must persuade the court that he has suffered a harm that is genuine, not speculative. (p. 98)

8. **CONTRIBUTORY AND COMPARATIVE NEGLIGENCE**   In a contributory negligence state, a plaintiff who is even slightly responsible for his own injury recovers nothing; in a comparative negligence state, the jury may apportion liability between plaintiff and defendant. (pp. 99–100)

EXAM Strategy

Question: There is a collision between cars driven by Candy and Zeke. The evidence is that Candy is about 25 percent responsible, for failing to stop quickly enough, and Zeke about 75 percent responsible, for making a dangerous turn. Candy is most likely to win:

(a)   A lawsuit for battery

(b)   A lawsuit for negligence, in a comparative negligence state

(c)   A lawsuit for negligence, in a contributory negligence state

(d)   A lawsuit for strict liability

(e)   A lawsuit for assault

Strategy: Battery and assault are intentional torts, which are irrelevant in a typical car accident. Are such collisions strict liability cases? No; therefore, the answer must be either (b) or (c). Apply the distinction between comparative and contributory negligence to the evidence here. (See the "Result" at the end of this section.)

9. **STRICT LIABILITY**   A defendant is strictly liable for harm caused by an ultrahazardous activity or a defective product. Ultrahazardous activities include using harmful chemicals, blasting, and keeping wild animals. Strict liability means that if the defendant's conduct led to the harm, the defendant is liable, even if she exercises extraordinary care. (pp. 100–101)

EXAM Strategy

Question: Marko owned a cat and allowed it to roam freely outside. In the three years he had owned the pet, the animal had never bitten anyone. The cat entered Romi's garage. When Romi attempted to move it outside, the cat bit her. Romi underwent four surgeries, was fitted with a plastic finger joint, and spent more than $39,000 on medical bills. She sued Marko, claiming both strict liability and ordinary negligence. Assume that state law allows a domestic cat to roam freely. Evaluate both of Romi's claims.

Strategy: Negligence requires proof that the defendant breached a duty to the plaintiff by behaving unreasonably and that the resulting harm was foreseeable. Was it? When would harm by a domestic cat be foreseeable? A defendant can be strictly liable for keeping a wild animal. Apply that rule as well. (See the "Result" at the end of this section.)

<u>8. Result:</u>   In a contributory negligence state, a plaintiff who is even 1 percent responsible for the harm loses. Candy was 25 percent responsible. She can win *only* in a comparative negligence state.

<u>9. Result:</u>   If Marko's cat had bitten or attacked people in the past, this harm was foreseeable and Marko is liable. If the cat had never done so, and state law allows domestic animals to roam, Romi probably loses her suit for negligence. Her strict liability case definitely fails: a housecat is not a wild animal.

MATCHING QUESTIONS

Match the following terms with their definitions:

_____ A. Breach

_____ B. Strict liability

_____ C. Compensatory damages

_____ D. Invitee

_____ E. Negligence

1. Money awarded to an injured plaintiff

2. Someone who has a legal right to enter upon land

3. A defendant's failure to perform a legal duty

4. A tort in which an injury or loss is caused accidentally

5. Legal responsibility that comes from performing ultrahazardous acts

TRUE/FALSE QUESTIONS

Circle true or false:

1. T F There are five elements in a negligence case, and a plaintiff wins who proves at least three of them.

2. T F Max, a 19-year-old sophomore, gets drunk at a fraternity party and then causes a serious car accident. Max can be found liable and so can the fraternity.

3. T F Some states are comparative negligence states, but the majority are contributory negligence states.

4. T F A landowner might be liable if a dinner guest fell on a broken porch step, but not liable if a trespasser fell on the same place.

5. T F A defendant can be liable for negligence even if he never intended to cause harm.

6. T F When Ms. Palsgraf sued the railroad, the court found that the railroad should have foreseen what might go wrong.

MULTIPLE-CHOICE QUESTIONS

1. In which case is a plaintiff most likely to sue based on strict liability?
   (a) Defamation
   (b) Injury caused on the job
   (c) Injury caused by a tiger that escapes from a zoo
   (d) Injury caused partially by the plaintiff and partially by the defendant
   (e) Injury caused by the defendant's careless driving

2. Martha signs up for a dinner cruise on a large commercial yacht. While the customers are eating dinner, the yacht bangs into another boat. Martha is thrown to the deck, breaking her wrist. She sues. At trial, which of these issues is likely to be the most important?
   (a) Whether the yacht company had permission to take Martha on the cruise
   (b) Whether the yacht company improperly restrained Martha
   (c) Whether Martha feared an imminent injury
   (d) Whether the yacht's captain did a reasonable job of driving the yacht
   (e) Whether Martha has filed similar suits in the past

3. Dolly, an architect, lives in Pennsylvania, which is a comparative negligence state. While she is inspecting a construction site for a large building she designed, she is injured when a worker drops a hammer from two stories up. Dolly was not wearing a safety helmet at the time. Dolly sues the construction company. The jury concludes that Dolly has suffered $100,000 in damages. The jury also believes that Dolly was 30 percent liable for the accident, and the construction company was 70 percent liable. Outcome?

(a) Dolly wins nothing.

(b) Dolly wins $30,000.

(c) Dolly wins $50,000.

(d) Dolly wins $70,000.

(e) Dolly wins $100,000.

4. A taxi driver, hurrying to pick up a customer at the airport, races through a 20 mph hospital zone at 45 mph and strikes May, who is crossing the street in a pedestrian crosswalk. May sues the driver and the taxi company. What kind of suit is this?

(a) Contract

(b) Remedy

(c) Negligence

(d) Assault

(e) Battery

ESSAY QUESTIONS

1. At approximately 7:50 p.m., bells at the train station rang and red lights flashed, signaling an express train's approach. David Harris walked onto the tracks, ignoring a yellow line painted on the platform instructing people to stand back. Two men shouted to Harris, warning him to get off the tracks. The train's engineer saw him too late to stop the train, which was traveling at approximately 66 mph. The train struck and killed Harris as it passed through the station. Harris's widow sued the railroad, arguing that the railroad's negligence caused her husband's death. Evaluate the widow's argument.

2. A new truck, manufactured by General Motors Corp. (GMC), stalled in rush-hour traffic on a busy interstate highway because of a defective alternator, which caused a complete failure of the truck's electrical system. The driver stood nearby and waved traffic around his stalled truck. A panel truck approached the GMC truck. Immediately behind the panel truck, Davis was driving a Volkswagen fastback. Because of the panel truck, Davis was unable to see the stalled GMC truck. The panel truck swerved out of the way of the GMC truck, and Davis drove straight into it. The accident killed him. Davis's widow sued GMC. GMC moved for summary judgment, alleging (1) no duty to Davis; (2) no factual causation; and (3) no foreseeable harm. Comment on the three defenses that GMC has raised.

3. Randy works for a vending machine company. One morning, he fills up a vending machine that is on the third floor of an office building. Later that day, Mark buys a can of Pepsi from that machine. He takes the full can to a nearby balcony and drops it three floors onto Carl, a coworker who recently started dating Mark's ex-girlfriend. Carl falls unconscious. Is Randy a cause in fact of Carl's injury? Is he a proximate cause? What about Mark?

4. **ETHICS**: Koby, age 16, works after school at FastFood from 4 p.m. until 11 p.m. On Friday night, the restaurant manager sees that Koby is exhausted, but insists that he remain until 4:30 a.m., cleaning up, then demands that he work Saturday morning from 8 a.m. until 4 p.m. On Saturday afternoon, as Koby drives home, he falls asleep at the wheel and causes a fatal car accident. Should FastFood be liable? What important values are involved in this issue? How does the Golden Rule apply?

5. Ryder leased a truck to Florida Food Service; Powers, an employee, drove it to make deliveries. He noticed that the door strap used to close the rear door was frayed, and he asked Ryder to fix it. Ryder failed to do so in spite of numerous requests. The strap broke, and Powers replaced it with a nylon rope. Later, when Powers was attempting to close the rear door, the nylon rope broke and he fell, sustaining severe injuries to his neck and back. He sued Ryder. The trial court found that Powers's attachment of the replacement rope was a superseding cause, relieving Ryder of any liability, and granted summary judgment for Ryder. Powers appealed. How should the appellate court rule?

DISCUSSION QUESTIONS

1. Imagine an undefeated high school football team on which the average lineman weighs 300 pounds. Also, imagine an 0–10 team on which the average lineman weighs 170 pounds. The undefeated team sets out to hit as hard as they can on every play and to run up the score as much as possible. Before the game is over, 11 players from the lesser team have been carried off the field with significant injuries. All injuries were the result of "clean hits"—none of the plays resulted in a penalty. Even late in the game, when the score is 70–0, the undefeated team continues to deliver devastating hits that are far beyond what would be required to tackle and block. The assumption of the risk doctrine exempts the undefeated team from liability. Is this reasonable?

2. Should the law hold landowners to different standards of care for trespassers, social guests, and invitees? Or do the few states that say, "Just always be reasonable" have a better rule?

3. Are strict liability rules fair? Someone has to dispose of chemicals. Someone has to use dynamite if road projects are to be completed. Is it fair to say to those companies, "You are responsible for all harm caused by your activities, even if you are as careful as you can possibly be?"

4. Steve is making copies. Lonnie, his coworker, politely asks, "When will you be done with the copier?" Steve punches Lonnie in the face. Later, Lonnie learns that Steve's last two employers fired him for punching coworkers. He also finds out that his company did not do a background check of any kind on Steve before hiring him. Would it be fair to hold Lonnie's company liable for the attack, or should Lonnie's only action be against Steve?

5. People who serve alcohol to others take a risk. In some circumstances, they can be held legally responsible for the actions of the people they serve. Is this fair? Should an intoxicated person be the only one liable if harm results? If not, in what specific circumstances is it fair to stretch liability to other people?

© r.nagy/Shutterstock.com

CRIME

Crime can take us by surprise. Stacey tucks her nine-year-old daughter, Beth, into bed. Promising her husband, Mark, that she will be home by 11:00 p.m., she jumps into her car and heads back to Be Patient, Inc. She plugs her iPhone into the player of her $85,000 sedan and tries to relax by listening to music. Be Patient is a health care organization that owns five geriatric hospitals. Most of its patients use Medicare, and Stacey supervises all billing to their largest client, the federal government.

She parks in a well-lighted spot on the street and walks to her building, failing to notice two men, collars turned up, watching from a parked truck. Once in her office, she goes straight to her computer and works on billing issues. Tonight's work goes more quickly than she expected, thanks to new software she helped develop. At 10:30, she emerges from the building with a quick step and a light heart, walks to her car—and finds it missing.

A major crime has occurred during the 90 minutes Stacey was at her desk, but she will never report it to the police. It is a crime that costs Americans countless dollars each year, yet Stacey will not even mention it to friends or family. Stacey is the criminal.

> **A major crime has occurred during the 90 minutes Stacey was at her desk, but she will never report it to the police.**

When we think of crime, we imagine the drug dealers and bank robbers endlessly portrayed on television. We do not picture corporate executives sitting at polished desks. "Street crimes" are indeed serious threats to our security and happiness. They deservedly receive the attention of the public and the law. But when measured only in dollars, street crime takes second place to white-collar crime, which costs society *tens of billions* of dollars annually.

The hypothetical about Stacey is based on many real cases and is used to illustrate that crime does not always dress the way we expect. Her car was never stolen; it was simply towed. Two parking bureau employees, watching from their truck, saw Stacey park illegally and did their job. It is Stacey who committed a crime—Medicare fraud. Every month, she has billed the government about $10 million for work that her company has not performed. Stacey's scheme was quick and profitable—and a distressingly common crime.

Crime, whether violent or white-collar, is detrimental to all society. It imposes a huge cost on everyone. Just the *fear* of crime is expensive—homeowners buy alarm systems and businesses hire security guards. But the anger and fear that crime engenders sometimes tempt us to forget that not all accused people are guilty. Everyone suspected of a crime should have the protections that you yourself would want in that situation. As the English jurist William Blackstone said, "Better that ten guilty persons escape than that one innocent suffer."

Thus, criminal law is a balancing act—between making society safe and protecting us all from false accusations and unfair punishment.

THE DIFFERENCE BETWEEN A CIVIL AND CRIMINAL CASE

In civil cases, the wrongdoing has harmed the safety or property of the parties, but it is not so serious that it threatens society as a whole. Conduct becomes criminal when society outlaws it. If a state legislature or Congress concludes that certain behavior harms *public* safety and welfare, it passes a statute forbidding that behavior; in other words, declaring it criminal. Medicare fraud, which Stacey committed, is a crime because Congress has outlawed it.

Prosecution

Suppose the police arrest Roger and accuse him of breaking into a store and stealing 50 computers. The owner of the store is the one harmed, and he has the right to sue the thief in civil court to recover money damages. But **only the government can prosecute a crime and punish Roger by sending him to prison.** The government may also impose a fine on Roger, but it keeps the fine and does not share it with the victim. (However, the court will sometimes order **restitution**, meaning that the defendant must reimburse the victim for harm suffered.)

Restitution
When a guilty defendant must reimburse the victim for the harm suffered.

Burden of Proof

In a civil case, the plaintiff must prove her case only by a preponderance of the evidence.[1] But because the penalties for conviction in a criminal case are so serious, the government has to prove its case **beyond a reasonable doubt**. In all criminal cases, if the jury has any significant doubt at all that Roger stole the computers, it *must* acquit him.

Beyond a reasonable doubt
The very high burden of proof in a criminal trial, demanding much more certainty than required in a civil trial.

---

[1]See the earlier discussion in Chapter 3, on dispute resolution.

Right to a Jury

The facts of a case are decided by a judge or jury. A criminal defendant has a right to a trial by jury for any charge that could result in a sentence of six months or longer. The defendant may demand a jury trial or may waive that right, in which case the judge will be the fact finder.

Felony/Misdemeanor

A **felony** is a serious crime, for which a defendant can be sentenced to one year or more in prison. Murder, robbery, rape, drug dealing, money laundering, wire fraud, and embezzlement are felonies. A **misdemeanor** is a less serious crime, often punishable by a year or less in a county jail. Public drunkenness, driving without a license, and simple possession of a single marijuana cigarette are considered misdemeanors in many states.

Felony
A serious crime, for which a defendant can be sentenced to one year or more in prison.

Misdemeanor
A less serious crime, often punishable by less than a year in a county jail.

CRIMINAL PROCEDURE

The title of a criminal case is usually the government versus someone: *The United States of America v. Simpson* or *The State of Texas v. Simpson*, for example. This name illustrates a daunting thought—if you are Simpson, the vast power of the government is against you. Because of the government's great power and the severe penalties it can impose, criminal procedure is designed to protect the accused and ensure that the trial is fair. Many of the protections for those accused of a crime are found in the first 10 amendments to the United States Constitution, known as the Bill of Rights.

Criminal procedure
The process of investigating, interrogating, and trying a criminal defendant.

> In the federal court system, about 75 percent of all prosecutions end in a plea bargain.

State of Mind

VOLUNTARY ACT

A defendant is not guilty of a crime if she was forced to commit it. In other words, she is not guilty if she acted under duress. However, the defendant bears the burden of proving by a preponderance of the evidence that she did act under duress. In 1974, a terrorist group kidnapped heiress Patricia Hearst from her college apartment. After being tortured for two months, she participated in a bank robbery with the group. Despite opportunities to escape, she stayed with the criminals until her capture by the police a year later. The State of California put on her on trial for bank robbery. One question for the jury was whether she had voluntarily participated in the crime. This was an issue on which many people had strong opinions. Ultimately Hearst was convicted, sent to prison, and then later pardoned.

Guilty
A judge or jury's finding that a defendant has committed a crime.

ENTRAPMENT

When the government induces the defendant to break the law, the prosecution must prove beyond a reasonable doubt that the defendant was predisposed to commit the crime. The goal is to separate the cases where the defendant was innocent before the government tempted him from those where the defendant was only too eager to break the law.

Kalchinian and Sherman met in the waiting room of a doctor's office where they were both being treated for drug addiction. After several more meetings, Kalchinian told Sherman that the treatment was not working for him and he was desperate to buy drugs. Could Sherman help him? Sherman repeatedly refused,, but ultimately agreed to help end Kalchinian's suffering by providing him with drugs. Little did Sherman know that Kalchinian was a police informer. Sherman sold drugs to Kalchinian a number of times. Kalchinian rewarded this act of friendship by getting Sherman hooked again and then turning him in to the police. A jury convicted Sherman of drug dealing, but the Supreme Court overturned the conviction on the grounds that Sherman had been entrapped.[2] The court felt there was no evidence that Sherman was predisposed to commit the crime.

Gathering Evidence: The Fourth Amendment

If the police suspect that a crime has been committed, they will need to obtain evidence. **The Fourth Amendment to the Constitution prohibits the government from making illegal searches and seizures of individuals, corporations, partnerships, and other organizations.** The goal of the Fourth Amendment is to protect the individual from the powerful state.

Warrant

As a general rule, the police must obtain a warrant before conducting a search. A warrant is written permission from a neutral official, such as a judge or magistrate, to conduct a search.[3] **The warrant must specify with reasonable certainty the place to be searched and the items to be seized.** Thus, if the police say they have reason to believe that they will find bloody clothes in the suspect's car in his garage, they cannot also look through his house and confiscate file folders.

Probable Cause

Probable cause

It is likely that evidence of crime will be found in the place to be searched.

The magistrate will issue a warrant only if there is probable cause. **Probable cause** means that based on all the information presented, **it is likely that evidence of a crime will be found in the place to be searched**.

Exclusionary Rule

Under the exclusionary rule, evidence obtained illegally may not be used at trial. The Supreme Court created the exclusionary rule to ensure that police conduct legal searches. The theory is simple: if police know in advance that illegally obtained evidence cannot be used in court, they will not be tempted to make improper searches. Is the exclusionary rule a good idea?

Opponents of the rule argue that a guilty person may go free because one police officer bungled. They are outraged by cases like *Coolidge v. New Hampshire*.[4] Pamela Mason, a 14-year-old babysitter, was brutally murdered. Citizens of New Hampshire were furious, and the state's attorney general personally led the investigation. Police found strong evidence that Edward Coolidge had done it. They took the evidence to the attorney general, who personally issued a search warrant. A search of Coolidge's car uncovered incriminating evidence, and he was found guilty of murder and sentenced to life in prison. But the United States Supreme Court reversed the conviction. The warrant had not been issued by a neutral magistrate. A law officer may not lead an investigation and simultaneously decide what searches are permissible.

After the Supreme Court reversed Coolidge's conviction, New Hampshire scheduled a new trial, attempting to convict him with evidence lawfully obtained. Before the trial began, Coolidge pleaded guilty to second degree murder. He was sentenced and remained in prison until his release years later.

---

[2]*Sherman v. United States*, 356 U.S. 369 (S. Ct., 1958).

[3]A magistrate is a judge who tries minor criminal cases or undertakes primarily administrative responsibilities.

[4]403 U.S. 443, 91 S. Ct. 2022, 1971 U.S. LEXIS 25 (S. Ct., 1971).

In fact, very few people do go free because of the exclusionary rule. One study showed that evidence is actually excluded in only 1.3 percent of all prosecutions; and in about one-half of *those* cases, the court convicted the defendant on other evidence. Only in 0.7 percent of all prosecutions did the defendant go free after the evidence was suppressed.[5]

The Fifth Amendment: Self-Incrimination

The Fifth Amendment bars the government from forcing any person to provide evidence against himself. This provision means that an accused cannot be forced to testify at trial. Indeed, many criminal defendants do not. After all, the burden of proof is on the prosecution, so the defendant may not testify if his lawyer feels the prosecution has not met this burden.

In addition, this provision means that the police may not use mental or physical coercion to force a confession or any other information out of someone. Society does not want a government that engages in torture. Such abuse might occasionally catch a criminal, but it would grievously injure innocent people and make all citizens fearful of the government that is supposed to represent them. Also, coerced confessions are inherently unreliable. The defendant may confess simply to end the torture. If the police do force a confession, the exclusionary rule prohibits the evidence from being admitted in court.

In the following landmark case, the Supreme Court established the requirement that police remind suspects of their right to protection against self-incrimination—with the very same warning that we have all heard so many times on television shows.

---

[5]See the discussion in *United States v. Leon* (Justice Brennan, dissenting), 468 U.S. 897, 1985 U.S. LEXIS 153 (S. Ct., 1984).

Landmark Case

MIRANDA V. ARIZONA

384 U.S. 436; 1966 U.S. LEXIS 2817
Supreme Court of the United States, 1966

CASE SUMMARY

Facts: Ernesto Miranda was a mentally ill, indigent citizen of Mexico. The Phoenix police arrested him at his home and brought him to a police station, where a rape victim identified him as her assailant. The police did not tell him that he had a right to have a lawyer present during questioning. After two hours of interrogation, Miranda signed a confession which said that it had been made voluntarily.

At Miranda's trial, the judge admitted this written confession into evidence over the objection of defense counsel. The officers testified that Miranda had also made an oral confession during the interrogation. The jury found Miranda guilty of kidnapping and rape. After the Supreme Court of Arizona affirmed the conviction, the U.S. Supreme Court agreed to hear his case.

Issues: *Was Miranda's confession admissible at trial? Should his conviction be upheld?*

Decision: Neither his written nor his oral confession was admissible. His conviction was overturned.

Reasoning: To maintain a fair balance between state power and individual rights, to respect human dignity, our system of criminal justice demands that the government seeking to punish an individual produce the evidence against him by its own independent labors rather than by the cruel, simple expedient of compelling it from his own mouth.

Therefore, once the police take a suspect into custody or otherwise deprive him of his freedom, they are required to protect his constitutional right to avoid self-incrimination. To do so, they must warn him that he has a right to remain silent, that any statement he does make may be used as evidence against him, and that he has a right to the presence of an attorney, either retained or appointed. If the police do not inform the accused of these rights, then nothing he says or writes can be admitted in court.

The defendant may waive these rights, provided the waiver is made voluntarily, knowingly, and intelligently.

If, however, he indicates in any manner and at any stage of the process that he does not want to be interrogated or wishes to consult with an attorney before speaking, then the police cannot question him. The mere fact that he may have answered some questions or volunteered some statements on his own does not deprive him of the right to refrain from answering any further inquiries until he has consulted with an attorney.

The Sixth Amendment: Right to a Lawyer

As we have seen in the *Miranda* case, the Sixth Amendment guarantees the **right to a lawyer** at all important stages of the criminal process. Because of this right, the government must *appoint* a lawyer to represent, free of charge, any defendant who cannot afford one.

The Patriot Act

In response to the devastating attacks of September 11, 2001, Congress passed a sweeping antiterrorist law known as the Patriot Act. This statute permits the FBI to issue a **national security letter** (NSL) to communications firms such as Internet service providers (ISPs) and telephone companies. An NSL typically demands that the recipient furnish to the government its customer records *without ever divulging* to anyone what it had done. NSLs can be used to obtain access to subscriber billing records, phone, financial, credit, and other information. However, an appeals court ruled that a secret NSL could be issued only if the government first demonstrated to a court's satisfaction that disclosure of the NSL would risk serious harm.[6]

After Arrest

INDICTMENT

Grand jury
A group of ordinary citizens that decides whether there is probable cause the defendant committed the crime with which she is charged.

Indictment
The government's formal charge that the defendant has committed a crime and must stand trial.

Once the police provide the prosecutor with evidence, he presents this evidence to a **grand jury** and asks its members to indict the defendant. It is the grand jury's job to determine whether there is probable cause that this defendant committed the crime with which she is charged. At the hearing in front of the grand jury, only the prosecutor presents evidence, not the defense attorney, because it is better for the defendant to save her evidence for the trial jury. Just because a defendant is indicted does not mean she is guilty.

If the grand jury determines that there is probable cause, an **indictment** is issued. An indictment is the government's formal charge that the defendant has committed a crime and must stand trial.

ARRAIGNMENT

At an arraignment, a clerk reads the formal charges of the indictment. The defendant must enter a plea. At this stage, most defendants plead not guilty.

---

[6]*Doe v. Mukasey*, 549 F.3d 861; 2008 U.S. App. LEXIS 25193, (2d Cir., 2008).

PLEA BARGAINING

Sometime before trial, the prosecutor and the defense attorney will meet to try to negotiate a plea bargain. A **plea bargain** is an agreement between prosecution and defense that the defendant will plead guilty to a reduced charge and the prosecution will recommend to the judge a relatively lenient sentence. In the federal court system, about 75 percent of all prosecutions end in a plea bargain. In state court systems, the number is often higher. A judge need not accept the bargain but usually does.

Plea bargain

An agreement in which the defendant pleads guilty to a reduced charge, and the prosecution recommends to the judge a relatively lenient sentence.

For example, astronaut Lisa Nowak drove across country dressed in a wig and trenchcoat to attack fellow astronaut Colleen Shipman, whom she viewed as a romantic rival. After Nowak's arrest, police found in her car a BB gun, a knife, and surgical tubing, which was thought to be evidence of her violent intent. Nowak was charged with attempted murder and attempted kidnapping, but much of the evidence was thrown out of court under the exclusionary rule because of police misconduct. Nowak ultimately pleaded guilty to battery and burglary of a car. At that point, she had served two days in jail. She did not receive further jail time, but she was required to complete 50 hours of community service and to attend anger-management classes.

TRIAL AND APPEAL

When there is no plea bargain, the case must go to trial. It is the prosecution's job to convince the jury beyond a reasonable doubt that the defendant committed every element of the crime charged. Convicted defendants have a right to appeal.

DOUBLE JEOPARDY

The prohibition against **double jeopardy** means that a defendant may be prosecuted only once for a particular criminal offense. The purpose is to prevent the government from destroying the lives of innocent citizens with repetitive prosecutions. Imagine that Rod and Lucy are accused of murdering a taxi driver. Rod is tried first and wins an acquittal. At Lucy's trial, Rod testifies that he is, indeed, the murderer. The jury acquits Lucy. The Double Jeopardy Clause prohibits the state from retrying Rod again for the same offense, even though he has now confessed to it.

Double jeopardy

A criminal defendant may be prosecuted only once for a particular criminal offense.

PUNISHMENT

The Eighth Amendment prohibits cruel and unusual punishment. The most dramatic issue litigated under this clause is the death penalty. The Supreme Court has ruled that capital punishment is not inherently unconstitutional.

As you might expect from the term "cruel and unusual," courts are generally unsympathetic to such claims unless the punishment is truly outrageous. For example, Mickle pleaded guilty to rape. The judge sentenced him to prison for five years and also ordered that he undergo a vasectomy. The appeals court ruled that this sentence was cruel and unusual. Although the operation in itself is not cruel (indeed, many men voluntarily undergo it), when imposed as punishment, it is degrading and in that sense cruel. It is also an unusual punishment.[7]

CRIMES THAT HARM BUSINESS

Businesses must deal with four major crimes: larceny, fraud, arson, and embezzlement.

Larceny

It is holiday season at the mall, the period of greatest profits—and the most crime. At the Foot Forum, a teenager limps in wearing ragged sneakers and sneaks out wearing Super Sneakers, valued at $145. Down the aisle at a home furnishing store, a man is so taken by a

---

[7]*Mickle v. Henrichs*, 262 F. 687 (1918).

$375 power saw that he takes it. Sweethearts swipe sweaters, pensioners pocket produce. All are committing larceny.

Larceny is the trespassory taking of personal property with the intent to steal it. "Trespassory taking" means that someone else originally has the property. The Super Sneakers are personal property (not real estate), they were in the possession of the Foot Forum, and the teenager deliberately left without paying, intending never to return the goods. That is larceny. By contrast, suppose Fast Eddie leaves Bloomingdale's in New York, descends to the subway system, and jumps over a turnstile without paying. Larceny? No. He has "taken" a service—the train ride—but not personal property.

Fraud

Robert Dorsey owned Bob's Chrysler in Highland, Illinois. When he bought cars, the First National Bank of Highland paid Chrysler, and Dorsey—supposedly—repaid the bank as he sold the autos. Dorsey, though, began to suffer financial problems, and the bank suspected he was selling cars without repaying his loans. A state investigator notified Dorsey that he planned to review all dealership records. One week later, a fire engulfed the dealership. An arson investigator discovered that an electric iron, connected to a timer, had been placed on a pile of financial papers doused with accelerant. Dorsey was convicted and imprisoned for committing two crimes that cost business billions of dollars annually—fraud (for failing to repay the loans) and arson (for burning down the dealership).[8]

Fraud

Deception for the purpose of obtaining money or property.

Fraud refers to various crimes, all of which have a common element: **the deception of another person for the purpose of obtaining money or property from him.** Robert Dorsey's precise violation was bank fraud, a federal crime.[9] It is bank fraud to use deceit to obtain money, assets, securities, or other property under the control of any financial institution.

WIRE FRAUD AND MAIL FRAUD

Wire and mail fraud are additional federal crimes involving the use of interstate mail, telegram, telephone, radio, or television to obtain property by deceit.[10] For example, if Marsha makes an interstate phone call to sell land that she does not own, that is wire fraud.

THEFT OF HONEST SERVICES

The theft of honest services statute prohibits public and private employees from taking bribes or kickbacks. Suppose that Theo has to choose a hotel chain to be his company's preferred provider. The salesperson from Bedstead Hotels agrees to pay Theo $100 each time a company employee stays in a Bedstead property. That payment is a kickback and is illegal under the honest services statute.

EXAM Strategy

Question: Eric mails glossy brochures to 25,000 people, offering to sell them a one-month time-share in a stylish apartment in Las Vegas. The brochure depicts an imposing building, an opulent apartment, and spectacular pools. To reserve a space, customers need only send in a $2,000 deposit. Three hundred people respond, sending in the money. In fact, there is no such building. Eric, planning to flee with the cash, is arrested and prosecuted. His sentence could be as long as 20 years. (1) With what crime

---

[8]*United States v. Dorsey*, 27 F.3d 285, 1994 U.S. App. LEXIS 15010 (7th Cir., 1994).
[9]18 U.S.C. §1344.
[10]18 U.S.C. §§1341–1346.

is he charged? (2) Is this a felony or misdemeanor prosecution? (3) Does Eric have a right to a jury trial? (4) What is the government's burden of proof?

Strategy: (1) Eric is deceiving people, and that should tell you the *type* of crime. (2, 3) The potential 20-year sentence determines whether Eric's crime is a misdemeanor or felony and whether or not he is entitled to a jury trial. (4) We know that the government has the burden of proof in criminal prosecutions—but *how much* evidence must it offer?

Result: Eric has committed fraud. A felony is one in which the sentence could be a year or more. The potential penalty here is 20 years, so the crime is a felony. Eric has a right to a jury, as does any defendant whose sentence could be six months or longer. The prosecution must prove its case beyond a reasonable doubt, a much higher burden than that in a civil case.

Arson

Robert Dorsey, the Chrysler dealer, committed a second serious crime. **Arson** is the malicious use of fire or explosives to damage or destroy any real estate or personal property. It is both a federal and a state crime. Dorsey used arson to conceal his bank fraud. Most arsonists hope to collect on insurance policies. Every year, thousands of buildings are burned as owners try to extricate themselves from financial difficulties. Everyone who purchases insurance ends up paying higher premiums because of this immorality.

Arson
The malicious use of fire or explosives to damage or destroy real estate or personal property.

Embezzlement

This crime also involves illegally obtaining property, but with one big difference: the culprit begins with legal possession. **Embezzlement** is the fraudulent conversion of property already in the defendant's possession.

This is a story without romance: for 15 years, Kristy Watts worked part time as a book-keeper for romance writer Danielle Steele, handling payroll and accounting. During that time, Watts stole $768,000 despite earning a salary of $200,000 a year. Watts said that she had been motivated by envy and jealousy. She was sentenced to three years in prison and agreed to pay her former boss almost $1 million.

Embezzlement
The fraudulent conversion of property already in the defendant's possession.

CRIMES COMMITTED BY BUSINESS

A corporation can be found guilty of a crime based on the conduct of any of its **agents**, who include anyone undertaking work on behalf of the corporation. An agent can be a corporate officer, an accountant hired to audit a statement, a sales clerk, or almost any other person performing a job at the company's request.

If an agent commits a criminal act within the scope of his employment and with the intent to benefit the corporation, the company is liable.[11] This means that the agent himself must first be guilty. If the agent is guilty, the corporation is, too.

---

[11]*New York Central & Hudson River R.R. Co. v. United States*, 212 U.S. 481, 29 S. Ct. 304, 1909 U.S. LEXIS 1832 (S. Ct., 1909). Note that what counts is the intention to benefit, not actual benefit. A corporation will not escape liability by showing that the scheme failed.

Critics believe that the criminal law has gone too far. It is unfair, they argue, to impose *criminal* liability on a corporation, and thus penalize the shareholders, unless high-ranking officers were directly involved in the illegal conduct. The following case concerns a corporation's responsibility for a death caused by its employee.

COMMONWEALTH V. ANGELO TODESCA CORP.

446 Mass. 128, 842 N.E. 2d 930
Supreme Judicial Court of Massachusetts, 2006

CASE SUMMARY

Facts: Brian Gauthier, an experienced truck driver, worked for Todesca, a paving company. After about a year driving a particular 10-wheel tri-axle dump truck, Gauthier noticed that the back-up alarm had stopped working. When he reported this, the company mechanic realized that the old alarm needed replacement. The mechanic had none in stock, so the company instructed Gauthier to drive the truck without the alarm.

About a month later, Gauthier and other Todesca drivers were delivering asphalt to a work site on a highway at the entrance to a shopping mall. A police officer directed the construction vehicles and the routine mall traffic. A different driver asked the officer to "watch our backs" as the trucks backed through the intersection. All of the other trucks were equipped with back-up alarms. When it was Gauthier's turn to back up, he struck the police officer, killing him.

The state charged the Todesca Corporation with motor vehicle homicide, and the jury found the company guilty. The trial judge imposed a fine—of $2,500. The court of appeals reversed the conviction, and the prosecution appealed to the state's highest court.

Issue: *Could the company be found guilty of motor vehicle homicide?*

Decision: Yes, the company was guilty of motor vehicle homicide.

Reasoning: The defendant maintains that a corporation never can be criminally liable for motor vehicle homicide because a corporation cannot "operate" a vehicle. We disagree. A corporation can act only through its agents. By the defendant's reasoning, a corporation never could be liable for any crime. A corporation can no more serve alcohol to minors, or bribe government officials, than operate a vehicle negligently. Only human agents are capable of these actions. Nevertheless, we consistently have held that a corporation may be criminally liable for such acts when performed by corporate employees, acting within the scope of their employment and on behalf of the corporation.

Gauthier's truck was not equipped with a functioning back-up alarm, and he knew the alarm was missing. The defendant had a written safety policy mandating that all its trucks be equipped with such alarms. An employee's violation of his employer's rules, intended to protect the safety of third persons, is evidence of the employee's negligence, for which the employer may be held liable.

Gauthier never informed the victim that his truck did not have an alarm. The jury could have inferred that the victim, a veteran police officer, knew that the defendant routinely equipped its trucks with backup alarms. The victim expected to hear a backup alarm and would have, almost right in his ear, had the truck been properly maintained.

Affirmed.

Selected Crimes Committed by Business

RICO

Racketeer Influenced and Corrupt Organizations Act (RICO)

A powerful Federal statute, originally aimed at organized crime, now used in many criminal prosecutions and civil lawsuits.

The **Racketeer Influenced and Corrupt Organizations Act (RICO)**[12] is one of the most powerful and controversial statutes ever written. Congress passed the law primarily to prevent gangsters from taking money they earned illegally and investing it in legitimate businesses. But

_____

[12]18 U.S.C. §§1961–1968.

RICO has expanded far beyond the original intentions of Congress and is now used more often against ordinary businesses than against organized criminals. Some regard this wide application as a tremendous advance in law enforcement, but others view it as an oppressive weapon used to club ethical companies into settlements they should never have to make.

What is a violation of this law? **RICO prohibits using two or more racketeering acts to accomplish any of these goals: (1) investing in or acquiring legitimate businesses with criminal money; (2) maintaining or acquiring businesses through criminal activity; or (3) operating businesses through criminal activity.**

What does that mean in English? It is a two-step process to prove that a person or an organization has violated RICO:

- The prosecutor must show that the defendant committed two or more **racketeering acts**, which are any of a long list of specified crimes: embezzlement, arson, mail fraud, wire fraud, and so forth. Thus, if a gangster ordered a building torched in January and then burned a second building in October, that would be two racketeering acts. If a stockbroker told two customers that Bronx Gold Mines was a promising stock when she knew that it was worthless, that would be two racketeering acts.

- The prosecutor must then show that the defendant used these racketeering acts to accomplish one of the three *purposes* listed above. If the gangster committed two arsons and then used the insurance payments to buy a dry cleaning business, that would violate RICO. If the stockbroker gave fraudulent advice and used the commissions to buy advertising for her firm, that would violate RICO.

Racketeering acts
Any of a long list of specified crimes, such as embezzlement, arson, mail fraud, and wire fraud.

The government may prosecute both individuals and organizations for violating RICO. For example, the government may prosecute a mobster, claiming that he has run a heroin ring for years. It may also prosecute an accounting firm, claiming that it lied about corporate assets in a stock sale to make the shares appear more valuable than they really were. If the government proves its case, the defendant can be hit with large fines and a prison sentence of up to 20 years. And the court may order a convicted defendant to hand over any property or money used in the criminal acts or derived from them.

In addition to criminal penalties, RICO also creates civil law liabilities. The government, organizations, and individuals all have the right to file civil lawsuits seeking damages and, if necessary, injunctions. For example, a physician sued State Farm Insurance, alleging that the company had hired doctors to produce false medical reports that the company used to cut off claims by injured policy holders. As a result of these fake reports, the company refused to pay the plaintiff for legitimate services he performed for the policy holders. RICO is powerful (and for defendants, frightening) in part because a civil plaintiff can recover **treble damages**, that is, a judgment for three times the harm actually suffered, as well as attorney's fees.

MONEY LAUNDERING

Money laundering consists of taking the proceeds of certain criminal acts and either (1) using the money to promote crime or (2) attempting to conceal the source of the money.[13]

Money laundering
Using the proceeds of criminal acts either to promote crime or conceal the source of the money.

Money laundering is an important part of major criminal enterprises. Successful criminals earn enormous sums, which they must filter back into the flow of commerce so that their crimes go undetected. Laundering is an essential part of the corrosive traffic in drugs. Profits, all in cash, may mount so swiftly that dealers struggle to use the money without attracting the government's attention. For example, Colombian drug cartels set up a sophisticated system in which they shipped money to countries such as Dubai that do not keep records on cash transactions. This money was then transferred to the United States disguised as offshore loans. Prosecution by the U.S. government led to the demise of some of the banks involved.

---

[13]18 U.S.C. §§1956 et seq.

EXAM Strategy

Question: Explain the difference between embezzlement and money laundering. Give an example of each.

Strategy: Both crimes involve money illegally obtained, but they are very different. As to embezzlement, how did the criminal obtain the funds? In a laundering case, to what use is the criminal trying to put the cash?

Result: Embezzlement refers to fraudulently taking money that is already in the defendant's possession. For example, if a financial advisor, *lawfully entrusted* with his client's funds for investing, uses some of the cash to buy himself a luxurious yacht, he has embezzled the client's money. Money laundering consists of taking *illegally obtained* money and either using the funds to promote additional crimes or attempting to *conceal* the source of the cash. Thus, an arms dealer might launder money so that he can use it to finance a terrorist organization.

HIRING ILLEGAL WORKERS

Employers are required to verify their workers' eligibility for employment in the United States. It is illegal to knowingly employ unauthorized workers. Within three days of hiring a worker, the employer must complete an I-9 form, which lists the items that can be used as documentation of eligibility. The government has the right to arrest illegal employees, but it can also bring charges against the business that hired them.

OTHER CRIMES

Additional crimes that affect business appear elsewhere in the text. An increasing number of federal and state statutes are designed to punish those who harm the environment. (See Chapter 26, on environmental law.) Antitrust violations, in which a corporation fixes prices, can lead to criminal prosecutions. (See Chapter 23 on government regulation.)

Punishing a Corporation

FINES

The most common punishment for a corporation is a fine, as demonstrated in the Todesca case. This makes sense in that the purpose of a business is to earn a profit, and a fine, theoretically, hurts. But most fines are modest by the present standards of corporate wealth. Does the $2,500 fine in the *Todesca* case force corporate leaders to be more cautious, or does it teach them that cutting corners makes economic sense because the penalties will be a tolerable cost of doing business?

Sometimes the fines are stiffer. British Petroleum (BP) was found guilty of two serious environmental violations. In 2005 in Texas, the company's failure to follow standard procedures for ensuring safe refineries caused a catastrophic explosion that killed 15 people and injured 170 more. In 2006 in Alaska, the company's failure to inspect and clean pipelines caused 200,000 gallons of crude oil to spill onto the tundra. The total fine for both criminal violations was $62 million.[14] Is that enough to change BP's practices? Evidently not. In the spring of 2010, a BP well called Deepwater Horizon exploded, killing 11 workers and releasing into the Gulf of Mexico the largest marine oil spill ever. The Deepwater rig had

---

[14]Source: **http://epa.gov/**

violated many safety requirements. As this book is going to press, another BP oil spill (of 2,000 to 4,000 gallons) has been reported in Alaska.

COMPLIANCE PROGRAMS

The **Federal Sentencing Guidelines** are the detailed rules that judges must follow when sentencing defendants convicted of federal crimes. The guidelines instruct judges to determine whether, at the time of the crime, the corporation had in place a serious **compliance program**, that is, a plan to prevent and detect criminal conduct at all levels of the company. A company that can point to a detailed, functioning compliance program may benefit from a dramatic reduction in the fine or other punishment meted out. Indeed, a tough compliance program may even convince federal investigators to curtail an investigation and to limit any prosecution to those directly involved rather than attempting to obtain a conviction against high-ranking officers or the company itself.

Federal Sentencing Guidelines

The detailed rules that judges must follow when sentencing defendants convicted of federal crimes.

Compliance program

A plan to prevent and detect criminal conduct at all levels of a company.

Chapter Conclusion

Crime has an enormous impact on business. Companies are victims of crimes, and sometimes they also commit criminal actions. Successful business leaders are ever-vigilant to protect their company from those who wish to harm it, whether from the inside or the outside.

EXAM REVIEW

EXAM Strategy

1. **BURDEN OF PROOF** In all prosecutions, the government must prove its case beyond a reasonable doubt. (p. 108)

Question: Arnie owns a two-family house in a poor section of the city. A fire breaks out, destroying the building and causing $150,000 in damage to an adjacent store. The state charges Arnie with arson. Simultaneously, Vickie, the store owner, sues Arnie for the damage to her property. Both cases are tried by juries, and the two juries hear identical evidence of Arnie's actions. But the criminal jury acquits Arnie, while the civil jury awards Vickie $150,000. How did that happen?

Strategy: The opposite outcomes are probably due to the different burdens of proof in a civil and criminal case. Make sure you know that distinction. (See the "Result" at the end of this section.)

2. **RIGHT TO A JURY** A criminal defendant has a right to a trial by jury for any charge that could result in a sentence of six months or longer. (p. 109)

3. **FOURTH AMENDMENT** The Fourth Amendment to the Constitution prohibits the government from making illegal searches and seizures of individuals, corporations, partnerships, and other organizations. (pp. 110–111)

4. **WARRANT**   As a general rule, the police must obtain a warrant before conducting a search. (pp. 110–111)

5. **THE EXCLUSIONARY RULE**   Under the exclusionary rule, evidence obtained illegally may not be used at trial. (pp. 110–111)

6. **FIFTH AMENDMENT**   The Fifth Amendment bars the government from forcing any person to provide evidence against himself. (pp. 111–112)

7. **SIXTH AMENDMENT**   The Sixth Amendment guarantees criminal defendants the right to a lawyer. (p. 112)

8. **DOUBLE JEOPARDY**   A defendant may be prosecuted only once for a particular criminal offense. (p. 113)

9. **EIGHTH AMENDMENT**   The Eighth Amendment prohibits cruel and unusual punishment. (p. 113)

10. **LARCENY**   Larceny is the trespassory taking of personal property with the intent to steal. (pp. 113–114)

11. **FRAUD**   Fraud refers to a variety of crimes, all of which involve the deception of another person for the purpose of obtaining money or property. (p. 114)

EXAM Strategy

Question: Chuck is a DJ for a radio station. A music company offers to pay him every time he plays one of its songs. Soon enough, Chuck is earning $10,000 a week in these extra payments, and his listeners love the music. In Chuck's view, this is a win-win situation. Is Chuck right?

Strategy: This is not traditional fraud because Chuck is not getting money from the people he is cheating—his listeners. Indeed, they are happy. Is there another type of fraud that applies in this situation? (See the "Result" at the end of this section.)

12. **ARSON**   Arson is the malicious use of fire or explosives to damage or destroy real estate or personal property. (p. 115)

13. **EMBEZZLEMENT**   Embezzlement is the fraudulent conversion of property already in the defendant's possession. (p. 115)

14. **CORPORATE LIABILITY**   If a company's agent commits a criminal act within the scope of her employment and with the intent to benefit the corporation, the company is liable. (pp. 115–119)

15. **RICO**   RICO prohibits using two or more racketeering acts to invest in legitimate business or carry on certain other criminal acts. RICO permits civil lawsuits as well as criminal prosecutions. (pp. 116–117)

16. **MONEY LAUNDERING**   Money laundering consists of taking profits from a criminal act and either using them to promote crime or attempting to conceal their source. (p. 117)

1. Result: The plaintiff offered enough proof to convince a jury by a preponderance of the evidence that Arnie had damaged her store. However that same evidence, offered in a criminal prosecution, was not enough to persuade the jury beyond a reasonable doubt that Arnie had lit the fire.

11. Result: Chuck has committed a theft of honest services because he has taken a bribe.

MATCHING QUESTIONS

Match the following terms with their definitions:

_____ A. Larceny

_____ B. RICO

_____ C. Money laundering

_____ D. Theft of honest services

_____ E. Embezzlement

1. A statute designed to prevent the use of criminal proceeds in legitimate businesses

2. Fraudulently keeping property already in the defendant's possession

3. Using the proceeds of criminal acts to promote crime

4. When employees take bribes or kickbacks.

5. The trespassory taking of personal property

TRUE/FALSE QUESTIONS

Circle true or false:

1. T F Both the government and the victim are entitled to prosecute a crime.

2. T F If police are interrogating a criminal suspect in custody and he says that he does not want to talk, the police must stop questioning him.

3. T F A misdemeanor is a less serious crime, punishable by less than a year in jail.

4. T F Corporate officers can be convicted of crimes; corporations themselves cannot be.

5. T F An affidavit is the government's formal charge of criminal wrongdoing.

MULTIPLE-CHOICE QUESTIONS

1. Cheryl is a bank teller. She figures out a way to steal $99.99 per day in cash without getting caught. She takes the money daily for eight months and invests it in a catering business she is starting with Floyd, another teller. When Floyd learns what she is doing, he tries it, but is caught in his first attempt. He and Cheryl are both prosecuted.

   (a) Both are guilty only of larceny.

   (b) Both are guilty of larceny and violating RICO.

   (c) Both are guilty of embezzlement; Cheryl is also guilty of violating RICO.

   (d) Both are guilty of embezzlement and violating RICO.

   (e) Both are guilty of larceny and violating RICO.

2. In a criminal case, which statement is true?

   (a) The prosecution must prove the government's case by a preponderance of the evidence.

   (b) The criminal defendant is entitled to a lawyer even if she cannot afford to pay for it herself.

   (c) The police are never allowed to question the accused without a lawyer present.

   (d) All federal crimes are felonies.

3. Benry asks his girlfriend, Alina, to drive his car to the repair shop. She drives his car, all right—to Las Vegas, where she hits the slots. Alina has committed

   (a) fraud.

   (b) embezzlement.

   (c) larceny.

   (d) a RICO violation.

4. Which of the following elements is required for a RICO conviction?

   (a) Investment in a legitimate business

   (b) Two or more criminal acts

   (c) Maintaining or acquiring businesses through criminal activity

   (d) Operating a business through criminal activity

5. Probable cause means

   (a) Substantial evidence that the person signing the affidavit has legitimate reasons for requesting the warrant

   (b) Substantial likelihood that a crime has taken place or is about to take place

   (c) Trustworthy evidence that the victim of the search is known to have criminal tendencies

   (d) That based on all of the information presented, it is likely that evidence of crime will be found in the place mentioned

Essay Questions

1. **YOU BE THE JUDGE WRITING PROBLEM** An undercover drug informant learned from a mutual friend that Philip Friedman "knew where to get marijuana." The informant asked Friedman three times to get him some marijuana, and Friedman agreed after the third request. Shortly thereafter, Friedman sold the informant a small amount of the drug. The informant later offered to sell Friedman three pounds of marijuana. They negotiated the price and then made the sale. Friedman was tried for trafficking in drugs. He argued entrapment. Was Friedman entrapped? **Argument for Friedman**: The undercover agent had to ask three times before Friedman sold him a small amount of drugs. A real drug dealer, predisposed to commit the crime, leaps at an opportunity to sell. **Argument for the government**: Government officials suspected Friedman of being a sophisticated drug dealer, and they were right. When he had a chance to buy three pounds, a quantity only a dealer would purchase, he not only did

so, but he bargained with skill, showing a working knowledge of the business. Friedman was not entrapped—he was caught.

2. Conley owned video poker machines. Although they are outlawed in Pennsylvania, he placed them in bars and clubs. He used profits from the machines to buy more machines. Is he guilty of money laundering?

3. An informant bought drugs from Dorian. The police obtained a search warrant to search Dorian's house. But before they acted on the warrant, they sent the informant back to try again. This time, Dorian said he did not have any drugs. The police then acted on the warrant and searched his house. Did the police have probable cause?

4. Shawn was caught stealing letters from mailboxes. After pleading guilty, he was sentenced to two months in prison and three years supervised release. One of the supervised release conditions required him to stand outside a post office for eight hours wearing a signboard stating, "I stole mail. This is my punishment." He appealed this requirement on the grounds that it constituted cruel and unusual punishment. Do you agree?

5. Karin made illegal firearm purchases at a gun show. At her trial, she alleged that she had committed this crime because her boyfriend had threatened to harm her and her two daughters if she did not. Her lawyer asked the judge to instruct the jury that the prosecution had an obligation to prove beyond a reasonable doubt that Karin had acted freely. Instead, the judge told the jury that Karin had the burden of proving duress by a preponderance of the evidence. Who is correct?

DISCUSSION QUESTIONS

1. Under British law, a police officer must now say the following to a suspect placed under arrest: "You do not have to say anything. But if you do not mention now something which you later use in your defense, the court may decide that your failure to mention it now strengthens the case against you. A record will be made of anything you say, and it may be given in evidence if you are brought to trial." What is the goal of this British law? What does a police officer in the United States have to say, and what difference does it make at the time of an arrest? Which approach is better?

2. **ETHICS** You are a prosecutor who thinks it is possible that Louisa, in her role as CEO of a brokerage firm, has stolen money from her customers, many of whom are not well off. If you charge her and her company with RICO violations, you know that she is likely to plea bargain because otherwise, her assets and those of the company may be frozen by the court. As part of the plea bargain, you might be able to get her to disclose evidence about other people who might have

taken part in this criminal activity. But you do not have any hard evidence at this point. Would such an indictment be ethical? Do the ends justify the means? Is it worth it to harm Louisa for the chance of protecting thousands of innocent investors?

3. Van is brought to the police station for questioning about a shooting at a mall. The police read him his Miranda rights. For the rest of the three-hour interrogation, he remains silent except for a few one-word responses. Has he waived his right to remain silent? Can those few words be used against him in court?

4. Andy was arrested for driving under the influence of alcohol (DUI). He had already been convicted of another driving offense. The court in the first offense was notified of this later DUI charge and took that information into consideration when determining Andy's sentence. Did the state violate Andy's protection against double jeopardy when it subsequently tried and convicted him for the DUI offense?

5. California passed a "three strikes" law, dramatically increasing sentences for repeat offenders. If defendants with two or more serious convictions were convicted of a third felony, the court had to sentence them to life imprisonment. Such a sentence required the defendant to actually serve a minimum of 25 years, and in some cases much more. Gary Ewing, on parole from a 9-year prison term, was prosecuted for stealing three golf clubs worth $399 each. Because he had prior convictions, the crime, normally a misdemeanor, was treated as a felony. Ewing was convicted and sentenced to 25 years to life. Did Ewing's sentence violate the Eighth Amendment?

CHAPTER 8

INTERNATIONAL LAW

© r.nagy/Shutterstock.com

The month after Anfernee graduates from business school, he opens a clothing store. Sales are brisk, but Anfernee is making little profit because his American-made clothes are expensive. Then an Asian company offers to sell him identical merchandise for 45 percent less than the American suppliers charge. Anfernee is elated, but he quickly begins to wonder. Why is the new price so low? Are the foreign workers paid a living wage? The sales representative requests a $50,000 cash "commission" to smooth the export process in his country. That sounds suspicious. The questions multiply . Will the contract be written in English or a foreign language? Must Anfernee pay in dollars or some other currency? The foreign company wants a letter of credit. What does that mean?

> The world is now one vast economy, and negotiations quickly cross borders.

Transnational business is growing with breathtaking speed. The United States now exports more than $1 trillion worth of goods and services each year. Leading exports include industrial machinery, computers, aircraft, electronic equipment, and chemicals. Anfernee should put this lesson under his cap: the world is now one vast economy, and negotiations quickly cross borders.

TRADE REGULATION: THE BIG PICTURE

Nations regulate international trade in many ways. In this section, we look at export and import controls that affect trade out of and into the United States. **Exporting** is shipping goods or services out of a country. The United States, with its huge farms, is the world's largest exporter of agricultural products. **Importing** is shipping goods and services into a country. The United States suffers trade deficits every year because the value of its imports exceeds that of its exports, as the following table demonstrates.[1]

Export

To ship goods or services out of a country.

Import

To ship goods or services into a country.

Rank	Country	Exports (in billions of U.S. dollars)	Imports (in billions of U.S. dollars)
	Total, All Countries	1,278	1,912
1	Canada	249	277
2	China	92	365
3	Mexico	163	230

Source: United States Census Bureau

Export Controls

You and a friend open an electronics business, intending to purchase goods in this country for sale abroad. A representative of Interlex stops in to see you. Interlex is an Asian electronics company, and the firm wants you to help it acquire a certain kind of infrared dome that helps helicopters identify nearby aircraft. You find a Pennsylvania company that manufactures the domes, and you realize that you can buy and sell them to Interlex for a handsome profit. Any reason not to? As a matter of fact, there is.

All nations limit what may be exported. In the United States, several statutes do this, including the **Arms Export Control Act** (AECA). This statute permits the president to create a list of controlled goods, all related to military weaponry. No one may export any listed item without a license.

Arms Export Control Act

Prohibits the export of specific weapons.

The AECA prohibits exports of the infrared domes. The equipment is used in the guidance system of one of the most sophisticated weapons in the American defense arsenal. Foreign governments have attempted to obtain the equipment through official channels, but the American government has placed the domes on the list of restricted military items. When a U.S. citizen did send such goods to a foreign country, he was convicted and imprisoned.

Import Controls

TARIFFS

Tariffs are the most widespread method of limiting what may be imported into a nation. A **tariff** is a tax imposed on goods when they enter a country. Tariffs are also called *duties*. Nations use tariffs primarily to protect their domestic industries. Because the company importing the goods must pay this duty, the importer's costs increase, making the merchandise more expensive for consumers. This renders domestic products more attractive. High

Tariff

A tax imposed on goods when they enter a country. Also called a *duty*.

---

[1]United States Census Bureau. Data is year-to-date through November 2010.

tariffs unquestionably help local industry, but they may harm local buyers. Consumers often benefit from zero tariffs, because the unfettered competition drives down prices.

Tariffs change frequently and vary widely from one country to another. For manufactured goods, the United States imposes an average tariff of less than 4 percent, about the same as that of the European Union (EU). However, some major trading partners around the world set tariffs of 10 to 30 percent for identical items, with those duties generally being highest in developing countries. Foodstuffs show even greater diversity. For agricultural products, average tariffs are about 25 percent in North America, but over 100 percent in South Asia. Tariffs count.[2]

Classification.   The U.S. Customs Service imposes tariffs at the point of entry into the United States. A customs official inspects the merchandise as it arrives and **classifies** it—in other words, decides precisely what the goods are. This decision is critical because the tariffs can vary greatly depending on the classification. Companies will often go to great lengths to convince a court to lower tariffs on their products. In the following case, Isotoner claimed that a tariff violated the Constitution.

Classification

The Customs Service decision about the precise nature of imported goods.

TOTES-ISOTONER CO. v. UNITED STATES

594 F.3d 1346
United States Court of Appeals for the Federal Circuit, 2010

CASE SUMMARY

Facts: Isotoner imports gloves for sale in the United States. The United States imposes a higher tariff on "men's" leather gloves than it does on gloves manufactured "for other persons." Isotoner argued that this difference violated the Constitution's Equal Protection Clause and amounted to illegal gender discrimination. The lower court dismissed the complaint, and Isotoner appealed.

Issue: *Do differing tariff rates for men's and women's gloves amount to illegal gender discrimination?*

Decision: No, the tariff rates do not violate the law.

Reasoning: The Constitution requires equal protection under the law, which means that the government must treat people the same. In this instance, plaintiff argues that the government treats men worse than women—with the result that men pay more for gloves. And that, says the plaintiff, is unacceptable discrimination.

But to be in violation of the Equal Protection Clause, the government must *intend* to discriminate. That intent does not appear to exist here. Tariff rates are set for a variety of reasons. Men's and women's gloves may be made by different companies, in different countries, with a different impact on American industry. The government has the discretion to set different tariff rates for gloves or any other kind of imported goods.

Valuation.   After classifying the imported goods, customs officials impose the appropriate duty *ad valorem,* meaning "according to the value of the goods." In other words, the Customs Service must determine the value of the merchandise before it can tax a percentage of that value. This step can be equally contentious since goods will have different prices at each stage of manufacturing and delivery. The question is supposed to be settled by the transaction value of the goods, meaning the price actually paid for the merchandise when sold for export to the United States (plus shipping and other minor costs). But there is often room for debate, so importers use customs agents to help negotiate the most favorable valuation.

Valuation

The Customs Service's determination of the tariff, based on the value of the goods.

---

[2]World Bank, Economic Research Service, United States Department of Agriculture.

Dumping
Selling merchandise at one price in the domestic market and at a cheaper, unfair price in the international market.

Dumping means selling merchandise at one price in the domestic market and at a cheaper, unfair price in an international market. Suppose a Singapore company, CelMaker, makes cellular telephones for $20 per unit and sells them in the United States for $12 each, vastly undercutting domestic American competitors. CelMaker may be willing to suffer short-term losses in order to bankrupt competitors. Once it has gained control of that market, it will raise its prices, more than compensating for its initial losses. And CelMaker may get help from its home government. Suppose the Singapore government prohibits foreign cellular phones from entering Singapore. CelMaker may sell its phones for $75 at home, earning such high profits that it can afford the temporary losses in America.

In the United States, the Commerce Department investigates suspected dumping. If the Department concludes that the foreign company is selling items at **less than fair value,** and that this harms an American industry, it will impose a **dumping duty** sufficiently high to put the foreign goods back on fair footing with domestic products.

Quotas

Quota
A limit on the quantity of a particular good that may enter a nation.

A **quota** is a limit on the quantity of a particular good that may enter a nation. For example, the United States, like most importing nations, has agreements with many developing nations, placing a quota on imported textiles. In some cases, textile imports from a particular country may grow by only a small percentage each year. Without such a limit, textile imports from the developing world would increase explosively because costs are so much lower there. As part of the GATT treaty (discussed below), the wealthier nations pledged to increase textile imports from the developing countries.

Treaties

The President makes treaties with foreign nations. To take effect, treaties must then be approved by at least 2/3 of the United States Senate. This section will examine three significant trade agreements.

General Agreement on Tariffs and Trade (GATT)

Money and politics are a volatile mix, as demonstrated by all recorded history from 3000 B.C. to the present. As long as nations have existed, they have engaged in disputes about quotas and tariffs. And that is why more than 100 countries negotiated and signed the GATT treaty.

What is GATT—the greatest boon to American commerce in a century, or the worst assault on the American economy in 200 years? It depends on whom you ask. Let's start where everyone agrees.

GATT
The General Agreement on Tariffs and Trade is a massive international treaty designed to eliminate trade barriers and bolster international commerce.

GATT is the General Agreement on Tariffs and Trade. This massive international treaty has been negotiated on and off since the 1940s as nations have sought to eliminate trade barriers and bolster commerce. GATT has already had considerable effect. In 1947, the worldwide average tariff on industrial goods was about 40 percent. Now it is about 4 percent (although agricultural duties still average over 40 percent). The world's economies have exploded over the past six decades.

Leading supporters of GATT suggest that its lower tariffs vastly increase world trade. The United States should be one of the biggest beneficiaries because this country has imposed lower duties than most other nations for decades. But opponents claim that the United States will be facing nations with unlimited pools of exploited labor. These countries will dominate labor-intensive merchandise such as textiles, eliminating millions of American jobs.

The World Trade Organization
A group created by GATT to resolve trade disputes.

GATT created the **World Trade Organization (WTO)** to resolve trade disputes. The WTO is empowered to hear arguments from any signatory nation about tariff violations or nontariff barriers. This international "court" may order compliance from any nation violating GATT and may penalize countries by imposing trade sanctions.

Here is how the WTO decides a trade dispute. Suppose that the United States believes that Brazil is unfairly restricting trade. The United States asks the WTO's Dispute Settlement Body (DSB) to form a panel, which consists of three nations uninvolved in the dispute. After the panel hears testimony and arguments from both countries, it releases its report. The DSB generally approves the report unless either nation appeals. If there is an appeal, the WTO Appellate Body hears the dispute and generally makes the final decision, subject to approval by the entire WTO. No single nation has the power to block final decisions. If a country refuses to comply with the WTO's ruling, affected nations may retaliate by imposing punitive tariffs.

Ethics   Child labor is a wrenching issue. The practice exists to some degree in all countries and is common throughout the developing world. The International Labor Organization estimates that more than 250 million children under the age of 14 work either full or part time. As the world generally becomes more prosperous, this ugly problem has actually increased. Children in developing countries typically work in agriculture and domestic work, but many toil in mines and factories.

The rug industry illustrates the international nature of this tragedy. In the 1970s, the shah of Iran banned child labor in rug factories, but many manufacturers simply packed up and moved to southern Asia. Today, tens of millions of children, some as young as four, toil in rug workrooms 12 hours a day, seven days a week.

Child labor raises compelling moral questions—and economic ones as well. In 1997, Congress passed a statute prohibiting the import of goods created by forced or indentured child labor. The first suit under the new law targeted the carpet factories of southern Asia and sought an outright ban on most rugs from that area. Is this statute humane legislation or cultural imperialism dressed as a nontariff barrier?

REGIONAL AGREEMENTS: NAFTA AND THE EUROPEAN UNION

Many regional agreements also regulate international trade. We will briefly describe the two that most closely affect the United States.

In 1993, the United States, Canada, and Mexico signed the **North American Free Trade Agreement** (NAFTA). The principal goal was to eliminate almost all trade barriers between the three nations. Like GATT, this treaty has been controversial. Unquestionably, trade between the three nations has increased enormously. Mexico now exports more goods to the United States than do Germany, Britain, and South Korea combined. Opponents of the treaty argue that NAFTA costs the United States jobs and lowers the living standards of American workers by forcing them to compete with low-paid labor. For example, Swingline Staplers closed a factory in Queens, New York, after 75 years of operation and moved to Mexico. Instead of paying its American workers $11.58 per hour, Swingline decided to pay Mexican workers 50 cents an hour to do the same job.

Proponents contend that although some jobs are lost, many others are gained, especially in fields with a bright future, such as high technology. They claim that as new jobs invigorate the Mexican economy, consumers there will be able to afford American goods for the first time, providing an enormous new market.

Twenty-seven countries belong to the **European Union** (EU), including Great Britain, Germany, France, Italy and Spain, as well as Latvia and Slovakia.

The EU is one of the world's most powerful associations, with a population of nearly half a billion people. Its sophisticated legal system sets union-wide standards for tariffs, dumping, subsidies, antitrust, transportation, and many other issues. The first goals of the EU were to eliminate trade barriers between member nations, establish common tariffs with

North American Free Trade Agreement
A treaty between Mexico, Canada, and the United States designed to eliminate almost all trade barriers among the three nations.

respect to external countries, permit the free movement of citizens across its borders, and coordinate agricultural and fishing policies for the collective good. The EU has largely achieved these goals. Most, but not all, of the EU countries have adopted a common currency, the euro. During the next decade, the union will focus on further economic integration and effective coordination of foreign policy.

EXAM Strategy

Question: California producers of sea salt protest to the American government that they cannot compete with the same product imported from China. How do the California producers want the government to respond? May the government legally oblige?

Strategy: Domestic producers who cannot compete with foreign competition typically ask their government to impose higher tariffs on the imported goods. However, the whole point of GATT and the WTO is to avoid trade wars. In what circumstances is the United States government free to levy increased duties on the Chinese goods?

Result: When a company *dumps* goods, it sells them overseas at an artificially low price, generally to destroy competition and gain a foothold. That is illegal, and the domestic (United States) government may impose dumping duties to protect local producers.

INTERNATIONAL SALES AGREEMENTS

> You must focus on two principal issues: the sales contract and letters of credit.

You own Big Heel, a company that manufactures boots in Dallas. Le Pied D'Or, a new, fast-growing French chain of shoe stores, is interested in buying 10,000 pairs of your boots, at $300 per pair. You must focus on two principal issues: the sales contract and letters of credit. You are wise enough to know that you must have a written contract— $3 million is a lot of money for Big Heel.

What Law Governs the Sale of Goods?

Potentially, three conflicting laws could govern your boot contract: Texas law, French law, and an international treaty. Each is different, and it is therefore essential to negotiate which law will control.

Texas lawyers are familiar with the Texas law and will generally prefer that it govern. French law is obviously different, and French lawyers and business executives are naturally partial to it. How to compromise? Perhaps by using a neutral law.

The **United Nations Convention on Contracts for the International Sale of Goods (CISG)** is the result of 50 years of work by various international groups, all seeking to create a uniform, international law on this important subject. The United States and most of its principal trading partners have adopted this important treaty.

The CISG applies automatically to any contract for the sale of goods between two parties from different countries if each operates in a country that is a signatory. (Goods are

The United Nations Convention on Contracts for the International Sale of Goods

A uniform, international law on trade that has been adopted by the United States and most of its principal trading partners.

moveable objects like boots.) France and the United States have both signed. Thus, the CISG automatically applies to the Big Heel–Pied D'Or deal unless the parties *specifically opt out*. If the parties want to be governed by other law, their contract must state very clearly that they exclude the CISG and elect, for example, French law.

Choice of Forum

The parties must decide not only what law governs, but where disagreements will be resolved. This can be a significant part of a contract because the French and American legal systems are dramatically different. In a French civil lawsuit, generally neither side is entitled to depose the other or to obtain interrogatories or even documents. This is in sharp contrast to the American system, where such discovery methods dominate litigation. American lawyers, accustomed to discovery to prepare a case and advance settlement talks, are sometimes frankly unnerved by the French system. Similarly, French lawyers are dismayed at the idea of spending two years taking depositions, exchanging paper, and arguing motions, all at great expense. At trial, the contrasts grow. In a French civil trial, there is generally no right to a jury. The rules of evidence are more flexible (and unpredictable), neither side employs its own expert witnesses, and the parties themselves never appear as witnesses.

Additional Choices

The parties must select a language for the contract and a currency for payment. Language counts because legal terms seldom translate literally. And currency is vital because the exchange rate may alter between the signing and payment.

The parties agree that the contract price will be paid in U.S. dollars. Pied D'Or is unfamiliar with U.S. law and absolutely refuses to make a deal unless either French law or the CISG governs. Your lawyer recommends accepting the CISG, provided that the contract is written in English and that any disputes will be resolved in Texas courts. Pied D'Or reluctantly agrees. You have a deal!

Letter of Credit

Because Pied D'Or is new and fast-growing, you are not sure it will be able to foot the bill. Pied D'Or provides a letter of reference from its bank, La Banque Bouffon, but this is a small bank that is unfamiliar to you. You need greater assurance of payment, and your lawyer recommends that payment be made by **letter of credit**. Here is how the letter will work.

Big Heel demands that the contract include a provision requiring payment by confirmed irrevocable letter of credit. Le Pied D'Or agrees. The French company now contacts its bank, La Banque Bouffon, and instructs Bouffon to issue a letter of credit to Big Heel. The letter of credit is a promise *by the bank itself* to pay Big Heel, if Big Heel presents certain documents. La Banque Bouffon, of course, expects to be repaid by Pied D'Or. The bank is in a good position to assess Pied D'Or's creditworthiness since it is local and can do any investigating it wants before issuing the credit. It may also insist that Pied D'Or give Bouffon a mortgage on property, or that Pied D'Or deposit money in a separate Bouffon account. Pied D'Or is the **account party** on the letter of credit, and Big Heel is the **beneficiary**.

But at Big Heel, you are still not entirely satisfied. You feel that a bank is unlikely to default on its promises, but still, you don't know anything about Bouffon. That is why you have required a *confirmed* letter of credit. Bouffon will forward its letter of credit to Big Heel's own bank, Wells Fargo. Wells Fargo examines the letter and then *confirms* the letter. This is *Wells Fargo's own legal guarantee* that it will pay Big Heel. Wells Fargo will do this only if it knows, through international banking contacts, that Bouffon is a sound and trustworthy bank. The risk has now been spread to two banks, and at Big Heel, you are finally confident of payment.

Why do banks do this? For a fee. When will Wells Fargo pay Big Heel? As soon as Big Heel presents documents indicating that the boots have been placed on board a ship bound for France.

The following case shows why sellers often demand a letter of credit.

CENTRIFUGAL CASTING MACHINE CO., INC. V. AMERICAN BANK & TRUST CO.

966 F.2d 1348, 1992 U.S. App. LEXIS 13089
United States Court of Appeals for the Tenth Circuit, 1992

CASE SUMMARY

Facts: Centrifugal Casting Machine Co. (CCM) entered into a contract with the State Machinery Trading Co. (SMTC), an agency of the Iraqi government. CCM agreed to manufacture cast-iron pipe plant equipment for a total price of $27 million. The contract specified payment of the full amount by confirmed irrevocable letter of credit. The Central Bank of Iraq then issued the letter, on behalf of SMTC (the "account party") to be paid to CCM (the "beneficiary"). The Banca Nazionale del Lavorov (BNL) confirmed the letter.

Following Iraq's invasion of Kuwait on August 2, 1990, President George H. W. Bush issued two executive orders blocking the transfer of property in the United States in which Iraq held any interest. In other words, no one could use, buy, or sell any Iraqi property or cash. When CCM attempted to draw upon the letter of credit, the United States government intervened. The government claimed that like all Iraqi money in the United States, this money was frozen by the executive order. The United States District Court rejected the government's claim, and the government appealed.

Issue: *Is CCM entitled to be paid pursuant to the letter of credit?*

Decision: CCM is entitled to payment. Affirmed.

Reasoning: United States claims that it is freezing Iraqi assets to punish international aggression. That is a legitimate foreign policy argument. However, no court has the power to rewrite basic principles of international trade.

A letter of credit has unique value for two reasons. First, the bank that issues the letter is substituting its credit for that of the buyer. Because the bank is promising to pay with its own funds, the seller is confident of receiving its money.

Second, the bank's obligation to pay on the letter of credit is entirely separate from the underlying bargain between buyer and seller. The bank must pay even if the seller has breached the contract or the buyer has gone bankrupt. The money in this case came from the bank that issued the letter; the government may not seize it. Any other ruling would undermine all letters of credit.

EXAM Strategy

Question: In an international contract for the sale of goods, Seller is to be paid by a confirmed irrevocable letter of credit. Buyer claims that the goods are defective and threatens to sue. If the parties are going to end up in court anyway, why bother with a letter of credit?

Strategy: A confirmed letter of credit is unique because the seller is assured of payment as soon as it presents a proper bill of lading to the appropriate local bank—regardless of the quality of the goods. Seller would much rather defend this lawsuit against Buyer than sue for its money in foreign courts.

Result: There *may* be a lawsuit, but Seller is not worried. It is Buyer who must sue, probably in Seller's home country. Buyer now risks substantial time and cash for an uncertain outcome. When the parties discuss a settlement, as surely they will, Seller is holding a big advantage—the cash.

INTERNATIONAL TRADE ISSUE

Extraterritoriality

The United States has many statutes designed to protect employees, such as those that prohibit discrimination on the basis of race, religion, gender, and so on. Do these laws apply overseas? This is an issue of **extraterritoriality**—the power of one nation to impose its laws in other countries.[3] Many American companies do business through international **subsidiaries**—foreign companies that they control. The subsidiary may be incorporated in a nation that denies workers the protection they would receive in the United States. What happens when an employee of a foreign subsidiary argues that his rights under an *American* statute have been violated? You make the call.

Extraterritoriality
The power of one nation to impose its laws in other countries.

Subsidiary
A company controlled by a foreign company.

[3]Extraterritoriality can also refer to exemption from local laws. For example, ambassadors are generally exempt from the law of the nation in which they serve.

You be the Judge

CARNERO V. BOSTON SCIENTIFIC CORPORATION

433 F.3d 1
First Circuit Court of Appeals, 2006

Facts: Boston Scientific (BSC) was an American company that manufactured medical equipment. The company had its headquarters in Massachusetts but did business around the world through foreign subsidiaries. One of the company's subsidiaries was Boston Scientific Argentina (BSA), and it was there that Ruben Carnero began working. His employment contract stated that he would work at BSA's headquarters in Buenos Aires and be paid in pesos. Argentine law was to govern the contract. Four years later, Carnero took an assignment to work as a country manager for a different BSC subsidiary, Boston Scientific Do Brasil (BSB). Carnero frequently traveled to Massachusetts to meet with company executives, but he did most of his work in South America.

About a year later, BSB fired Carnero, and BSA soon did the same. Carnero claimed that the companies terminated him in retaliation for his reporting to BSC executives that the Argentine and Brazilian subsidiaries inflated sales figures and engaged in other accounting fraud. Carnero filed suit in Massachusetts, alleging that his firing violated an American statute, the Sarbanes-Oxley Act of 2002 (SOX).

Congress passed that law in response to the massive fraud cases involving Enron, Arthur Andersen, and other companies. The law was passed primarily to protect investors, but it included a "whistleblower" provision. That section was designed to guard employees who informed superiors or investigating officials of fraud within the company. The law allows injured employees reinstatement and back pay.

BSC argued that SOX did not apply overseas and the District Court agreed, dismissing the case. Carnero appealed.

Issue: *Does SOX protect a whistleblower employed overseas by a subsidiary of an American company?*

Argument for Carnero: Congress passed SOX because the American people were appalled by the massive fraud in major corporations, and the resulting harm to employees, investors, the community, and the economy. The whistleblower protection is designed to encourage honest employees to come forward and report wrongdoing—an act that no employee wants to do, and one which has historically led to termination. Mr. Carnero knew his report would be poorly received but believed he had an ethical obligation to protect his company. For that effort, he was fired, and now Boston Scientific attempts to avoid liability using the technicality of corporate hierarchy.

Yes, Mr. Carnero was employed by BSB and BSA. But both of those companies are owned and operated by Boston Scientific. It is the larger company, with headquarters in the United States, which calls the shots. That is why executives in Massachusetts frequently asked Mr. Carnero to report to them—and why he brought them his unhappy news.

A whistleblower deserves gratitude and a pay raise. Mr. Carnero may well have saved his employer from massive losses and public disgrace. Would Boston Scientific like to wind up as Enron did—the company in bankruptcy court, its executives in prison? If Boston Scientific is too petty to acknowledge Mr. Carnero's contribution, the company should at least honor the purpose and intent of SOX by protecting his job.

Argument for Boston Scientific: First, we do not know whether there have been any accounting irregularities or not. Second, the fact that Mr. Carnero is employed by companies incorporated in Argentina and Brazil is more than a technicality. He is asking an American court to go into two foreign countries—sovereign nations with good ties to the United States—and investigate accounting and employment practices of companies incorporated and operating there. The very idea is offensive. No nation can afford to treat its allies and trading partners with such contempt.

If the United States can impose its whistleblowing law in foreign countries, may those nations impose their rules and values here? Suppose that a country forbids women to do certain work. May companies in those nations direct American subsidiaries to reject all female job applicants? Neither the citizens nor courts of this country would tolerate such interference for a moment.

Mr. Carnero's idea is also impractical. How would an American court determine why he was fired? Must the trial judge here subpoena Brazilian witnesses and demand documentary evidence from that country?

Finally, the SOX law does not apply overseas because Congress never said it did. The legislators—well aware that American corporations operate subsidiaries abroad—made no mention of those companies when they passed this statute.

Foreign Corrupt Practices Act

Foreign investment is another major source of international commerce. Assume that Fonlink is an American communications corporation that wants to invest in the growing overseas market. As a Fonlink executive, you travel to a small, new republic that was formerly part of the Soviet Union. You meet a trade official who tells you that Fonlink is the perfect company to install a new, nationwide telephone system for his young country. You are delighted with his enthusiasm. Over lunch, the official tells you that he can obtain an exclusive contract for Fonlink to do the work, but you will have to pay him a commission of $750,000. Such a deal would be worth millions of dollars for Fonlink, and a commission of $750,000 is economically sensible. Should you pay it?

Foreign Corrupt Practices Act

Prohibits an American businessperson from giving anything of value to a foreign official to influence an official decision.

The **Foreign Corrupt Practices Act (FCPA)** makes it illegal for an American businessperson to give "anything of value" to any foreign official in order to influence an official decision. The classic example of an FCPA violation is bribing a foreign official to obtain a government contract. You must find out exactly why the minister needs so much money, what he plans to do with it, and how he will obtain the contract.

You ask these questions, and the trade official responds, "I am a close personal friend of the minister of the interior. In my country, you must know people to make things happen. The minister respects my judgment, and some of my fee will find its way to him. Do not trouble yourself with details."

Bad advice. A prison sentence is not a detail. The FCPA permits fines of $100,000 for individuals and $1 million for corporations, as well as prison sentences of up to five years.

A company may also forfeit profits earned as a result of illegal bribes. In 2011, Johnson & Johnson agreed to pay $77 million to settle an FCPA action.

It is sad but true that in many countries, bribery is routine and widely accepted. When Congress investigated foreign bribes to see how common they were, more than 450 U.S. companies admitted paying hundreds of millions of dollars in bribes to foreign officials. Legislators concluded that such massive payments distorted competition among American companies for foreign contracts, interfered with the free market system, and undermined confidence everywhere in our way of doing business. In response, Congress passed the FCPA. This law has two principal requirements:

- *Bribes.* The statute makes it illegal for U.S. companies and citizens to bribe foreign officials to influence a governmental decision. It prohibits giving anything of value and also bars using third parties as a conduit for such payments. Interestingly, the bribe need not be actually paid. A *promise* to pay bribes violates the Act. Also, the bribe need not be successful. If an American company makes an unauthorized payment but never gains any benefit, the company has still violated the law.

- *Recordkeeping.* All publicly traded companies—whether they engage in international trade or not—must keep detailed records that prevent hiding or disguising bribes. These records must be available for inspection by U.S. officials.

Not all payments violate the FCPA. **A grease or facilitating payment is legal.** "Grease payments" are common in many foreign countries to obtain a permit, process governmental papers, or obtain utility service. For example, the cost of a permit to occupy an office building might be $100, but the government clerk suggests that you will receive the permit faster (that is, within this lifetime) if you pay $150, one-third of which he will pocket. Such small payments are legal. You cannot bribe the high-level decision makers who award contracts in the first place, but once a contract has been secured, you may often bribe lower-level government workers to encourage them to speed things along.

Chapter Conclusion

Overseas investment offers potentially great rewards but significant pitfalls. A working knowledge of international law is essential to any entrepreneur or executive seriously considering foreign commerce. As the WTO lowers barriers, international trade will increase, and your awareness of these principles will grow still more valuable.

EXAM REVIEW

1. **AECA** The Arms Export Control Act (AECA) restricts exports from the United States that would harm national security or foreign policy. (p. 126)

2. **TARIFF** A tariff is a tax imposed on goods when they enter a country. Tariffs are also known as *duties*. The U.S. Customs Service classifies goods when they enter the United States and imposes appropriate tariffs. (pp. 126–127)

Question: Sports Graphics, Inc. imports "Chill" brand coolers from Taiwan. Chill coolers have an outer shell of vinyl, with handles and pockets, and an inner layer of insulation. In a recent lawsuit, the issue was whether "Chill" coolers were "luggage" or "articles used for preparing, serving, or storing food or beverages," as Sports Graphics claimed. Who was the other party to the dispute, why did the two sides care about this, and what arguments did they make?

Strategy: The Customs Service (the other party) classifies goods and then imposes an appropriate *ad valorem* tax. What is at stake, of course, is money. (See the "Result" at the end of this section.)

3. **DUMPING**   Most countries, including the United States, impose duties for goods that have been dumped (sold at an unfairly low price in the international market). (p. 128)

4. **GATT**   The General Agreement on Tariffs and Trade is lowering the average duties worldwide. Proponents see it as a boon to trade; opponents see it as a threat to workers and the environment. (pp. 128–129)

5. **WTO**   GATT created the World Trade Organization, which resolves disputes between signatories to the treaty. (pp. 128–129)

6. **CISG**   A sales agreement between an American company and a foreign company may be governed by U.S. law, by the law of the foreign country, or by the United Nations Convention on Contracts for the International Sale of Goods. (pp. 130–131)

7. **LETTERS OF CREDIT**   A confirmed irrevocable letter of credit is an important means of facilitating international sales contracts because the seller is assured of payment by a local bank so long as it delivers the specified goods. (pp. 131–132)

Question: Flyby Knight (FK) contracts to sell 12 helicopters to Air Nigeria, for $8 million each. Payment is to be made by letter of credit, issued by the Bank of Nigeria, confirmed by Citibank in New York, and due when the confirming bank receives a bill of lading indicating that all helicopters are on board ship, ready for sailing to Nigeria. FK loads the aircraft on board ship and delivers the bill of lading to Citibank the next day. The same day, Air Nigeria informs FK that its inspectors onboard ship have discovered serious flaws in the rotator blades and the fuel lines. Air Nigeria states that it will neither accept nor pay for the helicopters. Is FK entitled to its $96 million?

   (a) FK is entitled to no money.
   (b) FK is entitled to no money, provided Air Nigeria can prove the helicopters are defective.
   (c) Air Nigeria is obligated to pay FK the full price.
   (d) Bank of Nigeria is obligated to pay FK the full price.
   (e) Citibank is obligated to pay FK the full price.

> **Strategy:** Payment is to be made by confirmed letter of credit. Ask yourself what that means. In such a case, the confirming bank is obligated to pay the seller when the bank receives a bill of lading indicating that conforming goods have been delivered. What about the fact that the goods seem defective? That is irrelevant. It is precisely to avoid long-distance arguments over such problems that sellers insist on these letters. (See the "Result" at the end of this section.)

8. **EXTRATERRITORIALITY**   The principle that refers to the power of one nation to impose its laws in other countries. (pp. 133–134)

9. **FCPA**   The Foreign Corrupt Practices Act makes it illegal for an American businessperson to bribe foreign officials. (pp. 134–135)

2. Result: Customs evidently claimed that the goods were luggage, which carries a much higher tariff than food storage articles. Customs argued that the handles and portability made the articles luggage. But Sports Graphics prevailed, convincing the court that the primary purpose of the containers was the storage of food. The lawsuit reduced the company's tariff from 20 percent to 3.4 percent.

7. Result: When Citibank receives the bill of lading, indicating delivery of the helicopters, it is obligated to pay. The correct answer is (e).

MATCHING QUESTIONS

Match the following terms with their definitions:

___A. Signatory
___B. NAFTA
___C. Tariff
___D. CISG
___E. Dumping

1. A trade agreement between Mexico, the United States, and Canada
2. Selling goods at a cheaper, unfair price internationally
3. An international convention that governs the sale of goods
4. A nation that signs a treaty
5. A duty imposed on imports

TRUE/FALSE QUESTIONS

Circle true or false:

1. T F A problem for many international merchants is that tariffs have been rising for the last decade.
2. T F The United States imports more goods and services (combined) than it exports.

3. T F "Valuation" is the process by which the Customs Service decides the nature of goods being imported into the United States.

4. T F The United States helped negotiate GATT, but ironically, it has refused to sign the agreement.

5. T F Decisions of the WTO are nonbinding recommendations.

MULTIPLE-CHOICE QUESTIONS

1. With which country does the United States trade more than any other?

(a) Mexico

(b) Germany

(c) China

(d) United Kingdom

(e) Canada

2. The Commerce Department alleges that Interlex, a foreign company, is selling Palm Pilots in the United States for less than the cost of production. The department is charging Interlex with

(a) A NAFTA violation

(b) Dumping

(c) An FCPA infraction

(d) An AECA violation

(e) A CISG violation

3. "Choice of forum" refers to

(a) The exporting venue

(b) The importing venue

(c) The country where legal disputes will be settled

(d) The method of payment in an international contract

(e) An inter-banking agreement designed to ensure payment for goods

4. The WTO rules that the nation of Lugubria must lower tariffs on software from the United States from 45 percent to 8 percent, but Lugubria refuses to comply. What can the United States do?

(a) Nothing, because the WTO's ruling is only a recommendation

(b) Appeal to the United Nations

(c) Appeal to the World Court

(d) Impose retaliatory tariffs

(e) File suit in federal court in the United States

5. Your Chicago company negotiates an agreement with a British company for the sale of goods. The contract does not specify the law that governs the agreement. If there is a dispute, what law *will* govern?

   (a) The UCC

   (b) The CISG

   (c) British law

   (d) Illinois law

   (e) EU law

Essay Questions

1. Jean-François, a French wine exporter, sues Bobby Joe, a Texas importer, claiming that Bobby Joe owes him $2 million for wine. Jean-François takes the witness stand to describe how the contract was created. What facts do you need to know in order to determine where this trial is taking place?

2. Blondek and Tull were two employees of an American company called Eagle Bus. They hoped that the Saskatchewan provincial government would award Eagle a contract for buses. To bolster their chances, they went to Saskatchewan and paid $50,000 to two government employees. Back in the United States, they were arrested and charged with a crime. Suppose they argue that even if they did something illegal, it occurred in Canada, and that Canada is the only nation that can prosecute them. Comment on the defense.

3. **ETHICS** Hector works in Zoey's importing firm. Zoey overhears Hector on the phone say, "OK, 30,000 ski parkas at $80 per parka. You've got yourself a deal. Thanks a lot." When Hector hangs up, Zoey is furious, yelling, "I told you not to make a deal on those Italian ski parkas without my permission! I think I can get a better price elsewhere." "Relax, Zoey," replies Hector. "I wanted to lock them in, to be sure we had some in case your deal fell through. It's just an oral contract, so we can always back out if we need to." Is that ethical? How far can a company go to protect its interests? Does it matter that another business might make serious financial plans based on the discussion? Apart from the ethics, is Hector's idea smart?

4. Continental Illinois National Bank issued an irrevocable letter of credit on behalf of Bill's Coal Company for $805,000, with the Allied Fidelity Insurance Co. as beneficiary. Bill's Coal Co. then went bankrupt, and subsequently Allied presented to Continental documents that were complete and conformed to the letter of credit. Continental refused to pay. Because Bill's Coal was bankrupt, there was no way Continental would collect once it had paid on the letter. Allied filed suit. Who should win?

5. Revisit the Totes-Isotoner case. Did the court make the correct decision? In your opinion, does setting different tariff rates on men's and women's gloves amount to unfair discrimination?

DISCUSSION QUESTIONS

1. The United States imports much more than it exports. The annual gap is consistently several hundred billion dollars. Does this concern you? If so, what should be done about it? If not, why not?

2. Does the FCPA seem sensible? Is fighting corruption the right thing to do, or does the statute place American companies at an unacceptable competitive disadvantage?

3. Generally speaking, should the United States pass laws that seek to control behavior outside the country? Or, when in Rome, should our companies and subsidiaries be allowed to do as the Romans do?

4. Do you favor free-trade agreements like NAFTA? Do you believe that free trade benefits everyone in the long run, or are you more concerned that American jobs may be lost?

5. Imagine that you read an article that reports the maker of your favorite brand of clothing uses child labor in its overseas factories. Being realistic, would you avoid buying that kind of clothing in the future? Why or why not?

Contracts

CHAPTER 9

INTRODUCTION TO CONTRACTS

© picsbyst/Shutterstock.com

Austin Electronics had a terrible year. John, the store's owner, decided to get out of the electronics business. Before closing his doors, he hung a sign reading "Everything Must Go!" and held a going out of business sale.

Customer #1—Fran

"Nice TV," Fran commented.

"Price says $400. I'll give you $250 for it."

"Sorry, but I need at least $400," John replied.

"Hmm. Nope, that's just too much."

"OK, OK, I'll let it go for $250."

"Well … no. No, I've changed my mind. No deal."

Customer #2—Ricky

"How much for that iPod, mister?" said Benny, a 10-year-old boy.

"Twenty bucks, kid," John said.

"Wow! I'll take it! Keep it for me while I ride home to get my money."

"Sure thing, kid."

> **"Well, how's about you sell them to me for $50 or I'll beat your face in for you."**

Customer #3—Carla

"That's a good-looking home theater projector," Carla said. "I don't see a price tag. How much?"

"Well," John replied, "how much are you offering?"

"Mmm…I could give you $700 for it."

John was pleasantly surprised. "You've got yourself a deal." The two shook hands.

"I'll be back with my checkbook later on today," Carla said.

Customer #4—Dave

As the sun set and the shadows lengthened, John waited patiently for his last customer to finish looking around. Truth be told, the guy looked kind of creepy.

"I'll give you $50 for these speakers," Dave said in a raspy voice.

"Sorry, man, but I can't let them go for less than $100," John replied.

"Well," Dave said, leaning closer, "how's about you sell them to me for $50 or I'll beat your face in for you."

"O…kay," John said, startled. "$50 it is, then."

Dave smiled. He slid a fifty dollar bill across the counter, picked up the speakers, and left without a word.

John has made four agreements, but are they contracts? Can he require Fran to buy the TV for $250? If Ricky and Carla never return to buy the iPod and the projector, can John take them to court and force them to follow through on the deals? Can John undo his transaction with Dave?

Throughout this unit on contracts, we will consider issues like these. It is vital for a businessperson to understand the difference between an ordinary promise and a legally enforceable contract.

Most contracts work out precisely as intended because the parties fulfill their obligations. Most—but not all. In this unit we will study contracts that have gone wrong. We look at these errant deals so that you can learn how to avoid problems.

CONTRACTS

Elements of a Contract

A contract is merely a legally enforceable agreement. People regularly make promises, but only some of them are enforceable. For a contract to be enforceable, seven key characteristics *must* be present. We will study this "checklist" at length in the next several chapters.

Contracts Checklist
- ☐ Offer
- ☐ Acceptance
- ☐ Consideration
- ☐ Legality
- ☐ Capacity
- ☐ Consent
- ☐ Writing

- ***Offer.*** All contracts begin when a person or a company proposes a deal. It might involve buying something, selling something, doing a job, or anything else. But only proposals made in certain ways amount to a legally recognized offer.

- ***Acceptance***. Once a party receives an offer, he must respond to it in a certain way. We will examine the requirements of both offers and acceptances in the next chapter.

- ***Consideration***. There has to be bargaining that leads to an *exchange* between the parties. Contracts cannot be a one-way street; both sides must receive some measureable benefit.

- ***Legality.*** The contract must be for a lawful purpose. Courts will not enforce agreements to sell cocaine, for example.

- ***Capacity.*** The parties must be adults of sound mind.

- ***Consent.*** Certain kinds of trickery and force can prevent the formation of a contract.

- ***Writing.*** While verbal agreements often amount to contracts, some types of contracts must be in writing to be enforceable.

Let's apply these principles to the opening scenario.

Fran is not obligated to buy the TV for $250 because John did not accept her offer. Ricky does not have to buy the iPod, because he is under 18. If he changes his mind, there is nothing John can do about it. Nor is Carla required to buy the projector. Agreements concerning a sale of goods valued at more than $500 must be in writing. John can successfully sue Dave. He accepted Dave's offer to buy the speakers for $50, but he did so under duress. Agreements made under threats of violence are not enforceable contracts.

Other Important Issues

Once we have examined the essential parts of contracts, the unit will turn to other important issues.

- *Third-party interests.* If Jerome and Tara have a contract, and if the deal falls apart, can Kevin sue to enforce the agreement? It depends.

- *Performance and discharge.* If a party fully accomplishes what the contract requires, his duties are discharged. But what if his obligations are performed poorly, or not at all?

- *Remedies.* A court will award money or other relief to a party injured by a breach of contract.

Contracts Defined

Contract
A promise that the law will enforce.

We have seen that a **contract** is a promise that the law will enforce. As we look more closely at the elements of contract law, we will encounter some intricate issues, but remember that we are usually interested in answering three basic questions of common sense, all relating to promises:

- Is it certain that the defendant promised to do something?

- If she did promise, is it fair to make her honor her word?

- If she did not promise, are there unusual reasons to hold her liable anyway?

TYPES OF CONTRACTS

Bilateral and Unilateral Contracts

Bilateral contract
A contract where both parties make a promise.

In a **bilateral contract**, both parties make a promise. Suppose a producer says to Gloria, "I'll pay you $2 million to star in my new romantic comedy, *A Promise for a Promise*, which we are shooting three months from now in Santa Fe." Gloria says, "It's a deal." That is a bilateral contract. Each party has made a promise to do something. The producer is now bound to pay Gloria $2 million, and Gloria is obligated to show up on time and act in the movie. The vast majority of contracts are bilateral contracts.

Unilateral contract
A contract where one party makes a promise that the other party can accept only by doing something.

In a **unilateral contract**, one party makes a promise that the other party can accept only by *doing* something. These contracts are less common. Suppose the movie producer tacks a sign to a community bulletin board. It has a picture of a dog with a phone number, and it reads, "I'll pay $100 to anyone who returns my lost dog." If Leo sees the sign, finds the producer, and merely promises to find the dog, he has not created a contract. Because of the terms on the sign, Leo must actually find and return the dog to stake a claim to the $100.

Executory and Executed Contracts

A contract is **executory** when it has been made, but one or more parties have not yet fulfilled their obligations. Recall Gloria, who agrees to act in the producer's film beginning in three months. The moment Gloria and the producer strike their bargain, they have an executory bilateral express contract. A contract is **executed** when all parties have fulfilled their obligations. When Gloria finishes acting in the movie and the producer pays her final fee, their contract will be fully executed.

Executory contract
A binding agreement in which one or more of the parties has not fulfilled its obligations.

Executed contract
An agreement in which all parties have fulfilled their obligations.

Valid, Unenforceable, Voidable, and Void Agreements

A **valid contract** is one that satisfies all of the law's requirements. It has no problems in any of the seven areas listed at the beginning of this chapter, and a court will enforce it. The contract between Gloria and the producer is a valid contract, and if the producer fails to pay Gloria, she will win a lawsuit to collect the unpaid fee.

An **unenforceable agreement** occurs when the parties intend to form a valid bargain but a court declares that some rule of law prevents enforcing it. Suppose Gloria and the producer orally agree that she will star in his movie, which he will start filming in 18 months. The law, as we will see in Chapter 15, requires that this contract be in writing because it cannot be completed within one year. If the producer signs up another actress two months later, Gloria has no claim against him.

A **voidable contract** occurs when the law permits one party to terminate the agreement. This happens, for example, when the other party has committed fraud, or when an agreement has been signed under duress. In the opening scenario, Dave threatened John when he would not sell the speakers for $50. The agreement is voidable at John's option. If John later decides that the $50 is acceptable, he may keep it. But if he decides that he wants to cancel the agreement and sue for the return of his speakers, he can do that as well.

A **void agreement** is one that neither party can enforce, usually because the purpose of the deal is illegal or because one of the parties had no legal authority to make a contract.

The following case illustrates the difference between voidable and void agreements.

Valid contract
A contract that satisfies all the law's requirements.

Unenforceable agreement
A contract where the parties intend to form a valid bargain but a court declares that some rule of law prevents enforcing it.

Voidable contract
An agreement that, because of some defect, may be terminated by one party, such as a minor, but not by both parties.

Void agreement
An agreement that neither party may legally enforce.

You be the Judge

Facts: Mr. W sells fireworks. Under Texas law, retailers may only sell fireworks to the public during the two weeks immediately before the Fourth of July and during the two weeks immediately before New Year's Day. And so, fireworks sellers like Mr. W tend to lease property.

Mr. W leased a portion of Ozuna's land. The lease contract contained two key terms:

> "In the event the sale of fireworks on the aforementioned property is or shall become unlawful during the period of this lease and the term granted, this lease shall become void.

MR. W FIREWORKS, INC.
v. OZUNA

2009 Tex. App. LEXIS 8237
Court of Appeals of Texas, Fourth District,
San Antonio, 2009

"Lessor(s) agree not to sell or lease any part of said property including any adjoining, adjacent, or contiguous property to any person(s) or corporation for the purpose of selling fireworks in competition to the Lessee during the term of this lease, *and for a period of ten years after lease is terminated.*" (Emphasis added.)

A longstanding San Antonio city ordinance bans the sale of fireworks inside city limits, and also within 5,000 feet of city limits. Like all growing cities, San Antonio sometimes annexes new land, and its city limits change.

One annexation caused the Ozuna property to fall within 5,000 feet of the new city limit, and it became illegal to sell fireworks from the property. Mr. W stopped selling fireworks and paying rent on Ozuna's land.

Two years later, San Antonio's border shifted again. This time, the city *disannexed* some property and *shrank*. The new city limits placed Ozuna's property just beyond the 5,000-foot no-fireworks zone. Ozuna then leased a part of his land to Alamo Fireworks, a competitor of Mr. W.

Mr. W sued for breach of contract, arguing that Ozuna had no right to lease to a competitor for a period of 10 years. The trial court granted Ozuna's motion for summary judgment. Mr. W appealed.

You Be the Judge: *Did Ozuna breach his contract with Mr. W by leasing his land to a competitor?*

Argument for Ozuna: Your honor, as soon as San Antonio's city limits changed and my client's land fell within 5,000 feet of the city, it became illegal to sell fireworks on his property. The lease is quite clear. By its own terms, it became void. Mr. W, therefore, had no continuing right to enforce any part of it.

Mr. W seeks to selectively enforce one portion of a void lease that it finds advantageous. The company shows no desire to pay rent or to live up to any other parts of the lease.

When the city's boundary changed again, my client was free to lease his property to any seller of fireworks he wished.

Argument for Mr. W: Your honor, my client paid for several things when he leased Ozuna's land. He was buying more than the right to sell fireworks; he was also paying for exclusive rights. The fact that selling fireworks became illegal on the property does not require that the court void the noncompete agreement.

Before San Antonio's city limits shifted, Mr. W lived up to its part of the bargain by paying rent each month. Mr. Ozuna has certainly not offered to return those payments. Yet he is trying to get out of his promise not to lease the land to any other fireworks company.

It is Ozuna who seeks to escape selected parts of the contract. He should be held to his agreement, and he should not be permitted to lease his land to a competitor of Mr. W. The court held that the agreement was in fact void, and that Ozuna was free to lease the land to another fireworks seller.

Express and Implied Contracts

Express contract
An agreement with all important terms explicitly stated.

In an **express contract**, the two parties explicitly state all important terms of their agreement. *The great majority* of binding agreements are express contracts. The contract between the producer and Gloria is an express contract because the parties explicitly state what Gloria will do, where and when she will do it, and how much she will be paid. Some express contracts are oral, as that one was, and some are written.

Implied contract
A contract where the words and conduct of the parties indicate that they intended an agreement.

In an **implied contract**, the words and conduct of the parties indicate that they intended an agreement. Suppose every Friday, for two months, the producer asks Leo to mow his lawn, and loyal Leo does so each weekend. Then for three more weekends, Leo simply shows up without the producer asking, and the producer continues to pay for the work done. But on the 12th weekend, when Leo rings the doorbell to collect, the producer suddenly says, "I never asked you to mow it. Scram." The producer is correct that there was no express contract because the parties had not spoken for several weeks. But a court will probably rule that the conduct of the parties has *implied* a contract. Not only did Leo mow the lawn every weekend, but the producer even paid on three weekends when they had not spoken. It was reasonable for Leo to assume that he had a weekly deal to mow and be paid. Naturally, there is no implied contract thereafter.

Today, the hottest disputes about implied contracts often arise in the employment setting. Many employees have "at will" agreements. This means that the employees are free to quit at any time and the company has the right to fire them at any time, for virtually any reason. Courts routinely enforce at-will contracts. But often a company provides its workers with personnel manuals that guarantee certain rights. The legal issue is whether the handbook implies a contract guaranteeing the specified rights, as the following case demonstrates.

DEMASSE V. ITT CORPORATION

194 Ariz. 500, 984 P.2d 1138, Supreme Court of Arizona, 1999

CASE SUMMARY

Facts: Roger Demasse and five others were employees at will at ITT Corporation, where they started working at various times between 1960 and 1979. Each was paid an hourly wage.

ITT issued an employee handbook, which it revised four times over two decades.

The first four editions of the handbook stated that within each job classification, any layoffs would be made in reverse order of seniority. The fifth handbook made two important changes. First, the document stated that "nothing contained herein shall be construed as a guarantee of continued employment. ITT does not guarantee continued employment to employees and retains the right to terminate or lay off employees."

Second, the handbook stated that "ITT reserves the right to amend, modify, or cancel this handbook, as well as any or all of the various policies [or rules] outlined in it." Four years later, ITT notified its hourly employees that layoff guidelines for hourly employees would be based not on seniority but on ability and performance. About 10 days later, the six employees were laid off, though less-senior employees kept their jobs. The six employees sued. ITT argued that because the workers were employees at will, the company had the right to lay them off at any time, for any reason. The case reached the Arizona Supreme Court.

Issue: *Did ITT have the right unilaterally to change the layoff policy?*

Decision: ITT did not have the right unilaterally to change the layoff policy because a valid implied contract prevented the company from doing so.

Reasoning: An employer has the right to lay off an at-will employee for virtually any reason. That means that the employer also has the right unilaterally to change the layoff policy. However, when the words or conduct of the parties establish an implied contract, the employee is no longer at will.

In deciding whether there is an implied contract concerning job security, the key issue is whether a reasonable person would conclude that the parties intended to limit the employer's right to terminate the employee. A company makes a contract offer when it puts in the handbook a statement about job security that a reasonable employee would consider a commitment. The worker can then accept that offer by beginning or continuing employment. At that point, the parties have created a binding implied contract. Here, the first handbook declared that layoffs would be based on seniority. The employees accepted that offer by working, and from that time on, an implied contract governed the employment relationship. ITT had no right to change the layoff policy unilaterally.

Promissory Estoppel and Quasi-Contracts

Now we turn away from "true" contracts and consider two unusual circumstances. Sometimes courts will enforce agreements even if they fail to meet the usual requirement of a contract. We emphasize that these remedies are uncommon exceptions to the general rules. Most of the agreements that courts enforce are the express contracts that we have already studied. Nonetheless, the next two remedies are still pivotal in some lawsuits. In each case, a sympathetic plaintiff can demonstrate an injury, but *there is no contract*. The plaintiff cannot claim that the defendant breached a contract because none ever existed. The plaintiff must hope for more "creative" relief.

The two remedies can be quite similar. The best way to distinguish them is this:

- In **promissory estoppel** cases, the defendant made a promise that the plaintiff relied on.

- In **quasi-contract** cases, the defendant did not make any promise, but did receive a benefit from the plaintiff.

Promissory estoppel

A doctrine in which a court may enforce a promise made by the defendant even when there is no contract.

Quasi-contract

A legal fiction in which, to avoid injustice, the court awards damages as if a contract had existed, although one did not.

Promissory Estoppel

A fierce fire swept through Dana and Derek Andreason's house in Utah, seriously damaging it. The good news was that agents for Aetna Casualty promptly visited the Andreasons and helped them through the crisis. The agents reassured the couple that all the damage was covered by their insurance, instructed them on which things to throw out and replace, and helped them choose materials for repairing other items. The bad news was that the agents were wrong: the Andreasons' policy had expired six weeks before the fire. When Derek Andreason presented a bill for $41,957 worth of meticulously itemized work that he had done under the agents' supervision, Aetna refused to pay.

The Andreasons sued—but not for breach of contract because the insurance agreement had expired. They sued Aetna under the legal theory of promissory estoppel. **Even when there is no contract, a plaintiff may use promissory estoppel to enforce the defendant's promise if he can show that:**

> ## Is enforcing the promise the only way to avoid injustice?

- The defendant made a promise knowing that the plaintiff would likely rely on it;

- The plaintiff did rely on the promise; and

- The only way to avoid injustice is to enforce the promise.

Aetna made a promise to the Andreasons; namely, its assurance that all the damage was covered by insurance. The company knew that the Andreasons would rely on that promise, which they did by ripping up a floor that might have been salvaged, throwing out some furniture, and buying materials to repair the house. Is enforcing the promise the only way to avoid injustice? Yes, ruled the Utah Court of Appeals.[1] The Andreasons' conduct was reasonable, based on what the Aetna agent said. Under promissory estoppel, the Andreasons received virtually the same amount they would have obtained had the insurance contract been valid.

Quasi-Contract

Don Easterwood leased more than 5,000 acres of farmland in Jackson County, Texas, from PIC Realty for one year. The next year he obtained a second one-year lease. During each year, Easterwood farmed the land, harvested the crops, and prepared the land for the following year's planting. Toward the end of the second lease, after Easterwood had harvested his crop, he and PIC began discussing the terms of another lease. As they negotiated, Easterwood prepared the land for the following year, cutting and plowing, the soil. But the negotiations for a new lease failed, and Easterwood moved off the land. He sued PIC Realty for the value of his work preparing the soil.

Easterwood had neither an express nor an implied contract for the value of his work. How could he make any legal claim? By relying on the legal theory of a quasi-contract: **Even when there is no contract, a court may use a quasi-contract to compensate a plaintiff who can show that:**

- The plaintiff gave some benefit to the defendant;

- The plaintiff reasonably expected to be paid for the benefit and the defendant knew this; and

- The defendant would be unjustly enriched if he did not pay.

---

[1] *Andreason v. Aetna Casualty & Surety Co.,* 848 P.2d 171, 1993 Utah App. LEXIS 26 (Utah App. 1993).

If a court finds all these elements present, it will generally award the value of the goods or services that the plaintiff has conferred. The damages awarded are called *quantum meruit*, meaning that the plaintiff gets "as much as he deserved." The court is awarding money that it believes the plaintiff *morally ought to have*, even though there was no valid contract entitling her to it. This is judicial activism. The purpose is justice; the term is contradictory.

Quantum meruit

"As much as he deserved." The damages awarded in a quasi-contract case.

Don Easterwood testified that in Jackson County, it was common for a tenant farmer to prepare the soil for the following year but then move. In those cases, he claimed, the landowner compensated the farmer for the work done. Other witnesses agreed. The court ruled that indeed there was no contract, but all elements of quasi-contract had been satisfied. Easterwood gave a benefit to PIC because the land was ready for planting. Easterwood reasonably assumed he would be paid, and PIC Realty knew it. Finally, said the court, it would be unjust to let PIC benefit without paying anything. The court ordered PIC to pay the fair market value of Easterwood's labors.

Almost all courts would agree with the result in the Easterwood case. But, once again, if a court "invents" a contract where none existed, it may have opened the door to an infinite variety of claims. When is the enrichment "unjust"? When would a defendant "reasonably know that the plaintiff expects compensation"? In the following case, the defendant knew nothing at all about what doctors did for him—how could he?

NOVAK V. CREDIT BUREAU COLLECTION SERVICE

877 N.E. 2d 1253, Court of Appeals of Indiana, 2007

CASE SUMMARY

Facts: David Novak was unconscious. He suffered a brain aneurysm, a weakness in the brain's blood vessels that can be life-threatening. An ambulance took him to Saint Regional Medical Center, where doctors operated successfully. He remained in the hospital for two months and was discharged, able to go about life's normal activities.

Novak did not pay the Medical Center's bill. The hospital assigned its claim to a credit bureau, meaning that the credit bureau acquired the right to sue Novak for the full debt—which it promptly did.

The trial court found that because Novak had been unconscious, he could not give consent to the treatment. The medical services had been necessary to avoid serious injury or death. When Novak recovered, he remained in the hospital and participated in his own recovery without objecting to the services he received. Based on all of that, the trial court gave judgment to the credit bureau on a theory of quasi-contract. Novak appealed.

Issue: *Was the credit bureau entitled to damages based on quasi-contract?*

Decision: Yes, the bureau was entitled to damages based on quasi-contract.

Reasoning: Novak argues that the credit bureau is entitled to nothing because he never expressly or impliedly requested medical services. However, the real issue in a case of quasi-contract is whether the plaintiff supplied a benefit under circumstances in which compensation is essential to avoid unjust enrichment.

A plaintiff who has supplied services to the defendant, although acting without the defendant's consent, is entitled to restitution if he expected to charge for his work, the services were necessary to prevent serious bodily harm, and it was impossible for the defendant to give consent.

The hospital saved Novak's life, and its doctors assumed they would be paid. Novak could not give consent because he was unconscious. Novak would be unjustly enriched if he received these vital services for free.

Affirmed.

Sources of Contract Law

Common Law

Express and implied contracts, promissory estoppel, and quasi-contract were all crafted, over centuries, by courts deciding one contract lawsuit at a time. Many contract lawsuits continue to be decided using common law principles developed by courts.

Uniform Commercial Code

Business methods changed quickly during the first half of the last century. Transportation speeded up. Corporations routinely conducted business across state borders and around the world. These developments presented a problem. Common law principles, whether related to contracts, torts, or anything else, sometimes vary from one state to another. New York and California courts often reach similar conclusions when presented with similar cases, but they are under no obligation to do so. Business leaders became frustrated that, to do business across the country, their companies had to deal with many different sets of common law rules.

Executives, lawyers, and judges wanted a body of law for business transactions that reflected modern commercial methods and provided uniformity throughout the United States. It would be much easier, they thought, if some parts of contract law were the same in every state. That desire gave birth to the Uniform Commercial Code (UCC), created in 1952. The drafters intended the UCC to facilitate the easy formation and enforcement of contracts in a fast-paced world. The Code governs many aspects of commerce, including the sale and leasing of goods, negotiable instruments, bank deposits, letters of credit, investment securities, secured transactions, and other commercial matters. Every state has adopted at least part of the UCC to govern commercial transactions within that state. For our purposes in studying contracts, the most important part of the Code is Article 2, which governs the sale of goods. **"Goods" means anything movable, except for money, securities, and certain legal rights.** Goods include pencils, commercial aircraft, books, and Christmas trees. Goods do not include land or a house because neither is movable, nor do they include a stock certificate. A contract for the sale of 10,000 sneakers is governed by the UCC; a contract for the sale of a condominium in Marina del Rey is governed by the California common law.

When analyzing any contract problem as a student or businessperson, you must note whether the agreement concerns the sale of goods. For many issues, the common law and the UCC are reasonably similar. But sometimes the law is quite different under the two sets of rules.

And so, the UCC governs contracts for a sale of goods. while common law principles govern contracts for sales of services and everything else. Most of the time it will be clear whether the UCC or the common law applies. But what if a contract involves both goods and services? When you get your oil changed, you are paying in part for the new oil and oil filter (goods) and in part for the labor required to do the job (services). In a mixed contract, Article 2 governs only if the *primary purpose* was the sale of goods.

Goods
Are things that are movable, other than money and investment securities.

EXAM Strategy

Question: Leila agrees to pay Kendrick $35,000 to repair windmills. Confident of this cash, Kendrick contracts to buy Derrick's used Porsche for $33,000. Then Leila informs Kendrick she does not need his help and will not pay him. Kendrick tells Derrick that he no longer wants the Porsche. Derrick sues Kendrick, and Kendrick files suit against Leila. What law or laws govern these lawsuits?

Strategy: Always be conscious of whether a contract is for services or the sale of goods. Different laws govern. To make that distinction, you must understand the term *goods*. If you are clear about that, the question is easily answered.

Result: *Goods* means anything movable, and a Porsche surely qualifies. The UCC will control Derrick's suit. Repairing windmills is a primarily a service. Kendrick's lawsuit is governed by the common law of contracts.

AGREEMENT

Meeting of the Minds

Parties form a contract only if they have a meeting of the minds. For this to happen, one side must make an **offer** and the other must make an **acceptance**. An offer proposes definite terms, and an acceptance unconditionally agrees to them.

Throughout the chapter, keep in mind that courts make *objective* assessments when evaluating offers and acceptances. A court will not try to get inside anyone's head and decide what she was thinking as she made a bargain.

Offer

Bargaining begins with an offer. The person who makes an offer is the **offeror**. The person to whom he makes that offer is the **offeree**. The terms are annoying but inescapable because, like handcuffs, all courts use them.

Two questions determine whether a statement is an offer:

- Do the offeror's words and actions indicate an *intention* to make a bargain?

- Are the terms of the offer reasonably definite?

Zachary says to Sharon, "Come work in my English-language center as a teacher. I'll pay you $800 per week for a 35-hour week, for six months starting Monday." This is a valid offer. Zachary's words seem to indicate that he intends to make a bargain and his offer is definite. If Sharon accepts, the parties have a contract that either one can enforce.

INVITATIONS TO BARGAIN

An invitation to bargain is not an offer. Suppose Martha telephones Joe and leaves a message on his answering machine, asking if Joe would consider selling his vacation condo on Lake Michigan. Joe faxes a signed letter to Martha saying, "There is no way I could sell the condo for less than $150,000." Martha promptly sends Joe a cashier's check for that amount. Does she own the condo? No. Joe's fax is not an offer. It is merely an invitation to bargain. Joe is indicating that he would be happy to receive an offer from Martha. He is not promising to sell the condo for $150,000 or for any amount.

PROBLEMS WITH DEFINITENESS

It is not enough that the offeror indicates that she intends to enter into an agreement. **The terms of the offer must also be definite.** If they are vague, then even if the offeree agrees to the deal, a court does not have enough information to enforce it, and there is no contract.

You want a friend to work in your store for the holiday season. This is a definite offer: "I offer you a job as a salesclerk in the store from November 1 through December 29, 40 hours per week at $10 per hour." But suppose, by contrast, you say: "I offer you a job as a

Offer

In contract law, an act or statement that proposes definite terms and permits the other party to create a contract by accepting those terms.

Contracts Checklist
- ☑ Offer
- ☐ Acceptance
- ☐ Consideration
- ☐ Legality
- ☐ Capacity
- ☐ Consent
- ☐ Writing

Offeror

The party in contract negotiations who makes the first offer.

Offeree

The party in contract negotiations who receives the first offer.

salesclerk in the store during the holiday season. We will work out a fair wage once we see how busy things get." Your friend replies, "That's fine with me." This offer is indefinite. What is a fair wage? $15 per hour? $20 per hour? What is the "holiday season"? How will the determination be made? There is no binding agreement.

The following case presents a problem with definiteness, concerning a famous television show. You want to know what happened? Go to the place. See the guy. No, not the guy in hospitality. Our friend in waste management. Don't say nothing. Then get out.

BAER V. CHASE

392 F.3d 609, Third Circuit Court of Appeals, 2004

CASE SUMMARY

Facts: David Chase was a television writer-producer with many credits, including a detective series called *The Rockford Files*. He became interested in a new program, set in New Jersey, about a "mob boss in therapy," a concept he eventually developed into *The Sopranos*. Robert Baer was a prosecutor in New Jersey who wanted to write for television. He submitted a *Rockford Files* script to Chase, who agreed to meet with Baer.

When they met, Baer pitched a different idea, concerning "a film or television series about the New Jersey Mafia." He did not realize Chase was already working on such an idea. Later that year, Chase visited New Jersey. Baer arranged meetings for Chase with local detectives and prosecutors, who provided the producer with information, material, and personal stories about their experiences with organized crime. Detective Thomas Koczur drove Chase and Baer to various New Jersey locations and introduced Chase to Tony Spirito. Spirito shared stories about loan sharking, power struggles between family members connected with the mob, and two colorful individuals known as Big Pussy and Little Pussy, both of whom later became characters on the show.

Back in Los Angeles, Chase wrote and sent to Baer a draft of the first *Sopranos* teleplay. Baer called Chase and commented on the script. The two spoke at least four times that year, and Baer sent Chase a letter about the script.

When *The Sopranos* became a hit television show, Baer sued Chase. He alleged that on three separate occasions, Chase had agreed that if the program succeeded, Chase would "take care of" Baer and would "remunerate Baer in a manner commensurate to the true value of his services." This happened twice on the phone, Baer claimed, and once during Chase's visit to New Jersey. The understanding was that if the show failed, Chase would owe nothing. Chase never paid Baer anything.

The district court dismissed the case, holding that the alleged promises were too vague to be enforced. Baer appealed.

Issue: *Was Chase's promise definite enough to be enforced?*

Decision: No, the promise was too indefinite to be enforced.

Reasoning: To create a binding agreement, the offer and acceptance must be definite enough that a court can tell what the parties were obligated to do. The parties need to agree on all of the essential terms; if they do not, there is no enforceable contract.

One of the essential terms is price. The agreement must either specify the compensation to be paid or describe a method by which the parties can calculate it. The duration of the contract is also basic: how long do the mutual obligations last?

There is no evidence that the parties agreed on how much Chase would pay Baer, or when or for what period. The parties never defined what they meant by the "true value" of Baer's services or how they would determine it. The two never discussed the meaning of "success" as applied to *The Sopranos*. They never agreed on how "profits" were to be calculated. The parties never discussed when the alleged agreement would begin or end.

Baer argues that the courts should make an exception to the principle of definiteness when the agreement concerns an "idea submission." The problem with his contention is that there is not the slightest support for it in the law. There is no precedent whatsoever for ignoring the definiteness requirement, in this type of contract or any other.

Affirmed.

Termination of Offers

As we have seen, the great power that an offeree has is to form a contract by accepting an offer. But this power is lost when the offer is terminated, which can happen in several ways.

REVOCATION

An offer is **revoked** when the offeror "takes it back" before the offeree accepts. In general, the offeror may revoke the offer any time before it has been accepted. Imagine that I call you and say, "I'm going out of town this weekend. I'll sell you my ticket to this weekend's football game for $75." You tell me that you'll think it over and call me back. An hour later, my plans change. I call you a second time and say, "Sorry, but the deal's off—I'm going to the game after all." I have revoked my offer, and you can no longer accept it.

In the next case, this rule was worth $100,000 to one of the parties.

NADEL v. TOM CAT BAKERY

2009 N.Y. Misc. LEXIS 5105
Supreme Court of New York, New York County, 2009

CASE SUMMARY

Facts: A Tom Cat Bakery delivery van struck Elizabeth Nadel as she crossed a street. Having suffered significant injuries, Nadel filed suit. Before the trial began, the attorney representing the bakery's owner offered a $100,000 settlement, which Nadel refused.

While the jury was deliberating, the bakery's lawyer again offered Nadel the $100,000 settlement. She decided to think about it during lunch. Later that day, the jury sent a note to the judge. The bakery owner told her lawyer that if the note indicated the jury had reached a verdict, that he should revoke the settlement offer.

Back in the courtroom, the bakery's lawyer said, "My understanding is that there's a note.... I was given an instruction that if the note is a verdict, my client wants to take the verdict."

Nadel's lawyer then said, "My client will take the settlement. My client will take the settlement."

The trial court judge allowed the forewoman to read the verdict, which awarded Nadel—nothing. She

appealed, claiming that a $100,000 settlement had been reached.

Issue: *Did Nadel's lawyer accept the settlement offer in time?*

Decision: No, the bakery owner's lawyer revoked the offer before acceptance.

Reasoning: An offer definitely existed. And the twice-repeated statement, "My client will take the settlement," indicates a clear desire to accept the proposal. The problem is that the acceptance came too late.

Analyzing the timeline, the bakery owner's attorney indicated that if a verdict had been returned, he revoked the offer. This notice was given before the attempted acceptance. And so, since a verdict had in fact been returned, the offer was no longer open.

The parties did not reach a binding settlement agreement.

REJECTION

If an offeree clearly indicates that he does not want to take the offer, then he has **rejected** it. A rejection immediately terminates the offer. Suppose a major accounting firm telephones you and offers a job, starting at $80,000. You respond, "Nah. I'm gonna work on my surfing for a year or two." The next day you come to your senses and write the firm, accepting its offer. No contract. Your rejection terminated the offer and ended your power to accept.

COUNTEROFFER

A party makes a **counteroffer** when it responds to an offer with a new and different proposal. Frederick faxes Kim, offering to sell a 50 percent interest in the Fab Hotel in New York for only $135 million. Kim faxes back, offering to pay $115 million. Moments later, Kim's business partner convinces her that Frederick's offer was a bargain, and she faxes an acceptance of his $135 million offer. Does Kim have a binding deal? No. A counteroffer is a rejection. The parties have no contract at any price.

EXPIRATION

When an offer specifies a time limit for acceptance, that period is binding. If the offer specifies no time limit, the offeree has a reasonable period in which to accept.

DESTRUCTION OF THE SUBJECT MATTER

A used car dealer offers to sell you a rare 1938 Bugatti for $7.5 million if you bring cash the next day. You arrive, suitcase stuffed with cash—just in time to see a stampeding herd of escaped circus elephants crush the Bugatti. The dealer's offer terminated.

Acceptance

Contracts Checklist
- [ ] Offer
- [x] Acceptance
- [ ] Consideration
- [ ] Legality
- [ ] Capacity
- [ ] Consent
- [ ] Writing

As we have seen, when there is a valid offer outstanding, it remains effective until it is terminated or accepted. An offeree accepts by saying or doing something that a reasonable person would understand to mean that he definitely wants to take the offer. Assume that Ellie offers to sell Gene her old iPod for $50. If Gene says, "I accept your offer, " then he has indeed accepted, but there is no need to be so formal. He can accept the offer by saying, "It's a deal" or "I'll take it," or any number of things. He need not even speak. If he hands her a $50 bill, he also accepts the offer.

It is worth noting that **the offeree must say or do *something* to accept.** Marge telephones Vick and leaves a message on his answering machine: "I'll pay $75 for your business law textbook from last semester. I'm desperate to get a copy, so I will assume you agree unless I hear from you by 6:00 tonight." Marge hears nothing by the deadline and assumes she has a deal. She is mistaken. Vick neither said nor did anything to indicate that he accepted.

MIRROR IMAGE RULE

If only he had known! A splendid university, an excellent position as department chair— gone. And all because of the mirror image rule. The Ohio State University wrote to Philip Foster offering him an appointment as a professor and chair of the art history department. His position was to begin July 1, and he had until June 2 to accept the job. On June 2, Foster telephoned the dean and left a message accepting the position, **effective July 15.** Later, Foster thought better of it and wrote the university, accepting the school's starting date of July 1. Too late! Professor Foster never did occupy that chair at Ohio State. The court held that since his acceptance varied the starting date, it was a counteroffer. And a counteroffer, as we know, is a rejection.[2]

---

[2]*Foster v. Ohio State University*, 41 Ohio App. 3d 86, 534 N.E.2d 1220, 1987 Ohio App. LEXIS 10761 (Ohio Ct. App. 1987).

The common law **mirror image rule** requires that acceptance be on precisely the same terms as the offer. If the acceptance contains terms that add to or contradict the offer, even in minor ways, courts generally consider it a counteroffer.

Mirror image rule
A contract doctrine that requires acceptance to be on exactly the same terms as the offer.

THE UCC AND THE BATTLE OF THE FORMS

Today, businesses use standardized forms to purchase most goods and services. This practice creates enormous difficulties. Sellers use forms they have prepared, with all conditions stated to their advantage, and buyers employ their own forms, with terms they prefer. The forms are exchanged in the mail or electronically, with neither side clearly agreeing to the other party's terms. The problem is known as the "battle of forms." Once again, the UCC has entered the fray, attempting to provide flexibility and common sense for those contracts involving the sale of goods. Under the UCC, an acceptance that adds additional or different terms often *will* create a contract. And, perhaps surprisingly, the additional terms will often become part of the contract.

UCC §2-207 dramatically modifies the mirror image rule for the sale of goods. Under this provision, an acceptance that adds additional or different terms **will often create a contract.** The rule is intricate, but it may be summarized this way:

- For the sale of goods, the most important factor is whether the parties believe they have a binding agreement. If their conduct indicates that they have a deal, they probably do.

- If the offeree *adds new terms* to the offer, acceptance by the offeror generally creates a binding agreement.

- If the offeree *changes* the terms of the offer, a court will probably rely on general principles of the UCC to create a fair contract.

- If a party wants a contract on its terms only, with no changes, it must clearly indicate that.

Suppose Wholesaler writes to Manufacturer, offering to buy "10,000 wheelbarrows at $50 per unit. Payable on delivery, 30 days from today's date." Manufacturer writes back, "We accept your offer of 10,000 wheelbarrows at $50 per unit, payable on delivery. Interest at normal trade rates for unpaid balances." Manufacturer clearly intends to form a contract. The company has added a new term, but there is still a valid agreement.

EXAM Strategy

Question: Elaine faxes an offer to Raoul. Raoul writes, "I accept. Please note, I will charge 2 percent interest per month for any unpaid money." He signs the document and faxes it back to Elaine. Do the two have a binding contract?

Strategy: Slow down—this is trickier than it seems. Raoul has added a term to Elaine's offer. In a contract for services, acceptance must mirror the offer, but not so in an agreement for the sale of goods.

Result: If this is an agreement for services, there is no contract. However, if this agreement is for goods, the additional term *may* become part of an enforceable contract.

Question: Assume that Elaine's offer concerns goods. Is there an agreement?

Strategy: Under UCC §2-207, an additional term will generally become part of a binding agreement for goods, unless … ?

Result: The parties have probably created a binding contract unless Elaine indicated in her offer that she would accept her terms only, with no changes.

Communication of Acceptance

The offeree must communicate his acceptance for it to be effective. The questions that typically arise concern the method, the manner, and the time of acceptance.

METHOD AND MANNER OF ACCEPTANCE

The "method" refers to whether acceptance is done in person or by mail, telephone, email, or fax. The "manner" refers to whether the offeree accepts by promising, by making a down payment, by performing, and so forth. **If an offer demands acceptance in a particular method or manner, the offeree must follow those requirements.** An offer might specify that it be accepted in writing, or in person, or before midnight on June 23. An offeror can set any requirements she wishes. Omri might say to Oliver, "I'll sell you my bike for $200. You must accept my offer by standing on a chair in the lunchroom tomorrow and reciting a poem about a cow." Oliver can only accept the offer in the exact manner specified if he wants to form a contract.

If the offer does not specify a type of acceptance, the offeree may accept in any reasonable manner and method. An offer generally may be accepted by performance or by a promise, unless it specifies a particular method. The same freedom applies to the method. If Masako faxes Eric an offer to sell 1,000 acres in Montana for $800,000, Eric may accept by mail or fax. Both are routinely used in real estate transactions, and either is reasonable.

TIME OF ACCEPTANCE: THE MAILBOX RULE

An acceptance is generally effective upon dispatch, meaning the moment it is out of the offeree's control. Terminations, on the other hand, are effective when received. When Masako faxes her offer to sell land to Eric and he mails his acceptance, the contract is binding the moment he puts the letter into the mail. In most cases, this **mailbox rule** is just a detail. But it becomes important when the offeror revokes her offer at about the same time the offeree accepts. Who wins? Suppose Masako's offer has one twist:

- On Monday morning, Masako faxes her offer to Eric.

- On Monday afternoon, Eric writes "I accept" on the fax, and Masako mails a revocation of her offer.

- On Tuesday morning, Eric mails his acceptance.

- On Thursday morning, Masako's revocation arrives at Eric's office

- On Friday morning, Eric's acceptance arrives at Masako's office.

Outcome? Eric has an enforceable contract. Masako's offer was effective when it reached Eric. His acceptance was effective on Tuesday morning, when he mailed it. Nothing that happens later can "undo" the contract.

Chapter Conclusion

Contracts govern countless areas of our lives, from intimate family issues to multibillion dollar corporate deals. Understanding contract principles is essential for a successful business or a professional career and is invaluable in private life. Courts no longer rubber-stamp any agreement that two parties have made. If we know the issues that courts scrutinize, the agreement we draft is likelier to be enforced. We thus achieve greater control over our affairs—the very purpose of a contract.

EXAM REVIEW

1. **CONTRACTS: DEFINITION AND ELEMENTS**   A contract is a legally enforceable promise. Analyzing whether a contract exists involves inquiring into these issues: offer, acceptance, consideration, capacity, legal purpose, consent, and sometimes, whether the deal is in writing. (pp. 143–144)

2. **UNILATERAL AND BILATERAL CONTRACTS**   In bilateral contracts, the parties exchange promises. In a unilateral contract, only one party makes a promise, and the other must take some action; his return promise is insufficient to form a contract. (p. 144)

3. **EXECUTORY AND EXECUTED CONTRACTS**   In an executory contract, one or both of the parties has not yet have not done everything that they promised to do. In an executed contract, all parties have fully performed. (p. 145)

4. **VALID, UNENFORCEABLE, VOIDABLE, AND VOID AGREEMENTS**   Valid contracts are fully enforceable. An unenforceable agreement is one with a legal defect. A voidable contract occurs when one party has an option to cancel the agreement. A void agreement means that the law will ignore the deal regardless of what the parties want. (pp. 145–146)

5. **EXPRESS AND IMPLIED CONTRACTS**   If the parties formally agreed and stated explicit terms, there is probably an express contract. If the parties did not formally agree but their conduct, words, or past dealings indicate they intended a binding agreement, there may be an implied contract. (pp. 146–147)

6. **PROMISSORY ESTOPPELS AND QUASI-CONTRACTS**   A claim of promissory estoppel requires that the defendant made a promise knowing that the plaintiff would likely *rely* on it, and the plaintiff did so. It would be wrong to deny recovery. A claim of quasi-contract requires that the defendant received a benefit, knowing that the plaintiff would expect compensation, and it would be unjust not to grant it. (pp. 147–149)

EXAM Strategy

Question: The Hoffmans owned and operated a successful small bakery and grocery store. They spoke with Lukowitz, an agent of Red Owl Stores, who told them that for $18,000, Red Owl would build a store and fully stock it for them. The Hoffmans sold their bakery and grocery store and purchased a lot on which Red Owl was to build the store. Lukowitz then told Hoffman that the price had gone up to $26,000. The Hoffmans borrowed the extra money from relatives, but then Lukowitz informed them that the cost would be $34,000. Negotiations broke off and the Hoffmans sued. The court determined that there was no contract because too many details had not been worked out—the size of the store, its design, and the cost of constructing it. Can the Hoffmans recover any money?

Strategy: Because there is no contract, the Hoffmans must rely on either promissory estoppel or quasi-contract. Promissory estoppel focuses on the defendant's promise and the plaintiff's reliance. Those suing in quasi-contract must show that the defendant received a benefit for which it should reasonably expect to pay. Does either fit here? (See the "Result" at the end of this section.)

7. SOURCES OF CONTRACT LAW
If a contract is for the sale of goods, the UCC is the relevant body of law. For anything else, the common law governs. If an contract involves both goods and services, a court will determine the agreement's primary purpose. (pp. 150–151)

8. MEETING OF THE MINDS
The parties can form a contract only if they have a meeting of the minds. (p. 151)

EXAM Strategy

Question: Norv owned a Ford dealership and wanted to expand by obtaining a BMW outlet. He spoke with Jackson and other BMW executives on several occasions. Norv now claims that those discussions resulted in an oral contract that requires BMW to grant him a franchise, but the company disagrees. Norv's strongest evidence of a contract is the fact that Jackson gave him forms on which to order BMWs. Jackson answered that it was his standard practice to give such forms to prospective dealers, so that if the franchise were approved, car orders could be processed quickly. Norv states that he was "shocked" when BMW refused to go through with the deal. Is there a contract?

Strategy: A court makes an *objective* assessment of what the parties did and said to determine whether they had a meeting of the minds and intended to form a contract. Norv's "shock" is irrelevant. Do the order forms indicate a meeting of the minds? Was there additional evidence that the parties had reached an agreement? (See the "Result" at the end of this section.)

9. OFFER
An offer is an act or a statement that proposes definite terms and permits the other party to create a contract by accepting. Offers may be terminated by revocation, rejection, expiration, or destruction of the agreement's subject matter. (pp. 151–154)

10. ACCEPTANCE
The offeree must say or do something to accept. The common law mirror image rule requires acceptance on precisely the same terms as the offer. Under the mailbox rule, acceptances are effective upon dispatch. (pp. 154–156)

6. Result: Red Owl received no benefit from the Hoffmans' sale of their store or purchase of the lot. However, Red Owl did make a promise and expected the Hoffmans to rely on it, which they did. The Hoffmans won their claim of promissory estoppel.

8. Result: The order forms are neither an offer nor an acceptance. Norv has offered no evidence that the parties agreed on price, date of performance, or any other key terms. There is no contract. Norv allowed eagerness and optimism to replace common sense.

MATCHING QUESTIONS

Match the following terms with their definitions:

_____ A. Implied contract   1. A party that makes an offer

_____ B. Mirror image rule   2. An agreement based on one promise in exchange for another

_____ C. Offeree   3. A party that receives an offer

_____ D. Offeror   4. An agreement based on the words and actions of the parties

_____ E. Bilateral contract   5. A common law principle requiring the acceptance to be on exactly the terms of the offer

TRUE/FALSE QUESTIONS

Circle true or false:

1. T F To be enforceable, all contracts must be in writing.
2. T F Abdul hires Sean to work in his store, and agrees to pay him $9 per hour. This agreement is governed by the Uniform Commercial Code.
3. T F If an offer demands a reply within a stated period, the offeree's silence indicates acceptance.
4. T F Without a meeting of the minds there cannot be a contract.
5. T F An agreement to sell cocaine is a voidable contract.

MULTIPLE-CHOICE QUESTIONS

1. Mark, a newspaper editor, walks into the newsroom and announces to a group of five reporters: "I'll pay a $2,000 bonus to the first reporter who finds definitive evidence that Senator Blue smoked marijuana at the celebrity party last Friday." Anna, the first reporter to produce the evidence, claims her bonus based on
   (a) Unilateral contract
   (b) Promissory estoppel
   (c) Quasi-contract
   (d) Implied contract
   (e) Express contract

2. Raul has finished the computer installation he promised to perform for Tanya, and she has paid him in full. This is
   (a) An express contract
   (b) An implied contract.
   (c) An executed contract.
   (d) A bilateral contract
   (e) No contract

3. Consider the following:

I. Madison says to a group of students, "I'll pay $35 to the first one of you who shows up at my house and mows my lawn."

II. Lea posts a flyer around town that reads, "Reward: $500 for information about the person who keyed my truck last Saturday night in the Wag-a-Bag parking lot. Call Lea at 555-5309."

Which of these proposes a *unilateral* contract?

(a) I only

(b) II only

(c) Both I and II

(d) None of the above

4. On Monday night, Louise is talking on her cell phone with Bill. "I'm desperate for a manager in my store," says Louise. "I'll pay you $45,000 per year, if you can start tomorrow morning. What do you say?"

"It's a deal," says Bill. "I can start tomorrow at 8 a.m. I'll take $45,000, and I also want 10 percent of any profits you make above last year's." Just then Bill loses his cell phone signal. The next morning he shows up at the store, but Louise refuses to hire him. Bill sues. Bill will

(a) Win, because there was a valid offer and acceptance

(b) Win, based on promissory estoppel

(c) Lose, because he rejected the offer

(d) Lose, because the agreement was not put in writing

(e) Lose, because Louise revoked the offer

5. Which of the following amounts to an offer?

(a) Ed says to Carmen, "I offer to sell you my pen for $1."

(b) Ed says to Carmen, "I'll sell you my pen for $1."

(c) Ed writes, "I'll sell you my pen for $1," and gives the note to Carmen.

(d) All of the above

ESSAY QUESTIONS

1. ETHICS John Stevens owned a dilapidated apartment that he rented to James and Cora Chesney for a low rent. The Chesneys began to remodel and rehabilitate the unit. Over a four-year period, they installed two new bathrooms, carpeted the floors, installed new septic and heating systems, and rewired, replumbed, and painted. Stevens periodically stopped by and saw the work in progress. The Chesneys transformed the unit into a respectable apartment. Three years after their work was done, Stevens served the Chesneys with an eviction notice. The Chesneys counterclaimed, seeking the value of the work they had done. Are they entitled to it? Comment on the law and the ethics.

2. Tindall operated a general contracting business in Montana. He and Konitz entered into negotiations for Konitz to buy the business. The parties realized that Konitz could succeed with the business only if Tindall gave support and assistance for a year or so after the purchase, especially by helping with the process of bidding for jobs and obtaining bonds to guarantee performance. Konitz bought the business, and Tindall helped with the bidding and bonding. Two years later, Tindall presented Konitz with a contract for his services up to that point. Konitz did not want to sign, but Tindall insisted. Konitz signed the agreement, which said: "Whereas Tindall sold his contracting business to Konitz and thereafter assisted Konitz in bidding and bonding, without which Konitz would have been unable to operate, NOW THEREFORE Konitz agrees to pay Tindall $138,629." Konitz later refused to pay. Comment.

3. The Tufte family leased a 260-acre farm from the Travelers Insurance Co. Toward the end of the lease, Travelers mailed the Tuftes an option to renew the lease. The option arrived at the Tuftes' house on March 30 and gave them until April 14 to accept. On April 13, the Tuftes signed and mailed their acceptance, which Travelers received on April 19. Travelers claimed there was no lease and attempted to evict the Tuftes from the farm. May they stay?

4. Sal says to Jennifer, "I'll trim all of your trees if you pay me $300." Jennifer replies, "It's a deal, if you'll also feed my dog next week when I go on vacation." Does the common law or the UCC apply to Sal's proposal? Is Jennifer's reply an acceptance? Why or why not?

5. Raul makes an offer to Tina. He says, "I'll sell you this briefcase for $100." Describe four ways in which this offer might be terminated.

DISCUSSION QUESTIONS

1. Someone offers to sell you a concert ticket for $50, and you reply, "I'll give you $40," The seller refuses to sell at the lower price, and you say, "OK, OK, I'll pay you $50." Clearly, no contract has been formed because you made a counteroffer. If the seller has changed her mind and no longer wants to sell for $50, she doesn't have to. But is this fair? If it is all part of the same conversation, should you be able to accept the $50 offer and get the ticket?

2. Have you ever made an agreement that mattered to you, only to have the other person refuse to follow through on the deal? Looking at the list of elements in the chapter, did your agreement amount to a contract? If not, which element did it lack?

3. Is it sensible to have two different sets of contract rules—one for sales of goods and another for everything else? Would it be better to have a single set of rules for all contracts?

4. Consider promissory estoppel and quasi-contracts. Do you like the fact that these doctrines exist? Should courts have "wiggle room" to enforce deals that fail to meet formal contract requirements, or should the rule be, "If it's not an actual contract, too bad"?

5. Return to the opening scenario. Fran, Ricky, Carla, and Dave each made an agreement with John. None is valid under contract law. For the sake of fairness, *should* any of them be legally enforceable? If so, which?

CHAPTER 10

CONTRACT IMPEDIMENTS

Soheil Sadri, a California resident, did some serious gambling at Caesar's Tahoe casino in Nevada. And lost. To keep gambling, he wrote checks to Caesar's and then signed two memoranda pledging to repay money advanced. After two days, with his losses totaling more than $22,000, he went home. Back in California, Sadri stopped payment on the checks and refused to pay any of the money he owed Caesar's. The casino sued and recovered … nothing. Sadri relied on an important legal principle to defeat the suit: a contract that is illegal is void and unenforceable.

A gambling contract is illegal unless it is specifically authorized by state statute. In California, as in many states, gambling on credit is not allowed. However, do not become too excited at the prospect of risk-free wagering. Casinos responded to cases like *Sadri* by changing their practices. Most now extend credit only to a gambler who agrees that disputes about repayment will be settled in *Nevada* courts. Because such contracts are legal in that state, the casino is able to obtain a judgment against a defaulting debtor.

Sometimes parties fail to create a valid contract even when they exchange an offer and acceptance. Sadri's agreement was not a binding contract because of a problem with legality. This is one of five "deal breakers" that we present in this chapter:

1. Consideration: each party must gain some value from a contract.

2. Legality: illegal contracts are not enforceable.

3. Capacity: both parties must have the legal ability to form a contract.

4. Fraud and certain types of mistake make a contract unenforceable.

5. Writing is required for some contracts.

If parties exchange an offer and acceptance, and if there are no problems in any of the five areas presented in this chapter, then a valid contract exists.

> "The casino sued and recovered … nothing."

CONSIDERATION

The central idea of consideration is simple: contracts must be a two-way street. If one side gets all the benefit and the other side gets nothing, then an agreement lacks consideration and is not an enforceable contract.

There are three rules of consideration:

1. Both parties must get something of measureable value from the contract. That thing can be money, boots, an agreement not to sue, or anything else that has real value.

2. A *promise* to give something of value counts as consideration. A *promise* to mow someone's lawn next week is the equivalent of actually *doing* the yardwork when evaluating whether consideration exists.

3. The two parties must have bargained for whatever was exchanged and struck a deal: "If you do this, I'll do that." If you just decide to deliver a cake to your neighbor's house without her knowing, that may be something of value, but since you two did not bargain for it, there is no contract, and she does not owe you the price of the cake.

Let's take an example: Sally's Shoe Store and Baker Boots agree that she will pay $20,000 for 100 pairs of boots. They both get something of value—Sally gets the boots, Baker gets the money. A contract is formed when the promises are made because a promise to give something of value counts. The two have bargained for this deal, so there is valid consideration.

Let's look at another example. Marvin works at Sally's. At 9 a.m., he is in a good mood and promises to buy his coworker a Starbucks during the lunch hour. The delighted coworker agrees. Later that morning, the coworker is rude to Marvin, who then changes his mind about buying the coffee. He is free to do so. His promise created a one-way street: the coworker stood to receive all of the benefit of the agreement, while Marvin got nothing. Because Marvin received no value, there is no contract.

What Is Value?

As we have seen, an essential part of consideration is that both parties must get something of value. That item of value can be either an "act" or a "forbearance."

ACT

A party commits an **act** when she does something she was not legally required to do in the first place. She might do a job, deliver an item, or pay money, for example. An act does not count if the party was simply complying with the law or fulfilling her obligations under an existing contract. Thus, for example, suppose that your professor tells the university that she will not post final grades unless she is paid an extra $5,000. Even if the university agrees to this outrageous demand, that agreement is not a valid contract because the professor is already under an obligation to post final grades.

FORBEARANCE

A **forbearance** is, in essence, the opposite of an act. A plaintiff forbears if he agrees *not* to do something he had a legal right to do. An entrepreneur might promise a competitor not to open a competing business, or an elderly driver (with a valid driver's license) might promise concerned family members that he will not drive at night.

In the movies, when a character wants to get serious about keeping a promise—*really* serious—he sometimes signs an agreement in blood. As it turns out, this kind of thing actually happens in real life. In the following case, did the promise of forbearance have value? Did a contract signed in blood count? You be the judge.

You be the Judge

KIM V. SON

2009 Cal. App. LEXIS 2011
Court of Appeal of California, 2009

Facts: Stephen Son was a part-owner and -operator of two corporations. Because the businesses were corporations, Son was not personally liable for the debts of either one.

Jinsoo Kim invested a total of about $170,000 in the companies. Eventually, both of them failed, and Kim lost his investment. Son felt guilty over Kim's losses.

Later, Son and Kim met in a sushi restaurant and drank heroic quantities of alcohol. At one point, Son pricked his finger with a safety pin and wrote the following in his own blood: "Sir, please forgive me. Because of my deeds, you have suffered financially. I will repay you to the best of my ability." In return, Kim agreed not to sue him for the money owed.

Son later refused to honor the bloody document and pay Kim the money. Kim filed suit to enforce their contract.

The judge determined that the promise did not create a contract because there had been no consideration.

You Be The Judge: *Was there consideration?*

Argument for Kim: As a part of the deal made at the sushi restaurant, Kim agreed not to sue Son. What could be more of a forbearance than that? Kim had a right to sue at any time, and he gave the right up. Even if Kim was unlikely to win, Son would still prefer not to be sued.

Besides, the fact that Son signed the agreement in blood indicates how seriously he took the obligation to repay his loyal investor. At a minimum, Son eased his guilty conscience by making the agreement, and surely that is worth something.

Argument for Son: Who among you has not at one point or another become intoxicated, experienced emotions more powerful than usual, and regretted them the next morning? Whether calling an ex-girlfriend and professing endless love while crying or writing out an agreement in your own blood, it is all the same.

A promise not to file a meritless lawsuit has no value at all. It did not matter to Son whether or not Kim filed suit because Kim could not possibly win. If this promise counts as value, then the concept of consideration is meaningless because anyone can promise not to sue any time. Son had no obligation to pay Kim. And the bloody napkin does not change that fact because it was made without consideration of any kind. It is an ordinary promise, not a contract that creates any legal obligation.

Adequacy of Consideration

Gold can make people crazy. At the turn of the twentieth century, John Tuppela joined the gold rush to Alaska. He bought a mine and worked it hard, a disciplined man in an unforgiving enterprise. Sadly, his prospecting proved futile, and mental problems overwhelmed him. In 1914, a court declared him insane and locked him in an institution in Portland, Oregon. Four years later, Tuppela emerged and learned to his ecstasy that gold had been discovered in his mine, now valued at over half a million dollars. Then the bad news hit: a court-appointed guardian had sold the mine for pennies while Tuppela was institutionalized. Destitute and forlorn, Tuppela turned to his lifelong friend, Embola, saying, "If you will give me $50 so I can go to Alaska and get my property back, I will pay you $10,000 when I win my property." Embola accepted the offer, advancing the $50.

After a long and bitter fight, Tuppela won back his mine, though a guardian would still supervise his assets. Tuppela asked the guardian to pay the full $10,000 to Embola, but the guardian refused. Embola sued, and the issue was whether his $50 was *adequate consideration* to support Tuppela's promise of $10,000. A happy ending: Embola won and recovered his money.

Courts seldom inquire into the *adequacy* of consideration. Although the difference between Embola's $50 and Tuppela's $10,000 was huge, it was not for a court to decide whether the parties had made an intelligent bargain. Embola undertook a risk, and his $50 *was valid consideration.* The question of adequacy is for the parties as they bargain, not for the courts.

Law professors often call this the "peppercorn rule," a reference to a Civil War–era case in which a judge mused, "What is a valuable consideration? A peppercorn." Even the tiniest benefit to a plaintiff counts, so long as it has a measureable value.[1]

EXAM Strategy

Question: 50 Cent has been rapping all day, and he is very thirsty. He pulls his Ferrari into the parking lot of a convenience store. The store turns out to be closed, but luckily for him, a Pepsi machine sits outside. While walking over to it, he realizes that he has left his wallet at home. Frustrated, he whistles to a 10-year-old kid who is walking by. "Hey kid!" he shouts. "I need to borrow fifty cents!" "I know you are!" the kid replies. Fiddy tries again. "No, no, I need to *borrow* fifty cents!" The kid walks over. "Well, I'm not going to just give you my last fifty cents. But maybe you can sell me something." 50 Cent cannot believe it, but he really is very thirsty. He takes off a Rolex, which is his least expensive bling. "How about this?" "Deal," the kid says, handing over two quarters. Can 50 Cent get his watch back?

Strategy: Even in extreme cases, courts rarely take an interest in *how much* consideration is given or whether everyone got a "good deal." Even though the Rolex is worth thousands of times more than the quarters, the quarters still count under the peppercorn rule.

Result: After this transaction, 50 Cent may have second thoughts, but they will be too late. The kid committed an act by handing over his money—he was under no legal obligation to do so. And 50 Cent received something of small, but measureable, value. So there is consideration to support this deal, and 50 Cent would not get his watch back.

LEGALITY

In the opening scenario, we saw that gambling agreements are illegal unless specifically authorized by a state statute. In this section, we examine a type of clause common in employment contracts. A **noncompete agreement** is a contract in which one party agrees not to compete with another in a stated type of business. For example, an anchorwoman for an NBC news affiliate in Miami might agree that she will not anchor any other Miami station's news for one year after she leaves her present employer. Noncompetes are often valid, but they are sometimes illegal and void.

Free trade is the basis of the American economy, and any bargain that restricts it is suspect. **To be valid, an agreement not to compete must be ancillary to a legitimate bargain.** "Ancillary" means that the noncompetition agreement must be part of a larger agreement.

Contracts Checklist
- ☐ Offer
- ☐ Acceptance
- ☐ Consideration
- ☑ Legality
- ☐ Capacity
- ☐ Consent
- ☐ Writing

---

[1] *Hobbs v. Duff* 23 Cal. 596 (1863).

Suppose Cliff sells his gasoline station to Mina, and the two agree that Cliff will not open a competing gas station within five miles any time during the next two years. Cliff's agreement not to compete is ancillary to the sale of his service station. His noncompetition promise is enforceable. But suppose that Cliff and Mina already had the only two gas stations within 35 miles. They agree between themselves not to hire each other's workers. Their agreement might be profitable to them because each could now keep wages artificially low. But their deal is ancillary to no legitimate bargain, and it is therefore void.

The two most common settings for legitimate noncompetition agreements are the *sale of a business* and an *employment relationship*.

Noncompete Agreements: Sale of a Business

Kory has operated a real estate office, Hearth Attack, in a small city for 35 years, building an excellent reputation and many ties with the community. She offers to sell you the business and its goodwill for $300,000. But you need assurance that Kory will not take your money and promptly open a competing office across the street. With her reputation and connections, she would ruin your chances of success. You insist on a noncompete clause in the sale contract. In this clause, Kory promises that for one year, she will not open a new real estate office or go to work for a competing company within a 10-mile radius of Hearth Attack. Suppose, six months after selling you the business, Kory goes to work for a competing realtor two blocks away. You seek an injunction (a court order) to prevent her from working. Who wins?

When a noncompete agreement is ancillary to the sale of a business, it is enforceable if reasonable in time, geographic area, and scope of activity. In other words, a court will not enforce a noncompete agreement that lasts an unreasonably long time, covers an unfairly large area, or prohibits the seller of the business from doing a type of work that she never had done before. Measured by this test, Kory is almost certainly bound by her agreement. One year is a reasonable time to allow you to get your new business started. A 10-mile radius is probably about the area that Hearth Attack covers, and realty is obviously a fair business from which to prohibit Kory. A court will grant the injunction, barring Kory from her new job.

If, on the other hand, the noncompete agreement had prevented Kory from working anywhere within 200 miles of Hearth Attack, and she started working 50 miles away, a court would refuse to enforce the contract.

Noncompete Agreements: Employment Contracts

When you sign an employment contract, the document may well contain a noncompete clause. Employers have legitimate worries that employees might go to a competitor and take with them trade secrets or other proprietary information. Some employers, though, attempt to place harsh restrictions on their employees, perhaps demanding a blanket agreement that the employee will never go to work for a competitor. Once again, courts look at the reasonableness of restrictions placed on an employee's future work. Because the agreement now involves the very livelihood of the worker, a court scrutinizes the agreement more closely.

A noncompete clause in an employment contract is generally reasonable—and enforceable— only to the extent necessary to protect (1) trade secrets, (2) confidential information, or (3) customer lists developed over an extended period. In general, other restrictions on future employment are unenforceable.[2] Suppose that Gina, an engineer, goes to work for Fission

---

[2] If the agreement restricts the employee from *starting a new business*, a court may apply the more lenient standard used for the sale of a business; the noncompete clause will be enforced if reasonable in time, geography, and scope of activity.

Chips, a silicon chip manufacturer that specializes in defense work. She signs a noncompete agreement promising never to work for a competitor. Over a period of three years, Gina learns some of Fission's proprietary methods of etching information onto the chips. She acquires a great deal of new expertise about chips generally. And she periodically deals with Fission Chips' customers, all of whom are well-known software and hardware manufacturers.

Gina accepts an offer from WriteSmall, a competitor. Fission Chips races into court, seeking an injunction to block Gina from working for WriteSmall. This injunction threatens Gina's career. If she cannot work for a competitor or use her general engineering skills, what will she do? And for exactly that reason, no court will grant such a broad order. The court will allow Gina to work for competitors, including WriteSmall. It will order her not to use or reveal any trade secrets belonging to Fission. She will, however, be permitted to use the general expertise she has acquired, and she may contact former customers because anyone could get their names from the yellow pages.

Was the noncompete in the following case styled fairly, or was the employee clipped?

KING V. HEAD START FAMILY HAIR SALONS, INC.

886 So.2d 769, Supreme Court of Alabama, 2004

CASE SUMMARY

Facts: Kathy King was a single mother supporting a college-age daughter. For 25 years, she had worked as a hairstylist. For the most recent 16 years, she had worked at Head Start, which provided haircuts, coloring, and styling for men and women. King was primarily a stylist, though she had also managed one of the Head Start facilities.

King quit Head Start and began working as manager of a Sports Clips shop, located in the same mall as the store she just left. Sports Clip offered only haircuts and primarily served men and boys. Head Start filed suit, claiming that King was violating the noncompetition agreement that she had signed. The agreement prohibited King from working at a competing business within a two-mile radius of any Head Start facility for 12 months after leaving the company. The trial court issued an injunction enforcing the noncompete. King appealed.

Issue: *Was the noncompete agreement valid?*

Decision: The agreement was only partly valid.

Reasoning: Head Start does business in 30 locations throughout Jefferson and Shelby counties. Virtually every hair-care facility in those counties is located within two miles of a Head Start business and is thus covered by the noncompetition agreement. The contract is essentially a blanket restriction, entirely barring King from this business.

King must work to support herself and her daughter. She is 40 years old and has worked in the hair-care industry for 25 years. She cannot be expected at this stage in life to learn new job skills. Enforcing the noncompetition agreement would create a grave hardship for her. The contract cannot be permitted to impoverish King and her daughter.

On the other hand, Head Start is entitled to some of the protection it sought in this agreement. The company has a valid concern that if King is permitted to work anywhere she wants, she could take away many customers from Head Start. The trial court should fashion a more reasonable geographic restriction, one that will permit King to ply her trade while ensuring that Head Start does not unfairly lose customers. For example, the lower court could prohibit King from working within two miles of the Head Start facility where she previously worked, or some variation on that idea.

Reversed and remanded.

Exculpatory Clauses

You decide to capitalize on your expert ability as a skier and open a ski school in Colorado called "Pike's Pique." But you realize that skiing sometimes causes injuries, so you require anyone signing up for lessons to sign this form:

> I agree to hold Pike's Pique and its employees entirely harmless in the event that I am injured in any way or for any reason or cause, including but not limited to any acts, whether negligent or otherwise, of Pike's Pique or any employee or agent thereof.

The day your school opens, Sara Beth, an instructor, deliberately pushes Toby over a cliff because Toby criticizes her color combinations. Eddie, a beginning student, "blows out" his knee attempting an advanced racing turn. And Maureen, another student, reaches the bottom of a steep run and slams into a snowmobile that Sara Beth parked there. Maureen, Eddie, and Toby's families all sue Pike's Pique. You defend based on the form you had them sign. Does it save the day?

Exculpatory clause

A contract provision that attempts to release one party from liability in the event the other party is injured.

The form on which you are relying is an **exculpatory clause,** that is, one that attempts to release you from liability in the event of injury to another party. Exculpatory clauses are common. Ski schools use them, and so do parking lots, landlords, warehouses, and daycare centers. All manner of businesses hope to avoid large tort judgments by requiring their customers to give up any right to recover. Is such a clause valid? Sometimes. Courts often—but not always—ignore exculpatory clauses, finding that one party was forcing the other party to give up legal rights that no one should be forced to surrender.

An exculpatory clause is generally unenforceable when it attempts to exclude an intentional tort or gross negligence. When Sara Beth pushes Toby over a cliff, that is the intentional tort of battery. A court will not enforce the exculpatory clause. Sara Beth is clearly liable.[3] As to the snowmobile at the bottom of the run, if a court determines that was gross negligence (carelessness far greater than ordinary negligence), then the exculpatory clause will again be ignored. If, however, it was ordinary negligence, then we must continue the analysis.

An exculpatory clause is generally unenforceable when the affected activity is in the public interest, such as medical care, public transportation, or some essential service. What about Eddie's suit against Pike's Pique? Eddie claims that he should never have been allowed to attempt an advanced maneuver. His suit is for ordinary negligence, and the exculpatory clause probably does bar him from recovery. Skiing is a recreational activity. No one is obligated to do it, and there is no strong public interest in ensuring that we have access to ski slopes.

An exculpatory clause is generally unenforceable when the parties have greatly unequal bargaining power. When Maureen flies to Colorado, suppose that the airline requires her to sign a form contract with an exculpatory clause. Because the airline almost certainly has much greater bargaining power, it can afford to offer a "take it or leave it" contract. But because the bargaining power is so unequal, the clause is probably unenforceable.

An exculpatory clause is generally unenforceable unless the clause is clearly written and readily visible. Thus, if Pike's Pique gave all ski students an eight-page contract, and the exculpatory clause was at the bottom of page 7 in small print, the average customer would never notice it. The clause would probably be void.

---

[3]Note that Pike's Pique is probably not liable under agency law principles that preclude an employer's liability for an employee's intentional tort.

EXAM Strategy

Question: Shauna flew a World War II fighter aircraft as a member of an exhibition flight team. While the team was performing in a delta formation, another plane collided with Shauna's aircraft, causing her to crash-land, leaving her permanently disabled. Shauna sued the other pilot and the team. The defendants moved to dismiss based on an exculpatory clause that Shauna had signed. The clause was one paragraph long and stated that Shauna knew team flying was inherently dangerous and could result in injury or death. She agreed not to hold the team or any members liable in case of an accident. Shauna argued that the clause should not be enforced against her if she could prove the other pilot was negligent. Please rule.

Strategy: The issue is whether the exculpatory clause is valid. Courts are likely to declare such clauses void if they concern vital activities like medical care, exclude an intentional tort or gross negligence, or arise from unequal bargaining power.

Result: This is a clear, short clause, between parties with equal bargaining power, and does not exclude an intentional tort or gross negligence. The activity is unimportant to the public welfare. The clause is valid. Even if the other pilot was negligent, Shauna will lose, meaning the court should dismiss her lawsuit.

CAPACITY

For Kevin Green, it was love at first sight. She was sleek, as quick as a cat, and a beautiful deep blue. He paid $4,600 cash for the used Camaro. The car soon blew a gasket, and Kevin demanded his money back. But the Camaro came with no guarantee, and Star Chevrolet, the dealer, refused. Kevin repaired the car himself. Next, some unpleasantness on the highway left the car a worthless wreck. Kevin received the full value of the car from his insurance company. Then he sued the dealer, seeking a refund of his purchase price. The dealer pointed out that it was not responsible for the accident, and that the car had no warranty of any kind. Yet the court awarded Kevin the full value of his car. How can this be?

The automobile dealer ignored *legal capacity*. Kevin Green was only 16 years old when he bought the car, and a minor, said the court, has the right to cancel any agreement he made, for any reason. **Capacity** is the legal ability of a party to enter a contract. Someone may lack capacity because of his young age or mental infirmity. Two groups of people usually lack legal capacity: minors and those with a mental impairment.

Contracts Checklist
- [ ] Offer
- [ ] Acceptance
- [ ] Consideration
- [ ] Legality
- [✓] Capacity
- [ ] Consent
- [ ] Writing

Capacity
The legal ability to enter into a contract.

Minors

A minor is someone under the age of 18. Because a minor lacks legal capacity, she normally can create only a voidable contract. **A voidable contract may be cancelled by the party who lacks capacity.** Notice that *only the party lacking capacity* may cancel the agreement. So a minor who enters into a contract generally may choose between enforcing the agreement or negating it. The other party, however, has no such right.

DISAFFIRMANCE

A minor who wishes to escape from a contract generally may **disaffirm** it; that is, he may notify the other party that he refuses to be bound by the agreement. Because Kevin was 16 when he signed, the deal was voidable. When the Camaro blew a gasket and the lad informed Star Chevrolet that he wanted his money back, he was disaffirming the contract, which he could do

Disaffirm
To give notice of refusal to be bound by an agreement.

for any reason at all. Kevin was entitled to his money back. If Star Chevrolet had understood the law of capacity, it would have towed the Camaro away and returned the young man's $4,600. At least the dealership would have had a repairable automobile.

RESTITUTION

Restitution
Restoring an injured party to its original position.

A minor who disaffirms a contract must return the consideration he has received, to the extent he is able. Restoring the other party to its original position is called **restitution**. The consideration that Kevin Green received in the contract was, of course, the Camaro. If Star Chevrolet had delivered a check for $4,600, Kevin would have been obligated to return the car.

What happens if the minor is not able to return the consideration because he no longer has it or it has been destroyed? Most states hold that the minor is still entitled to his money back. Kevin Green got his money and Star Chevrolet received a fine lesson.

Mentally Impaired Persons

A person suffers from a mental impairment if, by reason of mental illness or defect, he is unable to understand the nature and consequences of the transaction.[4] The mental impairment can be insanity that has been formally declared by a court, or mental illness that has never been ruled on but is now evident. The impairment may also be due to some other mental illness, such as schizophrenia, or to mental retardation, brain injury, senility, or any other cause that renders the person unable to understand the nature and consequences of the contract.

A party suffering a mental impairment generally creates only a voidable contract. The impaired person has the right to disaffirm the contract, just as a minor does. But again, the contract is voidable, not void. The mentally impaired party generally has the right to full performance if she wishes.

But the law creates an exception: if a person has been adjudicated insane, then all of his future agreements are void. "Adjudicated insane" means that a judge has made a formal finding that a person is mentally incompetent and has assigned the person a guardian.

Intoxication

Similar rules apply in cases of drug or alcohol **intoxication.** When one party is so intoxicated that he cannot understand the nature and consequences of the transaction, the contract is voidable.

We wish to stress that courts are *highly* skeptical of intoxication arguments. If you go out drinking and make a foolish agreement, you are probably stuck with it. Even if you are too drunk to drive, you are probably not nearly too drunk to make a contract. If your blood alcohol level is, say, .08, your coordination and judgment are poor. Driving in such a condition is dangerous. But you probably have a fairly clear awareness of what is going on around you.

To back out of a contract on the grounds of intoxication, you must be able to provide evidence that you did not understand the "nature of the agreement" or the basic deal that you made.

Contracts Checklist
☐ Offer
☐ Acceptance
☐ Consideration
☐ Legality
☐ Capacity
☑ Consent
☐ Writing

REALITY OF CONSENT

Smiley offers to sell you his house for $300,000, and you agree to buy in writing. After you move in, you discover that the house is sinking into the earth at the rate of six inches per week. In 12 months, your only access to the house may be through the chimney. You sue,

---

[4]Restatement (Second) of Contracts §15.

seeking to **rescind**, or cancel, the agreement. You argue that when you signed the contract, you did not truly consent because you lacked essential information. In this section, we look at fraud and mistake.

Fraud

Fraud begins when a party to a contract says something that is factually wrong. "This house has no termites," says a homeowner to a prospective buyer. If the house is swarming with the nasty pests, the statement is a misrepresentation. But does it amount to fraud? An injured person must show the following:

1. The defendant knew that his statement was false or he made the statement recklessly and without knowledge of whether it was false.

2. The false statement was material.

3. The injured party justifiably relied on the statement.

ELEMENT ONE: INTENTIONAL OR RECKLESS MISREPRESENTATION OF FACT

The injured party must show a false statement of fact. Notice that this does not mean the statement was necessarily a "lie." If a homeowner says that the famous architect Stanford White designed her house, but Bozo Loco actually did the work, it is a false statement.

Now, if the owner knows that Loco designed the house, she has committed the first element of fraud. And, if she has no idea who designed the house, her assertion that it was "Stanford White" also meets the first element.

But, the owner might have a good reason for the error. Perhaps a local history book identifies the house as a Stanford White. If she makes the statement with a reasonable belief that she is telling the truth, she has made an innocent misrepresentation (discussed in the next section) and not fraud.

Opinions and "puffery" do not amount to fraud. An opinion is not a statement of fact. A seller says, "I think land values around here will be going up 20 or 30 percent for the foreseeable future." That statement is pretty enticing to a buyer, but it is not a false statement of fact. The maker is clearly stating her own opinion, and the buyer who relies on it does so at his peril. A close relative of opinion is something called "puffery."

Get ready for one of the most astonishing experiences you've ever had! This paragraph on puffery is going to be the finest part of any textbook you have ever read! You're going to find the issue intriguing, the writing dazzling, and the legal summary unforgettable!! "But what happens," you might wonder, "if this paragraph fails to astonish? What if I find the issue dull, the writing mediocre, and the legal summary incomprehensible? Can I sue for fraud?" No. The promises we made were mere puffery. A statement is puffery when a reasonable person would realize that it is a sales pitch, representing the exaggerated opinion of the seller. Puffery is not a statement of fact.

ELEMENT TWO: MATERIALITY

The injured party must demonstrate that the statement was material, or important. A minor misstatement does not meet this second element of fraud. Was the misstatement likely to significantly influence the decision of the misled party? If so, it was material.

Imagine a farmer selling a piece of his land. He measures the acres himself and calculates a total of 200. If the actual acreage is 199, he has almost certainly not made a *material* misstatement. But if the actual acreage is 150, he has.

Rescind

To cancel a contract.

Fraud

Intending to induce the other party to contract, knowing the words are false or uncertain that they are true.

Misrepresentation

A statement that is factually wrong.

ELEMENT THREE: JUSTIFIABLE RELIANCE

The injured party must also show that she actually did rely on the false statement and that her reliance was reasonable. Suppose the seller of a gas station lies through his teeth about the structural soundness of the building. The buyer believes what he hears but does not much care because he plans to demolish the building and construct a day-care center. There was a material misstatement but no reliance, and the buyer may not rescind.

The reliance must be justifiable—that is, reasonable. If the seller of wilderness land tells Lewis that the area is untouched by pollution, but Lewis can see a large lake on the property covered with six inches of oily, red scum, Lewis is not justified in relying on the seller's statements. If he goes forward with the purchase, he may not rescind.

PLAINTIFF'S REMEDIES FOR FRAUD

In the case of fraud, the injured party generally has a choice of rescinding the contract or suing for damages or, in some cases, doing both. The contract is voidable, which meant that injured party is not *forced* to rescind the deal but may if he wants. Fraud *permits* the injured party to cancel. Alternatively, the injured party can sue for damages—the difference between what the contract promised and what it delivered.

Nancy learns that the building she bought has a terrible heating system. A new one will cost $12,000. If the seller told her the system was "like new," Nancy may rescind the deal. But it may be economically harmful for her to do so. She might have sold her old house, hired a mover, taken a new job, and so forth. What are her other remedies? She could move into the new house and sue for the difference between what she got and what was promised, which is $12,000, the cost of replacing the heating system.

In some states, a party injured by fraud may both rescind *and* sue for damages. In these states, Nancy could rescind her contract, get her deposit back, and then sue the seller for any damages she has suffered. Her damages might be, for example, a lost opportunity to buy another house or wasted moving expenses.

INNOCENT MISREPRESENTATION

If all elements of fraud are present except the misrepresentation of fact was not made intentionally or recklessly, then **innocent misrepresentation** has occurred. So, if a person misstates a material fact and induces reliance, but he had good reason to believe that his statement was true, then he has not committed fraud. Most states allow rescission of a contract, but not damages, in such a case.

Mistake

Contract law principles come from many sources, and in the area of "legal mistake," a cow significantly influenced the law. The cow was named Rose. She was a gentle animal that lived in Michigan in 1886. Rose's owner, Hiram Walker & Sons, bought her for $850. After a few years, the company concluded that Rose could have no calves. As a barren cow, she was worth much less than $850, so Walker contracted to sell her to T. C. Sherwood for a mere $80. But when Sherwood came to collect Rose, the parties realized that (surprise!) she was pregnant. Walker refused to part with the happy mother, and Sherwood sued. Walker defended, claiming that both parties had made a *mistake* and that the contract was voidable.

A mistake can take many forms. It may be a basic error about an essential characteristic of the thing being sold, as in Rose's case. It could be an erroneous prediction about future prices, such as an expectation that oil prices will rise. It might be a mechanical error, such as a builder offering to build a new home for $300 when he clearly meant to bid $300,000. Some mistakes lead to voidable contracts, others create enforceable deals. The first distinction is between bilateral and unilateral mistakes.

BILATERAL MISTAKE

A **bilateral mistake** occurs when both parties negotiate based on the same factual error. Sherwood and Walker both thought Rose was barren, both negotiated accordingly, and both were wrong. The Michigan Supreme Court gave judgment for Walker, the seller, permitting him to rescind the contract because the parties were *both* wrong about the essence of what they were bargaining for.

If the parties contract based on an important factual error, the contract is voidable by the injured party. Sherwood and Walker were both wrong about Rose's reproductive ability, and the error was basic enough to cause a tenfold difference in price. Walker, the injured party, was entitled to rescind the contract. Note that the error must be *factual*. Suppose Walker sold Rose thinking that the price of beef was going to drop when in fact the price rose 60 percent in five months. That would be simply a *prediction* that proved wrong, and Walker would have no right to rescind.

Conscious Uncertainty.   No rescission is permitted when one of the parties knows he is taking on a risk, that is, he realizes there is uncertainty about the quality of the thing being exchanged. Rufus offers 10 acres of mountainous land to Priscilla. "I can't promise you anything about this land," he says, "but they've found gold on every adjoining parcel." Priscilla, eager for gold, buys the land, digs long and hard, and discovers—mud. She may not rescind the contract. She understood the risk she was assuming, and there was no mutual mistake.

UNILATERAL MISTAKE

Sometimes only one party enters a contract under a mistaken assumption, a situation called **unilateral mistake**. In these cases, it is more difficult for the injured party to rescind a contract. This makes sense since in a bilateral error, neither side really knew what it was getting into, and rescission seems a natural remedy. But with a unilateral mistake, one side may simply have made a better bargain than the other. As we have seen throughout this unit on contracts, courts are unwilling to undo an agreement merely because someone made a foolish deal. Nonetheless, if her proof is strong, the injured party in a case of unilateral mistake still may sometimes rescind a contract.

To rescind for unilateral mistake, a party must demonstrate that she entered the contract because of a basic factual error and that *either* (1) enforcing the contract would be *unconscionable* or (2) the nonmistaken party *knew* of the error.

> **Bilateral mistake**
> Occurs when both parties negotiate based on the same factual error.

> **Unilateral mistake**
> Occurs when only one party negotiates based on a factual error.

> **Unconscionable contract**
> A contract that is shockingly one-sided and fundamentally unfair.

EXAM Strategy

Question: Joe buys an Otterhound named Barky from Purity Dog Shop. He pays $2,500 for the puppy, the high cost due to the certificate Purity gives him, indicating that the puppy's parents were both AKC champions (elite dogs). Two months later, Joe sells the hound to Emily for $2,800. Joe and Emily both believe that Barky is descended from champions. Then a state investigation reveals that Purity has been cheating and its certificates are fakes. Barky is a mixed-breed dog, worth about $100. Emily sues Joe. Who wins?

Strategy: Both parties are mistaken about the kind of dog Joe is selling, so this is an instance of bilateral mistake. What is the rule in such cases?

Result: If the two sides agree based on an important factual error, the contract is voidable by the injured party. A mutt is entirely different from a dog that might become a champion. The parties erred about the essence of their deal. Joe's good faith does not save him, and Emily is entitled to rescind.

CONTRACTS IN WRITING

> Perry moved out of their dorm room into a suite at the Ritz and refused to give Oliver one red cent.

Oliver and Perry were college roommates, two sophomores with contrasting personalities. They were sitting in the cafeteria with some friends, Oliver chatting away, Perry slumped on a plastic bench. Oliver suggested that they buy a lottery ticket, as the prize for that week's drawing was $3 million. Perry muttered, "Nah. You never win if you buy just one ticket." Oliver bubbled up, "OK, we'll buy a ticket every week. We'll keep buying them from now until we graduate. Come on, it'll be fun. This month, I'll buy the tickets. Next month, you will, and so on." Other students urged Perry to do it, and finally, grudgingly, he agreed. The two friends carefully reviewed their deal. Each party was providing consideration, namely, the responsibility for purchasing tickets during his month. The amount of each purchase was clearly defined at one dollar. They would start that week and continue until graduation day, two and a half years down the road. Finally, they would share equally any money won. As three witnesses looked on, they shook hands on the bargain. That month, Oliver bought a ticket every week, randomly choosing numbers, and won nothing. The next month, Perry bought a ticket with equally random numbers—and won $52 million. Perry moved out of their dorm room into a suite at the Ritz and refused to give Oliver one red cent. Oliver sued, seeking $26 million and the return of an Eric Clapton CD that he had loaned to Perry.

If the former friends had read this chapter, they would never have slid into such a mess. In the last chapter, we covered the basics of contract law, and now we put the icing on the cake. We will examine which contracts must be in writing, when third parties have rights or obligations under an agreement, what problems arise in the performance of contracts, and the remedies available when a deal goes awry. Oliver and Perry's case involves the Statute of Frauds, the law that tells us which contracts must be written.

Contracts Checklist
- ☐ Offer
- ☐ Acceptance
- ☐ Consideration
- ☐ Legality
- ☐ Capacity
- ☐ Consent
- ☑ Writing

The Statute of Frauds

The rule we examine in this chapter is not exactly news. Parliament passed the original **Statute of Frauds** in 1677. The purpose was to prevent lying (fraud) in civil lawsuits. The statute required that in several types of cases, a contract would be enforced only if it was in writing. Almost all states in our own country later passed their own statutes making the same requirements. It is important to remember, as we examine the rules and exceptions, that Parliament and the state legislatures all had a commendable, straightforward purpose in passing their respective statutes of fraud: *to provide a court with the best possible evidence of whether the parties intended to make a contract.*

A plaintiff may not enforce any of the following agreements unless the agreement, or some memorandum of it, is in writing and signed by the defendant. The agreements that must be in writing are those:

- For any interest in **land;**
- That **cannot be performed within one year;**
- To pay the **debt of another;**
- Made by an **executor of an estate;**
- Made in **consideration of marriage;** and
- For the **sale of goods worth $500 or more.**

Statute of Frauds
Requires certain contracts to be in writing.

UNENFORCEABLE (SORRY, OLIVER)

In other words, when two parties make an agreement covered by any one of these six topics, it must be in writing to be enforceable. Oliver and Perry made a definite agreement to purchase lottery tickets during alternate months and share the proceeds of any winning ticket. But their agreement was to last two and one-half years. As the second item on the list indicates, a contract must be in writing if it cannot be performed within one year. The good news is that Oliver gets back his Eric Clapton CD. The bad news is that he gets none of the lottery money. Even though three witnesses saw the deal made, it is unlikely to be enforced in any state. Perry the pessimist will probably walk away with all $52 million.[5]

Contracts That Must Be in Writing

AGREEMENTS FOR AN INTEREST IN LAND

A contract for the sale of any interest in land must be in writing to be enforceable. Notice the phrase "interest in land." This means any legal right regarding land. A house on a lot is an interest in land. A mortgage, an easement, and a leased apartment are all interests in land. As a general rule, leases must therefore be in writing, although many states have created an exception for short-term leases of a year or less.

Exception: Full Performance by the Seller. If the seller completely performs her side of a contract for an interest in land, a court is likely to enforce the agreement even if it was oral. Adam orally agrees to sell his condominium to Maggie for $150,000. Adam delivers the deed to Maggie and expects his money a week later, but Maggie fails to pay. Most courts will allow Adam to enforce the oral contract and collect the full purchase price from Maggie.

Exception: Part Performance by the Buyer. The buyer of land may be able to enforce an oral contract if she paid part of the purchase price and either entered upon the land or made improvements to it. Suppose that Eloise sues Grover to enforce an alleged oral contract to sell a lot in Happydale. She claims they struck a bargain in January. Grover defends based on the Statute of Frauds, saying that even if the two did reach an oral agreement, it is unenforceable. Eloise proves that she paid 10 percent of the purchase price, and that in February, she began excavating on the lot to build a house, and that Grover knew of the work. Eloise has established part performance and will be allowed to enforce her contract.

In the following case, the defendant seems to have acknowledged *in court* that she agreed to sell her property. Does that satisfy the Statute of Frauds?

---

[5]Perry might also raise *illegality* as a defense, claiming that a contract for gambling is illegal. That defense is likely to fail. Courts appear to distinguish between the simple purchase of a legal lottery ticket, which friends often share, and the more traditional—and socially dangerous—gambling contracts involving horse racing or casino betting. See, for example, *Pando v. Fernandez*, 118 A.D.2d 474, 499 N.Y.S.2d 950, 1986 N.Y. App. Div. LEXIS 54345 (N.Y. App. Div. 1986), finding no illegality in an agreement to purchase a lottery ticket, even where the purchaser was a minor! Because an illegality defense would probably fail Perry, it is all the more unfortunate that Oliver did not jot down their agreement in writing.

BAKER V. DAVES

83 Ark. App. 145, 119 S.W.3d 53, Court of Appeals of Arkansas, 2003

CASE SUMMARY

Facts: Tommy and Eleanor Daves had a daughter, Lisa Baker. The Daves gave Lisa a deed to a two-acre property with a house on it, keeping for themselves a *life interest* in the parcel. In other words, the Daves each had a half interest in the land for the rest of their lives; they could live in the house and use the land any way they wished. When they died, the property would go to their daughter.

Tommy and Eleanor divorced and settled their affairs amicably. In court, with Lisa watching from the second row, their lawyers informed the court of an agreement that all three parties had allegedly made to sell the two-acre property. Lisa would be reimbursed for taxes and insurance she had paid during the two years she owned the property, and the Daveses would split the rest of the money.

After the agreement was announced, Lisa put the property on the market but then withdrew it and refused to sell. Tommy Daves sued his daughter. Lisa defended based on the Statute of Frauds, saying she had never agreed in court to the deal and never signed any contract to sell. The trial court acknowledged that Lisa had signed nothing but found that the courtroom statements proved the parties had formed a binding contract. The judge ordered Lisa to sell the house, and she appealed.

Issue: *Was Lisa obligated to sell the house?*

Decision: No, Lisa was not obligated to sell the house.

Reasoning: In the trial court, the lawyers for Tommy and Eleanor Daves summarized what they considered to be an agreement to sell the property:

Attorney for Eleanor Daves: The parties have a joint life estate in 2.2 acres of property and a house on Vimy Ridge Road in Alexander, Arkansas. The parties have agreed to sell the house and 2.2 acres and split the pro-

ceeds. They have agreed that Mr. Daves will contact a real estate agency.

Attorney for Tommy Daves: They have a life estate. It was placed in her daughter's name and the daughter is the title owner. She is going to cooperate in listing the property for sale. They are actually selling the property, not just the life estate.

Attorney for Eleanor Daves: The daughter has agreed to sell her interest in the property as well as the life estate of the two parties.

Tommy Daves argues that because Lisa was in court while the statements were made, she implicitly agreed to them and is bound by the oral contract that was formed. Lisa argues that she made no such agreement.

Lisa Baker was not a party to the divorce proceedings. She was not represented by counsel during the trial. The trial court never asked whether she had heard the purported agreement or whether she agreed to it. In the absence of clear evidence that Lisa orally agreed in court to sell the property, the Statute of Frauds must control this case. There is no written evidence of a contract, and Lisa is not bound by any alleged oral agreement.

Reversed and remanded.

Reasoning of the Dissent: Lisa admitted she was present in the hallway with her mother at the time of the divorce hearing when the agreement was being discussed. She acknowledged that she was in the courtroom when the agreement was being read into the record, although she claimed she could not hear what the lawyers were saying. Lisa also admitted that she listed the property for sale pursuant to the agreement. Her conduct unequivocally demonstrates her assent to the agreement.

AGREEMENTS THAT CANNOT BE PERFORMED WITHIN ONE YEAR

Contracts that cannot be performed within one year are unenforceable unless they are in writing. This one-year period begins on the date the parties make the agreement. The critical phrase here is *"cannot* be performed within one year." If a contract could be completed within one year, it need not be in writing. Betty gets a job at Burger Brain, throwing fries in oil. Her boss tells her she can have Fridays off for as long as she works there. That oral contract is enforceable whether Betty stays one week or 57 years. It could have been performed within one year if, say, Betty quit the job after six months. Therefore, it does not need to be in writing.[6]

If the agreement will necessarily take longer than one year to finish, it must be in writing to be enforceable. If Betty is hired for three years as manager of Burger Brain, the agreement is unenforceable unless put in writing. She cannot perform three years of work in one year.

Type of Agreement	Enforceability
Cannot be performed within one year. *Example:* An offer of employment for three years.	Must be in writing to be enforceable.
Might be performed within one year, although could take many years to perform. *Example:* "As long as you work here at Burger Brain, you may have Fridays off."	Enforceable whether it is oral or written, because the employee might quit working a month later.

PROMISE TO PAY THE DEBT OF ANOTHER

When one person agrees to pay the debt of another as a favor to that debtor, it is called a collateral promise, and it must be in writing to be enforceable. A student applies for a $10,000 loan to help pay for college, and her father agrees to repay the bank if the student defaults. The bank will insist that the father's promise be in writing because his oral promise alone is unenforceable.

PROMISE MADE BY AN EXECUTOR OF AN ESTATE

An executor is the person who is in charge of an estate after someone dies. The executor's job is to pay debts of the deceased, obtain money owed to him, and disburse the assets according to the will. In most cases, the executor will use only the estate's assets to pay those debts, but occasionally she might offer her own money. An executor's promise to use her own funds to pay a debt of the deceased must be in writing to be enforceable.

PROMISE MADE IN CONSIDERATION OF MARRIAGE

Barney is a multimillionaire with the integrity of a gangster and the charm of a tax collector. He proposes to Li-Tsing, who promptly rejects him. Barney then pleads that if Li-Tsing will be his bride, he will give her an island he owns off the coast of California. Li-Tsing begins to see his good qualities and accepts. After they are married, Barney refuses to deliver the deed. Li-Tsing will get nothing from a court either, because a promise made in consideration of marriage must be in writing to be enforceable.

---

[6]This is the majority rule. In most states, if a company hires an employee "for life," the contract need not be in writing because the employee could die within one year. "Contracts of uncertain duration are simply excluded [from the Statute of Frauds]; the provision covers only those contracts whose performance cannot possibly be completed within a year." Restatement (Second) of Contracts §130, Comment a, at 328 (1981). However, a few states disagree. The Illinois Supreme Court ruled that a contract for lifetime employment is enforceable only if written. *McInerney v. Charter Golf, Inc.*, 176 Ill. 2d 482, 680 N.E.2d 1347, 1997 Ill. LEXIS 56 (Ill. 1997).

What the Writing Must Contain

Each of the five types of contract described earlier must be in writing in order to be enforceable. What must the writing contain? It may be a carefully typed contract, using precise legal terminology, or an informal memorandum scrawled on the back of a paper napkin at a business lunch. The writing may consist of more than one document, written at different times, with each document making a piece of the puzzle. However, there are some general requirements. The contract or memorandum:

- Must be signed by the defendant, and

- Must state with reasonable certainty the name of each party, the subject matter of the agreement, and all the essential terms and promises.[7]

SIGNATURE

A Statute of Frauds typically states that the writing must be "signed by the party to be charged therewith," in other words, the defendant. Judges define "signature" very broadly. Using a pen to write one's name, though sufficient, is not required. A secretary who stamps an executive's signature on a letter fulfills this requirement. Any other mark or logo placed on a document to indicate acceptance, even an "X," will likely satisfy the Statute of Frauds. Electronic commerce creates new methods of signing—and new controversies, discussed later in this chapter.

Electronic Contracts and Signatures.   E-commerce has grown at a dazzling rate—each year, U.S. enterprises buy and sell tens of billions of dollars worth of goods and services over the Internet. What happens to the writing requirement, though, when there is no paper? The present Statute of Frauds requires some sort of "signature" to ensure that the defendant committed to the deal. Today, an "electronic signature" could mean a name typed (or automatically included) at the bottom of an email message, a retinal or vocal scan, or a name signed by electronic pen on a writing tablet, among others.

E-signatures are valid in all 50 states. Almost all states have adopted the Uniform Electronic Transactions Act (UETA)[8]. UETA declares that *electronic* contracts and signatures are as enforceable as those on paper. In other words, the normal rules of contract law apply, and neither party can avoid such a deal merely because it originated in cyberspace. A federal statute, The Electronic Signatures in Global and National Commerce Act (E-SIGN), also declares that contracts cannot be denied enforcement simply because they are in electronic form or signed electronically. It applies in states that have not adopted UETA.

Note that, in many states, certain documents still require a traditional (non-electronic) signature. Wills, adoptions, court orders, and notice of foreclosure are common exceptions. If in doubt, get a hard copy, signed in ink.

REASONABLE CERTAINTY

Suppose Garfield and Hayes are having lunch, discussing the sale of Garfield's vacation condominium. They agree on a price and want to make some notation of the agreement even before their lawyers work out a detailed purchase and sales agreement. A perfectly adequate memorandum might say, "Garfield agrees to sell Hayes his condominium at 234 Baron Boulevard, apartment 18, for $350,000 cash, payable on June 18, 2004, and Hayes promises to pay the sum on that day." They should make two copies of their agreement and sign both.

---

[7]Restatement (Second) of Contracts §131.
[8]Except Illinois, New York, and Washington.

Sale of Goods

The UCC requires a writing for the sale of goods worth $500 or more. This is the sixth and final contract that must be written, although the Code's requirements are easier to meet than those of the common law. In some cases, the Code dispenses altogether with the writing requirement. The basic Statute of Frauds rule is §2-201(1). Important exceptions are found at §§2-201(2) and (3).

The essential UCC rule: a contract for the sale of goods worth $500 or more is not enforceable unless there is some writing, signed by the defendant, indicating that the parties reached an agreement. The key difference between the common law rule and the UCC rule is that the Code does not require all the terms of the agreement to be in writing. The Code demands only an indication that the parties reached an agreement. The two things that are essential are the signature of the defendant and the quantity of goods being sold. The quantity of goods is required because this is the one term for which there will be no objective evidence. Suppose a short memorandum between textile dealers indicates that Seller will sell to Buyer "grade AA, 100% cotton, white athletic socks." If the writing does not state the price, the parties can testify at court about what the market price was at the time of the deal. But how many socks were to be delivered? One hundred pairs or 100,000? The quantity must be written.

Chapter Conclusion

It is not enough to bargain effectively and obtain a contract that gives you exactly what you want. The deal must have consideration or it will not amount to a contract. Bargaining a contract with a noncompete or exculpatory clause that is too one-sided may lead a court to ignore it. Both parties must be adults of sound mind and must give genuine consent. Misrepresentation and mistakes indicate that at least one party did not truly consent. Some contracts must be in writing to be enforceable, and the writing must be clear and unambiguous.

EXAM REVIEW

1. **CONSIDERATION**   There are three rules of consideration:

   • Both parties must get something of measureable value from the contract.

   • A *promise* to give something of value counts as consideration.

   • The two parties must have bargained for whatever was exchanged. (pp. 163–165)

2. **ACT OR FORBEARANCE**   The item of value can be either an act or a forbearance. (p. 163)

3. **ADEQUACY**   The courts will seldom inquire into the adequacy of consideration. This is the "peppercorn rule." (pp. 164–165)

4. **ILLEGAL CONTRACTS**   Illegal contracts are void and unenforceable. Claims of illegality often arise concerning noncompete clauses and exculpatory clauses. (pp. 165–169)

Question: The purchaser of a business insisted on putting this clause in the sales contract: the seller would not compete, for five years, "anywhere in the United States, the continent of North America, or anywhere else on Earth." What danger does that contract represent *to the purchaser?*

Strategy: This is a noncompete clause based on the sale of a business. Such clauses are valid if reasonable. Is this clause reasonable? If it is unreasonable, what might a court do? (See the "Result" at the end of this section.)

5. **CAPACITY**   Minors, mentally impaired persons, and intoxicated persons generally may disaffirm contracts. (pp. 169–170)

6. **FRAUD**   Fraud is grounds for disaffirming a contract. The injured party must prove a false statement of fact, materiality, and justifiable reliance. (pp. 174–175)

7. **MISTAKE**   In a bilateral mistake, either party may rescind the contract. In a case of unilateral mistake, the injured party may rescind only in limited circumstances. (pp. 172–173)

8. **WRITING REQUIRED**   Contracts that must be in writing to be enforceable concern:

- The sale of any interest in land,
- Agreements that cannot be performed within one year,
- Promises to pay the debt of another,
- Promises made by an executor of an estate,
- Promises made in consideration of marriage, and
- The sale of goods worth $500 or more. (pp. 174–177)

Question: Donald Waide had a contracting business. He bought most of his supplies from Paul Bingham's supply center. Waide fell behind on his bills, and Bingham told Waide that he would extend no more credit to him. That same day, Donald's father, Elmer Waide, came to Bingham's store and said to Bingham that he would "stand good" for any sales to Donald made on credit. Based on Elmer's statement, Bingham again gave Donald credit, and Donald ran up $10,000 in goods before Bingham sued Donald and Elmer. What defense did Elmer make, and what was the outcome?

Strategy: This was an oral agreement, so the issue is whether the promise had to be in writing to be enforceable. Review the list of six contracts that must be in writing. Is this agreement there? (See the "Result" at the end of this section.)

9. **WRITING CONTENTS**   The writing must be signed by the defendant and must state the name of all parties, the subject matter of the agreement, and all essential terms and promises. (pp. 178–179)

4. Result: "Anywhere else on Earth"? This is almost certainly unreasonable. It is hard to imagine a purchaser who would legitimately need such wide-ranging protection. In some states, a court might rewrite the clause, limiting the effect to the seller's state or some other reasonable area. However, in other states, a court finding a clause unreasonable will declare it void in its entirety—enabling the seller to open a competing business next door.

8. Result: Elmer made a promise to pay the debt of another. He did so as a favor to his son. This is a collateral promise. Elmer never signed any such promise, and the agreement cannot be enforced against him.

MATCHING QUESTIONS

___A. Fraud

___B. Restitution

___C. Part performance

___D. Exculpatory clause

___E. Consideration

1. A contract clause intended to relieve one party from potential tort liability

2. The idea that contracts must be a two-way street

3. The intention to deceive the other party

4. Restoring the other party to its original position

5. Entry onto land, or improvements made to it, by a buyer who has no written contract

TRUE/FALSE QUESTIONS

1. T F A contract may not be rescinded based on puffery.

2. T F An agreement for the sale of a house does not need to be in writing if the deal will be completed within one year.

3. T F Noncompete clauses are suspect because they tend to restrain free trade.

4. T F A seller of property must generally disclose latent defects that he knows about.

5. T F A court is unlikely to enforce an exculpatory clause included in a contract for surgery.

6. T F An agreement for the sale of 600 plastic cups, worth $0.50 each, must be in writing to be enforceable.

MULTIPLE-CHOICE QUESTIONS

1. In which case is a court most likely to enforce an exculpatory clause?

   (a) Dentistry

   (b) Hang gliding

   (c) Parking lot

   (d) Public transportation

   (e) Accounting

2. Sarah, age 17, uses $850 of her hard-earned, summer-job money to pay cash for a diamond pendant for the senior prom. She has a wonderful time at the dance, but decides the pendant was an extravagance, returns it, and demands a refund. The store has a "no refund" policy that is clearly stated on a sign on the wall. There was no defect in the pendant. The store refuses the refund. When Sarah sues, she will

   (a) Win $850

   (b) Win $425

   (c) Win, but only if she did not notice the "no refund" policy

   (d) Win, but only if she did not think the "no refund" policy applied to her

   (e) Lose

3. Tobias is selling a surrealist painting. He tells Maud that the picture is by the famous French artist Magritte, although in fact Tobias has no idea whether that is true or not. Tobias's statement is

   (a) Bilateral mistake

   (b) Unilateral mistake

   (c) Fraud

   (d) Innocent misrepresentation

   (e) Legal, so long as he acted in good faith

4. Louise emails Sonya, "I will sell you my house at 129 Brittle Blvd. for $88,000, payable in one month. Best, Louise." Sonya emails back, "Louise, I accept the offer to buy your house at that price. Sonya." Neither party prints a copy of the two emails.

   (a) The parties have a binding contract for the sale of Louise's house.

   (b) Louise is bound by the agreement, but Sonya is not.

   (c) Sonya is bound by the agreement, but Louise is not.

   (d) Neither party is bound because the agreement was never put in writing.

   (e) Neither party is bound because the agreement was never signed.

5. In February, Chuck orally agrees to sell his hunting cabin, with 15 acres, to Kyle for $35,000, with the deal to be completed in July, when Kyle will have the money. In March, while Chuck is vacationing on his land, he permits Kyle to enter the land and dig the foundation for a new cottage. In July, Kyle arrives with the money, but Chuck refuses to sell. Kyle sues.

   (a) Chuck wins because the contract was never put in writing.

   (b) Chuck wins because the contract terms were unclear.

   (c) Kyle wins because a contract for vacation property does not need to be written.

   (d) Kyle wins because Chuck allowed him to dig the foundation.

   (e) Kyle wins because Chuck has committed fraud.

6. Ted's wallet is as empty as his bank account, and he needs $3,500 immediately. Fortunately, he has three gold coins that he inherited from his grandfather. Each is worth $2,500, but it is Sunday, and the local rare-coin store is closed.

When approached, Ted's neighbor Andrea agrees to buy the first coin for $2,300. Another neighbor, Cami, agrees to buy the second for $1,100. A final neighbor, Lorne, offers "all the money I have on me"—$100—for the last coin. Desperate, Ted agrees to the proposal. Which of the deals is supported by consideration?

(a) Ted's agreement with Andrea, only

(b) Ted's agreements with Andrea and Cami, only

(c) All three of the agreements

(d) None of the agreements

ESSAY QUESTIONS

1. Brockwell left his boat to be repaired at Lake Gaston Sales. The boat contained electronic equipment and other personal items. Brockwell signed a form stating that Lake Gaston had no responsibility for any loss to any property in or on the boat. Brockwell's electronic equipment was stolen and other personal items were damaged, and he sued. Is the exculpatory clause enforceable?

2. Guyan Machinery, a West Virginia manufacturing corporation, hired Albert Voorhees as a salesman and required him to sign a contract stating that if he left Guyan, he would not work for a competing corporation anywhere within 250 miles of West Virginia for a two-year period. Later, Voorhees left Guyan and began working at Polydeck Corp., another West Virginia manufacturer. The only product Polydeck made was urethane screens, which comprised half of 1 percent of Guyan's business. Is Guyan entitled to enforce its noncompete clause?

3. **ETHICS** Richard and Michelle Kommit traveled to New Jersey to have fun in the casinos. While in Atlantic City, they used their MasterCard to withdraw cash from an ATM conveniently located in the "pit," which is the gambling area of a casino. They ran up debts of $5,500 on the credit card and did not pay. The Connecticut National Bank sued for the money. What argument should the Kommits make? Which party, if any, has the moral high ground here? Should a casino offer ATM services in the gambling pit? If a credit card company allows customers to withdraw cash in a casino, is it encouraging them to lose money? Do the Kommits have any ethical right to use the ATM, attempt to win money by gambling, and then seek to avoid liability?

4. The McAllisters had several serious problems with their house, including leaks in the ceiling, a buckling wall, and dampness throughout. They repaired the buckling wall by installing I-beams to support it. They never resolved the leaks and the dampness. When they decided to sell the house, they said nothing to prospective buyers about the problems. They stated that the I-beams had been added for reinforcement. The Silvas bought the house for $60,000. Soon afterward, they began to have problems with leaks, mildew, and dampness. Are the Silvas entitled to any money damages? Why or why not?

5. Lonnie Hippen moved to Long Island, Kansas, to work at an insurance company owned by Griffiths. After he moved there, Griffiths offered to sell Hippen a house he owned, and Hippen agreed in writing to buy it. He did buy the house and moved in, but two years later, Hippen left the insurance company. He then claimed that at the time of the sale, Griffiths had orally promised to buy back his house at the selling price if Hippen should happen to leave the company. Griffiths defended based on the Statute of Frauds. Hippen argued that the Statute of Frauds did not apply because the repurchase of the house was essentially part of his employment with Griffiths. Comment.

DISCUSSION QUESTIONS

1. In the gold rush example, Embola gave Tuppela $50 in exchange for a promise of $10,000 later. Under the peppercorn rule, the deal was a contract. Is the peppercorn rule sensible? Should courts require a more *even* exchange of value?

2. Does the coverage of the Statute of Frauds make sense as it currently stands? Would it be better to expand the law and require that all contracts be in writing? Or should the law be done away with altogether?

3. Should noncompete agreements in employment contracts be illegal altogether? Is there equality of bargaining power between the company and the employee? Should noncompetes be limited to top officers of a company? Would you be upset if a prospective employer asked *you* to agree to a one-year covenant not to compete?

4. The Justice Department recently shut down three of the most popular online poker websites (Poker Stars, Absolute Poker, and Full Tilt Poker). State agencies take countless actions each year to stop illegal gaming operations. Do you believe that gambling by adults *should* be regulated? If so, which types? Rate the following types of gambling from most acceptable to least acceptable:

— online poker — state lotteries — horse racing

— casino gambling — bets on pro sports — bets on college sports

5. In the old Michigan case featuring Rose the Cow, the court refused to enforce the agreement. Was this a fair result? Should bilateral mistakes create voidable contracts, or should Walker have been required to sell the cow for $80?

CHAPTER 11

CONCLUSION TO CONTRACTS

© picsbyst/Shutterstock.com

Morty is 80, and a back injury makes it impossible for him to keep up with his yardwork. The weeds in his front yard are knee-high by the Fourth of July, when his son John comes to visit for a week.

Surprised at the condition of the lawn, John gets the old mower out of the garage and mows it himself. Later in the visit, John calls a local landscaping company. He agrees to pay $500 for the company to send workers to mow Morty's lawn every two weeks for the rest of the year.

The company bills John's credit card, but it never sends anyone to cut the grass. As the summer wears on, John and Morty make several angry phone calls to the landscaper, without result. The owner of the company seems not to care, and it may take a lawsuit to motivate him to refund John's money so that he can hire someone else to do the job.

But if John is too busy to take legal action, can *Morty* do so?

> If John is too busy to take legal action, can *Morty* do so?

The basic pattern in third party law is quite simple. Two parties make a contract, and their rights and obligations are subject to the rules that we have already studied: offer and acceptance, consideration, legality, and so forth. However, sometimes their contract affects a third party, one who had no role in forming the agreement itself. The two contracting parties may *intend* to benefit someone else. Those are cases of third party beneficiary. In other cases, one of the contracting parties may actually transfer his rights or responsibilities to a third party, raising issues of assignment or delegation. We consider the issues one at a time. Then we examine issues of contract performance and remedies.

THIRD PARTY BENEFICIARY

Third party beneficiary
Someone who is not a party to a contract but stands to benefit from it.

The two parties who make a contract always intend to gain some benefit for themselves. Often, though, their bargain will also benefit *someone else*. **A third party beneficiary is someone who was not a party to the contract but stands to benefit from it.** Many contracts create third party beneficiaries. In the opening scenario, Morty is a third party beneficiary of John's agreement with the landscaping company. As another example, suppose a major league baseball team contracts to purchase from Seller 20 acres of an abandoned industrial site to be used for a new stadium. The owner of a pizza parlor on the edge of Seller's land might benefit enormously. Forty thousand hungry fans in the neighborhood for 81 home games every season could turn her once-marginal operation into a gold mine of cheese and pepperoni.

But what if the contract falls apart? What if the team backs out of the deal to buy the land? Seller can certainly sue because it is a party to the contract. But what about the pizza parlor owner? Can she sue to enforce the deal, and recover lost profits for unsold sausage and green pepper?

The outcome in cases like these depends upon the intentions of the two contracting parties. If they *intended* to benefit the third party, she will probably be permitted to enforce their contract. If they did not intend to benefit her, she probably has no power to enforce the agreement.

Types of Beneficiaries

Promisor
The person who makes the promise that the third party beneficiary benefits from.

Promisee
The person to whom a promise is made.

A person is an **intended beneficiary** and may enforce a contract if the parties intended her to benefit *and if either* (a) enforcing the promise will satisfy a *duty* of the promisee to the beneficiary, or (b) the promisee intended to make a *gift* to the beneficiary. (The **promisor** is the one who makes the promise that the third party beneficiary is seeking to enforce. The **promisee** is the other party to the contract.)

In other words, a third party beneficiary must show two things in order to enforce a contract that two other people created. First, she must show that the two contracting parties were aware of her situation and knew that she would receive something of value from their deal. Second, she must show that the promisee wanted to benefit her for one of two reasons: either to satisfy some duty owed or to make her a gift.

If the promisee is fulfilling some duty, the third-party beneficiary is called a **creditor beneficiary**. Most often, the "duty" that a promisee will be fulfilling is a debt already owed to the beneficiary. If the promisee is making a gift, the third party is a **donee beneficiary**.[1] So long as the third party is either a creditor or a donee beneficiary, she may enforce the

---

[1]**Donee** comes from the word **donate,** meaning to give.

contract. If she fails to qualify as a creditor or donee beneficiary, then she is merely an **incidental beneficiary**, and she may not enforce the deal.

We will apply this rule to the dispute over Morty's lawn. Like most contracts, the deal between John and the landscaping company had two promises: the company's promise to mow the lawn every two weeks, and John's agreement to pay $500. The one that interests us is the promise to mow the lawn. The company is the promisor and John is the promisee.

Did the two parties intend to benefit Morty? Yes, they did. John wanted his father's property maintained. Did John owe Morty a legal duty? No. Did John intend to make a gift to Morty? Yes. So, Morty is an intended, donee beneficiary, and he can sue the landscaping company to enforce the contract himself.

By contrast, the pizza parlor owner will surely lose. A stadium is a multimillion-dollar investment, and it is most unlikely that the baseball team and the seller of the land were even aware of the owner's existence, let alone that they intended to benefit her. She probably cannot prove either the first element or the second element, and certainly not both.

In the following case, a dazzling diamond loses its luster. Who is entitled to sue?

SCHAUER V. MANDARIN GEMS OF CALIFORNIA, INC.

2005 WL 5730 Court of Appeal of California, 2005

CASE SUMMARY

Facts: Sarah Schauer and her fiance, Darin Erstad, went shopping for an engagement ring at Mandarin Gems, where they were captivated by an 3-carat diamond with a high clarity rating. Erstad bought the ring for $43,121. Later, Mandarin supplied Erstad with a written appraisal valuing the ring at $45,500. A certified gemologist signed the appraisal.

Diamonds may last forever but this marriage was short-lived. The divorce decree gave each party the right to keep whatever personal property they currently held, meaning that Schauer could keep the ring. She had the ring appraised by the Gem Trade Laboratory, which gave it a poor clarity rating and a value of only $20,000.

Schauer sued Mandarin for misrepresentation and breach of contract, but the jeweler defended by saying that it had never made a contract with her. The trial court dismissed Schauer's suit, and she appealed.

Issue *Does Schauer have any right to sue for breach of contract as a third party beneficiary?*

Decision: Yes, she is entitled to sue.

Reasoning: A true third party beneficiary may enforce a contract made by others unless they rescinded the agreement. Persons who expect to incidentally or remotely benefit from a bargain may not enforce it.

A plaintiff claiming status as a third party beneficiary must demonstrate that the promisor understood that the promisee intended to benefit the third party. It is not necessary that *both* parties intended to benefit the third party.

Schauer alleged that she and Erstad went shopping for an engagement ring. They were together when they looked at the ring, and they explained to the jeweler that Erstad was buying the diamond to give to Schauer as an engagement ring. The jeweler *must* have understood that Erstad was entering into a sales contract intending to benefit Schauer.

Schauer has alleged facts that, if found to be true, establish her as a third party beneficiary. She is entitled to proceed with her contract claim against Mandarin Gems.

Reversed and remanded.

ASSIGNMENT AND DELEGATION

After a contract is made, one or both parties may wish to substitute someone else for themselves. Six months before Maria's lease expires, an out-of-town company offers her a new job at a substantial increase in pay. After taking the job, she wants to sublease her apartment to her friend Sarah.

A contracting party may transfer his rights under the contract, which is called an **assignment** of rights. Or a party may transfer her obligations under the contract, which is a **delegation** of duties. Frequently, a party will make an assignment and delegation simultaneously, transferring both rights (such as the right to inhabit an apartment) and duties (like the obligation to pay monthly rent) to a third party.

Assignment

Lydia needs 500 bottles of champagne. Bruno agrees to sell them to her for $10,000, payable 30 days after delivery. He transports the wine to her.

Bruno owes Doug $8,000 from a previous deal. He says to Doug, "I don't have your money, but I'll give you my claim to Lydia's $10,000." Doug agrees. Bruno then *assigns* to Doug *his rights* to Lydia's money, and in exchange Doug gives up his claim against Bruno for $8,000. Bruno is the **assignor, the one making an assignment**, and Doug is the **assignee, the one receiving an assignment**.

Why would Bruno offer $10,000 when he owed Doug only $8,000? Because all he has is a *claim* to Lydia's money. Cash in hand is often more valuable. Doug, however, is willing to assume some risk for a potential $2,000 gain.

Bruno notifies Lydia of the assignment. Lydia, who owes the money, is called the **obligor;** that is, the one obligated to do something. At the end of 30 days, Doug arrives at Lydia's doorstep, asks for his money, and gets it since Lydia is obligated to him. Bruno has no claim to any payment.

Assignor
The person making an assignment.

Assignee
The person receiving an assignment.

Obligor
The person obligated to do something under a contract.

WHAT RIGHTS ARE ASSIGNABLE?

Any contractual right may be assigned unless the assignment

- would substantially change the obligor's rights or duties under the contract, or

- is forbidden by law or public policy, or

- is validly precluded by the contract itself.[2]

Substantial Change. An assignment is prohibited if it would substantially change the obligor's situation. For example, Bruno is permitted to assign to Doug his rights to payment from Lydia because it makes no difference to Lydia whether she writes a check to one person or another. But suppose that, before delivery, Lydia had wanted to assign her rights to the shipment of 500 bottles of champagne to a business in another country. In this example, Bruno would be the obligor, and his duties would substantially change. Shipping heavy items over long distances adds substantial costs, so Lydia would not be able to make the assignment.

Assignment is also prohibited when the obligor is agreeing to perform **personal services**. The close working relationship in such agreements makes it unfair to expect the obligor to work with a stranger. Warner, a feature film director, hires Mayer to be his assistant on a film

---

[2]Restatement (Second) of Contracts §317(2). And note that UCC §2-210(2) is, for our purposes, nearly identical.

to be shot over the next 10 weeks. Warner may not assign his right to Mayer's work to another director.

Public Policy.   Some assignments are prohibited by public policy. For example, someone who has suffered a personal injury may not assign her claim to a third person. Vladimir is playing the piano on his roof deck when the instrument rolls over the balustrade and drops 35 stories before smashing Wanda's foot. Wanda has a valid tort claim against Vladimir, but she may not assign the claim to anyone else. As a matter of public policy, all states have decided that the sale of personal injury claims could create an unseemly and unethical marketplace.

Contract Prohibition.   Finally, one of the contracting parties may try to prohibit assignment in the agreement itself. For example, most landlords include in the written lease a clause prohibiting the tenant from assigning the tenancy without the landlord's written permission.

How Rights Are Assigned

An assignment may be written or oral, and no particular formalities are required. However, when someone wants to assign rights governed by the Statute of Frauds, she must do it in writing. Suppose City contracts with Seller to buy Seller's land for a domed stadium and then brings in Investor to complete the project. If City wants to assign to Investor its rights to the land, it must do so in writing.

Rights of the Parties After Assignment

Once the assignment is made and the obligor notified, the assignee may enforce her contractual rights against the obligor. If Lydia fails to pay Doug for the champagne she gets from Bruno, Doug may sue to enforce the agreement. The law will treat Doug as though he had entered into the contract with Lydia.

But the reverse is also true. **The obligor may generally raise all defenses against the assignee that she could have raised against the assignor.** Suppose Lydia opens the first bottle of champagne—silently. "Where's the pop?" she wonders. All 500 bottles have gone flat. Bruno has failed to perform his part of the contract, and Lydia may use Bruno's nonperformance as a defense against Doug. If the champagne was indeed worthless, Lydia owes Doug nothing.

Delegation of Duties

Garret has always dreamed of racing stock cars. He borrows $250,000 from his sister, Maybelle, in order to buy a car and begin racing. He signs a promissory note in that amount, guaranteeing that he will repay Maybelle the full amount, plus interest, on a monthly basis over 10 years. Regrettably, during his first race, on a Saturday night, Garret discovers that he has a speed phobia. He finally finishes the race at noon on Sunday and quits the business. Garret transfers the car and equipment to Brady, who agrees in writing to pay all money owed to Maybelle. Brady sends a check for a few months, but the payments stop. Maybelle sues Garret, who defends based on the transfer to Brady. Will his defense work?

Most duties are delegable. But delegation does not by itself relieve the delegator of his own liability to perform the contract.

Garret was the **delegator** and Brady was the **delegatee**. Garret has legally delegated to Brady his duty to repay Maybelle. However, Garret remains personally obligated. When Maybelle sues, she will win. Garret, like many debtors, would have preferred to wash his hands of his debt, but the law is not so obliging.

Delegation of duties
A contracting party transfers her duties pursuant to a contract to someone else.

Delegator
A person who gives his obligation under a contract to someone else.

Delegatee
A person who receives an obligation under a contract from someone else.

Garret's delegation to Brady was typical in that it included an assignment at the same time. If he had merely transferred ownership, that would have been only an assignment. If he had convinced Brady to pay off the loan without getting the car, that would have been merely a delegation. He did both at once.

WHAT DUTIES ARE DELEGABLE

Assignment of rights
A contracting party transfers his rights under a contract to someone else.

The rules concerning what duties may be delegated mirror those about the **assignment of rights.**

An obligor may delegate his duties unless

1. delegation would violate public policy, or

2. the contract prohibits delegation, or

3. the **obligee** has a substantial interest in personal performance by the obligor.[3]

Obligee
The person who has an obligation coming to her.

Public Policy.   Delegation may violate public policy, for example in a public works contract. If City hires Builder to construct a subway system, state law may prohibit Builder from delegating his duties to Subcontractor. A public agency should not have to work with parties that it never agreed to hire.

Contract Prohibition.   The parties may forbid almost any delegation, and the courts will enforce the agreement. Hammer, a contractor, is building a house and hires Spot as his painter, including in his contract a clause prohibiting delegation. Just before the house is ready for painting, Spot gets a better job elsewhere and wants to delegate his duties to Brush. Hammer may refuse the delegation even if Brush is equally qualified.

Substantial Interest in Personal Performance.   Suppose Hammer had omitted the "nondelegation" clause from his contract with Spot. Could Hammer still refuse the delegation on the grounds that he has a substantial interest in having Spot do the work? No. Most duties are delegable. There is nothing so special about painting a house that one particular painter is required to do it. But some kinds of work do require personal performance, and obligors may not delegate these tasks. The services of lawyers, doctors, dentists, artists, and performers are considered too personal to be delegated. There is no single test that will perfectly define this group, but generally when the work will test *the character, skill, discretion, and good faith* of the obligor, she *may not* delegate her job.

PERFORMANCE AND DISCHARGE

A party is discharged when she has no more duties under a contract. Most contracts are discharged by full performance. In other words, the parties generally do what they promise. Sally agrees to sell Arthur 300 tulip-shaped wine glasses for his new restaurant. Right on schedule, Sally delivers the correct glasses and Arthur pays in full. Contract, full performance, discharge, end of case.

Rescind
To terminate a contract by mutual agreement.

Sometimes the parties discharge a contract by agreement. For example, the parties may agree to **rescind** their contract, meaning that they terminate it by mutual agreement. At times, a court may discharge a party who has not performed. When things have gone amiss, a judge must interpret the contract and issues of public policy to determine who in fairness should suffer the loss. We will analyze the most common issues of performance and discharge.

---

[3]Restatement (Second) of Contracts §318. And see UCC §2-210, establishing similar limits.

Performance

Caitlin has an architect draw up plans for a monumental new house, and Daniel agrees to build it by September 1. Caitlin promises to pay $900,000 on that date. The house is ready on time, but Caitlin has some complaints. The living room ceiling was supposed to be 18 feet high, but it is only 17 feet; the pool was to be azure, yet it is aquamarine; the maid's room was not supposed to be wired for cable television, but it is. Caitlin refuses to pay anything for the house. Is she justified? Of course not; it would be absurd to give her a magnificent house for free when it has only tiny defects. And that is how a court would decide the case. But in this easy answer lurks a danger. How much leeway will a court permit? Suppose the living room is only 14 feet high, or 12 feet, or 5 feet? What if Daniel finishes the house a month late? Six months late? Three years late? At some point, a court will conclude that Daniel has so thoroughly botched the job that he deserves little or no money. Where is that point? That is a question that businesses—and judges—face every day.

STRICT PERFORMANCE AND SUBSTANTIAL PERFORMANCE

Strict Performance.   Courts dislike strict performance because it enables one party to benefit without paying and sends the other one home empty-handed. **A party is generally not required to render strict performance unless the contract expressly demands it and such a demand is reasonable.** Caitlin's contract never suggested that Daniel would forfeit all payment if there were minor problems. Even if Caitlin had insisted on such a clause, a court would be unlikely to enforce it because the requirement is unreasonable.

In some cases, strict performance does make sense. Marshall agrees to deliver 500 sweaters to Leo's store, and Leo promises to pay $20,000 cash on delivery. If Leo has only $19,000 cash and a promissory note for $1,000, he has failed to perform, and Marshall need not give him the sweaters. Leo's payment represents 95 percent of what he promised, but there is a big difference between cash and a promissory note.

Substantial Performance.   Daniel, the house builder, won his case against Caitlin because he fulfilled most of his obligations, even though he did an imperfect job. Courts often rely on the substantial performance doctrine, especially in cases involving services as opposed to those concerning the sale of goods or land. **In a contract for services, a party that substantially performs its obligations will receive the full contract price, minus the value of any defects.** Daniel receives $900,000, the contract price, minus the value of a ceiling that is 1 foot too low, a pool the wrong color, and so forth. It will be for the trial court to decide how much those defects are worth. If the court decides the low ceiling is a $10,000 damage, the pool color worth $5,000, and the cable television issue worth $500, then Daniel receives $884,500.

On the other hand, a party that fails to perform substantially receives nothing on the contract itself and will only recover the value of the work, if any. If the foundation cracks in Caitlin's house and the walls collapse, Daniel will not receive his $900,000. In such a case, he collects only the market value of the work he has done, which is probably zero.

When is performance substantial? There is no perfect test, but courts look at these issues:

- How much benefit has the promisee received?

- If it is a construction contract, can the owner use the thing for its intended purpose?

- Can the promisee be compensated with money damages for any defects?

- Did the promisor act in good faith?

EXAM Strategy

Question: Jade owns a straight track used for drag racing. She hires Trevor to resurface it for $180,000, paying $90,000 down. When the project is completed, Jade refuses to pay the balance and sues Trevor for her down payment. He counterclaims for the $90,000 still due. At trial, Trevor proves that all of the required materials were applied by trained workers in an expert fashion, the dimensions were perfect, and his profit margin very modest. The head of the national drag racing association testifies that his group considers the strip unsafe. He noticed puddles in both asphalt lanes, found the concrete starting pads unsafe, and believed the racing surface needed to be ground off and reapplied. His organization refuses to sanction races at the track until repairs are made. Who wins the suit?

Strategy: When one party has performed imperfectly, we have an issue of substantial performance. To decide whether Trevor is entitled to his money, we apply four factors: (1) How much benefit did Jade receive? (2) Can she use the racing strip for its intended purpose? (3) Can Jade be compensated for defects? (4) Did Trevor act in good faith?

Result: Jade has received no benefit whatsoever. She cannot use her track for drag racing. Compensation will not help Jade—she needs a new strip. Trevor's work must be ripped up and replaced. Trevor may have acted in good faith, but he failed to deliver what Jade bargained for. Jade wins all of the money she paid. (As we will see later in this chapter, she may win additional sums for her lost profits.)

Good Faith

The parties to a contract must carry out their obligations in good faith. The difficulty, of course, is applying this general rule to the wide variety of problems that may arise when people or companies do business. The plaintiff in the following case argued that the owners of a shopping center failed to act in good faith. Did the court agree? Read on.

BRUNSWICK HILLS RACQUET CLUB INC. v. ROUTE 18 SHOPPING CENTER ASSOCIATES

182 N.J. 210, 864 A.2d 387, Supreme Court of New Jersey, 2005

CASE SUMMARY

Facts: Brunswick Hills Racquet Club (Brunswick) owned a tennis club on property that it leased from Route 18 Shopping Center Associates (Route 18). The lease ran for 25 years, and Brunswick had spent about $1 million in capital improvements. The lease expired March 30, 2002. Brunswick had the option of either buying the property or purchasing a 99-year lease, both on very favorable terms. To exercise its option, Brunswick had to notify Route 18 no later than September 30, 2001, and had to pay the option price of $150,000. If Brunswick

failed to exercise its options, the existing lease automatically renewed as of September 30, for 25 more years, but at more than triple the current rent.

In February 2000—19 months before the option deadline—Brunswick's lawyer, Gabriel Spector, wrote to Rosen Associates, the company that managed Route 18, stating that Brunswick intended to exercise the option for a 99-year lease. He requested that the lease be sent well in advance so that he could review it. He did not make the required payment of $150,000.

In March, Rosen replied that it had forwarded Spector's letter to its attorney, who would be in touch. In April, Spector again wrote, asking for a reply from Rosen or its lawyer.

Over the next six months, Spector continually asked for a copy of the lease, or for information, but neither Route 18's lawyer nor anyone else provided any data. In January 2001, Spector renewed his requests for a copy of the lease. Route 18's lawyer never replied. Sadly, in May 2001, after a long illness, Spector died. In August 2001, Spector's law partner, Arnold Levin, wrote to Rosen, again stating Brunswick's intention to buy the 99-year lease and requesting a copy of all relevant information. He received no reply, and the September deadline passed.

In February 2002, Route 18's lawyer dropped the hammer, notifying Levin that Brunswick could not exercise its option to lease because it had failed to pay the $150,000 by September 30, 2001.

Brunswick sued, claiming that Route 18 had breached its duty of good faith and fair dealing. The trial court found that Route 18 had no duty to notify Brunswick of impending deadlines, and it gave summary judgment for Route 18. The appellate court affirmed, and Brunswick appealed to the state supreme court.

Issue: *Did Route 18 breach its duty of good faith and fair dealing?*

Holding: Yes, Route 18 breached its duty of good faith and fair dealing.

Reasoning: Courts generally should not tinker with precisely drafted agreements entered into by experienced businesspeople. Nonetheless, every party to a contract is bound by a duty of good faith and fair dealing in its performance. Good faith is conduct that conforms to community standards of decency and reasonableness. Neither party may do anything that will prevent the other from receiving the contract benefits.

Route 18 and its agents acted in bad faith. Brunswick Hills notified the landlord 19 months before the deadline that it intended to exercise its option to purchase a 99-year lease. Brunswick Hills mistakenly believed that its payment was not due until closing. During that year and a half, Route 18 engaged in a pattern of evasion, sidestepping every request by Brunswick Hills to move forward on closing the lease. After Spector's death, Route 18's lawyer continued to play possum despite the obvious risk to Brunswick Hills. Route 18 acknowledged that it did not want the lease payment because the long-term lease was not in its financial interest.

Neither a landlord nor its attorney is required to act as his brother's keeper. However, there are ethical norms that apply even in the harsh world of commercial transactions. All parties must behave in good faith and deal fairly with the other side. Brunswick Hills' repeated letters and calls to close the lease placed an obligation on Route 18 to respond in a timely, honest manner. The company failed to do that, and Brunswick Hills is entitled to exercise the 99-year lease.

Breach

When one party *materially* breaches a contract, the other party is discharged. A material breach is one that substantially harms the innocent party. The discharged party has no obligation to perform and may sue for damages. Edwin promises that on July 1 he will deliver 20 tuxedos, tailored to fit male chimpanzees, to Bubba's circus for $300 per suit. After weeks of delay, Edwin concedes he hasn't a cummerbund to his name. This is a material breach and Bubba is discharged. Notice that a trivial breach, such as a one-day delay in delivering the tuxedos, would not have discharged Bubba.

STATUTE OF LIMITATIONS

A party injured by a breach of contract should act promptly. **A statute of limitations begins to run at the time of injury and will limit the time within which the injured party may file suit.** Statutes of limitation vary widely. In some states, for example, an injured party must sue on oral contracts within three years, on a sale of goods contract within four years, and on some written contracts within five years. Failure to file suit within the time limits discharges the breaching party.

Statute of limitations
Limits the time within which an injured party may file suit.

Impossibility

"Your honor, my client wanted to honor the contract. He just couldn't. Honest." Does the argument work? It depends. A court will discharge an agreement if performing a contract was truly impossible but not if honoring the deal merely imposed a financial burden. **True**

impossibility means that something has happened making it utterly impossible to do what the promisor said he would do. Francoise owns a vineyard that produces Beaujolais Nouveau wine. She agrees to ship 1,000 cases *of her wine* to Tyrone, a New York importer, as soon as this year's vintage is ready. Tyrone will pay $50 per case. But a fungus wipes out her entire vineyard. Francoise is discharged. It is theoretically impossible for Francoise to deliver wine from her vineyard, and she owes Tyrone nothing.

True impossibility is generally limited to these three causes:

- *Destruction of the subject matter.* This happened with Francoise's vineyard.

- *Death of the promisor in a personal services contract.* When the promisor agrees personally to render a service that cannot be transferred to someone else, her death discharges the contract.

- *Illegality.* If the purpose of a contract becomes illegal, that change discharges the contract.

It is rare for contract performance to be truly impossible but common for it to become a financial burden to one party. Suppose Bradshaw Steel in Pittsburgh agrees to deliver 1,000 tons of steel beams to Rice Construction in Saudi Arabia at a given price, but a week later, the cost of raw ore increases 30 percent. A contract once lucrative to the manufacturer is suddenly a major liability. Does that change discharge Bradshaw? Absolutely not. Rice signed the deal *precisely to protect itself against price increases.* The whole purpose of contracts is to enable the parties to control their futures.

REMEDIES

A remedy is the method a court uses to compensate an injured party. The most common remedy, used in the great majority of lawsuits, is money damages.

The first step that a court takes in choosing a remedy is to decide what interest it is trying to protect. An **interest** is a legal right in something. Someone can have an interest in property, for example, by owning it, or renting it to a tenant, or lending money so someone else may buy it. He can have an interest in a *contract* if the agreement gives him some benefit. There are four principal contract interests that a court may seek to protect:

Interest
A legal right in something.

- *Expectation interest.* This refers to what the injured party reasonably thought she would get from the contract.

- *Reliance interest.* The injured party may be unable to demonstrate expectation damages but may still prove that he expended money in reliance on the agreement.

- *Restitution interest.* An injured party may only be able to demonstrate that she has conferred a benefit on the other party. Here, the objective is to restore to the injured party the benefit she has provided.

- *Equitable interest.* In some cases, something more than money is needed, such as an order to transfer property to the injured party (specific performance) or an order forcing one party to stop doing something (an injunction).

Expectation Interest

This is the most common remedy. **The expectation interest is designed to put the injured party in the position she would have been in had both sides fully performed their obligations.** A court tries to give the injured party the money she would have made from the contract. If accurately computed, this should take into account all the gains she reasonably expected and all the expenses and losses she would have incurred. The injured party should not end up better off than she would have been under the agreement, nor should she suffer serious loss. If you ever go to law school, you will almost certainly encounter the following case during your first week of classes. It has been used to introduce the concept of damages in contract lawsuits for generations. Enjoy the famous "case of the hairy hand."

Landmark Case

HAWKINS V. MCGEE
84 N.H. 114; 146 A. 641
Supreme Court of New Hampshire, 1929

CASE SUMMARY

Facts: Hawkins suffered a severe electrical burn on the palm of his right hand. After years of living with disfiguring scars, he went to visit Dr. McGee, who was well known for his early attempts at skin-grafting surgery. The doctor told Hawkins "I will guarantee to make the hand a hundred percent perfect." Hawkins hired him to perform the operation.

McGee cut a patch of healthy skin from Hawkins's chest and grafted it over the scar tissue on Hawkins's palm. Unfortunately, the chest hair on the skin graft was very thick, and it continued to grow after the surgery. The operation resulted in a hairy palm for Hawkins. Feeling rather…embarrassed…Hawkins sued Dr. McGee.

The trial court judge instructed the jury to calculate damages in this way: "If you find the plaintiff entitled to anything, he is entitled to recover for what pain and suffering he has been made to endure and what injury he has sustained over and above the injury that he had before."

The jury awarded Hawkins $3,000, but the court reduced the award to $500. Dissatisfied, Hawkins appealed.

Issue: *How should Hawkins's damages be calculated?*

Holding: Hawkins should receive the difference between the benefit the contract promised and the benefit he actually received.

Reasoning: The lower court's jury instructions were improper. Damages in contract cases are designed to give the plaintiff the benefit he would have received if the contract had been properly performed.

Pain and suffering are not relevant. Almost any surgery involves some pain and suffering, but the benefits conferred can outweigh such harm. McGee could have performed his obligations perfectly and still caused Hawkins pain.

The correct determination of damages is related instead to the difference in value of the "100 percent perfect" hand Hawkins was promised and the hand as it was after the actual procedure.

Remanded for a new trial to calculate what these damages are.

Now let's consider a more modern example.

William Colby was a former director of the CIA. He wanted to write a book about his 15 years in Vietnam. He paid James McCarger $5,000 for help in writing an early draft and promised McCarger another $5,000 if the book was published. Then he hired Alexander Burnham to cowrite the book. Colby's agent secured a contract with Contemporary Books, which included a $100,000 advance. But Burnham was hopelessly late with the manuscript, and Colby missed his publication date. Colby fired Burnham and finished the book without him. Contemporary published *Lost Victory* several years late, and the book flopped, earning no significant revenue. Because the book was so late, Contemporary paid Colby a total of only $17,000. Colby sued Burnham for his lost expectation interest. The court awarded him $23,000, calculated as follows:

		$	100,000	advance, the only money Colby was promised
		–	10,000	agent's fee
		=	90,000	fee for the two authors, combined
divided by 2		=	45,000	Colby's fee (the other half went to the coauthor)
		–	5,000	owed to McCarger under the earlier agreement
		=	40,000	Colby's expectation interest
		–	17,000	fee Colby eventually received from Contemporary
		=	23,000	Colby's expectation damages—that is, the amount he would have received had Burnham finished on time

Compensatory damages
Are those that flow directly from the contract.

Consequential damages
Damages that result from the unique circumstances of the plaintiff. Also known as *special damages*.

Incidental damages
Are the relatively minor costs that the injured party suffers when responding to the breach.

The *Colby* case[4] presented a relatively easy calculation of damages. Other contracts are more complex. Courts typically divide the expectation damages into three parts: (1) direct (or **"compensatory"**) damages, which represent harm that flowed directly from the contract's breach; (2) **consequential** (or "special") damages, which represent harm caused by the injured party's unique situation; and (3) **incidental damages,** which are minor costs such as storing or returning defective goods, advertising for alternative goods, and so forth.

Note that punitive damages are absent from our list. The golden rule in contracts cases is to give successful plaintiffs "the benefit of the bargain," and not to punish defendants. Punitive damages are occasionally awarded in lawsuits that involve both a contract *and* either an intentional tort (such as fraud) or a breach of fiduciary duty, but they are not available in "simple" cases involving only a breach of contract.

DIRECT DAMAGES

Direct damages are those that flow directly from the contract. They are the most common monetary award for the expectation interest. These are the damages that inevitably result from the breach. Suppose Ace Productions hires Reina to star in its new movie, *Inside Straight*. Ace promises Reina $3 million, providing she shows up June 1 and works until the film is finished. But in late May, Joker Entertainment offers Reina $6 million to star in its new feature, and on June 1, Reina informs Ace that she will not appear. Reina has breached her contract, and Ace should recover direct damages.

What are the damages that flow directly from the contract? Ace has to replace Reina. If Ace hires Kayla as its star and pays her a fee of $4 million, Ace is entitled to the difference between what it expected to pay ($3 million) and what the breach forced it to pay ($4 million), or $1 million in direct damages.

CONSEQUENTIAL DAMAGES

In addition to direct damages, the injured party may seek consequential damages, or as they are also known, "special damages." **Consequential damages** reimburse for harm that results from the *particular* circumstances of the plaintiff. These damages are only available if they are a *foreseeable consequence* of the breach. Suppose, for example, Raould breaches two contracts—he is late picking both Sharon and Paul up for a taxi ride. His breach is the same for both parties, but the consequences are very different. Sharon misses her flight to

---

[4]*Colby v. Burnham*, 31 Conn. App. 707, 627 A.2d 457, 1993 Conn. App LEXIS 299 (Conn. App. Ct. 1993).

San Francisco and incurs a substantial fee to rebook the flight. Paul is simply late for the barber who manages to fit him in anyway. Thus, Raould's damages would be different for these two contracts.

The rule comes from a famous 1854 case, *Hadley v. Baxendale*. The Hadleys operated a flour mill, but a shaft broke and their business ground to a halt. The family hired Baxendale to cart the damaged part to a foundry, where a new one could be manufactured. Baxendale promised to make the delivery in one day, but he was late transporting the shaft, and as a result, the Hadleys' mill was shut for five extra days. They sued for their lost profit—and lost. The court declared: **the injured party may recover consequential damages only if the breaching party should have foreseen them when the two sides formed the contract.** Baxendale had no way of knowing that this was the Hadleys' only shaft, or that his delay in transport would cost them substantial profit. The Hadleys would have won had they *told* Baxendale this was their only shaft. They failed to do that, and they failed to win their profits.

Let us return briefly to *Inside Straight*. Suppose that, long before shooting began, Ace had sold the film's soundtrack rights to Spinem Sound for $2 million. Spinem believed it would make a profit only if Reina appeared in the film, so it demanded the right to discharge the agreement if Reina dropped out. When Reina quit, Spinem terminated the contract. Now, when Ace sues Reina, it will also seek $2 million in consequential damages for the lost music revenue. If Reina knew about Ace's contract with Spinem when she signed to do the film, she is liable for $2 million. If she never realized she was an essential part of the music contract, she owes nothing for the lost profits.

In the following case, the plaintiffs lost not only profits, but their entire business. Can they recover for harm that is so extensive? You decide.

You be the Judge

BI-ECONOMY MARKET, INC. v. HARLEYSVILLE INS. CO. OF NEW YORK

2008 WL 423451
New York Court of Appeals, 2008

Facts: Bi-Economy Market was a family-owned meat market in Rochester, New York. The company was insured by Harleysville Insurance. The "Deluxe Business Owner's" policy provided replacement cost for damage to buildings and inventory. Coverage also included "business interruption insurance" for one year, meaning the loss of pretax profit plus normal operating expenses, including payroll.

The company suffered a disastrous fire, which destroyed its building and all inventory. Bi-Economy immediately filed a claim with Harleysville, but the insurer responded slowly. Harleysville eventually offered a settlement of $163,000. A year later, an arbitrator awarded the Market $407,000. During that year, Harleysville paid for seven months of lost income but declined to pay more. The company never recovered or reopened.

Bi-Economy sued, claiming that Harleysville's slow, inadequate payments destroyed the company. The company also sought consequential damages for the permanent destruction of its business. Harleysville claimed that it was responsible only for damages specified in the contract: the building, inventory, and lost income. The trial court granted summary judgment for Harleysville. The appellate court affirmed, claiming that when they entered into the contract, the parties did not contemplate damages for termination of the business. Bi-Economy appealed to the state's highest court.

You Be the Judge: *Is Bi-Economy entitled to consequential damages for the destruction of its business?*

Argument for Bi-Economy: Bi-Economy is a small, family business. We paid for business interruption insurance for an obvious reason: in the event of a disaster, we lacked the resources to keep going while buildings were constructed and inventory purchased. We knew that in such a calamity, we would need prompt reimbursement—compensation covering the immediate damage and our ongoing lost income. Why else would we pay the premiums?

At the time we entered into the contract, Harleysville could easily foresee that if it responded slowly, with insufficient payments, we could not survive. They knew that is what we wanted to avoid—and it is just what happened. The insurer's bad faith offer of a low figure, and its payment of only seven months' lost income, ruined a fine family business. When the insurance company agreed to business interruption coverage, it was declaring that it would act fast and fairly to sustain a small firm in crisis. The insurer should now pay for the full harm it has wrought.

Argument for Harleysville: We contracted to insure the Market for three losses: its building, inventory, and lost income. After the fire, we performed a reasonable, careful evaluation and made an offer we considered fair. An arbitrator later awarded Bi-Economy additional money, which we paid. However, it is absurd to suggest that in addition to

that, we are liable for an open-ended commitment for permanent destruction of the business.

Consequential damages are appropriate in cases where a plaintiff suffers a loss that was not covered in the contract. In this case, though, the parties bargained over exactly what Harleysville would pay in the event of a major fire. If the insurer has underpaid for lost income, let the court award a fair sum. However, the parties never contemplated an additional, enormous payment for cessation of the business. There is almost no limit as to what that obligation could be. If Bi-Economy was concerned that a fire might put the company permanently out of business, it should have said so at the time of negotiating for insurance. The premium would have been dramatically higher.

Neither Bi-Economy nor Harleysville ever imagined such an open-ended insurance obligation, and the insurer should not pay an extra cent.

INCIDENTAL DAMAGES

Incidental damages are the relatively minor costs that the injured party suffers when responding to the breach. When Reina, the actress, breaches the film contract, the producers may have to leave the set and fly back to Los Angeles to hire a new actress. The cost of travel, renting a room for auditions, and other related expenses are incidental damages.

Reliance Interest

To win expectation damages, the injured party must prove the breach of contract caused damages that can be *quantified with reasonable certainty*. This rule sometimes presents plaintiffs with a problem.

George plans to manufacture and sell silk scarves during the holiday season. In the summer, he contracts with Cecily, the owner of a shopping mall, to rent a high-visibility stall for $100 per day. George then buys hundreds of yards of costly silk and gets to work cutting and sewing. Then in September, Cecily refuses to honor the contract. George sues and easily proves Cecily breached a valid contract. But what is his remedy?

George cannot establish an expectation interest in his scarf business. He hoped to sell each scarf for a $40 gross profit and wanted to make $2,000 per day. But how much would he actually have earned? Enough to retire on—or enough to buy a salami sandwich for lunch? A court cannot give him an expectation interest, so George will ask for *reliance damages*. **The reliance interest is designed to put the injured party in the position he would have been in had the parties *never entered* into a contract.** This remedy focuses on the time and money the injured party spent performing his part of the agreement.

> How much would he actually have earned? Enough to retire on—or enough to buy a salami sandwich for lunch?

Assuming he is unable to sell the scarves to a retail store (which is probable because retailers will have made purchases long ago), George should be able to recover the cost of the silk fabric he bought and perhaps something for the hours of labor he spent cutting and sewing. However, reliance damages can be difficult to win because *they are harder to quantify*. Judges dislike vague calculations. How much was

George's time worth in making the scarves? How good was his work? How likely were the scarves to sell? If George has a track record in the industry, he will be able to show a market price for his services. Without such a record, his reliance claim becomes a tough battle.

Restitution Interest

Jim and Bonnie Hyler bought an expensive recreational vehicle (RV) from Autorama. The salesman promised the Hylers that a manufacturer's warranty covered the entire vehicle for a year. The Hylers had a succession of major problems with their RV, including windows that wouldn't shut, a door that fell off, a loose windshield, and defective walls. Then they learned that the manufacturer had gone bankrupt. In fact, the Autorama salesman knew of the bankruptcy when he made the sales pitch. The Hylers returned the RV to Autorama and demanded their money back. They wanted restitution.

The restitution interest is designed to return to the injured party a benefit that he has conferred on the other party which would be unjust to leave with that person. Restitution is a common remedy in contracts involving fraud, misrepresentation, mistake, and duress. In these cases, restitution often goes hand in hand with **rescission**, which means to "undo" a contract and put the parties where they were before they made the agreement. The court declared that Autorama had misrepresented the manufacturer's warranty by omitting the small fact that the manufacturer itself no longer existed. Autorama was forced to return to the Hylers the full purchase price, plus the value of the automobile they had traded. The dealer, of course, was allowed to keep the defective RV and stare out the ill-fitting windows.[5]

Rescission
The undoing of a contract, which puts both parties in the positions they were in when they made the agreement.

Other Equitable Interests
SPECIFIC PERFORMANCE

Leona Claussen owned Iowa farmland. She sold some of it to her sister-in-law, Evelyn Claussen, and, along with the land, granted Evelyn an option to buy additional property at $800 per acre. Evelyn could exercise her option any time during Leona's lifetime or within six months of Leona's death. When Leona died, Evelyn informed the estate's executor that she was exercising her option. But other relatives wanted the property, and the executor refused to sell. Evelyn sued and asked for *specific performance*. She did not want an award of damages; she wanted the land itself. The remedy of **specific performance** forces the two parties to perform their contract.

Specific performance
Compels parties to perform the contract they agreed to when the contract concerns the sale of land or some other unique asset.

A court will award specific performance, ordering the parties to perform the contract, only in cases involving the sale of land or some other asset that is unique. Courts use this equitable remedy when money damages would be inadequate to compensate the injured party. If the subject is unique and irreplaceable, money damages will not put the injured party in the same position she would have been in had the agreement been kept. So a court will order the seller to convey the rare object and the buyer to pay for it.

Historically, every parcel of land has been regarded as unique, and therefore specific performance is always available in real estate contracts. Evelyn Claussen won specific performance. The Iowa Supreme Court ordered Leona's estate to convey the land to Evelyn for $800 per acre.[6] Generally speaking, either the seller or the buyer may be granted specific performance.

Other unique items, for which a court will order specific performance, include such things as rare works of art, secret formulas, patents, and shares in a closely held corporation. By contrast, a contract for a new Jeep Grand Cherokee is not enforceable by specific performance. An injured buyer can use money damages to purchase a virtually identical auto.

---

[5]*Hyler v. Garner*, 548 N.W.2d 864, 1996 Iowa Sup. LEXIS 322 (Iowa, 1966).
[6]*In re Estate of Claussen*, 482 N.W.2d 381, 1992 Iowa Sup. LEXIS 52 (Iowa 1992).

EXAM Strategy

Question: The Monroes, a retired couple who live in Illinois, want to move to Arizona to escape the northern winter. In May, the Monroes contract in writing to sell their house to the Temples for $450,000. Closing is to take place June 30. The Temples pay a deposit of $90,000. However, in early June, the Monroes travel through Arizona and discover it is too hot for them. They promptly notify the Temples they are no longer willing to sell and return the $90,000, with interest. The Temples sue, seeking the house. In response, the Monroes offer evidence that the value of the house has dropped from about $450,000 to about $400,000. They claim that the Temples have suffered no loss. Who will win?

Strategy: Most contract lawsuits are for money damages, but not this one. The Temples want the house. Because they want the house itself, and not money damages, the drop in value is irrelevant. What legal remedy are the Temples seeking? They are suing for specific performance. When will a court grant specific performance? Should it do so here?

Result: In cases involving the sale of land or some other unique asset, a court will grant specific performance, ordering the parties to perform the agreement. All houses are regarded as unique. The court will force the Monroes to sell their house, provided the Temples have sufficient money to pay for it.

INJUNCTION

Injunction
A court order to do something or to refrain from doing something.

An **injunction** is a court order that requires someone to refrain from doing something. It is another remedy that courts sometimes use when money damages would be inadequate. Bonnie has an employment contract that contains a noncompete clause. If she ever leaves her company, she has promised not to work for a competing firm for six months. But Bonnie breaks her word—she quits her job and immediately takes a job with a competitor. Her old firm might seek an injunction that prohibits her from working for her new firm until her noncompete has expired.

Mitigation of Damages

Mitigate
To keep damages as low as possible.

Note one limitation on *all* contract remedies: **A party injured by a breach of contract may not recover for damages that he could have avoided with reasonable efforts.** In other words, when one party perceives that the other has breached or will breach the contract, the injured party must try to prevent unnecessary loss. A party is expected to **mitigate** his damages—that is, to keep damages as low as he reasonably can.

Chapter Conclusion

A moment's caution! Often that is the only thing needed to avoid years of litigation. Yes, the broad powers of a court may enable it to compensate an injured party, but problems of proof and the uncertainty of remedies demonstrate that the best solution is a carefully drafted contract and socially responsible behavior.

EXAM REVIEW

1. **THIRD PARTY BENEFICIARY** A third party beneficiary is an intended beneficiary and may enforce a contract only if the parties intended her to benefit from the agreement and (1) enforcing the promise will satisfy a debt of the promisee to the beneficiary or (2) the promisee intended to make a gift to the beneficiary. (pp. 186–187)

2. **ASSIGNMENT AND DELEGATION** An assignment transfers the assignor's contract rights to the assignee. A delegation transfers the delegator's duties to the delegatee. (pp. 188–190)

3. **RIGHT TO ASSIGN** A party generally may assign contract rights unless doing so would substantially change the obligor's rights or duties, is forbidden by law, or is validly precluded by the contract. (pp. 188–189)

4. **RIGHT TO DELEGATE** Duties are delegable unless delegation would violate public policy, the contract prohibits delegation, or the obligee has a substantial interest in personal performance by the obligor. (pp. 189–190)

5. **DISCHARGE** Unless the obligee agrees otherwise, delegation does not discharge the delegator's duty to perform. (pp. 190–194)

6. **SUBSTANTIAL PERFORMANCE** Strict performance, which requires one party to fulfill its duties perfectly, is unusual. In construction and service contracts, substantial performance is generally sufficient to entitle the promisor to the contract price, minus the cost of defects. (pp. 191–192)

7. **GOOD FAITH** Good faith performance is required in all contracts. (pp. 192–193)

8. **IMPOSSIBILITY** True impossibility means that some event has made it impossible to perform an agreement. (pp. 193–194)

EXAM Strategy

Question: Omega Concrete had a gravel pit and factory. Access was difficult, so Omega contracted with Union Pacific Railroad (UP) for the right to use a private road that crossed UP property and tracks. The contract stated that use of the road was solely for Omega employees and that Omega would be responsible for closing a gate that UP planned to build where the private road joined a public highway. In fact, UP never constructed the gate; and Omega had no authority to construct the gate. Mathew Rogers, an Omega employee, was killed by a train while using the private road. Rogers's family sued Omega, claiming that Omega failed to keep the gate closed as the contract required. Is Omega liable?

Strategy: Impossibility means that the promisor cannot do what he promised to do. Is this such a case? (See the "Result" at the end of this section.)

9. **REMEDIES**   A remedy is the method a court uses to compensate an injured party. (pp. 194–200)

10. **EXPECTATION INTEREST**   The expectation interest puts the injured party in the position she would have been in had both sides fully performed. It has three components: direct, consequential, and incidental damages. (pp. 194–198)

EXAM Strategy

Question: Mr. and Ms. Beard contracted for Builder to construct a house on property he owned and sell it to the Beards for $785,000. The house was to be completed by a certain date, and Builder knew that the Beards were selling their own home in reliance on the completion date. Builder was late with construction, forcing the Beards to spend $32,000 in rent. Ultimately, Builder never finished the house, and the Beards moved elsewhere. They sued. At trial, expert testimony indicated the market value of the house as promised would have been $885,000. How much money are the Beards entitled to, and why?

Strategy: Normally, in cases of property, an injured plaintiff may use specific performance to obtain the land or house. However, there *is* no house, so there will be no specific performance. The Beards will seek their expectation interest. Under the contract, what did they reasonably expect? They anticipated a finished house, on a particular date, worth $885,000. They did not expect to pay rent while waiting. Calculate their losses. (See the "Result" at the end of this section.)

11. **RELIANCE INTEREST**   The reliance interest puts the injured party in the position he would have been in had the parties never entered into a contract. (pp. 198–199)

12. **RESTITUTION INTEREST**   The restitution interest returns to the injured party a benefit that she has conferred on the other party which would be unjust to leave with that person. (p. 199)

13. **SPECIFIC PERFORMANCE**   Specific performance, ordered only in cases of a unique asset, requires both parties to perform the contract. (pp. 199–200)

14. **INJUNCTION**   An injunction is a court order that requires someone to do something or refrain from doing something. (p. 200)

8. Result: There was no gate, and Omega had no right to build one. This is a case of true impossibility. Omega was not liable.

10. Result: The Beards' direct damages represent the difference between the market value of the house and the contract price. They expected a house worth $100,000 more than their contract price, and they are entitled to that sum. They also suffered consequential damages. Builder knew they needed the house as of the contract date, and he could foresee that his breach would force them to pay rent. He is liable for a total of $132,000.

MATCHING QUESTIONS

___A. Material

___B. Intended beneficiary

___C. Discharged

___D. Consequential

1. A type of breach that substantially harms the innocent party

2. When a party has no more obligations under a contract

3. Damages that can be recovered only if the breaching party should have foreseen them

4. A third party who should be able to enforce a contract between two others

TRUE/FALSE QUESTIONS

1. T F Contract dates and deadlines are strictly enforceable unless the parties agree otherwise.

2. T F Where one party has clearly breached, the injured party must mitigate damages.

3. T F Courts award the expectation interest more often than any other remedy.

4. T F A party who delegates duties remains liable for contract performance.

MULTIPLE-CHOICE QUESTIONS

1. Bob, a mechanic, claims that Cathy owes him $1,500 on a repair job. Bob wants to assign his claim to Hardknuckle Bank. The likeliest reason that Bob wants to do this is

   (a) Cathy also owes Hardknuckle Bank money.

   (b) Hardknuckle Bank owes Bob money on a consumer claim.

   (c) Hardknuckle Bank owes Bob money on a repair job.

   (d) Bob owes Hardknuckle Bank money.

   (e) Bob and Cathy are close friends.

2. The agreement between Bob and Cathy says nothing about assignment. May Bob assign his claim to Hardknuckle?

   (a) Bob may assign his claim, but only with Cathy's agreement.

   (b) Bob may assign his claim, but only if Cathy and Hardknuckle agree.

   (c) Bob may assign his claim without Cathy's agreement.

   (d) Bob may assign his claim, but Cathy may nullify the assignment.

   (e) Bob may not assign his claim because it violates public policy.

3. Jody is obligated under a contract to deliver 100,000 plastic bottles to a spring water company. Jody's supplier has just gone bankrupt; any other suppliers will charge her more than she expected to pay. This is

   (a) Consequential damages

   (b) Impossibility

   (c) Expectation interest

   (d) Substantial performance

   (e) Legally irrelevant

4. An example of true impossibility is

   (a) Strict performance

   (b) Failure of condition

   (c) Illegality

   (d) Material breach

   (e) Consequential interest

5. Museum schedules a major fundraising dinner, devoted to a famous Botticelli picture, for September 15. Museum then hires Sue Ellen to restore the picture, her work to be done no later than September 14. Sue Ellen is late with the restoration, forcing Museum to cancel the dinner and lose at least $500,000 in donations. Sue Ellen delivers the picture, in excellent condition, two weeks late. Museum sues.

   (a) Museum will win.

   (b) Museum will win if, when the parties made the deal, Sue Ellen knew the importance of the date.

   (c) Museum will win provided that it was Sue Ellen's fault she was late.

   (d) Museum will win provided that it was *not* Sue Ellen's fault she was late.

   (e) Museum will lose.

6. Tara is building an artificial beach at her lakefront resort. She agrees in writing to buy 1,000 tons of sand from Frank for $20 per ton, with delivery on June 1, at her resort. Frank fails to deliver any sand, and Tara is forced to go elsewhere. She buys 1,000 tons from Maureen at $25 per ton and then is forced to pay Walter $5,000 to haul the sand to her resort. Tara sues Frank. Tara will recover

   (a) Nothing

   (b) $5,000

   (c) $10,000

   (d) $15,000

   (e) $30,000

ESSAY QUESTIONS

1. Nationwide Discount Furniture hired Rampart Security to install an alarm in its warehouse. A fire would set off an alarm in Rampart's office, and the security company was then supposed to notify Nationwide immediately. A fire did break out, but Rampart allegedly failed to notify Nationwide, causing the fire to spread next

door and damage a building owned by Gasket Materials Corp. Gasket sued Rampart for breach of contract, and Rampart moved for summary judgment. Comment.

2. Evans built a house for Sandra Dyer, but the house had some problems. The garage ceiling was too low. Load-bearing beams in the "great room" cracked and appeared to be steadily weakening. The patio did not drain properly. Pipes froze. Evans wanted the money promised for the job, but Dyer refused to pay. Comment.

3. Racicky was in the process of buying 320 acres of ranchland. While that sale was being negotiated, Racicky signed a contract to sell the land to Simon. Simon paid $144,000, the full price of the land. But Racicky went bankrupt before he could complete the purchase of the land, let alone its sale. Which of these remedies should Simon seek: expectation, restitution, or specific performance?

4. **ETHICS:** The National Football League (NFL) owns the copyright to the broadcasts of its games. It licenses local television stations to telecast certain games and maintains a "blackout rule," which prohibits stations from broadcasting home games that are not sold out 72 hours before the game starts. Certain home games of the Cleveland team were not sold out, and the NFL blocked local broadcast. But several bars in the Cleveland area were able to pick up the game's signal by using special antennas. The NFL wanted the bars to stop showing the games. What did it do? Was it unethical of the bars to broadcast the games that they were able to pick up? Apart from the NFL's legal rights, do you think it had the moral right to stop the bars from broadcasting the games?

DISCUSSION QUESTIONS

1. A manufacturer delivers a new tractor to Farmer Ted on the first day of the harvest season. But the tractor will not start. It takes two weeks for the right parts to be delivered and installed. The repair bill comes to $1,000. During the two weeks, some acres of Farmer Ted's crops die. He argues in court that his lost profit on those acres is $60,000. The jury awards the full $1,000 for the tractor repairs, and $60,000 for the lost crops. Identify the two types of awards. Is it fair that Farmer Ted receives 60 times the value of the repair bill for his lost crops?

2. If a person promises to give you a gift, there is usually no consideration. The person can change his mind and decide not to give you the present, and there is nothing you can do about it. But if a person makes a contract with *someone else* and intends that you will receive a gift under the agreement, you are a donee beneficiary, and you *do* have rights to enforce the deal. Are these rules unacceptably inconsistent? If so, which rule should change?

3. Imagine that you hire your trusted friend Fran to paint your house and that you do not include a nondelegation clause in the agreement. Fran delegates the job to Sam, who is a stranger to you. The delegation is legal, but should it be? Is it reasonable that you must accept the substitute painter?

4. The death of a promisor in a *personal services* contract discharges an agreement. But if a promisor dies, other kinds of contracts live on. Is this sensible? Would it be better to discharge all kinds of agreements if one of the parties passes away?

5. If someone breaks a contract, the other party can generally sue and win some form of damages. But for centuries, the law has considered land to be unique, so a lawsuit that involves a broken agreement for a sale of land will usually result in an order of specific performance. Is this ancient rule still reasonable? If someone backs out of an agreement to sell an acre of land, should he be ordered to turn over the land itself? Why not just require him to pay an appropriate number of dollars in damages?

CHAPTER 12

PRACTICAL CONTRACTS

© picsbyst/Shutterstock.com

Two true stories:

One

Holly (on the phone to her client): So, Judd, Harry's lawyer just emailed me a letter that Harry says he got from you last year. I'm reading from the letter now: "Each year that you meet your revenue goals, you'll get a 1 percent equity interest." Is it possible you sent that letter?

Judd: I don't remember the exact wording, but probably something like that.

Holly: You told me, absolutely, positively, you had never promised Harry any stock. That he was making the whole thing up.

Judd: He was threatening to leave unless I gave him some equity, so I said what he wanted to hear. But that letter didn't *mean* anything. This is a family business, and no one but my children will ever get stock.

> I don't know what the *contract* says—that's just the legal stuff.

Two

Grace (on the phone with her lawyer): Providential has raised its price to $12 a pound. I can't afford to pay that! We had a deal that the price would never go higher than 10 bucks. I've talked to Buddy over there, but he is refusing to back down. We need to do something!

Lawyer: Let me look at the contract.

Grace (her voice rising): I don't know what the *contract* says—that's just the legal stuff. Our *business* deal was no more than $10 a pound!

Businesspeople, not surprisingly, tend to focus more on business than on the technicalities of contract law. However, *ignoring* the role of a written agreement can lead to serious trouble. Both of the clients in the opening scenario ended up being bound by a contract they did not want.

You have been studying the *theory* of contract law. This chapter is different—its purpose is to demonstrate how that theory operates in *practice*. We will look at the structure and content of a standard written agreement and answer questions such as: What do all these legal terms mean? Are any important provisions missing? By the end of the chapter, you will have a road map for understanding a written contract.[1]

To illustrate our discussion of specific contract provisions, we will use a real contract between an actor and a producer to make a movie. For reasons of confidentiality, however, we have changed the names.

Before we begin our discussion of written contracts, let's ask: **Do you need a written agreement at all?** Oral contracts can certainly be successful, but there are times when you should *definitely* sign an agreement:

1. The Statute of Frauds requires it.

2. The deal is crucial to your life or the life of your business.

3. The terms are complex.

4. You do not have an ongoing relationship with the other party.

Once you decide you need a written contract, then what?

THE LAWYER

Businesspeople sometimes refer to their lawyers with terms like *business prevention department.* They may be reluctant to ask an attorney to draft a contract for fear of the time and expense that lawyers can inject into the process. And they worry that the lawyers will interfere in the business deal itself, at best causing unnecessary hindrance, at worst killing the deal. Part of the problem is that lawyers and clients have different views of the future.

Lawyers and Clients

Businesspeople are optimists—they believe that they have negotiated a great deal and everything is going to go well—sales will boom, the company will prosper. **Lawyers have a different perspective—their primary goal is to protect their clients by avoiding litigation, now and in the future.** For this reason, lawyers are trained to be pessimists—they try to foresee and protect against everything that can possibly go wrong. Businesspeople sometimes view this lawyering as a waste of time and a potential deal-killer, but it may just save them from some dire failure.

Lawyers also prefer to negotiate touchy subjects at the beginning of a relationship, when everyone is on friendly terms and eager to make a deal, rather than waiting until trouble strikes. In the long run, nothing harms a relationship more than unpleasant surprises.

---

[1]For further reading on practical contracts, see Scott Burnham, *Drafting and Analyzing Contracts*, Lexis/Nexis, 2003; Charles M. Fox, *Working with Contracts*, Practical Law Institute, 2008; George W. Kuney, *The Elements of Contract Drafting*, Thomson/West, 2006.

One advantage of using lawyers to conduct these negotiations is that they can serve as the bad guys. Instead of the client raising tough issues, the lawyers do. Many a client has said, "but my lawyer insists …" If the lawyer takes the blame, the client is able to maintain a better relationship with the other party.

Of course, this lawyerly protection comes at a cost—legal fees, time spent bargaining, the hours used to read complex provisions, and the potential for goodwill to erode during negotiations.

Hiring a Lawyer

If you do hire a lawyer, be aware of certain warning signs. Although the lawyer's goal is to protect you, a good attorney should be a dealmaker, not a deal-breaker. She should help you do what you want and, therefore, should never (or, at least, hardly ever) say, "You cannot do this." Instead, she should say, "Here are the risks to this approach" or "Here is another way to achieve your goal."

Moreover, your lawyer's goal should not be to annihilate the other side. In the end, the contract will be more beneficial to everyone if the parties' relationship is harmonious. Trying to exact every last ounce of flesh, using whatever power you have to an abusive extreme, is not a sound long-term strategy. In the end, the best deals are those in which all the parties' incentives are aligned.

THE CONTRACT

In this section, we discuss how a contract is prepared and what provisions it should include.

Who Drafts It?

Once businesspeople have agreed to the terms of the deal, it is time to prepare a draft of the contract. Generally, both sides would prefer to *control the pen* (that is, to prepare the first draft of the contract) because the drafter has the right to choose a structure and wording that best represents his interests. Typically, the party with the most bargaining power prepares the drafts. In the movie contract, Producer's lawyer prepared the first draft. The contract then went to Artist's lawyer, who added the provisions that mattered to the client.

Mistakes

This author once worked with a lawyer who made a mistake in a contract. "No problem," he said. "I can win that one in court." Not a helpful attitude, given that the purpose of a contract is to *avoid* litigation. In this section, we look at the most common types of mistakes and how to avoid them.

VAGUENESS

Businesspeople sometimes *deliberately* choose vagueness. They do not want the terms of the contract to be clear. It may be that they are not sure what they can get from the other side, or in some cases, even what they really want. So they try to form a contract that leaves their options open. However, as the following case illustrates: **vagueness is your enemy.**

You be the Judge

Facts: Jones Brothers Construction was the general contractor on a job to expand American Airlines' facilities at O'Hare International Airport. After Quake bid on the project, Jones Brothers orally informed Quake that it had won the project and would receive a contract soon. Jones Brothers wanted the license numbers of the subcontractors that Quake would be using, but Quake could not furnish those numbers until it had assured its subcontractors that they had the job. Quake did not want to give that assurance until *it* was certain of its own work. So Jones Brothers sent a letter of intent that stated, among other things:

QUAKE CONSTRUCTION, INC. v. AMERICAN AIRLINES, INC.
141 Ill. 2d 281, 565 N.E.2d 990, 1990 Ill. LEXIS 151
Supreme Court of Illinois, 1990

> We have elected to award the contract for the subject project to your firm as we discussed on April 15. A contract agreement outlining the detailed terms and conditions is being prepared and will be available for your signature shortly.
>
> Your scope of work includes the complete installation of expanded lunchroom, restaurant, and locker facilities for American Airlines employees, as well as an expansion of American Airlines' existing Automotive Maintenance Shop. A sixty (60) calendar day period shall be allowed for the construction of the locker room, lunchroom, and restaurant area beginning the week of April 22. The entire project shall be completed by August 15.
>
> This notice of award authorizes the work set forth in the attached documents at a lump sum price of $1,060,568.00.

Jones Brothers Construction Corporation reserves the right to cancel this letter of intent if the parties cannot agree on a fully executed subcontract agreement.

The parties never signed a more detailed written contract, and ultimately Jones Brothers hired another company. Quake sued, seeking to recover the money it spent in preparation and its loss of anticipated profit.

You Be the Judge: *Was the letter of intent a valid contract?*

Argument for Quake: This letter was a valid contract. It explicitly stated that Jones awarded the contract to Quake. It also said, "This notice of award authorizes the work." The letter included significant detail about the scope of the contract, including the specific facilities Quake would be working on. Furthermore, the work was to commence approximately 4 to 11 days after the letter was written. This short period of time indicates that the parties intended to be bound by the letter so that work could begin quickly. And, the letter contained a cancellation clause. If it was not a contract, why would anyone need to cancel it?

Argument for Jones: This letter was not a contract. It referred several times to the execution of a formal contract by the parties, thus indicating that they did not intend to be bound by the letter. Look at the cancellation clause carefully: it could also be interpreted to mean that the parties did not intend to be bound by any agreement until they entered into a formal contract.

What a disaster for both parties that they have to litigate the meaning of this letter of intent. The problem is that they agreed to something so vague. Sometimes parties adopt vagueness as a *strategy*. One party may be trying to get a commitment from the other side without obligating itself. A party may feel *almost* ready to commit and yet still have reservations. It wants the *other* party to make a commitment so that planning can go forward. This approach is understandable but dangerous.

If you were negotiating for Jones Brothers and wanted to clarify negotiations without committing your company, how could you do it? State in the letter that it is *not a contract*, and that *neither side is bound by it*. State that it is a memorandum summarizing negotiations thus far, but that neither party will be bound until a full written contract is signed.

But what if Quake cannot get a commitment from its subcontractors until they are certain that it has the job? Quake should take the initiative and present Jones Brothers with its own letter of intent, stating that the parties *do* have a binding agreement for $1 million worth of work. Insist that Jones Brothers sign it. Jones Brothers would then be forced to decide whether it is willing to make a binding commitment. If it is not willing to commit, let it openly say so. At least both parties will know where they stand.

The movie contract provides another example of deliberate vagueness. In these contracts, nudity is always a contentious issue. Producers believe that nudity sells movie tickets; actors are afraid that it may tarnish their reputation. In the first draft of our contract, Artist's lawyer specified:

> Artist may not be photographed and shall not be required to render any services nude below the waist or in simulated sex scenes without Artist's prior written consent.

However, the script called for a scene in which Artist was swimming nude and the director wanted the option of showing him below the waist from the back. Ultimately, the nudity clause read as follows:

> Producer has informed Artist that Artist's role in the Picture might require Artist to appear and be photographed (a) nude, which nudity may include only above-the-waist nudity and rear below-the-waist nudity, but shall exclude frontal below-the-waist nudity; and (b) in simulated sex scenes. Artist acknowledges and agrees that Artist has accepted such employment in the Picture with full knowledge of Artist's required participation in nude scenes and/or in simulated sex scenes and Artist's execution of the Agreement constitutes written consent by Artist to appear in the nude scenes and simulated sex scenes and to perform therein as reasonably required by Producer. A copy of the scenes from the screenplay requiring Artist's nudity and/or simulated sex are attached hereto. Artist shall have a right of meaningful prior consultation with the director of the Picture regarding the manner of photography of any scenes in which Artist appears nude or engaged in simulated sex acts.
>
> Artist may wear pants or other covering that does not interfere with the shooting of the nude scenes or simulated sex scenes. Artist's buttocks and/or genitalia shall not be shown, depicted, or otherwise visible without Artist's prior written consent. Artist shall have the absolute right to change his mind and not perform in any nude scene or simulated sex scene, notwithstanding that Artist had prior thereto agreed to perform in such scene.

What does this provision mean? Has Artist agreed to perform in nude scenes or not? He has acknowledged that the script calls for nude scenes and he has agreed, in principle, that he will appear in them. However, he did not want to agree categorically, before shooting had even started and he had experience working with this director. Actor has a number of options—he can refuse to shoot nude scenes altogether, or he can shoot them and then, after viewing them, decide not to allow them in the movie. With a clause such as this one, the director shot different versions of the scene—some with nudity and some without—so that if Artist rejected the nude scene, the director still had options.

The true test of whether a vague clause belongs in a contract is this: Would you sign the contract if you knew that the other side's interpretation would prevail in litigation? In this example, each side was staking out its position, and deferring a final negotiation until there was an actual disagreement about a nude scene. If you would be happy enough with the other side's position in the end, the vague clause simply defers a fight that you can afford to lose. But if the point is really important to you, it may be wiser to resolve the issue before you sign the contract by writing the clause in a way that clearly reflects your desired outcome.

EXAM Strategy

Question: The nudity provision in the movie contract is vague. Rewrite it so that it accurately expresses the agreement between the parties.

Strategy: This is easy! Just say what the parties intended the deal to be.

Result: "The script for the Picture includes scenes showing Artist (a) with frontal nudity from the waist up and with rear below-the-waist nudity (but no frontal below-the-waist nudity); and (b) in simulated sex scenes. However, no scenes shall be shot in which Artist's buttocks and/or genitalia are shown, depicted, or otherwise visible without Artist's prior written consent. Artist shall have the absolute right not to perform in any nude scene or simulated sex scene. If shot, no nude or sex scenes may appear in the Picture without Artist's prior written consent."

AMBIGUITY

Vagueness occurs when the parties do not want the contract to be clear. Ambiguity is different—it means that the provision is *accidentally* unclear. It occurs in contracts when the parties think only about what *they* want a provision to mean, without considering the literal meaning or the other side's perspective. When reading a contract, try to imagine all the different ways a clause can be interpreted. Because you think it means one thing does not mean that the other side will share your view. For example, suppose that an employment contract says, "Employee agrees not to work for a competitor for a period of three years from employment." Does that mean three years from the date of hiring or the date of termination? Unclear, so who knows?

What happens if a contract does contain ambiguous language? **Any ambiguity is interpreted against the drafter of the contract**. Although both sides need to be careful in reading a contract—litigation benefits no one—the side that prepares the documents bears a special burden. This rule is meant to

- Protect laypeople from the dangers of form contracts that they have little power to change. The courts are especially sympathetic to laypeople if a company prepares a form contract and gives the other side only a "take it or leave it" option. (Think insurance policies.)

- Protect people who are unlikely to be represented by a lawyer. Most people do not hire a lawyer to read form contracts. And without an experienced lawyer, it is highly unlikely that an individual would be aware of ambiguities.

- Encourage those who prepare contracts to do so carefully.

TYPOS

Extell Development Corporation built the Rushmore, a luxury condominium complex in Manhattan. When Extell began selling the units, it agreed to refund any buyer's down payment if the first closing did not occur by September 1, 2009. (The goal was to protect buyers who might not have any place to live if the building was not finished on time.) In the end, the first closing occurred in February 2009. No problem, right? No problem except that, by accident, the purchase contract said September 1, *2008* rather than *2009*. In the meantime, the Manhattan real estate market tumbled, and many purchasers of Rushmore condominiums wanted to back out. After litigation all the way to the Federal Court of Appeals, Extell was required to refund the deposits.

What is the law of typos? First of all, the law has a fancier word than *typo*—it is **scrivener's error**. A scrivener is a clerk who copies documents. **In the case of a scrivener's error, a court will reform a contract if there is clear and convincing evidence that the mistake does not reflect the true intent of the parties.** In the Rushmore case, an arbitrator refused to reform the contract, ruling that there was no clear and convincing evidence that the parties intended something other than the contract term as written.

In the following case, even more money was at stake. What would you do if you were the judge?

Scrivener's error
A typo.

You be the Judge

HERITAGE TECHNOLOGIES, L.L.C. v. PHIBRO-TECH, INC.

2008 U.S. Dist. LEXIS 329
United States District Court for the Southern
District of Indiana, 2008

Facts: Heritage wanted to buy a substance called tribasic copper chloride (TBCC) from Phibro but, because of uncertainty in the industry, the two companies could not agree on a price for future years. It turned out, though, that the price of TBCC tended to rise and fall with that of copper sulfate, so Heritage proposed that the amount it paid for TBCC would increase an additional $15 per ton for each $0.01 increase in the cost of copper sulfate over $0.38 per pound.

At the end of a meeting between two top officers of Heritage and Phibro, the Phibro officer hand wrote a document stating the terms of their deal and agreeing to the Heritage pricing proposal. In a subsequent draft of the agreement prepared by Phibro, the $.01 number was changed to $0.10—that is, from 1 cent to 10 cents. In other words, in the original draft, Heritage agreed to a first increase if copper sulfate went above 39 cents per pound, an additional price rise at 40 cents, and so on. But in the Phibro draft, Heritage's first increase would not occur until the price of copper sulfate went to 48 cents a pound, with a second rise at 58 cents. In short, the Phibro draft was much more favorable to Heritage than the Heritage proposal had been.

At some point during the negotiations, the lawyer for Heritage asked his client if the $0.10 figure was accurate. The Heritage officer said that the increase in this amount was meant to be payment for other provisions that favored Phibro. There is no evidence that this statement was true. The contract went through eight drafts and numerous changes, but the two sides never again met or discussed the $0.10 figure.

After the execution of the agreement, Heritage discovered a different mistake. When Heritage brought the error to Phibro's attention, Phibro agreed to make the change, even though it was to Phibro's disadvantage to do so.

All was peaceful until the price of copper sulfate went to $0.478 per pound. Phibro believed that because the price was above $0.38 per pound, it was entitled to an increased payment. Heritage responded that the increase would not occur until the price went above $0.48. Phibro then looked at the agreement and noticed the $0.10 term for the first time. Phibro contacted Heritage to say that the $0.10 term was a typo and not what the two parties had originally agreed. Heritage refused to amend the agreement, and Phibro filed suit.

You Be the Judge: *Should the court enforce the contract as written or as the parties agreed in their meeting? Which number is correct—$0.10 or $0.01?*

Argument for Phibro: In their meeting, the two negotiators agreed to a $15 per ton increase in the price of TBCC for each 1-cent increase in copper sulfate price. Then by mistake, the contract said 10 cents. The two parties never negotiated the 10-cent provision, and there is no evidence that they had agreed to it. The court should revise this contract to be consistent with the parties' agreement, which was 1 cent.

Argument for Heritage: The parties conducted negotiations by sending drafts back and forth rather than by talking on the phone. Both parties were represented by a team of lawyers, the agreement went through eight drafts, and this pricing term was never altered despite several other changes and additions. Moreover, the change in price was in return for other provisions that benefited Phibro. There is no clear and convincing evidence that both parties were mistaken about what the document actually said. Ultimately, the parties agreed to 10 cents, and that is what the court should enforce.

Ethics

When Heritage found a different mistake in the contract, Phibro agreed to correct it, even though the correction was unfavorable to Phibro. But when a mistake occurred in Heritage's favor, Heritage refused to honor the intended terms of the agreement. Is Heritage behaving ethically? Does Heritage have an obligation to treat Phibro as well as Phibro behaved towards Heritage? Is it right to take advantage of other people's mistakes? What Life Principles would you apply in this situation?

What can you do to prevent mistakes? In theory, you should read every contract you sign very carefully. If, for whatever reason, that degree of care is not possible, be sure to at least **read the important terms carefully**. Before signing a contract, check *carefully* and *thoughtfully* the names of the parties, the dates, dollar amounts, and interest rates. If all these elements are correct, you are unlikely to go too far wrong. And, of course, having read this chapter, *you* will never mistake $0.10 for $0.01.

A contract is not only an agreement—it is also a reference document. During the course of your relationship with the other party, you may need to refer to the contract regularly to remind yourself what you agreed to. This brings us to our next topic—the structure of a contract. Once you understand the standard outline of a contract, it will be much easier for you to find your way through the thicket of provisions.

The Structure of a Contract

Traditional contracts tended to use archaic words—*whereas* and *heretofore* were common. Modern contracts are more straightforward, without as many linguistic flourishes. Our movie contract takes the modern approach.

TITLE

The title should be as descriptive as possible—a generic title such as AGREEMENT does not distinguish one contract from another. The title of our movie contract is MEMORANDUM OF AGREEMENT (not a particularly useful name), but in the upper right-hand corner, there is space for the date of the contract and the subject. The subject is Dawn Rising/Clay Parker.

INTRODUCTORY PARAGRAPH

The introductory paragraph includes the date, the names of the parties, and the nature of the contract. The names of the parties and the movie are defined terms, e.g., Clay Parker ("Artist"). By defining the names, the actual names do not have to be repeated throughout the agreement. In this way, a standard form contract can be used in different deals without worrying about whether the names of the parties are correct throughout the document.

The introductory paragraph should also include specific language indicating that the parties entered into an agreement. In our contract, the opening paragraph states:

> This shall confirm the agreement ("Agreement") between WINTERFIELD PRODUCTIONS ("Producer") and CLAY PARKER ("Artist") regarding the acting services of Artist in connection with the theatrical motion picture tentatively entitled "DAWN RISING" (the "Picture")[2], as follows:

COVENANTS

Now we get to the heart of the contract: what are the parties agreeing to do? Failure to perform these obligations constitutes a breach of the contract and damages will result. **Covenant** is a legal term that means a promise about what the parties will do in a contract.

Covenant
A promise in a contract.

At this stage, the relationship between lawyer and client is particularly important. They will obtain the best result if they work well together. And to achieve a successful outcome, both need to contribute. Clients should figure out what they need for the agreement to be successful. It is at this point that they have the most control over the deal, and they should exercise it. *It is a mistake to assume that everything will work itself out.* Instead, clients need to protect themselves now as best they can. Lawyers can help in this process because they have worked on other similar deals and they know what can go wrong. Listen to them—they are on your side.

Imagine you are an actor about to sign a contract to make a movie. What provisions would you want? Begin by asking what your goals are for the project. Certainly, to make a movie that

---

[2]These are not the parties' real names but are offered to illustrate the concepts.

> ## Both Artist and Producer want control over the final product. Who will win that battle?

gets good reviews and good box office. So you will ask for as much control over the process and product as you can get—selection of the director and co-stars, for instance. Maybe influence on the editing process. But you also want to make sure that the movie does not hurt your career. What provisions would you need to achieve that goal? And shooting a movie can be grueling work, so you want to ensure that your physical and emotional needs are met, particularly when you are on location away from home. Try to think of all the different events that could happen and how they would affect you. The contract should make provisions for these occurrences.

Now take the other side and imagine what you would want if you were the producer. The producer's goal is to make money—which means creating a quality movie while spending as little as possible and maintaining control over the process and final product. As you can see, some of the goals conflict—both Artist and Producer want control over the final product. Who will win that battle?

Here are the terms of the real movie contract.

The Artist negotiated:

1. A fixed fee of $1,800,000, to be paid in equal installments at the end of each week of filming.

2. Extra payment if the filming takes longer than 10 weeks.

3. 7.5 percent of the gross receipts of the movie.

4. Approval over (but approval shall not be unreasonably withheld):

   a. the director, costars, hairdresser, makeup person, costume designer, stand-ins, and the look of his role (although he lists one director and costar whom he has preapproved)

   b. any changes in the script that materially affect his role

   c. all product placements, but he preapproves the placement of Snickers candy bars

   d. locations where the filming takes place

   e. all videos, photos, and interviews of him

5. Approval (at his sole discretion) over the release of any blooper videos.

6. His name to be listed first in the movie credits, on a separate card (i.e., alone on the screen).

7. At least 12 hours off duty from the end of each day of filming to the start of the next day.

8. That he flies first class to any locations outside of Los Angeles.

9. That the producer pays for 10 first-class airline tickets for his friends to visit him on location.

10. A luxury hotel suite for himself and a room for his friends.

11. A driver and four-wheel-drive SUV to transport him to the set.

12. The right to keep some wardrobe items.

The Producer negotiated:

1. All intellectual property rights to the movie.

2. The right not to make the movie, although he would still have to pay Artist the fixed fee.

3. Control over the final cut of the movie.

4. That the Artist will show up on a certain date and work in good faith for

   a. 2 weeks in preproduction (wardrobe and rehearsals)

   b. 10 weeks shooting the movie

   c. 2 free weeks after the shooting ends, in case the director wants to reshoot some scenes. The Artist must in good faith make himself available whenever the director needs him.

5. The right to fire Artist if his appearance or voice materially changes before or during the filming of the movie.

6. That the Artist help promote the movie on dates subject to Artist's approval, which shall not be unreasonably withheld.

BREACH

Throughout the life of a contract, there could be many small breaches. Say, Artist shows up one day late for filming or he gains five pounds. To constitute a violation of the contract, though, the breach must be material. A **material breach** is important enough to defeat an essential purpose of the contract. Although a court would probably not consider one missed day to be a material breach, if Artist repeatedly failed to show up, that would be material.

Given that one goal of a contract is to avoid litigation, it is can be useful to define what a breach is. The movie contract uses this definition:

> "Artist fails or refuses to perform in accordance with Producer's instructions or is otherwise in material breach or material default hereof," and "Artist's use of drugs [other than prescribed by a medical doctor]."

The contract goes on, however, to give Artist one free pass:

> It being agreed that with regard to one instance of default only, Artist shall have 24 hours after receipt of notice to cure any alleged breach or default hereof.

Good faith. Note that many of the covenants in the movie contract provide that the right must be exercised *reasonably* or that a decision must be made in *good faith* (except for the right to approve blooper videos, over which Artist has *sole discretion*.) A party with **sole discretion** has the absolute right to make any decision on that issue. Sole discretion clauses are not entered into lightly. **Reasonable** means ordinary or usual under the circumstances. **Good faith** means an honest effort to meet both the spirit and letter of the contract.

In drafting covenants, there are two issues to keep in mind.

Reciprocal Promises and Conditions. Suppose that a contract provides:

1. Actor shall take part in the principal photography of Movie for 10 weeks, commencing on March 1.

2. Producer shall pay Artist $180,000 per week.

In this case, even if Artist does not show up for shooting, Producer is still required to pay him. These provisions are **reciprocal promises, which means that they are each enforceable independently.** Producer must make payment and then sue Artist, hoping to recover damages in court.

The better approach is for the covenants to be **conditional**—a party agrees to perform them only if the other side has first done what it promised. For example, in the real movie contract, Producer promises to pay Artist "On the condition that Artist fully performs all of Artist's services and obligations and agreements hereunder and is not in material breach or otherwise in material default hereof."

Material breach
A violation of a contract that defeats an essential purpose of the agreement.

Sole discretion
A party to a contract has the absolute right to make a decision on that issue.

Reasonable
Ordinary or usual under the circumstances.

Good faith
An honest effort to meet both the spirit and letter of a contract.

Reciprocal promises
Promises that are each enforceable independently.

Conditional promises
Promises that a party agrees to perform only if the other side has first done what it promised.

In short, if you do not expect to perform under the contract until the other side has met its obligations, be sure to say so.

Language of the covenants.   To clarify *who* exactly is doing what, covenants in a contract should use the active, not passive voice. In other words, a contract should say "Producer shall pay Artist $1.8 million," not "Artist shall be paid $1.8 million."

REPRESENTATIONS AND WARRANTIES

Covenants are the promises the parties make about what they will do in the future. Representations and warranties are statements of fact about the past or present; they are true when the contract is signed (or at some other specific, designated time).[3] These representations and warranties are important—without them, the other party might not have agreed to the contract. For example, in the movie contract, Artist warrants that he is a member of the Screen Actors Guild. This provision is important because, if it were not true, Producer would either have to obtain a waiver or pay a substantial penalty.

In a contract between two companies, each side will generally represent and warrant facts such as: (1) they legally exist, (2) they have the authority to enter into the contract, (3) their financial statements are accurate, and (4) they own all relevant assets. In a contract for the sale of goods, the contract will include warranties about the condition of the goods being sold.

> **Representations and warranties**
> Statements of fact about the past or present.

EXAM Strategy

Question: Producer does not want Artist to pilot an airplane during the term of the contract. Would that provision be a warranty and representation or a covenant? How would you phrase it?

Strategy: Warranties and representations are about events in the past or present. A covenant is a promise for the future. If, for example, Producer wanted to know that Artist had never used drugs in the past, that provision would be a warranty and representation.

Result: A promise not to pilot an airplane is a covenant. The contract could say, "Until Artist completes all services required hereunder, he shall not pilot an airplane."

BOILERPLATE

These standard previsions are typically placed in a section entitled *Miscellaneous*. Many people think that the term "boilerplate" is a synonym for "boring and irrelevant," but it is worth remembering that the word comes from the iron or steel that protects the hull of a ship—something that shipbuilders ignore to the passengers' peril. A contract without boilerplate is valid and enforceable—so it can be tempting to skip these provisions, but they do play an important protective role. In essence, boilerplate creates a private law that governs disputes between the parties. Courts can also play this role, and indeed, in the absence of boilerplate, they will. But remember that an important goal of a contract is to avoid court involvement.

Here are some standard, and important, boilerplate provisions.

---

[3]Although, technically, there is a slight difference between a representation and a warranty, many lawyers confuse the two terms, and the distinction is not important. We will treat them as synonyms, as many lawyers do.

Choice of Law and Forum. **Choice of law** provisions determine which state's laws will be used to interpret the contract. **Choice of forum** determines the state in which any litigation would take place. (One state's courts can apply another state's laws.) Lawyers often view these two provisions as the most important boilerplate because (1) individual states might have dramatically different laws and (2) it is a lot more convenient and cheaper to litigate a case in one's home courts.

The movie contract states: "This Agreement shall be deemed to have been made in the State of California and shall be construed and enforced in accordance with the law of the State of California." The contract did not, but might have, also specified the forum—that any litigation would be tried in California.

Modification. Contracts should contain a provision governing modification. The movie contract states: "This Agreement may not be amended or modified except by an instrument in writing signed by the party to be charged with such amendment or modification."

"Charged with such amendment" means the party who is adversely affected by the change. For example, if Producer agrees to pay Artist more, then Producer must sign the amendment. Without this provision, a conversation over beers between Producer and Artist about a change in pay might turn out to be an enforceable amendment.

Assignment of Rights and Delegation of Duties. An **assignment of rights** is a transfer of your benefits under a contract to another person, while **delegation of duties** is a transfer of your obligations. In the movie contract, Producer has the right to *assign* the contract, but he must stay secondarily liable on it. In other words, Producer can transfer to someone else the right to receive the benefits of the contract (that is, to make the movie with Artist), but he cannot transfer his obligations (to pay Artist). If the person who takes over the contract for him fails to pay Artist, then Producer is liable. Artist might be unhappy if another production company takes over the movie, but he is still required under the contract to perform his acting services. At least he knows that Producer is liable for his paycheck.

Delegation means that someone else performs the duties under the contract. It certainly matters to Producer which actor shows up to do the shooting. Artist cannot say, "I'm too busy— here's my cousin Jack." So the movie contract provides that Artist cannot delegate his services.

Arbitration. Some contracts prohibit the parties from suing in court and require that disputes be settled by an arbitrator. The parties to a contract do not have to arbitrate a dispute unless the contract specifically requires it.

Attorney's Fees. As a general rule, parties to a contract must pay their own legal fees. But contracts may override this general rule and provide that the losing party in a dispute must pay the attorney's fees for both sides. Such a provision tends to discourage the poorer party from litigating with a rich opponent for fear of having to pay two sets of attorney's fees. The movie contract provides:

> Artist hereby agrees to indemnify Producer from and against any and all losses, costs (including, without limitation, reasonable attorney's fees), liabilities, damages, and claims of any nature arising from or in connection with any breach by Artist of any agreement, representation, or warranty made by Artist under this Agreement.

There is no equivalent provision for breaches by Producer. What does that omission tell you about the relative bargaining power of the two parties?

Integration. During contract negotiations, the parties may discuss many ideas that are not ultimately included in the final version. The point of an integration clause is to prevent either side from later claiming that the two parties had agreed to additional provisions. The movie contract states:

> This Agreement, along with the exhibits attached hereto, shall constitute a binding contract between the parties hereto and shall supersede any and all prior negotiations and communications, whether written or oral, with respect hereto.

Choice of law provisions
Determine which state's laws will be used to interpret the contract.

Choice of forum provisions
Determines the state in which any litigation would take place.

Assignment of rights
A transfer of benefits under a contract to another person.

Delegation of duties
A transfer of obligations in a contract.

Severability.   If, for whatever reason, some part of the contract turns out to be unenforceable, a severability provision asks the court simply to delete the offending clause and enforce the rest of the contract. For example, courts will not enforce *unreasonable* non-compete clauses. (California courts will not enforce *any* non-competes, unless made in connection with the sale of a business.) In one case, a consultant signed an employment contract that prohibited him from engaging in his occupation "anyplace in the world." The court struck down this non-compete provision but ruled that the rest of the contract (which contained trade secret clauses) was valid.

The movie contract states:

> In the event that there is any conflict between any provision of this Agreement and any statute, law, or regulation, the latter shall prevail; provided, however, that in such event, the provision of this Agreement so affected shall be curtailed and limited only to the minimum extent necessary to permit compliance with the minimum requirement, and no other provision of this Agreement shall be affected thereby and all other provisions of this Agreement shall continue in full force and effect.

Force Majeure event

A disruptive, unexpected occurrence for which neither party is to blame that prevents one or both parties from complying with a contract.

Force Majeure.   A *force majeure* **event** is a disruptive, unexpected occurrence for which neither party is to blame that prevents one or both parties from complying with the contract. *Force majeure* events typically include wars, terrorist attacks, fires, floods, or general acts of God. If, for example, a major terrorist event were to halt air travel, Artist might not be able to appear on set as scheduled. The movie contract defines *force majeure* events thus:

> fire, war, governmental action or proceeding, third-party breach of contract, injunction, or other material interference with the production or distribution of motion pictures by Producer, or any other unexpected or disruptive event sufficient to excuse performance of this Agreement as a matter of law or other similar causes beyond Producer's control or by reason of the death, illness, or incapacity of the producer, director, or a member of the principal cast or other production personnel.

Notices.   After a contract is signed, there may be times when the parties want to send each other official notices—of a breach, an objection, or an approval, for example. In this section, the parties list the addresses where these notices can be sent. For Producer, it is company headquarters. For Artist, there are three addresses: his agent, his manager, and his lawyer. The notice provision also typically specifies when the notice is effective: when sent, when it would normally be expected to arrive, or when it actually does arrive.

Closing.   To indicate that the parties have agreed to the terms of the contract, they must sign it. When a party to the contract is a corporation, the signature lines should read like this:

Winterfield Productions Inc.

By:_____
Name:
Title:

In the end, both parties signed the contract and the movie was made. According to Rotten Tomatoes, the online movie site, professional reviewers rated it 7.9 out of 10.

Chapter Conclusion

You will undoubtedly sign many contracts in your life. The goal of this chapter is to help you understand the structure and meaning of the most important provisions so that you can read and analyze contracts more effectively.

EXAM REVIEW

1. **AMBIGUITY**   Any ambiguity in a contract is interpreted against the party that drafted the agreement. (p. 211)

2. **SCRIVENER'S ERROR**   A scrivener's error is a typo. In the case of a scrivener's error, a court will reform a contract if there is clear and convincing evidence that the mistake does not reflect the true intent of the parties. (p. 211)

EXAM Strategy

Question: Martha intended to transfer a piece of land to Paul. By mistake, she signed a contract transferring two parcels of land. Each piece was accurately described in the contract. Will the court reform this contract and transfer one piece of land back to her?

Strategy: Begin by asking if this was a scrivener's error. Then consider whether the court will correct the mistake. (See the "Result" at the end of this section.)

3. **MATERIAL BREACH**   A material breach is important enough to defeat an essential purpose of the contract. (p. 215)

4. **SOLE DISCRETION**   A party with sole discretion has the absolute right to make any decision on that issue. (p. 215)

EXAM Strategy

Question: A tenant rented space from a landlord for a seafood restaurant. Under the terms of the lease, the tenant could assign the lease only if the landlord gave her consent, which she had the right to withhold "for any reason whatsoever, at her sole discretion." The tenant grew too ill to run the restaurant and asked permission to assign the lease. The landlord refused. In court, the tenant argued that the landlord could not unreasonably withhold her consent. Is the tenant correct?

Strategy: A sole discretion clause grants the absolute right to make a decision. Are there any exceptions? (See the "Result" at the end of this section.)

5. **COVENANT**   Covenants are the promises the parties make about what they will do in the future. (pp. 213–215)

6. **REPRESENTATIONS AND WARRANTIES**   Representations and warranties are statements of fact about the present or past—they are true when the contract is signed (or at some other specific, designated time). (p. 216)

2. Result: The court ruled that it was not a scrivener's error because it was not a typo or clerical error. Therefore, the court did not reform the contract and the land was not transferred back to Martha.

4. Result: The court ruled for the landlord. She had the absolute right to make any decision, as long as the decision was not illegal. The moral: sole discretion clauses are serious business. Do not enter into one lightly

MATCHING QUESTIONS

___A. Assignment of rights

___B. Delegation of duties

___C. Covenant

___D. Reciprocal promise

___E. Conditional promise

___F. Representation

1. Promises that a party agrees to perform only if the other side has first done what it promised

2. Promises that are each enforceable independently

3. Statement of fact about the past or present

4. Transfer of obligations under a contract

5. Promise about what a party will do in the future

6. Transfer of benefits under a contract

TRUE/FALSE QUESTIONS

1. T F The same states must be named in the Choice of Law and Choice of Forum provisions.
2. T F For a modification to a contract to be valid, both parties must sign it.
3. T F A severability provision asks the court simply to delete the offending clause and enforce the rest of the contract.
4. T F A *force majeure* clause indicates who has the authority to write the first draft of the contract.
5. T F Unless the contract provides otherwise, both sides in a contract dispute pay their own legal fees.

MULTIPLE-CHOICE QUESTIONS

1. Daniel and Annie signed a contract providing that Annie would sell craft beers to Daniel's grocery stores at a price of $20 per case. During negotiations, Daniel and Annie agreed that the price would go up to $22 per case once he had bought 1,000 cases. This provision never made it into the contract. After the contract had been signed, Daniel agreed to a price of $23 per case once volume exceeded 1,000 cases. The contract had an integration provision but no modification clause. What price must Daniel pay for cases in excess of 1,000?

   (a) $20

   (b) $22

   (c) $23

   (d)   The contract is void because the terms are unclear.

2. A contract states (1) that Buzz Co. legally exists and (2) it will provide 2,000 pounds of wild salmon each week. Which of the following statements is true?

   (a) Clause 1 is a covenant and Clause 2 is a representation.

   (b) Clause 1 is a representation and Clause 2 is a covenant.

   (c) Both clauses are representations.

   (d) Both clauses are covenants.

3. The following list provides reasons why a party would strongly consider putting a contract in writing. Which of these reasons is *least* important?

   (a) The Statute of Frauds requires it.

   (b) The deal is crucial to your life or the life of your business.

   (c) The terms are complex.

   (d) The parties do not have an ongoing relationship.

   (e) The parties reside in different jurisdictions.

4. Michael and Scarlett cannot agree on the price he will pay her to manage his hotels in the third year of their contract. They agree to a provision stating that the price will be "reasonable." This provision is _____. Parties should never include such a provision in a contract unless _____.

   (a) ambiguous, they are sure they will be able to reach an agreement later

   (b) vague, they are sure they will be able to reach an agreement later

   (c) ambiguous, they would not mind if the other side's interpretation prevails in litigation

   (d) vague, they would not mind if the other side's interpretation prevails in litigation

5. Liesl purchased an insurance policy on her house. The policy stated that the insurance company was not liable for any damage to her house caused by vandalism or burglary. An arsonist burned down Liesl's house. Is the insurance company liable?

   (a) No, because arson is a form of vandalism.

   (b) Yes, because arson is not a form of vandalism.

   (c) Yes, because the language is ambiguous and should be interpreted against the insurance company.

   (d) No, because the language is vague and should be interpreted against Liesl.

ESSAY QUESTIONS

1. Make a list of provisions that you would expect in an employment contract.

2. List three provisions in a contract that would be material, and three that would not be.

3. Slimline and Distributor signed a contract which provided that Distributor would use reasonable efforts to promote and sell Slimline's diet drink. Slimline was already being sold in Warehouse Club. After the contract was signed, Distributor stopped conducting in-store demos of Slimline. It did not repackage the product as Slimline and Warehouse requested. Sales of Slimline continued to increase during the term of

the contract. Slimline sued Distributor, alleging a violation of the agreement. Who should win?

4. **YOU BE THE JUDGE WRITING PROBLEM** Chip bought an insurance policy on his house from Insurance Co. The policy covered damage from fire but explicitly excluded coverage for harm caused "by or through an earthquake." When an earthquake struck, Chip's house suffered no fire damage, but the earthquake caused a building some blocks away to catch on fire. That fire ultimately spread to Chip's house, burning it down. Is Insurance Co. liable to Chip? **Argument for Insurance Co.:** The policy could not have been clearer or more explicit. If there had been no earthquake, Chip's house would still be standing. The policy does not cover his loss. **Argument for Chip:** His house was not damaged by an earthquake; it burned down. The policy covered fire damage. If a contract is ambiguous, it must be interpreted against the drafter of the contract.

5. Laurie's contract to sell her tortilla chip business to Hudson contained a provision that she must continue to work at the business for five years. One year later, she quit. Hudson refused to pay her the amounts still owing under the contract. Laurie alleged that he is liable for the full amount because her breach was not material. Is Laurie correct?

DISCUSSION QUESTIONS

1. In the movie contract, which side was the more successful negotiator? Can you think of any terms that either party left out? Are any of the provisions unreasonable?

2. In a contract, should sole discretion clauses be enforced if the party with the discretion behaves unreasonably? Should everyone have an obligation to behave reasonably?

3. What are the advantages and disadvantages of hiring a lawyer to draft or review a contract?

4. **ETHICS** In the *Heritage* case, the two companies had agreed to a price change of $0.01. When Heritage's lawyer pointed out to his client the change to $0.10, the Heritage officer did not tell Phibro. The change was subtle in appearance but important in its financial impact. Was Heritage's behavior ethical? When the opposing side makes a mistake in a contract, do you have an ethical obligation to tell them? What Life Principles would you apply in this situation?

5. Blair Co.'s top officers approached an investment bank to find a buyer for the company. The bank sent an engagement letter to Blair with the following language:

   > If, within 24 months after the termination of this agreement, Blair is bought by anyone with whom Bank has had substantial discussions about such a sale, Blair must pay Bank its full fee.

   Is there any problem with the drafting of this provision? What could be done to clarify the language?

CHAPTER 13

SALES AND PRODUCT LIABILITY

He Sued, She Sued. Harold and Maude made a great couple because both were compulsive entrepreneurs. One evening, they sat on their penthouse roof deck, overlooking the twinkling Chicago skyline. Harold sipped a decaf coffee while negotiating, over the phone, with a real estate developer in San Antonio. Maude puffed a cigar as she bargained on a different line with a toy manufacturer in Cleveland. They hung up at the same time. "I did it!" shrieked Maude, "I made an incredible deal for the robots—five bucks each!" "No, *I* did it!" triumphed Harold, "I sold the 50 acres in Texas for $300,000 more than it's worth." They dashed indoors.

> "Confirming our deal—100,000 Psychopath Robots—you deliver Chicago—end of summer."

Maude quickly scrawled a handwritten memo, which read, "Confirming our deal—100,000 Psychopath Robots—you deliver Chicago—end of summer." She didn't mention a price, or an exact delivery date, or when payment would be made. She signed her memo and faxed it to the toy manufacturer. Harold took more time. He typed a thorough contract, describing precisely the land he was selling, the $2.3 million price, how and when each payment would be made, and what the deed conveyed. He signed the contract and faxed it, along with a plot plan showing the surveyed land. Then the happy couple grabbed a bottle of champagne, returned to the deck—and placed a side bet on whose contract would prove more profitable. The loser would have to cook and serve dinner for six months.

Neither Harold nor Maude ever heard again from the other parties. The toy manufacturer sold the robots to another retailer at a higher price. Maude was forced to buy comparable toys elsewhere for $9 each. She sued. And the Texas property buyer changed his mind, deciding to develop a Club Med in Greenland and refusing to pay Harold for his land. He sued. Only one of the two plaintiffs succeeded. Which one?

SALES

The adventures of Harold and Maude illustrate the Uniform Commercial Code (UCC) in action. The Code is the single most important source of law for people engaged in commerce and controls the vast majority of contracts made every day in every state. The Code is old in origin, contemporary in usage, admirable in purpose, and flawed in application. "Yeah, yeah, that's fascinating," snaps Harold, "but who wins the bet?" Relax, Harold, we'll tell you in a minute.

Development of the UCC

In the middle of the 20th century, contract law required a reinvention. Two problems had become apparent in the United States.

1. Old contract law principles often did not reflect modern business practices.

2. Laws had become different from one state to another.

On many legal topics, contract law included, the national government has had little to say and has allowed the states to act individually. Texas decides what kinds of agreements count as contracts in Texas, and next door in Oklahoma, the rules may be very different. On many issues, states reached essentially similar conclusions, and contract law developed in the same direction. But sometimes the states disagreed, and contract law took on the aspect of a patchwork quilt.

The UCC was created as an attempt to solve these two problems. It was a proposal written by legal scholars, not a law drafted by members of Congress or state legislatures. The scholars at the American Law Institute and the National Conference of Commissioners on Uniform State Laws had great ideas, but they had no legal authority to make anyone do anything.

Over time, lawmakers in all 50 states were persuaded to adopt many parts of the Uniform Commercial Code (UCC). They responded to these persuasive arguments:

- Businesses will benefit if most commercial transactions are governed by the modern and efficient contract law principles that are outlined in the UCC.

- Businesses everywhere will be able to operate more efficiently, and transactions will be more convenient, if the law surrounding most of their transactions is the same in all 50 states.

This chapter will focus on Article 2 of the UCC, which applies to the sale of goods. A **good** is any moveable physical object except for money and securities (like stock certificates). A house is not a good, but the *stuff* in the house—the car in the garage, the televisions, the furniture, and almost everything else—is. Article 2 applies to contracts that sell goods, and also to contracts that sell a mix of goods and services if the *predominant purpose* of the deal is to sell goods.

Assume that you take your car to a mechanic for repairs and that there are problems with the work. If a lawsuit ensues, a court will have to determine whether the predominant purpose of the contract was the parts (goods) which were replaced or the labor (service) involved in the work.

It is worth noting that the UCC is not a total replacement for older principles in contract law. Contract lawsuits not involving goods are still resolved using the older common law rules.

HAROLD AND MAUDE, REVISITED

Harold and Maude each negotiated what they believed was an enforceable agreement, and both filed suit: Harold for the sale of his land, Maude for the purchase of toy robots. Only one prevailed. The difference in outcome demonstrates why everyone in business needs a working knowledge of the Code. As we revisit the happy couple, Harold is clearing the dinner dishes. Maude sits back in her chair, lights a cigar, and compliments her husband on the apple tart.

Harold's contract was for the sale of land and was governed by the common law of contracts, which requires any agreement for the sale of land to be in writing and *signed by the defendant*, in this case the buyer in Texas. Harold signed it, but the buyer never did, so Harold's meticulously detailed document was worth less than a five-cent cigar.

Maude's quickly scribbled memorandum, concerning robot toys, was for the sale of goods and was governed by Article 2 of the UCC. The Code requires less detail and formality in a writing. Because Maude and the seller were both merchants, the document she scribbled could be enforced *even against the defendant*, who had never signed anything. The fact that Maude left out the price and other significant terms was not fatal to a contract under the UCC, though under the common law, such omissions would have made the bargain unenforceable.

MERCHANTS

The UCC evolved to provide merchants with rules that would meet their unique business needs. However, while the UCC offers a contract law that is more flexible than the common law, it also requires a higher level of responsibility from the merchants it serves. Those who make a living by crafting agreements are expected to understand the legal consequences of their words and deeds. Thus, many sections of the Code offer two rules: one for "merchants" and one for everybody else.

UCC Section 2-104: A merchant is someone who routinely deals in the particular goods involved, or who appears to have special knowledge or skill in those goods, or who uses agents with special knowledge or skill in those goods. A used car dealer is a "merchant" when it comes to selling autos because he routinely deals in them. He is not a merchant when he goes to a furniture store and purchases a new sofa.

Merchant
Someone who routinely deals in the particular goods involved.

The UCC frequently holds a merchant to a higher standard of conduct than a non-merchant. For example, a merchant may be held to an oral contract if she received written confirmation of it, even though the merchant herself never signed the confirmation. That same confirmation memo, arriving at the house of a non-merchant, would not create a binding deal.

Contract Formation

The common law expected the parties to form a contract in a fairly predictable and traditional way: the offeror made a clear offer that included all important terms, and the offeree agreed to all terms. Nothing was left open. The drafters of the UCC recognized that businesspeople frequently do not think or work that way and that the law should reflect business reality.

FORMATION BASICS: SECTION 2-204

UCC Section 2-204 provides three important rules that enable parties to make a contract quickly and informally:

1. *Any manner that shows agreement.* The parties may make a contract in any manner sufficient to show that they reached an agreement. They may show the agreement with words, writings, or even their conduct. Lisa negotiates with Ed to buy 300 barbecue grills. The parties agree on a price, but other business prevents them from finishing the deal. Six months later, Lisa writes, "Remember our deal for 300 grills? I still want to do it if you do." Ed does not respond, but a week later, a truck shows up at Lisa's store with the 300 grills, and Lisa accepts them. The combination of their original discussion, Lisa's subsequent letter, Ed's delivery, and her acceptance all adds up to show that they reached an agreement. The court will enforce their deal, and Lisa must pay the agreed-upon price.

2. *Moment of making is not critical.* The UCC will enforce a deal even though it is difficult, in common law terms, to say exactly when it was formed. Was Lisa's deal formed

when they orally agreed? When he delivered? She accepted? The Code's answer: it does not matter. The contract is enforceable.

3. *One or more terms may be left open.* The common law insisted that the parties clearly agree on all important terms. The Code changes that. **Under the UCC, a court may enforce a bargain even though one or more terms were left open.** Lisa's letter never said when she required delivery of the barbecue grills or when she would pay. Under the UCC, the omission is not fatal. As long as there is some certain basis for giving damages to the injured party, the court will do just that. If Lisa refused to pay, a court would rule that the parties assumed she would pay within a commercially reasonable time, such as 30 days.

In the following case, we can almost see the roller coasters, smell the cotton candy—and hear the carnival owners arguing.

Jannusch v. Naffziger

2008 WL 540877, Illinois Court of Appeals, 2008

Case Summary

Facts: Gene and Martha Jannusch owned Festival Foods, which served snacks at events throughout Illinois and Indiana. The business included a truck, servicing trailer, refrigerators, roasters, chairs, and tables.

Lindsey and Louann Naffziger orally agreed to buy Festival Foods for $150,000, the deal including all the assets and the opportunity to work at events secured by the Jannuschs. The Naffzigers paid $10,000 immediately, with the balance due when they received their bank loan. They took possession the next day and operated Festival Foods for the remainder of the season.

In a pretrial deposition, Louann Naffziger acknowledged orally agreeing to buy the business for $150,000. (Her admission under oath made the lack of a written contract irrelevant.) However, she could not recall making the agreement on any particular date. Gene Jannusch suggested the parties sign something, but the Naffzigers replied that they were "in no position to sign anything" because they had received no loan money from the bank and lacked a lawyer. Lindsey admitted taking possession of Festival Foods, receiving the income from the business, purchasing inventory, replacing equipment, and paying taxes and employees.

Two days after the business season ended, they returned Festival Foods to the Jannusches, stating that the income was lower than expected. The Jannusches sued. The trial court ruled that there had been no meeting of the minds and hence no contract. The Jannusches appealed.

Issue: *Did the parties form a contract?*

Decision: Yes, the parties formed a contract.

Reasoning: The Naffzigers argue that nothing was said in the contract about a price for good will, a covenant not to compete, the value of individual assets, release from earlier liens, or the consequences should their loan be denied.

Under the UCC, a contract may be enforced even though some contract terms are missing or left to be agreed upon. However, if the essential terms are so uncertain that a court cannot decide whether the agreement has been broken, there is no contract.

The essential terms were agreed upon. The purchase price was $150,000, and the parties specified all assets to be transferred. No essential terms remained to be agreed upon. The only action remaining was the performance of the contract, and the Naffzigers took possession and used all items as their own.

Louann Naffziger could not recall making the oral agreement on any particular date, but parties may form a binding agreement even though the moment of its making is undetermined. Returning the goods at the end of the season was not a rejection of the Jannusches' offer to sell; it was a breach of contract.

The parties agreed to a sale of Festival Foods for $150,000, and the Naffzigers violated the agreement. Reversed and remanded.

Based on the UCC, the Jannusches won a case they would have lost under the common law. Next, we look at changes the Code has made in the centuries-old requirement of a writing.

STATUTE OF FRAUDS

UCC Section 2-201 requires a writing for any sale of goods worth $500 or more. However, under the UCC, the writing need not completely summarize the agreement. The Code only requires a writing *sufficient to indicate* that the parties made a contract. In other words, the writing need not be a contract. A simple memo is enough, or a letter or informal note, mentioning that the two sides reached an agreement.

In general, the writing must be signed by the defendant—that is, whichever party is claiming there was no deal. Dick signs and sends to Shirley a letter saying, "This is to acknowledge your agreement to buy all 650 books in my rare book collection for $188,000." Shirley signs nothing. A day later, Louis offers Dick $250,000. Is Dick free to sell? No. He signed the memo, it indicates a contract, and Shirley can enforce it against him.

Now reverse the problem. Suppose that after Shirley receives Dick's letter, she decides against rare books in favor of original scripts from the *South Park* television show. Dick sues. Shirley wins because she signed nothing.

Enforceable Only to Quantity Stated. Because the writing only has to indicate that the parties agreed, it need not state every term of their deal. But one term is essential: quantity. **The Code will enforce the contract only up to the quantity of goods stated in the writing.** This is logical since a court can surmise other terms, such as price, based on market conditions. Buyer agrees to purchase pencils from Seller. The market value of the pencils is easy to determine, but a court would have no way of knowing whether Buyer meant to purchase 1,000 pencils or 100,000; the quantity must be stated.

Merchant Exception. This is a major change from the common law. **When two merchants make an oral contract, and one sends a confirming memo to the other within a reasonable time, and the memo is sufficiently definite that it could be enforced against the sender herself, then the memo is also valid against the merchant who receives it unless he objects within 10 days.** Laura, a tire wholesaler, signs and sends a memo to Scott, a retailer, saying, "Confm yr order today—500 tires cat #886—cat price." Scott realizes he can get the tires cheaper elsewhere and ignores the memo. Big mistake. Both parties are merchants, and Laura's memo is sufficient to bind her. So it also satisfies the Statute of Frauds against Scott unless he objects within 10 days.

EXAM Strategy

Question: Marko, a sporting goods retailer, speaks on the phone with Wholesaler about buying 500 footballs. After the conversation, Marko writes this message by hand: "Confirming our discussion—you will deliver to us 'Pro Bowl' model footballs—$45 per unit—arrival our store no later than July 20 this year." Marko signs and faxes the note to Wholesaler. Wholesaler reads the fax but then gets an order from Lana for the same model football at $51 per unit. Wholesaler never responds to Marko's fax and sells his entire supply to Lana. Two weeks later, Marko is forced to pay more from another seller and sues Wholesaler. Marko argues that under merchant exception, his fax was sufficient to satisfy the Statute of Frauds. Is he right?

Strategy: These two parties are merchants, and the merchant exception applies. Under this exception, a memo that could be enforced against the sender himself may bind the merchant who receives it. Could this memo be enforced against Marko? Make sure that you know what terms must be included to make a writing binding.

Result: The writing must indicate that the two parties reached an agreement. Marko's memo does so because he says he is confirming their discussion. Even if some terms are omitted, the writing may still suffice. However, the memo will be enforced only to the quantity of goods stated. Marko stated no quantity—a fatal error. His writing fails to satisfy the Statute of Frauds, and he loses the suit.

ADDED TERMS: SECTION 2-207

Under the common law's mirror image rule, when one party makes an offer, the offeree must accept those exact terms. If the offeree adds or alters any terms, the acceptance is ineffective, and the offeree's response becomes a counteroffer. In one of its most significant modifications of contract law, the UCC changes that outcome. **Under Section 2-207, an acceptance that adds or alters terms will often create a contract.** The Code has made this change in response to *battles of the form.* Every day, corporations buy and sell millions of dollars of goods using preprinted forms. The vast majority of all contracts involve such documents. Typically, the buyer places an order by using a preprinted form, and the seller acknowledges with its own preprinted acceptance form. Because each form contains language favorable to the party sending it, the two documents rarely agree. The Code's drafters concluded that the law must cope with real practices.

Intention. The parties must still *intend* to create a contract. Section 2-207 is full of exceptions, but there is no change in this basic requirement of contract law. If the differing forms indicate that the parties never reached agreement, there is no contract.

Additional or Different Terms. An offeree may include a new term in his acceptance and still create a binding deal. Suppose Breeder writes to Pet Shop, offering to sell 100 guinea pigs at $2 each. Pet Shop faxes a memo saying, "We agree to buy 100 g.p. We receive normal industry credit for any unhealthy pig." Pet Shop has added a new term, concerning unhealthy pigs, but the parties have created a binding contract because the writings show they intended an agreement. Now the court must decide what the terms of the contract are because there is some discrepancy. The first step is to decide whether the new language is an *additional term* or a *different term.*

Additional terms
Raise issues not covered in the offer.

Additional terms are those that raise issues not covered in the offer. The "unhealthy pig" issue is an additional term because the offer said nothing about it. **When both parties are *merchants,* additional terms generally become part of the bargain.**[1] Both Pet Shop and Breeder are merchants, and the additional term about credit for unhealthy animals does become part of their agreement.

Different terms
Contradict those in the offer.

Different terms *contradict* those in the offer. Suppose Brilliant Corp. orders 1,500 cell phones from Makem Co., for use by Brilliant's sales force. Brilliant places the order by using a preprinted form stating that the product is fully warranted for normal use and that seller is liable for compensatory *and consequential* damages. This means, for example, that Makem could be liable for lost profits if a salesperson's phone fails during a lucrative sales pitch. Makem responds with its own memo stating that in the event of defective phones, Makem is liable only to repair or replace and *is not liable for consequential damages, lost profits, or any other damages.*

Makem's acceptance has included a different term because its language contradicts the offer. **Different terms cancel each other out. The Code then supplies its own terms, called**

---

[1]There are three circumstances in which additional terms do *not* become part of the agreement: when the original offer *insisted on its own terms;* when the additional term *materially alters* the offer—that is, makes a dramatic change in the proposal; and when the offeror *promptly objects* to the new terms.

gap-fillers, which cover prices, delivery dates and places, warranties, and other subjects. The Code's gap-filler about warranties does permit recovery of compensatory and consequential damages. Therefore, Makem would be liable for lost profits.

Gap fillers
UCC rules for supplying missing terms.

Performance and Remedies

The Code's practical, flexible approach also shapes its rules about contract performance and remedy. As always, our goal in this chapter is to highlight doctrines that demonstrate a *change or an evolution in common law principles*.

BUYER'S REMEDIES

A seller is expected to deliver what the buyer ordered. **Conforming goods** satisfy the contract terms. Nonconforming goods do not.[2] Frame Shop orders from Wholesaler a large quantity of walnut wood, due on March 15, to be used for picture frames. If Wholesaler delivers, on March 8, high-quality *cherry* wood, it has shipped nonconforming goods.

Conforming goods
Satisfy the contract terms.

A buyer has the right to **inspect the goods** before paying or accepting[3] and may **reject nonconforming goods** by notifying the seller within a reasonable time.[4] Frame Shop may lawfully open Wholesaler's shipping crates before paying and is entitled to refuse the cherry wood. However, when the buyer rejects nonconforming goods, **the seller has the right to cure,** by delivering conforming goods before the contract deadline.[5] If Wholesaler delivers walnut wood by March 15, Frame Shop must pay in full. The Code even permits the seller to cure *after* the delivery date if doing so is reasonable. Notice the UCC's eminently pragmatic goal: to make contracts work.

Cover. If the seller breaches, the buyer may *cover* by reasonably obtaining substitute goods; it may then obtain the difference between the contract price and its cover price, plus incidental and consequential damages, minus expenses saved.[6] Retailer orders 10,000 pairs of ballet shoes from Shoemaker, at $55 per pair, to be delivered August 1. When no shoes dance through the door, Shoemaker explains that its workers in Europe are on strike and no delivery date can be guaranteed. Retailer purchases comparable shoes elsewhere for $70 and files suit. Retailer will win $150,000, representing the increased cost of $15 per pair.

Cover
To reasonably obtain substitute goods because another party has not honored a contract.

Incidental and Consequential Damages. An injured buyer is generally entitled to incidental and consequential damages. Incidental damages cover such costs as advertising for replacements, sending buyers to obtain new goods, and shipping the replacement goods. Consequential damages are those resulting from the unique circumstances of *this injured party*. They can be much more extensive and may include lost profits. **A buyer expecting to resell goods may obtain the loss of profit caused by the seller's failure to deliver.** In the ballet shoes case, suppose Retailer has contracts to resell the goods to ballet companies at an average profit of $10 per pair. Retailer is also entitled to those lost profits.

Consequential damages
Damages resulting from the unique circumstances of the injured party.

SELLER'S REMEDIES

Of course, a seller has rights, too. Sometimes a buyer breaches before the seller has delivered the goods, for example, by failing to make a payment due under the contract. If that happens, **the seller may refuse to deliver the goods.**[7]

---

[2]UCC Section 2-106(2).
[3]UCC Section 2-513.
[4]UCC Section 2-601, 602.
[5]UCC Section 2-508.
[6]UCC Section 2-712.
[7]UCC Section 2-705.

If a buyer unjustly refuses to accept or pay for goods, the injured seller may resell them. **If the resale is commercially reasonable, the seller may recover the difference between the resale price and contract price, plus incidental damages, minus expenses saved.**[8] Incidental damages are expenses the seller incurs in holding the goods and reselling them, costs such as storage, shipping, and advertising for resale. The seller must deduct expenses saved by the breach. For example, if the contract required the seller to ship heavy machinery from Detroit to San Diego, and the buyer's breach enables the seller to market its goods profitably in Detroit, the seller must deduct from its claimed losses the transportation costs that it saved.

Finally, the seller may simply sue **for the contract price** if the buyer has accepted the goods *or* if the goods are conforming and resale is impossible.[9] If the goods were manufactured to the buyer's unique specifications, there might be no other market for them, and the seller should receive the contract price.

WARRANTIES AND PRODUCT LIABILITY

You are sitting in a fast-food restaurant. Your friend Harley, who works for a state senator, is eating with one hand and gesturing with the other.

"I'm mostly working on product liability reform. We think it might actually pass this time," he proclaims, stabbing the air with his free hand. "Some of our constituents want it right now."

"What would be different?" you ask.

"Well, for starters, we'd cap lawsuit judgments. It's absurd, these multimillion-dollar verdicts, just because something has a *slight defect*."

"But if someone gets hurt," you reply, "shouldn't she get everything she's entitled to?"

Harley waves off your remark. "Ridiculous!" he exclaims. "Most of these 'victims' wouldn't have any problem if they'd just be more careful in the first place." Still feeling agitated, he takes a ferocious bite from his burger—and *CRACK*—he breaks a tooth.

> Still feeling agitated, he takes a ferocious bite from his burger—and *CRACK* – he breaks a tooth.

"Aaaahhhh! My toof! My *TOOF!*" Harley howls in pain and throws down the bun, revealing a large piece of bone in the meat. He tips his chair back in disbelief and says, loudly, "I'll sue these sons of aaaahhhh ..." Just then, his defective chair collapses, and Harley falls backwards and slams onto the tile floor, knocking himself unconscious. Hours later, when he revives in the hospital, he refuses to speak to you until he puts in a call to his lawyer.

Harley and his lawyer will be chatting about **product liability**, which refers to goods that have caused an injury. The harm may be physical, as it was in Harley's case. Sometimes, it is purely economic, as when a corporation buys a computer so defective it must be replaced, costing the buyer lost time and profits. The injured party's remedies may be derived from several legal ideas, including:

- *Warranty*, which is an assurance provided in a sales contract;

- *Negligence*, which refers to unreasonable conduct by the defendant; and

- *Strict liability*, which prohibits defective products whether the defendant acted reasonably or not.

---

[8]UCC Section 2-706.
[9]UCC Section 2-709.

What all product liability cases have in common is that a person or business has been hurt by goods.

Express Warranties

A warranty is a contractual assurance that goods will meet certain standards. It is normally a manufacturer or a seller who gives a warranty and a buyer who relies on it. A warranty might be explicit and written: "The manufacturer warrants that the light bulbs in this package will operate for an average of 2,000 hours." Or a warranty could be oral: "Don't worry, this machine can harvest any size of wheat crop ever planted in the state."

An express warranty is one that the seller creates with his words or actions.[10] Whenever a seller *clearly indicates* to a buyer that the goods being sold will meet certain standards, she has created an express warranty. For example, if the sales clerk for a paint store tells a professional house painter that "this exterior paint will not fade for three years, even in direct sunlight," that is an express warranty and the store is bound by it. The store is also bound by express warranty if the clerk gives the painter a brochure making the same promise or a sample that indicates the same thing.

In the following case, a ventilation company wrote a letter hoping to clear the air (and sell the product). Was the letter an express warranty? You decide.

Warranty
A guarantee that goods will meet certain standards.

Express warranty
A guarantee, created by the words or actions of the seller, that goods will meet certain standards.

[10]UCC Section 2-313.

You be the Judge

KELLER V. INLAND METALS ALL WEATHER CONDITIONING, INC.
139 Idaho 233, 76 P.3d 977
Supreme Court of Idaho, 2003

Facts: When Brian and Clarice Keller installed an indoor swimming pool in the athletic club they owned, customers began to complain that the air near the pool was hot, humid, and foul-smelling. The Kellers sought help from two contractors. Inland Metal submitted a bid to install a 7½-ton dehumidifier for about $30,000, and another company offered to install a 10-ton machine for about $40,000.

The Kellers were worried that the 7½-ton dehumidifier might be too small, so Inland's president visited the club, accompanied by a representative of the machine's manufacturer. The men assured the Kellers that the 7½-ton dehumidifier would work. Inland's president followed up with a letter to the Kellers, which said:

> As in any indoor pool, the air needs to be treated with outdoor fresh air, dehumidified, air conditioned in the summer, and heated in the winter. This ducted system will rid you of the sweating walls and eliminate those offensive odors, and overall "bad air." This is not an uncommon problem, and all commercial pool owners face the same thing until they install one of these systems.

Once you complete this installation, your air problems should be over, and your customers should be satisfied and happy.

The Kellers bought the system from Inland, but the dehumidifier did not improve the problem. The Kellers sued, and the trial court found that Inland had breached an express warranty. Inland appealed.

You Be the Judge: *Did Inland make an express warranty?*
Argument for Inland: Inland never made an express warranty. The company never said, "We guarantee that this unit will resolve all of the problems described." In its letter, the company described what it expected the dehumidifier to do and mentioned that customers "should be satisfied and happy" with the improved air. That is a far cry from promising to return the cost of the machine in the event that anyone claimed the machine was imperfect. Customers complain about many things, some legitimate, some not. Inland cannot prevent finicky clients from finding fault with a good dehumidifier. If Inland had intended its product to be guaranteed against any and all complaints, it would have said so—and charged much more.

Argument for the Kellers: When Inland representatives visited the health club, they assured the Kellers that the dehumidifier would do the job. An express warranty can be created orally, and that is exactly what Inland did. That is all the Kellers need to win, but they have more. Inland's follow-up letter repeated the reassurance: "This ducted system will rid you of the sweating walls and eliminate those offensive odors." That is a clear affirmation that the machine will meet certain standards—in other words, it is an express warranty. Inland made an oral and a written warranty and must be bound by its words.

Implied Warranties

Emily sells Sam a new jukebox for his restaurant, but the machine is so defective it never plays a note. When Sam demands a refund, Emily scoffs that she never made any promises. She is correct that she made no express warranties but is liable nonetheless. Many sales are covered by implied warranties. **Implied warranties are those created by the Code itself, not by any act or statement of the seller.**

IMPLIED WARRANTY OF MERCHANTABILITY

This is the most important warranty in the Code. **Unless excluded or modified, a warranty that the goods shall be merchantable is implied in a contract for their sale if the seller is a merchant with respect to goods of that kind.** *Merchantable* means that the goods are fit for the ordinary purposes for which they are used.[11] This rule contains several important principles:

- *Unless excluded or modified* means that the seller does have a chance to escape this warranty. A seller may disclaim this warranty, provided he actually mentions the word *merchantability*.

- *Merchantability* requires that goods be fit for their normal purposes. A ladder, to be merchantable, must be able to rest securely against a building and support someone who is climbing it. The ladder need not be serviceable as a boat ramp.

- *Implied* means that the law itself imposes this liability on the seller.

- A *merchant with respect to goods of that kind* means that the seller is someone who routinely deals in these goods or holds himself out as having special knowledge about these goods.

Dacor Corp. manufactured and sold scuba diving equipment. Dacor ordered air hoses from Sierra Precision, specifying the exact size and couplings so that the hose would fit safely into Dacor's oxygen units. Within a year, customers returned a dozen Dacor units, complaining that the hose connections had cracked and were unusable. Dacor recalled 16,000 units and refit them at a cost of $136,000. Dacor sued Sierra and won its full costs. Sierra was a merchant with respect to scuba hoses because it routinely manufactured and sold them. The defects were life-threatening to scuba divers, and the hoses could not be used for normal purposes.[12] The scuba equipment was not merchantable because a properly made scuba hose should never crack under normal use.

What if the product being sold is food, and the food contains something that is harmful—yet quite normal?

Implied warranty

Guarantees created by the Uniform Commercial Code and imposed on the seller of goods.

Implied warranty of merchantability

Goods must be of at least average, passable quality in the trade.

---

[11]UCC Section 2-314(1).
[12]*Dacor Corp. v. Sierra Precision*, 1993 U.S. Dist. LEXIS 8009 (N.D. Ill. 1993).

GOODMAN V. WENCO FOODS, INC.

333 N.C. 1, 423 S.E.2d 444, 1992 N.C. LEXIS 671
Supreme Court of North Carolina, 1992

CASE SUMMARY

Facts: Fred Goodman and a friend stopped for lunch at a Wendy's restaurant in Hillsborough, North Carolina. Goodman had eaten about half of his double hamburger when he bit down and felt immediate pain in his lower jaw. He took from his mouth a triangular piece of cow bone, about one-sixteenth to one-quarter inch thick and one-half inch long, along with several pieces of his teeth. Goodman's pain was intense, and his dental repairs took months.

The restaurant purchased all of its meat from Greensboro Meat Supply Company (GMSC). Wendy's required its meat to be chopped and "free from bone or cartilage in excess of 1/8 inch in any dimension." GMSC beef was inspected continuously by state regulators and was certified by the United States Department of Agriculture (USDA). The USDA considered any bone fragment less than three-quarters of an inch long to be "insignificant."

Goodman sued, claiming a breach of the implied warranty of merchantability. The trial court dismissed the claim, ruling that the bone was natural to the food and that the hamburger was therefore fit for its ordinary purpose. The appeals court reversed this, holding that a hamburger could be unfit even if the bone occurred naturally. Wendy's appealed to the state's highest court.

Issue: *Was the hamburger unfit for its ordinary purpose because it contained a harmful but natural bone?*

Decision: Affirmed. Even if the harmful bone occurred naturally, the hamburger could be unfit for its ordinary purpose.

Reasoning: When an object in food harms a consumer, the injured person may recover even if the substance occurred naturally, provided that a reasonable consumer would not expect to encounter it. A triangular, one-half-inch bone shaving may be inherent to a cut of beef, but whether a reasonable consumer would anticipate it is normally a question for the jury.

Wendy's hamburgers need not be perfect, but they must be fit for their intended purpose. It is difficult to imagine how a consumer could guard against bone particles, short of removing the hamburger from its bun, breaking it apart, and inspecting its small components.

Wendy's argues that since its meat complied with federal and state standards, the hamburgers were merchantable as a matter of law. However, while compliance with legal standards is evidence for juries to consider, it does not ensure merchantability. A jury could still conclude that a bone this size in hamburger meat was reasonably unforeseeable and that an injured consumer was entitled to compensation.

IMPLIED WARRANTY OF FITNESS FOR A PARTICULAR PURPOSE

The other warranty that the law imposes on sellers is the implied warranty of fitness for a particular purpose. This cumbersome name is often shortened to the *warranty of fitness*. **Where the seller at the time of contracting knows about a particular purpose for which the buyer wants the goods and knows that the buyer is relying on the seller's skill or judgment, there is (unless excluded or modified) an implied warranty that the goods shall be fit for such purpose.**[13]

Notice that the seller must know about some special use the buyer intends and realize that the buyer is relying on the seller's judgment. Suppose a lumber sales clerk knows that a buyer is relying on his advice to choose the best wood for a house being built in a swamp. The Code implies a warranty that the wood sold will withstand those special conditions.

Implied warranty of fitness for a particular purpose
If the seller knows that the buyer plans to use the goods for a particular purpose, the seller generally is held to warrant that the goods are in fact fit for that purpose.

---

[13]UCC Section 2-315.

Disclaimer
A statement that a particular warranty does not apply.

DISCLAIMERS

To make life easier, the Uniform Commercial Code permits a seller to disclaim *all* warranties by conspicuously stating that the goods are sold "as is" or "with all faults." But, as is often the case, we must point out two exceptions:

First, written express warranties generally *cannot* be disclaimed.

Second, many states prohibit a seller from disclaiming implied warranties in the sale of *consumer goods*. In these states, if a home furnishings store sells a bunk bed to a consumer and the top bunk tips out the window on the first night, the seller is liable.

As the following case illustrates, courts tend to impose high standards on defendants who try to disclaim warranties.

CCB OHIO, LLC v. CHEMQUE, INC.

649 F. Supp. 2d 757
United States District Court for the Southern District of Ohio, 2009

CASE SUMMARY

Facts: CCB Ohio specializes in upgrading power lines in a way that makes it possible to offer broadband service over an electrical grid. Chemque manufactures Q-gel.

Transformers reduce the 100,000 or more volts flowing through a typical power line to the 120 volts that actually arrive at the outlets in your home. But unfortunately, transformers completely block digital signals. And so, to offer broadband over an electrical grid, data must take a detour around transformers. Couplers allow for this detour.

CCB and its contractors purchased Q-gel. This substance was supposed to create a waterproof seal that would bind newly installed couplers to power lines. Unfortunately, the gel did not gel, at least not for long. Within 18 months, 40 percent of CCB Ohio's couplers were leaking liquefied Q-gel. Ultimately, 90 percent of the couplers throughout the Cincinnati area leaked and caused millions of dollars in losses.

CCB Ohio sued for breach of warranty. Chemque argued that it had disclaimed all implied warranties by giving CCB a specification sheet that read, "All information is given without warranty or guarantee." Chemque moved for summary judgment.

Issue: *Should Chemque's motion for a summary judgment on CCB's warranty claims be granted?*

Decision: No, the motion for summary judgment should not be granted.

Reasoning: In this state, companies that sell consumer goods may not disclaim implied warranties. However, the contract at issue here does not involve consumer goods.

To disclaim implied warranties for other kinds of transactions, the seller must show that the buyer actually received the disclaimer and that it was so conspicuous, a reasonable person would have noticed it. There is no evidence in the record that CCB did get the specification sheet in question. The company also argues that, even if it did receive the sheet, the disclaimer was not clear and conspicuous.

With these significant issues in dispute and unresolved, it would be inappropriate to grant Chemque's motion for summary judgment.

Motion for summary judgment denied.

Negligence

A buyer of goods may have remedies other than warranty claims. One is negligence. Here, we focus on how this law applies to the sale of goods. Negligence is notably different from contract law. In a contract case, the two parties have reached an agreement, and the terms of their bargain will usually determine how to settle any dispute. If the parties agreed that the seller disclaimed all warranties, then the buyer may be out of luck. But in a negligence case, there has been no bargaining between the parties, who may never have met. A consumer injured by an exploding cola bottle is unlikely to have bargained for her beverage with the CEO of the cola company. Instead, the law *imposes* a standard of conduct on everyone in society, corporation and individual alike. The two key elements of this standard, for present purposes, are *duty* and *breach*. A plaintiff injured by goods she bought must show that the defendant, usually a manufacturer or seller of a product, had a duty to her and breached that duty. A defendant has a duty of due care to anyone who could foreseeably be injured by its misconduct. Generally, it is the duty to act as *a reasonable person* would in like circumstances; a defendant who acts unreasonably has breached his duty.

In negligence cases concerning the sale of goods, plaintiffs most often raise one or more of these claims:

- *Negligent design.* The buyer claims that the product injured her because the manufacturer designed it poorly. Negligence law requires a manufacturer to design a product free of *unreasonable* risks. The product does not have to be absolutely safe. An automobile that guaranteed a driver's safety could be made but would be prohibitively expensive. Reasonable safety features must be built in if they can be included at a tolerable cost.

- *Negligent manufacture.* The buyer claims that the design was adequate but that failure to inspect or some other sloppy conduct caused a dangerous product to leave the plant.

- *Failure to warn.* A manufacturer is liable for failing to warn the purchaser or users about the dangers of normal use and also foreseeable misuse. However, there is no duty to warn about obvious dangers, a point evidently lost on some manufacturers. A Batman costume unnecessarily included this statement: "For play only: Mask and chest plate are not protective; cape does not enable user to fly."

Strict Liability

The other tort claim that an injured person can often bring against the manufacturer or seller of a product is strict liability. Like negligence, strict liability is a burden created by the law rather than by the parties. And, as with all torts, strict liability concerns claims of physical harm. But there is a key distinction between negligence and strict liability: in a negligence case, the injured buyer must demonstrate that the seller's conduct was unreasonable. Not so in strict liability.

In strict liability, the injured person need not prove that the defendant's conduct was unreasonable. The injured person must show only that the defendant manufactured or sold a product that was defective and that the defect caused harm. Almost all states permit such lawsuits, and most of them have adopted the following model:

1. One who sells any product in a defective condition unreasonably dangerous to the user or consumer or to his property is subject to liability for physical harm thereby caused to the ultimate user or consumer, or to his property, if

   a. the seller is engaged in the business of selling such a product, and

   b. it is expected to and does reach the user or consumer without substantial change in the condition in which it is sold.

2. The rule stated in Subsection (1) applies although

   a. the seller has exercised all possible care in the preparation and sale of his product, and

   b. the user or consumer has not bought the product from or entered into any contractual relation with the seller.[14]

---

[14]Restatement (Second) of Torts **Section 402A.**

These are the key terms in subsection (1):

- ***Defective condition unreasonably dangerous to the user.*** The defendant is liable only if the product is defective when it leaves his hands. There must be something wrong with the goods. If they are reasonably safe and the buyer's mishandling of the goods causes the harm, there is no strict liability. If you attempt to open a soda bottle by knocking the cap against a counter and the glass shatters and cuts you, the manufacturer owes nothing. A carving knife can produce a lethal wound, but everyone knows that, and a sharp knife is not unreasonably dangerous. On the other hand, prescription drugs may harm in ways that neither a layperson nor a doctor would anticipate. The manufacturer *must provide adequate warnings* of any dangers that are not apparent.

- ***In the business of selling.*** The seller is liable only if she normally sells this kind of product. Suppose your roommate makes you a peanut butter sandwich and, while eating it, you cut your mouth on a sliver of glass that was in the jar. The peanut butter manufacturer faces strict liability, as does the grocery store where your roommate bought the goods. But your roommate is not strictly liable because he is not in the food business.

- ***Reaches the user without substantial change.*** Obviously, if your roommate put the glass in the peanut butter thinking it was funny, neither the manufacturer nor the store would be liable.

And here are the important phrases in subsection (2).

- ***Has exercised all possible care.*** This is the heart of strict liability, which makes it a potent claim for consumers. *It is no defense that the seller used reasonable care.* If the product is dangerously defective and injures the user, the seller is liable even if it took every precaution to design and manufacture the product safely. Suppose the peanut butter jar did in fact contain a glass sliver when it left the factory. The manufacturer proves that it uses extraordinary care in keeping foreign particles out of the jars and thoroughly inspects each container before it is shipped. The evidence is irrelevant. The manufacturer has shown that it was not *negligent* in packaging the food, but reasonable care is irrelevant in strict liability cases.

- ***No contractual relation.*** Remember the word *privity*, from the warranty discussion? Privity exists only between the user and the person from whom she actually bought the goods, but in strict liability cases, *privity is not required*. Suppose the manufacturer that made the peanut butter sold it to a distributor, which sold it to a wholesaler, which sold it to a grocery store, which sold it to your roommate. You may sue the manufacturer, distributor, wholesaler, and store, even though you had no privity with any of them.

Contemporary Trends.   If the steering wheel on a brand-new car falls off and the driver is injured as a result, that is a clear case of defective manufacturing, and the company will be strictly liable. Those are the easy cases. But defective design cases have been more contentious. Suppose a vaccine that prevents serious childhood illnesses inevitably causes brain damage in a very small number of children because of the nature of the drug. Is the manufacturer liable? What if a racing sailboat, designed only for speed, is dangerously unstable in the hands of a less experienced sailor? Is the boat's maker responsible for fatalities? Suppose an automobile made of lightweight metal uses less fuel but exposes its occupants to more serious injuries in an accident. How is a court to decide whether the design was defective? Often, these design cases also involve issues of warnings: did the drug designer diligently detail dangers to doctors? Should a sailboat seller sell speedy sailboats solely to seasoned sailors?

Over the years, most courts have adopted one of two tests for design and warning cases. The first is *consumer expectation*. Here, a court finds the manufacturer liable for defective design if the product is less safe than a reasonable consumer would expect. If a smoke detector has a 3 percent failure rate, and the average consumer has no way of anticipating that danger, effective cautions must be included, though the design may be defective anyway.

Many other states use a *risk-utility test*. Here, a court must weigh the benefits for society against the dangers that the product poses. Principal factors in the risk-utility test include:

- The *value* of the product,

- The *gravity*, or *seriousness*, of the danger,

- The *likelihood* that such danger will occur,

- The mechanical feasibility of a *safer alternative* design, and

- The *adverse consequences* of an alternative design.

EXAM Strategy

Question: Warm, Inc. sells large, portable space heaters for industrial use. Warm sells Little Factory a unit and installs it. The sales contract states, "This heating unit is sold as is. There are no warranties, express or implied." On the third night the unit is used, it causes a fire and burns down the factory. Little sues Warm. At trial, the evidence indicates that a defect in the unit caused the fire, but also that this was unprecedented at Warm. The company employed more than the usual number of quality inspectors, and its safety record was the best in the entire industry. Discuss the effect of the sales contract and Warm's safety record. Predict who will win.

Strategy: The question raises three separate issues: warranty (the disclaimer), negligence (the safety record), and strict liability (the defect). What language most effectively disclaims warranties? What must a plaintiff prove to win a negligence case? To prove a strict liability case?

Result: A company may disclaim almost all warranties by stating the product is sold "as is," especially when selling to a corporate buyer. Warm's disclaimer is effective. The company's safety record is so good that there seems to be no case for negligence. However, Little Factory still wins its lawsuit. The product was unreasonably dangerous to the user. Warm was in the business of selling such heaters and installed the heater itself. In a strict liability case, Warm's safety efforts will not save it.

Chapter Conclusion

The development of the UCC was an enormous and ambitious undertaking. Its goal was to facilitate the free flow of commerce across this large nation. By any measure, the UCC has been a success. Remember, though: the terms of the UCC are precise. Failure to comply with these exacting provisions can close opportunities—and open courtroom doors.

EXAM REVIEW

1. **THE UCC**   The Code is designed to modernize commercial law and make it uniform throughout the country. Article 2 applies to the sale of goods. (pp. 224–230)

2. **MERCHANTS**   A merchant is someone who routinely deals in the particular goods involved, or who appears to have special knowledge or skill in those goods, or who uses agents with special knowledge or skill. (p. 225)

3. **CONTRACT FORMATION**   UCC Section 2-204 permits the parties to form a contract in any manner that shows agreement. (pp. 225–226)

4. **WRITING REQUIREMENT**   For the sale of goods worth $500 or more, UCC Section 2-201 requires some writing that indicates an agreement. (p. 227)

Question: To satisfy the UCC Statute of Frauds regarding the sale of goods, which of the following must generally be in writing?

a. Designation of the parties as buyer and seller

b. Delivery terms

c. Quantity of the goods

d. Warranties to be made

Strategy: O.K., this may be overkill. But the question illustrates two basic points of UCC law: first, the Code allows a great deal of flexibility in the formation of contracts. Second, there is one term for which no flexibility is allowed. Make sure you know which it is. (See the "Result" at the end of this section.)

EXAM Strategy

5. **MERCHANT EXCEPTION**   A merchant who receives a signed memo confirming an oral contract may become liable if he fails to object within 10 days. (p. 227)

6. **UCC §2-207**   UCC Section 2-207 governs an acceptance that does not "mirror" the offer. *Additional* terms usually become part of the contract. *Different* terms contradict the offer and are generally replaced by the Code's own gap-filler terms. (pp. 228–229)

EXAM Strategy

Question: Cookie Co. offered to sell Distrib Markets 20,000 pounds of cookies at $1 per pound, subject to certain specified terms for delivery. Distrib replied in writing as follows: "We accept your offer for 20,000 pounds of cookies at $1 per pound, weighing scale to have valid city certificate." Under the UCC:

a. A contract was formed between the parties.

b. A contract will be formed only if Cookie agrees to the weighing scale requirement.

c. No contract was formed because Distrib included the weighing scale requirement in its reply.

d. No contract was formed because Distrib's reply was a counteroffer.

Strategy: Distrib's reply included a new term. That means it is governed by UCC Section 2-207. Is the new term an additional term or a different term? An additional term goes beyond what the offeror stated. Additional terms become a part of the contract except in three specified instances. A different term contradicts one made by the offeror. Different terms generally cancel each other out. (See the "Result" at the end of this section.)

7. **REMEDIES** An injured seller may resell the goods and obtain the difference between the contract and resale prices. An injured buyer may buy substitute goods and obtain the difference between the contract and cover prices. (pp. 229–230)

8. **PRODUCT LIABILITY** Product liability may arise in various ways:

- A party may create an express warranty with words or actions. The Code may *imply* a warranty of merchantability or fitness for a particular purpose.

- A seller will be liable if her conduct is not that of a reasonable person.

- A seller may be strictly liable for a defective product that reaches the user without substantial change. (pp. 230–237)

4. Result: (C). The contract will be enforced only to the extent of the quantity stated.

6. Result: The "valid city certificate" phrase raises a new issue; it does not contradict anything in Cookie's offer. That means it is an additional term, and it becomes part of the deal unless Cookie insisted on its own terms, the additional term materially alters the offer, or Cookie promptly rejects it. Cookie did not insist on its terms, this is a minor addition, and Cookie never rejected it. The new term is part of a valid contract, and the answer is "a."

MATCHING QUESTIONS

___A. Additional terms

___B. Strict liability

___C. Merchantability

___D. Different terms

1. An implied warranty that goods are fit for their ordinary purpose

2. Generally become part of a contract between merchants

3. The reasonableness of defendant's conduct is irrelevant

4. Generally cancel each other out

TRUE/FALSE QUESTIONS

1. T F In a contract for the sale of goods, the offer may include any terms the offeror wishes; the offeree must accept on exactly those terms or reject the deal.

2. T F Sellers can be bound by written warranties but not by oral statements.

3. T F Under strict liability, an injured consumer could potentially recover damages from the product's manufacturer and the retailer who sold the goods.

4. T F A contract for the sale of $300 worth of decorative stone must be in writing to be enforceable.

MULTIPLE-CHOICE QUESTIONS

1. Which one of the following transactions is *not* governed by Article 2 of the UCC?
   (a) Purchasing an automobile for $35,000
   (b) Leasing an automobile worth $35,000
   (c) Purchasing a stereo worth $501
   (d) Purchasing a stereo worth $499

2. Marion orally agrees to sell Ashley her condominium in Philadelphia for $700,000. The parties have known each other for 20 years and do not bother to put anything in writing. Based on the agreement, Marion hires a moving company to pack up all her goods and move them to a storage warehouse. Ashley shows up with a cashier's check, and Marion says, "You're going to love it here." But at the last minute, Marion declines to take the check and refuses to sell. Ashley sues and wins
   (a) Nothing
   (b) The condominium
   (c) $700,000
   (d) The difference between $700,000 and the condominium's market value
   (e) Damages for fraud

3. Seller's sales contract states that "The model 8J flagpole will withstand winds up to 150 mph, for a minimum of 35 years." The same contract includes this: "This contract makes no warranties, and any implied warranties are hereby disclaimed." School buys the flagpole, which blows down six months later in a 105-mph wind.
   (a) Seller is not liable because it never made any express warranties.
   (b) Seller is not liable because it disclaimed any warranties.
   (c) Seller is liable because the disclaimer was invalid.
   (d) Seller is liable because implied warranties may not be disclaimed.

4. Manufacturer sells a brand-new, solar-powered refrigerator. Because the technology is new, Manufacturer sells the product "as is." Plaintiff later sues Manufacturer for breach of warranty and wins. Plaintiff is probably

(a)   A distributor with no understanding of legal terminology

(b)   A retailer who had previously relied on Manufacturer

(c)   A retailer who had never done business before with Manufacturer

(d)   A retailer who failed to notice the "as is" label

(e)   A consumer

5. **CPA QUESTION:** To establish a cause of action based on strict liability in tort for personal injuries resulting from using a defective product, one of the elements that the plaintiff must prove is that the seller (defendant)

(a)   Failed to exercise due care

(b)   Was in privity of contract with the plaintiff

(c)   Defectively designed the product

(d)   Was engaged in the business of selling the product

Essay Questions

1. Nina owns a used car lot. She signs and sends a fax to Seth, a used car wholesaler who has a huge lot of cars in the same city. The fax says, "Confirming our agrmt—I pick any 15 cars fr yr lot—30% below blue book." Seth reads the fax, laughs, and throws it away. Two weeks later, Nina arrives and demands to purchase 15 of Seth's cars. Is he obligated to sell?

2. **YOU BE THE JUDGE: WRITING PROBLEM** United Technologies advertised a used Beechcraft Baron airplane for sale in an aviation journal. Attorney Thompson Comerford spoke with a United agent who described the plane as "excellently maintained" and said it had been operated "under §135 flight regulations," meaning the plane had been subject to airworthiness inspections every 100 hours. Comerford arrived at a Dallas airport to pick up the plane, where he paid $80,000 for it. He signed a sales agreement stating that the plane was sold "as is" and that there were "no representations or warranties, express or implied, including the condition of the aircraft, its merchantability, or its fitness for any particular purpose." Comerford attempted to fly the plane home but immediately experienced problems with its brakes, steering, ability to climb, and performance while cruising. (Otherwise, it was fine.) He sued, claiming breach of express and implied warranties. Did United Technologies breach express or implied warranties? **Argument for Comerford:** United described the airplane as "excellently maintained," knowing that Mr. Comerford would rely. The company should not be allowed to say one thing and put the opposite in writing. **Argument for United Technologies:** Comerford is a lawyer, and we assume he can read. The contract clearly stated that the plane was sold as is. There were no warranties.

3. **ETHICS:** Texaco, Inc., and other oil companies sold mineral spirits in bulk to distributors, which then resold to retailers. Mineral spirits are used for cleaning and are harmful or fatal if swallowed. Texaco allegedly knew that the retailers, such as hardware stores, frequently packaged the mineral spirits (illegally) in used half-gallon milk containers and sold them to consumers, often with no warnings on the packages. David Hunnings, age 21 months, found a milk container in his home, swallowed the mineral spirits, and died. The Hunningses sued Texaco for negligence. The trial

court dismissed the complaint, and the Hunningses appealed. What is the legal standard in a negligence case? Have the plaintiffs made out a valid case of negligence? Assume that Texaco knew about the repackaging and the grave risk but continued to sell in bulk because doing so was profitable. (If the plaintiffs cannot prove those facts, they will lose even if they do get to a jury.) Would that make you angry? Should the case go to a jury? Or did the fault still lie with the retailer and/or the parents?

4. Lewis River Golf, Inc., grew and sold sod. It bought seed from the defendant, O. M. Scott & Sons, under an express warranty. But the sod grown from the Scott seeds developed weeds, a breach of Scott's warranty. Several of Lewis River's customers sued, unhappy with the weeds in their grass. Lewis River lost most of its customers, cut back its production from 275 acres to 45 acres, and destroyed all remaining sod grown from Scott's seeds. Eventually, Lewis River sold its business at a large loss. A jury awarded Lewis River $1,026,800, largely for lost profits. Scott appealed, claiming that a plaintiff may not recover for lost profits. Comment.

5. Boboli Co. wanted to promote its "California-style" pizza, which it sold in supermarkets. The company contracted with Highland Group, Inc., to produce 2 million recipe brochures, which would be inserted in the carton when the freshly baked pizza was still very hot. Highland contracted with Comark Merchandising to print the brochures. But when Comark asked for details concerning the pizza, the carton, and so forth, Highland refused to supply the information. Comark printed the first lot of 72,000 brochures, which Highland delivered to Boboli. Unfortunately, the hot bread caused the ink to run, and customers opening the carton often found red or blue splotches on their pizzas. Highland refused to accept additional brochures, and Comark sued for breach of contract. Highland defended by claiming that Comark had breached its warranty of merchantability. Please comment.

DISCUSSION QUESTIONS

1. Consider the scenario in which a diner cracked a tooth on a fragment of bone hidden in a hamburger. Would society be better off if lawsuits over such injuries were more difficult to win and yielded smaller damages? Or should the person with the cracked tooth have a good chance to get a large payday in court? Does your answer depend upon whether you are the person with the cracked tooth?

2. A seller can disclaim all implied warranties by stating that goods are sold "as is" (or by using other, more specific language). Is this fair? The UCC's implied warranties seem reasonable—that goods are fit for their normal purposes, for example. Should it be so easy for sellers to escape their obligations?

3. After learning more about implied warranties and disclaimers, would you ever buy an item sold "as is"? Imagine a car salesman who offers you a car for

$8,000, but who also says that he can knock the price down to $6,500 if you will buy the car "as is." If you live in a state that does not give consumers special protections, which deal would be more appealing?

4. Under the UCC's Statute of Frauds, sale-of-goods contracts for more than $500 must be in writing to be valid. But since Article 2 only covers sale-of-goods contracts, agreements to sell services are not subject to the rule. Should the common law change so that *all* contracts valued at more than $500 have a writing requirement, or would that place an undue burden on businesses?

5. When an acceptance contains additional terms, the UCC and the common law contain different rules. The common law's mirror image rule makes the acceptance ineffective, and no contract is formed. But the UCC rules "save" the contract. Which rule do you think is more sensible?

NEGOTIABLE INSTRUMENTS

As a freshman in college, Bemis was having lots of new experiences. For the first time in his life, he was living away from home, and he also had his own bank account and checkbook. He was discovering that being on his own offered new freedom, but it also imposed new responsibilities.

Bemis bought a combination refrigerator and microwave from a fellow selling them out on the sidewalk in front of the dorm. Since Bemis could not afford the entire $300 purchase price, he put down $100 in cash and signed a promissory note for the balance. When the microwave burst into flames, Bemis was relieved to think that at least he was out only $100. That was until a stranger named Samantha showed up at his door, demanding payment on the note. It turns out that the seller had sold the note to Samantha, and Bemis was liable to her for the full amount.

That night, Bemis went to a club to relax. When he left, a man followed him into an alley and threatened him with a knife. Bemis had no cash, but he offered to write the robber a check for $100. The bad guy took the check and ran away. The next morning, Bemis went to the bank, where he discovered to his relief that the check was not valid because he had signed it under duress.

> A man followed Bemis into an alley and threatened him with a knife. Bemis had no cash, but he offered to write the robber a check for $100.

Because Bemis's college distributed free iPods to all freshmen, he sold his old MP3 player to Vanessa. When she handed him the check, he glanced at it and saw "$50." What he failed to notice was that the *words* on the check said "five dollars." When Bemis took the check to the bank, he discovered that it was worth only five dollars because when words and numbers disagree, the words win.

COMMERCIAL PAPER

The law of commercial paper is important to anyone who writes checks or borrows money. Historically speaking, however, commercial paper is a relatively new development. In early human history, people lived on whatever they could hunt, grow, or make for themselves. Imagine what your life would be like if you had to subsist only on what you could make yourself. Over time, people improved their standard of living by bartering for goods and services they could not make themselves. But traders needed a method for keeping track of who owed how much to whom. That was the role of currency. Many items have been used for currency over the years, including silver, gold, copper, and cowrie shells. These currencies have two disadvantages—they are easy to steal and difficult to carry.

Paper currency weighs less than gold or silver, but it is even easier to steal. As a result, money had to be kept in a safe place, and banks developed to meet that need. However, money in a vault is not very useful unless it can be readily spent. Society needed a system for transferring paper funds easily. Commercial paper is that system. Electronic alternatives may ultimately dominate the marketplace, but for now, paper is still king.

TYPES OF NEGOTIABLE INSTRUMENTS

There are two kinds of commercial paper: negotiable and non-negotiable instruments. Article 3 of the Uniform Commercial Code (UCC) covers only negotiable instruments; non-negotiable instruments are governed by ordinary contract law. There are also two categories of negotiable instruments: notes and drafts.

A **note** (also called a **promissory note**) is your promise that you will pay money. A promissory note is used in virtually every loan transaction, whether the borrower is buying a multimillion-dollar company or a television. For example, when you borrow money from Aunt Leila to buy a car, you will sign a note promising to repay the money. You are the **maker** because you are the one who has made the promise. Aunt Leila is the **payee** because she expects to be paid.

Promissory note
The maker of the instrument promises to pay a specific amount of money.

Maker
The issuer of a promissory note.

Payee
Someone who is owed money under the terms of an instrument.

Draft
The drawer of this instrument orders someone else to pay money.

Check
An instrument in which the drawer orders the drawee bank to pay money to the payee.

Drawer
The person who issues a draft.

PROMISSORY NOTE

1,000.00 florins   Verona

16 . 2 . 1595

On or before the fifteenth day of April in the Year of Our Lord, 1595, the undersigned promises to pay to the order of Juliet, daughter of the house of Capulet, in Verona, the sum of 1,000 florins, with interest from the date hereof at five percent per annum, until paid.

_____
Romeo

© Cengage Learning 2013

In this note, Romeo is the maker and Juliet is the payee.

Drawee
The person who pays a draft. In the case of a check, the bank is the drawee.

A **draft** is an order directing someone else to pay money for you. A **check** is the most common form of a draft—it is an order telling a bank to pay money. In a draft, three people are involved: the **drawer** orders the **drawee** to pay money to the payee. Now before you slam the book shut in despair, let us sort out the players. Suppose that Serena Williams wins the River Oaks Club Open. River Oaks writes her a check for $500,000. This check is simply an order by River Oaks (the drawer) to its bank (the drawee) to pay money to Williams (the payee). The terms make sense if you remember that, when you take money out of your account, you *draw* it out. Therefore, when you write a check, you are the drawer and the bank is the drawee. The person to whom you make out the check is being paid, so she is called the payee.

The following table illustrates the difference between notes and drafts. Even courts sometimes confuse the terms *drawer* (the person who signs a check) and *maker* (someone who signs a promissory note). **Issuer** is an all-purpose term that means both maker and drawer.

Issuer
The maker of a promissory note or the drawer of a draft.

	Who Pays	Who Plays
Note	You make a promise that you will pay.	Two people are involved: maker and payee.
Draft	You order someone else to pay.	Three people are involved: drawer, drawee, and payee.

THE FUNDAMENTAL "RULE" OF COMMERCIAL PAPER

The possessor of a piece of commercial paper has an unconditional right to be paid, so long as (1) the paper is *negotiable*; (2) it has been *negotiated* to the possessor; (3) the possessor is a *holder in due course*; and (4) the issuer cannot claim a valid defense.

Negotiability

Holder in due course
Someone who has given value for an instrument, in good faith, without notice of outstanding claims or other defenses.

To work as a substitute for money, commercial paper must be freely transferable in the marketplace, just as money is. In other words, it must be *negotiable*.

The possessor of *non*-negotiable commercial paper has the same rights—no more, no less—as the person who made the original contract. With non-negotiable commercial paper, the transferee's rights are *conditional* because they depend upon the rights of the original party to the contract. If, for some reason, the original party loses his right to be paid, so does the transferee. The value of non-negotiable commercial paper is greatly reduced because the transferee cannot be absolutely sure what his rights are or whether he will be paid at all.

Suppose that Krystal buys a used car from the Trustie Car Lot for her business, Krystal Rocks. She cannot afford to pay the full $15,000 right now, but she is willing to sign a note promising to pay later. As long as Trustie keeps the note, Krystal's obligation to pay is contingent upon the validity of the underlying contract. If, for example, the car is defective, then Krystal might not be liable to Trustie for the full amount of the note. Trustie, however, does not want to keep the note. He needs the cash *now* so that he can buy more cars to sell to other customers. Reggie's Finance Co. is happy to buy Krystal's promissory note from Trustie, but the price Reggie is willing to pay depends upon whether her note is negotiable.

If Krystal's promissory note is non-negotiable, Reggie gets exactly the same rights that Trustie had. As the saying goes, he steps into Trustie's shoes. Suppose that Trustie tampered with the odometer and, as a result, Krystal's car is worth only $12,000. If, under contract law, she owes Trustie only $12,000, then that is all she has to pay Reggie, even though the note *says* $15,000.

The possessor of *negotiable* commercial paper has *more* rights than the person who made the original contract. With negotiable commercial paper, the transferee's rights are

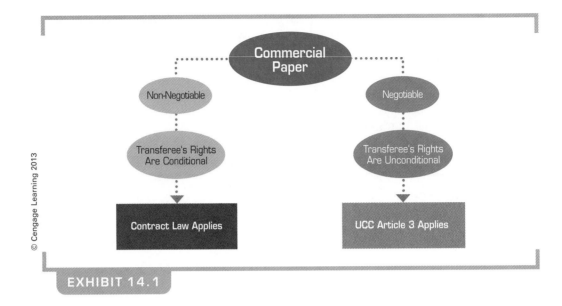

© Cengage Learning 2013

EXHIBIT 14.1

unconditional. He is entitled to be paid the full amount of the note, regardless of the relationship between the original parties. If Krystal's promissory note is a negotiable instrument, she must pay the full amount to whoever has possession of it, no matter what complaints she might have against Trustie.

Exhibit 14.1 illustrates the difference between negotiable and non-negotiable commercial paper.

Because negotiable instruments are more valuable than non-negotiable ones, it is important for buyers and sellers to be able to tell, easily and accurately, if an instrument is indeed negotiable. To be negotiable:

1. **The instrument must be in *writing*.**

2. **The instrument must be *signed* by the maker or drawer.**

3. **The instrument must contain an *unconditional promise* or *order to pay*.** If Krystal's promissory note says, "I will pay $15,000 as long as the car is still in working order," it is not negotiable because it is making a conditional promise. The instrument must also contain a promise or order to pay. It is not enough simply to say, "Krystal owes Trustie $15,000." She has to indicate that she owes the money and also that she intends to pay it. "Krystal promises to pay Trustie $15,000" would work.

4. **The instrument must state a *definite amount* of money which is clear "within its four corners."** "I promise to pay Trustie one-third of my profits this year" would not work because the amount is unclear. If Krystal's note says, "I promise to pay $15,000 worth of diamonds," it is not negotiable because it does not state a definite amount of *money.*

5. **The instrument must be payable on *demand* or at a *definite time*.** A demand instrument is one that must be paid whenever the holder requests payment. If an instrument is undated, it is treated as a demand instrument and is negotiable. An instrument can be negotiable even if it will not be paid until some time in the future, provided that the payment date can be determined when the document is made. A graduate of a well-known prep school wrote a generous check to his alma mater, but for payment date he put, "The day the headmaster is fired." This check is not negotiable because it is payable neither on demand nor at a definite time.

6. **The instrument must be payable to *order* or to *bearer*. Order paper** must include the words "Pay to the order of" someone. By including the word "order," the maker is indicating that the instrument is not limited to only one person. "Pay to the order of Trustie Car Lot" means that the money will be paid to Trustie *or to anyone Trustie designates*. If the note is made out "To bearer," it is **bearer paper** and can be redeemed by *any* holder in due course.

Order paper
An instrument that includes the words "pay to the order of" or their equivalent.

Bearer paper
An instrument payable "to bearer."

The rules for checks are different from other negotiable instruments. If properly filled out, checks are negotiable. And sometimes they are negotiable even if not filled out correctly. Most checks are preprinted with the words "Pay to the order of," but sometimes people inadvertently cross out "order of." Even so, the check is still negotiable. Checks are frequently received by consumers who, sadly, have not completed a course on business law. The drafters of the UCC did not think it fair to penalize them when the drawer of the check was the one who made the mistake.

EXAM Strategy

Question: Sam had a checking account at Piggy Bank. Piggy sent him special checks that he could use to draw down a line of credit. When Sam used these checks, Piggy did not take money out of his account; instead, the bank treated the checks as loans and charged him interest. Piggy then sold these used checks to Wolfe. Were the checks negotiable instruments?

Strategy: When faced with a question about negotiability, begin by looking at the list of six requirements. In this case, there is no reason to doubt that the checks are in writing, signed by the issuer, and with an unconditional promise to pay to order at a definite time. But do the checks state a definite amount of money? Can the holder "look at the four corners of the check" and determine how much Sam owes?

Result: Sam was supposed to pay Piggy the face amount of the check plus interest. Wolfe does not know the amount of the interest unless he reads the loan agreement. Therefore, the checks are not negotiable.

INTERPRETATION OF AMBIGUITIES

Perhaps you have noticed that people sometimes make mistakes. Although the UCC establishes simple and precise rules for creating negotiable instruments, people do not always follow these rules to the letter. It might be tempting simply to invalidate defective documents (after all, money is at stake here). But instead, the UCC favors negotiability and has rules to resolve uncertainty and supply missing terms.

Notice anything odd about the check pictured on the next page? Is it for $1,500 or $15,000? When the terms in a negotiable instrument contradict each other, three rules apply:

- Words take precedence over numbers.

- Handwritten terms prevail over typed and printed terms.

- Typed terms win over printed terms.

According to these rules, Krystal's check is for $15,000 because, in a conflict between words and numbers, words win.

In the following case, the amount of the check was not completely clear. Was it a negotiable instrument?

You be the Judge

BLASCO V. MONEY SERVICES CENTER

2006 Bankr. LEXIS 2899
United States Bankruptcy Court for the Northern District of Alabama, 2006

Facts: Christina Blasco ran out of money, so she went to the Money Services Center (MSC) and borrowed $500. To repay the loan, she gave MSC a check for $587.50, which it promised not to cash for two weeks. This kind of transaction is called a "payday loan" because it is made to someone who needs money to tide them over until the next paycheck. (Note that in this case, Blasco was paying 17.5 percent interest for a two-week loan, which is an annual compounded interest rate of 6,500 percent. This is the dark side of payday loans—interest rates are often exorbitant.)

Before MSC could cash the check, Blasco filed for bankruptcy protection. Although MSC knew about Blasco's filing, it deposited the check. It is illegal for creditors to collect debts after a bankruptcy filing, except that creditors are entitled to payment on negotiable instruments.

Ordinarily, checks are negotiable instruments, but only if they are for a definite amount. This check had a wrinkle: the numerical amount of the check was $587.50, but the amount in words was written as "five eighty-seven and 50/100 dollars." Did the words mean "five hundred eighty-seven" or "five thousand eighty-seven" or perhaps "five million eighty-seven"? Was the check negotiable despite this ambiguity?

You Be the Judge: *Was this check a negotiable instrument? Was it for a definite amount?*

Argument for Blasco: For a check to be negotiable, two rules apply:

1. The check must state a definite amount of money, which is clear within its four corners.

2. If there is a contradiction between the words and numbers, words take precedence over numbers.

Words prevail over numbers, which means that the check is for "five eighty-seven and 50/100 dollars." This amount is not definite. A holder cannot be sure of the precise amount of the check. Therefore, the check is not a negotiable instrument, and MSC had no right to submit it for payment.

Argument for MSC: Blasco is right about the two rules. However, she is wrong in their interpretation. If there is a contradiction between the words and numbers, words take precedence over numbers. In this case, there was no contradiction. The words were ambiguous, but they did not contradict the numbers. If the words had said "five thousand eighty-seven," that would have been a contradiction. Instead, the numbers simply clarified the words. Even someone who was a stranger to this transaction could safely figure out the amount of the check. Therefore, it is negotiable and MSC is not liable.

Negotiation

Negotiation means that an instrument has been transferred to the holder by someone *other than the issuer*. If the issuer has transferred the instrument to the holder, then it has not been negotiated and the issuer can refuse to pay the holder if there was some flaw in the underlying contract. Thus, if Jake gives Madison a promissory note for $2,000 in payment for a new computer, but the computer crashes and burns the first week, Jake has the right to refuse to pay the note. Jake was the issuer and the note was not negotiated. But if, before the computer self-destructs, Madison indorses and transfers the note to Kayla, then Jake is liable to Kayla for the full amount of the note, regardless of his claims against Madison.

> **If the computer crashes and burns the first week, Jake has the right to refuse to pay the note.**

To be negotiated, order paper must first be *indorsed* and then *delivered* to the transferee. Bearer paper must simply be *delivered* to the transferee; no indorsement is required.[1]

An **indorsement** is the signature of the payee. Tess writes a rent check for $475 to her landlord, Larnell. If Larnell signs the back of the check and delivers it to Patty, he has met the two requirements for negotiating order paper: indorsement and delivery. If Larnell delivers the check to Patty but forgets to sign it, the check has not been indorsed and therefore cannot be negotiated—it has no value to Patty.

Negotiation
An instrument has been transferred to the holder by someone other than the issuer.

Indorsement
The signature of the payee.

EXAM Strategy

Question: Antoine makes a check out to cash and delivers it to Barley. He writes on the back, "Pay to the order of Charlotte." She signs her name. Is this check bearer paper or order paper? Has it been negotiated?

Strategy: Whenever a negotiable instrument is transferred, it is important to ask if the instrument has been properly negotiated. To be negotiated, order paper must be indorsed and delivered; bearer paper need only be delivered, but in both cases by someone other than the issuer.

Result: This check changes back and forth between order and bearer paper, depending on what the indorsement says. When Antoine makes out a check to cash, it is bearer paper. When he gives it to Barley, it is not negotiated because he is the issuer. When Barley writes on the back "Pay to the order of Charlotte," it becomes order paper. When he gives it to Charlotte, it is properly negotiated because he is not the issuer and he has both indorsed the check and transferred it to her. When she signs it, the check becomes bearer paper. And so it could go on forever.[2]

Holder in Due Course

A holder in due course has an automatic right to receive payment for a negotiable instrument (unless the issuer can claim a valid defense). If the possessor of an instrument is not a holder in due course, then his right to payment depends upon the relationship between the

---

[1] §3-201. The UCC spells the word *indorsed*. Outside the UCC, the word is more commonly spelled *endorsed*.

[2] Even when all the space on the back of the check is filled, the holder can attach a separate paper for indorsements, which is called an **allonge**.

issuer and payee. He inherits whatever claims and defenses arise out of that contract. Clearly, then, holder in due course status dramatically increases the value of an instrument because it enhances the probability of being paid.

REQUIREMENTS FOR BEING A HOLDER IN DUE COURSE

A holder in due course is a *holder* who has given *value* for the instrument, in *good faith*, *without notice* of outstanding claims or other defects.[3]

Holder.   For order paper, a **holder** is anyone in possession of the instrument if it is payable to or indorsed to her. For bearer paper, a holder is anyone in possession. Tristesse gives Felix a check payable to him. Because Felix owes his mother money, he indorses the check and delivers it to her. This is a valid negotiation because Felix has both indorsed the check (which is order paper) and delivered it. Therefore, Felix's mother is a holder.

Value.   A holder in due course must give value for an instrument. **Value** means that the holder has *already* done something in exchange for the instrument. Felix's mother has already lent him money, so she has given value.

Good Faith.   There are two tests to determine if a holder acquired an instrument in good faith. The holder must meet *both* these tests:

- **Subjective test.** Did the holder *believe* the transaction was honest in fact?

- **Objective test.** Did the transaction *appear* to be commercially reasonable?

Felix persuades his elderly neighbor, Faith, that he has invented a fabulous beauty cream guaranteed to remove wrinkles. She gives him a $10,000 promissory note, payable in 90 days, in return for exclusive sales rights in Pittsburgh. Felix sells the note to his old friend, Griffin, for $2,000. Felix never delivers the sales samples to Faith. When Griffin presents the note to Faith, she refuses to pay on the grounds that Griffin is not a holder in due course. She contends that he did not buy the note in good faith.

Griffin fails both tests. Any friend of Felix knows he is not trustworthy, especially when presenting a promissory note signed by an elderly neighbor. Griffin did not believe the transaction was honest in fact. Also, $10,000 notes are not usually discounted to $2,000; $8,000 or $9,000 would be more normal. This transaction is not commercially reasonable, and Griffin should have realized immediately that Felix was up to no good.

In the following case, the plaintiff passed the subjective test but failed the objective one.

Holder
For order paper, anyone in possession of the instrument if it is payable to or indorsed to her. For bearer paper, anyone in possession.

Value
The holder has *already* done something in exchange for the instrument.

BUCKEYE CHECK CASHING, INC. V. CAMP

159 Ohio App. 3d 784; 825 N.E.2d 644; 2005 Ohio App. LEXIS 929
Court of Appeals of Ohio, 2005

CASE SUMMARY

Facts: On October 12, Shawn Sheth and James Camp agreed that Camp would provide services to Sheth by October 15. In payment, Sheth gave Camp a check for $1,300 that was postdated October 15. On October 13, Camp sold the check to Buckeye Check Cashing for $1,261.31. On October 14, fearing that Camp would vio-late the contract, Sheth stopped payment on the check. That same day, Buckeye deposited the check with its bank, believing that the check would reach Sheth's bank on October 15. Buckeye was unaware of the stop payment order. Sheth's bank refused to pay the check. Buckeye filed suit against Sheth.

---

[3]UCC §3-302.

The trial court ruled that because Buckeye was a holder in due course, the check was valid and Sheth had to pay Buckeye. Sheth appealed.

Issues: *Was Buckeye a holder in due course? Must Sheth pay Buckeye?*

Decision: Sheth is not required to pay Buckeye because the company was not a holder in due course.

Reasoning: To be a holder in due course, Buckeye must have acted in good faith when it bought Sheth's check. In determining good faith, we apply two standards:

1. A subjective test, also called the "pure heart and empty head doctrine." The holder meets this test if he subjectively believed he was negotiating an instrument in good faith. In the absence of obviously fraudulent behavior, an innocent party is assumed to have acted in good faith.

2. An objective test, which requires the observance of reasonable commercial standards of fair dealing.

Check cashing is unlicensed and unregulated in Ohio. Thus, there are no concrete commercial standards by which check-cashing businesses must operate. Buckeye argues that its own internal operating policies did not require that it verify the availability of funds, and apparently the company did not have any guidelines for the acceptance of postdated checks.

Under the purely subjective test, it is clear that Buckeye accepted the check in good faith. But Buckeye fails the objective test because it did not act in a commercially reasonable manner. A postdated check is an obvious sign of trouble, and Buckeye should have realized that there was at least some possibility that the instrument was invalid. Therefore, it should have taken reasonable steps to verify the check before cashing it.

Notice of Outstanding Claims or Other Defects.   In certain circumstances, a holder is on notice that an instrument has an outstanding claim or other defect:

1. **The instrument is overdue.** An instrument is overdue the day after its due date. At that point, the recipient ought to wonder why no one has bothered to collect the money owed. A check is overdue 90 days after its date. Any other demand instrument is overdue (1) the day after a request for payment is made or (2) a reasonable time after the instrument was issued.

2. **The instrument is dishonored.** To dishonor an instrument is to refuse to pay it. For example, once a check has been stamped "Insufficient Funds" by the bank, it has been dishonored, and no one who obtains it afterward can be a holder in due course.

3. **The instrument is altered, forged, or incomplete.** Anyone who knows that an instrument has been altered or forged cannot be a holder in due course. Suppose Joe wrote a check to Tony for $200. While showing the check to Liza, Tony cackles to himself and says, "Can you believe what that goof did? Look, he left the line blank after the words 'two hundred.' " Taking his pen out with a flourish, Tony changes the zeroes to nines and adds the words "ninety-nine." He then indorses the check over to Liza, who is definitely not a holder in due course.

4. **The holder has notice of certain claims or disputes.** No one can qualify as a holder in due course if she is on notice that (1) someone else has a claim to the instrument or (2) there is a dispute between the original parties to the instrument. Matt hires Sheila to put aluminum siding on his house. In payment, he gives her a $15,000 promissory note with the due date left blank. They agree that the note will not be due until 60 days after completion of the work. Despite the agreement, Sheila fills in the date immediately and sells the note to Rupert at American Finance Corp., who has bought many similar notes from Sheila. Rupert knows that the note is not supposed to be due until after the work is finished. Usually, before he buys a note from her, he demands a signed document from the homeowner certifying that the work is complete. Not only

that, but he lives near Matt and can see that Matt's house is only half finished. Rupert is not a holder in due course because he has reason to suspect there is a dispute between Sheila and Matt.

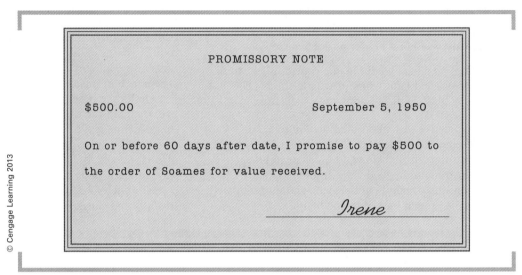

PROMISSORY NOTE

$500.00   September 5, 1950

On or before 60 days after date, I promise to pay $500 to the order of Soames for value received.

Irene

The holder of this note should realize that there may be a problem.

DEFENSES AGAINST A HOLDER IN DUE COURSE

Negotiable instruments are meant to be a close substitute for money, and, as a general rule, holders expect to be paid. **However, the issuer of a negotiable instrument is not required to pay if:**

1. His signature on the instrument was forged.

2. After signing the instrument, his debts were discharged in bankruptcy.

3. He was underage (typically younger than 18) at the time he signed the instrument.

4. The amount of the instrument was altered after he signed it. (However, if he left the instrument blank, he is liable for any amounts later filled in.)

5. He signed the instrument under duress, while mentally incapacitated, or as part of an illegal transaction.

6. He was tricked into signing the instrument without knowing what it was and without any reasonable way to find out.

Consumer Exception

In the 18th and 19th centuries, negotiable instruments often circulated through several hands. The business community treated them as money. The concept of holder in due course was essential because the instruments had little use if they could not be transferred for value. In the modern banking system, however, instruments are much less likely to circulate. Currently, the most common use for negotiable instruments is in consumer transactions. A consumer pays for a refrigerator by giving the store a promissory note. The store promptly sells the note to a finance company. Even if the refrigerator is defective, under Article 3 the consumer must pay full value on the note because the finance company is a holder in due course.

© Cengage Learning 2013

Some commentators have argued that the concept of holder in due course no longer serves a useful purpose and that it should be eliminated once and for all (and with it, Article 3 of the UCC). No state has yet taken such a dramatic step. Instead, some states require promissory notes given by a consumer to carry the words "consumer paper." Notes with this legend are non-negotiable.

Meanwhile, the Federal Trade Commission (FTC) has special rules for consumer credit contracts. A **consumer credit contract** is one in which a consumer borrows money from a lender to purchase goods and services from a seller who is affiliated with the lender. If Sears loans money to Gerald to buy a television at Sears, that is a consumer credit contract. It is not a consumer credit contract if Gerald borrows money from his cousin Vinnie to buy the TV from Sears. The FTC requires all promissory notes in consumer credit contracts to contain the following language:

> NOTICE
> ANY HOLDER OF THIS CONSUMER CREDIT CONTRACT IS SUBJECT TO ALL CLAIMS AND DEFENSES WHICH THE DEBTOR COULD ASSERT AGAINST THE SELLER OF GOODS OR SERVICES OBTAINED WITH THE PROCEEDS HEREOF.

The UCC, provides that no one can be a holder in due course of an instrument with this language.[4] If the language is omitted from a consumer note, it is possible to be a holder in due course, but the seller is subject to a fine.

In the following case, consumers found that a home improvement contract, far from improving their home, almost caused them to lose it.

Consumer credit contract
A contract in which a consumer borrows money from a lender to purchase goods and services from a seller who is affiliated with the lender.

ANTUNA V. NESCOR, INC.

2002 Conn. Super. Lexis 1003
Superior Court of Connecticut, 2002

CASE SUMMARY

Facts: NESCOR was, in theory, a home improvement company. One of its salespeople signed a contract with the Antunas to install vinyl siding and windows. The contract contained the required FTC language: "Any holder of this consumer credit contract is subject to all claims and defenses which the debtor could assert against the Seller of the goods or services pursuant hereto or with the proceeds hereof." NESCOR assigned this contract to The Money Store (TMS).

Under Connecticut law, a home improvement contract is invalid and unenforceable if it is entered into by a salesperson or contractor who has not registered with the state. The NESCOR salesperson was unregistered.

Unhappy with NESCOR's work, the Antunas stopped making payments under the contract. TMS filed suit, seeking to foreclose on their house. The Antunas moved for summary judgment, arguing that TMS could not enforce the contract because it was not a holder in due course.

Issue: *Was TMS a holder in due course? Does it have the right to foreclose on the Antunas' home?*

Decision: TMS has no right to foreclose because it was not a holder in due course.

Reasoning: Because the NESCOR salesperson was not registered, state law gives the Antunas the right to invalidate the home improvement contract with NESCOR. The FTC language explicitly gives the Antunas the right to assert against TMS whatever defenses they have against NESCOR. Accordingly, because the home improvement contract is invalid, neither NESCOR nor TMS can benefit from it. TMS may not enforce the consumer credit contract by foreclosing on the Antunas' house.

---

[4]UCC §3-106(d).

Chapter Conclusion

Commercial paper provides essential grease to the wheels of commerce. It is worth remembering, however, that the terms of the UCC are precise and that failure to comply with these exacting provisions can lead to unfortunate consequences.

Exam Review

1. **NEGOTIABILITY** The possessor of non-negotiable commercial paper has the same rights—no more, no less—as the person who made the original contract. The possessor of negotiable commercial paper has more rights than the person who made the original contract. (pp. 244–245)

2. **THE FUNDAMENTAL RULE OF COMMERCIAL PAPER** The possessor of a piece of commercial paper has an unconditional right to be paid, so long as:

   - The paper is negotiable,

   - It has been negotiated to the possessor,

   - The possessor is a holder in due course, and

   - The issuer cannot claim a valid defense. (pp. 245–253)

3. **REQUIREMENTS FOR NEGOTIABILITY** To be negotiable, an instrument must:

   - Be in writing,

   - Be signed by the maker or drawer,

   - Contain an unconditional promise or order to pay,

   - State a definite amount of money which is clear "within its four corners,"

   - Be payable on demand or at a definite time, and

   - Be payable to order or to bearer. (pp. 246–247)

4. **AMBIGUITY** When the terms in a negotiable instrument contradict each other, three rules apply:

   - Words take precedence over numbers.

   - Handwritten terms prevail over typed and printed terms.

   - Type terms win over printed terms. (p. 247)

5. **NEGOTIATION** To be negotiated, order paper must first be indorsed and then delivered to the transferee. Bearer paper must simply be delivered to the transferee; no indorsement is required. (p. 249)

6. **HOLDER IN DUE COURSE** A holder in due course is a holder who has given value for the instrument, in good faith, without notice of outstanding claims or other defects. (pp. 249–252)

Question: After Irene fell behind on her mortgage payments, she answered an advertisement from Best Financial Consultants offering attractive refinancing opportunities. During a meeting at a McDonald's restaurant, a Best representative told her that the company would arrange for a complete refinancing of her home, pay off two of her creditors, and give her an additional $5,000 in spending money. Irene would only have to pay Best $4,000. Irene signed a blank promissory note that was filled in later by Best representatives for $14,986.61. Best did not fulfill its promises to Irene, but within two weeks, it sold the note to Robin for just under $14,000. Irene refused to pay the note, alleging that Robin was not a holder in due course. Is Irene liable to Robin?

Strategy: Review the requirements for being a holder in due course. Is this person a *holder* who has given *value* for the instrument, in *good faith*, without *notice* of outstanding claims or other defects? (See the "Result" at the end of this section.)

7. **DEFENSES** The issuer of a negotiable instrument is not required to pay if:

- His signature was forged.

- After signing the instrument, his debts were discharged in bankruptcy.

- He was underage (typically under 18) at the time he signed the instrument.

- The amount of the instrument was altered after he signed it.

- He signed the instrument under duress, while mentally incapacitated, or as part of an illegal transaction.

- He was tricked into signing the instrument without knowing what it was and without any reasonable way to find out. (p. 252)

8. **CONSUMER EXCEPTION** The Federal Trade Commission requires all promissory notes in consumer credit contracts to contain language preventing any subsequent holder from being a holder in due course. (pp. 252–253)

Question: Gina and Douglas Felde purchased a Chrysler car with a 70,000-mile warranty. They signed a loan contract with the dealer to pay for the car in monthly installments. The dealer sold the contract to the Chrysler Credit Corp. The car soon developed a tendency to accelerate abruptly and without warning. Two Chrysler dealers were unable to correct the problem. The Feldes filed suit against Chrysler Credit Corp., but the company refused to rescind the loan contract. The company argued that, as a holder in due course on the note, it was entitled to be paid regardless of any defects in the car. How would you decide this case if you were the judge?

Strategy: Whenever consumers are involved, consider the possibility that there is a consumer credit contract. The plaintiffs in this case are consumers who have borrowed money from a lender to purchase goods from a seller who is affiliated with the lender (both seller and lender are owned by Chrysler). Thus, the contract is a consumer credit contract. (See the "Result" at the end of this section.)

6. Result: In this case, Robin is a holder who has given value. Did she act in good faith? We don't know if she actually *believed* the transaction was honest, but the court held that the transaction did not *appear* to be commercially reasonable because Robin's profit was so high. She paid $14,000 for a note worth $14,986.61. Thus, Robin was not a holder in due course, and Irene was not liable to her.

8. Result: Chrysler Credit was not a holder in due course. Therefore, it is subject to any defenses the Feldes might have against the dealer, including that the car was defective.

Matching Questions

Match the following terms with their definitions:

___A. Drawer
___B. Drawee
___C. Issuer
___D. Maker
___E. Holder

1. Someone who issues a promissory note
2. The person who issues a draft
3. The person who pays a draft
4. Anyone in possession of an instrument if it is indorsed to her
5. The maker of a promissory note or the drawer of a draft

True/False Questions

Circle true or false:

1. T F The possessor of a piece of commercial paper always has an unconditional right to be paid.
2. T F Three parties are involved in a draft.
3. T F To be negotiable, bearer paper must be indorsed and delivered to the transferee.
4. T F Negotiation means that an instrument has been transferred to the holder by the issuer.
5. T F A promissory note may be valid even if it does not have a specific due date.

Multiple-Choice Questions

1. **CPA QUESTION:** In order to negotiate bearer paper, one must:
   (a) Indorse the paper
   (b) Indorse and deliver the paper with consideration
   (c) Deliver the paper
   (d) Deliver and indorse the paper

2. The possessor of a piece of order paper does *not* have an unconditional right to be paid if:

    (a) The paper is negotiable.

    (b) The possessor is the payee.

    (c) The paper has been indorsed to the possessor.

    (d) The possessor is a holder in due course.

    (e) The issuer changed his mind after signing the instrument.

3. An instrument is negotiable unless:

    (a) It is in writing.

    (b) It is signed only by the drawee.

    (c) It contains an order to pay.

    (d) It is payable on demand.

    (e) It is payable only to bearer.

4. Chloe buys a motorcycle on eBay from Junior. In payment, she gives him a promissory note for $7,000. He immediately negotiates the note to Terry. After the motorcycle arrives, Chloe discovers that it is not as advertised. One week later, she notifies Junior. She still has to pay Terry because:

    (a) On eBay, the rule is "buyer beware."

    (b) Terry's rights are not affected by Junior's misdeeds.

    (c) Terry indorsed the note.

    (d) Chloe is the drawee.

    (e) Chloe waited too long to complain.

5. Donna gives a promissory note to C. J. Which of the following errors would make the note invalid?

    (a) The instrument was written on a dirty sock.

    (b) The instrument promised to pay 15,000 euros.

    (c) The note stated that Donna owed C. J. "$1,500: One thousand and five dollars."

    (d) Donna signed the note without reading it.

    (e) The due date was specified as "three months after Donna graduates from college."

Essay Questions

1. Kay signed a promissory note for $220,000 that was payable to Investments, Inc. The company then indorsed the note over to its lawyers to pay past and future legal fees. Were the lawyers holders in due course?

2. Shelby wrote the check shown on the next page to Dana. When is it payable and for how much?

3. In the prior question, who are the drawer, drawee, and payee of this check?

4. Duncan Properties, Inc. agrees to buy a car from Shifty for $25,000. The company issues a promissory note in payment. The car that Duncan bought is defective. If Shifty still has the note, does Duncan have to pay it?

```
                                                              4201
SHELBY CASE
3020 CREST DRIVE                              July 27, 2002
ALVIN, TX
                                          August 3, 20 02

PAY TO THE
ORDER OF    Dana Locke                        |$   352.00

            Three Hundred Eighty-Two                  DOLLARS

            LAST NATIONAL BANK OF ALVIN
            ALVIN, TX 77511
            5-14/111
                                          Shelby Case
MEMO _____          _____

  ⑆010110456⑆  286  72566  4201
```

© Cengage Learning 2013

5. Shifty sells that note to Honest Abe for $22,000. Does Duncan have to pay Abe?

6. Abe gives the note to his daughter, Prudence, for her birthday. Is Prudence a holder in due course? Does Duncan have to pay Prudence?

DISCUSSION QUESTIONS

1. In the *Buckeye* case, the court ruled that Buckeye was not a holder in due course and the check was not valid because Buckeye should have checked with Sheth's bank before buying the check. Would this remedy have worked? What could Buckeye have done to protect itself?

2. In the *Antuna* case, the Antunas were foolish to sign an agreement with an unlicensed contractor to install aluminum siding. There is no evidence that TMS was acting in bad faith. Why should it suffer for the Antunas' mistake? What could TMS have done to protect itself?

3. Catherine suffered serious physical injuries in an automobile accident and became acutely depressed as a result. One morning, she received a check for $17,400 in settlement of her claims arising from the accident. She indorsed the check and placed it on the kitchen table. She then called Robert, her longtime roommate, to tell him the check had arrived. That afternoon, she jumped from the roof of her apartment building, killing

herself. The police found the check and a note from her stating that she was giving it to Robert. Had Catherine negotiated the check to Robert?

4. **ETHICS** In desperate financial trouble and fearful of losing his house, Abbott asked his friend Taylor for help. Taylor had been an officer of the Bank, so she put Abbott in touch with some of her former colleagues there. When a $300,000 loan was ready for closing, Taylor informed Abbott that she expected a commission of $15,000. Taylor threatened to block the loan if her demands were not met. Abbott was desperate, so he agreed to give Taylor $4,000 in cash and a promissory note for $11,000. On what grounds might Abbott claim that the note is invalid? Would this be a valid defense? Even if Taylor was in the right legally, was she in the right ethically? What is her Life Principle?

5. The *Blasco* case involved a payday loan, for which she was paying 6,500 percent interest. Some states outlaw such loans or heavily regulate the interest rates. Should the law permit these loans?

CHAPTER 15

SECURED TRANSACTIONS

© picsbyst/Shutterstock.com

To: Allison@credit-help-for-all.com

From: Sam12345@yahoo.com

Hi, Allison.

Look, this just doesn't make any sense. When I got out of school, I paid a guy $18,000 for my Jeep. I made every payment on my loan—*every one*—for over two years. I paid out over 9,000 bucks for that thing. Then I got laid off and I missed a few payments and the bank repossessed the car. And OK, fair enough, I can see why they have to do that.

So they auctioned off the Jeep and somebody else owns it. But now the bank's lawyer called me and said I still owe $5,000. What is that, a joke? I owe money for a Jeep I don't even have anymore? That can't be right. I look forward to your advice.

Sam

> I owe money for a Jeep I don't even have anymore?

To: Sam12345@yahoo.com

From: Allison@credit-help-for-all.com

Dear Sam,

I am sympathetic with your story, but unfortunately the bank is entitled to its money. Here is how the law sees your plight. When you bought the Jeep, you signed two documents: a note, in which you promised to pay the full balance owed, and a security agreement, which said that if you stopped making payments, the bank could repossess the vehicle and sell it.

There are two problems. First, even after two years of writing checks, you might still have owed about $10,000 (because of interest). Second, cars depreciate quickly. Your $18,000 vehicle probably had a market value of about $8,000 thirty months later. The security agreement allowed the bank to sell the Jeep at auction, where prices are still lower. Your car evidently fetched about $5,000. That leaves a deficiency of $5,000—for which you are legally responsible, regardless of who is driving the car.

I hope you have a good weekend.

Allison

SECURED TRANSACTIONS

We can sympathize with Sam but the bank is entitled to its money. The buyer and the bank had entered into a secured transaction, meaning that one party gave credit to another, insisting on full repayment and the right to seize certain property if the debt went unpaid. It is essential to understand the basics of this law because we live and work in a world economy based solidly on credit.

Article 9 of the Uniform Commercial Code (UCC) governs secured transactions in personal property. Article 9 employs terms not used elsewhere, so we must lead off with some definitions:

- **Fixtures** are goods that have become attached to real estate. For example, heating ducts are goods when a company manufactures them, but they become fixtures when installed in a house.

- **Security interest** means an interest in personal property or fixtures that secures the performance of some obligation. If an automobile dealer sells you a new car on credit and retains a security interest, it means she is keeping legal rights in your car, including the right to drive it away if you fall behind in your payments.

- **Secured party** is the person or company that holds the security interest. The automobile dealer who sells you a car on credit is the secured party.

- **Collateral** is the property subject to a security interest. When a dealer sells you a new car and keeps a security interest, the vehicle is the collateral.

- **Debtor** For our purposes, debtor refers to a person who has some original ownership interest in the collateral. If Alice borrows money from a bank and uses her Mercedes as collateral, she is the debtor because she owns the car.

- **Security agreement** is the contract in which the debtor gives a security interest to the secured party. This agreement protects the secured party's rights in the collateral.

- **Perfection** is a series of steps the secured party must take to protect its rights in the collateral against people other than the debtor.

- **Financing statement** is a record intended to notify the general public that the secured party has a security interest in the collateral.

- **Record** refers to information written on paper or stored in an electronic or other medium.

- **Authenticate** means to sign a document or to use any symbol or encryption method that identifies the person and clearly indicates she is adopting the record as her own. You authenticate a security agreement when you sign the papers at an auto dealership. A company may authenticate by using the Internet to transmit an electronic signature.

Fixtures

Goods that have become attached to real estate.

Security interest

An interest in personal property or fixtures that secures the performance of an obligation.

Secured party

A person or company that holds a security interest.

Collateral

Property that is subject to a security interest.

Debtor

A person who has original ownership interest in the collateral.

Security agreement

A contract in which the debtor gives a security interest to the secured party.

Perfection

A series of steps the secured party must take to protect its rights in the collateral against people other than the debtor.

Financing statement

A document that the secured party files to give the general public notice that it has a secured interest in the collateral.

Record

Information written on paper or stored in an electronic or other medium.

Authenticate

To sign a document or to use any symbol or encryption method that identifies the person and clearly indicates she is adopting the record as her own.

AN EXAMPLE

Here is an example using the terms just discussed. A medical equipment company manufactures a CT scanner and sells it to a clinic for $2 million, taking $500,000 cash and the clinic's promise to pay the rest over five years. The clinic simultaneously authenticates a security agreement, giving the manufacturer a security interest in the CT scanner. The manufacturer then electronically files a financing statement in an appropriate state agency. This perfects the manufacturer's rights, meaning that its security interest in the CT scanner is now valid against all the world. Exhibit 15.1 illustrates this transaction.

If the clinic goes bankrupt and many creditors try to seize its assets, the manufacturer has first claim to the CT scanner. The clinic's bankruptcy is of great importance. When a debtor has money to pay all of its debts, there are no concerns about security interests. A creditor insists on a security interest to protect itself in the event the debtor cannot pay all of its debts.

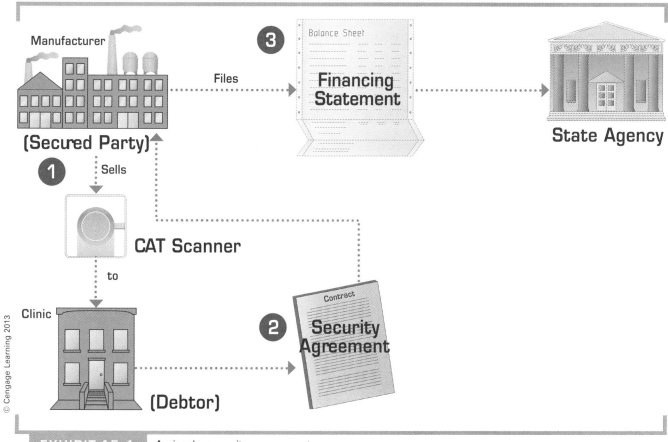

EXHIBIT 15.1   A simple security agreement:
(1) The manufacturer sells a CT scan machine to a clinic, taking $500,000 and the clinic's promise to pay the balance over five years.
(2) The clinic simultaneously authenticates a security agreement.
(3) The manufacturer perfects by electronically fi ling a financing statement.

© Cengage Learning 2013

Scope of Article 9

Article 9 applies to any transaction intended to create a security interest in personal property or fixtures.

TYPES OF COLLATERAL

The personal property that may be used as collateral includes:

- Goods, which are things that are movable.

- Inventory, meaning goods held by someone for sale or lease, such as all the beds and chairs in a furniture store.

- Instruments, such as drafts, checks, certificates of deposit, and notes.

- Investment property, which refers primarily to securities and related rights.

- Other property, including documents of title, accounts, general intangibles (copyrights, patents, goodwill, and so forth), and chattel paper (for example, a sales document indicating that a retailer has a security interest in goods sold to a consumer). Slightly different rules apply to some of these forms of property, but the details are less important than the general principles on which we shall focus.

Article 9 applies any time the parties intended to create a security interest in any of the items listed above.

ATTACHMENT OF A SECURITY INTEREST

Attachment
A three-step process that creates an enforceable security interest.

Attachment is a vital step in a secured transaction. This means that the secured party has taken three steps to create an enforceable security interest:

- The two parties made a security agreement and either the debtor has authenticated a security agreement describing the collateral, or the secured party has obtained possession;

- The secured party has given value to obtain the security agreement; and

- The debtor has rights in the collateral.[1]

Agreement

Without an agreement, there can be no security interest. Generally, the agreement must be either written on paper and signed by the debtor, or electronically recorded and authenticated by the debtor. The agreement must reasonably identify the collateral. For example, a security agreement may properly describe the collateral as "all equipment in the store at 123 Periwinkle Street."

A security agreement at a minimum might:

- State that Happy Homes, Inc., and Martha agree that Martha is buying an Arctic Co. refrigerator, and identify the exact unit by its serial number;

- Give the price, the down payment, the monthly payments, and interest rate;

---

[1]UCC Section 9-203.

- State that because Happy Homes is selling Martha the refrigerator on credit, it has a security interest in the refrigerator; and

- Provide that if Martha defaults (fails to make payments when due), Happy Homes is entitled to repossess the refrigerator.

Possession

In certain cases, the security agreement need not be in writing if the parties have an oral agreement and the secured party has possession. For some kinds of collateral, for example stock certificates, it is safer for the secured party actually to take the item than to rely upon a security agreement.

EXAM Strategy

Question: Hector needs money to keep his business afloat. He asks his uncle for a $1 million loan. The uncle agrees, but he insists that his nephew grant him a security interest in Hector's splendid gold clarinet, worth over $2 million. Hector agrees. The uncle prepares a handwritten document summarizing the agreement and asks his nephew to sign it. Hector hands the clarinet to his uncle and receives his money, but he forgets to sign the document. Has a security agreement attached?

Strategy: Attachment occurs if the parties made a security agreement and there was authentication or possession, the secured party has given value, and the debtor had rights in the collateral.

Result: Hector agreed to give his uncle a security interest in the instrument. He never authenticated (signed) the agreement, but the uncle did take possession of the clarinet. The uncle gave Hector $1 million, and Hector owned the instrument. Yes, the security interest attached.

Value

For the security interest to attach, the secured party must give value. Usually, the value will be apparent. If a bank loans $400 million to an airline, that money is the value, and the bank may therefore obtain a security interest in the planes that the airline is buying.

Debtor Rights in the Collateral

The debtor can only grant a security interest in goods if he has some legal right to those goods himself. Typically, the debtor owns the goods. But a debtor may also give a security interest if he is leasing the goods or even if he is a bailee, meaning that he is lawfully holding them for someone else.

Result

Once the security interest has attached to the collateral, the secured party is protected against the debtor. If the debtor fails to pay, the secured party may repossess the collateral, meaning take it away.

Attachment to Future Property

After-acquired property
Items that the debtor obtains
after the parties have made
their security agreement.

After-acquired property refers to items that the debtor obtains after the parties have made their security agreement. The parties may agree that the security interest attaches to after-acquired property. Basil is starting a catering business but owns only a beat-up car. He borrows $55,000 from the Pesto Bank, which takes a security interest in the car. But Pesto also insists on an after-acquired clause. When Basil purchases a commercial stove, cooking equipment, and freezer, Pesto's security interest attaches to each item as Basil acquires it.

A security agreement automatically applies to proceeds—whatever a debtor obtains who sells the collateral or otherwise disposes of it. The secured party obtains a security interest in the proceeds of the collateral unless the security agreement states otherwise.[2]

PERFECTION

Nothing Less Than Perfection

Once the security interest has attached to the collateral, the secured party is protected against the debtor. Pesto Bank loaned money to Basil and has a security interest in all of his property. If Basil defaults on his loan, Pesto may insist he deliver the goods to the bank. If he fails to do that, the bank can seize the collateral. But Pesto's security interest is valid only against Basil; if a third person claims some interest in the goods, the bank may never get them. For example, Basil might have taken out another loan, from his friend Olive, and used the same property as collateral. Olive knew nothing about the bank's original loan. To protect itself against Olive, and all other parties, the bank must perfect its interest.

There are several kinds of perfection, including:

- Perfection by filing;
- Perfection by possession; and
- Perfection of consumer goods.

In some cases, the secured party will have a choice of which method to use; in other cases, only one method works.

Perfection by Filing

The most common way to perfect is by filing a financing statement with the appropriate state agency. A financing statement gives the names of all parties, describes the collateral, and outlines the security interest, enabling any interested person to learn about it. Suppose the Pesto Bank obtains a security interest in Basil's catering equipment and then perfects by filing with the secretary of state in the state capital. When Basil asks his friend Olive for a loan, she will check the records to see if anyone has a security interest in the catering equipment. Olive's search uncovers Basil's previous security agreement, and she realizes it would be unwise to make the loan. If Basil were to default, the collateral would go straight to Pesto Bank, leaving Olive empty-handed. See Exhibit 15.2.

Article 9 prescribes one form, to be used nationwide for financing statements. The financing form is available online at many websites. Remember that the filing may be done on paper or electronically.

---

[2]UCC Section 9-204 and Section 9-203.

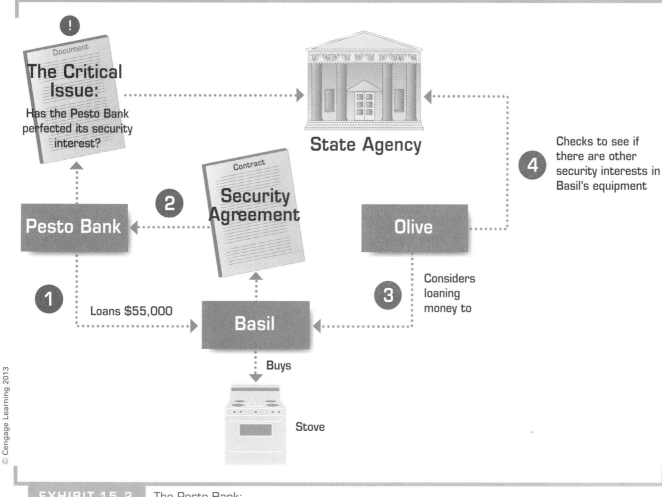

!

Document

The Critical Issue:

Has the Pesto Bank perfected its security interest?

State Agency

Contract

Security Agreement

2

Pesto Bank

Olive

4

Checks to see if there are other security interests in Basil's equipment

1

Loans $55,000

Basil

3

Considers loaning money to

Buys

Stove

© Cengage Learning 2013

EXHIBIT 15.2   The Pesto Bank:
(1) Loans money to Basil and
(2) Takes a security interest in his equipment.
Later, when Olive:
(3) Considers loaning Basil money, she will
(4) Check to see if any other creditors already have a security interest in his goods.

The most common problems that arise in filing cases are (1) whether the financing statement contained enough information to put other people on notice of the security interest; and (2) whether the secured party filed the papers in the right place.

CONTENTS OF THE FINANCING STATEMENT

A financing statement is sufficient if it provides the name of the debtor, the name of the secured party, and an indication of the collateral.[3]

The name of the debtor is critical because that is what an interested person will use to search among the millions of other financing statements on file. Faulty descriptions of the debtor's name have led to thousands of disputes and untold years of litigation, as

---

[3]UCC Section 9-502(a).

subsequent creditors have failed to locate any record of an earlier claim on the debtor's property. In response, the Uniform Commercial Code is now very precise about what name must be used. If the debtor is a "registered organization," such as a corporation, limited partnership, or limited liability company, the official, registered name of the company is the only one acceptable. If the debtor is a person or an unregistered organization (such as a club), then the *correct* name is required. Trade names are not sufficient. Because misnamed debtors have created so much conflict, the Code now offers a straightforward test: a financing statement is effective if a computer search run under the debtor's correct name produces it. That is true even if the financing statement used the *incorrect* name. If the search does not reveal the document, then the financing statement is ineffective as a matter of law. The burden is on the secured party to file accurately, not on the searcher to seek out erroneous filings.[4]

The collateral must be described reasonably so that another party contemplating a loan to the debtor will understand which property is already secured. A financing statement could properly state that it applies to "all inventory in the debtor's Houston warehouse." If the debtor has given a security interest in everything he owns, then it is sufficient to state simply that the financing statement covers "all assets" or "all personal property." The filing must be done by the debtor's last name. But which name is the last? The answer is not always entirely straightforward, as the following case indicates. Did the court get it right?

Corona Fruits & Veggies, Inc. v. Frozsun Foods, Inc.

143 Cal. App. 4th 319, 48 Cal. Rptr. 3d 868
California Court of Appeals, 2006.

CASE SUMMARY

Facts: Corona Fruits & Veggies (Corona) leased farmland to a strawberry farmer named Armando Munoz Juarez. He signed the lease, "Armando Munoz." Corona advanced money for payroll and farm production expenses. The company filed a UCC-1 financing statement, claiming a security interest in the strawberry crop. The financing statement listed the debtor's name as "Armando Munoz." Six months later, Armando Munoz Juarez contracted with Frozsun Foods, Inc., to sell processed strawberries. Frozsun advanced money and filed a financing statement listing the debtor's name as "Armando Juarez."

By the next year, the strawberry farmer owed Corona $230,000 and Frozsun $19,600. When he was unable to make payments on Corona's loan, the company repossessed the farmland. And, while it may sound a bit … lame … it also repossessed the strawberries.

Both Corona and Frozsun claimed the proceeds of the crop. The trial court awarded the money to Frozsun, finding that Corona had filed its financing statement under the wrong last name and therefore had failed to perfect its security interest in the strawberry crop. Corona appealed.

Issue: *Did Corona correctly file its financing statement?*

Decision: No, Corona did not correctly file. Affirmed.

Reasoning: Because UCC-1 financing statements are indexed by last name, it is essential that a creditor use the correct surname. This debtor's true last name was "Juarez," not "Munoz." Corona's own business records, receipts, and checks all refer to him as "Juarez," as do his green card and photo ID.

The record indicates that Frozsun's agent conducted a "Juarez" debtor name search and did not discover appellants'

---

[4]UCC Section 9-506(c).

UCC-1 financing statement. The secured party, not the debtor or uninvolved third parties, has the duty of ensuring proper filing and indexing of the notice.

Corona contends that since the debtor is from Mexico, we should follow the traditions of that country, where the surname is formed by listing the father's name, then the mother's. But the strawberries were planted in California, not Mexico. This is where the debt arose and the UCC-1 was filed. The state cannot organize a filing system that will accommodate naming practices in all foreign countries.

Corona failed to file properly, and its security interest never perfected.

Article 9—2010 Amendments.   In 2010, the authors of the UCC—the National Conference of Commissioners on Uniform State Laws (NCCUSL)—created a set of amendments to Article 9. Remember that the NCCUSL has no power to make law. Once it creates a set of model rules, it is up to the states to decide whether or not to actually enact the proposals.

At the time of this writing, six states have adopted the changes to Article 9 as law, and several others are actively considering doing the same. It appears likely that many states will adopt the changes soon. For all adopting states, the amendments will take effect on July 1, 2013.

While most of these changes are so technical as to be beyond the scope of this chapter, one of the amendments addresses the issue of what name must appear on a financing statement. Under the proposed 2010 amendments, states will require that for an individual, the name on a financing statement must be the same as that *on the person's driver's license, if one exists.* If a state also issues official identification cards from a driver's license office to non-drivers, then the name on such an ID card will be acceptable. If a person has neither kind of state ID card, then her surname and first personal name will be required to perfect by filing.

PLACE AND DURATION OF FILING

Article 9 specifies where a secured party must file. These provisions may vary from state to state, so it is essential to check local law: a misfiled record accomplishes nothing. Generally speaking, a party must file in a central filing office located in the state where an individual debtor lives or where an organization has its executive office.[5]

Once a financing statement has been filed, it is effective for five years (except for a manufactured home, where it lasts 30 years). After five years, the statement will expire and leave the secured party unprotected unless she files a continuation statement within six months prior to expiration. The continuation statement is valid for an additional five years, and a secured party may file such a statement periodically, forever.

Perfection by Possession

For most types of collateral, in addition to filing, a secured party generally may perfect by possession. So if the collateral is a diamond brooch or 1,000 shares of stock, a bank may perfect its security interest by holding the items until the loan is paid off. **However, possession imposes one important duty: a secured party must use reasonable care in the custody and preservation of collateral in her possession.**[6] Reliable Bank holds 1,000 shares of stock as collateral for a loan it made to Grady. Grady instructs the bank to sell the shares and use the proceeds to pay off his debt in full. If Reliable neglects to sell the stock for five days and the share price drops by 40 percent during that period, the bank will suffer the loss, not Grady.

---

[5]UCC Section 9-307.
[6]UCC Section 9-207.

Perfection of Consumer Goods

The UCC gives special treatment to security interests in most consumer goods. Merchants cannot realistically file a financing statement for every bed, television, and stereo for which a consumer owes money. To understand the UCC's treatment of these transactions, we need to know two terms. The first is *consumer goods*, which are those used primarily for personal, family, or household purposes. The second term is *purchase money security interest*.

Purchase money security interest (PMSI)

An interest taken by the person who sells the collateral or advances money so the debtor can buy it.

A **purchase money security interest (PMSI)** is one taken by the person who sells the collateral or by the person who advances money so the debtor can buy the collateral.[7] Assume the Gobroke Home Center sells Marion a $5,000 stereo system. The sales document requires a payment of $500 down and $50 per month for the next three centuries and gives Gobroke a security interest in the system. Because the security interest was "taken by the seller," the document is a PMSI. It would also be a PMSI if a bank had loaned Marion the money to buy the system and the document gave the bank a security interest. See Exhibit 15.3.

But aren't all security interests PMSIs? No, many are not. Suppose a bank loans a retail company $800,000 and takes a security interest in the store's present inventory. That is not a PMSI, since the store did not use the money to purchase the collateral.

What must Gobroke Home Center do to perfect its security interest? Nothing. **A PMSI in consumer goods perfects** *automatically*, **without filing.**[8] Marion's new stereo is clearly consumer goods because she will use it only in her home. Gobroke's security interest is a PMSI, so the interest has perfected automatically.

The Code provisions about perfecting generally do not apply to motor vehicles, trailers, mobile homes, boats, or farm tractors. These types of secured interests are governed by state law, which frequently require a security interest to be noted directly on the vehicle's certificate of title.

EXAM Strategy

Question: Winona owns a tropical fish store. To buy a spectacular new aquarium, she borrows $25,000 from her sister, Pauline, and signs an agreement giving Pauline a security interest in the tank. Pauline never files the security agreement. Winona's business goes belly up, and both Pauline and other creditors angle to repossess the tank. Does Pauline have a perfected interest in the tank?

Strategy: Generally, a creditor obtains a perfected security interest by filing or possession. However, a PMSI in consumer goods perfects automatically, without filing. Was Pauline's security agreement a PMSI? Was the fish tank a consumer good?

Result: A PMSI is one taken by the person who sells the collateral or advances money for its purchase. Pauline advanced the money for Winona to buy the tank, so Pauline does have a PSMI. Consumer goods are those used primarily for personal, family, or household purposes, so this was *not* a consumer purchase. Pauline failed to perfect and is unprotected against other creditors.

---

[7]UCC Section 9-103.
[8]UCC Section 9-309(1).

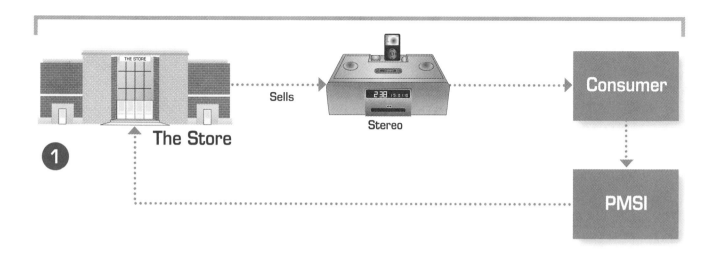

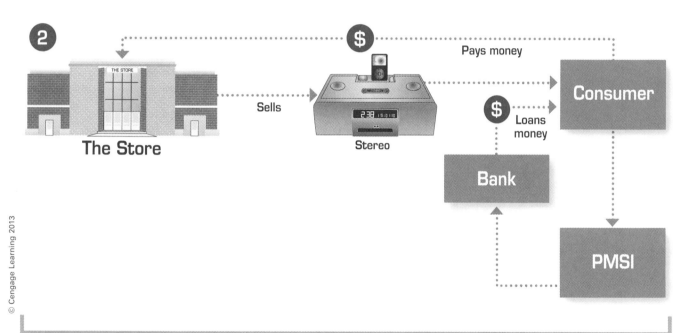

EXHIBIT 15.3   A purchase money security interest can arise in either of two ways. In the first example, a store sells a stereo to a consumer on credit; the consumer in turn signs a PMSI, giving the store a security interest in the stereo. In the second example, the consumer buys the stereo with money loaned from a bank; the consumer signs a PMSI giving the *bank* a security interest in the stereo.

PROTECTION OF BUYERS

Generally, once a security interest is perfected, it remains effective regardless of whether the collateral is sold, exchanged, or transferred in some other way. Bubba's Bus Co. needs money to meet its payroll, so it borrows $150,000 from Francine's Finance Co., which takes a security interest in Bubba's 180 buses and perfects its interest. Bubba, still short of cash, sells 30 of his buses to Antelope Transit. But even that money is not enough to keep Bubba solvent: he defaults on his loan to Francine and goes into bankruptcy. Francine pounces on Bubba's buses. May she repossess the 30 that Antelope now operates? Yes. The security interest continued in the buses even after Antelope purchased them, and Francine can whisk them away.

But there are some exceptions to this rule. The UCC gives a few buyers special protection.

Buyers in Ordinary Course of Business

Buyer in ordinary course of business (BIOC)

Someone who buys goods in good faith from a seller who routinely deals in such goods.

A **buyer in ordinary course of business (BIOC)** is someone who buys goods in good faith from a seller who routinely deals in such goods. For example, Plato's Garden Supply purchases 500 hemlocks from Socrates' Farm, a grower. Plato is a BIOC: he is buying in good faith, and Socrates routinely deals in hemlocks. This is an important status because a BIOC is generally not affected by security interests in the goods. However, if Plato realized that the sale violated another party's rights in the goods, there would be no good faith. If Plato knew that Socrates was bankrupt and had agreed with a creditor not to sell any of his inventory, Plato would not achieve BIOC status.

A BIOC takes the goods free of a security interest created by his seller, even though the security interest is perfected.[9] Suppose that, a month before Plato made his purchase, Socrates borrowed $200,000 from the Athenian Bank. Athenian took a security interest in all of Socrates' trees and perfected by filing. Then Plato purchased his 500 hemlocks. If Socrates defaults on the loan, Athenian will have no right to repossess the 500 trees that are now at the Garden Supply. Plato took them free and clear. (Of course, Athenian can still attempt to repossess other trees from Socrates.) The BIOC exception is designed to encourage ordinary commerce. A buyer making routine purchases should not be forced to perform a financing check before buying.

But the rule creates its own problems. A creditor may extend a large sum of money to a merchant based on collateral, such as inventory, only to discover that by the time the merchant defaults, the collateral has been sold. Because the BIOC exception undercuts the basic protection given to a secured party, the courts interpret it narrowly. BIOC status is available only if the seller created the security interest. Often, a buyer will purchase goods that have a security interest created by someone other than the seller. If that happens, the buyer is not a BIOC. However, should that rule be strictly enforced even when the results are harsh? You make the call.

---

[9]UCC Section 9-320(a). In fact, the buyer takes free of the security interest *even if the buyer knew of it*. Yet a BIOC, by definition, must be acting in good faith. Is this a contradiction? No. Plato might know that a third party has a security interest in Socrates' crops yet not realize that his purchase violates the third party's rights. Generally, for example, a security interest will permit a retailer to sell consumer goods, the presumption being that part of the proceeds will go to the secured party. A BIOC cannot be expected to determine what a retailer plans to do with the money he is paid.

You be the Judge

CONSECO FINANCE SERVICING CORP. v. LEE

2004 WL 1243417
Court of Appeals of Texas, 2004

Facts: Lila Williams purchased a new Roadtrek 200 motor home from New World R.V. Inc. She paid about $14,000 down and financed $63,000, giving a security interest to New World. The RV company assigned its security interest to Conseco Finance, which perfected. Two years later, Williams returned the vehicle to New World (the record does not indicate why), and New World sold the RV to Robert and Ann Lee for $42,800. A year later, Williams defaulted on her payments to Conseco.

The Lees sued Conseco, claiming to be BIOCs and asking for a court declaration that they had sole title to the Roadtrek. Conseco counterclaimed, seeking title based on its perfected security interest. The trial court ruled that the Lees were BIOCs, with full rights to the vehicle. Conseco appealed.

You Be the Judge: *Were the Lees BIOCs?*

Argument for Conseco: Under the UCC, a buyer in ordinary course takes free of a security interest *created by the buyer's seller.* The buyers were the Lees. The seller was New World. New World did not create the security interest—Lila Williams did. There is no security interest created by New World. The security interest held by Conseco was created by someone else (Williams) and is not affected by the Lees' status as BIOCs. The law is clear, and Conseco is entitled to the Roadtrek.

Argument for the Lees: Conseco weaves a clever argument, but let's look at what they are really saying. Two honest buyers, acting in perfect good faith, can walk into an RV dealership, spend $42,000 for a used vehicle, and end up with—nothing. Conseco claims it is entitled to an RV that the Lees paid for because someone that the Lees have never dealt with, never even heard of, gave *to this RV seller* a security interest which the seller, years earlier, passed on to a finance company. Conseco's argument defies common sense and the goals of Article 9.

PRIORITIES AMONG CREDITORS

What happens when two creditors have a security interest in the same collateral? The party who has **priority** in the collateral gets it. Typically, the debtor lacks assets to pay everyone, so all creditors struggle to be the first in line. After the first creditor has repossessed the collateral, sold it, and taken enough of the proceeds to pay off his debt, there may be nothing left for anyone else. (There may not even be enough to pay the first creditor all that he is due, in which case that creditor will sue for the deficiency.) Who gets priority? There are three principal rules.[10]

The first rule is easy: a party with a perfected security interest takes priority over a party with an unperfected interest. This is the whole point of perfecting: to ensure that your security interest gets priority over everyone else's. On August 15, Meredith's Market, an antique store, borrows $100,000 from the Happy Bank, which takes a security interest in all of Meredith's inventory. Happy Bank does not perfect. On September 15, Meredith uses the same collateral to borrow $50,000 from the Suspicion Bank, which files a financing statement the same day. On October 15, as if on cue, Meredith files for bankruptcy and stops paying both creditors. Suspicion wins because it holds a perfected interest, whereas the Happy Bank holds merely an unperfected interest.

[10]UCC Section 9-322(a)(2), UCC Section 9-322(a)(3), and UCC Section 9-322(a)(1).

The second rule: if neither secured party has perfected, the first interest to attach gets priority. Suppose that Suspicion Bank and Happy Bank had both failed to perfect. In that case, Happy Bank would have the first claim to Meredith's inventory since Happy's interest attached first.

And the third rule follows logically: between perfected security interests, the first to file or perfect wins. Diminishing Perspective, a railroad, borrows $75 million from the First Bank, which takes a security interest in Diminishing's rolling stock (railroad cars) and immediately perfects by filing. Two months later, Diminishing borrows $100 million from Second Bank, which takes a security interest in the same collateral and also files. When Diminishing arrives, on schedule, in bankruptcy court, both banks will race to seize the rolling stock. First Bank gets the railcars because it perfected first.

March 1	**April 2**	**May 3**	**The Winner:**
First Bank lends money and perfects its security interest by filing a financing statement.	Second Bank lends money and perfects its security interest by filing a financing statement.	Diminishing goes bankrupt, and both banks attempt to take the rolling stock.	First Bank, because it perfected first.

In the example above, it is easy to apply the rules. But sometimes courts must sort through additional complications. We know that a perfected security interest takes priority over others. But sometimes it is not clear exactly when the security interest was perfected. In the following case, the creditor got in just under the wire.

In Re Roser

613 F.3d 1240; 2010 U.S. App. LEXIS 14817
United States Court of Appeals for the Tenth Circuit, 2010

Case Summary

Facts: Robert Roser obtained a loan from Sovereign Bank, which he promptly used to buy a car. Nineteen days later, Sovereign filed a lien with the state of Colorado. The bank expected that with a perfected interest, it would have priority over everyone else.

Unknown to Sovereign Bank, Roser had declared bankruptcy only *12* days after he purchased the car. Later, the bankruptcy trustee argued that he had priority over Sovereign because the bankruptcy filing happened *before Sovereign perfected* its security interest. When the court found for the trustee, Sovereign Bank appealed.

Issue: *Did Sovereign Bank, a PMSI holder, obtain priority over the bankruptcy trustee?*

Decision: Yes, the PMSI holder obtained priority.

Reasoning: On the day that Roser entered bankruptcy, Sovereign Bank had not filed its financing statement, which means that its security interest was not yet perfected. Ordinarily, a bankruptcy trustee would take priority over all security interests that are unperfected on the day that a debtor files a bankruptcy petition. However, there is an exception to this rule: if the creditor files a financing statement for a PMSI within 20 days after the debtor receives the collateral, that security interest is deemed to have been perfected as of the date of the debtor receives the collateral, not the day on which the financing statement was filed. In this case, the bank filed within that 20-day grace period, so its security interest took priority over the bankruptcy trustee.

Reversed and remanded.

DEFAULT AND TERMINATION

We have reached the end of the line. Either the debtor has defaulted, or it has performed its obligations and may terminate the security agreement.

Default

The parties define "default" in their security agreement. Generally, a debtor defaults when he fails to make payments due or enters bankruptcy proceedings. The parties can agree that other acts will constitute default, such as the debtor's failure to maintain insurance on the collateral. When a debtor defaults, the secured party has two principal options: (1) it may take possession of the collateral; or (2) it may file suit against the debtor for the money owed. The secured party does not have to choose between these two remedies; it may try one after the other, or both simultaneously.

TAKING POSSESSION OF THE COLLATERAL

When the debtor defaults, the secured party may take possession of the collateral.[11] The secured party may act on its own, without any court order, and simply take the collateral, provided this can be done without a breach of the peace. Otherwise, the secured party must file suit against the debtor and request that the court order the debtor to deliver the collateral.

DISPOSITION OF THE COLLATERAL

Once the secured party has obtained possession of the collateral, it has two choices. The secured party may (1) dispose of the collateral; or (2) retain the collateral as full satisfaction of the debt. Notice that until the secured party disposes of the collateral, the debtor has the right to redeem it, that is, to pay the full value of the debt and retrieve her property.

A secured party may sell, lease, or otherwise dispose of the collateral in any commercially reasonable manner.[12] Typically, the secured party will sell the collateral in either a private or a public sale. First, however, the debtor must receive reasonable notice of the time and place of the sale so that she may bid on the collateral.

When the secured party has sold the collateral, it applies the proceeds of the sale: first, to its expenses in repossessing and selling the collateral, and second, to the debt. Sometimes the sale leaves a deficiency; that is, insufficient funds to pay off the debt. The debtor remains liable for the deficiency, and the creditor will sue for it. On the other hand, the sale of the collateral may yield a surplus; that is, a sum greater than the debt. The secured party must pay the surplus to the debtor.

Termination

Finally, we need to look at what happens when a debtor does not default, but pays the full debt. (You are forgiven if you have lost track of the fact that things sometimes work out smoothly.) Once that happens, the secured party must complete a termination statement, a document indicating that it no longer claims a security interest in the collateral.[13]

---

[11]UCC Section 9-609.
[12]UCC Section 9-610.
[13]UCC Section 9-513.

Chapter Conclusion

Borrowed money is the lubricant that keeps a modern economy motoring smoothly. Without it, many consumers would never own a car or stereo, and many businesses would be unable to grow. But unless these debts are repaid, the economy will falter. Secured transactions are one method for ensuring that creditors are paid.

EXAM REVIEW

1. **ARTICLE 9** Article 9 applies to any transaction intended to create a security interest in personal property or fixtures. (pp. 260–262)

2. **ATTACHMENT** Attachment means that (1) the two parties made a security agreement and either the debtor has authenticated a security agreement describing the collateral or the secured party has obtained possession; (2) the secured party gave value in order to get the security agreement; and (3) the debtor has rights in the collateral. (pp. 262–264)

3. **PERFECTION** Attachment protects against the debtor. Perfection of a security interest protects the secured party against parties other than the debtor. (pp. 264–269)

4. **FILING** Filing is the most common way to perfect. For many forms of collateral, the secured party may also perfect by obtaining either possession or control. (pp. 264–267)

5. **PMSI** A purchase money security interest is one taken by the person who sells the collateral or advances money so the debtor can buy the collateral. A PMSI in consumer goods perfects automatically. (pp. 268–269)

EXAM Strategy

Question: John and Clara Lockovich bought a 22-foot Chaparrel Villian II boat from Greene County Yacht Club for $32,500. They paid $6,000 cash and borrowed the rest of the purchase price from Gallatin National Bank, which took a security interest in the boat. Gallatin filed a financing statement in Greene County, Pennsylvania, where the bank was located. But Pennsylvania law requires financing statements to be filed in the county of the debtor's residence, and the Lockoviches lived in Allegheny County. The Lockoviches soon washed up in bankruptcy court. Other creditors demanded that the boat be sold, claiming that Gallatin's security interest had been filed in the wrong place. Who wins?

Strategy: Gallatin National Bank obtained a special kind of security interest in the boat. Identify that type of interest. What special rights does this give to the bank? (See the "Result" at the end of this section.)

6. **BIOC** A buyer in ordinary course of business takes the goods free of a security interest created by his seller even though the security interest is perfected. (pp. 270–271)

7. **PRIORITY** Priority among secured parties is generally as follows:

   a. A party with a perfected security interest takes priority over a party with an unperfected interest.
   b. If neither secured party has perfected, the first interest to attach gets priority.
   c. Between perfected security interests, the first to file or perfect wins. (pp. 271–272)

EXAM Strategy

Question: Barwell, Inc., sold McMann Golf Ball Co. a "preformer," a machine that makes golf balls, for $55,000. Barwell delivered the machine on February 20. McMann paid $3,000 down, the remainder to be paid over several years, and signed an agreement giving Barwell a security interest in the preformer. Barwell did not perfect its interest. On March 1, McMann borrowed $350,000 from First of America Bank, giving the bank a security interest in McMann's present and after-acquired property. First of America perfected by filing on March 2. McMann, of course, became insolvent, and both Barwell and the bank attempted to repossess the preformer. Who gets it?

Strategy: Two parties have a valid security interest in this machine. When that happens, there is a three-step process to determine which party gets priority. Apply them. (See the "Result" at the end of this section.)

8. **DEFAULT** When the debtor defaults, the secured party may take possession of the collateral and then sell, lease, or otherwise dispose of the collateral in any commercially reasonable way, or it may ignore the collateral and sue the debtor for the full debt. (p. 273)

5. Result: Gallatin advanced the money that the Lockoviches used to buy the boat, meaning the bank obtained a PMSI. A PMSI in consumer goods perfects automatically, without filing. The boat was a consumer good. Gallatin's security interest perfected without any filing at all, and so the bank wins.

7. Result: This question is resolved by the first of those three steps. A party with a perfected security interest takes priority over a party with an unperfected interest. The bank wins because its perfected security interest takes priority over Barwell's unperfected interest.

MATCHING QUESTIONS

Match the following terms with their definitions:

___A. Attachment

___B. BIOC

___C. Perfection

___D. PMSI

___E. Priority

1. Someone who buys goods in good faith from a seller who deals in such goods

2. Steps necessary to make a security interest valid against the whole world

3. A security interest taken by the person who sells the collateral or advances money so the debtor can buy it

4. The order in which creditors will be permitted to seize the property of a bankrupt debtor

5. Steps necessary to make a security interest valid against the debtor, but not against third parties

TRUE/FALSE QUESTIONS

Circle true or false:

1. T F A party with a perfected security interest takes priority over a party with an unperfected interest.

2. T F A buyer in ordinary course of business takes goods free of an unperfected security interest but does not take them free of a perfected security interest.

3. T F When a debtor defaults, a secured party may seize the collateral and hold it, using reasonable care, but may not sell or lease it.

4. T F A party may take a security interest in tangible things, such as goods, but not in intangible things, such as bank accounts.

5. T F Without an agreement of the parties, there can be no security interest.

MULTIPLE-CHOICE QUESTIONS

1. **CPA QUESTION:** Under the UCC Secured Transactions Article, perfection of a security interest by a creditor provides added protection against other parties if the debtor does not pay its debts. Which of the following parties is not affected by perfection of a security interest?

   (a) Other prospective creditors of the debtor

   (b) The trustee in a bankruptcy case

   (c) A buyer in the ordinary course of business

   (d) A subsequent personal injury judgment creditor

2. **CPA QUESTION:** Mars, Inc., manufactures and sells Blu-ray players on credit directly to wholesalers, retailers, and consumers. Mars can perfect its security interest in the goods it sells without having to file a financing statement or take possession of the Blu-ray players if the sale is made to which of the following:

(a) Retailers

(b) Wholesalers that sell to distributors for resale

(c) Consumers

(d) Wholesalers that sell to buyers in ordinary course of business

3. Bank has loaned unsecured money to Retailer, which still owes $700,000. Nervous that Retailer is on the verge of bankruptcy, Bank sends a "notice of security interest" to Retailer, claiming a security interest in all the inventory and real estate of Retailer. Retailer does not respond. Bank files its notice in the state's central filing office. When Retailer goes bankrupt, Bank

(a) Has a perfected security interest in the inventory, but not the real estate

(b) Has a perfected security interest in the real estate, but not the inventory

(c) Has a perfected security interest in both the real estate and the inventory

(d) Has no security interest in either the real estate or the inventory

(e) Has an unperfected security interest in both the real estate and the inventory

4. Which case does *not* represent a purchase money security interest?

(a) Auto Dealer sells Consumer a car on credit.

(b) Wholesaler sells Retailer 5,000 pounds of candy on credit.

(c) Bank lends money to Retailer, using Retailer's existing inventory as collateral.

(d) Bank lends money to Auto Dealer to purchase 150 new cars, which are the collateral.

(e) Consumer applies to Credit Agency for a loan with which to buy a yacht.

5. Millie lends Arthur, her next-door neighbor, $25,000. He gives her his diamond ring as collateral for the loan. Which statement is true?

(a) Millie has no valid security interest in the ring because the parties did not enter into a security agreement.

(b) Millie has no valid security interest in the ring because she has not filed appropriate papers.

(c) Millie has an attached, unperfected security interest in the ring.

(d) Millie has an attached, unperfected security interest in the ring, but she can perfect her interest by filing.

(e) Millie has an attached, perfected security interest in the ring.

Essay Questions

1. The Copper King Inn, Inc., had money problems. It borrowed $62,500 from two of its officers, Noonan and Patterson, but that did not suffice to keep the inn going. So Noonan, on behalf of Copper King, arranged for the inn to borrow $100,000 from Northwest Capital, an investment company that worked closely with Noonan in other ventures. Copper King signed an agreement giving Patterson, Noonan, and Northwest a security interest in the inn's furniture and equipment. But the financing statement that the parties filed made no mention of Northwest. Copper King went

bankrupt. Northwest attempted to seize assets, but other creditors objected. Is Northwest entitled to Copper King's furniture and equipment?

2. Sears sold a lawn tractor to Cosmo Fiscante for $1,481. Fiscante paid with his personal credit card. Sears kept a valid security interest in the lawnmower but did not perfect. Fiscante had the machine delivered to his business, Trackers Raceway Park, the only place he ever used the machine. When Fiscante was unable to meet his obligations, various creditors attempted to seize the lawnmower. Sears argued that because it had a PMSI in the lawnmower, its interest had perfected automatically. Is Sears correct?

3. **ETHICS:** The Dannemans bought a Kodak copier worth over $40,000. Kodak arranged financing by GECC and assigned its rights to that company. Although the Dannemans thought they had purchased the copier on credit, the papers described the deal as a lease. The Dannemans had constant problems with the machine and stopped making payments. GECC repossessed the machine and, without notifying the Dannemans, sold it back to Kodak for $12,500, leaving a deficiency of $39,927. GECC sued the Dannemans for that amount. The Dannemans argued that the deal was not a lease, but a sale on credit. Why does it matter whether the parties had a sale or a lease? Is GECC entitled to its money? Finally, comment on the ethics. Why did the Dannemans not understand the papers they had signed? Who is responsible for that? Are you satisfied with the ethical conduct of the Dannemans? Kodak? GECC?

4. Alpha perfects its security interest by properly filing a financing statement on January 1, 2010. Alpha files a continuation statement on September 1, 2014. It files another continuation statement on September 1, 2018. When will Alpha's financing statement expire? Why?

5. The state of Kentucky filed a tax lien against Panbowl Energy, claiming unpaid taxes. Six months later, Panbowl bought a powerful drill from Whayne Supply, making a down payment of $11,500 and signing a security agreement for the remaining debt of $220,000. Whayne perfected the next day. Panbowl defaulted. Whayne sold the drill for $58,000, leaving a deficiency of just over $100,000. The state filed suit, seeking the $58,000 proceeds. The trial court gave summary judgment to the state, and Whayne appealed. Who gets the $58,000?

DISCUSSION QUESTIONS

1. In the opening scenario, the bank demanded $5,000 from poor Sam for his Jeep that had been repossessed and sold to someone else. As we have seen, Article 9 gives the bank the right to demand this payment. But is that fair? Should Article 9 change so that a person like Sam does not have to pay? Or is the law reasonable now?

2. After reading this chapter, will your behavior as a consumer change? Are there any types of transactions that you might be more inclined to avoid?

3. After reading this chapter, will your future behavior as a businessperson change? What specific steps will you be most careful to take to protect your interests?

4. A perfected security interest is far from perfect. We examined several exceptions to normal perfection rules involving BIOCs, consumer goods, and so on. Are the exceptions reasonable? Should the UCC change to give the holder of a perfected interest absolute rights against absolutely everyone else?

5. Do you agree with the court's decision in the *Corona Fruits & Veggies* case? Did the court resolve the confusion over the farmer's name *fairly*, or should Corona's interest have perfected?

CHAPTER 16

BANKRUPTCY

Three bankruptcy stories:

1. Tim's account: "It happened all at once. My daughter's basketball team qualified for the nationals at Disney World. The kids had never gone to Disney World. How could we say no? Then my car died. And I didn't get a bonus this year. Next thing you know, we had $27,000 in credit card debt. Then we had some uninsured medical bills. There was just no way we could pay all that money back."

© picsbyst/Shutterstock.com

2. Kristen had always loved flowers. When the guy who owned the local flower shop wanted to retire, it seemed a great opportunity to buy the business. Everything went really well at first. Then the recession hit, and people cut back on nonessentials like flowers. How could she pay her loans?

3. General Motors (GM), once a symbol of American business, filed for bankruptcy in 2009. At the time, its liabilities were $90 billion more than its assets. It also had 325,000 employees and even more stakeholders: retired employees, car owners, suppliers, investors, and communities in which it operated and its employees lived and paid taxes. A mere 40 days after the filing, GM emerged from bankruptcy. The next year, the company was profitable.

> The kids had never gone to Disney World. How could we say no?

Bankruptcy laws are controversial. Typically, in other countries, their goal is to protect creditors and punish debtors, but American laws are more lenient towards the bankrupt.

The General Motors example illustrates the good news about American bankruptcy. It is efficient (taking only 40 days!) and effective at reviving ailing companies. Everyone—investors, employees, the country—benefits from GM's survival. And, although Kristen's flower shop did not survive, bankruptcy laws will protect her so that she is not afraid to try entrepreneurship again. New businesses fail more often than not, but they are nonetheless important engines of growth for our country.

Tim represents the bad news in bankruptcy laws. Unfortunately, he is often the type of person who first comes to mind when people think about bankrupts. And people do not like Tim very much. They think: why should he be rewarded for his irresponsibility, when I get stuck paying all my bills? But a more difficult bankruptcy process will probably not discourage Tim. He is the kind of guy who cares a lot about current pleasures and little about future pain. No matter what bankruptcy laws are in place, he will not say no to Disney World. Should the laws become too onerous, businesses will fail, entrepreneurs will be discouraged, and the Tims of the world will continue to spend more than they should.

But maybe America has too much of a good thing. This nation has the highest bankruptcy rate in the world. In the most recent year, there was one bankruptcy filing for every 200 Americans.[1] Clearly, bankruptcy laws play a vital role in our economy. At the same time, it is important not to enable irresponsible spendthrifts. Do American bankruptcy laws strike the right balance?

OVERVIEW OF BANKRUPTCY

The U.S. Bankruptcy Code (the Code) has three primary goals:

- To preserve as much of the debtor's property as possible,

- To divide the debtor's assets fairly between the debtor and creditors, and

- To divide the creditors' share of the assets fairly among them.

The following options are available under the Bankruptcy Code:

Number	Topic	Description
Chapter 7	Liquidation	The bankrupt's assets are sold to pay creditors. If the debtor owns a business, it terminates. The creditors have no right to the debtor's future earnings.
Chapter 11	Reorganization	This chapter is designed for businesses and wealthy individuals. Businesses continue to operate, and creditors receive a portion of both current assets and future earnings.
Chapter 13	Consumer reorganization	Chapter 13 offers reorganization for the typical consumer. Creditors usually receive a portion of the individual's current assets and future earnings.

---

[1]Some of these filings are by businesses, although that percentage is small. In the last 15 years, more than 95 percent of all bankruptcy filings have been by consumers.

The goal of Chapters 11 and 13 is to rehabilitate the debtor. These chapters hold creditors at bay while the debtor develops a payment plan. In return for retaining some of their assets, debtors typically promise to pay creditors a portion of their future earnings. However, when debtors are unable to develop a feasible plan for rehabilitation under Chapter 11 or 13, Chapter 7 provides for liquidation (also known as a **straight bankruptcy**). Most of the debtor's assets are distributed to creditors, but the debtor has no obligation to share future earnings.

Debtors are sometimes eligible to file under more than one chapter. No choice is irrevocable because both debtors and creditors have the right to ask the court to convert a case from one chapter to another at any time during the proceedings.

Straight bankruptcy

Also known as liquidation, this form of bankruptcy mandates that the bankrupt's assets be sold to pay creditors, but the bankrupt has no obligation to share future earnings.

CHAPTER 7 LIQUIDATION

All bankruptcy cases proceed in a roughly similar pattern, regardless of chapter. We use Chapter 7 as a template to illustrate common features of all bankruptcy cases. Later on, the discussions of the other Chapters will indicate how they differ from Chapter 7.

Filing a Petition

Any individual, partnership, corporation, or other business organization that lives, conducts business, or owns property in the United States can file under the Code. (Chapter 13, however, is available only to individuals.) The traditional term for someone who could not pay his debts was **bankrupt**, but the Code uses the term **debtor** instead. We use both terms interchangeably.

A case begins with the filing of a bankruptcy petition in federal district court. Debtors may go willingly into the bankruptcy process by filing a voluntary petition, or they may be dragged into court by creditors who file an involuntary petition.

Bankrupt

Someone who cannot pay his debts and files for protection under the Bankruptcy Code.

Debtor

Another term for bankrupt.

VOLUNTARY PETITION

Any debtor (whether a business or individual) has the right to file for bankruptcy. It is not necessary that the debtor's liabilities exceed assets. Debtors sometimes file a bankruptcy petition because cash flow is so tight they cannot pay their debts, even though they are not technically insolvent. However, *individuals* must meet two requirements before filing:

- Within 180 days before the filing, an individual debtor must undergo credit counseling with an approved agency.

- Individual debtors may file under Chapter 7 only if they earn less than the median income in their state *or* they cannot afford to pay back at least $7,025 over five years.[2] Generally, all other debtors must file under Chapters 11 or 13. (These Chapters require the bankrupt to repay some debt.)

---

[2]In some circumstances, debtors with income higher than $7,025 may still be eligible to file under Chapter 7, but the formula is highly complex and more than most readers want to know. The formula is available at 11 USC Section 707(b)(2)(A). Also, you can google "bapcpa means test" and then click on the Department of Justice website. The dollar amounts are updated every three years. You can find them by googling "federal register bankruptcy revision of dollar amounts."

The voluntary petition must include the following documents:

Document	Description
Petition	Begins the case. Easy to fill out, it requires checking a few boxes and typing in name, address, and social security number.
List of Creditors	The names and addresses of all creditors.
Schedule of Assets and Liabilities	A list of the debtor's assets and debts.
Claim of Exemptions	A list of all assets that the debtor is entitled to keep.
Schedule of Income and Expenditures	The debtor's job, income, and expenses.
Statement of Financial Affairs	A summary of the debtor's financial history and current financial condition. In particular, the debtor must list any recent payments to creditors and any other property held by someone else for the debtor.

INVOLUNTARY PETITION

Creditors may force a debtor into bankruptcy by filing an involuntary petition. The creditors' goals are to preserve as much of the debtor's assets as possible and to ensure that all creditors receive a fair share. Naturally, the Code sets strict limits—debtors cannot be forced into bankruptcy every time they miss a credit card payment. An involuntary petition must meet all of the following requirements:

- The debtor must owe at least $14,425 in unsecured claims to the creditors who file.

- If the debtor has at least 12 creditors, 3 or more must sign the petition. If the debtor has fewer than 12 creditors, any of them may file a petition.

- The creditors must allege either that a custodian for the debtor's property has been appointed in the prior 120 days or that the debtor has generally not been paying debts that are due.

What does "a custodian for the debtor's property" mean? *State* laws sometimes permit the appointment of a custodian to protect a debtor's assets. The Code allows creditors to pull a case out from under state law and into federal bankruptcy court by filing an involuntary petition.

Once a voluntary petition is filed or an involuntary petition approved, the bankruptcy court issues an **order for relief**. This order is an official acknowledgment that the debtor is under the jurisdiction of the court, and it is, in a sense, the start of the bankruptcy process. An involuntary debtor must now make all the filings that accompany a voluntary petition.

Order for relief

An official acknowledgment that a debtor is under the jurisdiction of the bankruptcy court.

Trustee

The trustee is responsible for gathering the bankrupt's assets and dividing them among creditors. The creditors have the right to elect a trustee, but often they do not bother. In this case, the **U.S. Trustee** makes the selection. The U.S. Attorney General appoints a U.S. Trustee for each region of the country to administer the bankruptcy law.

U.S. Trustee

Oversees the administration of bankruptcy law in a region.

Creditors

After the order for relief, the U.S. Trustee calls a meeting of all of the creditors. At this meeting, the bankrupt must answer (under oath) any question the creditors pose about his financial situation. If the creditors want to elect a trustee, they do so now.

After the meeting of creditors, unsecured creditors must submit a **proof of claim**. The proof of claim is a simple form stating the name of the creditor and the amount of the claim. Secured creditors do not file proofs of claim.

Proof of claim
A form stating the name of an unsecured creditor and the amount of the claim against the debtor.

Automatic Stay

A fox chased by hounds has no time to make rational long-term decisions. What that fox needs is a safe burrow. Similarly, it is difficult for debtors to make sound financial decisions when hounded night and day by creditors shouting, "Pay me! Pay me!" The Code is designed to give debtors enough breathing space to sort out their affairs sensibly. An **automatic stay** is a safe burrow for the bankrupt. It goes into effect as soon as the petition is filed. An automatic stay prohibits creditors from collecting debts that the bankrupt incurred before the petition was filed. Creditors may not sue a bankrupt to obtain payment nor may they take other steps, outside of court, to pressure the debtor for payment. The following case illustrates how persistent creditors can be.

Automatic stay
Prohibits creditors from collecting debts that the bankrupt incurred before the petition was filed.

Jackson v. Holiday Furniture

309 B.R. 33, 2004 Bankr. LEXIS 548
United States Bankruptcy Court for the Western District of Missouri, 2004

Case Summary

Facts: In April, Cora and Frank Jackson purchased a recliner chair on credit from Dan Holiday Furniture. They made payments until November. That month, they filed for protection under the Bankruptcy Code. Dan Holiday received a notice of the bankruptcy. This notice stated that the store must stop all efforts to collect on the Jacksons' debt.

Despite this notice, a Dan Holiday collector telephoned the Jacksons' house 10 times between November 15 and December 1 and left a card in their door threatening repossession of the chair. On December 1, Frank, without Cora's knowledge, went to Dan Holiday to pay the $230.00 owed for November and December. He told the store owner about the bankruptcy filing but allegedly added that he and his wife wanted to continue making payments directly to Dan Holiday.

In early January, employees at Dan Holiday learned that Frank had died the month before. Nevertheless, after Cora failed to make the payment for the month of January, a collector telephoned her house 26 times between January 14 and February 19. The store owner's sister left the following message on Cora's answering machine:

Hello. This is Judy over at Dan Holiday Furniture. And this is the last time I am going to call you. If you do not call me, I will be at your house. And I expect you to call me today. If there is

a problem, I need to speak to you about it. You need to call me. We need to get this thing going. You are a January and February payment behind. And if you think you are going to get away with it, you've got another thing coming.

When Cora returned home on February 18, she found seven bright yellow slips of paper in her doorjamb stating that a Dan Holiday truck had stopped by to repossess her furniture. The cards read:

OUR TRUCK was here to REPOSSESS Your furniture [sic]. 241-6933 Dan Holiday Furn. & Appl. Co.

The threat to send a truck was merely a ruse designed to frighten Cora. In truth, Dan Holiday did not really want the recliner back. The owner just wanted to talk directly with Cora about making payments.

Also on February 18, Dan Holiday sent Cora a letter stating that she had 24 hours to bring her account current or else "Repossession Will Be Made and Legal Action Will Be Taken." That same day, Cora's bankruptcy attorney contacted Dan Holiday. Thereafter, all collection activity ceased.

Issues: *Did Dan Holiday violate the automatic stay provisions of the Bankruptcy Code? What is the penalty for a violation?*

Decision: Dan Holiday was in violation of the Bankruptcy Code. The court awarded the Jacksons their actual damages, attorney's fees, court costs, and punitive damages.

Reasoning: Creditors who violate the automatic stay provisions must pay both actual damages (including court costs and attorney's fees) as well as punitive damages where appropriate. In this case, the court awarded actual damages of $230.00, because that is how much Dan Holiday coerced from Frank Jackson on December 1. The court also awarded the Jacksons their attorney's fees and court costs in the amount of $1,142.42.

In addition, the Jacksons were entitled to punitive damages because Dan Holiday intentionally and flagrantly violated the automatic stay provision. Dan Holiday's conduct was remarkably bad—employees called the Jackson household no less than 26 times in January and February.

The court did not know how much to award in punitive damages because no evidence was presented at trial about how much Dan Holiday could afford. But assuming that it was a relatively small business, the court awarded $2,800 in punitive damages. That was $100 for each illegal contact with the Jacksons after December 1—the date when it was crystal clear that Dan Holiday knew about the bankruptcy filing. This penalty was designed to sting the pocketbook of Dan Holiday and impress upon the company the importance of complying with the provisions of the Bankruptcy Code.

Bankruptcy Estate

The filing of the bankruptcy petition creates a new legal entity separate from the debtor—the **bankruptcy estate**. All of the bankrupt's assets pass to the estate, except exempt property and new property that the debtor acquires after the petition is filed.

Bankruptcy estate
The new legal entity created when a debtor files a bankruptcy petition. All of the debtor's existing assets pass into the estate.

EXEMPT PROPERTY

The Code permits *individual* debtors (but not organizations) to keep some property for themselves. This exempt property saves the debtor from destitution during the bankruptcy process and provides the foundation for a new life once the process is over.

In this one area of bankruptcy law, the Code defers to state law. Although the Code lists various types of exempt property, it permits states to opt out of the federal system and define a different set of exemptions. However, debtors can take advantage of state exemptions only if they have lived in that state for two years prior to the bankruptcy.

Under the *federal* Code, a debtor is allowed to exempt only $21,625 of the value of her home. Many *states* exempt items such as the debtor's home, household goods, cars, work tools, disability and pension benefits, alimony, and health aids. Both Florida and Texas permit debtors to keep homes of unlimited value and a certain amount of land. But the federal statute limits this state exemption to $146,450 for any house that was acquired during the 40 months before the bankruptcy.

VOIDABLE PREFERENCES

A major goal of the bankruptcy system is to divide the debtor's assets fairly among creditors. It would not be fair if debtors were permitted to pay off some of their creditors immediately before filing a bankruptcy petition. Such a payment is called a **preference** because it gives unfair preferential treatment to a creditor. **The trustee can void any transfer to a creditor that took place in the 90-day period before the filing of a petition.**

Preference
When a debtor unfairly pays creditors immediately before filing a bankruptcy petition.

FRAUDULENT TRANSFERS

Suppose that a debtor sees bankruptcy approaching across the horizon like a tornado. He knows that, once the storm hits and he files a petition, everything he owns except a few items of exempt property will become part of the bankruptcy estate. Before that happens, he may be tempted to give some of his property to friends or family to shelter it from the tornado. If he succumbs to that temptation, however, he is committing a fraudulent transfer. **A transfer is fraudulent if it is made within the year before a petition is filed and its purpose is to hinder, delay, or defraud creditors.** The trustee can void any fraudulent transfer. The debtor has committed a crime and may be prosecuted.

EXAM Strategy

Question: Lawrence and his wife, Diana, enjoyed a luxurious lifestyle while his investment bank flourished. But when the bank failed, Lawrence was faced with debts of $6 million. On the eve of the bankruptcy filing, Diana suddenly announced that she wanted a divorce. In what had to be the most amicable breakup ever, Lawrence willingly transferred all of his assets to her. The unhappy couple went on to obtain their divorce in only two months, a speed that the bankruptcy court referred to as "astonishing." Was this transfer a voidable preference or a fraudulent transfer? What difference does it make?

Strategy: Begin by looking at the differences between these two types of wrongful transfers. Fraudulent transfers sound similar to voidable preferences, but there is an important distinction: voidable preferences pay legitimate debts, while fraudulent transfers protect the debtor's assets from legitimate creditors. A voidable transfer is a civil offense; a fraudulent transfer is a crime.

Result: The court found that Lawrence had committed a fraudulent transfer because he was attempting to protect his assets from creditors.

Payment of Claims

Imagine a crowded delicatessen on a Saturday evening. People are pushing and shoving because they know there is not enough food for everyone; some customers will go home hungry. The delicatessen could simply serve whoever pushes to the front of the line, or it could establish a number system to ensure that the most deserving customers are served first. The Code has, in essence, adopted a number system to prevent a free-for-all fight over the bankrupt's assets. Indeed, one of the Code's primary goals is to ensure that creditors are paid in the proper order, not according to who pushes to the front of the line.

All claims are placed in one of three classes: (1) secured claims, (2) priority claims, and (3) unsecured claims. **The trustee pays the bankruptcy estate to the various classes of claims in order of rank.** A higher class is paid in full before the next class receives any payment at all. The debtor is entitled to any funds remaining after all claims have been paid. The payment order is shown in Exhibit 16.1.

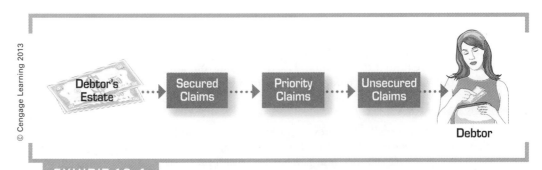

© Cengage Learning 2013

EXHIBIT 16.1

SECURED CLAIMS

Creditors whose loans are secured by specific collateral are paid first. Secured claims are fundamentally different from all other claims because they are paid not out of the general funds of the estate but by selling a specific asset.

PRIORITY CLAIMS

Each category of priority claims is paid in order, with the first group receiving full payment before the next group receives anything. Priority claims include:

- Alimony and child support,

- Administrative expenses (such as fees to the trustee, lawyers, and accountants),

- Back wages to the debtor's employees for work performed during the 180 days prior to the date of the petition, and

- Income and property taxes.

UNSECURED CLAIMS

Last, and frequently very much least, unsecured creditors have now reached the delicatessen counter. They can only hope that some assets remain.

Discharge

Filing a bankruptcy petition is embarrassing and time-consuming. It can affect the debtor's credit rating for years, making the simplest car loan a challenge. To encourage debtors to file for bankruptcy despite the pain involved, the Code offers a powerful incentive: the **fresh start**. Once a bankruptcy estate has been distributed to creditors, they cannot make a claim against the debtor for money owed before the filing, *whether or not they actually received any payment*. These prepetition debts are **discharged**. All is forgiven, if not forgotten.

Discharge is an essential part of bankruptcy law. Without it, debtors would have little incentive to take part. To avoid abuses, however, the Code limits both the type of debts that can be discharged and the circumstances under which discharge can take place. In addition, a debtor must complete a course on financial management before receiving a discharge.

Fresh start
After the termination of a bankruptcy case, creditors cannot make a claim against the debtor for money owed before the initial bankruptcy petition was filed.

Discharge
The bankrupt no longer has an obligation to pay a debt.

DEBTS THAT CANNOT BE DISCHARGED

The following debts are among those that can never be discharged. The debtor remains liable in full until they are paid:

- Recent income and property taxes;

- Money obtained by fraud;

- Cash advances on a credit card totaling more than $875 that an individual debtor takes out within 70 days before the order of relief;

- Debts omitted from the Schedule of Assets and Liabilities;

- Money owed for alimony, maintenance, or child support;

- Debts stemming from intentional and malicious injury;

- Debts that result from a violation of securities laws; and

- Student loans (unless repayment would cause undue hardship to the debtor).

EXAM Strategy

Question: Someone stole a truck full of cigarettes. Zeke found the vehicle abandoned at a truck stop. Not being a thoughtful fellow, he took the truck and sold it with its cargo. Although Tobacco Company never found out who stole the truck originally, it did discover Zeke's role. A court ordered Zeke to pay Tobacco $50,000. He also owed his wife $25,000 in child support. Unfortunately, he only had $20,000 in assets. After he files for bankruptcy, who will get paid what?

Strategy: There are two issues: the order in which the debts are paid and whether they will be discharged.

Result: Child support is a priority claim, so that will be paid first. In a similar case, the court refused to discharge the claim over the theft of the truck, ruling that that was an intentional and malicious injury. Nor will a court discharge the child support claim. So Zeke will be on the hook for both debts, but the child support must be paid first.

CIRCUMSTANCES THAT PREVENT DEBTS FROM BEING DISCHARGED

The Code also prohibits the discharge of debts under the following circumstances:

- *Business organizations.* Under Chapter 7 (but not the other Chapters), only the debts of individuals can be discharged, not those of business organizations. Once its assets have been distributed, an organization must cease operation. If the company resumes business again, it becomes responsible for all its prefiling debts.

- *Revocation.* A court can revoke a discharge within one year if it discovers the debtor engaged in fraud or concealment.

- *Dishonesty or bad-faith behavior.* The court may deny discharge altogether if the debtor has made fraudulent transfers, hidden assets, or otherwise acted in bad faith.

- *Repeated filings for bankruptcy.* A debtor who has received a discharge under Chapter 7 or 11 cannot receive another discharge under Chapter 7 for at least eight years after the prior filing. And a debtor who received a prior discharge under Chapter 13, cannot in most cases receive one under Chapter 7 for at least six years.

Ethics Banks and credit card companies lobbied Congress hard to insert the prohibition against repeat bankruptcy filings. They argued that irresponsible consumers run up debt and then blithely walk away. You might think that, if this were true, lenders would avoid customers with a history of bankruptcy. New research indicates, though, that lenders actually target those consumers, repeatedly sending them offers to borrow money. The reason is simple: these consumers are much more likely to take cash advances, which carry very high interest rates. And this is one audience that must repay its loans, for the simple reason that these borrowers cannot obtain a discharge again anytime soon.[3] Is this strategy ethical?

---

[3]See Porter, Katherine M., "Bankrupt Profits: The Credit Industry's Business Model for Postbankruptcy Lending," *Iowa Law Review*, Vol. 94, 2008.

REAFFIRMATION

Sometimes debtors are willing to **reaffirm** a debt, meaning they promise to pay even after discharge. They may want to reaffirm a secured debt to avoid losing the collateral. For example, a debtor who has taken out a loan secured by a car may reaffirm that debt so that the finance company will not repossess it. Sometimes debtors reaffirm because they feel guilty or want to maintain a good relationship with the creditor. They may have borrowed from a family member or an important supplier.

Because discharge is a fundamental pillar of the bankruptcy process, creditors are not permitted to unfairly pressure the bankrupt. A reaffirmation must be approved by the court if the debtor is not represented by an attorney or if, as a result of the reaffirmed debt, the bankrupt's expenses exceed his income.

In the following case, the debtor sought to reaffirm the loan on his truck. He may have been afraid that if he did not, the lender would repossess it, leaving him stranded. It is hard to get around Dallas without a car. Should the court permit the reaffirmation?

Reaffirm

To promise to pay a debt even after it is discharged.

In Re: Grisham

436 B.R. 896; 2010 Bankr. LEXIS 2907
United States Bankruptcy Court for the Northern District of Texas, 2010

CASE SUMMARY

Facts: William Grisham owned a Dodge truck. When he filed for bankruptcy, the vehicle was worth $16,000, but he owed $17,500 on it. The monthly payments were $400. In addition, Grisham owed $200,000 in non-dischargeable debt and $70,000 in unsecured loans.

Grisham sought to reaffirm the truck loan. Should the court allow him to do so?

Issue: *Would reaffirmation of this debt create an undue hardship for the debtor?*

Decision: The court did not approve the reaffirmation.

Reasoning: The debtor's expenses are $1,100 a month higher than his income. He owns no real estate and is living rent-free with a relative. The truck is worth less than he owes on it. The debtor also has enormous non-dischargeable debts. While the monthly payments on the vehicle are not eye-popping, they are nonetheless unduly burdensome for him.

The whole point of a bankruptcy filing is to obtain a fresh start. It is about belt-tightening and shedding past bad habits. Too often, bankrupts do not understand this principle and instead want to go forward in a manner that will impair their fresh start and perpetuate bad habits from the past.

The court presumes that the debtor wants to reaffirm the debt to prevent the lender from repossessing the truck. But the debtor never explained why he especially needed this vehicle. The time has come simply to say "good riddance" to it.

The court will not stamp its seal of approval on the debtor's reaffirmation of the debt. To do so would create a hardship on this debtor and does not otherwise seem justified.

CHAPTER 11 REORGANIZATION

For a business, the goal of a Chapter 7 bankruptcy is euthanasia—putting it out of its misery by shutting it down and distributing its assets to creditors. Chapter 11 has a much more complicated and ambitious goal—resuscitating a business so that it can ultimately emerge as a viable economic concern, as GM did.

Both individuals and businesses can use Chapter 11. Businesses usually prefer Chapter 11 over Chapter 7 because Chapter 11 does not require them to dissolve at the end, as Chapter 7 does. The threat of death creates a powerful incentive to try rehabilitation under Chapter 11. Individuals, however, tend to prefer Chapter 13 because it is specifically designed for them.

A Chapter 11 proceeding follows many of the same steps as Chapter 7: a petition (either voluntary or involuntary), an order for relief, a meeting of creditors, proofs of claim, and an automatic stay. There are, however, some significant differences.

Debtor in Possession

Chapter 11 does not require a trustee. The bankrupt is called the **debtor in possession** and, in essence, serves as trustee. The debtor in possession has two jobs: to operate the business and to develop a plan of reorganization. A trustee is chosen only if the debtor is incompetent or uncooperative. In that case, the creditors can elect the trustee, but if they do not choose to do so, the U.S. Trustee appoints one.

Creditors' Committee

In a Chapter 11 case, the creditors' committee is important because typically there is no neutral trustee to watch over the committee's interests. The committee may play a role in developing the plan of reorganization. The U.S. Trustee typically appoints the seven largest *un*secured creditors to the committee, although the court has the right to require the appointment of some small-business creditors as well.

Plan of Reorganization

Once the bankruptcy petition is filed, an automatic stay goes into effect to provide the debtor with temporary relief from creditors. The next stage is to develop a plan of reorganization that provides for the payment of debts and the continuation of the business. For the first 120 days after the order for relief, the debtor has the exclusive right to propose a plan. If the shareholders and creditors accept it, then the bankruptcy case terminates. If the creditors or shareholders reject the debtor's plan, they may file their own version.

Confirmation of the Plan

All the creditors and shareholders have the right to vote on the plan of reorganization. In preparation for the vote, each creditor and shareholder is assigned to a class. Chapter 11 classifies claims in the same way as Chapter 7: (1) secured claims, (2) priority claims, and (3) unsecured claims.

The bankruptcy court will approve a plan if a majority of *each* class votes in favor of it *and* if the "yes" votes hold at least two-thirds of the total debt in that class. Even if some classes vote against the plan, the court can still confirm it under what is called a **cramdown** (as in, "the plan is crammed down the creditors' throats"). If the court rejects the plan of reorganization, the creditors must develop a new one.

Discharge

A confirmed plan of reorganization is binding on the debtor and creditors. **The debtor now owns the assets in the bankrupt estate, free of all obligations except those listed in the plan.** Under a typical plan of reorganization, the debtor gives some current assets to creditors and also promises to pay them a portion of future earnings. In contrast, the Chapter 7 debtor typically relinquishes all assets (except exempt property) to creditors

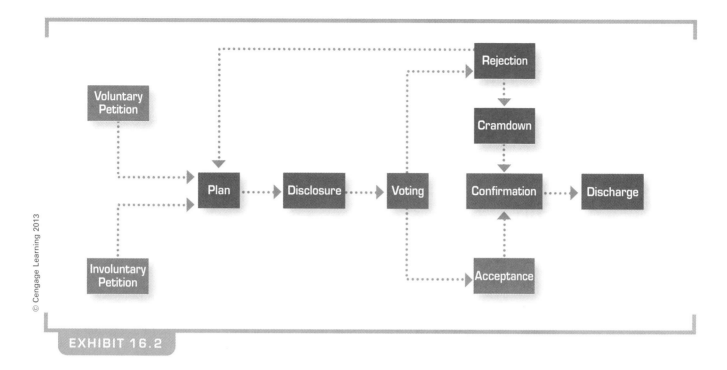

© Cengage Learning 2013

EXHIBIT 16.2

but then has no obligation to turn over future income. Exhibit 16.2 illustrates the steps in a Chapter 11 bankruptcy.

Small-Business Bankruptcy

Out of concern that the lengthy procedure in Chapter 11 was harming the creditors of small businesses, Congress decided to speed up the bankruptcy process for businesses with less than $2 million in debt. After the order of relief, the bankrupt has the exclusive right to file a plan for 180 days. The court must confirm or reject the plan within 45 days after its filing. If these deadlines are not met, the case can be converted to Chapter 7 or dismissed.

CHAPTER 13 CONSUMER REORGANIZATIONS

The purpose of Chapter 13 is to rehabilitate an individual debtor. It is not available at all to businesses or to individuals with more than $360,475 in unsecured debts or $1,081,400 in secured debts. Under Chapter 13, the bankrupt consumer typically keeps most of her assets in exchange for a promise to repay some of her debts using future income. Therefore, to be eligible, the debtor must have a regular source of income. Individuals usually choose this chapter because it is easier and cheaper than Chapters 7 and 11.

A bankruptcy under Chapter 13 generally follows the same course as Chapter 11: the debtor files a petition, creditors submit proofs of claim, the court imposes an automatic stay, the debtor files a plan, and the court confirms the plan. But there are some differences.

Beginning a Chapter 13 Case

To initiate a Chapter 13 case, the debtor must file a voluntary petition. Creditors cannot use an involuntary petition to force a debtor into Chapter 13. In all Chapter 13 cases, the U.S. Trustee appoints a trustee to supervise the debtor. The trustee also serves as a central clearinghouse for the debtor's payments to creditors. The debtor pays the trustee who, in turn, transmits these funds to creditors. For this service, the trustee is allowed to keep up to 10 percent of the payments.

Plan of Payment

The debtor must file a plan of payment within 15 days after filing the voluntary petition. Only the bankruptcy court has the authority to confirm or reject a plan of payment. Creditors have no right to vote on it. However, to confirm a plan, the court must ensure that:

- The plan is feasible and the bankrupt will be able to make the promised payments;
- The plan does not extend beyond three years without good reason and in no event lasts longer than five years;
- If the plan does not provide for the debtor to pay off creditors in full, then all of the debtor's disposable income for the next five years must go to creditors; and
- The debtor is acting in good faith, making a reasonable effort to pay obligations.

Discharge

Once confirmed, a plan is binding on all creditors whether they like it or not. **The debtor is washed clean of all prepetition debts except those provided for in the plan.** But if the debtor violates the plan, all of the debts are revived, and the creditors have a right to recover them under Chapter 7. The debts become permanently discharged only when the bankrupt fully complies with the plan. Note, however, that any debtor who has received a discharge under Chapter 7 or 11 within the prior four years or under Chapter 13 within the prior two years is not eligible for discharge under Chapter 13.

If the debtor's circumstances change, the debtor, the trustee, or unsecured creditors can ask the court to modify the plan. Most such requests come from debtors whose income has declined. However, if the debtor's income rises, the creditors or the trustee can ask that payments increase, too.

Chapter Conclusion

Bankruptcy law is the safety net that catches those who are not able to meet their financial obligations. Bankruptcy laws cannot create assets where there are none, but they can ensure that the debtor's assets, however limited, are fairly divided between the debtor and creditors. Any bankruptcy system that accomplishes this goal must be deemed a success.

EXAM REVIEW

The following chart sets out the important elements of each bankruptcy chapter.

	Chapter 7	**Chapter 11**	**Chapter 13**
Objective	Liquidation	Reorganization	Consumer reorganization
Who May Use It	Individual or organization	Individual or organization	Individual
Type of Petition	Voluntary or involuntary	Voluntary or involuntary	Only voluntary
Administration of Bankruptcy Estate	Trustee	Debtor in possession (trustee selected only if debtor is unable to serve)	Trustee
Selection of Trustee	Creditors have right to elect trustee; otherwise, U.S. Trustee makes appointment	Usually no trustee	Appointed by U.S. Trustee
Participation in Formulation of Plan	No plan is filed	Both creditors and debtor can propose plans	Only debtor can propose a plan
Creditor Approval of Plan	Creditors do not vote	Creditors vote on plan, but court may approve plan without the creditors' support	Creditors do not vote
Impact on Debtor's Post-Petition Income	Not affected; debtor keeps all future earnings	Must contribute toward payment of pre-petition debts	Must contribute toward payment of pre-petition debts

1. Question: Mark Milbank's custom furniture business was unsuccessful, so he repeatedly borrowed money from his wife and her father. He promised that the loans would enable him to spend more time with his family. Instead, he spent more time in bed with his next-door neighbor. After the divorce, his ex-wife and her father demanded repayment of the loans. Milbank filed for protection under Chapter 13. What could his ex-wife and her father do to help their chances of being repaid?

Strategy: First ask yourself what kind of creditor they are: secured or unsecured. Then think about what creditors can do to get special treatment. (See the "Result" at the end of this section.)

2. Question: After a jury ordered actor Kim Basinger to pay $8 million for violating a movie contract, she filed for bankruptcy protection, claiming $5 million in assets and $11 million in liabilities. Under which Chapter should she file? Why?

Strategy: Look at the requirements for each Chapter. Was Basinger eligible for Chapter 13? What would be the advantages and disadvantages of Chapters 7 and 11? (See the "Result" at the end of this section.)

<u>**1. Result**</u>:   The father and the ex-wife were unsecured creditors who, as a class, come last on the priority list. The court granted their request not to discharge their loans on the grounds that Milbank had acted in bad faith.

<u>**2. Result**</u>:   Basinger was not eligible to file under Chapter 13 because she had debts of $11 million. She first filed under Chapter 11 in a effort to retain some of her assets, but then her creditors would not approve her plan of reorganization, so she converted to liquidation under Chapter 7.

MATCHING QUESTIONS

Match the following terms with the correct description:

___A. Discharge

___B. Fraudulent transfer

___C. Exempt property

___D. Reaffirmation

___E. Voidable preference

1. Property that individual debtors can keep for themselves
2. Debtors are not liable for money owed before the filing
3. Debtor's promise to pay a debt after discharge
4. Payment to a creditor immediately before filing
5. Payment made within the year before a petition is filed with the goal of hindering creditors

TRUE/FALSE QUESTIONS

Circle true or false:

1. T F One of the primary goals of the Code is to teach the debtor a lesson.
2. T F Each of the Code's Chapters has one of two objectives—rehabilitation or liquidation.
3. T F A creditor is not permitted to force a debtor into bankruptcy.
4. T F The bankruptcy court issues an order for relief to give the debtor a chance to file a petition.
5. T F The Code permits *individual* debtors (but not organizations) to keep some property for themselves.

MULTIPLE-CHOICE QUESTIONS

1. **CPA QUESTION:** Decal Corp. incurred substantial operating losses for the past three years. Unable to meet its current obligations, Decal filed a petition of reorganization under Chapter 11 of the federal Bankruptcy Code. Which of the following statements is correct?

   (a) A creditors' committee, if appointed, will consist of unsecured creditors.

   (b) The court must appoint a trustee to manage Decal's affairs.

   (c) Decal may continue in business only with the approval of a trustee.

   (d) The creditors' committee must select a trustee to manage Decal's affairs.

2. **CPA QUESTION:** A voluntary petition filed under the liquidation provisions of Chapter 7 of the federal Bankruptcy Code:

   (a) Is not available to a corporation unless it has previously filed a petition under the reorganization provisions of Chapter 11 of the Code

   (b) Automatically stays collection actions against the debtor except by secured creditors

   (c) Will be dismissed unless the debtor has 12 or more unsecured creditors whose claims total at least $5,000

   (d) Does not require the debtor to show that the debtor's liabilities exceed the fair market value of assets

3. **CPA QUESTION:** Unger owes a total of $50,000 to eight unsecured creditors and one fully secured creditor. Quincy is one of the unsecured creditors and is owed $6,000. Quincy has filed a petition against Unger under the liquidation provisions of Chapter 7 of the federal Bankruptcy Code. Unger has been unable to pay debts as they become due. Unger's liabilities exceed Unger's assets. Unger has filed papers opposing the bankruptcy petition. Which of the following statements regarding Quincy's petition is correct?

   (a) It will be dismissed because the secured creditor failed to join in the filing of the petition.

   (b) It will be dismissed because three unsecured creditors must join in the filing of the petition.

   (c) It will be granted because Unger's liabilities exceed Unger's assets.

   (d) It will be granted because Unger is unable to pay Unger's debts as they become due.

4. A debtor is not required to file the following document with his voluntary petition:

   (a) Budget statement for the following three years

   (b) Statement of financial affairs

   (c) List of creditors

   (d) Claim of exemptions

   (e) Schedule of income and expenditures

5. Grass Co. is in bankruptcy proceedings under Chapter 11. _____ serves as trustee. In the case of _____, the court can approve a plan of reorganization over the objections of the creditors.

   (a) The debtor in possession, a cramdown

   (b) A person appointed by the U.S. Trustee, fraud

   (c) The head of the creditors' committee, reaffirmation

   (d) The U.S. Trustee, voidable preference

ESSAY QUESTIONS

1. James, the owner of an auto parts store, told his employee, Rickey, to clean and paint some tires in the basement. Highly flammable gasoline fumes accumulated in the poorly ventilated space. James threw a firecracker into the basement as a joke, intending only to startle Rickey. Sparks from the firecracker caused an explosion and fire that severely burned him. Rickey filed a personal injury suit against James for $1 million. Is this debt dischargeable under Chapter 7?

2. Mary Price went for a consultation about a surgical procedure to remove abdominal fat. When Robert Britton met with her, he wore a name tag that identified him as a doctor, and was addressed as "doctor" by the nurse. Britton then examined Price, touching her stomach and showing her where the incision would be made. It turned out that Britton was the office manager, not a doctor. Although a doctor actually performed the surgery on Price, Britton was present. The doctor left a tube in Price's body at the site of the incision. The area became infected, requiring corrective surgery. A jury awarded Price $275,000 in damages in a suit against Britton. He subsequently filed a Chapter 7 bankruptcy petition. Is this judgment dischargeable in bankruptcy court?

3. Lydia D'Ettore received a degree in computer programming at DeVry Institute of Technology, with a grade point average of 2.51. To finance her education, she borrowed $20,500 from a federal student loan program. After graduation, she could not find a job in her field, so she went to work as a clerk at a salary of $12,500. D'Ettore and her daughter lived with her parents free of charge. After setting aside $50 a month in savings and paying bills that included $233 for a new car (a Suzuki Samurai) and $50 for jewelry from Zales, her disposable income was $125 per month. D'Ettore asked the bankruptcy court to discharge the debts she owed for her DeVry education. Should the court do so?

4. Dr. Ibrahim Khan caused an automobile accident in which a fellow physician, Dolly Yusufji, became a quadriplegic. Khan signed a contract for the lifetime support of Yusufji. When he refused to make payments under the contract, she sued him and obtained a judgment for $1,205,400. Khan filed a Chapter 11 petition. At the time of the bankruptcy hearing, five years after the accident, Khan had not paid Yusufji anything. She was dependent on a motorized wheelchair; he drove a Rolls-Royce. Is Khan's debt dischargeable under Chapter 11?

5. After filing for bankruptcy, Yvonne Brown sought permission of the court to reaffirm a $6,000 debt to her credit union. The debt was unsecured, and she was under no obligation to pay it. The credit union had published the following notice in its newsletter:

> If you are thinking about filing bankruptcy, THINK about the long-term implications. This action, filing bankruptcy, closes the door on TOMORROW. Having no credit means no ability to purchase cars, houses, credit cards. Look into the future—no loans for the education of your children.

Should the court approve Brown's reaffirmation?

DISCUSSION QUESTIONS

1. ETHICS On November 5, Hawes, Inc., a small subcontractor, opened an account with Basic Corp., a supplier of construction materials. Hawes promised to pay its bills within 30 days of purchase. Although Hawes purchased a substantial quantity of goods on credit from Basic, it made few payments on the accounts until the following March, when it paid Basic over $21,000. On May 14, Hawes filed a voluntary petition under Chapter 7. Does the bankruptcy trustee have a right to recover this payment? Is it fair to Hawes's other creditors if Basic is allowed to keep the $21,000 payment?

2. Look on the web for your state's rules on exempt property. Compared with other states and the federal government, is your state generous or stingy with exemptions? In considering a new bankruptcy statute, Congress struggled mightily over whether or not to permit state exemptions at all. Is it fair for exemptions to vary by state? Why should someone in one state fare better than his her neighbor across the state line?

3. Some states permit debtors an unlimited exemption on their homes. Is it fair for bankrupts to be allowed to keep multimillion-dollar homes while their creditors remain unpaid? But other states allow an exemption of as little as $5,000. Should bankrupts be thrown out on the street? What amount is fair?

4. What about the rules regarding repeated bankruptcy filings? Debtors cannot obtain a discharge under Chapter 7 within eight years of a prior filing. Under Chapter 13, no discharge is available within four years of a prior Chapter 7 or 11 filing and within two years of a prior Chapter 13 filing. Are these rules too onerous, too lenient, or just right?

5. A bankrupt who owns a house has the option of either paying the mortgage or losing his home. The only advantage of bankruptcy is that his debt to the bank is discharged. The U.S. House of Representatives passed a bill permitting a bankruptcy judge to adjust the terms of mortgages to aid debtors in holding on to their houses. Proponents argued that this change in the law would reduce foreclosures and stabilize the national housing market. Opponents said that it was not fair to reward homeowners for being irresponsible. How would you vote if you were in the Senate?

6. In the *Grisham* case, the debtor had virtually no income but owed about $200,000 in debts that could not be discharged. What kind of fresh start is that? Should limits be placed on the total debt that cannot be discharged? Is the list of non-dischargeable debts appropriate?

Agency and Employment Law

CHAPTER 17

AGENCY

The first time Bella walked into the store, my heart flipped. A lot of hot girls just know you can't keep your eyes off them. But not Bella. She had the shyest, sweetest smile you ever saw. From the beginning, I knew she was out of my league. But it didn't matter. Just to be in the same room with her was awesome. I would have folded shirts forever if I could do it standing next to her. She smelled like flowers and her skin was beautiful.

© Ivan Cholakov Gostock-dot-net/Shutterstock.com

Of course, she didn't last long at the store. How could she? All she had to do was walk down the street and good things would happen to her. She got picked to be on one of those reality shows.

Being on TV and all, she had to look good, so a couple of weeks after she left, she texted me: "Need clothes 4 show. Can u help?"

I like to think I wouldn't have murdered someone if Bella had asked me to, but I guess it depends on who the someone was. So I came up with a pretty good idea. I issued merchandise credits made out to fake people, which she used to buy clothes. I also let her use my employee discount. Look, Desert Sand is a big company—it's not like they would miss the clothes or anything. Besides, having Bella wear them on that TV show was great advertising.

But you know what those guys at corporate did? Sued me for violating my duty of loyalty! To some big company! Are they kidding?? Like they would ever be loyal to me.

> I like to think I wouldn't have murdered someone if Bella had asked me to, but I guess it depends on who the someone was.

Is this sales clerk liable to the company that employed him? As you will see in the *Otsuka* case later in the chapter, *all* employees owe a duty of loyalty to their employers.

Thus far, this book has primarily dealt with issues of individual responsibility: what happens if *you* knock someone down or *you* sign an agreement? Agency law, on the other hand, is concerned with your responsibility for the actions of others. What happens if your agent assaults someone or enters into an agreement? Agency law presents a significant trade-off: once you hire other people, you can accomplish a great deal more, but your risk of legal liability increases immensely.

CREATING AN AGENCY RELATIONSHIP

Principals have substantial liability for the actions of their agents.[1] Therefore, disputes about whether an agency relationship exists are not mere legal quibbles but important issues with potentially profound financial consequences. According to the Restatement of Agency:

> Agency is the fiduciary relationship that arises when one person (a principal) manifests assent to another person (an agent) that the agent shall act on the principal's behalf and subject to the principal's control, and the agent manifests assent or otherwise consents so to act.[2]

To create an agency relationship, there must be:

- A **principal** and
- An **agent**
- Who mutually **consent** that the agent will act on behalf of the principal and
- Be subject to the principal's **control,**
- Thereby creating a **fiduciary relationship**.

Principal
In an agency relationship, the person for whom an agent is acting.

Agent
In an agency relationship, the person who is acting on behalf of a principal.

Consent

To establish consent, the principal must ask the agent to do something, and the agent must agree. In the most straightforward example, you ask a neighbor to walk your dog, and she agrees. Matters were more complicated, however, when Steven James met some friends one evening at a restaurant. During the two hours he was there, he drank four to six beers. (It is probably a bad sign that he cannot remember how many.) From then on, one misfortune piled upon another. After leaving the restaurant at about 7:00 p.m., James sped down a highway and crashed into a car that had stalled on the roadway, thereby killing the driver. James told the police at the scene that he had not seen the parked car (another bad sign). In a misguided attempt to help his client, James's lawyer took him to the local hospital for a blood test. Unfortunately, the test confirmed that James had indeed been drunk at the time of the accident.

---

[1]The word "principal" is always used when referring to a person. "Principle," on the other hand, refers to a fundamental idea.
[2]Section 1.01 of the Restatement (Third) of Agency (2006), prepared by the American Law Institute.

The attorney knew that if this evidence was admitted at trial, his client would soon be receiving free room and board from the Massachusetts Department of Corrections. So the lawyer argued that the blood test was protected by the client-attorney privilege because the hospital had been his agent and therefore a member of the defense team. The court disagreed, however, holding that the hospital employees were not agents for the lawyer because they had not consented to act in that role. James was convicted of murder in the first degree by reason of extreme atrocity or cruelty.[3]

Control

Principals are liable for the acts of their agents because they exercise control over the agents. If principals direct their agents to commit an act, it seems fair to hold the principal liable when that act causes harm. How would you apply that rule to the following situation?

William Stanford was an employee of the Agency for International Development. While on his way home to Pakistan to spend the holidays with his family, his plane was hijacked and taken to Iran, where he was killed. Stanford had originally purchased a ticket on Northwest Airlines but had traded it in for a seat on Kuwait Airways (KA). The airlines had an agreement permitting passengers to exchange tickets from one to another. Stanford's widow sued Northwest on the theory that KA was Northwest's agent. The court found, however, that no agency relationship existed because Northwest had no *control* over KA.[4] Northwest did not tell KA how to fly planes or handle terrorists; therefore, it should not be liable when KA made fatal errors.

Fiduciary Relationship

A fiduciary relationship is a special relationship with high standards. The beneficiary places special confidence in the fiduciary, who in turn is obligated to act in good faith and candor, putting his own needs second. The purpose of a fiduciary relationship is for one person to benefit another. **Agents have a fiduciary duty to their principals.** Suppose, for example, that you hire a real estate agent to help you find a house. She shows you a great house but does not reveal to you the brutal murder that took place there because she is afraid that you would not buy it and she would not receive a commission. She has violated her fiduciary duty to put your interests first.

DUTIES OF AGENTS TO PRINCIPALS

Duty of Loyalty

An agent has a fiduciary duty to act loyally for the principal's benefit in all matters connected with the agency relationship.[5] As the following case illustrates, this duty applies to all employees, no matter what their level in the organization.

---

[3]*Commonwealth v. James*, 427 Mass. 312, 693 N.E.2d 148, 1998 Mass. LEXIS 175.
[4]*Stanford v. Kuwait Airways Corp.*, 648 F. Supp. 1158, 1986 U.S. Dist. LEXIS 18880 (S.D.N.Y. 1986).
[5]Restatement (Third) of Agency Section 8.01.

OTSUKA V. POLO RALPH LAUREN CORPORATION

2007 U.S. Dist. LEXIS 86523
United States District Court for the Northern District of California, 2007

CASE SUMMARY

Facts: Justin Kiser and Germania worked together at a Ralph Lauren Polo store in San Francisco. After she left the job, he let her buy clothing using merchandise credits made out to nonexistent people. He also let her use his employee discount. Not surprisingly, both of these activities were against store policies. Polo sued Kiser, alleging that he had violated his duty of loyalty.

Issue: Do all *employees owe a duty of loyalty to their employer?*

Decision: Yes, all employees owe a duty of loyalty.

Reasoning: The cases cited by Polo to support its claim all involved higher-level employees than Kiser, who was simply a clerk in a Polo store. No matter—the Restatement (Third) of Agency clearly states that all employees are agents and owe a duty of loyalty to their employers. *All* employees must put their employer's interests first.

OUTSIDE BENEFITS

An agent may not receive profits unless the principal knows and approves. Suppose that Hope is an employee of the agency Big Egos and Talents, Inc. (BEAT). She has been representing Will Smith in his latest movie negotiations.[6] Smith often drives her to meetings in his new Maybach. He is so thrilled that she has arranged for him to star in the new movie *Little Men* that he buys her a Maybach. Can Hope keep this generous gift? Only with BEAT's permission. She must tell BEAT about the Maybach; the company may then take the vehicle itself or allow her to keep it.

CONFIDENTIAL INFORMATION

The ability to keep secrets is important in any relationship, but especially a fiduciary relationship. **Agents can neither disclose nor use for their own benefit any confidential information they acquire during their agency.** For example, after the Beatles fired an employee, he passed on to a competitor confidential information about the royalties on a George Harrison song. The court held that the agent's obligation to keep information confidential continued even after the agency relationship ended.[7]

COMPETITION WITH THE PRINCIPAL

Agents are not allowed to compete with their principal in any matter within the scope of the agency business. Michael Jackson bought the copyright to many of the Beatles' songs. If, before he made that purchase, one of his employees had bought the songs instead, that employee would have violated her duty to Jackson. Once the agency relationship ends, however, so does the rule against competition. After the employee's job with Jackson ended, she could have bid against him for the Beatles' songs.

---

[6]Do not be confused by the fact that Hope works as an agent for movie stars. As an employee of BEAT, her duty is to the company. She is an agent of BEAT, and BEAT works for the celebrities.

[7]*Abkco Music, Inc. v. Harrisongs Music, Ltd.*, 722 F.2d 988, 1983 U.S. App. LEXIS 15562.

CONFLICT OF INTEREST BETWEEN TWO PRINCIPALS

Unless otherwise agreed, an agent may not act for two principals whose interests conflict. Suppose Travis represents both director Steven Spielberg and actress Angelina Jolie. Spielberg is casting the title role in his new movie, *Nancy Drew: Girl Detective,* a role that Jolie covets. Travis cannot represent these two clients when they are negotiating with each other unless they both know about the conflict and agree to ignore it.

SECRETLY DEALING WITH THE PRINCIPAL

If a principal hires an agent to arrange a transaction, the agent may not become a party to the transaction without the principal's permission. Suppose that actor Matt Damon hired Trang to read scripts for him. Unbeknownst to Damon, Trang has written her own script. She may not sell it to him without revealing that she wrote it herself. Damon may be perfectly happy to buy Trang's script, but he has the right, as her principal, to know that she is the person selling it.

APPROPRIATE BEHAVIOR

An agent may not engage in inappropriate behavior that reflects badly on the principal. This rule applies even to *off-duty* conduct. For example, a coed trio of flight attendants went wild at a hotel bar in London. They kissed and caressed each other, showed off their underwear, and poured alcohol down their trousers. The airline fired two of the employees and gave a warning letter to the third.

Other Duties of an Agent

Before Taylor left for a five-week trip to England, he hired Claudia to rent his vacation house. Claudia never got around to listing his house on Multiple Listing Service, used by all the area brokers, nor did she post it on the Web herself, but when the Fords contacted her looking for rental housing, she did show them Taylor's place. They offered to rent it for $750 per month.

Claudia called Taylor in England to tell him. He responded that he would not accept less than $850 a month, which Claudia thought the Fords would be willing to pay. He told Claudia to call back if there was any problem. The Fords decided that they would go no higher than $800 a month. Although Taylor had told Claudia that he could not receive text messages in England, she texted him the Fords' counteroffer. Taylor never received it, so he never responded. When the Fords pressed Claudia for an answer, she said she could not get in touch with Taylor. Not until Taylor returned home did he learn that the Fords had rented another house. Did Claudia violate any of the duties that agents owe to their principals?

DUTY TO OBEY INSTRUCTIONS

An agent must obey her principal's instructions unless the principal directs her to behave illegally or unethically. Taylor instructed Claudia to call him if the Fords rejected the offer. When Claudia failed to do so, she violated this duty.

DUTY OF CARE

An agent has a duty to act with reasonable care. In other words, an agent must act as a reasonable person would, under the circumstances. A reasonable person would not have texted Taylor while he was in England.

DUTY TO PROVIDE INFORMATION

An agent has a duty to provide the principal with all information in her possession that she has reason to believe the principal wants to know. She also has a duty to provide accurate information. Claudia knew that the Fords had counteroffered for $800 a month. She had a duty to pass this information on to Taylor.

EXAM Strategy

Question: Jonah tells his friend Derek that he would like to go parasailing. Derek is very enthusiastic and suggests they try an outfit called "Wind Beneath Your Wings," because he has heard good things about them. Derek makes a reservation, puts the $600 bill on his credit card, and picks Jonah up to drive him to the Wings location. What a friend! But the day does not turn out as Jonah had hoped. While he is soaring up in the air over the Pacific Ocean, his sail springs a leak, he goes plummeting into the sea and breaks both legs. During his recuperation in the hospital, he learns that Wings is unlicensed. He also sees an ad for Wings offering parasailing for only $350. And Derek is listed in the ad as one of the company's instructors. Is Derek an agent for Jonah? Has he violated his fiduciary responsibility?

Strategy: There are two issues to consider in answering this question: (1) was there an agency relationship? This requires consent, control, and a fiduciary relationship. (2) Has the agent fulfilled his duties?

Result: There is an agency relationship: Derek had agreed to help Jonah; it was Jonah who set the goal for the relationship (parasailing); the purpose of this relationship is for one person to benefit another. It does not matter if Derek was not paid or the agreement not written. Derek has violated his duty to exercise due care. He should not have taken Jonah to an unlicensed company. He has also violated his duty to provide information: he should have told Jonah the true cost for the lessons and also revealed that he was a principal of the company. And he violated his duty of loyalty when he worked for two principals whose interests were in conflict.

Principal's Remedies when the Agent Breaches a Duty

A principal has three potential remedies when an agent breaches her duty:

- The principal can recover from the agent any **damages** the breach has caused. Thus, if Taylor can rent his house for only $600 a month instead of the $800 the Fords offered, Claudia would be liable for $2,400—$200 a month for one year.

- If an agent breaches the duty of loyalty, he must turn over to the principal any **profits** he has earned as a result of his wrongdoing.

- If the agent has violated her duty of loyalty, the principal may **rescind** the transaction. When Trang sold a script to her principal, Matt Damon, without telling him that she was the author, she violated her duty of loyalty. Damon could rescind the contract to buy the script.

DUTIES OF PRINCIPALS TO AGENTS

The principal must (1) pay the agent as required by the agreement, (2) reimburse the agent for reasonable expenses, and (3) cooperate with the agent in performing agency tasks. The respective duties of agents and principals can be summarized as follows:

Duties of Agents to Principals	Duty of Principals to Agents
Duty of loyalty	Duty to compensate as provided by the agreement
Duty to obey instructions	Duty to reimburse
Duty of care	Duty to cooperate
Duty to provide information	

TERMINATING AN AGENCY RELATIONSHIP

> Hiring an agent is not like buying a book. You might not care which copy of the book you buy, but you do care which agent you hire.

Either the agent or the principal can terminate the agency relationship at any time. Here are their options:

- *Term agreement.* The principal and agent can agree in advance how long their relationship will last. Alexandra hires Nicholas to help her purchase guitars previously owned by rock stars. If they agree that the relationship will last two years, they have a term agreement.

- *Achieving a purpose.* The principal and agent can agree that the agency relationship will terminate when the principal's goals have been achieved. Alexandra and Nicholas might agree that their relationship will end when Alexandra has purchased 10 guitars.

- *Mutual agreement.* No matter what the principal and agent agree at the start, they can always change their minds later on, so long as the change is mutual. If Nicholas and Alexandra originally agree to a two-year term, but Nicholas decides he wants to go back to business school and Alexandra runs out of money after only one year, they can decide together to terminate the agency.

- *Agency at will.* If they make no agreement in advance about the term of the agreement, either principal or agent can terminate at any time.

- *Wrongful termination.* An agency relationship is a personal relationship. Hiring an agent is not like buying a book. You might not care which copy of the book you buy, but you do care which agent you hire. If an agency relationship is not working out, the courts will not force the agent and principal to stay together. **Either party always has the *power* to walk out. They may not, however, have the *right*.** If one party's departure from the agency relationship violates the agreement and causes harm to the other party, the wrongful party must pay damages. Nonetheless, he will be permitted to leave. If Nicholas has agreed to work for Alexandra for two years but he wants to leave after one, he can leave, provided he pays Alexandra the cost of hiring and training a replacement.

The agency agreement also terminates if either the principal or the agent becomes unable to perform his required duties. For example, if either the principal or the agent dies, the agency agreement automatically terminates. And the agreement terminates if the activity becomes illegal. Andrew and Zach hired Lucia to perform their marriage ceremony in California, but then the voters changed the law to make gay marriage illegal. The agency agreement automatically ended.

LIABILITY

Although an agent can greatly increase his principal's ability to accomplish her goals, an agency relationship also dramatically increases the risk of the principal's legal liability to third parties.

Principal's Liability for Contracts

A principal is liable on contracts entered into on her behalf by her agent, if the agent is authorized. She may even be liable if the agent is not authorized but appeared to be so. There are three types of authority: express, implied, and apparent.

Express Authority. The principal grants **express authority** by words or conduct that, reasonably interpreted, cause the agent to believe the principal desires her to act on the principal's account.[8] In other words, the principal asks the agent to do something and the agent does it. Craig calls his stockbroker, Alice, and asks her to buy 100 shares of Banshee Corp. for his account. She has *express authority* to carry out this transaction.

> **Express authority**
> Either by words or conduct, the principal grants an agent permission to act.

Implied Authority. **Unless otherwise agreed, authority to conduct a transaction includes authority to perform acts that are reasonably necessary to accomplish it.**[9] The principal does not have to micromanage the agent. David has recently inherited a house from his grandmother. He hires Nell to auction off the house and its contents. She hires an auctioneer, advertises the event, rents a tent, and generally does everything necessary to conduct a successful auction. After withholding her expenses, she sends the tidy balance to David. Totally outraged, he calls her on the phone, "How dare you hire an auctioneer and rent a tent? I never gave you permission! I *refuse* to pay these expenses!"

> **Implied authority**
> The agent has authority to perform acts that are reasonably necessary to accomplish an authorized transaction, even if the principal does not specify them.

David is wrong. A principal almost never gives an agent absolutely complete instructions. Unless some authority is implied, David would have had to say, "Open the car door, get in, put the key in the ignition, drive to the store, buy stickers, mark an auction number on each sticker . . ." and so forth. To solve this problem, the law assumes that the agent has authority to do anything that is reasonably necessary to accomplish her task.

Apparent Authority. **A principal can be liable for the acts of an agent who is not, in fact, acting with authority if the *principal's* conduct causes a third party reasonably to believe that the agent is authorized.** Because the principal has done something to make an innocent

> **Apparent authority**
> A principal does something to make an innocent third party believe that an agent is acting with the principal's authority, even though the agent is not authorized.

---

[8] Restatement (Third) of Agency Section 2.01.
[9] Restatement (Third) of Agency Section 2.02.

third party *believe* the agent is authorized, the principal is every bit as liable to the third party as if the agent did have authority.

For example, two stockbrokers sell fraudulent stock out of their offices at a legitimate brokerage house, using firm email accounts and making presentations to investors in the firm conference rooms. Although the two brokers do not have *actual* or *implied* authority to sell the stock, their employer is nonetheless liable on the grounds that the brokers *appeared* to have authority. Of course, the company has the right to recover from the two brokers if it can compel them to pay.

Agent's Liability for Contracts

The agent's liability on a contract depends upon how much the third party knows about the principal. Disclosure is the agent's best protection against liability.

FULLY DISCLOSED PRINCIPAL

An agent is not liable for any contracts she makes on behalf of a *fully* disclosed principal. A principal is fully disclosed if the third party knows of his *existence* and his *identity*. Augusta acts as agent for Parker when he buys Tracey's prize-winning show horse. Tracey does not know Parker, but she figures any friend of Augusta's must be OK. She figures wrong— Parker is a charming deadbeat. He injures Tracey's horse, fails to pay the full contract price, and promptly disappears. Tracey angrily demands that Augusta make good on Parker's debt. Unfortunately for Tracey, Parker was a fully disclosed principal—Tracey knew of his *existence* and his *identity*. Augusta is not liable because Tracey knew who the principal was and could have investigated him. Tracey's only recourse is against the principal, Parker (wherever he may be).

UNIDENTIFIED PRINCIPAL

Jointly and severally liable
An injured third party has the right to recover the full amount of her damages from one, some, or all of those who caused her harm. She may not recover more than 100 percent of her damages.

In the case of an unidentified principal, the third party can recover from either the agent or the principal. A principal is unidentified if the third party knew of his *existence* but not his *identity*. Suppose Augusta had simply said, "I have a friend who is interested in buying your champion." Parker is an unidentified principal because Tracey knows only that he exists, not who he is. She cannot investigate him because she does not know his name. Tracey relies solely on what she is able to learn from the agent, Augusta. Both Augusta and Parker are liable to Tracey. (They are **jointly and severally liable**, which means that Tracey can recover from either or both of them. She cannot, however, recover more than the total that she is owed: if her damages are $100,000, she can recover that amount from either Augusta or Parker, or partial amounts from both, but in no event more than $100,000.)

UNDISCLOSED PRINCIPAL

In the case of an *undisclosed* principal, the third party can recover from either the agent or the principal. A principal is undisclosed if the third party did not know of his existence. Suppose that Augusta simply asks to buy the horse herself, without mentioning that she is purchasing it for Parker. In this case, Parker is an undisclosed principal because Tracey does not know that Augusta is acting for someone else. Both Parker and Augusta are jointly and severally liable. As Exhibit 17.1 illustrates, the principal is always liable, but the agent is not unless the principal's identity is a mystery.

It is easy to understand why the principal and agent are liable on these contracts, but what about the third party? Is it fair for her to be liable on a contract if she does not even know the identity of the principal? The courts have found these contracts valid for reasons of commercial necessity. For instance, the United Nations headquarters in New York City is located on land purchased secretly. If sellers had known the identity of the purchaser (a wealthy real estate developer), the price of the land would have skyrocketed.

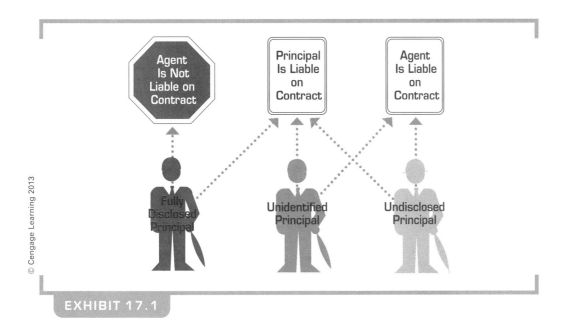

EXHIBIT 17.1

Principal's Liability for Torts

An employer is liable for a tort committed by his employee acting within the scope of employment or acting with authority.[10] This principle of liability is called **respondeat superior**, which is a Latin phrase that means "let the master answer." Under the theory of *respondeat superior*, the employer (i.e., the principal) is liable for misbehavior by the employee (that is, the agent) whether or not the employer was at fault. Indeed, the employer is liable even if he forbade or tried to prevent the employee from misbehaving. This sounds like a harsh rule. The logic is that, because the principal controls the agent, he should be able to *prevent* misbehavior. If he cannot prevent it, at least he can *insure* against the risks. Furthermore, the principal may have deeper pockets than the agent or the injured third party and thus be better able to *afford* the cost of the agent's misbehavior.

Respondeat superior

The principle that an employer is liable for a tort committed by an employee acting within the scope of employment or acting with authority.

EMPLOYEE

There are two kinds of agents: (1) *employees* and (2) *independent contractors*. **A principal *may be* liable for the torts of an employee but generally is *not* liable for the torts of an independent contractor.**

Employee or Independent Contractor?   The more control the principal has over an agent, the more likely that the agent will be considered an employee. Therefore, when determining if agents are employees or independent contractors, courts consider whether:

- The principal supervises details of the work.
- The principal supplies the tools and place of work.
- The agents work full time for the principal.
- The agents receive a salary or hourly wages, not a fixed price for the job.
- The work is part of the regular business of the principal.

---

[10]Restatement (Third) of Agency Section 7.07.

- The principal and agents believe they have an employer-employee relationship.
- The principal is in business.

Negligent Hiring. As a general rule, principals are not liable for the torts of an independent contractor. There is, however, one exception to this rule: **the principal is liable for the torts of an independent contractor *if* the principal has been negligent in hiring or supervising her.** Thus, an employment agency would be liable if it failed to run a background check on a nanny with a criminal record who then harmed a child in her care.

Exhibit 17.2 illustrates the difference in liability between an employee and an independent contractor.

SCOPE OF EMPLOYMENT

Principals are liable only for torts that an employee commits within the *scope of employment*. If an employee leaves a pool of water on the floor of a store and a customer slips and falls, the employer is liable. But if the same employee leaves water on his own kitchen floor and a friend falls, the employer is not liable because the employee is not acting within the scope of employment. An employee is acting within the scope of employment if the act:

- Is one that employees are generally responsible for,
- Takes place during hours that the employee is generally employed,
- Is part of the principal's business,
- Is similar to the one the principal authorized,
- Is one for which the principal supplied the tools, and
- Is not seriously criminal.

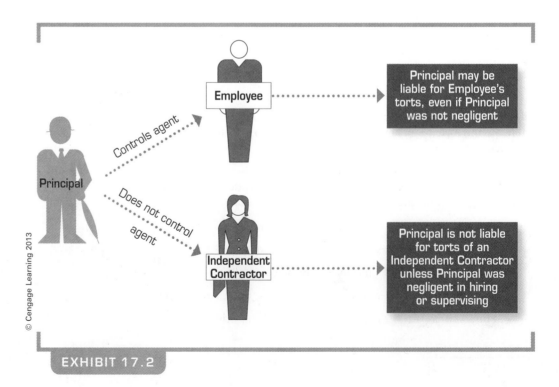

© Cengage Learning 2013

EXHIBIT 17.2

Authorization.   An act is within the scope of employment, even if expressly forbidden, if it is of the same general nature as that authorized or if it is incidental to the conduct authorized.[11] Although Jane has often told Hank not to speed when driving the delivery van, Hank ignores her instructions and plows into Bernadette. Hank was authorized to drive the van but not to speed. However, his speeding was of the same general nature as the authorized act, so Jane is liable to Bernadette.

Abandonment.   The principal is liable for the actions of the employee that occur while the employee is at work, but not for actions that occur after the employee has *abandoned* the principal's business. The employer is liable if the employee is simply on a *detour* from company business, but the employer is not liable if the employee is off on a *frolic of his own*. Suppose that Hank, the delivery van driver, speeds during his afternoon commute home. An employee is generally not acting within the scope of his employment when he commutes to and from work, so his principal, Jane, is not liable. On the other hand, if Hank stops at the Burger Box drive-in window en route to making a delivery, Jane is liable when he crashes into Anna on the way out of the parking lot because this time, he is simply making a detour.

Was the employee in the following case acting within the scope of his employment while driving to work? You be the judge.

---

[11]Restatement (Third) of Agency Section 7.07.

You be the Judge

ZANKEL V. UNITED STATES OF AMERICA

2008 U.S. Dist. LEXIS 23655
United States District Court for the Western District
of Pennsylvania, 2008

Facts: Staff Sergeant William E. Dreyer was a recruiter for the United States Marine Corps, working 16 to 18 hours a day, seven days a week. He was required to ask permission before using his Marine Corps car to commute to or from work. Late one night, Dreyer's personal car would not start, so he drove his government car home. He did not ask permission because he thought it was too late to call his boss. Dreyer believed that, had he called, his boss would have said it was OK because he had given approval in similar situations in the past. Driving to work in the government car at 6:40 the next morning on the way to an early training session, Dreyer struck and killed 12-year-old Justin Zankel.

You Be the Judge: *Was Dreyer acting within the scope of his employment? Was the federal government liable for Zankel's death?*

Argument for the Zankels: At the time of the accident, Dreyer was driving a government vehicle. Although he had not requested permission to drive the car, if he had done so, permission certainly would have been granted.

Moreover, even if Dreyer was not authorized to drive the Marine Corps car, the government is still liable because his activity was of the same general nature as that authorized and it was incidental to the conduct authorized. Also, Dreyer was on the road early so that he could attend a required training session. The Marine Corps must bear responsibility for this tragic accident.

Argument for United States: The government had a clear policy stating that recruiters were not authorized to drive a government car without first requesting permission. Dreyer had not done so.

Moreover, it is well established that an employee commuting to and from work is not within the scope of employment. If Dreyer had been driving from one recruiting effort to another, that would be a different story. But in this case, he had not yet started work for the Marine Corps, and therefore the government is not liable.

INTENTIONAL TORTS

A principal is *not* liable for the *intentional* torts of the employee unless the employee intended to serve some purpose of the employer or (2) the employer was negligent in hiring or supervising this employee.[12] A Catholic priest engaged in a sexual relationship with one of his students. In response, the bishop in charge transferred the priest to a parish church. In this new job, the priest sexually abused a child. This child sued the Church, alleging that it was liable for the priest's intentional tort. The court held that the sexual abuse of a child did not serve any purpose of the Church—indeed, it was harmful to the Church. Nor had the Church been negligent in hiring the priest because when it hired him, it had no reason to believe that he was likely to commit this tort. However, the Church was liable for the negligence of the bishop in supervising the priest.[13]

NONPHYSICAL HARM

Nonphysical torts are those that that harm only reputation, feelings, or wallet. Nonphysical torts are treated like a contract claim, and the principal is liable if the employee acted with actual, implied, or apparent authority.[14] For example, suppose that Dwayne buys a house insurance policy from Andy, who is an agent of the Balls of Fire Insurance Company. Andy throws away Dwayne's policy and pockets his premiums. When Dwayne's house burns down, Balls of Fire is liable because Andy was acting with apparent authority.

EXAM Strategy

Question: Daisy was the founder of an Internet start-up company. Mac was her driver. One day, after he had dropped her at a board meeting, he went to the car wash. There, he told an attractive woman that he worked for a money management firm. She gave him money to invest. He was so excited that, on the way out of the car wash, he hit another customer's expensive car. Who is liable for Mac's misdeeds?

Strategy: In determining a principal's liability, begin by figuring out whether the agent has committed a physical or nonphysical tort. Remember that the principal is liable for physical torts within the scope of employment, but for nonphysical torts, she is liable only if the employee acted with authority.

Result: In this case, Daisy is liable for the damage to the car because that was a physical tort within the scope of employment. But she is not liable for the investment money because Mac did not have authority from her to take those funds.

Agent's Liability for Torts

The focus of the prior section was on the *principal's* liability for the agent's torts. But it is important to remember that **agents are always liable for their own torts.** Agents who commit torts are personally responsible whether or not their principal is also liable. Even if the tort was committed to benefit the principal, the agent is still liable.

This rule makes obvious sense. If the agent were not liable, he would have little incentive to be careful. Imagine Hank driving his delivery van for Jane. If he were not

---

[12]Restatement (Third) of Agency Section 7.07.
[13]*Doe v. Liberatore*, 478 F. Supp. 2d 742; 2007 U.S. Dist. LEXIS 19067.
[14]Restatement (Third) of Agency Section 7.08.

personally liable for his own torts, he might think, "If I drive fast enough, I can make it through that light even though it just turned red. And if I don't, what the heck, it'll be Jane's problem, not mine." Agents, as a rule, may have fewer assets than their principal, but it is important that their personal assets be at risk in the event of their negligent behavior.

If the agent and principal are *both* liable, which does the injured third party sue? The principal and the agent are *jointly and severally liable*, which means, as we have seen, that the injured third party can sue either one or both, as she chooses. If she recovers from the principal, he can sue the agent.

Chapter Conclusion

Agency is an area of the law that affects us all because each of us has been and will continue to be both an agent and a principal many times in our lives.

EXAM REVIEW

1. **CREATING AN AGENCY RELATIONSHIP**   A principal and an agent mutually consent that the agent will act on behalf of the principal and be subject to the principal's control, thereby creating a fiduciary relationship. (pp. 301–302)

2. **AN AGENT'S DUTIES TO THE PRINCIPAL**   An agent owes these duties to the principal: duty of loyalty, duty to obey instructions, duty of care, and duty to provide information. (pp. 302–305)

EXAM Strategy

> **Question:** When Bessie signed up for a fancy trip, she emphasized to her travel agent that she was seriously allergic to lead paint, and therefore, she could stay only in new hotels. The agent assumed that Hotel Augustine would be fine because it had been renovated at a time after lead paint was banned. However, the renovation had not removed all the lead paint, and Bessie became ill after staying at the hotel.
>
> **Strategy:** An agent has four duties. Which of these might the travel agent have violated? (See the "Result" at the end of this section.)

3. **THE PRINCIPAL'S REMEDIES IN THE EVENT OF A BREACH**   The principal has three potential remedies when the agent breaches her duty: recovery of damages the breach has caused, recovery of any profits earned by the agent from the breach, and rescission of any transaction with the agent. (p. 305)

4. **THE PRINCIPAL'S DUTIES TO THE AGENT**   The principal has three duties to the agent: to compensate as provided by the agreement, to reimburse legitimate expenses, and to cooperate with the agent. (p. 306)

5. **POWER AND RIGHT TO TERMINATE**   Both the agent and the principal have the power to terminate an agency relationship, but they may not have the right. If the termination violates the agency agreement and causes harm to the other party, the wrongful party must pay damages. (pp. 306–307)

6. **AUTOMATIC TERMINATION**   An agency relationship automatically terminates if the principal or agent no longer can perform the required duties or if the activity becomes illegal. (p. 306)

7. **A PRINCIPAL'S LIABILITY FOR CONTRACTS**   A principal is liable for the contracts of the agent if the agent has express, implied, or apparent authority. (pp. 307–308)

8. **EXPRESS AUTHORITY**   The principal grants express authority by words or conduct that, reasonably interpreted, cause the agent to believe that the principal desires her to act on the principal's account. (p. 307)

9. **IMPLIED AUTHORITY**   Implied authority includes authority to perform acts that are reasonably necessary to accomplish the designated task. (p. 307)

10. **APPARENT AUTHORITY**   A principal can be liable for the acts of an agent who is not, in fact, acting with authority if the principal's conduct causes a third party reasonably to believe that the agent is authorized. (pp. 307–308)

EXAM Strategy

Question: Dr. James Leonard wrote Dr. Edward Jacobson to offer him a position at a hospital. In the letter, Leonard stated that this appointment would have to be approved by the promotion committee. Jacobson believed that the promotion committee acted only as a "rubber stamp" and its approval was certain. Jacobson accepted the offer, sold his house, and quit his old job. Two weeks later, the promotion committee voted against Jacobson, and the offer was rescinded. Did Leonard have apparent authority?

Strategy: In cases of apparent authority, begin by asking what the principal did to make the third party believe that the agent was authorized. Did the hospital do anything? (See the "Result" at the end of this section.)

11. **AN AGENT'S LIABILITY FOR A CONTRACT**   In the case of a fully disclosed principal, the principal is liable for any contract the agent makes on her behalf, but the agent is not. In the case of a unidentified or undisclosed principal, both the agent and the principal are liable on the contract. (pp. 308–309)

12. **A PRINCIPAL'S LIABILITY FOR TORTS**   An employer is liable for a tort committed by its employee acting within the scope of employment or acting with authority. (pp. 309–312)

13. **INDEPENDENT CONTRACTOR**   The principal is liable for the torts of an independent contractor if the principal has been negligent in hiring or supervising her. (pp. 309–310)

14. **INTENTIONAL TORTS**   A principal is not liable for the intentional torts of the employee unless (1) the employee intended to serve some purpose of the employer or (2) the employer was negligent in hiring or supervising the employee. (p. 312)

15. **AGENT'S LIABILITY FOR TORTS**   Agents are always liable for their own torts. (pp. 312–313)

16. **NONPHYSICAL TORTS**   A principal is liable only for the nonphysical torts of an employee who is acting with actual, implied, or apparent authority. (p. 312)

> **2. Result:**   From this set of facts, there is no reason to believe that the travel agent was disloyal, disobeyed instructions, or failed to provide information. But the agent did violate his duty of care when choosing hotels for Bessie. He should have made sure that there was no lead paint.
>
> **10. Result:**   No. Indeed, Leonard had told Jacobson that he did not have authority. If Jacobson chose to believe otherwise, that was his problem.

Matching Questions

Match the following terms with their definitions:

___A. Term agreement

___B. Apparent authority

___C. Agency at will

___D. A duty of an agent

___E. Implied authority

1. When two parties make no agreement in advance about the duration of their agreement

2. When an agent has authority to perform acts that are necessary to accomplish an assignment

3. When two parties agree in advance on the duration of their agreement

4. When behavior by a principal convinces a third party that the agent is authorized, even though she is not

5. Duty of loyalty

True/False Questions

Circle true or false:

1. T F A principal is always liable on a contract, whether he is fully disclosed, unidentified, or undisclosed.

2. T F When a contract goes wrong, a third party can always recover damages from the agent, whether the principal is fully disclosed, unidentified, or undisclosed.

3. T F An agent may receive profits from an agency relationship even if the principal does not know about the profits, so long as the principal is not harmed.

4. T F An agent may never act for two principals whose interests conflict.

5. T F An agent has a duty to provide the principal with all information in her possession that she has reason to believe the principal wants to know, even if he does not specifically ask for it.

MULTIPLE-CHOICE QUESTIONS

1. Someone painting the outside of a building you own crashed through a window, injuring a visiting executive. Which of the following questions would your lawyer *not* need to ask to determine if the painter was your employee?

   (a) Did the painter work full time for you?

   (b) Had you checked the painter's references?

   (c) Was the painter paid by the hour or by the job?

   (d) Were you in the painting business?

   (e) Did the painter consider herself your employee?

2. Which of the following duties does an agent *not* owe to her principal?

   (a) Duty of loyalty

   (b) Duty to obey instructions

   (c) Duty to reimburse

   (d) Duty of care

   (e) Duty to provide information

3. Finn learns that, despite his stellar record, he is being paid less than other salespeople at Barry Co. So he decides to start his own company. During his last month on the Barry payroll, he tells all of his clients about his new business. He also tells them that Barry is a great company, but his fees will be lower. After he opens the doors of his new business, most of his former clients come with him. Is Finn liable to Barry?

   (a) No, because he has not been disloyal to Barry—he praised the company.

   (b) No, because Barry was underpaying him.

   (c) No, because his clients have the right to hire whichever company they choose.

   (d) Yes, Finn has violated his duty of loyalty to Barry.

4. Kurt asked his car mechanic, Quinn, for help in buying a used car. Quinn recommends a Ford Focus that she has been taking care of its whole life. Quinn was working for the seller. Which of the following statements is true?

   (a) Quinn must pay Kurt the amount of money she received from the Ford's prior owner.

   (b) After buying the car, Kurt finds out that it needs $1,000 in repairs. He can recover that amount from Quinn, but only if Quinn knew about the needed repairs before Kurt bought the car.

   (c) Kurt cannot recover anything because Quinn had no obligation to reveal her relationship with the car's seller.

   (d) Kurt cannot recover anything because he had not paid Quinn for her help.

5. Figgins is the dean of a college. He appointed Sue acting dean while he was out of the country and posted a message on the college website announcing that she was authorized to act in his place. He also told Sue privately that she did not have the right to make admissions decisions. While Figgins was gone, Sue overruled the admissions committee to admit the child of a wealthy alumnus. Does the child have the right to attend this college?

   (a) No, because Sue was not authorized to admit him.

   (b) No, because Figgins was an unidentified principal.

   (c) Yes, because Figgins was a fully disclosed principal.

   (d) Yes, because Sue had apparent authority.

6. **CPA QUESTION** A principal will not be liable to a third party for a tort committed by an agent:

   (a) Unless the principal instructed the agent to commit the tort

   (b) Unless the tort was committed within the scope of the agency relationship

   (c) If the agency agreement limits the principal's liability for the agent's tort

   (d) If the tort is also regarded as a criminal act

Essay Questions

1. An elementary school custodian hit a child who wrote graffiti on the wall. Is the school district liable for this intentional tort by its employee?

2. What if the custodian hit one of the schoolchildren for calling him a name? Is the school district liable?

3. A soldier was drinking at a training seminar. Although he was told to leave his car at the seminar, he disobeyed orders and drove to a nightclub. On the way to the club, he was in an accident. Is the military liable for the damage he caused?

4. One afternoon while visiting friends, tennis star Vitas Gerulaitis fell asleep in their pool house. A mechanic had improperly installed the swimming pool heater, which leaked carbon monoxide fumes into the house where he slept, killing him. His mother filed suit against the owners of the estate. On what theory would they be liable?

5. **YOU BE THE JUDGE WRITING PROBLEM** Sarah went to an auction at Christie's to bid on a tapestry for her employer, Fine Arts Gallery. The good news is that she purchased a Dufy tapestry for $77,000. The bad news is that it was not the one her employer had told her to buy. In the excitement of the auction, she forgot her instructions. Fine Art refused to pay, and Christie's filed suit. Is Fine Arts liable for the unauthorized act of its agent? **Argument for Christie's:** Christie's cannot possibly ascertain in each case the exact nature of a bidder's authority. Whether or not Sarah had actual authority, she certainly had apparent authority, and Fine Arts is liable. **Argument for Fine Arts:** Sarah was not authorized to purchase the Dufy tapestry, and therefore, Christie's must recover from her, not Fine Arts.

DISCUSSION QUESTIONS

1. **ETHICS** Mercedes has just begun work at Photobook.com. What a great place to work! Although the salary is not high, the company has fabulous perks. The dining room provides great food from 7 a.m. to midnight, five days a week. There is also a free laundry and dry-cleaning service. Mercedes's social life has never been better. She invites her friends over for Photobook meals and has their laundry done for free. And because her job requires her to be online all the time, she has plenty of opportunity to stay in touch with her friends by g-chatting, tweeting, and checking Facebook updates. However, she is shocked that one of her colleagues takes paper home from the office for his children to use at home. Are these employees behaving ethically?

2. Kevin was the manager of a radio station, WABC. A competing station lured him away. In his last month on the job at WABC, he notified two key on-air personalities that if they were to leave the station, he would not hold them to their noncompete agreements. What can WABC do?

3. Jesse worked as a buyer for the Vegetable Co. Rachel offered to sell Jesse 10 tons of tomatoes for the account of Vegetable. Jesse accepted the offer. Later, Jesse discovered that Rachel was an agent for Sylvester Co. Who is liable on this contract?

4. The Pharmaceutical Association holds an annual convention. At the convention, Brittany, who was president of the association, told Luke that Research Corp. had a promising new cancer vaccine. Luke was so excited that he chartered a plane to fly to Research's headquarters. On the way, the plane crashed and Luke was killed. Is the Pharmaceutical Association liable for Luke's death?

5. Betsy has a two-year contract as a producer at Jackson Movie Studios. She produces a remake of the movie *Footloose*. Unfortunately, it bombs, and Jackson is so furious that he fires her on the weekend the movie opens. Does he have the power to do this?

EMPLOYMENT LAW

"On the killing beds you were apt to be covered with blood, and it would freeze solid; if you leaned against a pillar, you would freeze to that, and if you put your hand upon the blade of your knife, you would run a chance of leaving your skin on it. The men would tie up their feet in newspapers and old sacks, and these would be soaked in blood and frozen, and then soaked again, and so on, until by nighttime a man would be walking on great lumps the size of the feet of an elephant. Now and then, when the bosses were not looking, you would see them plunging their feet and ankles into the steaming hot carcass of the steer.... The cruelest thing of all was that nearly all of them—all of those who used knives—were unable to wear gloves, and their arms would be white with frost and their hands would grow numb, and then of course there would be accidents."[1]

> ... you would see them plunging their feet and ankles into the steaming hot carcass of the steer.

[1]From Upton Sinclair, *The Jungle* (New York: Bantam Books, 1981), p. 80, a 1906 novel about the meat-packing industry.

INTRODUCTION

For most of history, the concept of career planning was unknown. By and large, people were born into their jobs. Whatever their parents had been—landowner, soldier, farmer, servant, merchant, or beggar—they became, too. Few people expected that their lives would be better than their parents'. The primary English law of employment reflected this simpler time. Unless the employee had a contract that said otherwise, he was hired for a year at a time. This rule was designed to prevent injustice in a farming society. If an employee worked through harvest time, the landowner could not fire him in the winter. Likewise, a worker could not stay the winter and then leave for greener pastures in the spring.

In the 18th and 19th centuries, the Industrial Revolution profoundly altered the employment relationship. Many workers left the farms and villages for large factories in the city. Bosses no longer knew their workers personally, so they felt little responsibility toward them. Since employees could quit their factory jobs whenever they wanted, it was thought to be only fair for employers to have the same freedom to fire a worker. Unless workers had an explicit employment contract, they were employees at will. **An *employee at will* could be fired for a good reason, a bad reason, or no reason at all.** For nearly a century, this was the basic common law rule of employment.[2]

However evenhanded this rule may have sounded in theory, in practice, it could lead to harsh results. The lives of factory workers were grim. It was not as if they could simply pack up and leave; conditions were no better elsewhere. Courts and legislatures began to recognize that individual workers were generally unable to negotiate fair contracts with powerful employers. Since the beginning of the 20th century, employment law has changed dramatically. Now, the employment relationship is more strictly regulated by statutes and by the common law.

Note well, though: **in the absence of a specific legal exception, the rule in the United States is that an employee at will can be fired for any reason.** But, there *are* many exceptions to this rule. They take the form of statutes and common law. Many of the statutes discussed in this chapter were passed by Congress and therefore apply nationally. The common law, however, comes from state courts and only applies locally. We will look at a sampling of cases that illustrates national trends, even though the law may not be the same in every state.

This chapter covers three topics in employment law: (1) employment security; (2) safety and privacy in the workplace; and (3) financial protection. Another important topic, employment discrimination, is covered in Chapter 19.

EMPLOYMENT SECURITY

National Labor Relations Act

Without unions to represent employee interests, employers could simply fire any trouble-making workers who complained about conditions in factories or mines. By joining together, workers could bargain with their employers on more equal terms. Naturally, the owners fought against the unions, firing organizers and even hiring goons to beat them up. Distressed by anti-union violence, Congress passed the National Labor Relations Act in 1935. Known as the NLRA or the Wagner Act, this statute:

- Prohibits employers from penalizing workers who engage in union activity (for example, joining or forming a union); and

- Requires employers to "bargain in good faith" with unions.

---

[2]You remember that common law rules are those created by the courts.

Family and Medical Leave Act

The Family and Medical Leave Act (FMLA) guarantees both men and women up to 12 weeks of *unpaid* leave each year for childbirth, adoption, or a serious health condition of their own or in their immediate family. A family member is a spouse, child, or parent—but not a sibling or an in-law. An employee who takes a leave must be allowed to return to the same or an equivalent job with the same pay and benefits. The FMLA applies only to companies with at least 50 workers and to employees who have been with the company full time for at least a year. This is about 60 percent of all employees.

Kevin Knussman was the first person to win a lawsuit under the FMLA. While a Maryland state trooper, he requested eight weeks of leave to care for his pregnant wife, who was suffering severe complications. His boss granted only two weeks. After Knussman's daughter was born, his boss again denied leave, saying that "God made women to have babies." Knussman ultimately recovered $40,000.[3]

Health Insurance

Companies are *not* required to provide their employees with health insurance. However, current legislation specifies that starting in 2014, employers who have more than 50 full-time employees must pay a penalty if they do not provide basic health insurance. In addition, company insurance policies must cover employees' children up to the age of 26. At this writing, however, some judges have found this statute to be unconstitutional, while others have upheld it. Almost inevitably, the Supreme Court will decide the statute's fate. (For updates, visit bizlawupdate.com.)

Losing your job does not mean that you must also give up your health insurance—at least not right away. Under the Consolidated Omnibus Budget Reconciliation Act (COBRA), **former employees must be allowed to continue their health insurance for 18 months after leaving their job.** The catch is that employees must pay for it themselves, up to 102 percent of the cost. (The extra 2 percent covers administrative expenses.) COBRA applies to any company with 20 or more workers.

Common Law Protections

The common law employment-at-will doctrine was created by the courts. Because that rule has sometimes led to absurdly unfair results, the courts have now created a major exception to the rule—**wrongful discharge.**

WRONGFUL DISCHARGE: VIOLATING PUBLIC POLICY

Wrongful discharge
An employer may not fire a worker for a reason that violates basic social rights, duties or responsibilities.

Olga Monge was a schoolteacher in her native Costa Rica. After moving to New Hampshire, she attended college in the evenings to earn a U.S. teaching degree. At night, she worked at the Beebe Rubber Co. During the day, she cared for her husband and three children. When she applied for a better job at her plant, the foreman offered to promote her if she would be "nice" and go out on a date with him. When she refused, he assigned her to a lower-wage job, took away her overtime, made her clean the washrooms, and ridiculed her. Finally, she collapsed at work, and he fired her.

At that time, an employee at will could be fired for any reason. But the New Hampshire Supreme Court decided to change the rule. It held that Monge's firing was a wrongful discharge. Under the doctrine of **wrongful discharge,** an employer cannot fire a worker for a reason that violates public policy.

Although the public policy rule varies from state to state, in essence, it prohibits an employer from firing a worker for refusing to violate the law, performing a legal duty, exercising a legal right, or supporting basic societal values. Here are some examples of the public policy doctrine.

---

[3]Eyal Press, "Family-Leave Values," *New York Times*, July 29, 2007.

Refusing to Violate the Law.   Larry Downs went to Duke Hospital for surgery on his cleft palate. When he came out of the operating room, the doctor instructed a nurse, Marie Sides, to give Downs enough anesthetic to immobilize him. Sides refused because she thought the anesthetic was wrong for this patient. The doctor angrily administered the anesthetic himself. Shortly thereafter, Downs stopped breathing. Before the doctors could resuscitate him, he suffered permanent brain damage. When Downs's family sued the hospital, Sides was called to testify. A number of Duke doctors told her that she would be "in trouble" if she testified. She did testify, and after three months of harassment, was fired. When she sued Duke University, the court held that the university could not fire an employee for telling the truth in court.

As a general rule, employees may not be discharged for refusing to break the law. For example, courts have protected employees who refused to participate in an illegal price-fixing scheme, fake pollution control records required by state law, pollute waters in violation of federal law, or assist a supervisor in stealing from customers.

Exercising a Legal Right.   Dorothy Frampton injured her arm while working at the Central Indiana Gas Co. Her employer (and its insurance company) paid her medical expenses and her salary during the four months she was out of work. When she discovered that she also qualified for benefits under the state's workers' compensation plan, she filed a claim and received payment. One month later, the company fired her. When she sued, the court held the company liable on the theory that if employees can be penalized for filing workers' compensation claims, they will not file, and the whole purpose of the statute will be undermined. As a general rule, an employer may not fire a worker for exercising a legal right.

Performing a Legal Duty.   Courts have consistently held that an employee may not be fired for serving on a jury. Jury duty is an important civic obligation that employers are not permitted to undermine.

Supporting Societal Values.   Courts are sometimes willing to protect employees who do the right thing, even if they violate the boss's orders. For example, a company fired the driver of an armored truck because he disobeyed company policy by leaving his vehicle to go to the aid of two women who were being attacked by a bank robber. A court ruled for the driver on the grounds that, although he had no affirmative legal duty to intervene in such a situation, society values those who aid people in danger.[4] This issue is, however, one on which the courts are divided. Not all would have made the same decision.

In the following case, employees objected when their company supplied defective human tissue for transplantation into live patients. Should the court protect them from termination?

KOZLOSKI v. AMERICAN TISSUE SERVICES FOUNDATION

2006 U.S. Dist. LEXIS 95435
United States District Court for the District of Minnesota, 2006

CASE SUMMARY

Facts: American Tissue Services Foundation (ATSF) was in the business of supplying human tissue from cadavers for transplantation into live patients. Mike Slack, an employee of ATSF, revealed to his boss that he had falsified a donor medical record and changed the donor's blood type on the form. This falsification was not only dangerous to recipients of the tissue, it violated Food and Drug Administration (FDA) regulations. Slack was fired and the infractions were reported to the FDA, as required by law.

---

[4]*Gardner v. Loomis Armored, Inc.*, 913 P.2d 377, 1996 Wash. LEXIS 109 (1996).

It turned out, however, that Slack was the foster child of the company's chairman. And, in this case, (foster) blood was thicker than water. The chairman not only hired Slack at another company as a quality assurance specialist (believe it or not), but he fired Slack's boss and the two men who had reported the problem to the FDA. The men filed suit against ATSF for wrongful discharge, but the company filed a motion to dismiss on the grounds that the public policy doctrine in Minnesota applied only to employees who had refused to violate the law.

Issues: *Does the public policy doctrine in Minnesota apply only to employees who refuse to violate the law? Do the plaintiffs have the right to proceed with their lawsuit?*

Decision: The wrongful discharge doctrine also applies to situations in which an employee is fired for a reason that clearly violates public policy. The defendants may proceed with their lawsuit.

Reasoning: These plaintiffs were fired because they reported to their employer and the FDA their concerns that human tissue was wrongly labeled. This wrongdoing not only created grave risks for the recipients but also violated federal law. ATSF alleges that under Minnesota law, employees can bring a wrongful discharge claim only if they were fired for refusing to violate the law. This reading of the law is incorrect. Wrongful discharge also applies when the termination is for a reason that *clearly* violates public policy. This termination meets that standard. The safe use of human tissue in live patients is *clearly* a matter of public safety and, therefore, public policy.

CONTRACT LAW

Traditionally, many employers (and employees) thought that only a formal, signed document qualified as an employment contract. Increasingly, however, courts have been willing to enforce an employer's more casual promises, whether written or oral.

Truth in Hiring. When the Tanana Valley Medical-Surgical Group, Inc. hired James Eales as a physician's assistant, it promised him that so long as he did his job, he could stay there until retirement age. Six years later, the company fired him without cause. The Alaska Supreme Court held oral promises made during the hiring process are enforceable.

Employee Handbooks. The employee handbook at Blue Cross & Blue Shield stated that employees could be fired only for just cause and then only after warnings, notice, a hearing, and other procedures. Charles Toussaint was fired without warning five years after he joined the company. The court held that an employee handbook creates a contract.

In the following case, an agent of the Federal Bureau of Investigation (FBI) engaged in appalling behavior that affected the morale of his branch. Does the agency's employee handbook protect him from being fired?

You be the Judge

DOE V. DEPARTMENT OF JUSTICE

565 F.3d 1375, 2009 U.S. App. LEXIS 10031
United States Court of Appeals for the Federal Circuit, 2009

Facts: Doe was an FBI agent who was dating a member of the agency's support staff (#1). At her suggestion, he videotaped their sexual encounters. He was so taken with this idea that he also videotaped sexual activity with another FBI employee (#2) and a woman who did not work for the FBI (#3). But he did so without telling #2 and #3. While Doe was out of town, #1 went to his house, where she found all of the tapes. She and Doe saw a therapist. She also consulted a counselor in the FBI's Employee Assistance Program (EAP), who assisted #1 by spreading this news around the office. As the court blandly notes, these rumors were "upsetting to Female #1 and Female #2."

The FBI's personnel handbook provides that employees will not be disciplined because of their morality in romantic or intimate relationships unless there is (1) a violation of criminal law, (2) an adverse impact on the agency's ability to perform its responsibilities, or (3) a violation of an internal regulation. The handbook also states that agents must maintain high standards of conduct "not only when they are engaged in their official duties, but while off duty" and that agents must act with integrity and honesty.

The FBI subsequently fired Doe. He filed suit for wrongful termination.

You Be the Judge: *Could the FBI fire Doe?*

Argument for Doe: The FBI's rules are vague and unclear. How is an agent supposed to know what misconduct adversely affects the "agency's ability to perform its responsibilities"? "Integrity" and "honesty" are imprecise guides to behavior. Could anyone who has an affair be fired? What about someone who cheats during a Friday-night poker game? It seems that the result will depend solely on the supervisor's moral compass. That standard is hardly fair or predictable.

Doe made a choice that many of us would not make. But he and #1 sought help and solved their issues. It is hardly his fault that someone in the EAP violated rules and spread rumors.

Argument for the FBI: Doe did not commit some minor mistake—he was videotaping intimate activities without his partners' consent. And he was not just having an affair—he was having affairs with three women, two of whom worked at his branch. Did he honestly think that they would not find out? Was he truly surprised that news of his activities disrupted work at his branch? Doe's fellow workers felt that they could no longer trust his judgment. Who would? No matter what definition of integrity and honesty you use, Doe did not meet it.

Also, Doe was working at arguably the most important law enforcement agency in the country. Damaged morale could put lives at risk.

TORT LAW

Workers have successfully sued their employers under the following tort theories.

Defamation.   Employers may be liable for defamation when they give false and unfavorable references about a former employee. In his job as a bartender at the Capitol Grille restaurant, Christopher Kane often flirted with customers. After he was fired from his job, his ex-boss claimed that Kane had been "fired from every job he ever had for sexual misconduct." In fact, Kane had never been fired before. He recovered $300,000 in damages for this defamation.

More than half of the states, however, recognize a *qualified privilege* **for employers who give references about former employees.** A **qualified privilege** means that employers are liable only for false statements that they know to be false or that are primarily motivated by ill will. After Becky Chambers left her job at American Trans Air, Inc., she discovered that her former boss was telling anyone who called for a reference that Chambers "does not work good with other people," is a "troublemaker," and "would not be a good person to rehire." However, Chambers was unable to prove that her boss had been primarily motivated by ill will. Neither Trans Air nor the boss was held liable for these statements because they were protected by the qualified privilege.

Even if the employer wins, a trial is expensive and takes time. Therefore, many companies tell their managers that when asked for a reference, they should only reveal the person's salary and dates of employment and not offer an opinion on job performance.

On the flip side, do employers have any obligation to warn about risky workers? **Generally, courts have held that employers do not have a legal obligation to disclose information about former employees.** For example, while Jeffrey St. Clair worked at the St. Joseph Nursing Home, he was disciplined 24 times for actions ranging from extreme violence to drug and alcohol use. When he applied for a job with Maintenance Management Corp., St. Joseph refused to give any information other than St. Clair's dates of employment. After he savagely murdered a security guard at his new job, the guard's family sued, but the court dismissed the case.

Qualified privilege
Employers are liable only for false statements that they know to be false or that are primarily motivated by ill will.

In some recent cases, however, courts have held that, when a former worker is potentially dangerous, employers do have an obligation to disclose this information. For example, officials from two junior high schools gave Robert Gadams glowing letters of recommendation, without mentioning that he had been fired for inappropriate sexual conduct with students. While an assistant principal at a new school, he molested a 13-year-old. Her parents sued the former employers. The court held that the writer of a letter of recommendation has "a duty not to misrepresent the facts in describing the qualifications and character of a former employee, if making these misrepresentations would present a substantial, foreseeable risk of physical injury to the third persons." As a result of cases such as this, it makes sense to disclose past violent behavior.

Ethics What if someone calls you to check references on a former employee who had a drinking problem? The job is driving a van for junior high school sports teams. What is the manager's ethical obligation in this situation? Many managers say that, in the case of a serious problem such as alcoholism, sexual harassment, or drug use, they will find a way to communicate that an employee is unsuitable. What if the ex-employee says she is reformed? Are people entitled to a second chance? Is it right to risk a defamation suit against your company to protect others from harm?

Intentional Infliction of Emotional Distress. **Employers who permit cruel treatment of their workers face liability under the tort of intentional infliction of emotional distress.** For example, when a 57-year-old social work manager at Yale–New Haven Hospital was fired, she was forced to place her personal belongings in a plastic bag and was escorted out the door by security guards, in full view of gaping coworkers. A supervisor told her that she would be arrested for trespassing if she returned. A jury awarded her $105,000.

Whistleblowing

FMC Corp. sold 9,000 Bradley Fighting Vehicles to the U.S. Army at a price of $1.5 million each. Designed to carry soldiers around battlefields in Eastern Europe, this vehicle was supposed to "swim" across water. But Henry Boisvert, an FMC supervisor, charged that when a test Bradley entered a pond, it immediately filled with water. FMC workers had no time to weld gaps properly, so they filled them in with putty instead. FMC fired Boisvert for raising these quality issues, but the jury sided with him, finding FMC liable for $171.6 million.

No one likes to be accused of wrongdoing even if (or, perhaps, especially if) the accusations are true. **This is exactly what whistleblowers do: they are employees who disclose illegal behavior on the part of their employer.** Not surprisingly, many companies, when faced with such an accusation by an employee, prefer to shoot the messenger.

Whistleblowers are protected in the following situations:

- *Defrauding the government.* Henry Boisvert recovered under the federal False Claims Act, a statute that permits anyone to bring suit against someone who defrauds the government. The government and the whistleblower share any recovery. The Act also prohibits employers from firing workers who file suit under the statute.

- *Violations of securities or commodities laws.* Under the Dodd-Frank Act, anyone who provides information to the government about violations of securities or commodities laws is entitled to a portion of whatever award the government receives, provided that the award tops $1 million. If a company retaliates against tipsters, they are entitled to reinstatement, double back pay, and attorney's fees.

- *Employees of public companies.* The Sarbanes-Oxley Act of 2002 protects employees of public companies who provide evidence of fraud to investigators. A successful plaintiff must be rehired and given back pay.

- *Common law.* Most state courts do not permit employers to fire workers who report illegal activity. For example, a Connecticut court held a company liable when it fired a quality control director who reported to his boss that some products had failed quality tests.

EXAM Strategy

Question: When Shiloh interviewed for a sales job at a medical supply company, the interviewer promised that she could work exclusively selling medical devices and would not have to be involved in the sale of drugs. Once she began work (as an employee at will), Shiloh discovered that the sales force was organized around regions, not products, so she had to sell both devices and drugs. When she complained to her boss over lunch in the employee lunchroom, he said in a loud voice, "You are a big girl now—it's time you learned that you don't always get what you want." That afternoon, she was fired. Does she have a valid claim against the company?

Strategy: First: We know that Shiloh is an employee at will. Is she protected by a *statute*? So far, we have learned about two statutes: the FMLA and COBRA. Neither applies here.
  Second: Does the *common law* apply? Shiloh has had two interactions with the company—being hired and being fired. What protections does the common law provide during the hiring process? The employer's promises are enforceable. Here, the company is liable because the interviewer clearly made a promise that the company did not keep. What about the way in which Shiloh was fired? Is it intentional infliction of emotional distress? Was this treatment cruel? Probably not cruel enough to constitute intentional infliction of emotional distress.

Result: The company is liable to Shiloh for making false promises to her during the hiring process but not for the manner in which she was fired.

SAFETY AND PRIVACY IN THE WORKPLACE

Workplace Safety

Congress passed the Occupational Safety and Health Act (OSHA) to ensure safe working conditions. Under OSHA:

- Employers are under a general obligation to keep their workplace free from hazards that could cause serious harm to employees.

- Employers must comply with specific health and safety standards. For example, health care personnel who work with blood are not permitted to eat or drink in areas where the blood is kept and must not put their mouths on any instruments used to store blood.

- Employers must keep records of all workplace injuries and accidents.

- The Occupational Safety and Health Administration (also known as OSHA) may inspect workplaces to ensure that they are safe. OSHA may assess fines for violations and order employers to correct unsafe conditions.

OSHA has done a lot to make the American workplace safer. In 1900, roughly 35,000 workers died at work. A century later, the workforce had grown five times larger, but the number of annual deaths had fallen to about 5,500.

Employee Privacy

Upon opening the country's first moving assembly line in the early 1900s, Henry Ford issued a booklet, "Helpful Hints and Advice to Employees," that warned against drinking, gambling, borrowing money, taking in boarders, and practicing poor hygiene. Ford also created a department of 100 investigators for door-to-door checks on his employees' drinking habits, sexual practices, and housekeeping skills. It may be surprising, but in modern times, employees have been fired or disciplined for such extracurricular activities as playing dangerous sports, dating coworkers, or even having high cholesterol. What protection do workers have against intrusive employers?

Employees are entitled under the common law to a reasonable expectation of privacy. This protection means that an employer could not, for instance, search an employee's home even if looking for items that the employee might have stolen from the company. What other privacy protections do workers have?

OFF-DUTY CONDUCT

A worker's off-duty conduct may affect her employer. For instance, a smoker may have lower productivity and higher healthcare expenses. As a result, some employers refuse to hire smokers or even threaten to fire current workers who smoke.

> Can a boss fire a worker for smoking at home?

But more than half of the states have passed statutes prohibiting job bans on smokers. Indeed, some states have passed laws that protect the right of employees to engage in any *lawful* activity when off duty, including smoking, drinking socially, having high cholesterol, being overweight, or engaging in dangerous hobbies—bungee jumping or rollerblading, for instance. In the absence of such a statute, however, an employer does have the right to fire an employee for off-duty conduct.

ALCOHOL AND DRUG TESTING

Government employees can be tested for drug and alcohol use only if they show signs of use or if they are in a job where this type of abuse endangers the public. The federal government and most states permit *private* employers to administer alcohol and drug tests, and a substantial number do. However, the Equal Employment Opportunity Commission (EEOC), which is the federal agency charged with enforcing federal employment laws, prohibits testing for prescription drugs unless a worker seems impaired.

LIE DETECTOR TESTS

Under the Employee Polygraph Protection Act of 1988, employers may not require, or even suggest, that an employee or job candidate submit to a lie detector test, except as part of an "ongoing investigation" into crimes that have occurred.

ELECTRONIC MONITORING OF THE WORKPLACE

Technological advances in communications have raised a host of new privacy issues. The Electronic Communications Privacy Act of 1986 (ECPA) permits employers to monitor workers' telephone calls and email messages if (1) the employee consents; (2) the monitoring occurs in the ordinary course of business; or (3) in the case of email, the employer provides the email system. However, bosses may not disclose any private information revealed by the monitoring.

Sending personal emails through a company server is dangerous. In one case, the court upheld the firing of two workers who exchanged joking (they claimed) emails threatening violence to sales managers. The company had an explicit policy stating that emails were confidential and would not be intercepted or used against an employee.[5] A few courts have ruled for employees on this issue, but unless you enjoy the prospect of engaging in years of litigation to clarify the point, it is a good idea to consider all email you send through a company server to be public.

SOCIAL MEDIA

Social media are the newest challenge facing both employers and workers alike. Companies may find themselves liable for statements that their workers make electronically. For example, Cisco Systems Inc. has settled two lawsuits brought against the company for statements made by a company lawyer on his blog. Not surprisingly, employers have fired workers who posted inappropriate information in cyberspace. But companies may find themselves liable for violations of employee privacy if a boss reads workers' Facebook or MySpace pages.

In short, the law is uncertain and varies by state, so employees at will should err on the side of caution and consider anything they publish on the Internet to be public. As for companies, it makes sense to establish policies that protect them from liability for their employees' cyber words. At a minimum, they should not permit employees to reveal confidential information or even their company's name on a blog or social website such as Facebook.

IMMIGRATION

Once a new worker has been hired, the employer must complete an I-9 form—Employment Eligibility Verification—within three days. The I-9 must be kept for three years after the worker is hired or one year after termination.

EXAM Strategy

Question: To ensure that its employees did not use illegal drugs in or outside the workplace, Marvel Grocery Store required all employees to take a lie detector test. Moreover, managers began to screen the company email system for drug references. Jagger was fired for refusing to take the polygraph test. Jonathan was sacked when a search of his email revealed that he had used marijuana during the prior weekend. Has the company acted legally?

Strategy: First: As employees at will, are Jagger and Jonathan protected by a statute? The Employee Polygraph Protection Act permits employers to require a lie detector test as part of an ongoing investigation into crimes that have occurred. Here, Marvel has no reason to believe that a crime occurred, so it cannot require a polygraph test. Second: What about Jonathan's marijuana use? The ECPA permits Marvel to monitor email messages on its own system. But can the company fire Jonathan for illegal off-duty conduct? Some statutes protect employees for *legal* behavior outside the workplace, but no state protects employees for behavior that violates the law.

Result: The company is liable to Jagger for requiring him to take the lie detector test, but not to Jonathan for monitoring his email or firing him for illegal drug use.

---

[5] *Smyth v. Pillsbury*, 914 F. Supp. 97, 1996 U.S. Dist. LEXIS 776, (Fed. Dist. Ct., 1996)

FINANCIAL PROTECTION

Congress and the states have enacted laws that provide employees with a measure of financial security. All of the laws in this section were created by statute, not by the courts.

Fair Labor Standards Act

The Fair Labor Standards Act (FLSA) regulates wages and limits child labor nationally. It provides that hourly workers must be paid a minimum wage of $7.25 per hour, plus time and a half for any hours over 40 in one week. These wage provisions do not apply to managerial, administrative, or professional staff. More than half the states set a higher minimum wage, so it is important to check state guidelines as well.

The FLSA also prohibits "oppressive child labor," which means that children under 14 may work only in agriculture and entertainment. Fourteen- and fifteen-year-olds are permitted to work limited hours after school in nonhazardous jobs. Sixteen- and seventeen-year-olds may work unlimited hours in nonhazardous jobs.

Workers' Compensation

Workers' compensation statutes provide payment to employees for injuries incurred at work. In return, employees are not permitted to sue their employers for negligence. The amounts allowed (for medical expenses and lost wages) under workers' comp statutes are often less than a worker might recover in court, but the injured employee trades the certainty of some recovery for the higher risk of rolling the dice at trial.

Social Security

The federal social security system began in 1935, during the depths of the Great Depression, to provide a basic safety net for the elderly, ill, and unemployed. The social security system pays benefits to workers who are retired, disabled, or temporarily unemployed and to the spouses and children of disabled or deceased workers. It also provides medical insurance to the retired and disabled. The social security program is financed through a tax on wages that is paid by employers, employees, and the self-employed.

Although the social security system has done much to reduce poverty among the elderly, many worry that it cannot survive in its current form. The system was designed to be "pay as you go," that is, when workers pay taxes, the proceeds do not go into a savings account for their retirement but instead are used to pay benefits to current retirees. In 1940, there were 40 workers for each retiree; currently, there are 3.3. By 2025, when the last Baby Boomers retire, there will be only two workers to support each retiree—a prohibitive burden. No wonder Baby Boomers are often cautioned not to count on social security when making their retirement plans.

The Federal Unemployment Tax Act (FUTA) is the part of the social security system that provides support to the unemployed. FUTA establishes some national standards, but states are free to set their own benefit levels and payment schedules. While receiving payments, a worker must make a good-faith effort to look for other employment. A worker who quits voluntarily or is fired for just cause is not entitled to benefits.

Chapter Conclusion

Although managers sometimes feel overwhelmed by the long list of laws that protect workers, the United States guarantees its workers fewer rights than virtually any other industrialized nation. For instance, Japan, Great Britain, France, Germany, and Canada all require employers to show just cause before terminating workers. Although American employers are no longer insulated from minimum standards of fairness, reasonable behavior, and compliance with important policies, they still have great freedom to manage their employees.

Exam Review

1. **TRADITIONAL COMMON LAW RULE** Traditionally, an employee at will could be fired for a good reason, a bad reason, or no reason at all. This right is now modified by common law and by statute. (p. 320)

2. **NLRA** The National Labor Relations Act prohibits employers from penalizing workers for union activity. (p. 320)

3. **FMLA** The Family and Medical Leave Act guarantees workers up to 12 weeks of unpaid leave each year for childbirth, adoption, or a serious health condition of their own or in their immediate family. (p. 321)

4. **HEALTH INSURANCE** Starting in 2014, employers who have more than 50 full-time employees must pay a penalty if they do not provide basic health insurance. (p. 321)

5. **COBRA** Former employees must be allowed to continue their health insurance for 18 months after being terminated from their job, but they must pay for it themselves. (p. 321)

6. **WRONGFUL DISCHARGE** Under the doctrine of wrongful discharge, an employer cannot fire a worker for a reason that violates public policy. (pp. 321–323)

7. **PUBLIC POLICY** Generally, an employee may not be fired for refusing to violate the law, performing a legal duty, exercising a legal right, or supporting basic societal values. (p. 321)

8. **TRUTH IN HIRING** Promises made during the hiring process are enforceable. (p. 323)

EXAM Strategy

Question: When Phil McConkey interviewed for a job as an insurance agent with Alexander & Alexander, the company did not tell him that it was engaged in secret negotiations to merge with Aon. When the merger went through soon thereafter, Aon fired McConkey. Was Alexander liable for not telling McConkey about the possible merger?

Strategy: Was McConkey protected by a statute? No. Did the company make any promises to him during the hiring process? (See the "Result" at the end of this section.)

9. **HANDBOOKS**   An employee handbook creates a contract. (pp. 323–324)

10. **DEFAMATION**   Employers may be liable for defamation if they give false and unfavorable references. More than half of the states, however, recognize a qualified privilege for employers who give references about former employees. (pp. 324–325)

EXAM Strategy

Question: Jack was a top salesperson but a real pain in the neck. He argued with everyone, especially his boss, Ross. Finally, Ross had had enough and abruptly fired Jack. But he was worried that if Jack went to work for a competitor, he might take business away. So Ross told everyone who called for a reference that Jack was a difficult human being. Is Ross liable for these statements?

Strategy: Ross would be liable for making untrue statements. (See the "Result" at the end of this section.)

11. **INTENTIONAL INFLICTION OF EMOTIONAL DISTRESS**   Employers are liable if they treat their workers cruelly. (p. 325)

12. **WHISTLEBLOWERS**   Whistleblowers receive some protection under both federal and state laws. (pp. 325–326)

13. **OSHA**   The goal of the Occupational Safety and Health Act is to ensure safe conditions in the workplace. (pp. 326–327)

14. **EMPLOYEE PRIVACY**   An employer may not violate a worker's reasonable expectation of privacy. However, unless a state has passed a statute to the contrary, employers may monitor many types of off-duty conduct (even legal activities such as smoking). (pp. 327–328)

15. **THE ECPA**   The Electronic Communications Privacy Act of 1986 permits employers to monitor workers' telephone calls and email messages if (1) the employee consents, (2) the monitoring occurs in the ordinary course of business, or (3) in the case of email, the employer provides the email system. (p. 327)

16. **IMMIGRATION**   Once a new worker has been hired, the employer must complete an I-9 form—Employment Eligibility Verification—within three days. (p. 328)

17. **THE FLSA**   The Fair Labor Standards Act regulates minimum and overtime wages. It also limits child labor. (p. 329)

18. **WORKERS' COMPENSATION**   Workers' compensation statutes ensure that employees receive payment for injuries incurred at work. (p. 329)

19. **SOCIAL SECURITY**   The social security system pays benefits to workers who are retired, disabled, or temporarily unemployed and to the spouses and children of disabled or deceased workers. (p. 329)

8. Result: The court held that when Alexander hired him, it was making an implied promise that he would not be fired immediately. The company was liable for not having revealed the merger negotiations.

10. Result: These statements were true, so Ross would not be liable. Before making the statements, though, he should ask himself if he wanted the burden of having to prove them true in court.

MATCHING QUESTIONS

Match the following terms with their definitions:

___A. Employee at will

___B. Public policy rule

___C. FLSA

___D. Wrongful discharge

___E. OSHA

___F. Whistleblower

1. A federal statute that ensures safe working conditions

2. Happens when an employee is fired for a bad reason

3. An employee who discloses illegal behavior on the part of his employer

4. An employee without an explicit employment contract

5. A federal statute that regulates wages and limits child labor

6. States that an employer may not fire a worker for refusing to violate the law, performing a legal duty, exercising a legal right, or supporting basic societal values.

TRUE/FALSE QUESTIONS

Circle true or false:

1. T F An employee may be fired for a good reason, a bad reason, or no reason at all.

2. T F An employee may be fired if she disobeys a direct order from her boss not to join a labor union.

3. T F Promises made by the employer during the hiring process are not enforceable.

4. T F In some states, employers are not liable for false statements they make about former employees unless they know these statements are false or are primarily motivated by ill will.

5. T F The federal government has the right to inspect workplaces to ensure that they are safe.

6. T F Any employer has the right to insist that employees submit to a lie detector test.

7. T F Federal law limits the number of hours every employee can work.

8. T F Children under 16 may not hold paid jobs.

9. T F Only workers, not their spouses or children, are entitled to benefits under the social security system.

MULTIPLE-CHOICE QUESTIONS

1. Brook moved from Denver to San Francisco to take a job with an advertising agency. His employment contract stated that he was "at will and could be terminated at any time." After 28 months with the company, he was fired without explanation. Which of the following statements is true?

    (a) His contract implied that he could only be fired for cause.

    (b) Because he had a contract, he was not an employee at will.

    (c) He could only be fired for a good reason.

    (d) He could be fired for any reason.

    (e) He could be fired for any reason except a bad reason.

2. Under the FMLA:

    (a) Both men and women are entitled to take a leave of absence from their jobs for childbirth, adoption, or a serious health condition of their own or in their immediate family.

    (b) An employee is entitled to 12 weeks of paid leave.

    (c) An employee is entitled to leave to care for any member of his household, including pets.

    (d) An employee who takes a leave is entitled to return to the exact job she left.

    (e) All employees in the country are covered.

3. Which of the following statements is true under the public policy doctrine?

    (a) An employee can be fired for any reason.

    (b) An employee can be fired for threatening a coworker.

    (c) An employee can be fired for filing a workers' compensation claim.

    (d) An employee can be fired for violating company policy, even if he does so to save someone's life.

    (e) An employee can be fired for refusing to lie under oath on the witness stand.

4. A whistleblower is

    (a) always protected by the law

    (b) never protected by the law

    (c) always protected when filing suit under the False Claims Act

    (d) always protected if she is an employee of the federal government

    (e) always protected if she works for a private company

5. George was furious when Hermione left the company in the middle of a very busy sales period. He vowed that he would get even with her. Another employer called to check Hermione's references. Which of the following statements should George make, if his goal is to limit his company's potential liability?

    (a) Hermione was generally a good worker, but she was often late arriving at the office. (This is true.)

    (b) Hermione tried to run over a coworker with her car. (This is true.)

    (c) Hermione wore inappropriate clothing. (This is not true.)

(d) Hermione doesn't know her debits from her credits. (This is not true.)

(e) Hermione worked for this company for a year and a half. Her title was chief knowledge officer. (This is true.)

6. **CPA QUESTION:** An unemployed CPA generally would receive unemployment compensation benefits if the CPA:

   (a) Was fired as a result of the employer's business reversals

   (b) Refused to accept a job as an accountant while receiving extended benefits

   (c) Was fired for embezzling from a client

   (d) Left work voluntarily without good cause

Essay Questions

1. Reginald Delaney managed a Taco Time restaurant in Portland, Oregon. Some of his customers told Mr. Ledbetter, the district manager, that they would not be eating there so often because there were too many black employees. Ledbetter told Delaney to fire Ms. White, who was black. Delaney did as he was told. Ledbetter's report on the incident said: "My notes show that Delaney told me that White asked him to sleep with her and that when he would not, that she started causing dissension within the crew. She asked him to come over to her house and that he declined." Delaney refused to sign the report because it was untrue, so Ledbetter fired him. What claim might Delaney make against his former employer?

2. Debra Agis worked as a waitress in a Ground Round restaurant. The manager, Roger Dionne, informed the waitresses that "there was some stealing going on." Until he found out who was doing it, he intended to fire all the waitresses in alphabetical order, starting with the letter "A." Dionne then fired Agis. Does she have a valid claim against her employer?

3. Kay Smith was Catherine Wagenseller's supervisor at Scottsdale Memorial Hospital. Wagenseller was an employee at will. While on a camping trip with other nurses, Wagenseller refused to join in a parody of the song "Moon River," which concluded with members of the group "mooning" the audience. Prior to the trip, Wagenseller had received consistently favorable performance evaluations. Six months after the outing, Wagenseller was fired. She contends that she was fired for reasons that violated public policy. Should the hospital be able to fire Wagenseller for refusing to moon?

4. **ETHICS:** When Walton Weiner interviewed for a job with McGraw-Hill, Inc., he was assured that the company would not terminate an employee without "just cause." McGraw-Hill's handbook said, "[The] company will resort to dismissal for just and sufficient cause only, and only after all practical steps toward rehabilitation or salvage of the employee have been taken and failed. However, if the welfare of the company indicates that dismissal is necessary, then that decision is arrived at and is carried out forthrightly." After eight years, Weiner was fired suddenly for "lack of application." Does Weiner have a valid claim against McGraw-Hill? Apart from the legal issue, did McGraw-Hill do the right thing? Was the process fair? Did the company's behavior violate important values?

5. FedEx gave Marcie Dutschmann an employment handbook stating that: (1) she was an at-will employee, (2) the handbook did not create any contractual rights, and (3) employees who were fired had the right to a termination hearing. The company fired Dutschmann, claiming that she had falsified delivery records. She said that FedEx was retaliating against her because she had complained of sexual harassment. FedEx refused her request for a termination hearing. Did the employee handbook create an implied contract guaranteeing Dutschmann a hearing?

DISCUSSION QUESTIONS

1. School officials fired a teacher after they saw a photo on her Facebook page that showed her looking sober, but holding a glass of wine in her hand. Her school was combating an epidemic of binge drinking, and they feared her photo set a bad example for students. Should they be allowed to fire her?

2. Most smokers begin as teenagers, and an addiction to nicotine is very hard to break. On the other hand, the federal government estimates that it costs $3,400 a year to employ a worker who smokes. Should employers be allowed to discriminate against smokers?

3. Workers who are tested after accidents in the workplace were four times more likely to have opiates in their system than job applicants. Many of these opiates are from legal drug prescriptions, often prescribed to treat pain from work-related injuries. The EEOC prohibits testing for prescription drugs unless a worker seems impaired. It has filed suit against a company that randomly tested employees for prescription drugs, but the court has not yet issued an opinion. What would be the right result in this case?

4. Most shoplifting in retail stores is done by employees. Should employers be allowed to perform routine polygraphs to weed out thieves?

5. In many countries, employers must show just cause before firing an employee. Should the United States have such a law?

CHAPTER 19

EMPLOYMENT DISCRIMINATION

Imagine that you are on the hiring committee of a top San Francisco law firm. You come across a resume from a candidate who grew up on an isolated ranch in Arizona. Raised in a house without electricity or running water, he had worked alongside the ranch hands his entire childhood. At the age of 16, he left home for Stanford University and from there had gone on to Stanford Law School, where he finished third in his class. You think to yourself, "This sounds like a real American success story. A great combination of hard work and intelligence." But without hesitation, you toss the resume into the wastebasket.

This is a true story. Indeed, there was a candidate with these credentials who was unable to find a job in any San Francisco law firm. The only jobs on offer were as a secretary because this candidate was a woman— Sandra Day O'Connor, who went on to become one of the most influential lawyers of her era and the first woman Supreme Court Justice. But when she graduated from law school, that is the way the world was. It was a terrible waste of resources—so many talented people who were unable to use their skills. In the last four decades, Congress has enacted important legislation to prevent discrimination in the workplace.

> You think, "This sounds like a real American success story." But you toss the resume into the wastebasket.

EQUAL PAY ACT OF 1963

Under the Equal Pay Act, an employee may not be paid at a lesser rate than employees of the opposite sex for equal work. "Equal work" means tasks that require equal skill, effort, and responsibility under similar working conditions. If the employee proves that she is not being paid equally, the employer will be found liable unless the pay difference is based on merit, productivity, seniority, or some factor other than sex. A "factor other than sex" includes prior wages, training, profitability, performance in an interview, and value to the company. For example, female agents sued Allstate Insurance Co. because its salary for new agents was based, in part, on prior salary. The women argued that this system was unfair because it perpetuated the historic wage differences between men and women. The court, however, held for Allstate.

TITLE VII

Prior to 1964, it was legal to treat men and women, whites and people of color, differently in the workplace. Women, for example, could be paid less than men for the same job and could be fired if they got married or pregnant. Newspapers had different pages for men's and women's job ads. Under Title VII of the Civil Rights Act of 1964, it is illegal for employers to discriminate on the basis of race, color, religion, sex, or national origin. More specifically, Title VII prohibits (1) discrimination in the workplace; (2) sexual harassment; and (3) discrimination because of pregnancy. It also permits employers to develop affirmative action plans under certain circumstances.

Discrimination under Title VII means firing, refusing to hire, failing to promote, or otherwise reducing a person's employment opportunities because of race, color, religion, sex, or national origin. This protection applies to every stage of the employment process from job ads to postemployment references and includes placement, wages, benefits, and working conditions.

Proof of Discrimination

Plaintiffs in Title VII cases can prove discrimination two different ways: disparate treatment and disparate impact.

DISPARATE TREATMENT

To prove a disparate treatment case, the plaintiff must show that she was *treated* differently because of her sex, race, color, religion, or national origin. The required steps in a disparate treatment case are:

Step 1. The plaintiff presents evidence that the defendant has discriminated against her because of a protected trait. This is called a ***prima facie*** case. The plaintiff is not required to prove discrimination; she need only create a *presumption* that discrimination occurred.

Suppose that Louisa applies for a job coaching a boys' high school ice hockey team. She was an All-American hockey star in college. Although Louisa is obviously qualified for the job, Harry, the school principal, rejects her and continues to interview other people. This is not proof of discrimination because Harry may have a perfectly good, nondiscriminatory explanation. However, his behavior *could have been* motivated by discrimination.

Step 2. The defendant must present evidence that its decision was based on *legitimate, nondiscriminatory* reasons. Harry might say, for example, that he wanted someone with prior coaching experience. Although Louisa is clearly a great player, she has never coached before.

Step 3. To win, the plaintiff must now prove that the employer discriminated. She may do so by showing that the reasons offered were simply a *pretext*. Louisa might show that Harry had recently hired a male to coach the tennis team who had no prior coaching experience. Or Harry's assistant might testify that Harry said, "No way I'm going to put a woman on the ice with those guys." If she can present evidence such as this, Louisa wins.

In the following case, was the bartender treated differently because of her sex?

You be the Judge

JESPERSEN V. HARRAH'S

444 F.3d 1104, 2006 U.S. App. LEXIS 9307
United States Court of Appeals for
the Ninth Circuit, 2006

Facts: Darlene Jespersen was a bartender at the sports bar in Harrah's Casino in Reno, Nevada. She was an outstanding employee, frequently praised by both her supervisors and customers.

When Jespersen first went to work for Harrah's, female bartenders were encouraged, but not required, to wear makeup. Jespersen tried for a short period of time, but she did not like it. Moreover, she felt that wearing makeup interfered with her ability to deal with unruly, intoxicated guests because it "took away [her] credibility as an individual and as a person."

After Jespersen had been at Harrah's for almost 20 years, the casino implemented a program that required bartenders to be "well groomed, appealing to the eye." More explicitly, for men:

- Hair must not extend below top of shirt collar. Ponytails are prohibited.

- Hands and fingernails must be clean and nails neatly trimmed at all times.

- No colored polish is permitted.

- Eye and facial makeup is not permitted.

- Shoes will be solid black leather or leather type with rubber (nonskid) soles.

The rules for women were:

- Hair must be teased, curled, or styled. Hair must be worn down at all times, no exceptions.

- Nail polish can be clear, white, pink, or red color only. No exotic nail art or length.

- Shoes will be solid black leather or leather type with rubber (non-skid) soles.

- Makeup (foundation/concealer and/or face powder, as well as blush and mascara) must be worn and applied neatly in complimentary colors, and lip color must be worn at all times.

An expert was brought in to show the employees (both male and female) how to dress. The workers were then photographed and told that they must look like the photographs every day at work.

When Jespersen refused to wear makeup, Harrah's fired her. She sued under Title VII. The district court granted Harrah's motion for summary judgment. Jespersen appealed.

You Be the Judge: *Did Harrah's requirement that women wear makeup violate Title VII?*

Argument for Jespersen: Jespersen refused to wear makeup to work because the cost—in time, money, and personal dignity—was too high.

Employers are free to adopt different appearance standards for each sex, but these standards may not impose a greater burden on one sex than the other. Men were not required to wear makeup; women were. That difference meant a savings for men of hundreds of dollars and hours of time. Harrah's did not have the right to fire Jespersen for violating a rule that applies only to women, with no equivalent for men.

Argument for Harrah's: Employers are permitted to impose different appearance rules on women than on men as long as the overall burden on employees is the same. For example, it is not discriminatory to require men to wear their hair short. On balance, Harrah's rules did not impose a heavier burden on women than on men.

EXAM Strategy

Question: Although Kim was an able accountant, she offended a lot of her male colleagues because she was unattractive and had a loud, masculine voice. She was also aggressive about demanding raises. Kim was denied promotion. Has the firm violated Title VII?

Strategy: Was Kim being treated differently because of her sex?

Result: The firm had to have the same expectations for men as it did for women. If it promoted only attractive men with soft voices, then it had the right not to promote Kim, either. But if the standards were different for men and women, then the firm was in violation.

DISPARATE IMPACT

Disparate impact applies if the employer has a rule that, *on its face,* is not discriminatory, but *in practice* excludes too many people in a protected group. The following landmark case illustrates this principle.

Landmark Case

GRIGGS V. DUKE POWER CO.

401 U.S. 424, 91 S. Ct. 849, 1971 U.S. LEXIS 134
United States Supreme Court, 1971

CASE SUMMARY

Facts: Before Title VII, Duke Power hired black employees only in the Labor department, where the highest pay was less than the lowest earnings in the other departments. After Title VII, the company required all new hires for jobs in the desirable departments to have a high school education or satisfactory scores on two tests that measured intelligence and mechanical ability. Neither test gauged the ability to perform a particular job. The pass rate for whites was much higher than for blacks and whites were also more likely than blacks to have a high school diploma. The new policy did not apply to the (exclusively white) employees who were already working in the preferred departments. These "unqualified" whites all performed their jobs satisfactorily.

Black employees sued Duke Power, alleging that this hiring policy violated Title VII.

Issue: *Does a policy violate Title VII if it has the* **effect of** *discriminating, even though the* **intent** *was not discriminatory?*

whites, but only if the requirements are *necessary* to do that *particular* work. In this case, there was no evidence that either a high school diploma or the two tests bore any relationship to the job in question. Indeed, white employees without any of these qualifications had been doing the jobs well for years and had even been promoted.

Whether or not Duke Power intended to discriminate is irrelevant. Title VII is concerned with the *consequences* of an employer's practices, not its motivation. The burden is on the employer to show that all job requirements have an important relationship to the work in question. Any tests must measure the person for the job and not the person in the abstract.

Decision: Yes, a policy violates Title VII if it has a discriminatory impact, regardless of intent.

Reasoning: Under Title VII, employers may establish job requirements that exclude more blacks than

The steps in a disparate impact case are:

Step 1. The plaintiff must present a *prima facie* case. The plaintiff is not required to prove discrimination; he need only show a disparate impact—that the employment practice in question excludes a disproportionate number of people in a protected group (women and minorities, for instance). In the *Griggs* case, a higher percentage of whites than blacks passed the tests required for a job in one of the desirable departments.

Step 2. The defendant must offer some evidence that the employment practice was a *job-related business necessity*. Duke Power would have to show that the tests predicted job performance.

Step 3. To win, the plaintiff must now prove either that the employer's reason is a *pretext* or that other, *less discriminatory* rules would achieve the same results.

The plaintiffs in *Griggs* showed that the tests were not a job-related business necessity—after all, whites who had not passed any of these tests performed the jobs well. Duke Power could no longer use them as a hiring screen. If the power company wanted to use tests, it would have to find some that measured an employee's ability to perform particular jobs.

Hiring tests remain controversial. In a recent case, a group of white firefighters sued the city of New Haven, Connecticut, for discarding promotion tests on which twice as many whites as blacks passed. The Supreme Court upheld the use of the examination on the grounds that it was job-related and consistent with business necessity, and there was no strong evidence that an equally valid, less-discriminatory test existed. In short, the mere existence of a disparate impact does not mean that an employment practice violates the law.

Color

Title VII prohibits discrimination based on both race and color. Although many people assume that they are essentially the same, that is not necessarily the case. For example, Dwight Burch alleged that his coworkers at an Applebee's restaurant called him hateful names because of his dark skin color. These colleagues were also African American but were lighter-skinned. Burch sued on the basis of "color discrimination."

Title VII prohibits the type of treatment that Burch allegedly suffered. While denying any wrongdoing, Applebee's settled the case by paying Burch $40,000 and agreeing to conduct antidiscrimination training.

Transgender

David Schroer was in the Army for 25 years, including a stint tracking terrorists. The Library of Congress offered him a job as a specialist in terrorism. (Who knew that libraries needed terrorism specialists?) However, when he revealed that he was in the process of becoming Diane Schroer, the Library of Congress withdrew the offer. As you can guess, he sued under Title VII.

Traditionally, courts took the view that sex under Title VII applied only to how people were born, not what they chose to become. Employers could and did fire workers for changing sex. However, a federal court recently found the Library of Congress in violation of Title VII for withdrawing Schroer's offer. Only time will tell if other federal courts will follow this lead.

Retaliation

Title VII not only prohibits discrimination, it also penalizes employers who retaliate against workers for *complaining* about discrimination. Retaliation in this circumstance means that the employer has done something so bad it would deter a reasonable worker from complaining about discrimination. For example, when a woman was demoted to a less desirable job after she complained about sexual harassment by her boss, the company was liable.

Religion

Employers must make *reasonable accommodation* for a worker's religious beliefs unless the request would cause *undue hardship* for the business. What would you do in the following cases if you were the boss:

1. A Christian says he cannot work at Wal-Mart on Sundays—his Sabbath. It also happens to be one of the store's busiest days.

2. A Jewish police officer wants to wear a beard and yarmulke as part of his religious observance. Facial hair and headgear are banned by the force.

3. Muslim workers at a meat-packing plant want to pray at sundown but break times were specified in the labor contract and sundown changes from day to day. The workers begin to take bathroom breaks at sundown, stopping work on the production line.

Disputes such as these are on the rise and are not easy to handle fairly. In the end, Wal-Mart fired the Christian, but when he sued on the grounds of religious discrimination, the company settled the case. A judge ruled that the police officer could keep his beard because the force allowed other employees with medical conditions to wear facial hair, but the headcovering had to go. The boss at the meat-packing plant fired the Muslim employees who walked off the job.

Defenses to Charges of Discrimination

Under Title VII, the defendant has three possible defenses.

MERIT

A defendant is not liable if he shows that the person he favored was the most qualified. Test results, education, or productivity can all be used to demonstrate merit, provided they relate to the job in question. Harry can show that he hired Bruce for the coaching job instead of Louisa because Bruce has a master's degree in physical education and seven years of coaching experience. On the other hand, the fact that Bruce scored higher on the National Latin Exam in the eighth grade is not a good reason to hire him over Louisa for a coaching job.

SENIORITY

A legitimate seniority system is legal even if it perpetuates past discrimination. Suppose that Harry has always chosen the most senior assistant coach to take over as head coach when a vacancy occurs. Since the majority of the senior assistant coaches are male, most of the head coaches are, too. Such a system does not violate Title VII.

BONA FIDE OCCUPATIONAL QUALIFICATION

An employer is permitted to establish discriminatory job requirements if they are *essential* to the position in question. The business must show that it cannot fulfill its primary function unless it discriminates in this way. Such a requirement is called a **bona fide occupational qualification (BFOQ)**. Catholic schools may, if they choose, refuse to hire non-Catholic teachers; clothing companies may refuse to hire men to model women's attire. Generally, however, courts are not sympathetic to claims of BFOQ. They have, for example, almost always rejected BFOQ claims that are based on customer preference.

Bona fide occupational qualification (BFOQ)
An employer is permitted to establish discriminatory job requirements if they are *essential* to the position in question.

Thus, airlines could not refuse to hire male flight attendants even if they believed that travelers prefer female attendants. The major exception to this customer preference rule is sexual privacy: an employer may refuse to hire women to work in a men's bathroom, and vice versa.

Affirmative Action

Affirmative action is not required by Title VII, nor is it prohibited. Affirmative action programs have three different sources:

- *Litigation.* Courts have the power under Title VII to order affirmative action to remedy the effects of past discrimination.

- *Voluntary action.* Employers can voluntarily introduce an affirmative action plan to remedy the effects of past practices or to achieve equitable representation of minorities and women.

- *Government contracts.* In 1965, President Lyndon Johnson signed Executive Order 11246, which prohibits discrimination by federal contractors. This order had a profound impact on the American workplace because one-third of all workers are employed by companies that do business with the federal government. If an employer found that women or minorities were underrepresented in its workplace, it was required to establish goals and timetables to correct the deficiency.

In 1995, however, the Supreme Court ruled that these affirmative action programs are permissible only if (1) the government can show that the programs are needed to overcome specific past discrimination; (2) they have time limits; and (3) nondiscriminatory alternatives are not available.

> Everyone has heard of sexual harassment, but few people know exactly what it is.

Sexual harassment

Involves unwelcome sexual advances, requests for sexual favors, and other verbal or physical conduct of a sexual nature.

Quid pro quo

A Latin phrase that means "one thing in return for another."

Sexual Harassment

Everyone has heard of sexual harassment, but few people know exactly what it is. Men fear that a casual comment or glance will be met with career-ruining charges; women claim that men "just don't get it." So what is sexual harassment, anyway? **Sexual harassment involves unwelcome sexual advances, requests for sexual favors, and other verbal or physical conduct of a sexual nature.** There are two major categories of sexual harassment:

- *Quid Pro Quo.* From a Latin phrase that means "one thing in return for another," *quid pro quo* harassment occurs if any aspect of a job is made contingent upon sexual activity. In other words, when a banker says to an assistant, "You can be promoted to teller if you sleep with me," that is *quid pro quo* sexual harassment.

- **Hostile Work Environment.** An employee has a valid claim of sexual harassment if sexual talk and innuendo are so pervasive that they interfere with her (or his) ability to work. Courts have found that offensive jokes, comments about clothes or body parts, and public displays of pornographic pictures create a hostile environment. In a landmark case, the Supreme Court found a company liable because its president frequently made inappropriate sexual comments to female employees. He called one worker "a dumb-ass woman" and suggested that the two of them "go to the Holiday Inn to negotiate her raise." He also insisted that women employees pick up objects he had thrown on the ground.[1]

Text messages have become a new frontier in sexual harassment—so-called *textual harassment.* In behavior that can only make you ask, "What were they thinking?" bosses have sent wildly inappropriate text messages to their subordinates—offering promotions for sex or providing evidence of a sexual relationship. News flash: text messages can be recovered and juries can read. "She said, he said" cases are a lot harder to win than "She said, he texted."

Employees who commit sexual harassment are liable for their own wrongdoing. But is their company also liable? The Supreme Court has held that:

- If the victimized employee has suffered a "tangible employment action" such as firing, demotion, or reassignment, the company is liable to her for sexual harassment by a supervisor.

- Even if the victimized employee has *not* suffered a tangible employment action, the company is liable unless it can prove that (1) it used reasonable care to prevent and correct sexually harassing behavior; and (2) the employee unreasonably failed to take advantage of the company's complaint procedures.

In an effort to develop practical guidelines for its employees, Corning Consumer Products Co. asks them to apply four tests in judging whether their behavior constitutes sexual harassment:

- Would you say or do this in front of your spouse or parents?

- What about in front of a colleague of the opposite sex?

- Would you like your behavior reported in your local newspaper?

- Does it need to be said or done at all?

Procedures and Remedies

Before a plaintiff in a Title VII case brings suit, she must first file a complaint with the federal Equal Employment Opportunity Commission (EEOC). Note, however, that the plaintiff must file within 180 days of the wrongdoing. The EEOC then has the right to sue on behalf of the plaintiff. This arrangement is favorable for the plaintiff because the government pays the legal bill. If the EEOC decides not to bring the case or does not make a decision within six months, it issues a **right to sue letter,** and the plaintiff may proceed on her own in court. Many states also have their own version of the EEOC.

Remedies available to the successful plaintiff include hiring, reinstatement, retroactive seniority, back pay, reasonable attorney's fees, and damages of up to $300,000. However, employers now often require new hires to agree in advance to arbitrate, not litigate, any future employment claims. Typically, employees receive worse results in the arbitrator's office than in the courtroom.

Pregnancy

Lucasfilm Ltd. (owned by filmmaker George Lucas) offered Julie Veronese a job as a manager on his California estate, but then withdrew the offer when she revealed she was pregnant. Is that a problem? Under the Pregnancy Discrimination Act of 1978, **an employer may not fire or refuse to hire a woman because she is pregnant.** An employer must also treat

---

[1]*Harris v. Forklift Systems,* 510 U.S. 17, 114 S. Ct. 367, 1993 U.S. LEXIS 7155.

pregnancy as any other temporary disability. If, for example, employees are allowed time off from work for other medical disabilities, women must also be allowed a maternity leave. A jury ordered Lucasfilm to pay Veronese $113,800.

The Pregnancy Discrimination Act also protects a woman's right to terminate a pregnancy. An employer cannot fire a woman for having an abortion.

Parenthood

Suppose that you are in charge of hiring at your company. You receive applications from four people: a mother, a father, a childless woman, and a childless father. All have equivalent qualifications. Which one would you hire? In studies, participants repeatedly rank mothers as less qualified than other employees, and fathers as most desirable, even when their credentials are exactly the same.

Increasingly, courts have held that unequal treatment of mothers is a violation of Title VII. For example, after Dawn Gallina, an associate at the Mintz, Levin law firm, revealed to her boss that she had a young child, he began to treat her differently from her male colleagues and spoke to her "about the commitment differential between men and women." The court ruled that her belief of illegal discrimination was reasonable.[2] The EEOC has issued guidelines indicating that stereotypes are not a legitimate basis for personnel decisions.

AGE DISCRIMINATION

The Age Discrimination in Employment Act (ADEA) of 1967 prohibits age discrimination against employees or job applicants who are at least 40 years old. An employer may not fire, refuse to hire, fail to promote, or otherwise reduce a person's employment opportunities because he is 40 or older. Employers may not require workers to retire at any age (with a few exceptions, such as police officers and top-level corporate executives).

The procedure for an age-bias claim is similar to that under Title VII—plaintiffs must first file a charge with the EEOC. If the EEOC does not take action, they can file suit themselves. However, the standard of proof is tougher in an age discrimination case than in Title VII litigation. To win a case under the ADEA, the plaintiff must show that age was not just one factor, it was the *deciding* factor.

Another issue in age discrimination cases: what happens if a company fires older workers because they are paid more? Circuit City Stores fired 8 percent of its employees because they could be replaced with people who would work for less. The fired workers were more experienced—and older. This action is legal under the ADEA. As the court put it in one case, "An action based on price differentials represents the very quintessence of a legitimate business decision."[3] Indeed, economists argue that the U.S. economy's strength is based at least in part on its flexibility—an American employer can hire workers without fear of being stuck with them until retirement.

What protection does the ADEA provide? In passing this statute, Congress was particularly concerned about employers who relied on unfavorable stereotypes rather that job performance. The following case illustrates this issue.

---

[2]*Gallina v. Mintz, Levin, Cohn, Ferris, Glovsky, and Popeo*; 2005 U.S. App. LEXIS 1710 (4th Cir., 2005).
[3]*Marks v. Loral Corp.*, 57 Cal. App. 4th 30, 1997 Cal. App. LEXIS 611 (Cal. Ct. App. 1997).

REID V. GOOGLE, INC.

50 Cal. 4th 512, 2010 Cal. LEXIS 7544;
Supreme Court of California, 2010

CASE SUMMARY

Facts: Google's vice-president of engineering, Wayne Rosing (aged 55), hired Brian Reid (52) as director of operations and director of engineering. At the time, the top executives at Google were CEO Eric Schmidt (47), vice-president of engineering operations Urs Hölzle (38), and founders Sergey Brin (28) and Larry Page (29).

During his two years at Google, Reid's only written performance review stated that he had consistently met expectations. The comments indicated that Reid had an extraordinarily broad range of knowledge, an aptitude and orientation towards operational and IT issues, an excellent attitude, and that he projected confidence when dealing with fast-changing situations, was very intelligent and creative, and was a terrific problem solver. The review also commented that "Adapting to Google culture is the primary task. Right or wrong, Google is simply different: Younger contributors, inexperienced first line managers, and the super fast pace are just a few examples of the environment."

According to Reid, even as he received a positive review, Hölzle and other employees made derogatory age-related remarks such as his ideas were "obsolete," "ancient," and "too old to matter," that he was "slow," "fuzzy," "sluggish," and "lethargic," an "old man," an "old guy," and an "old fuddy-duddy," and that he did not "display a sense of urgency" and "lacked energy."

Nineteen months after Reid joined Google, he was fired. Google says it was because of his poor performance. Reid alleges he was told it was based on a lack of "cultural fit."

Reid sued Google for age discrimination. The trial court granted Google's motion for summary judgment on the grounds that Reid did not have sufficient evidence of discrimination. He appealed.

Issues: *Did Reid have enough evidence of age discrimination to warrant a trial? Should the summary judgment motion be granted?*

Decision: The trial court was overruled and summary judgment denied.

Reasoning: Google argued that the trial court should have ignored the ageist comments about Reid because they were "stray remarks," made neither by decision-makers nor during the decision process. But stray remarks may be relevant, circumstantial evidence of discrimination. The jury should decide how relevant.

An ageist remark, in and of itself, does not prove discrimination. But when combined with other testimony, it may provide enough evidence to find liability.

AMERICANS WITH DISABILITIES ACT

The Americans with Disabilities Act (ADA) prohibits employers from discriminating on the basis of disability. As with Title VII, a plaintiff under the ADA must first file a charge with the EEOC. If the EEOC decides not to file suit, the individual may do so himself.

A disabled person is someone with a physical or mental impairment that substantially limits a major life activity or someone who is regarded as having such an impairment. The definition of major life activity includes caring for oneself, performing manual tasks, seeing, hearing, eating, sleeping, walking, standing, lifting, bending, speaking, breathing, learning, reading, concentrating, thinking, communicating, and working. Cell growth and digestive, bowel, bladder, neurological, brain, respiratory, circulatory, endocrine, reproductive, and immune system functions are also considered major life activities. However, the definition does not include the *current* use of drugs, sexual disorders, pyromania, exhibitionism, or compulsive gambling.

Disabled person
Someone with a physical or mental impairment that substantially limits a major life activity, or someone who is regarded as having such an impairment.

An employer may not refuse to hire or promote a disabled person so long as she can, with *reasonable accommodation,* **perform the** *essential functions* **of the job. An accommodation is not reasonable if it would create** *undue hardship* **for the employer.**

- *Reasonable accommodation:* This includes buying necessary equipment, providing readers or interpreters, or permitting employees to work a part-time schedule.

- *Undue hardship:* In determining what this term means, relative cost, not absolute cost, is the issue. Even an expensive accommodation—such as hiring a full-time reader—is not considered an undue hardship unless it imposes a significant burden on the overall finances of the company.

- *Essential functions:* In one case, a court held that a welder who could perform 88 percent of a job was doing the essential functions.

An employer may not ask about disabilities before making a job offer. The interviewer may ask only whether an applicant can perform the work. **Before making a job offer, an employer cannot require applicants to take a medical exam** unless the exam is (1) job-related, and (2) required of all applicants for similar jobs. However, drug testing is permitted. **After a job offer has been made, an employer may require a medical test, but it must be related to the essential functions of the job.** For example, an employer could not test the cholesterol of someone applying for an accounting job because high cholesterol is no impediment to good accounting.

An employer may not discriminate against someone because of his relationship with a disabled person. For example, an employer cannot refuse to hire an applicant because he has a child with Down's syndrome or a spouse with AIDS.

Under EEOC rules, physical and mental disabilities are to be treated the same. The difficulty is that physical ailments such as diabetes and deafness may be easy to diagnose, but what does a supervisor do when an employee is chronically late, rude, or impulsive? Does this mean the worker is mentally disabled or just a lazy, irresponsible jerk? Among other accommodations, the EEOC rules indicated that employers should be willing to put up barriers to isolate people who have difficulty concentrating, provide detailed day-to-day feedback to those who need greater structure in performing their jobs, or allow workers on antidepressants to come to work later if they are groggy in the morning.

While lauding the ADA's objectives, many managers have been apprehensive about its impact on the workplace. Most acknowledge, however, that society is clearly better off if every member has the opportunity to work. And as advocates for the disabled point out, we are all, at best, only temporarily able-bodied.

GENETIC INFORMATION NONDISCRIMINATION ACT

Suppose you want to promote someone to chief financial officer, but you know that her mother and sister both died young of breast cancer. Is it legal to consider that information in making a decision? Not since Congress passed the Genetic Information Nondiscrimination Act (GINA). **Under this statute, employers (with 15 or more workers) may not require genetic testing or discriminate against workers because of their genetic makeup.** Nor may health insurers use such information to decide coverage or premiums. Thus, neither employers nor health insurers may require you to provide your family medical history—who has died of cancer or heart disease, for instance. And if they find this information out from another source (such as a newspaper obituary), they may not use it in making an employment decision.

Every applicant feels slightly apprehensive before a job interview, but now the interviewer may be even more nervous—fearing that every question is a potential landmine of liability. Most interviewers (and students who have read this chapter) would know better than Delta

Airlines interviewers, who allegedly asked applicants about their sexual preference, birth control methods, and abortion history. The following list provides guidelines for interviewers.

Don't Even Consider Asking	Go Ahead and Ask
Can you perform this function with or without reasonable accommodation?	Would you need reasonable accommodation in this job?
How many days were you sick last year?	How many days were you absent from work last year?
What medications are you currently taking?	Are you currently using drugs illegally?
Where were you born? Are you a United States citizen?	Are you authorized to work in the United States?
How old are you?	What work experience have you had?
How tall are you? How much do you weigh?	Could you carry a 100-pound weight, as required by this job?
When did you graduate from college?	Where did you go to college?
How did you learn this language?	What languages do you speak and write fluently?
Have you ever been arrested?	Have you ever been convicted of a crime that would affect the performance of this job?
Do you plan to have children? How old are your children? What method of birth control do you use?	Can you work weekends? Travel extensively? Would you be willing to relocate?
What is your corrected vision?	Do you have 20/20 corrected vision?
Are you a man or a woman? Are you single or married? What does your spouse do? What will happen if your spouse is transferred? What clubs, societies, or lodges do you belong to?	Talk about the weather!

The most common gaffe on the part of interviewers? Asking women about their child-care arrangements. That question assumes the woman is responsible for child care.

EXAM Strategy

Question: For Michael, it was the job of his dreams—editor of *Literature* magazine. When Cyrus, the owner of the magazine, offered him the position, Michael accepted immediately. But he also revealed a secret few people knew—he had Parkinson's, a neurological disorder that affects the patient's ability to move. That symptom of the disease is controllable with medication, but about 40 percent of Parkinson's patients suffer severe dementia and become unable to work. Michael had no signs of dementia—he was the host of a popular television talk show. Fifteen minutes after

Michael returned to his hotel room, Cyrus called to withdraw the job offer. He said he did not like some of Michael's ideas for changing the magazine. Has Cyrus violated the ADA? Could he fire Michael if dementia set in?

Strategy: Is Michael covered by the ADA? Can he perform the essential functions of the job?

Result: Michael is covered by the ADA. He has an impairment that substantially limits a major life activity—movement. But Michael is able to perform the essential functions of the job, so Cyrus violated the law when he withdrew the offer. If Michael becomes demented in the future and can no longer run a magazine, Cyrus could fire him then.

Chapter Conclusion

The statutes in this chapter have changed America—it is far different now than when Sandra Day O'Connor first looked for a job. People are more likely to be offered employment because of their efforts and talents rather than their age, appearance, faith, family background, or health.

Exam Review

1. **EQUAL PAY ACT**   Under the Equal Pay Act, an employee may not be paid for equal work at a lesser rate than employees of the opposite sex. (p. 337)

2. **TITLE VII**   Title VII of the Civil Rights Act of 1964 prohibits employers from discriminating on the basis of race, color, religion, sex, or national origin. (pp. 337–344)

3. **DISPARATE TREATMENT**   To prove a disparate treatment case under Title VII, the plaintiff must show that she was treated differently because of her sex, race, color, religion, or national origin. (pp. 337–339)

4. **DISPARATE IMPACT**   To prove disparate impact under Title VII, the plaintiff must show that the employer has a rule that on its face is not discriminatory, but in practice excludes too many people in a protected group. (pp. 339–340)

EXAM Strategy

Question: Ladies Plus refuses to hire Eric for a job as a sales associate because his credit score is too low to meet the store's hiring standards. Men, on average, have worse credit ratings than women. Has the store violated Title VII?

Strategy: Is there evidence that men and women are being treated differently? No, the same rule applies to both. Do the rules have a disparate impact? Yes, many more women have acceptable credit ratings. Is sex a protected category under Title VII? Yes. Are the standards essential for the job? Would other, less discriminatory rules have achieved the same result? (See the "Result" at the end of this section.)

5. **RETALIATION** Title VII penalizes employers who retaliate against workers for *complaining* about discrimination. (pp. 340–341)

6. **RELIGION** Employers must make reasonable accommodation for a worker's religious beliefs unless the request would cause undue hardship for the business. (p. 341)

7. **SENIORITY** A legitimate seniority system is legal even if it perpetuates past discrimination. (p. 341)

8. **BONA FIDE OCCUPATIONAL QUALIFICATION (BFOQ)** An employer is permitted to establish discriminatory job requirements if they are *essential* to the position in question. (pp. 341–342)

EXAM Strategy

Question: You are the vice president of administration at a hospital. A hospital study reveals that both male and female patients prefer to have a male neurosurgeon, while men prefer male urologists and women prefer female gynecologists. Can you act on this information when hiring doctors?

Strategy: To hire based on sex would be a violation of Title VII unless sex is a BFOQ for the job. (See the "Result" at the end of this section.)

9. **AFFIRMATIVE ACTION** Affirmative action is not required by Title VII, nor is it prohibited. (p. 342)

10. **SEXUAL HARASSMENT** Sexual harassment involves unwelcome sexual advances, requests for sexual favors, and other verbal or physical conduct of a sexual nature. (pp. 342–343)

11. **PREGNANCY DISCRIMINATION** Under the Pregnancy Discrimination Act of 1978, an employer may not fire or refuse to hire a woman because she is pregnant. (pp. 343–344)

12. **AGE DISCRIMINATION** The Age Discrimination in Employment Act of 1967 prohibits age discrimination against employees or job applicants who are at least 40 years old. (pp. 344–345)

13. **ADA** Under the Americans with Disabilities Act an employer may not refuse to hire or promote a disabled person as long as she can, with reasonable accommodation, perform the essential functions of the job. A disabled person is someone with a physical or mental impairment that substantially limits a major life activity. An accommodation is not reasonable if it would create undue hardship for the employer. (pp. 345–346)

4. Result: The store is in violation of Title VII unless it can show that (1) credit ratings directly relate to a sales associate's job performance and (2) no other requirement would accurately evaluate applicants for this work.

8. Result: Customer preference does not justify discrimination except in cases of sexual privacy. You cannot consider sex when hiring neurosurgeons, but you can when selecting urologists and gynecologists.

MATCHING QUESTIONS

Match the following terms with their definitions:

___A. Equal Pay Act

___B. Right to sue letter

___C. ADEA

___D. Title VII

___E. ADA

1. Statute that prohibits an employee from being paid at a lesser rate than employees of the opposite sex for equal work

2. Statute that prohibits discrimination on the basis of race, color, religion, sex, or national origin

3. Permission from the EEOC for a plaintiff to proceed with a case

4. Statute that prohibits age discrimination

5. Statute that prohibits discrimination against the disabled

TRUE/FALSE QUESTIONS

Circle true or false:

1. T F In a disparate impact case, an employer may be liable for a rule that is not discriminatory on its face.

2. T F Title VII applies to all aspects of the employment relationship, including hiring, firing, and promotion.

3. T F If more whites than Native Americans pass an employment test, the test necessarily violates Title VII.

4. T F Employers that have contracts with the federal government are required to fill a quota of women and minority employees.

5. T F Employers do not have to accommodate an employee's religious beliefs if doing so would impose an undue hardship on the business.

MULTIPLE-CHOICE QUESTIONS

1. Which of the following steps is *not* required in a disparate treatment case?

   (a) The plaintiff must file with the EEOC.

   (b) The plaintiff must submit to arbitration.

   (c) The plaintiff must present evidence of a *prima facie* case.

   (d) The defendant must show that its action had a nondiscriminatory reason.

   (e) The plaintiff must show that the defendant's excuse was a pretext.

2. An employer can legally require all employees to have a high school diploma if:

   (a) All of its competitors have such a requirement.

   (b) Most of the applicants in the area have a high school diploma.

   (c) Shareholders of the company are likely to pay a higher price for the company's stock if employees have at least a high school diploma.

   (d) The company intends to branch out into the high-tech field, in which case a high school diploma would be needed by its employees.

   (e) The nature of the job requires those skills.

3. Which of the following employers has violated Title VII?

   (a) Carlos promoted the most qualified employee.

   (b) Hans promoted five white males because they were the most senior.

   (c) Luke refused to hire a Buddhist to work on a Christian Science newspaper.

   (d) Max hired a male corporate lawyer because his clients had more confidence in male lawyers.

   (e) Dylan refused to hire a woman to work as an attendant in the men's locker room.

4. Which of the following activities would *not* be considered sexual harassment?

   (a) Shannon tells Connor that she will promote him if he will sleep with her.

   (b) Kailen has a screen saver that shows various people having sex.

   (c) Paige says she wants "to negotiate Owen's raise at the Holiday Inn."

   (d) Nancy yells "Crap!" at the top of her lungs every time her Rotisserie Baseball team loses.

   (e) *Quid pro quo.*

5. Which of the following activities is legal under Title VII?

   (a) When Taggart comes to a job interview, he has a white cane. Ann asks him if he is blind.

   (b) Craig refuses to hire Ben, who is blind, to work as a playground supervisor because it is essential to the job that the supervisor be able to see what the children are doing.

   (c) Concerned about his company's health insurance rates, Matt requires all job applicants to take a physical.

   (d) Concerned about his company's health insurance rates, Josh requires all new hires to take a physical so that he can encourage them to join some of the preventive treatment programs available at the company.

   (e) Jennifer refuses to hire Alexis because her child is ill and she frequently has to take him to the hospital.

ESSAY QUESTIONS

1. When Michelle told her boss that she was pregnant, his first comment was, "Congratulations on your pregnancy. My sister vomited for months." Then he refused to speak to her for a week. A month later, she was fired. Her boss told her the business was shifting away from her area of expertise. Does Michelle have a valid claim? Under what law?

2. The Lillie Rubin boutique in Phoenix would not permit Dick Kovacic to apply for a job as a salesperson. It hired only women to work in sales because fittings and alterations took place in the dressing room or immediately outside. The customers were buying expensive clothes and demanded a male-free dressing area. Has the Lillie Rubin store violated Title VII? What would its defense be?

3. After the terrorist attacks of 9/11, the United States tightened its visa requirements. In the process, baseball teams discovered that 300 foreign-born professional players had lied about their age. (A talented 16-year-old is much more valuable than a 23-year-old with the same skills.) In some cases, the players had used birth certificates that belonged to other (younger) people. To prevent this fraud, baseball teams began asking for DNA tests on prospects and their families to make sure they were not lying about their identity. Is this testing legal?

4. Ronald Lockhart, who was deaf, worked for FedEx as a package handler. Although fluent in American Sign Language, he could not read lips. After 9/11, the company held meetings to talk about security issues. Lockhart complained to the EEOC that he could not understand these discussions. FedEx fired him. Has FedEx violated the law?

5. When the boss fired Clarence from his job at a moving company, she said it was because he could no longer lift heavy furniture, his salary was too high, and as he got older, he would have a hard time remembering stuff. Clarence is 60. Has the boss violated the law?

DISCUSSION QUESTIONS

1. **ETHICS** Mary Ann Singleton was the librarian at a maximum-security prison located in Tazewell County, Virginia. About four times a week, Gene Shinault, assistant warden for operations, persistently complimented Singleton and stared at her breasts when he spoke to her. On one occasion, he measured the length of her skirt to judge its compliance with the prison's dress code and told her that it looked "real good"; constantly told her how attractive he found her; made references to his physical fitness, considering his advanced age; asked Singleton if he made her nervous (she answered "yes"); and repeatedly remarked to Singleton that if he had a wife as attractive as Singleton, he would not permit her to work in a prison facility around so many inmates. Shinault told Singleton's supervisor in her presence, "Look at her. I bet you have to spank her every day." The supervisor then laughed and said, "No. I probably should, but I don't." Shinault replied, "Well, I know I would." Shinault also had a security camera installed in her office in a way that permitted him to observe her as she worked. Singleton reported this behavior to her supervisor, who simply responded, "Boys will be boys." Did Shinault sexually harass Singleton? Whether or not Shinault violated the law, what *ethical* obligation did Singleton's supervisor have to protect her from this type of behavior?

2. When Thomas Lussier filled out a Postal Service employment application, he did not admit that he had twice pleaded guilty to charges of disorderly conduct. Lussier suffered from Post-Traumatic Stress Disorder (PTSD) acquired during military service. Because of this disorder, he sometimes had panic attacks that required him to leave meetings. He was also a recovered alcoholic and drug user. During his stint with the Postal Service, he had some personality conflicts with other employees. Once, another employee hit him. He also had one episode of "erratic emotional behavior and verbal outburst." In the meantime, a postal employee in Ridgewood, New Jersey, killed four colleagues. The postmaster general encouraged all supervisors to identify workers who had dangerous propensities. Lussier's boss discovered that he had lied on his employment application about the disorderly conduct charges and fired him. Is the Postal Service in violation of the law?

3. Gregg Young, the CEO of BJY Inc. insisted on calling Mamdouh El-Hakem "Manny" or "Hank." Does this behavior violate the law?

4. FedEx refused to promote José Rodriguez to a supervisor's position because of his accent and "how he speaks." Is FedEx in violation of the law?

5. Title VII does not prohibit discrimination against people who are unattractive. Should it be amended to include looks?

CHAPTER 20

LABOR LAW

A strike! For five weeks, the union workers have been walking picket lines at JMJ, a manufacturer of small electrical engines. An entire town of 70,000 citizens, most of them blue-collar workers, is sharply divided, right down to the McNally kitchen table. Buddy, age 48, has worked on the assembly lines at JMJ for more than 25 years. Now he's sipping coffee in the house where he grew up. His sister Kristina, age 46, is a vice president for personnel at JMJ. The two have always been close, but today, the conversation is halting.

© Ivan Cholakov Gostock-dot-net/Shutterstock.com

"It's time to get back together, Buddy," Kristina murmurs. "The strike is hurting the whole company—and the town."

"Not the *whole* town, Kristina," he replies. "Your management pals still have fat incomes and nice houses."

"Oh yeah? You haven't seen our porch lately."

"Go talk to Tony Falcione. He can't pay his rent."

"Talk to the Ericksons," Kristina snaps back. "They don't even work for JMJ. Their sandwich shop is going under because none of you guys stop in for lunch. Come back to work."

"Not with that clause on the table."

That clause is management's proposal for the new union contract—one that Kristina helped draft. The company officers want the right to subcontract work; that is, to send it out for other companies to perform.

"Buddy, we need the flexibility. K-Ball is underselling us by 35 percent. If we can't compete, there won't be *any* jobs or *any* contract!"

"The way to save money is not by sending our jobs overseas, where people will work for 50 bucks a month."

"OK, fine. Tell me how we *should* save money."

"How you can sit at this table and say these things? In this house? You never would have gone to college if Dad hadn't made union wages."

> An entire town of 70,000 citizens, most of them blue-collar workers, is sharply divided, right down to the McNally kitchen table.

"If we can't cut costs, we're out of business. *Then* what's your union going to do for you? All we're asking is the right to subcontract some of the smallest components. Everything else gets built here."

"This is just the start. Next it'll be the wiring, then the batteries, then you'll assemble the whole thing over there—and that'll be it for me. You take that clause off the table, we'll be back in 15 minutes."

"You know I can't do that."

Buddy stands up. They stare silently, sadly, at each other, and then Kristina says, in a barely audible voice, "I have to tell you this. My boss is starting to talk about hiring replacement workers."

Buddy walks out.

UNIONS DEVELOP

During the 19th century, as industrialization spread across America, workers found employment conditions unbearable and wages inadequate. In factories, workers, often women and children, worked 60 to 70 hours per week and sometimes more, standing at assembly lines in suffocating, dimly lit factories, performing monotonous yet dangerous work with heavy machinery for pennies a day. Mines were different—they were worse.

Workers began to band together into unions, but courts and Congress were hostile. From the 1800s through the 1920s, judges routinely issued injunctions against strikes, ruling that unions were either criminal conspiracies or illegal monopolies. With the economic collapse of 1929, however, and the vast suffering of the Great Depression, public sympathy shifted to the workers.

Key Statutes

In 1932, Congress passed the **Norris-LaGuardia Act**, which prohibited federal court injunctions in nonviolent labor disputes. Congress was declaring that workers should be permitted to organize unions and to use their collective power to achieve legitimate economic ends.

In 1935 Congress passed the Wagner Act, generally known as the **National Labor Relations Act (NLRA)**. This is the most important of all labor laws. A fundamental aim of the NLRA is the establishment and maintenance of industrial peace, to preserve the flow of commerce. **Section 7 guarantees employees the right to organize and join unions, bargain collectively through representatives of their own choosing, and engage in other concerted activities.** Section 8 reinforces these rights by outlawing unfair labor practices.

Section 8 prohibits employers from engaging in the following unfair labor practices (ULPs):

- Interfering with union organizing efforts,

- Dominating or interfering with any union,

- Discriminating against a union member, or

- Refusing to bargain collectively with a union.

The NLRA also established the **National Labor Relations Board (NLRB)** to administer and interpret the statute and to adjudicate labor cases. For example, when a union charges that an employer has committed an unfair labor practice—say, by refusing to bargain—the charge goes first to the NLRB.

Norris-LaGuardia Act
Prohibits federal court injunctions in peaceful labor disputes.

National Labor Relations Act (NLRA)
Ensures the right of workers to form unions and encourages management and unions to bargain collectively.

National Labor Relations Board (NLRB)
Administers and interprets the NLRA and adjudicates labor cases.

The Board, which sits in Washington, D.C., has five members, all appointed by the president. The NLRB makes final agency decisions about representation and ULP cases. But the Board has no power to *enforce* its orders. If it is evident that the losing party will not comply, the Board must petition a federal appeals court to enforce the order. Typically, the steps resulting in an appeal follow this pattern: the Board issues a decision (for example, finding that a company has unfairly refused to bargain with a union). The Board orders the company to bargain. The Board then appeals to the United States Court of Appeals to enforce its order, and the company cross-appeals, requesting the court not to enforce the Board's order. Throughout the 1930s and 1940s, unions grew in size and power, but employers complained of union abuse. In 1947 Congress responded with the Taft-Hartley Act, also known as the **Labor-Management Relations Act**. The statute amended Section 8 of the NLRA to outlaw certain unfair labor practices *by unions*.

Labor-Management Relations Act

A statute designed to curb union abuses.

Section 8(b) makes it an unfair labor practice for a union to:

- Interfere with employees who are exercising their labor rights under Section 7,

- Encourage an employer to discriminate against a particular employee because of a union dispute,

- Refuse to bargain collectively, or

- Engage in an illegal strike or boycott, particularly secondary boycotts.

Finally, in the 1950s, the public became aware that certain labor leaders were corrupt. Some officers stole money from large union treasuries, rigged union elections, and stifled opposition within the organization. In 1959 Congress responded by passing the Landrum-Griffin Act, generally called the **Labor-Management Reporting and Disclosure Act (LMRDA).** The LMRDA requires union leadership to make certain financial disclosures and guarantees free speech and fair elections within a union.

These landmark federal labor laws are outlined below.

Four Key Labor Statutes

Norris-LaGuardia Act (1932)	Prohibits federal court injunctions in peaceful strikes.
National Labor Relations Act (1935)	Guarantees workers' right to organize unions and bargain collectively. Prohibits an employer from interfering with union organizing or discriminating against union members. Requires an employer to bargain collectively.
Labor-Management Relations Act (1947)	Prohibits union abuses such as coercing employees to join. Outlaws secondary boycotts.
Labor-Management Reporting and Disclosure Act (1959)	Requires financial disclosures by union leadership. Guarantees union members free speech and fair elections.

© Cengage Learning 2013

Labor Unions Today

Organized labor is in flux in the United States. In the 1950s, about 1 in 4 workers belonged to a union. Today, only about 1 in 8, or 15 million total U.S. workers, are union members. Employers point to this figure with satisfaction and claim that it shows that unions have failed their memberships. In an increasingly high-tech, service-oriented economy, employers argue, there is no place for organized labor. Union supporters respond that although the country has shed many old factories, workers have not benefited. Throughout the last 20 years, they assert, compensation for executives has soared into the stratosphere while wages for the average worker, in real dollars, have fallen.

Unions continue to attract political attention. In 2011, legislators in Wisconsin voted to strip most collective bargaining rights from schoolteachers and other state government workers. Public employees are five times more likely to be union members than private sector workers, but they are generally not protected by the NLRA.

Crowds of as many as 100,000 gathered in Madison to protest. Commentators on the left forecast significant political consequences for the Wisconsin lawmakers, while editorialists on the right predict that many states will soon follow the Wisconsin model.

Although overall membership is down, unions still matter.

ORGANIZING A UNION

Exclusivity

Under Section 9 of the NLRA, a validly recognized union is the exclusive representative of the employees. This means that the union will represent all of the designated employees, regardless of whether a particular worker *wants* to be represented. The company may not bargain directly with any employee in the group, nor with any other organization representing the designated employees. A **collective bargaining unit** is the precisely defined group of employees who will be represented by a particular union.

Collective bargaining unit
The precisely defined group of employees represented by a particular union.

Organizing: Stages

A union organizing effort generally involves the following pattern.

CAMPAIGN

Union organizers talk with employees and try to interest them in forming a union. The organizers may be employees of the company, who simply chat with fellow workers about unsatisfactory conditions. Or a union may send nonemployees of the company to hand out union leaflets to workers as they arrive and depart from work.

AUTHORIZATION CARDS

Union organizers ask workers to sign authorization cards, which state that the particular worker requests the specified union to act as her sole bargaining representative. If a union obtains authorization cards from a sizable percentage of workers, it seeks recognition as the exclusive representative for the bargaining unit. The union may ask the employer to recognize it as the bargaining representative, but most of the time, employers refuse to recognize the union voluntarily. The NLRA permits an employer to refuse recognition.

PETITION

Assuming that the employer does not voluntarily recognize a union, the union generally petitions the NLRB for an election. It must submit to the NLRB authorization cards signed by at least 30 percent of the workers. If the NLRB determines that the union has identified an appropriate bargaining unit and has enough valid cards, it orders an election.

ELECTION

The NLRB closely supervises the election to ensure fairness. All members of the proposed bargaining unit vote on whether they want the union to represent them. If more than 50 percent of the workers vote for the union, the NLRB designates that union as the exclusive representative of all members of the bargaining unit. When unions hold elections in private corporations, they win about half the time. Labor organizations claim that management typically uses company time to campaign against the union. Employers respond that labor loses elections because workers fear that a union will hurt them, not help them.

THE "CARD-CHECK" DEBATE

Before becoming president, then-Senator Barack Obama co-introduced a bill called the Employee Free Choice Act. This bill provides that when more than 50 percent of workers sign an authorization card, the NLRB must immediately designate that union as the exclusive representative of all members in the bargaining unit *without an election*.

Supporters argue that, if a majority of workers return authorization cards, an election is unnecessary and only gives companies an opportunity to intimidate workers. Those who dislike the bill argue that workers may feel bullied into signing an authorization card and should always have the right to a final vote by secret ballot.

The bill has generated much debate but has not passed Congress at the time of this writing.

Organizing: Actions
WHAT WORKERS MAY DO

The NLRA guarantees employees the right to talk among themselves about forming a union, to hand out literature, and ultimately to join a union.[1] Workers may urge other employees to sign authorization cards and may vigorously push their cause. When employees hand out leaflets, the employer generally may not limit the content. In one case, a union distributed leaflets urging workers to vote against political candidates who opposed minimum-wage laws. The employer objected to the union distributing the information on company property, but the Supreme Court upheld the union's right. Even though the content of the writing was not directly related to the union, the connection was close enough that the NLRA protected the union's activity.[2]

There are, of course, limits to what union organizers may do. The statute permits an employer to restrict organizing discussions if they interfere with discipline or production. A worker on a moving assembly line has no right to walk away from his task to talk with other employees about organizing a union.[3]

WHAT EMPLOYERS MAY DO

An employer may prohibit employees from organizing if the efforts interfere with the company's work. In a retail store, for example, management may prohibit union discussions in the presence of customers because the discussions could harm business.

May the employer speak out against a union organizing drive? Yes. **Management is entitled to communicate to the employees why it believes a union will be harmful to the company.** But the employer's efforts must be limited to explanation and advocacy. The employer may not use either threats or promises of benefits to defeat a union drive.[4] The company is prohibited not only from threatening reprisals, such as firing a worker who favors the union, but also from offering benefits designed to defeat the union. A company that has vigorously rejected employee demands for higher wages may not suddenly grant a 10 percent pay increase in the midst of a union campaign.

---

[1]NLRA Section 7.
[2]*Eastex, Inc. v. NLRB*, 434 U.S. 1045, 98 S. Ct. 888, 1978 U.S. LEXIS 547 (1978).
[3]*NLRB v. Babcock & Wilcox Co.*, 351 U.S. 105, 76 S. Ct. 679, 1956 U.S. LEXIS 1721 (1956).
[4]*NLRB v. Gissel Packing Co.*, 395 U.S. 575, 89 S. Ct. 1918, 1969 U.S. LEXIS 3172 (1969).

It is an unfair labor practice for an employer to interfere with a union organizing effort. Normally, a union claiming such interference will file a ULP charge. If the Board upholds the union's claim, it will order the employer to stop its interference and permit a fair election.

Here is a case illustrating the tensions and crude language that so often arise during organizing efforts.

PROGRESSIVE ELECTRIC, INC. v. NATIONAL LABOR RELATIONS BOARD

453 F.3d 538,
District of Columbia Court of Appeals, 2006

CASE SUMMARY

Facts: Progressive Electric, Inc. was a non-union electrical contractor. The International Brotherhood of Electrical Workers (IBEW) targeted the company for organizing. Progressive did not go quietly.

Progressive advertised in the local paper that it was accepting applications for electrician/technicians. Without revealing his IBEW membership, David Cousins responded to the ad and was hired. A month later, eight more union members went as a group to Progressive to apply. They carried video and tape recording equipment. Randy Neeman, Progressive's president, realized that they were union members and told them, "You guys, we are not hiring. We are not taking no [sic] applications. We hired a couple of people and filled the spots. So I would love to put you all on and as soon as I get an opening, I will give you guys a call." The union members filled out job applications and Neeman said he would call when there was an opening. In fact, he immediately threw away the applications.

Don Hildreth, a Progressive foreman, told Cousins and one other employee that Neeman "didn't want any union crap around here." Hildreth continued, "If the unions got into Progressive, Progressive would lose contracts and would go out of business because Progressive couldn't afford the union wages and benefits."

Neeman held a company meeting, where he told the assembled employees: "All right, I've been quiet up 'til now, which is strange for me, I know. But now we're gonna talk about this dirty word—*union*." Neeman's presentation was punctuated by phrases such as "Mr. Asshole Union Rep" and "bunch of dummies." At one point in the presentation, Neeman wrote the word "union" on the board, drew a circle around it, and put a slash through it.

Progressive later filled various positions with non-union members, never advertising the jobs nor contacting the IBEW applicants.

The IBEW filed charges with the NLRB, which concluded that Progressive had committed a ULP by threatening job loss and plant closure if the union organized the company. The Board found in favor of the union, and Progressive appealed.

Issue: *Did the company commit a ULP?*

Holding: Yes, the company committed a ULP.

Reasoning: An employer may not use discriminatory hiring to discourage union membership. After Neeman accepted a sheet containing the union applicants' information, he lied to them, assuring them he would call them as soon as there was an opening, when in fact he had no such intention. The Board pointed to various other events over the next year indicating anti-union bias, including multiple union letters, which Progressive received but never responded to; the company's decision to use blind advertisements; and its failure to hire union applicants for any of the seven suitable positions. At the company meeting, Neeman showed overt hostility to the union, describing it in crude terms. Perhaps none of these actions in itself would be a ULP, but the Board reasonably found they were collectively part and parcel of Progressive's overall scheme to refuse to consider and hire the union applicants.

The Board's order is enforced.

EXAM Strategy

Question: We Haul is a trucking company. The Teamsters Union is attempting to organize the drivers. Workers who favor a union have been using the lunchroom to hand out petitions and urge other drivers to sign authorization cards. The company posts a notice in the lunchroom: "No Union Discussions. Many employees do not want unions discussed in the lunchroom. Out of respect for them, we are prohibiting further union efforts in this lunchroom." Comment.

Strategy: The NLRA guarantees employees the right to talk among themselves about forming a union and to hand out literature. Union workers may vigorously push their cause. Management is entitled to communicate to the employees why it believes a union will be harmful to the company, but the employer's efforts must be limited to explanation and advocacy.

Result: We Haul has violated the NLRA. The company has the right to urge employees not to join the union. However, it is not entitled to block the union from its organizing campaign. Even assuming the company is correct that some employees do not want unions discussed, it has no right to prohibit such advocacy.

APPROPRIATE BARGAINING UNIT

When a union petitions the NLRB for an election, the Board determines whether the proposed bargaining unit is appropriate. **The Board generally certifies a proposed bargaining unit if and only if the employees share a "community of interest."** Employers frequently assert that the bargaining unit is inappropriate. If the Board agrees with the employer and rejects the proposed bargaining unit, it dismisses the union's request for an election.

Managerial employees must be excluded from the bargaining unit.[5] An employee is managerial if she is so closely aligned with management that her membership in the bargaining unit would create a conflict of interest between her union membership and her actual work. For example, a factory worker who spends one-third of his time performing assembly work but two-thirds of his time supervising a dozen other workers could not fairly be part of the bargaining unit.

Once the Board has excluded managerial employees, it looks at various criteria to decide whether the remaining employees should logically be grouped in one bargaining unit; that is, whether they share a **community of interest.** The Board looks for rough similarity of training, skills, hours of work, and pay. The Board either certifies the bargaining unit or rejects the unit and dismisses the union's petition.

COLLECTIVE BARGAINING

Collective bargaining agreement (CBA)
A contract between a union and management.

The goal of bargaining is to create a new contract, which is called a **collective bargaining agreement (CBA)**. Problems can arise as union and employer advocate their respective positions. Three of the most common conflicts are (1) whether an issue is a mandatory subject of bargaining; (2) whether the parties are bargaining in good faith; and (3) how to enforce the agreement.

---

[5]*NLRB v. Bell Aerospace Co., Div. of Textron, Inc.*, 416 U.S. 267, 94 S. Ct. 1757, 1974 U.S. LEXIS 35 (1974).

Subjects of Bargaining

The NLRA *permits* the parties to bargain almost any subject they wish but *requires* them to bargain certain issues. **Mandatory subjects include wages, hours, and other terms and conditions of employment.** Either side may propose to bargain other subjects, but neither side may insist upon bargaining them.

Management and unions often disagree as to whether a particular topic is mandatory or not. Courts generally find these subjects to be mandatory: pay, benefits, order of layoffs and recalls, production quotas, work rules (such as safety practices), retirement benefits, and in-plant food service and prices (e.g., cafeteria food). Courts usually consider these subjects to be nonmandatory: product type and design, advertising, sales, financing, corporate organization, and location of plants.

Today, some of the most heated disputes between management and labor arise from a company's desire to subcontract work or to move plants to areas with cheaper costs. **Subcontracting** means that a manufacturer, rather than producing all parts of a product and then assembling them, contracts for other companies, frequently overseas, to make some of the parts. Is a business free to subcontract work? That depends on management's motive. A company that subcontracts in order to maintain its economic viability is probably not required to bargain first; however, **bargaining is mandatory if the subcontracting is designed to replace union workers with cheaper labor.**

EMPLOYER AND UNION SECURITY

Both the employer and the union will seek clauses making their positions more secure. Management, above all, wants to be sure that there will be no strikes during the course of the agreement. For its part, the union tries to ensure that its members cannot be turned away from work during the CBA's term and that all newly hired workers will affiliate with the union. We look next at two specific union security issues.

No Strike/No Lockout.   Most agreements include some form of no-strike clause, meaning that the union promises not to strike during the term of the contract. In turn, unions insist on a no-lockout clause, meaning that in the event of a labor dispute, management will not prevent union members from working. **No-strike and no-lockout clauses are both legal.**

Union Shop.   In a union shop, membership in the union becomes compulsory after the employee has been hired. Thus management retains an unfettered right to hire whom it pleases, but all new employees who fit into the bargaining unit must affiliate with the union. **A union shop is generally legal,** with two limitations. First, new members need not join the union for 30 days. Second, the new members, after joining the union, can only be required to pay initiation fees and union dues. If the new hire decides he does not want to participate in the union, the union may not compel him to do so.

Duty to Bargain

Both the union and the employer must bargain in good faith. However, they are *not* obligated to reach an agreement. In the end, this means that the two sides must meet with open minds and make a reasonable effort to reach a contract. Each side must listen to the other's proposals and consider possible compromises.

In the following case, the Supreme Court examined these requirements. Did the company fail to bargain in good faith? You be the judge.

You be the Judge

NLRB v. Truitt Manufacturing Co.

351 U.S. 149
United States Supreme Court, 1956

Facts: A union representing workers at Truitt Manufacturing Company requested a raise of 10 cents per hour for all members. The company offered an additional 2.5 cents per hour and argued that a larger increase would bankrupt the company. The union demanded to examine Truitt's books, and when the company refused, the union complained to the National Labor Relations Board.

The NLRB determined that the company had failed to bargain in good faith and ordered it to allow union representatives to examine its finances. A court of appeals found no unfair labor practices and refused to enforce the Board's order. The Supreme Court granted *certiorari*.

You Be the Judge: *Did the company refuse to bargain in good faith?*

Argument for the Union: The NLRA requires that management bargain in good faith, but Truitt has failed to meet this obligation. It refuses to show evidence that it cannot afford our request for a small increase in hourly wages. We have absolutely no desire to bankrupt an employer. But we are skeptical that Truitt is so close to going out of business.

We simply ask for information. If the evidence shows that our proposed wage increase will in fact destroy the company, we will reduce or abandon it.

We wish to make reasonable demands, but we cannot do so without an opportunity to review the company's finances. By keeping us in the dark, Truitt acts in bad faith.

Argument for the Company: We have made an honest claim. The union's demands, if met, will cause great harm to the company.

The NLRA requires that we bargain in good faith, but it does not require proof of all assertions. Our precise financial position is not relevant to the issue of whether we are making reasonable efforts to reach a new agreement. We have listened to the union's request, considered it, and made a counteroffer. We are not refusing to negotiate.

The Court of Appeals ruled correctly. We have not engaged in an unfair labor practice.

Sometimes an employer will attempt to make changes without bargaining the issues at all. However, **management may not unilaterally change wages, hours, or terms and conditions of employment without bargaining the issues to impasse.** "Bargaining to impasse" means that both parties must continue to meet and bargain in good faith until it is clear that they cannot reach an agreement. The goal in requiring collective bargaining is to bring the parties together to reach an agreement that brings labor peace. In one case, the union won an election, but before bargaining could begin, management changed the schedule from five 8-hour days to four 10-hour days a week. The company also changed its layoff policy from one of strict seniority to one based on ability and began laying off employees based on alleged poor performance. The court held that each of these acts violated the company's duty to bargain. The employer ultimately might be allowed to make every one of these changes, but first it had to bargain the issues to impasse.[6]

Enforcement

Virtually all collective bargaining agreements provide for their own enforcement, typically through **grievance-arbitration.** Suppose a company transfers an employee from the day shift to the night shift, and the worker believes the contract prohibits such a transfer for any employee with her seniority. The employee complains to the union, which files a **grievance;** that is, a formal complaint with the company notifying management that the union claims a contract violation. Generally, the CBA establishes some kind of informal hearing, usually

Grievance
A formal complaint alleging a
contract violation.

---

[6]*Adair Standish Corp. v. NLRB*, 912 F.2d 854, 1990 U.S. App. LEXIS 14670 (6th Cir. 1990).

conducted by a member of management, at which the employee, represented by the union, may state her case.

After the manager's decision, if the employee is still dissatisfied, the union may file for **arbitration,** that is, a formal hearing before a neutral arbitrator. In the arbitration hearing, each side is represented by its lawyer. The arbitrator is required to decide the case based on the CBA. An arbitrator finds either for the employee, and orders the company to take certain corrective action, or for the employer, and dismisses the grievance.

In the vast majority of grievances, the arbitrator's decision is final. The following case demonstrates how reluctant courts are to interfere with an arbitrator's award.

Arbitration

A formal hearing before a neutral party to resolve a contract dispute between a union and a company.

BRENTWOOD MEDICAL ASSOCIATES v. UNITED MINE WORKERS OF AMERICA

396 F.3d 237
United States Court of Appeals for the Third Circuit, 2005

CASE SUMMARY

Facts: Brentwood Medical Associates operated a hospital. The United Mine Workers of America represented one unit of employees, which included Denise Cope, a phlebotomist (someone who draws blood). Exercising her seniority rights, Cope changed jobs to Charge Entry Associate. A year and a half later, BMA announced it was terminating the position. Cope asked to return to her old job. This would have required "bumping" the least-senior phlebotomist out of a job. BMA refused, claiming that bumping was not allowed under the collective bargaining agreement (CBA). Cope filed a grievance, which an arbitrator heard.

The arbitrator ruled in Cope's favor. In his decision, he asked rhetorically why, if the CBA disallowed bumping, did it include the following language:

> . . . employees who exercise seniority rights and bump must have the skill to perform all of the work [in the new job].

The problem with the quoted language was that it did not in fact exist anywhere in the CBA. BMA filed suit, asking a federal court to overturn the arbitration decision. The trial court upheld the award, and BMA appealed.

Issue: *Should the arbitration award be affirmed even though the arbitrator relied on language that cannot be found in the CBA?*

Decision: Yes, the decision is affirmed.

Reasoning: The parties wanted arbitration, bargained for it, and included it in their CBA. Full-blown judicial review of the arbitrator's decision would contravene their agreement, injecting a judicial interpretation that neither side expected.

Although the arbitrator did cite language he should not have, his decision relied on several provisions of the agreement. For example, Section 1 defines seniority as "bargaining unit-wide" and not within classification. Section 2 provides that the principle of seniority is a factor in layoffs and recalls. Section 5 specifies that in filling vacancies when the qualifications of two or more applicants are relatively equal, preference will be based on seniority.

The arbitrator's award does not rest solely upon the aberrant language that he unfortunately added. He attempted to give effect to all provisions of the agreement. His decision is affirmed.

CONCERTED ACTION

Concerted action refers to any tactics union members take in unison to gain some bargaining advantage. It is this power that gives a union strength. The NLRA guarantees the right of employees to engage in concerted action for mutual aid or protection.[7] The most common forms of concerted action are strikes and picketing.

Concerted action

Tactics taken by union members to gain bargaining advantage.

---

[7]NLRA Section 7.

Strikes

The NLRA guarantees employees the right to strike, but with some limitations.[8] A union has a guaranteed right to call a strike if the parties are unable to reach a collective bargaining agreement. A union may call a strike to exert economic pressure on management, to protest an unfair labor practice, or to preserve work that the employer is considering sending elsewhere.

This right to strike can be waived. Management will generally insist that the CBA include a no-strike clause, which prohibits the union from striking while the CBA is in force. Other restrictions include a 60-day cooling-off period before many strikes, and in many states, a flat prohibition on strikes by public employees (police, teachers, and so forth). Violent strikes are always illegal.

Ethics Suppose state law prohibits teachers from striking, but the teachers' union is angry. Their contract expired a year ago, and the Board of Education has refused any pay raises. The teachers decide they will "work to rule," meaning they will teach classes, issues grades, and so forth ... but will not write any college recommendations. Is the teachers' refusal to perform any "extras" a reasonable tactic?

Replacement Workers

When employees go on strike, management generally wants to replace them to keep the company operating. Are replacement workers legal? Yes. **Management has the right to hire replacement workers during a strike.** May the employer offer the replacement workers permanent jobs, or must the company give union members their jobs back when the strike is over? It depends on the type of strike.

After an *economic strike,* an employer may not discriminate against a striker, but the employer is not obligated to lay off a replacement worker to give a striker his job back. An economic strike is one intended to gain wages or benefits. When a union bargains for a pay raise but fails to get it and walks off the job, that is an economic strike. During such a strike, an employer may hire permanent replacement workers. When the strike is over, the company has no obligation to lay off the replacement workers to make room for the strikers. However, if the company does hire more workers, it may not discriminate against the strikers.

After an *unfair labor practice strike,* a union member is entitled to her job back, even if that means the employer must lay off a replacement worker. Suppose management refuses to bargain in good faith by claiming poverty without producing records to substantiate its claim. The union strikes. Management's refusal to bargain was an unfair labor practice, and the strike is a ULP strike. When it ends, the striking workers must get their jobs back.

Picketing

Picketing the employer's workplace in support of a strike is generally lawful. Striking workers are permitted to establish picket lines at the employer's job site and to urge all others—employees, replacement workers, and customers—not to cross the line. But the picketers are not permitted to use physical force to prevent anyone from crossing the line.

Secondary boycotts are generally illegal. A secondary boycott is a picket line established not at the employer's premises, but at the workplace of a *different* company that does

---

[8]NLRA Section 13.

business with the union's employer. Such a boycott is designed to put pressure on the union's employer by forcing other companies to stop doing business with it.

Lockouts

The workers have bargained with management for weeks, and discussions have turned belligerent. It is 6 a.m., the start of another day at the factory. But as 150 employees arrive for work, they are amazed to find the company's gate locked and armed guards standing on the other side. What is this? A lockout.

> 150 employees find the company's gate locked and armed guards standing on the other side.

The power of a union comes ultimately from its potential to strike. But management, too, has weapons. In a lockout, management prohibits workers from entering the premises, denying the employees work and a chance to earn a paycheck.

A lockout is legal if the parties have reached a bargaining impasse. Management, bargaining a new CBA with a union, may wish to use a lockout to advance its position. It is allowed to do so provided the parties have reached an impasse. If there is no impasse, a lockout will probably be illegal. Most courts consider that a lockout before impasse indicates hostility to the union.

EXAM Strategy

Question: Union workers are striking at Cheesey, a restaurant, forming picket lines in front of the restaurant during the lunch and dinner hours, but at no other times. The union members chant slogans denouncing their wages and working conditions, urging diners not to enter. There is no violence, but the picketers cause many prospective customers to stay away, and Cheesey suffers a substantial drop in business. The restaurant files a charge with the NLRB, claiming that the union has committed a ULP by (1) deliberately harming its business and (2) engaging in a secondary boycott. Who will win?

Strategy: Striking workers are allowed to picket. May they *urge* non-union members to stay out of the business? May they *prohibit* others from entering? Secondary boycotts are illegal. Is this one?

Result: Striking workers may urge the public not to cross the picket line. The union may not use violence to keep people out, but this union has not done so. This is not a secondary boycott, which is a picket line established at a *different* company that does business with the employer. The company's loss of business is one possible—and legal—consequence of a strike. The union has committed no ULP.

Chapter Conclusion

Contemporary clashes between union and management are less likely to stem from sweltering temperatures in a mine than from a management decision to subcontract work or from a teacher's refusal to write college recommendations. But although the flash points have changed, labor law is still dominated by issues of organizing, collective bargaining, and concerted action.

EXAM REVIEW

1. **RIGHT TO ORGANIZE** Section 7 of the National Labor Relations Act (NLRA) guarantees employees the right to organize and join unions, bargain collectively, and engage in other concerted activities. (p. 355)

2. **INTERFERENCE WITH ORGANIZING** Section 8(a) of the NLRA makes it an unfair labor practice (ULP) for an employer to interfere with union organizing, discriminate against a union member, or refuse to bargain collectively. (p. 355)

3. **DISCRIMINATION** Section 8(b) of the NLRA makes it a ULP for a union to interfere with employees who are exercising their rights under Section 7 or to engage in an illegal strike or boycott. (p. 356)

4. **EXCLUSIVITY** Section 9 of the NLRA makes a validly recognized union the exclusive representative of the employees. (p. 357)

5. **EMPLOYER OPPOSITION** During a union organizing campaign, an employer may vigorously present anti-union views to its employees, but it may not use threats or promises of benefits to defeat the union effort. (pp. 358–359)

EXAM Strategy

Question: Power, Inc., which operated a coal mine, suffered financial losses and had to lay off employees. The United Mine Workers of America (UMWA) began an organizing drive. Power's general manager warned miners that if the company was unionized, it would be shut down. An office manager told one of the miners that the company would get rid of union supporters. Shortly before the election was to take place, Power laid off 13 employees, all of whom had signed union cards. A low-seniority employee who had not signed a union card was not laid off. The union claimed that Power had committed ULPs. Comment.

Strategy: Section 7 of the NLRA guarantees employees the right to organize. An employer may vigorously advocate against a union organizing campaign. However, Section 8(a) makes it a ULP to interfere with union organizing or discriminate against a union member. (See the "Result" at the end of this section.)

6. **CERTIFICATION** The National Labor Relations Board (NLRB) will certify a proposed bargaining unit only if the employees share a community of interest. (p. 360)

7. **BARGAINING** The employer and the union must bargain over wages, hours, and other terms and conditions of employment. (pp. 360–363)

8. **GOOD FAITH** The union and the employer must bargain in good faith, but they are not obligated to reach an agreement. (pp. 361–362)

Question: Concrete Company was bargaining a CBA with the drivers' union. Negotiations went on for many months. Concrete made its final offer of $9.50 per hour, with step increases of $0.75 per hour in a year, and the same the following two years. The union refused to accept the offer, and the two sides reached an impasse. Concrete then implemented its plan, minus the step increases. Was its implementation legal?

Strategy: Management may unilaterally change wages and so forth only if the parties have reached an impasse. At all stages, the two sides must bargain in good faith. The goal of the NLRA is to achieve labor peace through productive negotiations. (See the "Result" at the end of this section.)

9. **STRIKES**   The NLRA guarantees employees the right to strike, with some limitations. (p. 364)

10. **REPLACEMENT WORKERS**   During a strike, management may hire replacement workers. (p. 364)

11. **PICKETING**   Picketing the employer's workplace in support of a strike is generally lawful, but secondary boycotts are usually illegal. (pp. 364–365)

12. **LOCKOUTS**   Lockouts are lawful if the parties have bargained to impasse. (p. 365)

5. Result: Each of the acts described was a ULP. Threatening layoffs or company closure are classic examples of ULPs. Laying off those who had signed union cards, but not those who refused, was clear discrimination. The NLRB found the violations so extreme that it certified the union and issued an order to bargain.

8. Result: The implementation was illegal. Because the parties had reached an impasse, the company was entitled to implement the last proposal it had made at the bargaining table. But it did not do so. By implementing a reduced plan that it had never proposed, management showed bad faith. To allow the company to implement something that it had never offered would defeat the whole purpose of bargaining.

MATCHING QUESTIONS

Match the following terms with their definitions:

___A. ULP

___B. Exclusivity

___C. Collective bargaining unit

___D. Union shop

___E. Concerted action

1. A specific group of employees that a union will represent

2. The union's right to be the sole representative of workers

3. Management interference with a union organizing effort

4. Picketing and strikes

5. The requirement that workers within specified categories join the union

TRUE/FALSE QUESTIONS

Circle true or false:

1. T F The union and management are both obligated to bargain until they reach a CBA or a court declares the bargaining futile.

2. T F Health benefits are a mandatory subject of bargaining.

3. T F During the last two decades, labor unions have grown by about 15 percent in the United States.

4. T F Workers are entitled to form a union whether management wants them to or not.

5. T F While organizing, workers may not discuss union issues on company property but may do so off the premises.

MULTIPLE-CHOICE QUESTIONS

1. During a union organizing drive, management urges workers not to join the union and discusses a competing company that lost business after a union was formed. Management
   (a) Committed a ULP by urging workers to reject the union, but did not do so by discussing a competing company
   (b) Committed a ULP by discussing a competing company, but did not do so by urging workers to reject the union
   (c) Committed a ULP both by urging workers to reject the union and by discussing a competitor
   (d) Committed no ULP
   (e) Has violated other sections of the NLRA

2. Which of these does the NLRA *not* protect?
   (a) The right to form a union
   (b) The right to picket
   (c) The right to strike
   (d) The right to block non-union workers from company property
   (e) The right to bargain collectively

3. The CBA at Grey Corp. has expired, as has the CBA at Blue Corp. At Grey, union and management have bargained a new CBA to impasse. Suddenly, Grey locks out all union workers. The next day, during a bargaining session at Blue, management announces that it will not discuss pay increases.
   (a) Grey has committed a ULP, but Blue has not.
   (b) Blue has committed a ULP, but Grey has not.
   (c) Both Blue and Grey have committed ULPs.
   (d) Neither company has committed a ULP.
   (e) Grey and Blue have violated labor law, but not by committing ULPs.

4. When the union went on strike, the company replaced Ashley, a union member, with Ben, a non-union member. The strike is now over, and a federal court has ruled that this was a ULP strike. Does Ashley get her job back?

   (a) The company is obligated to hire Ashley, even if that requires laying off Ben.

   (b) The company is obligated to hire Ashley *unless* that would require laying off Ben.

   (c) The company is obligated to hire Ashley only if Ben voluntarily leaves.

   (d) The company's only obligation is to notify Ashley of future job availability.

   (e) The company has no obligation at all to Ashley.

5. When new hires are forced to join an existing union, a union shop _____ exist. This kind of arrangement _____ legal under the NLRA.

   (a) does; is

   (b) does; is not

   (c) does not; is

   (d) does not; is not

ESSAY QUESTIONS

1. Gibson Greetings, Inc., had a plant in Berea, Kentucky, where the workers belonged to the International Brotherhood of Firemen & Oilers. The old CBA expired, and the parties negotiated a new one, but they were unable to reach an agreement on economic issues. The union struck. At the next bargaining session, the company claimed that the strike violated the old CBA, which had a no-strike clause and which stated that the terms of the old CBA would continue in force as long as the parties were bargaining a new CBA. The company refused to bargain until the union at least agreed that by bargaining, the company was not giving up its claim of an illegal strike. The two sides returned to bargaining, but meanwhile the company hired replacement workers. Eventually, the striking workers offered to return to work, but Gibson refused to rehire many of them. In court, the union claimed that the company had committed a ULP by (1) insisting the strike was illegal; and (2) refusing to bargain until the union acknowledged the company's position. Why is it very important to the union to establish the company's act as a ULP? *Was* it a ULP?

2. Fred Schipul taught English at the Thomaston High School in Connecticut for 18 years. When the position of English Department chairperson became vacant, Schipul applied, but the Board of Education appointed a less-senior teacher. Schipul filed a grievance based on a CBA provision that required the Board to promote the most-senior teacher where two or more applicants were equal in qualification. Before the arbitrator ruled on the grievance, the Board eliminated all department chairpersons. The arbitrator ruled in Schipul's favor. The Board then reinstated all department chairs—all but the English Department. Comment.

3. **ETHICS:** This chapter refers in several places to the contentious issue of subcontracting. Make an argument for management in favor of a company's ethical right to subcontract, and another for unions in opposition.

4. Triec, Inc., is a small electrical contracting company in Springfield, Ohio, owned by executives Yeazell, Jones, and Heaton. Employees contacted the International Brotherhood of Electrical Workers, which began an organizing drive, and 6 of the 11 employees in the bargaining unit signed authorization cards. The company declined to recognize the union, which petitioned the NLRB to schedule an election. The company then granted several new benefits for all workers, including higher wages, paid vacations, and other measures. When the election was held, only 2 of the 11 bargaining unit members voted for the union. Did the company violate the NLRA?

5. Eads Transfer, Inc., was a moving and storage company with a small workforce represented by the General Teamsters, Chauffeurs, and Helpers Union. When the CBA expired, the parties failed to reach agreement on a new one, and the union struck. As negotiations continued, Eads hired temporary replacement workers. After 10 months of the strike, some union workers offered to return to work, but Eads made no response to the offer. Two months later, more workers offered to return to work, but Eads would not accept any of the offers. Eventually, Eads notified all workers that they would not be allowed back to work until a new CBA had been signed. The union filed ULP claims against the company. Please rule.

DISCUSSION QUESTIONS

1. Once a union is recognized, it acts as the exclusive representative for all workers in a bargaining unit, even if some of them do not want the union to represent them. Is this reasonable? Should individual employees be able to "opt out," or would it be unfair for workers to get all the benefit of the union without having to pay dues?

2. Union workers earn an average of $200 per week more than non-union workers. Many people believe that unions are an essential part of creating a broad middle class, while others argue that they create undeserved windfalls for members. Do you have a favorable or unfavorable view of unions?

3. Union membership has fallen steadily in recent decades, in part because many unionized manufacturing jobs have been shipped overseas. Do you believe that unions will make a comeback in new industries? Would you prefer to be a member of a union if you had a choice? Why or why not?

4. Weigh in on the "card check" controversy. Imagine a company with 100 workers. After union organizers talk to the employees, 55 of them sign an authorization card. Should that be enough to establish the union, or should the employees also have to vote in a secret ballot before the union is designated as the employees' representative?

5. Strikes and lockouts frequently make the news, especially when a professional sports league is involved. Pro athletes tend to be highly compensated. Does that fact change your opinions about labor disputes? In the recent NFL lockout, did you side with the players or the owners?

© Evan Meyer/Shutterstock.com

Business
Organizations

CHAPTER 21

STARTING A BUSINESS: LLCS AND OTHER OPTIONS

© Evan Meyer/Shutterstock.com

Poor Jeffrey Horning. If only he had understood business law. Horning owned a thriving construction company, which operated as a corporation—Horning Construction Company, Inc. To lighten his crushing workload, he decide to bring in two partners to handle more day-to-day responsibility. It seemed a good idea at the time.

Horning transferred the business to Horning Construction, LLC, and then gave one-third ownership each to two trusted employees, Klimowski and Holdsworth. But Horning did not pay enough attention to the legal formalities—the new LLC had no operating agreement.

> Jeffrey Horning was stuck in purgatory, with two business partners he loathed and no way out.

Nothing worked out as he had planned. The two men did not take on extra work. Horning's relationship with them went from bad to worse, with the parties bickering over every petty detail and each man trying to sabotage the others. It got to the point that Klimowski sent Horning a letter full of foul language. At his wit's end, Horning proposed that the LLC buy out his share of the business. Klimowski and Holdsworth refused. Really frustrated, Horning asked a court to dissolve the business on the grounds that Klimowski despised him, Holdsworth resented him, and neither of them trusted him. In his view, it was their goal "to make my remaining time with Horning, LLC so unbearable that I will relent and give them for a pittance the remainder of the company for which they have paid nothing to date."

Although the court was sympathetic, it refused to help. Because Horning, LLC, did not have an operating agreement that provided for a buyout, it had to depend upon the LLC statute, which only permitted dissolution "whenever it is not reasonably practicable to carry on the business." Unfortunately, Horning, LLC, was very successful, grossing over

$25 million annually. Jeffrey Horning was stuck in purgatory, with two business partners he loathed and no way out.[1]

The law affects virtually every aspect of business. Wise (and successful) entrepreneurs know how to use the law to their advantage.

To begin, entrepreneurs must select a form of organization. The correct choice can reduce taxes, liability, and conflict while facilitating outside investment.

Sole Proprietorships

A sole proprietorship is an unincorporated business owned by one person. For example, Linda runs ExSciTe (which stands for Excellence in Science Teaching), a company that helps teachers prepare hands-on science experiments for the classroom.

If an individual runs a business without taking any formal steps to create an organization, she automatically has a sole proprietorship. It is, if you will, the default option. She is not required to hire a lawyer or register with the government. The company is not even required to file a separate tax return—all profits and losses flow through to the owner and are reported on her personal return.

However, sole proprietorships have some serious disadvantages:

- The owner of the business is responsible for all of the business's debts. If ExSciTe cannot pay its suppliers or if a student is injured while doing an experiment, Linda is *personally* liable.

- The owner of a sole proprietorship has limited options for financing her business. Debt is generally her only source of working capital because she has no stock or memberships to sell. If someone else brings in capital and helps with the management of the business, then it is a partnership, not a sole proprietorship. For this reason, sole proprietorships work best for small businesses without large capital needs.

> **Sole proprietorship**
> An unincorporated business owned by one person.

Corporations

Corporations are the dominant form of organization for a simple reason—they have been around for a long time and, as a result, they are numerous and the law that regulates them is well developed.

Corporations in General

Limited Liability

Shareholders of a corporation have limited liability, which means that if a corporation cannot pay its bills, shareholders lose their investment in the company, but not their other assets. Be aware, however, that **individuals are always responsible for their** *own* **acts**. Suppose that a careless employee who is also a company shareholder causes an accident at work. Being a shareholder does not protect him from liability for his own misdeeds. Both he and the company would be liable.

Transferability of Interests

Ownership interests in a partnership are not transferable without the permission of the other partners, whereas corporate stock can be easily bought and sold.

---

[1] *In the Matter of Jeffrey M. Horning*, 816 N.Y.S.2d 877; 2006 N.Y. Misc. LEXIS 555.

DURATION

When a sole proprietor dies, legally so does the business. But corporations have perpetual existence: they can continue without their founders.

LOGISTICS

Corporations require substantial expense and effort to create and operate. The cost of establishing a corporation includes legal and filing fees, not to mention the cost of the annual filings that states require. Corporations must also hold annual meetings for both shareholders and directors. Minutes of these meetings must be kept indefinitely in the company minute book.

TAXES

Because corporations are taxable entities, they must pay taxes and file returns. This is a simple sentence that requires a complex explanation. Originally, there were only three ways to do business: a sole proprietorship, a partnership, or a corporation. The sole proprietor pays taxes on all of the business's profits. A partnership is not, as we say, a taxable entity, which means it does not pay taxes itself. All income and losses are passed through to the partners and reported on their personal income tax returns. Corporations, by contrast, are taxable entities and pay income tax on their profits. Shareholders must then pay tax on dividends from the corporation. Thus, a dollar is taxed only once before it ends up in a partner's bank account, but twice before it is deposited by a shareholder.

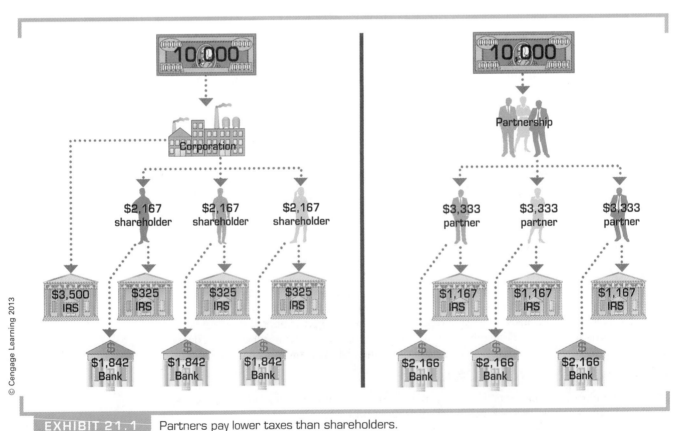

© Cengage Learning 2013

EXHIBIT 21.1   Partners pay lower taxes than shareholders.

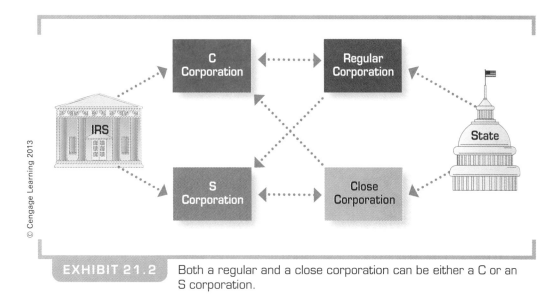

© Cengage Learning 2013

EXHIBIT 21.2 | Both a regular and a close corporation can be either a C or an S corporation.

Exhibit 21.1 compares the single taxation of partnerships with the double taxation of corporations. Suppose, as shown in the exhibit, that a corporation and a partnership each receive $10,000 in additional income. The corporation pays tax at a top rate of 35 percent.[2] Thus, the corporation pays $3,500 of the $10,000 in tax. The corporation pays out the remaining $6,500 as a dividend of $2,167 to each of its three shareholders. Then the shareholders are taxed at the special dividend rate of 15 percent, which means they each pay a tax of $325. They are each left with $1,842. Of the initial $10,000, almost 45 percent ($4,475) has gone to the Internal Revenue Service (IRS).

Compare the corporation to a partnership. The partnership itself pays no taxes, so it can pass on $3,333 to each of its partners. At a 35 percent individual rate, they will each pay an income tax of $1,167. As partners, they pocket $2,166, which is $324 more than they could keep as shareholders. Of the partnership's initial $10,000, 35 percent ($3,501) has gone to the IRS, compared with the corporation's 45 percent.

One further tax issue: corporations are created and regulated by state law but must pay both federal and state taxes. Federal law gives favorable tax treatment to some small corporations, which it calls "S corporations." Many states also treat small corporations differently but call them "close corporations." Federal tax law and state corporation statutes are completely independent. Thus, an organization could be a close corporation under state law and not qualify as an S corporation or, conversely, could be an S corporation under federal law but may or may not be a close corporation for state purposes. Exhibit 21.2 illustrates the difference between state corporate law and federal taxation of corporations

S Corporations

The majority of new businesses lose money in their early years. Congress created S corporations (aka "S corps") to encourage entrepreneurship by offering tax breaks. **Shareholders of S corps have both the limited liability of a corporation and the tax status of a partnership.** Like a partnership, an S corp is not a taxable entity—all of the company's profits and losses pass through to the shareholders, who pay tax at their individual rates. It avoids the double taxation of a regular corporation (called a "C corporation"). If, as is often the case, the start-up loses money, investors can deduct these losses against their other income.

---

[2]This is the federal tax rate; states also levy a corporate tax.

S corps do face some major restrictions:

- There can be only one class of stock.

- There can be no more than 100 shareholders.

- Shareholders must be individuals, estates, charities, pension funds, or trusts, not partnerships or corporations.

- Shareholders must be citizens or residents of the United States, not nonresident aliens.

- All shareholders must agree that the company should be an S corporation.

Close Corporations

Close corporation
A company whose stock is not publicly traded. Also known as a *closely held corporation.*

Generally, a **close corporation** is a company whose stock is not publicly traded. However, some states make special provisions for small close corporations. These provisions vary from state to state, but they tend to have certain common themes:

- **Protection of minority shareholders.** As there is no public market for the stock of a close corporation, a minority shareholder who is being mistreated by the majority cannot simply sell his shares and depart. Therefore, close corporation statutes often provide some protection for minority shareholders. For example, the charter of a close corporation could require a unanimous vote of all shareholders to choose officers, set salaries, or pay dividends. It could grant each shareholder veto power over all important corporate decisions.

- **Transfer restrictions.** The shareholders of a close corporation often need to work closely together in the management of the company. Therefore, statutes typically permit the corporation to require that a shareholder first offer shares to the other owners before selling them to an outsider. In that way, the remaining shareholders have some control over who their new co-owners will be.

- **Flexibility.** Close corporations can typically operate without a board of directors, a formal set of bylaws, or annual shareholder meetings.

- **Dispute resolution.** The shareholders are allowed to agree in advance that any one of them can dissolve the corporation if some particular event occurs or, if they choose, for any reason at all. If the shareholders are in a stalemate, the problem can be solved by dissolving the corporation. Even without such an agreement, a shareholder can ask a court to dissolve a close corporation if the other owners behave "oppressively" or "unfairly."

EXAM Strategy

Question: Consider these two entrepreneurs: Judith formed a corporation to publish a newsletter that will not generate substantial revenues. Drexel operated his construction and remodeling business as a sole proprietorship. Were these forms of organization right for these businesses?

Strategy: Prepare a list of the advantages and disadvantages for each form of organization. Sole proprietorships are best for businesses without substantial capital needs. Corporations can raise capital but are expensive to operate.

Result: Judith would be better off with a sole proprietorship—her revenues will not support the expenses of a corporation. Also, her debts are likely to be small, so she will not need the limited liability of a corporation. And no matter what her form of organization, she would be personally liable for any negligent acts she commits, so a corporation would not provide any additional protection. But for Drexel, a sole proprietorship could be disastrous because his construction company will have substantial expenses and a large number of employees. If an employee causes an injury, Drexel might be personally liable. And if his business fails, the court might liquidate his personal assets.

LIMITED LIABILITY COMPANIES

An LLC offers the limited liability of a corporation and the tax status of a partnership.

LIMITED LIABILITY

Members are not personally liable for the debts of the company. They risk only their investment, as if they were shareholders of a corporation. Are the members of the LLC liable in the following case? You be the judge.

You be the Judge

RIDGAWAY V. SILK
2004 Conn. Super. LEXIS 548
Superior Court of Connecticut, 2004

Facts: Norman Costello and Joseph Ruggiero were members of Silk, LLC, which owned a bar and adult entertainment nightclub in Groton, Connecticut, called Silk Stockings. Anthony Sulls went drinking there one night—and drinking heavily. Although he was obviously drunk, employees at Silk Stockings continued to serve him. Giordano and Costello were working there that night. They both greeted customers (who numbered in the hundreds), supervised employees, and performed "other PR work." When Sulls left the nightclub at 1:45 a.m. with two friends, he drove off the highway at high speed, killing himself and one of his passengers, William Ridgaway, Jr.

Ridgaway's estate sued Costello and Giordano personally. The defendants filed a motion for summary judgment.

You Be the Judge: *Are Costello and Giordano personally liable to Ridgaway's estate?*

Argument for Costello and Giordano: The defendants did not own Silk Stockings; they were simply members of an LLC that owned the nightclub. The whole point of an LLC is to protect members against personal liability. The assets of Silk, LLC, are at risk, but not the personal assets of Costello and Giordano.

Argument for Ridgaway's Estate: The defendants are not liable for being *members* of Silk, LLC, they are liable for their own misdeeds as *employees* of the LLC. They were both present at Silk Stockings on the night in question, meeting and greeting customers and supervising employees. It is possible that they might actually have served drinks to Sulls, but in any event, they did not adequately supervise and train their employees to prevent them from serving alcohol to someone who was clearly drunk. The world would be an intolerable place to live if employees were free to be as careless as they wished, knowing that they were not liable because they were members of an LLC.

TAX STATUS

As in a partnership, **income flows through the company to the individual members, avoiding the double taxation of a corporation.**

FORMATION

To organize an LLC, you must have a charter and you should have an operating agreement. The charter contains basic information, such as name and address. It must be filed with the Secretary of State in the jurisdiction in which the company is being formed. An operating agreement sets out the rights and obligations of the owners, called *members*. Although some states do not require an operating agreement, lawyers recommend them as a way to avoid disputes. The *Horning* case that began the chapter illustrates one of the many things that can go wrong without an operating agreement. But as the following case illustrates, not just any operating agreement will do.

WYOMING.COM, LLC V. LIEBERMAN

2005 WY 42; 109 P.3d 883; 2005 Wyo. LEXIS 48
Supreme Court of Wyoming, 2005

CASE SUMMARY

Facts: Lieberman was a member of an LLC called Wyoming.com. After he withdrew, he and the other members disagreed about what his membership was worth. Wyoming.com filed a lawsuit asking the court to determine the financial rights and obligations of the parties, if any, upon the withdrawal of a member.

The Supreme Court of Wyoming reached a decision that may have sounded logical but left Lieberman in a sad twilight zone—neither in nor out of the LLC. The court ruled that Lieberman still owned part of the business despite his withdrawal as a member. So far, so good. But neither the LLC statute nor the company's operating agreement required the LLC to pay a member the value of his share. In other words, Lieberman was still an owner, but he was not entitled to any payment for his ownership. Not quite understanding the implications of this ruling,

Lieberman filed a motion seeking financial information about the company. The original trial court denied the request on the theory that, since Lieberman had no rights to a payout, the company had no obligation to give him financial data.

Issue: *Does Lieberman have a right to any financial data about Wyoming.com?*

Decision: Wyoming.com has no obligation to provide Lieberman with financial data about the company.

Reasoning: The court in the prior Lieberman case ruled that Lieberman was not entitled to any payment from Wyoming.com. Thus, there is no point in requiring the company to give him financial information. He still owns a share of the company, but he has no further rights.

FLEXIBILITY

Unlike S corporations, LLCs can have members that are corporations, partnerships, or nonresident aliens. LLCs can also have different classes of membership. Unlike corporations, LLCs are not required to hold annual meetings or maintain a minute book.

TRANSFERABILITY OF INTERESTS

Unless the operating agreement provides otherwise, the members of the LLC must obtain the unanimous permission of the remaining members before transferring their ownership rights. This is yet another reason to have an operating agreement.

LLCs cannot issue stock options, which is potentially a serious problem because options may be an essential lure in attracting and retaining top talent.

DURATION

It used to be that LLCs automatically dissolved upon the withdrawal of a member (owing to death, resignation, or bankruptcy, for example). The current trend in state laws, however, is to permit an LLC to continue in operation even after a member withdraws.

Going Public

Once an LLC goes public, it loses its favorable tax status and is taxed as a corporation, not a partnership.[3] Thus, there is no advantage to using the LLC form of organization for a publicly traded company. And there are some disadvantages: unlike corporations, publicly traded LLCs do not enjoy a well-established set of statutory and case law that is relatively consistent across the many states. For this reason, privately held companies that begin as LLCs usually change to corporations when they go public.

Piercing the LLC Veil

It has long been the case that, if corporate shareholders do not comply with the technicalities of corporation law, they may be held personally liable for the debts of the organization. As the following case illustrates, under these circumstances, members of an LLC are also liable.

BLD Products, Ltd. v. Technical Plastics of Oregon, LLC

2006 U.S. Dist. LEXIS 89874
United States District Court for the District of Oregon, 2006

CASE SUMMARY

Facts: Mark Hardie was the sole member of Technical Plastics of Oregon, LLC (TPO). He operated the business out of an office in his home. Hardie regularly used TPO's accounts to pay such expenses as landscaping and housecleaning. TPO also paid some of Hardie's personal credit card bills, loan payments on his Ford truck, the cost of constructing a deck on his house, his stepson's college bills, and the expenses of family vacations to Disneyland. At the same time, Hardie deposited cash advances from his personal credit cards into the TPO checking account. Hardie did not take a salary from TPO. When TPO filed for bankruptcy, it owed BLD Products approximately $120,000.

In some cases, a court will "pierce the veil" of a corporation and hold its shareholders personally liable for the debts of the business. BLD argued that the same doctrine should apply to LLCs and the court should hold Hardie personally liable for TPO's debts.

Issues: *Does the doctrine of "piercing the veil" apply to LLCs? Is Hardy personally liable for TPO's debts?*

Decision: Yes, an LLC's veil can be pierced. Hardy is personally liable for TPO's debts.

Reasoning: An LLC's veil can be pierced if the following three tests are met:

1. The member (that is, Hardie) controlled the LLC;

2. The member engaged in improper conduct; and

3. As a result of that improper conduct, the plaintiff was unable to collect on a debt against the insolvent LLC.

Hardie, as the sole member and manager of TPO, clearly controlled the company. In addition, he engaged in improper conduct when he paid his personal expenses from the TPO business account. These amounts were more than occasional dips into petty cash—they indicated a disregard of TPO's separate LLC identity. Moreover, he did not keep records of these personal payments.

It is not clear whether Hardie's improper conduct prevented BLD from collecting its entire $120,000 debt. A jury will have to determine the amount that Hardie owes BLD.

---

[3]26 U.S.C. Section 7704.

LEGAL UNCERTAINTY

As we have observed, LLCs are a relatively new form of organization without a consistent and widely developed body of law. As a result, members of an LLC may find themselves in the unhappy position of litigating issues of law which, although well established for corporations, are not yet clear for LLCs. Win or lose, lawsuits are expensive in both time and money.

An important area of legal uncertainty involves managers' duties to the members of the organization. For example, is not clear in many jurisdictions if managers of an LLC have a legal obligation to act in the best interest of members. Under Delaware law, managers do have a fiduciary duty to an LLC's members unless the operating agreement provides otherwise. (In that state, an operating agreement can limit any duty except the requirement of good faith and fair dealing.) However, this uncertainty means that, before becoming a member of an LLC, it is important to understand both state law and the terms of the operating agreement. Likewise, a Delaware court recently ruled that creditors have fewer rights against LLCs than they do against corporations. In short, many issues of law that are well established for corporations still reside in foggy territory when it comes to LLCs.

CHOICES: LLC v. CORPORATION

When starting a business, which form makes the most sense—LLC or corporation? The tax status of an LLC is a major advantage over a corporation. Although an S corporation has the same tax status as an LLC, it also has all the annoying rules about classes of stock and number of shareholders. Once an LLC is established, it does not have as many housekeeping rules as corporations—for example, it does not have to make annual filings or hold annual meetings. However, the LLC is not right for everyone. If done properly, an LLC is more expensive to set up than a corporation because it needs to have a thoughtfully crafted operating agreement. Also, venture capitalists almost always refuse to invest in LLCs, preferring C corporations instead. There are four reasons for this preference:

- Complex tax issues,

- C corporations are easier to merge, sell, or take public,

- Corporations can issue stock options, and

- The general legal uncertainty involving LLCs.

EXAM Strategy

Question: Hortense and Gus are each starting a business. Hortense's business will be an Internet start-up. Gus will be opening a yarn store. Hortense needs millions of dollars in venture capital and expects to go public soon. Gus has borrowed $10,000 from his girlfriend, which he hopes to pay back promptly. Should either of these businesses organize as an LLC?

Strategy: Sole proprietorships may be best for businesses without substantial capital needs and without significant liability issues. Corporations are best for businesses that will need substantial outside capital and expect to go public shortly.

Result: An LLC is not the best choice for either of these businesses. Venture capitalists will insist that Hortense's business be a corporation, especially if it is going public soon. A yarn store has few liability issues, and Gus does not expect to have any outside investors. Hence, a sole proprietorship would be more appropriate.

GENERAL PARTNERSHIPS

Partnerships have two important advantages: they are *easy to form* and they do not pay *taxes*. Partnerships, however, also have some major disadvantages:

- *Liability.* Each partner is personally liable for the debts of the enterprise, whether or not she caused them.

- *Funding.* Financing a partnership may be difficult because the firm cannot sell shares as a corporation does. The capital needs of the partnership must be met by contributions from partners or by borrowing.

- *Management.* Managing a partnership can also be difficult because in the absence of an agreement to the contrary, all partners have an equal say in running the business.

- *Transferability.* A partner only has the right to transfer the *value* of her partnership interest, not the interest itself. Thus, a mother who is a partner in a law firm can pass to her son the value of her partnership interest, not the right to be a partner in the firm (or even the right to work there).

Formation

A partnership is an association of two or more co-owners who carry on a business for profit. Each co-owner is called a *general partner*. Like sole proprietorships, partnerships are easy to form. Although, practically speaking, a partnership *should* have a written agreement, the law generally does not require anything in the way of forms, filings, or agreements. If two or more people do business together, sharing management, profits and losses, they have a partnership whether they know it or not. They are subject to all the rules of partnership law.

Partnership
An unincorporated association of two or more co-owners who operate a business for profit.

Taxes

As we have seen above, a partnership is not a taxable entity, which means it does not pay taxes itself.

Liability

Every partner is an agent of the partnership. Thus, the entire partnership is liable for the act of one partner in, say, signing a contract. **A partnership is also liable for any torts that a partner commits in the ordinary course of the partnership's business.**

It gets worse. **If a partnership does not have enough assets to pay its debts, creditors may go after the personal property of individual partners whether or not they were in any way responsible for the debt.** Because partners have **joint and several liability**, creditors can sue the partnership and the partners together, or in separate lawsuits, or in any combination of the two. The partnership and the partners are all individually liable for the full amount of the debt, but, obviously, the creditor cannot keep collecting after he has already received the total amount owed. **Also note that, even if creditors have a judgment against an individual partner, they cannot go after that partner's assets until all the partnership's assets are exhausted.**

Letitia, one of the world's wealthiest people, enters into a partnership with penniless Harry to drill for oil on her land. While driving on partnership business, Harry crashes into Rama, seriously injuring him. Rama can sue any combination of the partnership, Letitia, and Harry for the full amount, even though Letitia was 2,000 miles away on her Caribbean island when the accident occurred and she had cautioned Harry many times to drive carefully. Even if Rama obtains a judgment against Letitia, however, he cannot recover

Joint and several liability
An injured third party has the right to recover the full amount of his damages from one, some, or all of those who caused his harm. He may not recover more than 100 percent of his damages.

against her while the partnership still has assets. So, for all practical purposes, he must try to collect first against the partnership. If the partnership is bankrupt and he manages to collect the full amount from Letitia, he cannot then try to recover against Harry.

Management

The management of a partnership can be a significant challenge.

MANAGEMENT RIGHTS

Unless the partnership agrees otherwise, partners share both profits and losses equally, and each partner has an equal right to manage the business.

In a large partnership, with hundreds of partners, too many cooks can definitely spoil the firm's profitability. That is why large partnerships are almost always run by one or a few partners who are designated as **managing partners** or **members of the executive committee.**

> In a large partnership, too many cooks can definitely spoil the firm's profitability.

MANAGEMENT DUTIES

Partners have a **fiduciary duty** to the partnership. This duty means that:

- *Partners are liable to the partnership for gross negligence or intentional misconduct.*

- *Partners cannot compete with the partnership.* Each partner must turn over to the partnership all earnings from any activity that is related to the partnership's business. Thus, law firms would typically expect a partner to turn over any fees he earned as a director of a company, but he could keep royalties from his novel on scuba diving.

- *A partner may not take an opportunity away from the partnership unless the other partners consent.* If the partnership wants to buy an office building and a partner hears of one for sale, she must give the partnership an opportunity to buy it before she purchases it herself.

- *If a partner engages in a conflict of interest, he must turn over to the partnership any profits he earned from that activity.* Thus, someone who bid on partnership assets (in this case, a racehorse) at auction without telling his partner was in violation of his fiduciary duty to the partnership.

Terminating a Partnership

A partnership begins with an *association* of two or more people. Appropriately, the end of a partnership begins with a *dissociation*. **A dissociation occurs when a partner quits.**

DISSOCIATION

A partner always has the *power* to leave a partnership but may not have the *right*. In other words, a partner can always dissociate, but she may have to pay damages for any harm that her departure causes.

A dissociation is a fork in the road: **the partnership can either buy out the departing partner(s) and continue in business or wind up the business and terminate the partnership.** If the partnership chooses to terminate the business, it must follow three steps: dissolution, winding up, and termination.

THREE STEPS TO TERMINATION

Dissolution.   The rules on dissolution depend, in part, on the type of partnership. If the partners have agreed in advance how long the partnership will last, it is a **term partnership.** At the end of the specified term, the partnership automatically ends. Otherwise, it is a **partnership at will**, which means that any of the partners can leave at any time, for any reason.

A partnership *automatically* dissolves:

- In a partnership at will, when a partner withdraws

- In a term partnership, when:

  - A partner is dissociated and half of the remaining partners vote to wind up the partnership business,

  - All the partners agree to dissolve, or

  - The term expires or the partnership achieves its goal.

- In any partnership, when:

  - An event occurs that the partners had agreed would cause dissolution,

  - The partnership business becomes illegal or,

  - A court determines that the partnership is unlikely to succeed. If the partners simply cannot get along or they cannot make a profit, any partner has the right to ask a court to dissolve the partnership.

Winding Up.   During the winding-up process, all debts of the partnership are paid, and the remaining proceeds are distributed to the partners.

Termination.   Termination happens automatically once the winding up is finished. The partnership is not required to do anything official; it can go out of the world even more quietly and simply than it came in.

LIMITED LIABILITY PARTNERSHIPS

A limited liability partnership (LLP) is a type of general partnership that most states now permit. There is a very important distinction, however, between these two forms of organization: **in an LLP, the partners are not liable for the debts of the partnership.** They are, naturally, liable for their own misdeeds, just as if they were a member of an LLC or a shareholder of a corporation.

To form an LLP, the partners must file a statement of qualification with state officials. LLPs must also file annual reports. The other attributes of a partnership remain the same. Thus, an LLP is not a taxable entity.

Although an LLP can be much more advantageous for partners than a general partnership, it is absolutely crucial to comply with all the technicalities of the LLP statute. Otherwise, the partners lose protection against personal liability. Note the sad result for Michael Gaus and John West, who formed a Texas LLP. Unfortunately, they did not renew the LLP registration each year, as the statute required. Four years after its initial registration, the partnership entered into a lease. When the partners ultimately stopped paying rent and abandoned the premises, they were both were held personally liable for the rent because the LLP registration had expired. As the court pointed out, the statute did not contain a "substantial compliance" section, nor did it contain a grace period for filing a renewal application. In short, close counts in horseshoes and hand grenades, but not in LLPs.

LIMITED PARTNERSHIPS AND LIMITED LIABILITY LIMITED PARTNERSHIPS

Although limited partnerships and limited liability limited partnerships sound confusingly similar to limited liability partnerships and general partnerships, like many siblings, they operate very differently. And truth to tell, limited partnerships and limited liability limited partnerships are relatively rare—they are generally only used for estate planning purposes (usually, to reduce estate taxes) and for highly sophisticated investment vehicles. You should be aware of their existence, but you may not see them very often in your business life. Here are the major features:

STRUCTURE

Limited partnerships must have at least one *limited* partner and one *general* partner.

LIABILITY

Limited partners are not *personally* liable, but general partners are. Like corporate share-holders, limited partners risk only their investment in the partnership (which is called their "capital contribution"). In contrast, general partners of the limited partnership are personally liable for the debts of the organization.

However, the revised version of the Uniform Limited Partnership Act (ULPA) permits a limited partnership, in its certificate of formation and partnership agreement, simply to declare itself a *limited liability* limited partnership.[4] **In a limited liability limited partnership, the general partner is not personally liable for the debts of the partnership.** This provision effectively removes the major disadvantage of limited partnerships. Although at this writing, fewer than half the states have actually passed the revised version of the ULPA, this revision would seem to indicate the trend for the future.

TAXES

Limited partnerships are not taxable entities. Income is taxed only once before landing in a partner's pocket.

FORMATION

The general partners must file a **certificate of limited partnership** with their Secretary of State. Although most limited partnerships do have a partnership agreement, it is not required.

MANAGEMENT

General partners have the right to manage a limited partnership. Limited partners are essentially passive investors with few management rights beyond the right to be informed about the partnership business.

TRANSFER OF OWNERSHIP

Limited partners have the right to transfer the *value* of their partnership interest, but they can only sell or give away the interest itself if the partnership agreement permits.

DURATION

Unless the partnership agreement provides otherwise, limited partnerships enjoy perpetual existence—they continue even as partners come and go.

---

[4]ULPA Section 102(9).

PROFESSIONAL CORPORATION

Traditionally, most professionals (such as lawyers and doctors) were not permitted to incorporate their businesses, so they organized as partnerships. Now professionals are allowed to incorporate in "professional corporations" or "PCs." **PCs provide more liability protection than a general partnership.** If a member of a PC commits malpractice, the corporation's assets are at risk but not the personal assets of the innocent members. If Drs. Sharp, Payne, and Graves form a *partnership*, all the partners will be personally liable when Dr. Payne accidentally leaves her scalpel inside a patient. If the three doctors have formed a *PC* instead, Dr. Payne's Aspen condo and the assets of the PC will be at risk, but not the personal assets of the two other doctors.

Generally, the shareholders of a PC are not personally liable for the contract debts of the organization, such as leases or bank loans. Thus, if Sharp, Payne, & Graves, P.C. is unable to pay its rent, the landlord cannot recover from the personal assets of any of the doctors.

PCs have some limitations:

- All shareholders of the corporation must be members of the same profession. For Sharp, Payne, & Graves, P.C., that means all shareholders must be licensed physicians.

- The required legal technicalities for forming and maintaining a PC are expensive and time-consuming.

- Tax issues can be complicated. A PC is a separate taxable entity, like any other corporation. It must pay tax on its profits, and then its shareholders pay tax on any dividends they receive. Salaries, however, are deductible from firm profits. Thus, the PC can avoid paying taxes on its profits by paying out all the profits as salary. But any profits remaining in firm coffers at the end of the year are taxable. To avoid tax, PCs must be careful to calculate their profits accurately and pay them out before year's end. This chore can be time-consuming, and any error may cause unnecessary tax liability.

FRANCHISES

Franchises are not, strictly speaking, a separate form of organization. They are included here because they represent an important option for entrepreneurs. Most franchisors and franchisees are corporations, although they could legally choose to be any of the forms discussed in this chapter.

Although franchises can be a great opportunity for entrepreneurs, historically they have also been a great opportunity for fraudsters to trick the unwary. And franchise agreements, which the franchisor drafts, tend to be one-sided. For these reasons, the Federal Trade Commission (FTC) regulates franchises. In addition, some states also impose their own franchise requirements.

Under FTC rules, a franchisor must deliver to a potential purchaser a so-called Franchise Disclosure Document (FDD) at least 14 calendar days before any contract is signed or money is paid. The FDD must provide information about the franchise that includes history, litigation, expenses, restrictions on products, suppliers and territory, other franchisees, and audited financials. Earnings information is not required, but if disclosed, the franchisor must reveal the basis for this information

The purpose of the FDD is to ensure that the franchisor discloses all relevant facts. It is not a guarantee of quality because the FTC does not investigate to make sure that the information is accurate. Suppose you obtain an FDD for Shrinking Cats, a franchise that offers psychiatric services for neurotic felines. The company has lost money on all the outlets it operates itself; it has sold only three franchises, two of which have gone out of business; and all the required contracts are ridiculously favorable to the franchisor. Nevertheless, the FTC will still permit sales, so long as the franchisor discloses all the information required in the FDD.

As the following case illustrates, the franchisor has much of the power in a franchise relationship.

NATIONAL FRANCHISEE ASSOCIATION v. BURGER KING CORPORATION

2010 U.S. Dist. LEXIS 123065
United States District Court for the Southern District of Florida, 2010

CASE SUMMARY

Facts: The Burger King Corporation (BKC) would not allow franchisees to have it their way. Instead, BKC forced them to sell double-cheeseburgers (DCB) for $1.00, which was below cost. BKC franchisees filed suit alleging that (1) BKC did not have the right to set maximum prices; and (2) that even if BKC had such a right, it had violated its obligation under the franchise agreement to act in good faith.

The court dismissed the first claim because the franchise agreement unambiguously permitted BKC to set whatever prices it wanted. But the court allowed the plaintiffs to proceed with the second claim.

Issue: *Was BKC acting in good faith when it forced franchisees to sell items below cost?*

Decision: Yes, BKC was acting in good faith.

Reasoning: This case hinges on BKC's motives. To show bad faith, plaintiffs must present evidence that

BKC's goal, in setting these prices, was to harm the franchisees. For example, the franchisees could show that BKC's motive was to weaken them so much that the company could take them over itself.

Alternatively, the plaintiffs could show (1) that no reasonable person would have set the price of a DCB at $1.00 and (2) this pricing caused severe harm to the franchises. Clearly, the plaintiffs would never have agreed to a contract that permitted unreasonable and harmful behavior.

The franchisees cannot meet any of these tests. First, there is no evidence that BKC had any motive other than helping the franchisees. Second, selling below cost is not necessarily irrational. Indeed, there are lots of good reasons why stores might adopt such a strategy—to build customer loyalty, lure customers away from competitors, or serve as loss leaders to generate increased sales on other, higher-priced products. Third, there is no evidence that the franchises were unprofitable or in danger of bankruptcy.

Chapter Conclusion

The process of starting a business is immensely time-consuming. Not surprisingly, entrepreneurs are sometimes reluctant to spend their valuable time on legal issues that, after all, do not contribute directly to the bottom line. No customer buys more fried chicken because the business is a limited liability company instead of a corporation. Wise entrepreneurs know, however, that careful attention to legal issues is an essential component of success. The idea for the business may come first, but legal considerations occupy a close second place.

EXAM REVIEW

	Separate Taxable Entity	Personal Liability for Owners	Ease of Formation	Transferable Interests (Easily Bought and Sold)	Perpetual Existence	Other Features
Sole Proprietorship	No	Yes	Very easy	No, can only sell entire business	No	
Corporation	Yes	No	Difficult	Yes	Yes	
Close Corporation	Yes, for C corporation No, for S corporation	No	Difficult	Transfer restrictions	Yes	Protection of minority shareholders. No board of directors required.
S Corporation	No	No	Difficult	Transfer restrictions	Yes	Only 100 shareholders. Only one class of stock. Shareholders must be individuals, estates, trusts, charities, or pension funds and be citizens or residents of the United States. All shareholders must agree to S status.
Limited Liability Company	No	No	Difficult	Yes, if the operating agreement permits	Varies by state, but generally, yes	No limit on the number of shareholders, the number of classes of stock, or the type of shareholder.
General Partnership	No	Yes	Easy	No	Depends on the partnership agreement	Management can be difficult.
Limited Liability Partnership	No	No	Difficult	No	Depends on the partnership agreement	
Limited Partnership	No	Yes, for general partner No, for limited partners	Difficult	Yes (for limited partners), if partnership agreement permits	Yes	
Limited Liability Limited Partnership	No	No	Difficult	Yes (for limited partners), if partnership agreement permits	Yes	
Professional Corporation	Yes	No	Difficult	Shareholders must all be members of same profession	Yes, as long as it has shareholders	Complex tax issues.
Franchise	All these issues depend on the form of organization chosen by participants.					

MATCHING QUESTIONS

Match the following terms with their definitions:

_____ A. S corporation
_____ B. Dissociation
_____ C. Close corporation
_____ D. Dissolution
_____ E. Limited partnership

1. The first step in the process of terminating a partnership
2. Created by federal law
3. The general partner is liable
4. Created by state law
5. A partner leaves the partnership

TRUE/FALSE QUESTIONS

Circle true or false:

1. T F Sole proprietorships must file a tax return.
2. T F Ownership in a partnership is not transferable.
3. T F Creditors of a partnership must first seek recovery from partnership assets before going after the personal assets of a partner.
4. T F In both a limited partnership and a limited liability limited partnership, the partners are not personally liable for the debts of the partnership.
5. T F Venture capitalists often require companies they own to become LLCs before going public.

MULTIPLE-CHOICE QUESTIONS

1. **CPA QUESTION:** Assuming all other requirements are met, a corporation may elect to be treated as an S corporation under the Internal Revenue Code if it has:
   (a) Both common and preferred stockholders
   (b) A partnership as a stockholder
   (c) 100 or fewer stockholders
   (d) The consent of a majority of the stockholders

2. A limited liability partnership:
   (a) Has ownership interests that cannot be transferred
   (b) Protects the partners from liability for the debts of the partnership
   (c) Must pay taxes on its income
   (d) Requires no formal steps for its creation
   (e) Permits a limited number of partners

3. A limited liability company:
   (a) Is regulated by a well-established body of law
   (b) Pays taxes on its income
   (c) May issue stock options
   (d) Must register with state authorities
   (e) Protects the owners from personal liability for their own misdeeds

4. Joint and several liability means that:
   (a) A creditor of the partnership must sue all of the partners together.
   (b) A creditor of the partnership must sue the partnership and all of the partners together.
   (c) A creditor of the partnership can recover the full amount owed from the partnership or from any of the partners.
   (d) A creditor of the partnership can recover the full amount owed from the partnership and from each partner, even if this results in the creditor receiving more than his original debt.
   (e) A creditor of the partnership can recover from the partners individually, but not from the partnership.

5. While working part time at a Supercorp restaurant, Jenna spills a bucket of hot French fries on a customer. Who is liable to the customer?
   (a) Supercorp alone
   (b) Jenna alone
   (c) Both Jenna and Supercorp
   (d) Jenna, Supercorp, and the president of Supercorp
   (e) Jenna, Supercorp, and the shareholders of Supercorp

ESSAY QUESTIONS

1. The Logan Wright Foundation (LWF), an Oklahoma corporation, was a partner in a partnership formed to operate two Sonic drive-in restaurants. LWF argued that it was not responsible for Sonic's taxes because LWF was merely a limited partner, with limited liability to the partnership's creditors, including the IRS. The partnership had never filed a certificate of limited partnership with the Secretary of State. Is LWF liable to the IRS?

EXAM Strategy

2. **Question:** Alan Dershowitz, a law professor famous for his wealthy clients (O. J. Simpson, among others), joined with other lawyers to open a kosher delicatessen, Maven's Court. Dershowitz met with greater success at the bar than in the kitchen—the deli failed after barely a year in business. One supplier sued for overdue bills. What form of organization would have been the best choice for Maven's Court?

Strategy: A sole proprietorship would not have worked because there was more than one owner. A partnership would have been a disaster because of unlimited liability. They could have met all the requirements of an S corporation or an LLC. (See the "Result" at the end of this section.)

EXAM Strategy

3. **Question:** Mrs. Meadows opened a biscuit shop called The Biscuit Bakery. The business was not incorporated. Whenever she ordered supplies, she was careful to sign the contract in the name of the business, not personally: "The Biscuit Bakery by Daisy Meadows," for instance. Unfortunately, she had no money to pay her flour bill. When the vendor threatened to sue her, Mrs. Meadows told him that he could only sue the business because all the contracts were in the business's name. Will Mrs. Meadows lose her dough?

Strategy: The first step is to figure out what type of organization her business is. Then recall what liability protection that organization offers. (See the "Result" at the end of this section.)

4. Kristine bought a Rocky Mountain Chocolate Factory franchise. Her franchise agreement required her to purchase a cash register that cost $3,000, with an annual maintenance fee of $773. The agreement also provided that Rocky Mountain could change to a more expensive system. Within a few months after signing the agreement, Kristine learned that she would have to buy a new cash register that cost $20,000, with annual maintenance fees of $2,000. Does Kristine have to buy this new cash register? Did Rocky Mountain act in bad faith?

5. What is the difference between close corporations and S corporations?

2. Result: Maven's Court would have chosen an LLC or an S corporation.

3. Result: The Biscuit Bakery was a sole proprietorship. No matter how Mrs. Meadows signed the contracts, she is still personally liable for the debts of the business.

DISCUSSION QUESTIONS

1. **ETHICS** Lee McNeely told Hardee's officials that he was interested in purchasing multiple restaurants in Arkansas. A Hardee's officer assured him that any of the company-owned stores in Arkansas would be available for purchase. However, the company urged him to open a new store in Maumelle and sent him a letter estimating first-year sales at around $800,000. McNeely built the Maumelle restaurant, but gross sales the first year were only $508,000. When McNeely asked to buy an existing restaurant, a Hardee's officer refused, informing him that Hardee's rarely sold company-owned restaurants. The disclosure document contained no misstatements, but McNeely brought suit alleging fraud in the sale of the Maumelle franchise. Does McNeely have a valid claim against Hardee's? Apart from the legal issues, did Hardee's officers behave ethically? Is all fair in love, war, and franchising?

2. Leonard, an attorney, was negligent in his representation of Anthony. In settlement of Anthony's claim against him, Leonard signed a promissory note for $10,400 on behalf of his law firm, an LLC. When the law firm did not pay, Anthony filed suit against Leonard personally for payment of the note. Is a member personally liable for the debt of an LLC that was caused by his own negligence?

3. Think of a business concept that would be appropriate for each of the following: a sole proprietorship, a corporation, and a limited liability company.

4. As you will see in Chapter 22, Facebook began life as a corporation, not an LLC. Why did the founder, Mark Zuckerberg, make that decision?

5. Corporations developed to encourage investors to contribute the capital needed to create large-scale manufacturing enterprises. But LLCs are often start-ups or other small businesses. Why do their members deserve limited liability? And is it fair that LLCs do not have to pay income taxes?

CHAPTER 22

CORPORATIONS

On July 26, 2004, Mark Zuckerberg signed a Certificate of Incorporation for his company, which he called TheFacebook, Inc. At 11:34 a.m. on July 29, 2004, that Certificate was filed with the Secretary of State for Delaware, and TheFacebook began its life as a corporation. Zuckerberg had started this social networking Internet site the previous February in his dorm room at Harvard. By December 2004, TheFacebook had almost 1 million users. By the beginning of 2006, the company was estimated to be worth between $750 million and $2 billion. Today, TheFacebook is valued at more than $50 billion. As Zuckerberg built his company, what did he need to know about the law?

© Evan Meyer/Shutterstock.com

Zuckerberg started
TheFacebook in his
dorm room at Harvard.
Within 10 months,
it had almost 1 million
users.

PROMOTER'S LIABILITY

TheFacebook operated for five months before it was incorporated. During this period, Zuckerberg needed to be careful to avoid liability as a promoter. **A promoter is someone who organizes a corporation.**

Zuckerberg had moved company headquarters to Palo Alto, California, before the certificate of incorporation was filed. Suppose that he finds the perfect location for his headquarters. He is eager to sign the lease before someone else snatches the opportunity away, but TheFacebook does not yet legally exist—it is not incorporated. What would happen if he signed the lease anyway? **As promoter, he is personally liable on any contract he signs before the corporation is formed.** If Zuckerberg signs the lease before TheFacebook, Inc. legally exists, he is personally liable for the rent due. After formation, the corporation can **adopt** the contract, in which case, both it and the promoter are liable. Adoption means either that the board of directors approves the contract or the corporation accepts the benefits under the contract. The promoter can get off the hook personally only if the landlord agrees to a **novation**—that is, a new contract with the corporation alone.

Promoter
Someone who organizes a corporation.

Novation
A new contract.

EXAM Strategy

Question: Warfield hired Wolfe, a young carpenter, to build his house. A week or so after they signed the contract, Wolfe filed Articles of Incorporation for Wolfe Construction, Inc. Warfield made payments to the corporation. Unfortunately, the work on the house was shoddy—the architect said he did not know whether to blow up the house or try to salvage what was there. Warfield sued Wolfe and Wolfe Construction, Inc. for damages. Wolfe argued that if he was liable as a promoter, then the corporation must be absolved and that, conversely, if the corporation was held liable he, as an individual, must not be. Who is liable to Warfield? Does it matter if Wolfe signed the contract in his own name or in the name of the corporation?

Strategy: Wolfe's argument is wrong—Warfield does not have to choose between suing him individually or suing the corporation. He can sue both.

Result: Wolfe is personally liable on any contract signed before the corporation is filed, no matter whose name is on the contract. The corporation is liable only if it adopts the contract. Did it do so here? The fact that the corporation cashed checks that were made out to it means that the corporation is also liable. So Warfield can sue both Wolfe and the corporation.

INCORPORATION PROCESS

The mechanics of incorporation are easy: simply download the form and mail or fax it to the Secretary of State for your state. But do not let this easy process fool you; the incorporation document needs to be completed with some care. The corporate charter defines the corporation, including everything from the company's name to the number of shares it will issue. States use different terms to refer to a charter; some call it the *articles of incorporation*, others use *articles of organization*, and still others say *certificate* instead of *articles*. All these terms mean the same thing. Similarly, some states use the term *shareholders*, and others use *stockholders;* they are both the same.

There is no federal corporation code, which means that a company can incorporate only under state, not federal, law. No matter where a company actually does business, it may incorporate in any state. This decision is important because the organization must live by the laws of whichever state it chooses for incorporation. To encourage similarity among state corporation statutes, the American Bar Association drafted the Model Business Corporation Act (the Model Act) as a guide. Many states do use the Model Act as a guide, although Delaware does not. Therefore, in this chapter we will give examples from both the Model Act and specific states, such as Delaware. Why Delaware? Despite its small size, it has a disproportionate influence on corporate law. More than half of all public companies have incorporated there, including 60 percent of Fortune 500 companies.

Where to Incorporate?

A company is called a **domestic corporation** in the state where it incorporates and a **foreign corporation** everywhere else. Companies generally incorporate either in the state where they do most of their business or in Delaware. They typically must pay filing fees and franchise taxes in their state of incorporation, as well as in any state in which they do business. To avoid this double set of fees, a business that will be operating primarily in one state would probably select that state for incorporation rather than Delaware. But if a company is going to do business in several states, it might consider choosing Delaware.

Delaware offers corporations several advantages:

- *Laws that favor management.* For example, if the shareholders want to take a vote in writing instead of holding a meeting, many other states require the vote to be unanimous; Delaware requires only a majority to agree.

- *An efficient court system.* Delaware has a special court (called "Chancery Court") that hears nothing but business cases and has judges who are experts in corporate law.

- *An established body of precedent.* Because so many businesses incorporate in this state, its courts hear a vast number of corporate cases, creating a large body of precedent. This precedent makes the outcome of litigation more predictable.

The Charter

NAME

The Model Act imposes two requirements in selecting a name. First, all corporations must use one of the following words in their name: *corporation, incorporated, company,* or *limited.* Delaware also accepts some additional terms, such as *association* or *institute.* Second, under both the Model Act and Delaware law, a new corporate name must be different from that of any corporation, limited liability company, or limited partnership that already exists in that state. If your name is Freddy Dupont, you cannot name your corporation "Freddy Dupont, Inc.," because Delaware already has a company named E. I. DuPont de Nemours & Co. It does not matter that Freddy Dupont is your real name or that the existing company is a large chemical business, whereas you want to open a frozen yogurt shop. The names are too similar. Zuckerberg chose "TheFacebook" because that was what Harvard students called their freshman directory.

ADDRESS AND REGISTERED AGENT

A company must have an official address in the state in which it is incorporated so that the Secretary of State knows where to contact it and so that anyone who wants to sue the corporation can serve the complaint in-state. Because most companies incorporated in Delaware do not actually have an office there, they hire a registered agent to serve as their official presence in the state.

INCORPORATOR

The incorporator signs the charter and delivers it to the Secretary of State for filing. Mark Zuckerberg was the incorporator for TheFacebook, but lawyers often serve this role.

PURPOSE

The corporation is required to give its purpose for existence. Most companies use a very broad purpose clause, such as TheFacebook's:

> The purpose of the Corporation is to engage in any lawful act or activity for which corporations may be organized under the General Corporation Law of Delaware.

STOCK

The charter must provide three items of information about the company's stock.

Par Value.   Par value does not relate to market value; it is usually some nominal figure such as 1¢ or $1 per share, or it is even possible to have no par value for stock. TheFacebook stock has a par value of $0.0001 per share.

Number of Shares.   Before stock can be sold, it must first be authorized in the charter. The corporation can authorize as many shares as the incorporators choose, but the more shares, the higher the filing fee. The charter for TheFacebook authorizes 10 million shares. After incorporation, a company can add authorized shares by simply amending its charter and paying the additional fee. Stock that the company has sold but later bought back is **treasury stock**.

Treasury stock
Stock that a company has sold, but later bought back.

Classes of Stock.   Shareholders often make different contributions to a company. Some may be involved in management, whereas others may simply contribute financially. To reflect these varying contributions, a corporation can issue different classes of stock, such as preferred or common stock. Owners of **preferred stock** are in line before common shareholders to receive dividends and any liquidation payments after a company goes into bankruptcy.

Preferred stock
The owners of preferred stock have preference on dividends and also, typically, in liquidation.

AFTER INCORPORATION

Directors and Officers

Under the Model Act, a corporation is required to have at least one director, unless (1) all the shareholders sign an agreement that eliminates the board, or (2) the corporation has 50 or fewer shareholders. To elect directors, the shareholders may hold a meeting, or, in the more typical case for a small company, they elect directors by **written consent.** A typical written consent looks like this:

Classic American Novels, Inc.
Written Consent

The undersigned shareholders of Classic American Novels, Inc., a corporation organized and existing under the General Corporation Law of the State of Wherever, hereby agree that the following action shall be taken with full force and effect as if voted at a validly called and held meeting of the shareholders of the corporation:

Agreed: That the following people are elected to serve as directors for one year or until their successors have been duly elected and qualified:

Herman Melville
Louisa May Alcott
Mark Twain

Dated: _____   Signed: _____

Willa Cather

Dated: _____   Signed: _____

Nathaniel Hawthorne

Dated: _____   Signed: _____

Harriet Beecher Stowe

The directors then elect the officers of the corporation. They can use a consent form if they wish. The Model Act requires a corporation to have whatever officers are described in the bylaws. The same person can hold more than one office.

The written consents and any records of actual meetings are kept in a **minute book**, which is the official record of the corporation. Entrepreneurs sometimes feel they are too busy to bother with all these details, but if a corporation is ever sold, the lawyers for the buyers will *insist* on a well-organized and complete minute book.

Minute book

A book that contains a record of a firm's official meetings.

Bylaws

The **bylaws** list all the "housekeeping" details for the corporation. For example, bylaws set the date of the annual shareholders' meeting, define what a **quorum** is (i.e., what percentage of stock must be represented for a meeting to count), give titles to officers, set the number of directors, and establish the fiscal (i.e., tax) year of the corporation.

Bylaws

A document that specifies the organizational rules of a corporation such as the date of the annual meeting and the required number of directors.

Quorum

The percentage of stock that must be represented for a meeting to count.

DEATH OF THE CORPORATION

Sometimes business ideas are not successful, and the corporation fails. This death can be voluntary (the shareholders elect to terminate the corporation) or forced (by court order). Sometimes a court takes a step that is much more damaging to shareholders than simply dissolving the corporation—it removes the shareholders' limited liability.

Piercing the Corporate Veil

One of the major purposes of a corporation is to protect its owners—the shareholders—from personal liability for the debts of the organization. Sometimes, however, a court will **pierce the corporate veil**; that is, the court will hold shareholders personally liable for the debts of the corporation. Courts generally pierce a corporate veil in four circumstances:

Pierce the corporate veil

A court holds shareholders personally liable for the debts of the corporation.

- *Failure to observe formalities.* If an organization does not act like a corporation, it will not be treated like one. It must, for example, hold required shareholders' and directors' meetings (or sign consents), keep a minute book as a record of these meetings, and make all the required state filings. In addition, officers must be careful to sign all corporate documents with a corporate title, not as an individual. An officer should sign like this:

Classic American Novels, Inc.

By: *Stephen Crane*

Stephen Crane, President

- *Commingling of assets.* Nothing makes a court more willing to pierce a corporate veil than evidence that shareholders have mixed their assets with those of the corporation. Sometimes, for example, shareholders may use corporate assets to pay their personal debts. If shareholders commingle assets, it is genuinely difficult for creditors to determine which assets belong to whom. This confusion is generally resolved in favor of the creditors—all assets are deemed to belong to the corporation.

- *Inadequate capitalization.* If the founders of a corporation do not raise enough capital to give the business a fighting chance of paying its debts, courts may require shareholders to pay corporate obligations. For example, Oriental Fireworks Co. had hundreds of thousands of dollars in annual sales, but only $13,000 in assets. The company did not bother to obtain any liability insurance, keep a minute book, or defend lawsuits. There was no need because the company had so few assets. But then a court pierced the corporate veil and found the owner of the company personally liable.[1]

- *Fraud.* If fraud is committed in the name of a corporation, victims can make a claim against the personal assets of the shareholders who profited from the fraud.

Termination

Terminating a corporation is a three-step process:

- *Vote.* The directors recommend to the shareholders that the corporation be dissolved, and a majority of the shareholders agree.

- *Filing.* The corporation files "Articles of Dissolution" with the Secretary of State.

- *Winding up.* The officers of the corporation pay its debts and distribute the remaining property to shareholders. When the winding up is completed, the corporation ceases to exist.

The Secretary of State may dissolve a corporation that violates state law by, for example, failing to pay the required annual fees. Indeed, many corporations, particularly small ones, do not bother with the formal dissolution process. They simply cease paying their required annual fees and let the Secretary of State act. In addition, a court may dissolve a corporation if it is insolvent or if its directors and shareholders cannot resolve conflict over how the corporation should be managed.

THE ROLE OF CORPORATE MANAGEMENT

Before the Industrial Revolution in the 18th and 19th centuries, a business owner typically supplied both capital and management. However, the cash needs of the great manufacturing enterprises spawned by the Industrial Revolution were larger than any small group of individuals could supply. To find capital, firms sought outside investors, who often had neither the knowledge nor the desire to manage the enterprise. Investors without management skills complemented managers without capital. (The term *manager* includes both directors and officers.)

---

[1] *Rice v. Oriental Fireworks Co.*, 75 Or. App. 627, 707 P.2d 1250, 1985 Ore. App. LEXIS 3928.

Modern businesses still have the same vast need for capital and the same division between managers and investors. As businesses grow, shareholders are too numerous and too uninformed to manage the enterprises they own. Therefore, they elect directors to manage for them. The directors set policy and then appoint officers to implement corporate goals.

Managers have a fiduciary duty to act in the best interests of the corporation's shareholders. Because shareholders are primarily concerned about their return on investment, managers must *maximize shareholder value,* which means providing shareholders with the highest possible financial return from dividends and stock price. However, reality is more complicated than this simple rule indicates. It is often difficult to determine which strategy will best maximize shareholder value. And what about other **stakeholders,** such as employees, customers, creditors, suppliers, and neighbors? A number of states have adopted statutes that permit directors to take into account the interests of stakeholders as well as stockholders.

THE BUSINESS JUDGMENT RULE

Officers and directors have a fiduciary duty to act in the best interests of their stockholders, but under the **business judgment rule,** the courts allow managers great leeway in carrying out this responsibility. The business judgment rule is two shields in one: it protects both the manager and her decision. If a manager has complied with the rule, a court will not hold her personally liable for any harm her decision has caused the company, nor will the court rescind her decision. If the manager violates the business judgment rule, then she has the burden of proving that her decision was entirely fair to the shareholders. If it was not fair, she may be held personally liable, and the decision may be rescinded.

To be protected by the business judgment rule, managers must act in good faith:

Duty of Loyalty	1. Without a conflict of interest
Duty of Care	2. With the care that an ordinarily prudent person would take in a similar situation, and
	3. In a manner they reasonably believe to be in the best interests of the corporation.

Analysis of the business judgment rule is divided into two parts. The obligation of a manager to act without a conflict of interest is called the **duty of loyalty**. The requirements that a manager act with care and in the best interests of the corporation are referred to as the **duty of care**.

Duty of Loyalty

The duty of loyalty prohibits managers from making a decision that benefits them at the expense of the corporation.

SELF-DEALING

Self-dealing **means that a manager makes a decision benefiting either himself or another company with which he has a relationship.** While working at the Blue Moon restaurant, Zeke signs a contract on behalf of the restaurant to purchase bread from Rising Sun Bakery. Unbeknownst to anyone at Blue Moon, he is a part owner of Rising Sun. Zeke has engaged in self-dealing, which is a violation of the duty of loyalty.

Duty of loyalty
The obligation of a manager to act without a conflict of interest.

Duty of care
The requirement that a manager act with care and in the best interests of the corporation.

Once a manager engages in self-dealing, the business judgment rule no longer applies. This does not mean the manager is automatically liable to the corporation or that his decision is automatically void. All it means is that the court will no longer presume that the transaction was acceptable. Instead, the court will scrutinize the deal more carefully. A self-dealing transaction is valid in any one of the following situations:

- **The disinterested members of the board of directors approve the transaction.** Disinterested directors are those who do not themselves benefit from the transaction.

- **The disinterested shareholders approve it.** The transaction is valid if the shareholders who do not benefit from it are willing to approve it.

- **The transaction was entirely fair to the corporation.** In determining fairness, the courts will consider the impact of the transaction on the corporation and whether the price was reasonable.

> Corporate officers sometimes forget that they do not have the right to do whatever they want.

Exhibit 22.1 illustrates the rules on self-dealing.

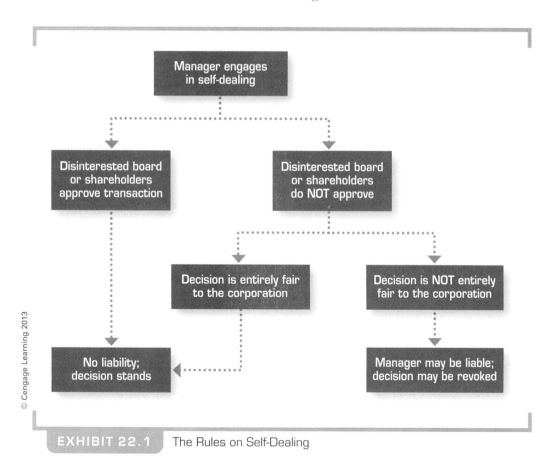

© Cengage Learning 2013

EXHIBIT 22.1   The Rules on Self-Dealing

Corporate officers, especially in family businesses, sometimes forget that they do not have the right to do whatever they want. The following case illustrates the business judgment rule, as well as the enduring principle that litigation is a very sad method for resolving family disputes.

LIPPMAN V. SHAFFER

15 Misc. 3d 705; 836 N.Y.S.2d 766; 2006 N.Y. Misc. LEXIS 4212
Supreme Court of New York, 2006

CASE SUMMARY

Facts: Years ago, Harry Lippman purchased Despatch Industries, Inc., which manufactured hardware for cabinets. His son, James, worked for the company. Later, James's son, Wade, and son-in-law, Alan Shaffer, also went on the company payroll. Both young men signed identical employment contracts. After Wade and James had a falling out, Wade resigned from the company. The Despatch board agreed to pay $1.3 million to both Wade and Alan. Company tax returns referred to these as "severance" payments, although Alan continued to work for the company and receive a salary.

Wade filed suit against Alan and Despatch, alleging that the payments to Alan were improper and should be returned. The defendants argued that the payments were protected by the business judgment rule. Wade filed a motion for summary judgment.

Issue: *Were the payments to Alan protected by the business judgment rule?*

Decision: No, these payments were not protected and Wade's motion was granted.

Reasoning: The purpose of the business judgment rule is to prevent courts from second-guessing corporate decision making. But that does not mean managers can do whatever they want. The business judgment rule does not apply if (1) the directors were self-dealing and (2) the decision was not entirely fair to the corporation. Here, Alan engaged in self-dealing: not only was he on the board that approved the payment to himself, he signed the check. The decision was not fair because Alan had no right to receive the money—it was a "severance" payment, but he still worked for the company. The payment to Wade, on the other hand, was fair because he had left the company. Alan received something he was not entitled to, while Wade simply got what he was owed under his contract.

CORPORATE OPPORTUNITY

Managers are in violation of the corporate opportunity doctrine if they compete against the corporation without its consent. Long ago, Charles Guth was president of Loft, Inc., which operated a chain of candy stores. These stores sold Coca-Cola. Guth purchased the Pepsi-Cola Company personally, without offering the opportunity to Loft. The Delaware court found that Guth had violated the corporate opportunity doctrine and ordered him to transfer all his shares in PepsiCo to Loft.[2] That was in 1939, and Pepsi-Cola was bankrupt; today, PepsiCo, Inc. is worth more than $100 billion.

Duty of Care

In addition to the *duty of loyalty*, managers also owe a *duty of care*. **The duty of care requires officers and directors to act in the best interests of the corporation and to use the same care that an ordinarily prudent person would in a similar situation.** To meet this duty of care:

- The decision must be legal;

- It must have a rational business purpose; and

- The manager must have made an informed decision.

Even if she violates the duty of care, a manager is not liable under the business judgment rule as long as the decision is entirely fair to the corporation.

---

[2]*Guth v. Loft*, 5 A2d 503, 1939 Del. Lexis 13 (Del. 1939).

EXAM Strategy

Question: You are the CEO of a software company. You will only allow your engineers to create software for Apple computers, not for PCs, because you think Apple is cooler. Some of your shareholders disagree with this policy. Is your decision protected by the business judgment rule?

Strategy: Remember that you owe a duty of care to the corporation. This means that you must have a rational business purpose for your decision.

Result: The courts are very generous in defining a rational business purpose. They would probably uphold your decision as long as it was not in some way personally benefiting you, e.g., as long as you are not a major shareholder of Apple.

THE ROLE OF SHAREHOLDERS

As we have seen, *directors*, not *shareholders*, have the right to manage the corporate business. What rights do shareholders have over the enterprises they own?

The topic of shareholder rights is a contentious, controversial topic. In this century, we have already experienced two financial meltdowns—one at the beginning of the 2000s and one at the end—that starkly revealed the different incentives faced by shareholders and managers. Too often, managers earned exorbitant compensation from highly risky short-term decisions that in the longer run left shareholders holding an empty bag. If CEOs made a risky decision that paid off, they profited enormously. If the decision failed, they might be fired, but even then, they were likely to have received generous compensation all along. On the way out the door, many also got severance payments that left them wealthy beyond most people's dreams. For example, in the two years before investment banks Bear Stearns Companies, Inc. and Lehman Brothers Holdings Inc failed, their top five executives took home $1.4 billion and $1 billion respectively, even as their shareholders were left with nothing.

Even worse, investigations after the fact revealed that compliant boards had been little more than rubber stamps, approving whatever the officers wanted. In anger and frustration, shareholders, Congress, the Securities and Exchange Commission (SEC) and stock exchanges undertook an unprecedented effort to rebalance corporate power. Yet these changes are little more than a shot in the dark, without compelling evidence that they will enhance financial stability or improve shareholder results. The rest of this chapter examines that balance of power.

Rights of Shareholders

Shareholders have neither the right nor the obligation to manage the day-to-day business of the enterprise. If you own stock in Starbucks Corp., your share of stock plus $6.25 entitles you to a triple grande soy vanilla latte, the same as everyone else. By the same token, if the pipes freeze and the local Starbucks store floods, the manager has no right to call you, as a shareholder, to help clean up the mess.

Right to Information

Under the Model Act, shareholders acting in good faith and with a proper purpose have the right to inspect and copy the corporation's minute book, accounting records, and shareholder lists. A proper purpose is one that aids the shareholder in managing and protecting her investment. If, for example, Celeste is convinced that the directors of Devil Desserts, Inc., are mismanaging the company, she might demand a list of other shareholders so that she can ask them to join her in a lawsuit. This purpose is proper—although the company may not like it—and the company is required to give her the list. If, however, Celeste wants to use the shareholder list as a potential source for her new online business featuring exercise equipment, the company could legitimately turn her down.

Right to Vote

A corporation must have at least one class of stock with voting rights.

SHAREHOLDER MEETINGS

Annual shareholder meetings are the norm for publicly traded companies. Although technically not all states require public companies to hold an annual meeting of shareholders, the New York Stock Exchange (NYSE) does. Companies whose stock is not publicly traded can either hold an annual meeting or use written consents from their shareholders.

PROXIES

Shareholders who do not wish to attend a shareholders' meeting may appoint someone else to vote for them. Confusingly, both this person and the card the shareholder signs to appoint the substitute voter are called a **proxy.** Companies are not required to solicit proxies. However, a meeting is invalid without a certain percentage of shareholders in attendance, either in person or by proxy. As a practical matter, if a public company with thousands of investors does not solicit proxies, it will not obtain a quorum and the meeting will be invalid. Therefore, virtually all public companies do solicit proxies. Along with the proxy, the company must also give shareholders a **proxy statement** and an **annual report.** The proxy statement provides information on everything from management compensation to a list of directors who miss too many meetings. The annual report contains detailed financial data.

ELECTION AND REMOVAL OF DIRECTORS

The process of electing directors to the board of a publicly traded company is different from what most people think. Shareholders do *not* have the automatic right to use the company's proxy statement to propose nominees for director. Instead, the nominating committee of the board of directors produces a slate of directors, with one name per opening. Typically, the names are approved by the CEO. This slate is then placed in the proxy statement and sent to shareholders whose only choice is to vote in favor of a nominee or to withhold their vote (i.e., not vote at all). If shareholders want to vote for someone who was not selected by the company, they have to nominate their own slate, prepare and distribute a proxy statement to other shareholders, and then communicate why their slate is superior, all the while fighting against the company's almost unlimited financial resources. Not surprisingly, only a few shareholder groups undertake this effort each year.

This traditional corporate voting method is called **plurality voting**. A successful candidate does not need to receive a majority vote; he must simply receive more than any competitor. Since there are no competitors, one vote is sufficient (and that vote could be his own).

Congress, other regulators, and major shareholders are now reforming corporate democracy in an effort to rebalance the relationship between managers and shareholders.

Independent Directors. Independent directors are those who are *not employees of the company* and, therefore, presumably not in the pocket of the CEO. Congress passed the Sarbanes-Oxley Act (SOX), which requires that all members of a board's audit committee must be independent. Likewise, the NYSE and NASDAQ require that, for their listed companies, independent directors must comprise a majority of the board, and only independent directors can serve on audit, compensation, or nominating committees.

Plurality voting

To be elected, a candidate only needs to receive more votes than her opponent, not a majority of the votes cast.

Shareholder Activists.   Proxy advisors, such as Institutional Shareholder Services, Inc. (ISS) are a new development in corporate democracy. They advise institutional investors (pension plans, mutual funds, insurance companies, banks, foundations, and university endowments) on how to vote their shares. ISS alone can affect up to 20 to 40 percent of the vote at a company. Corporate managers argue that it is too much power—that activists may well have an agenda that is contrary to that of other shareholders. In any event, boards have become more responsive to the demands of shareholder activists and, as a result, are more likely to replace executives who perform badly.

Majority Voting Systems.   Because of pressure from shareholder activists, two-thirds of the S&P 500 (large companies) now refuse to seat a director if fewer than half of the shares that vote tick off her name on the ballot.

Proxy Access.   By a 3-2 vote of the Commissioners, the SEC approved a proxy access rule that required companies to include on the ballot that is provided with the proxy material the names of board nominees selected by large shareholders (that is, those who have owned 3 percent of the company for three years). But when business groups sued the SEC to prevent implementation, a federal appeals court invalidated the proxy access rule on the grounds that the SEC had not followed required procedures in adopting it. The SEC elected not to appeal this decision. However, proxy access survives in a weakened form because the SEC amended Rule 14a-8 so that shareholders can now make proposals which would amend company bylaws to permit proxy access.[3] This two-step process is more complicated, and less likely to succeed, than the one-step version the SEC originally proposed.

The effectiveness of any of these developments is uncertain. At this stage, none of them has changed the reality that for most companies, shareholders have little say on board nominations.

COMPENSATION FOR OFFICERS AND DIRECTORS—THE PROBLEM

Given that directors have little fear of being voted off the board by shareholders, it is not surprising that when the board sets the CEO's compensation, the results can sometimes appear to unfairly favor the CEO over the shareholders whose money is being used to pay her. Between 2001 and 2003, public companies spent 9.8 percent of their net income on compensation for top executives. In 1975, the top 100 CEOs earned 39 times as much as the average worker. By 2005, that ratio was over 400. See Exhibit 22.2 for an illustration of this trend.

The ratio in Japan is 11 to 1; in Britain, it is 22 to 1. Or, to look at it another way, the average salary of the CEO of a Fortune 500 company in 1960 was twice that of the president of the United States. In 2006, the ratio was 30 to 1. Here are some examples of executive compensation that particularly agitated shareholders:

- Michael Eisner was the head of Walt Disney Corporation for 20 years. At the beginning of his tenure, the company did very well, and few complained when he was exceedingly well paid. But for the final 13 years, he earned $800 million while the stock performed worse than government bonds (a low-risk, low-return investment).

- The CEO of Fannie Mae earned $90 million during a time when the company's accounting system was so flawed that it overstated its earnings by $11 billion.

- Executives whose companies survived the 2008 financial crisis only because of taxpayer bailouts still received enormous bonuses. For example, taxpayers spent $180 billion to save American International Group, Inc. even as the company awarded bonuses of $165 million to its executives.

Why did executive pay become so lavish?

---

[3]*Business Roundtable v. SEC*, 2011 U.S. App. LEXIS 14988 (D.C. Cir, 2011).

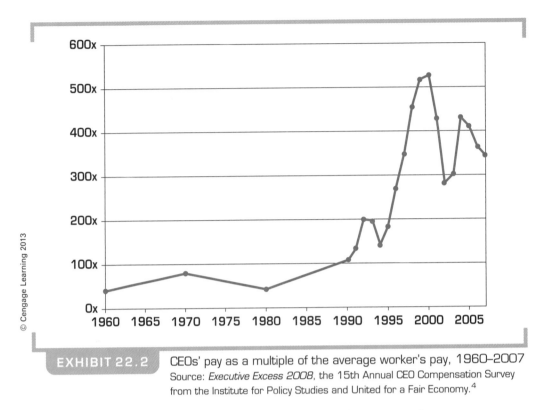

© Cengage Learning 2013

EXHIBIT 22.2   CEOs' pay as a multiple of the average worker's pay, 1960–2007
Source: *Executive Excess 2008*, the 15th Annual CEO Compensation Survey
from the Institute for Policy Studies and United for a Fair Economy.[4]

Directors, Not Shareholders, Set Executive Compensation.   Directors set
the CEO's compensation, but shareholders are the ones who pay the money. People tend to
spend someone else's money more generously than their own. Also, directors and the CEO
are often friends. Imagine if you got to decide how much your friend could spend dining
out, knowing that someone else, whom you had never met, would have to pay the bill. It
would be easy to be generous.

Benchmarking Games.   Compensation is rarely linked closely to individual performance,
but instead to overall industry or stock market performance, which is defined in a way to favor
executives. Two-thirds of the largest 1,000 U.S. companies report that they performed better
than their peers.[5]

The CEO Gets All the Credit.   Compensation committees sometimes act as if the CEO
and (maybe a few other top executives) are solely responsible for a company's success. Although
there is much talk about "pay for performance," the reality is that luck can be as important a
determinant of executive compensation as good performance.[6] After James Kilts became CEO of
Gillette Co., the stock price went up 61 percent. He had added $20 billion in shareholder value,
and therefore, to many it seemed only fair when he was rewarded with a $153 million payout. But
was it? About half the increase in Gillette revenues during the time that Kilts was running the
show were attributable to currency fluctuations. A cheaper dollar increased revenue overseas. If
the dollar had moved in the opposite direction, there might not have been any increase in revenue.

---

[4]Prepared by Professor G. William Miller, University of California at Santa Cruz, *http://sociology.ucsc.edu/
whorulesamerica/power/wealth.html.*
[5]Kevin J. Murphy, "Politics, Economics and Executive Compensation," reported in Lucian Bebchuk
and Jesse Fried, *Pay Without Performance*, Harvard University Press, 2004, p. 71.
[6]See, for example, Marianne Bertrand and Sendhil Mullainathan, "Are CEOs Rewarded for Luck?
The Ones Without Principals Are," *The Quarterly Journal of Economics*, August 2001.

Most Executives Are Above Average.   Of course, not everyone can be above average, but most directors believe that their executives are. No one wants to admit to hiring incompetents. Each time one company raises its pay so that its executive will be above average, the industrywide average rises and other companies feel they must respond by increasing their pay, too.

Compensation Consultants Often Have Conflicts of Interest.   Many companies hire compensation consultants to offer advice on executive pay. These same consultants may also provide other services to the company—such as human resource management—for which the fees can be substantial. The consultants have every incentive to suggest generous packages. In any event, it is not their money.

COMPENSATION FOR OFFICERS AND DIRECTORS—A SOLUTION?

The federal government has begun to respond to these perceived abuses.

Proxy Rules.   Proxy statements must now include a summary table setting out the full amount of compensation for the five highest-earning executives.

SOX.   Under SOX, if a company has to restate its earnings, its CEO and CFO must reimburse the company for any bonus or profits they received from selling company stock within a year of the release of the flawed financials. This is a so-called clawback provision. (See bizlawupdate.com for an article about how this clawback provision is working.)

Dodd-Frank.   The Dodd-Frank Wall Street Reform and Consumer Protection Act requires so-called say-on-pay. At least once every three years, companies must take a *non-binding* shareholder vote on executive compensation. In addition, companies must disclose the CEO's compensation and the median compensation of all other company employees plus the ratio of these two numbers.

Even with these new protections in place, shareholder influence over executive compensation is far from guaranteed. Note that the shareholder resolutions are non-binding. And, as the following case demonstrates, for shareholders to successfully challenge executive compensation in the courts, they must prove that the board violated the business judgment rule.

BREHM V. EISNER

2006 Del. LEXIS 307
Supreme Court of Delaware, 2006

CASE SUMMARY

Facts: Michael Ovitz founded Creative Artists Agency (CAA), the premier talent agency in Hollywood. As a partner at this agency, he earned between $20 and $25 million per year. He was also a longtime friend of Michael Eisner, who recommended that Disney hire him as president. Upon the advice of Graef Crystal, a compensation consultant, the board approved Ovitz's contract.

After 14 months, all parties agreed that the experiment had failed, so Ovitz left Disney—but not empty-handed. Under his contract, he was entitled to $130 million in severance pay.

Shareholders of Disney sued the board, alleging that it had violated the business judgment rule by failing to exercise due care.

Issues: *Did Disney directors violate the business judgment rule?*

Decision: No, the board did not violate the business judgment rule.

Reasoning: The board's choice of Graef Crystal as a compensation advisor was reasonable. He is well known and highly regarded in this field. Once the board had hired him, it was reasonable to rely on his advice. It is true that the behavior of the board did not meet a "best practices" standard—it could have done a more thorough job of understanding the contract. But the business judgment rule does not require best practices. Its purpose is to protect directors who act in good faith and the board did meet that standard. Moreover, the contract had a rational business purpose: to induce Ovitz to leave CAA and join Disney. For these two reasons, the board did not breach its duty of care.

FUNDAMENTAL CORPORATE CHANGES

A corporation must seek shareholder approval before undergoing any of the following fundamental changes: a merger, a sale of major assets, dissolution of the corporation, or an amendment to the charter or bylaws.

Chapter Conclusion

How can shareholders ensure that the corporation will operate in their best interest? How can managers make tough decisions without being second-guessed by shareholders? Balancing the interests of managers and shareholders is a complex problem the law struggles to resolve.

EXAM REVIEW

1. **PROMOTERS** Promoters are personally liable for contracts they sign before the corporation is formed unless the corporation and the third party agree to a novation. (p. 393)

2. **STATE OF INCORPORATION** Companies generally incorporate in the state in which they will be doing business. However, if they intend to operate in several states, they may choose to incorporate in a jurisdiction known for its favorable corporate laws, such as Delaware. (p. 394)

3. **CHARTER** A corporate charter must generally include the company's name, address, registered agent, purpose, and a description of its stock. (pp. 394–395)

4. **PIERCING THE CORPORATE VEIL** A court may, under certain circumstances, pierce the corporate veil and hold shareholders personally liable for the debts of the corporation. (pp. 396–397)

5. **TERMINATION** Termination of a corporation is a three-step process requiring a shareholder vote, the filing of Articles of Dissolution, and the winding up of the enterprise's business. (p. 397)

6. **FIDUCIARY DUTY** Officers and directors have a fiduciary duty to act in the best interests of the shareholders of the corporation. (p. 398)

7. **BUSINESS JUDGMENT RULE** If managers comply with the business judgment rule, a court will not hold them personally liable for any harm their decisions cause the company, nor will the court rescind the decision. (pp. 398–401)

EXAM Strategy

Question: Employees of Exxon Corp. paid some $59 million in corporate funds as bribes to Italian political parties to secure special favors and other illegal commitments. The board of directors decided not to sue the employees who had committed the illegal acts. Were these decisions protected by the business judgment rule?

Strategy: Two decisions are at issue here: illegal payments and the decision not to sue. (See the "Result" at the end of this section.)

8. **DUTY OF LOYALTY: SELF-DEALING** Under the duty of loyalty, managers may not enter into an agreement on behalf of their corporation that benefits them personally unless the disinterested directors or shareholders have first approved it. If the manager does not seek the necessary approval, the business judgment rule no longer applies, and the manager will be liable unless the transaction was entirely fair to the corporation. (pp. 398–399)

9. **DUTY OF LOYALTY: CORPORATE OPPORTUNITY** Managers are in violation of the corporate opportunity doctrine if they compete against the corporation without its consent. (p. 400)

EXAM Strategy

Question: Vern owned 32 percent of Coast Oyster Co. and served as president and director. Coast was struggling to pay its debts, so Vern suggested that the company sell some of its oyster beds to Keypoint Co. After the sale, officers at Coast discovered that Vern owned 50 percent of Keypoint. They demanded that he give the Keypoint stock to Coast. Did Vern violate his duty to Coast?

Strategy: Vern has violated the duty of loyalty not once, but twice. (See the "Result" at the end of this section.)

10. **DUTY OF CARE** Under the duty of care, managers must make decisions that are legal, informed and have a rational business purpose. (p. 400)

11. **DIRECTORS** Directors, not shareholders, have the right to manage the corporate business. (p. 401)

12. **PROXY** Virtually all publicly held companies solicit proxies from their shareholders. A proxy authorizes someone else to vote in place of the shareholder. (p. 402)

13. **SHAREHOLDER RIGHTS** Shareholders have the right to:

- Receive annual financial statements (if their company is publicly traded),

- Inspect and copy the corporation's records (for a proper purpose),

- Elect and remove directors, and

- Approve fundamental corporate changes, such as a merger or a major sale of assets. (pp. 401–403)

14. EXECUTIVE COMPENSATION

- Under SOX, If a company has to restate its earnings, its CEO and CFO must reimburse the company for any bonus or profits they received from selling company stock within a year of the release of the flawed financials.

- Dodd-Frank requires shareholder "say-on-pay." In addition, companies must disclose the CEO's compensation and the median compensation of all other company employees plus the ratio of these two numbers. (pp. 403–405)

7. Result: The business judgment rule would not protect the underlying illegal payments, but it did protect the decision not to sue. In other words, anyone who *made* an illegal payment had violated the business judgment rule, but the people who had decided not to pursue the violators had not themselves breached the business judgment rule because they had not violated the duty of care or the duty of loyalty.

9. Result: If the shareholders and directors did not know of Vern's interest in Keypoint, they could not properly evaluate the contract. By not telling them, he violated the rule against self-dealing. Also, by purchasing stock in Keypoint, Vern took a corporate opportunity. He had to turn over to Coast any profits he had earned on the transaction, as well as his stock in Keypoint.

MATCHING QUESTIONS

Match the following terms with their definitions:

___A. Duty of loyalty

___B. Duty of care

___C. Promoter

___D. Incorporator

___E. Registered agent

1. Requires managers to act in the best interests of the corporation

2. The company's representative in its state of incorporation

3. Someone who organizes a corporation

4. The person who prepares and files the charter

5. Prohibits managers from making a decision that benefits them at the expense of the corporation

TRUE/FALSE QUESTIONS

Circle true or false:

1. T F A corporation can be formed in any state or under the federal corporate code.
2. T F Shareholders and stockholders are the same thing.
3. T F Most companies use a very broad purpose clause in their charter.
4. T F Shareholders have the right to manage the corporate business.
5. T F A company must include in its proxy materials the names of all shareholder nominees for the board of directors.

MULTIPLE-CHOICE QUESTIONS

1. A promoter is liable for any contract he signs on behalf of a corporation before it is formed, unless:

(a) The corporation adopts the contract.

(b) The promoter notifies the other party that the corporation has not yet been formed.

(c) The promoter signs the contract on behalf of the corporation.

(d) The promoter forms the corporation within 72 hours of signing the contract.

(e) The other party agrees to a novation.

2. CPA QUESTION: A corporate stockholder is entitled to which of the following rights?

(a) Elect officers

(b) Receive annual dividends

(c) Approve dissolution

(d) Prevent corporate borrowing

3. CPA QUESTION: Generally, a corporation's articles of incorporation must include all of the following except:

(a) The name of the corporation's registered agent

(b) The name of each incorporator

(c) The number of authorized shares

(d) Quorum requirements

4. Generally, a corporation's bylaws include all of the following except:

(a) Par value of the stock

(b) The date of the shareholders meeting

(c) The number of directors

(d) The titles of officers

(e) The date of the fiscal year

5. Under the duty of care, directors will be liable if they:

(a) Make a decision that has a rational business purpose

(b) Use the same care as an ordinarily prudent person

(c) Make informed decisions

(d) Engage in illegal behavior that is profitable to the company

(e) Make an informed decision that ultimately harms the company

ESSAY QUESTIONS

1. Michael incorporated Erin Homes, Inc., to manufacture mobile homes. He issued himself a stock certificate for 100 shares, for which he made no payment. He and his wife served as officers and directors of the organization, but during the eight years of its existence, the corporation held only one meeting. Erin always had its own checking account, and all proceeds from the sales of mobile homes were deposited there. It filed federal income tax returns each year, using its own federal identification number. John and Thelma paid $17,500 to purchase a mobile home from Erin, but the company never delivered it to them. John and Thelma sued Erin Homes and Michael, individually. Should the court "pierce the corporate veil" and hold Michael personally liable?

2. Davis signed an employment contract with William. The contract stated: "… whatever company, partnership, or corporation that William may form for the purpose of manufacturing shall succeed William and exercise the rights and assume all of William's obligations as fixed by this contract." Two months later, William formed Auto-Soler Company. Davis entered into a new contract with Auto-Soler providing that the company was liable for William's obligations under the old contract. Neither William nor the company ever paid Davis the sums owed him under the contracts. Davis sued William personally. Does William have any obligations to Davis?

3. **ETHICS:** Edgar Bronfman, Jr., dropped out of high school to go to Hollywood and write songs and produce movies. Eventually, he left Hollywood to work in the family business—the Bronfmans owned 36 percent of Seagram Co., a liquor and beverage conglomerate. Promoted to president of the company at the age of 32, Bronfman seized a second chance to live his dream. Seagram received 70 percent of its earnings from its 24 percent ownership of DuPont Co. Bronfman sold this stock at less than market value to purchase (at an inflated price) 80 percent of MCA, a movie and music company that had been a financial disaster for its prior owners. Some observers thought Bronfman had gone Hollywood, others that he had gone crazy. After the deal was announced, the price of Seagram shares fell 18 percent. Was there anything Seagram shareholders could have done to prevent what to them was not a dream but a nightmare? Apart from legal issues, was Bronfman's decision ethical? What ethical obligations did he owe Seagram's shareholders?

4. Angelica is planning to start a home security business in McGehee, Arkansas. She plans to start modestly but hopes to expand her business within 5 years to neighboring towns and, perhaps, within 10 years, to neighboring states. Her inclination is to incorporate her business in Delaware. Is her inclination correct?

5. Ulrick and Birger started an air taxi service in Berlin, Germany, under the name Berlinair, Inc. Birger was approached by a group of travel agents who were interested in hiring an air charter business to take German tourists on vacation. Birger formed Air Berlin Charter Co. (ABC) and was its sole owner. On behalf of ABC, he entered into a contract with the Berlin travel agents. Birger concealed his negotiations from Ulrick, even though he used Berlinair working time, staff, money, and facilities. Birger defended his behavior on the grounds that Berlinair could not afford to enter into a contract with the travel agents. Has Birger violated the corporate opportunity doctrine?

DISCUSSION QUESTIONS

1. States compete for lucrative filing fees by passing corporate statutes that favor management. One proposed solution to this problem would be a federal system of corporate registration. Is this a good idea? What are the impediments to such a system?

2. Congressional Airlines was highly profitable operating flights between Washington D.C. and New York City. The directors approved a plan to offer flights from Washington to Boston. This decision turned out to be a major mistake and the airline ultimately went bankrupt. Under what circumstances would shareholders be successful in bringing suit against the directors?

3. An appraiser valued a subsidiary of Signal Co. at between $230 million and $260 million. Six months later, Burmah Oil offered to buy the subsidiary at $480 million, giving Signal only three days to respond. The board of directors accepted the offer without obtaining an updated valuation of the subsidiary or determining if other companies would offer a higher price. Members of the board were sophisticated, with a great deal of experience in the oil industry. A Signal Co. shareholder sued to prevent the sale. Is the Signal board protected by the business judgment rule?

4. For several years, CSK Auto, Inc., fraudulently reported inflated earnings. During this period, Maynard Jenkins was CEO. He was not involved in the fraud, however, and he was never charged with a crime. Nonetheless, using a SOX provision, the SEC sought to claw back some of his earnings during this period. Should Jenkins be financially responsible for fraud that occurred on his watch, even though he did not participate?

5. Would the following initiatives improve corporate governance? Can you think of others that would?

   - Proxy access: As originally proposed by the SEC

   - Majority vote: Prohibit boards of directors from seating directors who fail to receive a majority vote of shares cast

   - Compensation: Base compensation on the company's growth in earnings compared with those of its competitors, not just increases in earnings (that might be caused by a general market rise)

CHAPTER 23

GOVERNMENT REGULATION: SECURITIES AND ANTITRUST

© Evan Meyer/Shutterstock.com

Sandy is a director of a public company. He tells his girlfriend, Carly, that the company is about to receive a takeover offer. Sandy does not buy any stock himself, but Carly does. When the offer is announced, the stock zooms up in price and Carly makes a tidy profit.

Steve and Joe coach college wrestling teams that are in the same conference, and have very tight budgets. Both men are also about to hire an assistant coach. One day at a meet, Steve suggests to Joe that they each agree to limit their new coach's salary to $52,000. That way, neither of them will break their budget and they might even have more money to give for athletic scholarships. Joe thinks this is a great plan and agrees on the spot.

> **Each of these people is about to find out, in a very unpleasant way, about government regulation.**

Each of these people is about to find out, in a very unpleasant way, about government regulation. Sandy and Carly have violated securities laws on insider trading. Steve and Joe have engaged in price fixing that is illegal under antitrust laws. The moral of the story? It is important to be familiar with the most crucial government regulations. Ignorance can not only harm your business but also lead to fines and even imprisonment.

SECURITIES LAWS

There are two major securities laws: the Securities Act of 1933 (the 1933 Act) and the Securities Exchange Act of 1934 (the 1934 Act).

What Is a Security?

Both the 1933 and the 1934 Acts regulate securities. **A security is any transaction in which the buyer (1) invests money in a common enterprise and (2) expects to earn a profit predominantly from the efforts of others.**

This definition covers investments that are not necessarily called *securities*. Besides the obvious stocks, bonds, or notes, the definition of security can even include items such as orange trees. W. J. Howey Co. owned large citrus groves in Florida. It sold these trees to investors, most of whom were from out of state and knew nothing about farming. Purchasers were expected to hire someone to take care of their trees. Someone like Howey-in-the-Hills, Inc., a related company that just happened to be in the service business. Customers were free to hire any service company, but 85 percent of the acreage was covered by service contracts with Howey-in-the-Hills. The court held that Howey was selling a security (no matter how orange or tart), because the purchaser was investing in a common enterprise (the orange grove) expecting to earn a profit from Howey's farmwork.

Other courts have interpreted the term *security* to include animal breeding arrangements (chinchillas, silver foxes, or beavers, take your pick); condominium purchases in which the developer promises the owner a certain level of income from rentals; and even investments in whiskey.

Security
Any transaction in which the buyer invests money in a common enterprise and expects to earn a profit predominantly from the efforts of others.

Securities Act of 1933

The 1933 Act requires that, before offering or selling securities in a *public* offering, the issuer must register the securities with the Securities and Exchange Commission (SEC). An issuer is the company that sells the stock initially.

It is important to remember that **when an issuer registers securities, the SEC does not investigate the quality of the offering.** Permission from the SEC to sell securities does not mean that the company has a good product or will be successful. SEC approval simply means that, on the surface, the company has provided all required information about itself and its major products. For example, the Green Bay Packers football team sold an offering of stock to finance stadium improvements. The prospectus admitted:

Issuer
A company that sells its own stock.

> IT IS VIRTUALLY IMPOSSIBLE that any investor will ever make a profit on the stock purchase. The company will pay no dividends, and the shares cannot be sold.

This does not sound like a stock you want in your retirement fund; on the other hand, the SEC will not prevent Green Bay from selling it, or you from buying it, so long as you understand what the risks are.

LIABILITY

Under the 1933 Act, the seller of a security is liable for making any material misstatement or omission, either oral or written, in connection with the offer or sale of a security. Anyone who issues fraudulent securities is in violation of the 1933 Act, whether or not the securities are registered. Both the SEC and any purchasers of the stock can sue the issuer. In addition, the Justice Department can bring criminal charges against anyone who willfully violates this statute.

Material
Important enough to affect an investor's decision.

Initial public offering (IPO)
A company's first public sale of securities.

PUBLIC OFFERINGS

A company's first public sale of securities is called an **initial public offering** or an **IPO.** Any subsequent public sale is called a **secondary offering**.

Secondary offering
Any public sale of securities by a company after the initial public offering.

Registration Statement.   To make a public offering, the company must file a registration statement with the SEC. The **registration statement** has two purposes: to notify the SEC that a sale of securities is pending and to disclose information of interest to prospective purchasers. The registration statement must include detailed information about the issuer and its business, a description of the stock, the proposed use of the proceeds from the offering, and two years of audited balance sheets and income statements. Preparing a registration statement is neither quick nor inexpensive—it can cost as much as $8 million for an IPO.

Prospectus.   Typically, buyers never see the registration statement; they are given the **prospectus** instead. (The prospectus is part of the registration statement that is sent to the SEC.) The prospectus includes all of the important disclosures about the company, while the registration statement includes additional information that is of interest to the SEC but not to the typical investor, such as the names and addresses of the lawyers for the issuer and underwriter. **All investors must receive a copy of the prospectus before purchasing stock.**

Sales Effort.   Even before the final registration statement and prospectus are completed, the investment bank representing the issuer begins its sales effort. It cannot actually make sales during this period, but it can solicit offers. The SEC closely regulates an issuer's sales effort to ensure that it does not hype the stock by making public statements about the company before the stock is sold. For example, the SEC delayed an offering of stock by Google, Inc., after *Playboy* magazine published an interview with its founders.

Going Effective.   Once the SEC finishes its review of the registration statement, it sends the issuer a **comment letter,** listing required changes. An issuer almost always has to amend the registration statement at least once, and sometimes more than once. Remember that the SEC does not assess the *value* of the stock or the *merit* of the investment. Its role is to ensure that the company has disclosed enough information to enable investors to make an informed decision. After the SEC has approved a final registration statement (which includes, of course, the final prospectus), the issuer and underwriter agree on a price for the stock and the date to **go effective,** that is, to begin the sale.

Registering securities with the SEC for a public offering is very time-consuming and expensive, but the 1933 Act also permits issuers to sell stock in a private offering, which is much simpler (and cheaper).

PRIVATE OFFERINGS

Under the 1933 Act, an issuer is not required to register securities that are sold in a *private* offering, that is, an offering with a relatively small number of investors or a limited amount of money involved. Tens of thousands of these offerings take place each year, compared with only about 130 IPOs. The most common and important type of private offering is under **Regulation D** (often referred to as "Reg D"). Rule 505 under Reg D permits a company to sell up to $5 million of stock during each 12-month period, subject to the following restrictions:

- The issuer can sell to an unlimited number of accredited investors, but to only 35 unaccredited investors. **Accredited investors** are institutions (such as banks and insurance companies) or wealthy individuals (with a net worth of more than $1 million, not counting their homes, or an annual income of more than $200,000).

- The company may not advertise the stock publicly.

- The company need not provide information to accredited investors but must make some disclosure to unaccredited investors.

Accredited investors

Are institutions (such as banks and insurance companies) or wealthy individuals (with a net worth of more than $1 million or an annual income of more than $200,000).

Securities Exchange Act of 1934

REGISTRATION

Most buyers do not purchase new securities from the issuer in an IPO. Rather, they buy stock that is publicly traded in the open market. This stock is, in a sense, secondhand because other people—perhaps many others—have already owned it. The purpose of the 1934 Act is to provide investors with ongoing information about public companies (that is, companies with publicly traded stock).

Under the 1934 Act, an issuer must register with the SEC if (1) it completes a public offering under the 1933 Act, or (2) its securities are traded on a national exchange (such as the New York Stock Exchange), or (3) it has at least 500 shareholders *and* total assets that exceed $10 million.

The 1934 Act requires public companies to file the following documents:

- **Annual reports** on Form 10-K, containing audited financial statements, a detailed analysis of the company's performance, and information about officers and directors. A public company must also deliver its annual report to shareholders.

- **Quarterly reports** on Form 10-Q, which are less detailed than 10-Ks and contain unaudited financials.

- **Form 8-K** to report any significant developments, such as a change in control, the resignation of a director over a policy dispute, or a change in auditing firms.

In response to corporate scandals, Congress passed the Sarbanes-Oxley Act of 2002. This statute requires each company's CEO and CFO to certify that:

- The information in the quarterly and annual reports is true,

- The company has effective internal controls, and

- The officers have informed the company's audit committee and its auditors of any concerns that they have about the internal control system.

LIABILITY

Section 10(b) (and Rule 10b-5) prohibit fraud in connection with the purchase and sale of any security, whether or not the security is registered under the 1934 Act. Under these rules, anyone who fails to disclose material information or makes incomplete or inaccurate disclosure is liable, so long as the statement or omission was made willfully, knowingly, or recklessly. Thus, an accounting firm that certified financials in a company's annual report, knowing that it had not in fact adequately audited the firm's books, would be liable under Section 10(b).

Short-Swing Trading—Section 16

Section 16 of the 1934 Act was designed to prevent corporate insiders—officers, directors, and shareholders who own more than 10 percent of the company—from taking unfair advantage of privileged information to manipulate the market.

Section 16 takes a two-pronged approach:

- First, insiders must **report** their trades within two business days.

- Second, insiders must **turn over to the corporation** any profits they make from the purchase and sale or sale and purchase of company securities in a six-month period. Section 16 is a strict liability provision. It applies even if the insider did not actually take advantage of secret information or try to manipulate the market; if she bought and sold or sold and bought stock in a six-month period, she is liable for any profits she earned.

Suppose that Manuela buys 20,000 shares of her company's stock in June at $10 a share. In September, her (uninsured) winter house in Florida is destroyed by a hurricane. To raise money for rebuilding, she sells the stock at $12 per share, making a profit of $40,000. But she has violated Section 16 and must turn over the profit to her company.

Insider Trading

Insider trading is immensely tempting. Anyone with reliable secret information can earn millions of dollars overnight. The downside? Insider trading is a crime punishable by fines and imprisonment. The guilty party may also be forced to turn over to the SEC three times the profit made. Ivan Boesky paid $100 million and spent two years in prison. Dennis Levine suffered an $11.6 million penalty and three years in prison.

The following Landmark Case established one of the most important rules on insider trading.

Landmark Case

CHIARELLA V. UNITED STATES

445 U.S. 222; 1980 U.S. LEXIS 88
Supreme Court of the United States, 1980

CASE SUMMARY

Facts: Chiarella was a printer at Pandick Press, a company that printed the documents used to announce corporate takeover bids. He secretly bought shares in some of the target companies, selling them at a profit once the takeover was publicly announced.

When the SEC found out what he had done, it brought civil charges against him. To settle those charges, he agreed to turn over his profits to the sellers of the shares. Then Pandick Press fired him, he was convicted of the crime of insider trading, sentenced to a year in prison, and the Court of Appeals affirmed his conviction. But the Supreme Court granted *certiorari*.

Issue: *Did Chiarella violate securities laws when he traded on secret information that he acquired in his job as a printer?*

Decision: Chiarella was not guilty.

Reasoning: The Court of Appeals ruled that anyone who trades on material, secret information has violated federal securities laws, but this holding is wrong. Insider trading is illegal only if the person with secret information has a *duty* to disclose to those with whom he trades. In this case, there was no such duty because the sellers had not placed their trust in Chiarella—he was neither their agent nor their fiduciary. He was, in fact, a complete stranger who dealt with the sellers only through impersonal market transactions.

The result would have been different if Chiarella had been an insider of the companies whose stock he bought because corporate insiders do have a relationship of trust with shareholders and must, therefore, place the shareholder's welfare before their own. But Chiarella was not a corporate insider, and he received no confidential information from the companies whose stock he traded. His secret information related to the plans of the acquiring company, not the operations or earnings of the target enterprise. His use of that information was not fraudulent because he did not have a duty to disclose it.

The judgment of the Court of Appeals is reversed.

These are the rules on insider trading:

- *Fiduciaries.* As we saw in the *Chiarella* case, **someone who trades on inside information is liable only if he breaches a fiduciary duty.** Anyone who works for a company is a fiduciary. If the director of research for MediSearch learns of the company's promising new treatment for AIDS and buys stock in MediSearch before the information is public, she is guilty of insider trading. But suppose that, while looking in a Dumpster, Harry finds correspondence indicating that MediSearch will shortly announce a major breakthrough in the treatment of AIDS. Harry buys the stock, which promptly quadruples in value. Harry will be dining at the Ritz, not in the Dumpster nor in federal prison, because he has no fiduciary duty to MediSearch.

- *Temporary insiders.* Even outsiders who work for a company temporarily, such as lawyers and accountants, are considered to be fiduciaries.

- *Possession* versus *use* of information. Suppose that an insider sells stock just after learning that her company is about to report lower earnings but before this information is public. When challenged by the SEC, she argues that she sold her stock for other reasons—say, to buy a new house, or set her son up in business. To deal with this issue, the SEC ruled **that an insider may trade while in possession of material, nonpublic information, if she has committed in advance to a plan to sell those securities.** Thus, if an insider knows that she will want to sell stock to pay college tuition, she can establish such a sales plan in advance. (And, then, despite any change in circumstances, she must sell according to the plan.) She will then not be liable for the sales, no matter what inside information she ultimately learns.

- *Tippers.* What about people who do not trade themselves but pass on information to someone who does? **Insiders who pass on important, secret information are liable, even if they do not trade themselves, so long as (1) they know the information is confidential; and (2) they expect some personal gain.** Personal gain is loosely defined. Essentially, any gift to a friend counts as personal gain. W. Paul Thayer was a corporate director, deputy secretary of defense, and former fighter pilot ace who gave stock tips to his girlfriend in lieu of paying her rent. That counted as personal gain, and he spent a year and a half in prison.

- *Tippees.* **Those who receive tips—tippees—are liable for trading on inside information,** even if they do not have a fiduciary relationship to the company, so long as (1) they know the information is confidential; (2) they know it came from an insider who was violating his fiduciary duty; and (3) the insider expected some personal gain. Barry Switzer, then head football coach at the University of Oklahoma, went to a track meet to see his son compete. While sunbathing on the bleachers, he overheard someone talking about a company that was going to be acquired. Switzer bought the stock, but was acquitted of insider trading charges because the insider had not breached his fiduciary duty. He had not tipped anyone on purpose—he had simply been careless. Also, Switzer did not know that the insider was breaching a fiduciary duty, and the insider expected no personal gain from releasing the information.[1]

- *Misappropriation.* A person is liable if he trades in securities (1) for personal profit; (2) using confidential information; and (3) in breach of a fiduciary duty to the *source of the information.* This rule applies even if that source was not the company whose stock was traded. For example, James O'Hagan was a lawyer in a firm that represented a company attempting to take over Pillsbury Co. Although O'Hagan did not work on the case, he heard about it and then bought stock in Pillsbury. After the takeover attempt was publicly announced, O'Hagan sold his stock in Pillsbury at a profit of more than $4.3 million.[2] The Supreme Court ruled that O'Hagan had violated insider trading laws. While it was true that he had no fiduciary duty to Pillsbury, he did owe one to his law firm, which was the source of the information. According to the court, what he had done was the same thing as embezzlement.[3]

---

[1]*SEC v. Switzer,* 590 F. Supp. 756, 1984 U.S. Dist. LEXIS 15303 (W.D. Okla. 1984).
[2]O'Hagan used the profits that he gained through this trading to conceal his previous embezzlement of client funds. There is a moral here.
[3]521 U.S. 642, 117 S. Ct. 2199, 1997 U.S. LEXIS 4033.

EXAM Strategy

Question: Paul was an investment banker who sometimes bragged about deals he was working on. One night, he told a bartender, Ryanne, about an upcoming deal. Ryanne bought stock in the company Paul had mentioned. Both were prosecuted for insider trading. Ryanne was acquitted but Paul was convicted, even though Ryanne was the one who made money. How is that possible?

Strategy: Note that there are different standards for tippers and tippees.

Result: Paul is liable if he knew the information was confidential and he expected some personal gain. A gift counts as personal gain. (The courts have an expansive definition of gifts—practically anything counts. Here, the information could be interpreted as a tip to the bartender.) Ryanne would not be liable unless she knew the information was confidential and had come from an insider who was violating his fiduciary duty.

Why is insider trading a crime? Who is harmed? Insider trading is illegal because:

- It offends our fundamental sense of fairness. No one wants to be in a poker game with marked cards.

- Investors will lose confidence in the market if they feel that insiders have an unfair advantage.

- Investment banks typically "make a market" in stocks, meaning that they hold extra shares so that orders can be filled smoothly. These marketmakers expect to earn a certain profit, but inside traders skim some of it off. So marketmakers simply raise the commission they charge. As a result, everyone who buys and sells stock pays a slightly higher price.

Blue Sky Laws

Currently, all states and the District of Columbia also regulate the sale of securities. These state statutes are called **blue sky laws** (because crooks were willing to sell naive investors a "piece of the great blue sky").

ANTITRUST

Congress passed the Sherman Act in 1890 to prevent extreme concentrations of economic power. Because this statute was aimed at the Standard Oil Trust, which then controlled the oil industry throughout the country, it was termed **antitrust** legislation.

Per se violation
An automatic breach of antitrust laws.

Rule of reason violation
An action that breaches antitrust laws only if it has an anticompetitive impact.

Violations of the antitrust laws are divided into two categories: *per se* and **rule of reason**. *Per se* violations are automatic. Defendants charged with this type of violation cannot defend themselves by saying, "But the impact wasn't so bad" or "No one was hurt." The court will not listen to excuses, and violators may be sent to prison.

Rule of reason violations, on the other hand, are illegal only if they have an anticompetitive impact on the market. For example, mergers are illegal only if they harm competition in their industry. Those who commit rule of reason violations are not sent to prison.

Both the Justice Department and the Federal Trade Commission (FTC) have authority to enforce the antitrust laws. In addition to the government, anyone injured by an antitrust violation has the right to sue for damages. The United States is unusual in this regard—in most other countries, only the government is able to sue antitrust violators. A successful plaintiff can recover treble (that is, triple) damages from the defendant.

The Sherman Act

PRICE-FIXING

Section 1 of the Sherman Act prohibits all agreements "in restraint of trade." The most common—and one of the most serious—violations of this provision involves horizontal price-fixing. **When competitors agree on the prices at which they will buy or sell products, their price-fixing is a *per se* violation of Section 1 of the Sherman Act.**

In the following Landmark Case, the defendants argued that price-fixing was wrong only if the prices were *unfair*. Did the Supreme Court agree?

Landmark Case

UNITED STATES V. TRENTON POTTERIES COMPANY

273 U.S. 392; 1927 U.S. LEXIS 975
Supreme Court of the United States, 1927

CASE SUMMARY

Facts: This case involved dirty behavior in the bathroom fixture business. The federal government alleged that 23 of the corporations that manufactured these fixtures had agreed on the prices they would charge their customers. The defendants argued that they had not violated the law because their prices had been reasonable.

They were found guilty at trial, but the appeals court overturned their convictions. The Supreme Court granted *certiorari*.

Issue: *Is price-fixing legal so long as the prices are reasonable?*

Decision: Price-fixing is a *per se* violation, even if the prices are reasonable.

Reasoning: The goal of the Sherman Act is to promote competition, but price-fixing automatically eliminates one form of it. Indeed, the power to fix prices is the power to control a market, an outcome that the Sherman Act prohibits.

Moreover, even if the prices were fair when set, the reasonable price today may, through economic and business changes, become the unreasonable price of tomorrow. And it would be wrong to require the government to prove that prices are unreasonable, especially since economists may not be able to agree.

For these reasons, the judgment of the appeals court is reversed.

The Supreme Court has referred to this type of collusion as "the supreme evil of antitrust," and it has been illegal for the better part of a century.[4] But it never seems to go away. Samsung Electronics Co. paid a $300 million fine for having conspired to fix prices of computer chips. Other companies engaged in the conspiracy have paid $346 million in fines. These penalties were topped by F. Hoffmann-La Roche, which paid $500 million for conspiring to fix the prices of vitamins. Executives went to prison for their roles in these conspiracies.

---

[4]*Verizon Communs., Inc. v. Trinko, LLP*, 540 U.S. 398 (S.Ct. 2004).

RESALE PRICE MAINTENANCE

Resale price maintenance (RPM), also called *vertical price fixing*, means the manufacturer sets the *minimum* prices that retailers may charge. In other words, it prevents retailers from discounting. Why does the manufacturer care, though? After all, once the retailer purchases the item, the manufacturer has made its profit. The only way the manufacturer makes more money is to raise its wholesale price, not the retail price. RPM guarantees a profit margin for the retailer.

Manufacturers care about retail prices because pricing affects the product's image with consumers. Armani men's suits sell for around $2,000. What conclusion do you draw about the quality of those suits? Would your opinion change if you saw Armani suits being sold at discounted prices? You can understand that Armani might want to prohibit retailers from lowering the prices on its suits. Consumer advocates contend, however, that manufacturers such as Armani are simply protecting dealers from competition. Discounting may or may not harm products, but, they insist, RPM certainly hurts consumers.

Should RPM be a *per se* or rule of reason violation of the antitrust laws? The Supreme Court answered this question in the following case.

LEEGIN CREATIVE LEATHER PRODUCTS, INC. v. PSKS, INC.

127 S. Ct. 2705, 2007 U.S. LEXIS 8668
Supreme Court of the United States, 2007

CASE SUMMARY

Facts: Leegin manufactured belts and other women's fashion accessories under the brand name "Brighton." It sold these products only to small boutiques and specialty stores. Sales of the Brighton brand accounted for about half the profits at Kay's Kloset, a boutique in Lewisville, Texas.

Leegin decided it would no longer sell to retailers who discounted Brighton prices. It wanted to ensure that stores could afford to offer excellent service. It was also concerned that discounting harmed Brighton's image. Despite warnings from Leegin, Kay's Kloset persisted in marking down Brighton products by 20 percent. So Leegin cut the store off.

Kay's sued Leegin, alleging that RPM was a *per se* rule violation of the law. The trial court found for Kay's and entered judgment against Leegin for almost $4 million. The Court of Appeals affirmed. The Supreme Court granted *certiorari*. On appeal, Leegin did not dispute that it had entered into RPM agreements with retailers. Rather, it contended that the rule of reason should apply to those agreements.

Issue: *Is resale price maintenance a* **per se** *or rule of reason violation of the Sherman Act?*

Decision: RPM is a rule of reason violation.

Reasoning: To be a *per se* violation, an activity must not only be anticompetitive, it must also lack any redeeming virtue. Recent research indicates that resale price maintenance may offer some benefits:

- *Retailers can provide better service.* Without RPM, consumers might go *look* at a product at the retailer who hires experienced sales help or offers product demonstrations, but then go *buy* the item from a discounter who provides none of these services. In short order, the upscale retailer will either go out of business or cut back on service and consumers will have fewer options.

- *If retailers do not have to compete with others who sell the same brand, they can focus instead on competing against other brands.* For example, retailers selling the same brand may pool their marketing dollars to have greater impact.

It is worth noting, though, that RPM can have an anticompetitive effect. A manufacturer with market power could, for example, use resale price maintenance to give retailers an incentive not to sell the products of smaller rivals. Courts must be diligent in recognizing and preventing any RPM that has an anticompetitive impact.

MONOPOLIZATION

Under Section 2 of the Sherman Act, it is illegal to monopolize or attempt to monopolize a market. To monopolize means to acquire control over a market in the wrong way. *Having* a monopoly is legal unless it is *gained* or *maintained* by using wrongful tactics.

To determine if a defendant has illegally monopolized, we must ask two questions:

> Possessing a monopoly is not necessarily illegal; using *"bad acts"* to acquire or maintain one is.

- **Does the company control the market?** No matter what its market share, a company does not have a monopoly unless it can exclude competitors or control prices. For example, the Justice Department sued a movie theater chain that possessed a 93 percent share of the box office in Las Vegas. But the court ruled against the Justice Department because the chain's market share decreased to 75 percent within three years. This decline indicated that the company did not control the market and that barriers to entry were low.[5]

- **How did the company acquire or maintain its control?** If the law prohibited the mere possession of a monopoly, it might discourage companies from producing excellent products or offering low prices. So possessing a monopoly is not necessarily illegal; using *"bad acts"* to acquire or maintain one is. For example, Microsoft insisted that computer manufacturers who wanted to install the Windows operating system on *any* computer had to purchase a license for *every* machine they made. This requirement meant that a manufacturer would not even consider offering consumers another operating system because it had already paid for Microsoft's on all of its machines. The Justice Department ordered Microsoft to halt this arrangement.

Predatory pricing is another example of a bad act.

PREDATORY PRICING

Predatory pricing occurs when a company lowers its prices below cost to drive competitors out of business. Once the predator has the market to itself, it raises prices to make up lost profits—and more besides. Typically, the goal of a predatory pricing scheme is either to win control of a market or to maintain it. Therefore, it is illegal under Section 2 of the Sherman Act. **To win a predatory pricing case, the plaintiff must prove three elements:**

- The defendant is selling its products *below cost.*

- The defendant *intends* that the plaintiff go out of business.

- If the plaintiff does go out of business, the defendant will be able to earn sufficient profits to *recover* its prior losses.

The classic example of predatory pricing is a large grocery store that comes into a small town offering exceptionally low prices that are subsidized by profits from its other branches. Once all the "Ma and Pa" corner groceries go out of business, MegaGrocery raises its prices to much higher levels.

Predatory pricing cases can be difficult to win. For example, it is hard for Ma and Pa to prove that MegaGrocery intended for them to go out of business. It is also difficult for Ma and Pa to show that MegaGrocery will be able to make up all its lost profits once the corner

---

[5]*United States v. Syufy Enterprises,* 903 F.2d 659, 1990 U.S. App. LEXIS 7396, (9th Cir, 1990).

grocery is out of the way. They need to prove, for example, that no other grocery chain will come to town. It is difficult to prove a negative proposition like that, especially in the grocery business, where barriers to entry are low.

The Clayton Act

MERGERS

The Clayton Act prohibits mergers that are anticompetitive. Companies with substantial assets must notify the Federal Trade Commission (FTC) before undertaking a merger.[6] This notification gives the government an opportunity to prevent a merger ahead of time, rather than trying to untangle one after the fact.

TYING ARRANGEMENTS

A tying arrangement is an agreement to sell a product on the condition that the buyer also purchases a different (or tied) product. A tying arrangement is illegal under the Clayton Act if:

- The two products are clearly separate,

- The seller requires the buyer to purchase the two products together,

- The seller has significant power in the market for the tying product, and

- The seller is shutting out a significant part of the market for the tied product.

Six movie distributors refused to sell individual films to television stations. Instead, they insisted that a station buy an entire package of movies. To obtain classics such as *Treasure of the Sierra Madre* and *Casablanca* (the **tying product**), the station also had to purchase such forgettable films as *Gorilla Man* and *Tugboat Annie Sails Again* (the **tied product**).[7] The distributors engaged in an illegal tying arrangement. These are the questions that the court asked:

- *Are the two products clearly separate?* A left and right shoe are not separate products, and a seller can legally require that they be purchased together. *Gorilla Man*, on the other hand, is a separate product from *Casablanca*.

- *Is the seller requiring the buyer to purchase the two products together?* Yes, that is the whole point of these "package deals."

- *Does the seller have significant power in the market for the tying product?* In this case, the tying products are the classic movies. Since they are copyrighted, no one else can show them without the distributor's permission. The six distributors controlled a great many classic movies. So, yes, they do have significant market power.

- *Is the seller shutting out a significant part of the market for the tied product?* In this case, the tied products are the undesirable films like *Tugboat Annie Sails Again*. Television stations forced to take the unwanted films did not buy "B" movies from other distributors. These other distributors were effectively foreclosed from a substantial part of the market.

Tying arrangement

An agreement to sell a product on the condition that a buyer also purchases another, usually less desirable, product.

Tying product

In a tying arrangement, the product offered for sale on the condition that another product be purchased as well.

Tied product

In a tying arrangement, the product that a buyer must purchase as the condition for being allowed to buy another product.

---

[6]For example, a notice must be filed if the acquiring company is purchasing stock or assets of the acquired company that are worth more than $212 million (adjusted annually for inflation).
[7]*United States v. Loew's Inc.*, 371 U.S. 38, 1962 U.S. LEXIS 2332 (1962).

EXAM Strategy

Question: Two medical supply companies in the San Francisco area provide oxygen to homes of patients. The companies are owned by the doctors who prescribe the oxygen. These doctors make up 60 percent of the lung specialists in the area. Does this arrangement create an antitrust problem?

Strategy: Does the seller have significant power in the market for the tying product (lung patients)? Is it shutting out a significant part of the market for the tied product (oxygen)?

Result: The FTC charged the doctors with an illegal tying arrangement. Because the doctors effectively controlled such a high percentage of the patients needing the service, other oxygen companies could not enter the market.

The Robinson-Patman Act

Under the Robinson-Patman Act (RPA), it is illegal to charge different prices to different purchasers if:

- The items are the same, and
- The price discrimination lessens competition.

However, it is legal to charge a lower price to a particular buyer if:

- The costs of serving this buyer are lower, or
- The seller is simply meeting competition.

Congress passed the RPA in 1936 to prevent large chains from driving small, local stores out of business. Owners of these Ma and Pa stores complained that the large chains could sell goods cheaper because suppliers charged them lower prices. As a result of the RPA, managers who would otherwise like to develop different pricing strategies for specific customers or regions may hesitate to do so for fear of violating this statute. In reality, however, they have little to fear.

Under the RPA, a plaintiff must prove both that price discrimination occurred and that it lessened competition. It is perfectly permissible, for example, for a supplier to sell at a different price to its Texas and California distributors, or to its health care and educational distributors, so long as the distributors are not in competition with each other.

The RPA also permits price variations that are based on differences in cost. Thus, Kosmo's Kitchen would be perfectly within its legal rights to sell its frozen cheese enchiladas to Giant at a lower price than to Corner Grocery if Kosmo's costs are lower to do so. Giant often buys shipments the size of railroad containers, which cost less to deliver than smaller boxes.

Chapter Conclusion

In this chapter, you have learned about some of the important government regulations that affect business. They can have a profound impact on your business—and on your life.

EXAM REVIEW

1. **SECURITY**   A security is any transaction in which the buyer (1) invests money in a common enterprise and (2) expects to earn a profit predominantly from the efforts of others. (p. 413)

EXAM Strategy

Question: As a pitcher for the Cleveland Indians farm team, Randy Newsom had dreams of glory, but a paycheck that was a nightmare—$8,000 for the season. Newsom came up with a clever solution: he set up a website that offered fans the opportunity to buy a share of his future. For only $20, the buyer was entitled to .002 percent of his career pay. Any problems with this plan?

Strategy: Remember that even orange trees can be securities. (See the "Result" at the end of this section.)

2. **THE 1933 ACT**   The 1933 Act requires that, before offering or selling securities in a public offering, the issuer must register the securities with the Securities and Exchange Commission (SEC). (pp. 413–414)

3. **PROSPECTUS**   All investors must receive a copy of the prospectus before purchasing stock in a public offering. (p. 414)

4. **PRIVATE OFFERING**   Under the 1933 Act, an issuer is not required to register securities that are sold in a private offering, but the issuer may have to meet certain disclosure requirements. (p. 414)

5. **REGULATION D**   The most common and important type of private offering is under Regulation D. It permits issuers to sell stock to a small number of investors and for a limited amount of money. (p. 414)

6. **THE 1934 ACT**   The 1934 Act requires public companies to make regular filings with the SEC, including annual reports, quarterly reports, and Form 8-Ks. (pp. 415–416)

7. **REGISTRATION**   Under the 1934 Act, an issuer must register with the SEC if (1) it completes a public offering under the 1933 Act, or (2) its securities are traded on a national exchange (such as the New York Stock Exchange), or (3) it has at least 500 shareholders *and* total assets that exceed $10 million. (p. 415)

8. **SARBANES-OXLEY**   Sarbanes-Oxley requires each company's CEO and CFO to certify that the information in the quarterly and annual reports is true. (p. 415)

9. **SECTION 16**   Insiders must report their trades in company stock within two business days. They must turn over to the corporation any profits they make from the purchase and sale or sale and purchase of company securities in a six-month period. (pp. 415–416)

10. **INSIDER TRADING**   Insider trading is illegal. (pp. 416–418)

11. **BLUE SKY LAWS**   State securities statutes are called blue sky laws. (p. 418)

12. **PRICE-FIXING**   When competitors agree on the prices at which they will buy or sell products, their price-fixing is a *per se* violation of Section 1 of the Sherman Act. (p. 419)

13. **RPM**   Resale price maintenance means the manufacturer sets minimum prices that retailers may charge. It is a rule of reason violation of Section 1 of the Sherman Act. (p. 420)

14. **MONOPOLIZATION**   Under Section 2 of the Sherman Act, it is illegal to monopolize or attempt to monopolize a market. *Having* a monopoly is legal unless it is *gained* or *maintained* by using wrongful tactics. (p. 421)

EXAM Strategy

Question: BAR/BRI was the largest bar review company in the country, with branches in 45 states. Barpassers was a much smaller company located only in Arizona and California. BAR/BRI distributed pamphlets on campuses that falsely suggested Barpassers was near bankruptcy. Enrollments in Barpassers' courses dropped, and the company was forced to postpone plans for expansion. Did Barpassers have an antitrust claim against BAR/BRI?

Strategy: It did not matter if BAR/BRI *had* a monopoly. These "bad acts" could have helped the company *acquire* one. (See the "Result" at the end of this section.)

15. **PREDATORY PRICING**   Predatory pricing occurs when a company lowers its prices below cost to drive competitors out of business. (pp. 421–422)

16. **THE CLAYTON ACT**   The Clayton Act prohibits mergers that are anticompetitive. (p. 422)

17. **TYING ARRANGEMENTS**   A tying arrangement is an agreement to sell a product on the condition that the buyer also purchases a different (or tied) product. Certain tying arrangements are illegal under the Clayton Act. (p. 422)

18. **RPA**   Under the Robinson-Patman Act, it is illegal to charge different prices to different purchasers if the items are the same and the price discrimination lessens competition. (p. 423)

1. Result: Newsom was selling securities: buyers were investing in him, hoping that they could earn a profit from his efforts. He needed to comply with the provisions of the 1933 Act.

14. Result: A jury found that BAR/BRI had violated Section 2 of the Sherman Act by attempting to create an illegal monopoly. The jury ordered BAR/BRI to pay Barpassers more than $3 million, plus attorney's fees.

MATCHING QUESTIONS

Match the following terms with their definitions:

___ A. Securities Act of 1933

___ B. Section 16

___ C. Sarbanes-Oxley

___ D. Section 10(b)

___ E. Securities Exchange Act of 1934

1. Prohibits fraud in connection with the purchase and sale of a security

2. Regulates companies once they have gone public

3. Requires officers to certify their company's financial statements

4. Regulates the issuance of securities

5. Requires an insider to turn over profits she has earned from buying and selling or selling and buying company stock in a six-month period

TRUE/FALSE QUESTIONS

Circle true or false:

1. T F Before permitting a company to issue new securities, the SEC investigates to ensure that the company has a promising future.

2. T F Small offerings of securities do not need to be registered with the SEC.

3. T F Horizontal price-fixing is legal as long as it does not have an anticompetitive impact.

4. T F Only the federal government regulates securities offerings; the states do not.

5. T F It is legal for a company to sell its product at a price below cost so long as it does not intend to drive competitors out of business.

MULTIPLE-CHOICE QUESTIONS

1. Under Regulation D, an issuer:
   (a) May not sell to 1,000 accredited investors
   (b) May not sell to 27 unaccredited investors
   (c) Must make disclosure to accredited investors
   (d) Must make disclosure to unaccredited investors
   (e) May advertise the stock publicly

2. Which of the following statements is *not* true about a public offering?
   (a) The issuer files a registration statement with the SEC.
   (b) The issuer files a prospectus with the SEC.
   (c) Company officers may make public statements about the offering before the stock is sold.
   (d) Company officers may make public statements about the offering after the stock is sold.
   (e) The issuer may solicit offers for the stock before the effective date.

3. To have an illegal monopoly, a company must:

I. Control the market

II. Maintain its control improperly

III. Have a market share greater than 50 percent

(a) I, II, and III

(b) I and II

(c) II and III

(d) I and III

(e) Neither I, II, nor III

4. Lloyd sold car floor mats to Mercedes dealerships. Then Mercedes began to include floor mats as standard equipment. Mercedes has a 10 percent share of the luxury car market.

(a) Mercedes has created an illegal tying arrangement because floor mats and cars are separate products.

(b) Mercedes has not created an illegal tying arrangement because it does not have significant power in the luxury car market.

(c) Mercedes has not created an illegal tying arrangement because it is not tying the two products together.

(d) Mercedes has created an illegal tying arrangement because it controls the market in floor mats for its cars.

5. Mike is director of sales for his company. He negotiates prices with Paige and Lauren, who work for two of his biggest customers. Paige tells him that she can buy the same product cheaper elsewhere. He cuts the price for her, but not for his other customers. At the same time, he develops a crush on Lauren, so offers to sell her the product at a lower price. In subsequent months, these two customers come to dominate the market. Which statement is correct?

(a) Mike can charge whatever price he wants to any customer.

(b) Mike must charge all his customers the same price.

(c) The price cut to Paige, but not Lauren, is legal.

(d) The price cut to Lauren, but not Paige, is legal.

(e) Mike is not required to charge all his customers the same price, but neither of these price cuts is legal.

ESSAY QUESTIONS

1. Jonah bought 12 paintings from Theo's Art Gallery, at a total cost of $1 million. Theo told Jonah that the paintings were a safe investment that could only go up in value. The gallery permitted any purchaser to trade in a painting for any other artwork the gallery owned. In the trade-in, the purchaser would get credit for the amount of the original painting and then pay the difference if the new painting was worth more. When Jonah's paintings did not increase in value, he sued Theo for a violation of the securities laws. Were these paintings securities?

2. You're in line at the movie theater when you overhear a stranger say: "The FDA has just approved Hernstrom's new painkiller. When the announcement is made on Monday, Hernstrom stock will take off." Have you violated the law if you buy stock in the company before the announcement on Monday?

3. In New York City, 50 bakeries agreed to raise the retail price of bread. All the association's members printed the new price on their bread sleeves. Are the bakeries in violation of the antitrust laws?

4. Suppose that Disney insists that retailers cannot sell DVDs of *Ratatouille* for less than $16.99. The company threatens to cut off any retailers who discount that price. But video stores would like to use these movies as a loss leader, selling them at a very low price to lure customers. Is it legal for Disney to cut off retailers who discount prices?

5. Reserve Supply Corp., a cooperative of 379 lumber dealers, charged that Owens-Corning Fiberglass Corp. violated the Robinson-Patman Act by selling at lower prices to Reserve's competitors. Owens-Corning had granted lower prices to a number of Reserve's competitors to meet, but not beat, the prices of other insulation manufacturers. Is Owens-Corning in violation of the Robinson-Patman Act?

DISCUSSION QUESTIONS

1. Federal security laws are based on the assumption that investors are knowledgable enough to assess the quality of a stock, so long as the issuer provides adequate disclosure. Is this assumption reasonable, or should securities laws provide greater protection to investors?

2. **ETHICS:** David Sokol worked at Berkshire Hathaway for legendary investor Warren Buffett, who is renowned not only for his investment skills but also his ethics. Bankers suggested to both Sokol and the CEO of Lubrizol that the company might be a good buy for Berkshire. Sokol then found out that the CEO of Lubrizol planned to ask his board for permission to approach Berkshire about a possible acquisition. Sokol purchased $10 million worth of Lubrizol stock before recommending Lubrizol to Buffett. Sokol mentioned to Buffett "in passing" that he owned shares of Lubrizol. Buffett did not ask any questions about the timing or amount of Sokol's purchases. Sokol made a $3 million profit when Berkshire acquired Lubrizol. Did Sokol violate insider trading laws? Did he behave ethically? What about Buffett?

3. The SEC believes that anyone in possession of nonpublic material information about a company should be required to disclose it before trading on the stock of that enterprise. Instead, the courts have developed a more complex set of rules. Do you agree with the SEC or the courts on this issue?

4. Resale price maintenance used to be a *per se* violation of the antitrust laws, but now it is a rule of reason violation. Will this change in the law lead to higher or lower prices for consumers? Will it provide other benefits for consumers? Do you agree with the Supreme Court's decision?

5. **ETHICS:** Clarice, a young woman with a mental disability, brought a malpractice suit against a doctor at the Medical Center. As a result, the Medical Center refused to treat her on a nonemergency basis. Clarice then went to another local clinic, which was later acquired by the Medical Center. Because the new clinic also refused to treat her, Clarice had to seek medical treatment in another town 40 miles away. Has the Medical Center violated the antitrust laws? Was is it ethical to deny treatment to a patient?

CHAPTER 24

ACCOUNTANTS' LIABILITY

© Evan Meyer/Shutterstock.com

> The firm collapsed in disgrace, the first major accounting firm ever to be convicted of a crime.

The accounting firm Arthur Andersen prided itself on its ethics. Old-timers would tell new recruits the legend of the firm's founder: how in 1914, the young Arthur Andersen had refused a client's request to certify a dubious earnings report. Although Andersen knew his firm would be fired and he might not be able to meet payroll, he nonetheless stood on principle. He was vindicated a few months later, when the client went bankrupt. For its first 35 years, Andersen was primarily in the business of auditing public companies. Although its partners did not become rich, they made a good living. Then the firm entered the consulting business. Soon the consultants in the firm were generating much higher profits—and earning much higher salaries—than the auditors. Audits were fast becoming loss leaders to attract consulting business. Lower prices led to lower quality, as Andersen (and other auditors) felt they could not afford to invest as many hours in their audits. And the audits were becoming less effective because partners were increasingly afraid to deliver bad news for fear of losing both audit and consulting fees.

To save money, the firm began to force partners to retire at 56. This system reduced the general level of experience and expertise. At the same time, accounting was becoming more complicated. Predictably, mistakes happened, lawsuits were filed, settlements were made.

Andersen's name was soiled by its role in a number of financial disasters, such as Global Crossing and WorldCom. And then there was Enron. Andersen opened an office in Enron's headquarters staffed with more than 150 Andersen employees. When the federal government began investigating Enron's bankruptcy, panicked Andersen employees shredded documents, leading to the firm's conviction on a criminal charge of obstructing justice. And so, the firm that began as a model of ethics in the accounting profession collapsed in disgrace, the first major accounting firm ever to be convicted of a crime.[1] The conviction was ultimately overturned by the Supreme Court, but by then it was too late. Andersen was dead.

INTRODUCTION

To begin our study of the accounting industry, it is important to understand what accountants do.

Audits

Accountants serve two masters—company management and the investing public. Management hires the accountants, but investors and creditors rely upon them to offer an independent evaluation of the financial statements that management issues.

When conducting an audit, accountants verify information provided by management. Since it is impossible to check each and every transaction, they verify a *sample* of various types of transactions. If these are accurate, they assume all are. To verify transactions, accountants use two mirror image processes—vouching and tracing.

In **vouching**, accountants choose a transaction listed in the company's books and check backwards to make sure that there are original data to support it. They might, for example, find in accounts payable a bill for the purchase of 1,000 reams of photocopy paper. They would check to ensure that all the paper had actually arrived and that the receiving department had properly signed and dated the invoice. The auditors would also check the original purchase order to ensure that the acquisition was properly authorized in the first place.

In **tracing**, the accountant begins with an item of original data and traces it forward to ensure that it has been properly recorded throughout the bookkeeping process. For example, the sales ledger might report that 1,000 copies of a software program were sold to a distributor. The accountant checks the information in the sales ledger against the original invoice to ensure that the date, price, quantity, and customer's name all match. The auditor then verifies each step along the paper trail until the software leaves the warehouse.

In performing their duties, accountants must follow two sets of rules: (1) generally accepted accounting principles (GAAP); and (2) generally accepted auditing standards (GAAS). **GAAP** are the rules for preparing financial statements, and **GAAS** are the rules for conducting audits. These two sets of standards include broadly phrased general principles, as well as specific guidelines and illustrations. The application and interpretation of these rules require acute professional skill.

The Securities and Exchange Commission (SEC) has proposed a set of rules that would ultimately require U.S. companies to use **international financial reporting standards (IFRS)** instead of GAAP.[2] As businesses become more global, there is something to be said for a worldwide, consistent set of accounting rules. If everyone used IFRS (as more than 100 countries now do), cross-country comparisons would be easier. It may be, too, that foreign companies would be more willing to invest in the United States if they could use international accounting rules. Accounting firms have urged adoption of IFRS in the United States.

The downside? Because IFRS rules generally offer greater flexibility, some commentators worry that cross-company comparisons will be *more* difficult because observers will not

Vouching
Auditors choose a transaction listed in a company's books and check backwards for original data to support it.

Tracing
An auditor takes an item of original data and tracks it forward to ensure that it has been properly recorded throughout the bookkeeping process.

GAAP
"Generally accepted accounting principles" are the rules for preparing financial statements.

GAAS
"Generally accepted auditing standards" are the rules for conducting audits.

IFRS
"International financial reporting standards" are a set of international accounting principles that U.S. companies may ultimately be required to follow in preparing financial statements.

---

[1]Based in part on information in Ken Brown and Ianthe Jeanne Dugan, "Andersen's Fall from Grace Is a Tale of Greed and Miscues," *The Wall Street Journal*, June 7, 2002, p. 1.

[2]IFRS are established by the International Accounting Standards Board, a privately funded organization located in London.

know how each company interpreted the guidelines. Some experts worry that allowing the use of IFRS is the equivalent of outsourcing financial safety standards. Also, companies must report financial information to other places besides the SEC—to parties with whom they have contracted, banks, and other regulators. Unless everyone accepts IFRS, companies could end up having to prepare two sets of financials.

Opinions

After an audit is complete, the accountant issues an opinion on the financial statements that indicates how accurately those statements reflect the company's true financial condition. The auditor has four choices:

- **Unqualified opinion.** Also known as a **clean opinion,** this indicates that the company's financial statements fairly present its financial condition in accordance with GAAP. A less-than-clean opinion is a warning to potential investors and creditors that something may be wrong.

- **Qualified opinion.** This opinion indicates that although the financial statements are generally accurate, there is nonetheless an outstanding, unresolved issue. For example, the company may face potential liability from environmental law violations, but the liability cannot yet be estimated accurately.

- **Adverse opinion.** In the auditor's view, the company's financial statements do not accurately reflect its financial position. In other words, the company is being less than totally truthful about its finances.

- **Disclaimer of opinion.** Although not as damning as an adverse opinion, a disclaimer is still not good news. It is issued when the auditor does not have enough information to form an opinion.

Congress Responds to Enron: Sarbanes-Oxley

As the stock market tumbled after the verdict in the Arthur Andersen case, Congress acted to restore investor confidence by passing the Sarbanes-Oxley Act of 2002 (SOX). The major provisions of this act as it relates to auditors are as follows.

THE PUBLIC COMPANY ACCOUNTING OVERSIGHT BOARD

Congress established the Public Company Accounting Oversight Board (PCAOB) to ensure that investors receive accurate and complete financial information. The board has the authority to regulate public accounting firms, establishing everything from audit rules to ethics guidelines. All accounting firms that audit public companies must register with the board, and the board must inspect them regularly. The PCAOB has the authority to revoke an accounting firm's registration or prohibit it from auditing public companies.

In an effort to keep the foxes out of the henhouse, the statute provides that no more than two of the five PCAOB board members may be certified public accountants. This board has the authority and, it is hoped, will have the political will to revise lax accounting rules, including those that contributed to the Enron financial earthquake. The PCAOB's first inspection of the Big Four accounting firms found audit and accounting problems at all of them, but the board still expressed confidence in the general quality of their work.

REPORTS TO THE AUDIT COMMITTEE

Traditionally, auditors reported to the senior management of a client. This reporting relationship created obvious conflicts of interest—the auditors were reporting concerns to the very people who could be causing, or at least benefiting from, these problems. Under SOX, auditors must report to the audit committee of the client's board of directors, not to senior management. The accountants must inform the audit committee of any (1) significant flaws they find in the company's internal controls; (2) alternative options that the firm considered in preparing the financial statements; and (3) accounting disagreements with management.

CONSULTING SERVICES

For years, the SEC tried to restrict consulting by accounting firms, but the firms found powerful allies in Congress to protect them. SOX prohibits accounting firms that audit public companies from providing consulting services to their audit clients on topics such as bookkeeping, financial information systems, human resources, and legal issues (unrelated to the audit). Any consulting agreements must be approved by a client's audit committee. Auditing firms cannot base their employees' compensation on sales of consulting services to clients. Some observers believe that these conflict-of-interest rules are too lenient—that auditors should do nothing but audit. They argue that even providing advice on taxes or internal control systems, as SOX permits, could warp an accountant's objectivity about auditing issues. Also, SOX rules on these issues apply only in the United States. Globally, the Big Four earn between a sixth and a quarter of their income from consulting.

CONFLICTS OF INTEREST

An accounting firm cannot audit a company if one of the client's top officers has worked for that accounting firm within the prior year and was involved in the company's audit. In short, a client cannot hire one of its auditors to ensure a friendly attitude.

TERM LIMITS ON AUDIT PARTNERS

After five years with a client, the lead audit partner must rotate off the account for at least five years. Other partners must rotate off an account every seven years for at least two years.

LIABILITY TO CLIENTS

Contract

Engagement letter
A written contract by which a client hires an accountant.

A written contract between accountants and their clients is called an **engagement letter**. The contract has both express and implied terms. The accountant *expressly* promises to perform a particular project by a given date. The accountant also *implies* that she will work as carefully as an ordinarily prudent accountant would under the circumstances. If she fails to do either, she has breached her contract and may be liable for any damages that result.

Negligence

An accountant is liable for negligence to a client who can prove both of the following elements:

- **The accountant breached his duty to his client by failing to exercise the degree of skill and competence that an ordinarily prudent accountant would under the circumstances.** For example, if the accountant fails to follow GAAP or GAAS, he has almost certainly breached his duty.

- **The accountant's violation of duty caused harm to the client.** In the following case, the accounting firm had clearly breached its duty. But had this wrongdoing actually caused harm to the client?

You be the Judge

Facts: Oregon Steel Mills, Inc., was a publicly traded company whose financial statements were audited by Coopers & Lybrand, LLP. When Oregon sold the stock in one of its subsidiaries, Coopers advised Oregon that the transaction should be reported as a $1 million gain. This advice was wrong, and Coopers was negligent in giving it.

> ### OREGON STEEL MILLS, INC. v. COOPERS & LYBRAND, LLP
> 336 Ore. 329, 83 P.3d 322, 2004 Ore. LEXIS 55
> Supreme Court of Oregon, 2004

Two years later, Oregon began a public offering of additional shares of stock. It intended to sell these shares to the public on May 2. Shortly before Oregon filed the stock offering with the SEC, Coopers told the company that the sale of its subsidiary had been misreported and that it would have to revise its financial statements. As a result, the offering was delayed from May 2 to June 13. During this period of delay, the price of the stock fell.

Oregon filed suit against Coopers, seeking as damages the difference between what Oregon actually received for its stock and what it would have received if the offering had occurred on May 2—an amount equal to approximately $35 million.

Issue: *Did Coopers' negligence cause the loss to Oregon?*

Argument for Oregon: Coopers was negligent in giving advice to Oregon. As a result, Oregon had to delay its securities offering for six weeks. During this time, the market price of Oregon stock fell, with the result that the company sold the new stock for $35 million less than it would have received on the original sale date. Someone is going to suffer a $35 million loss. It should be Coopers, which caused the loss, rather than Oregon, which was blameless.

Argument for Coopers: It is true that Coopers was negligent, the market price of the stock fell, and Oregon suffered a loss. However, to recover for negligence, the plaintiff must show that the loss was reasonably foreseeable.[3] When Coopers made its error, no one could foresee that, as a result, Oregon would suffer a loss two years later because its securities offering was delayed by six weeks. At the time of its mistake, Coopers did not know when the offering would take place, nor that one date would be more favorable than another. The decline in stock price was unrelated to Oregon's financial condition or Coopers' conduct. Coopers is not liable.

Common Law Fraud

An accountant is liable for fraud if (1) she makes a false statement of a material fact, (2) she either knows it is not true or recklessly disregards the truth, (3) the client justifiably relies on the statement, and (4) the reliance results in damages. For example, Kurt deliberately inflated numbers in the financial statements he prepared for Tess so that she would not discover that he had made some disastrous investments for her. Because of these errors, Tess did not realize her true financial position for some years, which caused her to make some poor investment choices. Kurt committed fraud.

A fraud claim is an important weapon because it permits the client to ask for punitive damages, which can be substantially higher than a compensatory claim.

Breach of Trust

Accountants occupy a position of enormous trust because financial information is often sensitive and confidential. Clients may put as much trust in their accountant as they do in their lawyer, clergy, or psychiatrist. **Accountants have**

> Clients may put as much trust in their accountant as they do in their lawyer, clergy, or psychiatrist.

---

[3]See Chapter 6 for a discussion of negligence.

a legal obligation to (1) keep all client information confidential; and (2) use client information only for the benefit of the client. For example, Alexander Grant & Co. did accounting work for Consolidata Services, Inc. (CDS), a company that provided payroll services. The two firms had a number of clients in common. When Alexander Grant discovered discrepancies in CDS's client funds accounts, it notified those companies that were clients of both firms. Not surprisingly, these mutual clients fired CDS, which then went out of business. The court held that Alexander Grant had violated its duty of trust to CDS.[4]

Fiduciary Duty

In a **fiduciary relationship**, one party has an obligation (1) to act in a trustworthy fashion for the benefit of the other person and (2) to put that person's interests first. As a general rule, accountants do *not* have a fiduciary duty to their clients. However, clients often do put great faith in their accountants and sometimes accountants take on responsibilities that extend beyond the typical scope of an accountant-client relationship. As the following case illustrates, in such situations, accountants may be deemed a fiduciary and held to a high standard of accountability.

LEBER V. KONIGSBERG

2010 U.S. Dist. LEXIS 128910
United States District Court for the Southern District of Florida, 2010

CASE SUMMARY

Facts: Steven Leber was the trustee of a trust worth $4 million (the Trust). Paul Konigsberg was a certified public accountant in the firm of Konigsberg Wolf & Co., P.C.

Konisberg not only recommended that Leber invest all the Trust's assets with Bernard Madoff, he promised to personally supervise and monitor this account. Sadly, it turned out that Madoff was running a $65 billion Ponzi scheme.[5] The trust's investment turned out to be virtually worthless.

Leber filed suit against Konigsberg and the accounting firm on the grounds that they breached their fiduciary duty to him and the Trust. He sought payment of $4 million. Defendants filed a motion for summary judgment on the grounds that accountants do not have a fiduciary relationship with their clients.

Issue: *Do accountants owe a fiduciary duty to their clients?*

Decision: Although accountants *generally* do not owe a fiduciary duty, they do in this case.

Reasoning: Accountants do not have a fiduciary relationship with their clients unless they take on additional responsibilities beyond the typical role. However, a fiduciary duty does exist if an accountant assumes the duties of a financial advisor, has control and influence over the client, and the client trusts the accountant's integrity.

Konigsberg not only recommended this fraudulent investment, he indicated that if the Trust did not hire his firm as its tax accountants, he would cut off access to Madoff. Konigsberg charged a monthly fee for "analyzing" the reports that Madoff sent the Trust each month. These actions created a fiduciary relationship.

---

[4]*Wagenheim v. Alexander Grant & Co.*, 19 Ohio App. 3d 7, 482 N.E.2d 955, 1983 Ohio App. LEXIS 11194 (App. Ct., Ohio, 1983).

[5]In a Ponzi scheme, the fraudster uses money from new investors to pay large returns to prior victims. The scheme can be very profitable for all involved until the fraudster runs out of new "investors." Indeed, investors often attract new victims for the fraudster by bragging about their incredible returns (which are, indeed, incredible). For years, Madoff had been well known in the investment community as someone who earned implausibly steady returns, no matter the market conditions.

EXAM Strategy

Question: Zapper, Inc., hired the accounting firm PriceTouche to determine if building an apartment building was financially feasible. After PriceTouche determined that the building would be profitable, Zapper started construction. Before the structure was complete, it burned to the ground. Although Zapper rebuilt it, the apartment building turned out not to be profitable, at least in part because of the delay in construction. Is PriceTouche liable to Zapper?

Strategy: There are four potential bases for liability—contract, negligence, breach of trust, and violation of a fiduciary duty. Which apply here?

Result: If PriceTouche did not perform as carefully as an ordinarily prudent accountant would under the circumstances, then it has violated its contract with Zapper and would be liable under contract law. It would also be negligent. But it would only be liable if its negligence caused the harm. It might be that the apartment building was not profitable because of the delays caused when it burned down during construction. If this is the case, PriceTouche would not be liable for negligence. There is no breach of trust because it has not violated client confidentiality. It has not violated a fiduciary duty because there was no evidence that PriceTouche gave bad advice or that Zapper had placed exceptional trust in PriceTouche's advice.

LIABILITY TO THIRD PARTIES

No issue in the accounting field is more controversial than liability to third parties (those who are not clients, but nonetheless rely on audits). Plaintiffs argue that auditors owe an important duty to a trusting public. The job of the auditor, they say, is to provide an independent, professional source of assurance that a company's audited financial statements are accurate. If the auditors do their job properly, they have nothing to fear. The accounting profession says in response, however, that if everyone who has ever been harmed, even remotely, by a faulty audit can recover damages, there will soon be no auditors left.

Negligence

Accountants who fail to exercise due care are liable to (1) anyone they knew would rely on the information and (2) anyone else in the same class. Suppose, for example, that Adrienne knows she is preparing financial statements for the BeachBall Corp. to use in obtaining a bank loan from the First National Bank of Tucson. If Adrienne is careless in preparing the statements and BeachBall bursts, she will be liable to First Bank. Suppose, however, that the company takes its financial statements to the Last National Bank of Tucson instead. She would also be liable because Last Bank is in the same class as First Bank. Once Adrienne knows that a bank will rely on the statements she has prepared, the identity of the particular bank should not make any difference to her when doing her work.

Suppose, however, that BeachBall uses the financial statements to persuade a landlord to rent it a manufacturing facility. In this case, Adrienne would not be liable because the landlord is not in the same class as First Bank, for whom Adrienne knew she was preparing the documents.

In the following case, a potential employee relied on audited financial statements that proved to be faulty. Was the accounting firm liable?

ELLIS V. GRANT THORNTON

2008 U.S. App. Lexis 13379
United States Court of Appeals for the Fourth Circuit, 2008

CASE SUMMARY

Facts: For five years, the First National Bank of Keystone issued a lot of risky mortgage loans on which the borrowers defaulted. Keystone management also lied about the value of the loans. When the Office of the Comptroller of the Currency (OCC) first began to smell trouble, it required Keystone to hire a nationally recognized, independent accounting firm to audit its books. The bank hired Grant Thornton. Stan Quay was the lead partner on the account. On a theory of what can go wrong will go wrong, he was negligent in conducting the audit and failed to notice a discrepancy of $515 million between the reported and actual value of the loans.

As Quay was finishing his audit, the board began talking with Gary Ellis about becoming president of the bank. Ellis already had a perfectly good job, so he was understandably reluctant to move to a bank that the OCC was investigating. To reassure him, the Keystone board suggested he talk with Quay and look at the bank's financials. Quay told Ellis that Keystone would receive a clean, unqualified opinion.

Quay did ultimately issue a clean opinion reporting shareholder's equity of $184 million when, in fact, the bank was insolvent. The first page of the report stated: "This report is intended for the information and use of the Board of Directors and Management of The First National Bank of Keystone and its regulatory agencies and should not be used by third parties for any other purpose." A week later, the Board voted to hire Ellis, who then quit his job elsewhere to join Keystone.

Five months later, the OCC declared Keystone insolvent and shut it down. Ellis was out of work. He filed suit against Grant Thornton, seeking compensation for his lost wages. The district court ruled in favor of Ellis and granted him $2.5 million in damages. Grant Thornton appealed.

Issue: *Was Grant Thornton liable to Ellis for its negligence in preparing Keystone's financial statements?*

Decision: Grant Thornton was not liable.

Reasoning: Grant Thornton prepared its audit for the benefit of Keystone and the OCC. It did not know that Ellis, or any other potential employee, would be relying on the report. Keystone did not pay Grant Thornton to review the bank's financial position with potential employees and, indeed, the accountants did not know about Ellis's involvement until *after* it had decided to issue the clean opinion. Grant Thornton was not aware that it might be held liable for Ellis's lost wages. If the accountant is unaware of the risk, he cannot be held liable.

Fraud

Courts consider fraud to be much worse than negligence because it is *intentional*. Therefore, the penalty is heavier. **An accountant who commits fraud is liable to any foreseeable user of the work product who justifiably relied on it.** Take the example of TechDisk, a manufacturer of disk drives. Customers were buying disk drives faster than the company could make them. Afraid that the stock price would plummet if investors found out about the shortage, company officers helped their sales numbers by shipping out bricks wrapped up to look like disk drives. Company accountants altered the financial statements to pretend that the bricks were indeed computer parts. These accountants would be liable to any foreseeable users—including investors, creditors, and customers.

Securities Act of 1933

The Securities Act of 1933 (1933 Act) requires a company to register securities before offering them for sale to the public. To do this, the company files a registration statement with the SEC. This registration statement must include audited financial statements.

Auditors are liable for any important misstatement or omission in the financial statements that they prepare for a registration statement if the investors lose money.

The plaintiff must prove only that (1) the registration statement contained an important misstatement or omission and (2) she lost money. Ernst & Young served as the auditor for FP Investments, Inc., a company that sold tax shelter partnerships. These partnerships were formed to cultivate tropical plants in Hawaii. The prospectus for this investment neglected to mention that the partnerships did not have enough cash on hand to grow the plants. The investors lost their money. A jury ordered Ernst & Young to pay damages of $18.9 million.[6]

However, auditors can avoid liability by showing that they made a reasonable investigation of the financial statements in a registration statement. This investigation is called **due diligence**. Typically, auditors will not be liable if they can show that they complied with GAAP and GAAS.

Due diligence
An investigation of the registration statement.

Securities Exchange Act of 1934

Under the Securities Exchange Act of 1934 (1934 Act), public companies must file an annual report containing audited financial statements and quarterly reports with unaudited financials.

FRAUD

In these filings under the 1934 Act, an auditor is liable for making (1) a misstatement or omission of an important fact; (2) knowingly or recklessly; (3) that the plaintiff relies on in purchasing or selling a security. Note that accountants are liable only if they are know their statement is wrong or they are reckless in checking the accuracy of their reports. The following Landmark Case established these principles of liability.

---

[6]*Hayes v. Haushalter*, 1994 U.S. App. LEXIS 23608 (9th Cir. 1994).

Landmark Case

ERNST & ERNST V. HOCHFELDER

425 U.S. 185; 96 S. Ct. 1375; 1976 U.S. LEXIS 2
Supreme Court of the United States, 1976

CASE SUMMARY

Facts: For 19 years, Ernst & Ernst audited a small brokerage firm, First Securities Company of Chicago (First Securities). Leston B. Nay was president of the firm and owned 92 percent of its stock. He convinced some customers to invest funds in "escrow" accounts that would yield a high rate of return. And, indeed, from 1942 through 1966, they did. The investments were unusual in that the customers wrote their checks to Nay personally, not to First Securities. None of these escrow accounts appeared in First Securities' records.

As you perhaps have guessed, there were no escrow accounts. Nay was spending much of the customers' money on himself. The fraud came to light when he killed himself.

In investigating the fraud, customers discovered that Nay had had a rigid rule prohibiting anyone else from ever opening mail addressed to him, even if it arrived in his absence. The customers alleged that if Ernst had done a proper audit, they would have found out about this mail rule, which would have led to an investigation of Nay and discovery of the fraud.

The customers sued Ernst under the 1934 Act. The accounting firm filed a motion for summary judgment, alleging that liability under this statute requires **scienter;** that is, an intent to deceive, manipulate, or defraud. Ernst admitted that it had been negligent but denied any *intentional* wrongdoing. The trial court granted Ernst's motion, the Court of Appeals reversed, and the Supreme Court granted *certiorari.*

Issue: *Was Ernst liable under the 1934 Act when it acted negligently but not intentionally?*

Decision: Liability under the 1934 Act requires scienter. Ernst was not liable.

Reasoning: The language of the statute prohibits the use or employment of "any manipulative or deceptive device or contrivance." These words indicate that the goal of the statute was to prohibit intentional misconduct.

A look at the legislative history of the statute confirms this interpretation. A spokesman for the drafters interpreted this provision thus: "Thou shalt not devise any cunning devices." It is difficult to believe that any lawyer or legislator would use these words if the intent was to create liability for merely negligent acts or omissions.

WHISTLEBLOWING

Auditors who suspect that a client has committed an illegal act must notify the client's board of directors. If the board fails to take appropriate action, the auditors must issue an official report to the board. If the board receives such a report from its auditors, it must notify the SEC within one business day (and send a copy of this notice to its accountant). If the auditors do not receive this copy, they must notify the SEC themselves.

JOINT AND SEVERAL LIABILITY

Traditionally, liability under the 1934 Act was joint and several. When several different participants were potentially liable, a plaintiff could sue any one defendant or any group of defendants for the full amount of the damages. If a company committed fraud and then went bankrupt, its accounting firm might well be the only defendant with assets. Even if the accountants had caused only, say, 5 percent of the damages, they could be liable for the full amount.

Congress amended the 1934 Act to provide that accountants are **liable *jointly and severally*** only if they *knowingly* violate the law. Otherwise, the defendants are *proportionately* liable, meaning that they are liable only for the share of the damages that they themselves caused.

Joint and several liability
All members of a group are liable. They can be sued as a group, or any of them can be sued individually for the full amount owing. But the plaintiff may not recover more than 100 percent of her damages.

CRIMINAL LIABILITY

Some violations by accountants are criminal acts for which the punishment may be a fine and imprisonment:

- The Justice Department has the right to prosecute **wilful violations** under either the 1933 Act or the 1934 Act.

- The Internal Revenue Code imposes various criminal penalties on accountants for **wrongdoing in the preparation of tax returns.**

- Many states prosecute violations of their securities laws.

<table>
<tr><td>

EXAM **Strategy**

Question: When Benjamin hired Howard to prepare financial statements for American Equities, he gave Howard a handwritten sheet of paper entitled "Pro Forma Balance Sheet." It contained a list of real estate holdings and the balance sheets of two corporations that Benjamin claimed were owned by American Equities. From this one piece of paper, without any examination of books and records, Howard prepared an Auditor's Report for the company. Benjamin used the Auditor's Report to sell stock in American Equities. Has Howard committed a criminal offense?

Strategy: Willful violations of the securities laws are criminal offenses.

Result: A court held that Howard's actions were willful. He was found guilty of a criminal violation.

</td></tr>
</table>

OTHER ACCOUNTANT-CLIENT ISSUES

The Accountant-Client Relationship

The SEC has long been concerned about the relationship between accountants and the companies they audit. Its rules require accountants to maintain independence from their clients. **For example, an auditor or her family must not maintain a financial or business relationship with the client.**

SEC rules on independence specifically prohibit accountants or their families from owning stock in a company that their firm audits. To take one woeful example, the SEC discovered that most of PricewaterhouseCoopers's partners were in violation of this rule, including half of the partners who were charged with enforcing it. Even worse, the firm had been caught violating the same rule only a few years before. The SEC notified 52 of the firm's clients that there were potential concerns about the integrity of their financial statements and even requested that some of the companies select a new auditor.

SEC rules of practice specify that an accountant who engages in "unethical or improper professional conduct" may be banned from practice before the SEC. Auditors who are banned or suspended cannot perform the audits that are required by the 1933 and 1934 Acts—quite a professional blow.

Accountant-Client Privilege

Traditionally, an accountant-client privilege did not exist under federal law. Accountants were under no obligation to keep confidential any information they received from their clients. In one notorious case, the IRS suspected that the owner of a chain of pizza parlors was underreporting his income. The agency persuaded the owner's certified public accountant, James Checksfield, to spy on him for eight years. (The IRS agreed to drop charges against Checksfield, who had not paid his own taxes for three years.) Thanks to the information that Checksfield passed to the IRS, his client was indicted on criminal charges of evading taxes.

Congress passed the Internal Revenue Service Restructuring and Reform Act to reduce IRS abuse of taxpayers. This statute provides limited protection for tax advice that accountants give their clients. That is the good news. The bad news is the word *limited*. **This privilege applies only in civil cases involving the IRS or the U.S. government.** It does not apply to criminal cases, civil cases not involving the U.S. government, or cases with other federal agencies such as the SEC, nor does it apply to advice about tax shelters. Thus, for example, this new accountant-client privilege would not have protected Checksfield's client because he was charged with a criminal offense.

Working Papers

When working for a client, accountants use the client's own documents and also prepare working papers of their own—notes, memoranda, and research. In theory, each party owns whatever it has prepared itself. Thus, accountants own the working papers they have created. In practice, however, the client controls even the accountant's working papers. **The accountant (1) cannot show the working papers to anyone without the client's permission (or a valid court order); and (2) must allow the client access to the working papers.** Under the Sarbanes-Oxley Act, accountants for public companies must keep all audit work papers for at least seven years.

Chapter Conclusion

Accountants serve many masters and, therefore, face numerous potential conflicts. Clients, third parties, and the government all rely on their work. The wrong decision may destroy the client, impoverish its shareholders, and subject its auditors to substantial penalties.

Exam Review

1. **SOX**   The Sarbanes-Oxley Act:

   - Establishes the Public Company Accounting Oversight Board (PCAOB);

   - Requires an accounting firm to make regular and complete reports to the audit committees of its clients;

   - Prohibits accounting firms that audit public companies from providing consulting services to those companies on certain topics, such as bookkeeping, financial information systems, human resources, and legal issues (unrelated to the audit);

   - Prohibits an accounting firm from auditing a company if one of the company's top officers has worked for the firm within the last year and was involved in the company's audit; and

   - Provides that a lead audit partner cannot work for a client in any auditing role for more than five years at a time. (pp. 431–432)

2. **LIABILITY TO CLIENTS FOR NEGLIGENCE**   Accountants are liable to their clients for negligence if:

   - They breach their duty to their clients by failing to exercise the degree of skill and competence that an ordinarily prudent accountant would under the circumstances; and

   - The violation of this duty causes harm to the client. (pp. 432–433)

CPA Question: A CPA's duty of due care to a client most likely will be breached when a CPA:

(a) Gives a client an oral instead of a written report

(b) Gives a client incorrect advice based on an honest error judgment

(c) Fails to give tax advice that saves the client money

(d) Fails to follow generally accepted auditing standards

Strategy: Accountants are not liable for every error they make, only if they fail to act like an ordinarily prudent accountant. (See the "Result" at the end of this section.)

3. **LIABILITY TO CLIENTS FOR COMMON LAW FRAUD** Accountants are liable for fraud if:

- They make a false statement of a material fact;

- They know it is not true or recklessly disregard the truth;

- The client justifiably relies on the statement; and

- The reliance results in damages. (p. 433)

4. **BREACH OF TRUST** Accountants have a legal obligation to:

- Keep all client information confidential; and

- Use client information only for the benefit of the client. (pp. 433–434)

5. **FIDUCIARY DUTY** As a general rule, accountants do *not* have a fiduciary duty to their clients. However, accountants sometimes take on responsibilities that extend beyond the typical scope of an accountant-client relationship, such as when they serve as a financial advisor. In these situations, they may have a fiduciary duty. (p. 434)

6. **LIABILITY TO THIRD PARTIES FOR NEGLIGENCE** Accountants who fail to exercise due care are liable to (1) any third party they knew would rely on the information; and (2) anyone else in the same class. (pp. 435–436)

7. **LIABILITY TO THIRD PARTIES FOR FRAUD** An accountant who commits fraud is liable to any foreseeable user of the work product who justifiably relies on it. (p. 436)

Question: When Jeff told one of the general partners of the Edge Energies limited partnerships that he did not wish to invest in these ventures, the general partner suggested he call Jackson, the partnerships' accountant. Jackson told Jeff that these partnerships were a "good deal," that they were "good moneymakers," and "they were expecting something like a two-year payoff." In fact, Jackson knew that the operators were mismanaging these ventures and that the partnerships were bad investments. Jeff relied on Jackson's recommendation and invested in Edge Energies. He subsequently lost his entire investment. Is Jackson liable to Jeff?

Strategy: Whenever there is intentional wrongdoing, think fraud. (See the "Result" at the end of this section.)

8. **SECURITIES ACT OF 1933**   Auditors are liable for any important misstatement or omission in the financial statements that they provide for a registration statement if investors lose money. (pp. 436–437)

9. **SECURITIES EXCHANGE ACT OF 1934**   Under the 1934 Act, an auditor is liable for making (1) any misstatement or omission of a material fact in financial statements; (2) knowingly or recklessly; (3) that the plaintiff relies on in purchasing or selling a security. (pp. 437–438)

10. **WHISTLEBLOWING**   Auditors who suspect that a client has committed an illegal act must notify the client's board of directors. (p. 438)

11. **JOINT AND SEVERAL LIABILITY**   Under the 1934 Act, accountants are liable jointly and severally only if they knowingly violate the law. Otherwise, they are proportionately liable. (p. 438)

12. **CRIMINAL LIABILITY**   The Justice Department has the right to prosecute willful violations under either the 1933 Act or the 1934 Act. The Internal Revenue Code imposes various criminal penalties on accountants for wrongdoing in the preparation of tax returns. (pp. 438–439)

13. **AUDITOR INDEPENDENCE**   Public accountants or their families may not own stock in a company that their firm audits. (p. 439)

14. **ACCOUNTANT-CLIENT PRIVILEGE**   A *limited* accountant-client privilege exists under federal law. (pp. 439–440)

15. **WORKING PAPERS**   An accountant cannot show working papers to anyone without the client's permission (or a valid court order); and must allow the client access to the working papers. (p. 440)

> **2. Result:**   The correct answer is (d) because an ordinarily prudent accountant follows GAAS.
>
> **7. Result:**   Jackson was liable to Jeff for fraud because Jeff was a foreseeable user of the information and justifiably relied on it.

Matching Questions

Match the following terms with their definitions:

___A. GAAS

___B. Tracing

___C. Qualified opinion

___D. GAAP

___E. Vouching

___F. Unqualified opinion

1. Rules for preparing financial statements
2. When accountants check backward to ensure there are data to support a transaction
3. Clean opinion
4. Rules for conducting audits
5. When accountants check a transaction forward to ensure it has been properly recorded
6. When there is some uncertainty in the financial statements

TRUE/FALSE QUESTIONS

Circle true or false:

1. T F Auditors are liable under the 1933 Act only if they intentionally misrepresent financial statements.
2. T F Auditors generally are not liable if they follow GAAP and GAAS.
3. T F Under the 1934 Act, accountants are liable for negligent behavior.
4. T F If auditors discover that company officers have committed an illegal act, they must report this wrongdoing to the SEC.
5. T F Under federal law, accounting firms may not provide any consulting services to companies that they audit.

MULTIPLE-CHOICE QUESTIONS

1. To be successful in a suit under the Securities Act of 1933, the plaintiff must prove

	Important Mistake in the Registration Statement	**Plaintiff Lost Money**
A.	No	Yes
B.	No	No
C.	Yes	No
D.	Yes	Yes

2. An accountant is liable to a client for conducting an audit negligently if the accountant:
   (a) Acted with intent
   (b) Was a fiduciary of the client
   (c) Failed to exercise due care
   (d) Executed an engagement letter

3. Which of the following statements about Sarbanes-Oxley is *not* true?
   (a) All accounting firms that audit public companies must register with the PCAOB.
   (b) Auditors must report to the CEO of the company they are auditing.
   (c) Auditing firms cannot base their employees' compensation on sales of consulting services to clients.
   (d) An accounting firm cannot audit a company if one of the client's top officers has worked for that firm within the prior year and was involved in the company's audit.
   (e) Every five years, the lead audit partner must rotate off an audit account.

4. For a client to prove a case of fraud against an accountant, the following element is *not* required:

   (a) The client lost money.

   (b) The accountant made a false statement of fact.

   (c) The client relied on the false statement.

   (d) The accountant knew the statement was false.

   (e) The accountant was reckless.

5. Dusty is trying to buy an office building to house his growing consulting firm. When Luke, a landlord, asks to see a set of financials, Dusty asks his accountant, Ellen, to prepare a set for Luke. Dusty shows these financials to a number of landlords, including Carter. Dusty rents from Carter. Ellen has been careless, and the financials are inaccurate. Dusty cannot pay his rent, and Carter files suit against Ellen. Which of the following statements is true?

   (a) Carter will win because Ellen was careless.

   (b) Carter will win because Ellen was careless and she knew that landlords would see the financials.

   (c) Carter will lose because Ellen did not know that he would see the financials.

   (d) Carter will lose because he had no contract with Ellen.

6. Ted prepared fraudulent financial statements for the Arbor Corp. Lacy read these statements before purchasing stock in the company. When Arbor goes bankrupt, Lacy sues Ted.

   (a) Lacy will win because it was foreseeable that she would rely on these statements.

   (b) Lacy will win because Ted was negligent.

   (c) Lacy will lose because she did not rely on these statements.

   (d) Lacy will lose because it was not foreseeable that she would rely on these statements.

ESSAY QUESTIONS

1. After reviewing Color-Dyne's audited financial statements, the plaintiffs provided materials to the company on credit. These financial statements showed that Color-Dyne owned $2 million in inventory. The audit failed to reveal, however, that the company had loans outstanding on all of this inventory. The accountant did not know that the company intended to give the financial statements to plaintiffs or any other creditors. Color-Dyne went bankrupt. Is the accountant liable to plaintiffs?

2. James and Penelope Monroe purchased securities offered by Hughes Homes, Inc., a retailer of manufactured housing in Tacoma, Washington. During its audit, Deloitte & Touche found that Hughes Homes' internal controls had flaws. As a result, the accounting firm adjusted the scope of its audit to perform independent testing to verify the accuracy of the company's financial records. Satisfied that the internal controls were functional, Deloitte issued a clean opinion. After Hughes Homes went bankrupt, the Monroes sued Deloitte for violating the 1933 Act. They alleged that Deloitte's failure to disclose that it had found flaws in Hughes's internal control system was a material omission. GAAS did not require disclosure. Is Deloitte liable?

3. The British Broadcasting Corp. (BBC) broadcast a TV program alleging that Terry Venables, a former professional soccer coach, had fraudulently obtained a £1 million loan by misrepresenting the value of his company. Venables had been a sportscaster for the BBC but had switched to a competing network. The source of the BBC's story was "confidential working papers" from Venables's accountant. According to the accountant, the papers had been stolen. Who owns these working papers? Does the accountant have the right to disclose the content of working papers?

4. Medtrans, an ambulance company, was unable to pay its bills. In need of cash, it signed an engagement letter with Deloitte & Touche to perform an audit that could be used to attract investors. Unfortunately, the audit had the opposite effect. The unaudited statements showed earnings of $1.9 million, but the accountants calculated that the company had actually lost about $500,000. While in the process of negotiating adjustments to the financials, Deloitte resigned. Some time passed before Medtrans found another auditor, and, in that interim, a potential investor withdrew its $10 million offer. Is Deloitte liable for breach of contract?

5. A partnership of doctors in Billings, Montana, sought to build a larger office building. It decided to finance this project using industrial revenue bonds under a complex provision of the Internal Revenue Code. It hired Peat Marwick to do the required financial work. The deal was all set to close when it was discovered that the accountants had made an error in structuring the deal. As a result, the partnership was forced to pay a significantly higher rate of interest. When the partnership sued Peat for breach of contract, the accounting firm asked the court to dismiss the claim on the grounds that the client could only sue in tort. Peat argued that it had performed its duties under the contract. The statute of limitations had expired for a tort case, but not for a contract case. Should the doctors' case be dismissed?

DISCUSSION QUESTIONS

1. Accountants do not have a fiduciary duty to their clients when performing accounting services. Why not?

2. **ETHICS** Pete, an accountant, recommended that several of his clients invest in Competition Aircraft. These clients passed this recommendation on to Arlene, who did invest. Unfortunately, Competition was a fraudulent company that pretended to sell airplanes. After the company went bankrupt, she sought to recover from Pete. Is Pete liable to Arlene? Whether or not Pete faces legal liability, is it a good idea for accountants to recommend investments to clients? Does that practice create any potential conflicts of interest?

3. Should the IFRS be adopted in the United States? What result would be best for companies? For investors?

4. Are the SOX rules on consulting services sufficiently strict? Should auditing firms be prohibited from performing *any* consulting services to companies that they audit?

5. Some argue that investors have unrealistic expectations about what an audit can accomplish, especially at the prices companies are willing to pay their accountants. Critics respond that this view is just another way of saying: "Given how much money firms want to earn each year, they may not spend as much time as they should on an audit, especially in a complex situation." Arthur Andersen got in trouble, in part, because of its desire to maintain high levels of profitability. Should the government create new regulations for audits, or are current rules sufficient?

Property and Consumer Law

CHAPTER 25

CONSUMER LAW

Three women signed up for a lesson at the Arthur Murray dance studio in Washington, D.C. Expecting a session of quiet fun, they instead found themselves in a nightmare of humiliation and coercion:

- I tried to say no and get out of it and I got very, very upset because I got frightened at paying out all that money and having nothing to fall back on. I remember I started crying and couldn't stop crying. All I thought of was getting out of there. So finally after—I don't know how much time, Mr. Mara said, well, I could sign up for 250 hours, which was half the 500 Club, which would amount to $4,300. So I finally signed it. After that, I tried to raise the money from the bank and found I couldn't get a loan for that amount and I didn't have any savings and I had to get a bank loan to pay for it. That was when I went back and asked him to cancel that contract. But Mr. Mara said that he couldn't cancel it.

> I started crying and couldn't stop crying. All I thought of was getting out of there.

- I did not wish to join the carnival, and while it was only an additional $55, I had no desire to join. [My instructor] asked everyone in the room to sit down in a circle around me and he stood me up in that circle, in the middle of the circle, and said, "Everybody, I want you to look at this woman here who is too cheap to join the carnival. I just want you to look at a woman like that. Isn't it awful?"

Because of abuses such as these, the Federal Trade Commission (FTC) ordered the Arthur Murray dance studio to halt its high-pressure sales techniques, limit each contract to no more than $1,500 in dance lessons, and permit all contracts to be canceled within seven days.[1]

---

[1] *In re Arthur Murray Studio of Washington, Inc.*, 78 F.T.C. 401, 1971 FTC LEXIS 75 (1971).

© Steve Allen/Jupiterimages

INTRODUCTION

Years ago, consumers typically dealt with merchants they knew well. A dance instructor in a small town would not stay in business long if he tormented his elderly clients. As the population of the country grew and cities expanded, however, merchants became less and less subject to community pressure. The law has supplemented, if not replaced, these informal policing mechanisms. Both Congress and the states have passed statutes that protect consumers. But the legal system is generally too slow and expensive to handle small cases. The women who fell into the web of Arthur Murray had neither the wealth nor the energy to sue the studio themselves. To aid consumers such as these, Congress empowered federal agencies to enforce consumer laws. The FTC is the most important of these agencies. In addition, Congress recently created the Consumer Financial Protection Bureau (CFPB) to regulate consumer financial products and services, including mortgages, credit cards, and private student loans.

SALES

Section 5 of the Federal Trade Commission Act (FTC Act) prohibits "unfair and deceptive acts or practices."

Deceptive Acts or Practices

Many deceptive acts or practices involve advertisements. **Under the FTC Act, an advertisement is deceptive if it contains an important misrepresentation or omission that is likely to mislead a reasonable consumer.** Nestlé sold a drink called Boost Kid Essentials, which contained probiotics—good bacteria that aid digestion and fight bad germs. But Nestlé claimed that Boost would prevent children from getting sick or missing school, assertions for which the company had no evidence. In a settlement with the FTC, Nestlé promised to stop making such claims.

In the following case, the court discussed the type of scientific evidence required to support health claims.

FEDERAL TRADE COMMISSION v. DIRECT MARKETING CONCEPTS, INC.

624 F.3d 1; 2010 U.S. App. LEXIS 21743
United States Court of Appeals for the First Circuit, 2010

CASE SUMMARY

Facts: Direct Marketing Concepts, Inc. broadcast an infomercial for Coral Calcium that featured a spokesperson named Robert Barefoot. In the ad, his claims were as bare as his feet. He asserted that these pills could cure virtually all diseases, including heart disease, cancer, lupus, multiple sclerosis, and Parkinson's. To bolster these claims, Barefoot cited unspecified articles from prominent medical journals.

During an 18-month period, this infomercial generated $54 million in sales.

The FTC filed suit against the company and Barefoot, alleging that the infomercials were deceptive. The trial court granted the FTC's motion for summary judgment, ruling that the infomercials were misleading as a matter of law and, therefore, there was no need for a trial. The defendants appealed.

Issue: *Were the infomercials misleading as a matter of law?*

Decision: Yes, the infomercials were misleading and no trial was needed.

Reasoning: To make claims such as these, the defendants must have some scientific evidence. But medical experts for the FTC testified that there is no evidence that calcium cures any of the diseases listed in the infomercial. Nor have there ever been any articles in serious medical journals that would support such claims.

The only evidence for these infomercials are excerpts from Barefoot's books, his deposition testimony, and some popular science and pseudoscientific articles, which include references to magazines such as *Reader's Digest*. But none of these sources (other than his own writings) support Barefoot's claims. Therefore, the defendant has engaged in deceptive advertising as a matter of law.

The defendants also allege that the claims were nothing but puffery and that the disclaimers in the ads were sufficient to defeat a deceptive advertising claim. However, specific and measurable claims are not puffery. And the only disclaimer was the notice that the ads were paid advertising.

Unfair Practices

The FTC Act also prohibits unfair acts or practices. For example, a furnace repair company dismantled home furnaces for "inspection" and then refused to reassemble them until the consumers agreed to buy services or replacement parts.

Bait and Switch

Bait and switch
A practice where sellers advertise products that are not generally available but are being used to draw interested parties in so that they will buy other items.

FTC rules prohibit bait and switch advertisements: A merchant may not advertise a product and then disparage it to consumers in an effort to sell a different (more expensive) item. In addition, merchants must have enough stock on hand to meet reasonable demand for any advertised product.

Seven websites, such as Best Price Photo and 86th Street Photo, engaged in a classic bait-and-switch operation. They advertised products at a much lower price than competitors. That was the **bait**—an alluring offer that is too good to be true. Once a customer placed an order, the company tried to sell an upgraded product at a much higher price. That is the **switch**. The real purpose of the advertisement was simply to find customers who were interested in buying. If customers refused the new item, they would be told that the original product was backordered and the sale was cancelled. This practice violated FTC rules.

Merchandise Bought by Mail, Telephone, or Online

The FTC has established the following guidelines on merchandise bought by mail, telephone, or online:

- Sellers must ship an item within the time stated or, if no time is given, within 30 days after receipt of the order.

- If a company cannot ship the product when promised, it must send the customer a notice with the new shipping date and an opportunity to cancel. If the new shipping date is within 30 days of the original one, and the customer does not cancel, the order is still valid.

- If the company cannot ship by the second shipment date it must send the customer another notice. This time, however, the company must cancel the order unless the customer returns the notice, indicating that he still wants the item.

Staples, Inc., violated these FTC rules when it told customers that they were viewing "real-time" inventory and that products would be delivered in one day, even on weekends.

In fact, the website was not updated in real time and one-day delivery only applied to customers who lived within 20 miles of a Staples store and never happened on weekends. The company paid a fine of $850,000 to settle these charges.

Telemarketing

The telephone rings: "Could I speak with Alexander Johannson? This is Denise from Master Chimney Sweeps." It is 7:30 p.m.; you have just straggled in from work and are looking forward to a peaceful dinner of takeout cuisine. You are known as Sandy, your last name is pronounced Yohannson, and you live in a modern apartment without a chimney. A telemarketer has struck again! What can you do to protect your peace and quiet?

The FTC prohibits telemarketers from calling any telephone number listed on its do-not-call registry. You can register your home and cell numbers with the FTC online or by telephone at (888) 382-1222. FTC rules also prohibit telemarketers from blocking their names and telephone numbers on Caller ID systems. In addition, robocalls (prerecorded commercial telemarketing calls) from a machine are illegal unless the telemarketer obtains written permission from the person being called. You can file a complaint by going to the **ftc.gov** website.

Unordered Merchandise

Under §5 of the FTC Act, anyone who receives unordered merchandise in the mail can treat it as a gift. She can use it, throw it away, or do whatever else she wants with it.

There you are, watching an infomercial for Anushka products, guaranteed to fight that scourge of modern life—cellulite! Rushing to your phone, you place an order. The Anushka cosmetics arrive, but for some odd reason, the cellulite remains. A month later another bottle arrives, like magic, in the mail. The magic spell is broken, however, when you get your credit card bill and see that, without your authorization, the company has charged you for the new supply of Anushka. This company was in violation of FTC rules because it did not notify customers that they were free to treat the unauthorized products as a gift, to use or throw out as they wished.[2]

Door-to-Door Sales

Consumers at home need special protection from salespeople. In a store, customers can simply walk out, but at home, they may feel trapped. **Under the FTC door-to-door rules, a salesperson is required to notify the buyer that she has the right to cancel the transaction prior to midnight of the third business day thereafter.** This notice must be given both orally and in writing; the actual cancellation must be in writing. The seller must return the buyer's money within 10 days.

EXAM Strategy

Question: Mantra Films sold "Girls Gone Wild" DVDs on the Internet. When customers ordered one DVD, the company would automatically enroll them in a "continuity program" and send them unordered DVDs each month on a "negative-option" basis, charging consumers' credit cards for each DVD until consumers took action to stop the shipments. Is Mantra's marketing plan legal?

---

[2]*In the Matter of Synchronal Corp.*, 116 F.T.C. 1189, 1993 FTC LEXIS 280 (1993).

Strategy: Review the various sales regulations—more than one is involved in this case.

Result: This marketing plan was deceptive because customers were not told that they would be enrolled in the continuity program. Also, Mantra could not legally bill for the unordered DVDs. Under the unordered merchandise rule, consumers had the right to treat them as gifts.

CONSUMER CREDIT

Most states limit the maximum interest rate a lender may charge consumers. These laws are called **usury statutes.** (Note, though, that usury laws typically do not apply to credit card debt, mortgages, consumer leases, or commercial loans.) The penalty for violating usury statutes varies among the states. Depending upon the jurisdiction, the borrower may be allowed to keep (1) the interest above the usury limit; (2) all of the interest; or (3) all of the loan and the interest.

Truth in Lending Act

The federal Truth in Lending Act (TILA) does not regulate interest rates or the terms of a loan; these are set by state law. It simply requires lenders to disclose the terms of a loan in an understandable and complete manner. Thus, credit card companies must still comply with TILA, even though they are not governed by state usury statutes.

Under TILA:

- *The disclosure must be clear and in a sensible order.* A finance company violated TILA when it loaned money to Dorothy Allen. The company made all the required disclosures but scattered them throughout the loan document and intermixed them with confusing terms that were not required by TILA.[3]

- *The lender must disclose the finance charge.* The finance charge is the amount, in dollars, the consumer will pay in interest and fees over the life of the loan.

- *The creditor must disclose the annual percentage rate (APR).* This number is the actual rate of interest the consumer pays on an annual basis. Without this disclosure, it would be easy in a short-term loan to disguise a very high APR because the finance charge is low. Boris borrows $5 for lunch from his employer's credit union. Under the terms of the loan, he must repay $6 the following week. His finance charge is only $1, but his APR is astronomical—20 percent per week—which is over 1,000 percent for a year.

Home Mortgage Loans

TILA prohibits unfair, abusive, or deceptive home mortgage lending practices. Under TILA (as amended by the Dodd-Frank Wall Street Reform and Consumer Protection Act), lenders:

- Must make a good faith effort to determine whether a borrower can afford to repay the loan. (Do lenders really have to be told this? History indicates that they do.)

---

[3]*Allen v. Beneficial Fin. Co. of Gary,* 531 F.2d 797, 1976 U.S. App. LEXIS 12935 (7th Cir. 1976).

- May not coerce or bribe an appraiser into misstating a home's value.

- Cannot charge prepayment penalties on adjustable rate mortgages.

These statutes also regulate so-called **subprime loans** (also known as *higher-priced mortgage loans*). These are loans that have an above-market interest rate because they involve high-risk borrowers.[4] For subprime loans, a lender:

Subprime loan
A loan that has an above-market interest rate because the borrower is high-risk.

- May not make loans that have balloon payments (very large payments at the end of the loan term), and

- May not charge excessive late fees.

Credit Cards

BILL PAYMENT

During the economic crisis that began in 2008, many consumers struggled to pay their credit card bills. In response, Congress increased oversight of credit card companies. Under the new rules, these companies:

- Cannot increase the interest rate, fees, or charges on balances a consumer has already run up unless she is more than 60 days late in making the minimum payment.

- Must give 45 days' notice before increasing a card's APR.

- Cannot charge late payment fees of more than $25 (unless one of the consumer's last six payments was late, in which case the fee may be up to $35).

- Cannot charge late fees that are greater than the minimum payment owed.

- Cannot charge interest on fees or on a bill that is paid on time or during a grace period.

- Must apply any payments to whichever debt on the card has the highest interest rate (say, a cash advance rather than a new purchase).

- Must offer consumers the right to set a fixed credit limit. Consumers cannot be charged a fee if the company accepts charges above that limit unless the consumer has agreed to the fee.

- Cannot issue credit cards to people under 21 unless the young person has income or the application is co-signed by someone who can afford to pay the bills, such as a parent or spouse.

Ethics Each of the rules in this section was aimed at eliminating existing abuses. Should Congress really have to tell credit card companies that they cannot charge interest and fees on a bill that is paid on time? What Life Principles might the employees of credit card companies use when setting policies?

---

[4]In the official definition, subprime loans are first mortgages that have an APR 1.5 percentage points or more above the average prime offer rate or second mortgages that have an APR 3.5 percentage points or more above that index.

STOLEN CARDS

Your wallet is missing, and with it your cash, your driver's license, a photo of your dog, a Groupon, and—oh! no!—all your credit cards! It is a disaster, to be sure. But it could have been worse. There was a time when you would have been responsible for every charge a thief rang up. **Now, under TILA, you are liable only for the first $50 in charges the thief makes before you notify the credit card company.** If you call the company before any charges are made, you have no liability at all. But if, by the time you contact the company, a speedy robber has completely furnished her apartment on your card, you are still liable only for $50.

DISPUTES WITH MERCHANTS

You use your credit card to buy a new tablet at ShadyComputers, but when you take it out of the box, it will not even turn on. You have a major problem with a $600 price tag. But all is not lost. **In the event of a dispute between a customer and a merchant, the credit card company cannot bill the customer if** (1) she makes a good faith effort to resolve the dispute, (2) the dispute is for more than $50, and (3) the merchant is in the same state where she lives or is within 100 miles of her house. These are the circumstances under which a credit card company *cannot* bill customers, but most *will not* seek payment from cardholders who seem to have a reasonable claim against a merchant.

DISPUTES WITH THE CREDIT CARD COMPANY

Is there anyone in America who has not sometime or other discovered an error in a credit card bill? Before Congress passed the Fair Credit Billing Act (FCBA), a dispute with a credit card company often deteriorated into an avalanche of threatening form letters that ignored any response from the hapless cardholder. But under the FCBA:

- If, within 60 days of receipt of a bill, a consumer writes to a credit card company to complain about the bill, the company must acknowledge receipt of the complaint within 30 days.

- Within two billing cycles (but no more than 90 days), the credit card company must investigate the complaint and respond.

- The credit card company cannot try to collect the disputed debt or close or suspend the account until it has responded to the consumer complaint.

- The credit card company cannot report to credit agencies that the consumer has an unpaid bill until 10 days after the response. If the consumer still disputes the charge, the credit card company may report the amount to a credit agency but must disclose that it is disputed.

> **Debit cards look and feel like credit cards, but legally they are a different plastic altogether.**

Debit Cards

STOLEN CARDS

So your wallet is missing, and with it your *debit* card. No problem—it is just like a credit card, right? Wrong. Debit cards look and feel like credit cards, but legally they are a different plastic altogether. Debit cards work like checks (which is why they are also called **check cards**). When you use your debit card, the bank deducts money directly from your account, which means there is no bill to pay at the end of the month (and no interest charges on unpaid bills). That is the good news.

The bad news is that your liability for a stolen debit card is much greater. If you report the loss before anyone uses your card, you are not liable for any unauthorized withdrawals. If you report the theft within two days of discovering it, the bank will make good on all losses above $50. If you wait until after two days, your bank will only replace stolen funds above $500. After 60 days of receipt of your bank statement, all losses are yours: the bank will not repay any stolen funds.

FEES

Many people like to use debit cards to help keep track of their spending and to avoid paying the interest rates on credit cards. However, traditionally there was a large downside to debit cards: banks would charge a flat fee of $20 to $30 *each time* cardholders overdrew their bank account, no matter how small the overdraft. A customer could easily be charged $150 in fees on $50 worth of overdrafts. Suppose that someone makes a $20 overdraft that he repays in two weeks, but in the meantime, he incurs a $27 fee. He has paid an interest rate of 3,520 percent.

Under new rules, though, banks are not allowed to overdraw an account and charge the fee unless the consumer signs up for an overdraft plan. Of course, this rule means that consumers who do not "opt in" to the overdraft plan will not be able to overdraw their account, no matter how desperate they are. (The same rule applies to ATM withdrawals.)

Credit Reports

Most adults rely on credit— to acquire a house, credit cards, overdraft privileges at the bank, or even obtain a job or rent an apartment. A number of statutes, including the Fair Credit Reporting Act (FCRA) and the Fair and Accurate Credit Transactions Act (FACTA), regulate credit reports. Consumer reporting agencies are businesses that supply consumer reports to third parties such as credit card companies, banks, and employers.

Under the FCRA:

- A consumer report can be used only for a legitimate business need.

- A consumer reporting agency cannot report information that is more than 7 years old. (In the case of bankruptcies, the limit is 10 years.)

- An employer cannot request a consumer report on an employee or potential employee without the employee's permission.

- Anyone who penalizes a consumer because of a credit report must reveal the name and address of the reporting agency that supplied the information.

- Upon request from a consumer, a reporting agency must disclose all information in his file.

- If a consumer tells an agency that some of the information in his file is incorrect, the agency must investigate. The consumer also has the right to give the agency a short report telling his side of the story.

FACTA also created the National Fraud Alert System, which permits consumers who fear they may be the victim of identity theft to place an alert in their credit files, warning financial institutions to investigate carefully before issuing any new credit.

Under FACTA, consumers are entitled by law to one free credit report every year from each of the three major reporting agencies: Equifax, Experian, and TransUnion. You can order these reports at **https://www.annualcreditreport.com**.

Although your credit report is valuable information, you do not know how creditors will evaluate it. For that, you need to know your credit score (usually called a FICO score).[5] This

---

[5]It is called a FICO score because it was developed by the Fair Isaac Corporation.

number (which ranges between 300 and 850) is based on your credit report and is supposed to predict your ability to pay your bills. However, it is not automatically included as part of your credit report. But now, anyone who penalizes you because of your score has to give it to you for free, as well as information about how your score compares with others.

Debt Collection

Debt collectors can be ruthless in tracking down their victims. Their practices can even disrupt Super Bowl Sunday. Debt collectors seek to catch their prey off guard, and what better time than when the entire nation is at home, glued to the television? If the phone rings, sports fans assume it is a friend calling to gab about the game. Congress passed the Fair Debt Collection Practices Act (FDCPA) because it was concerned that abusive practices could contribute to the number of personal bankruptcies, to marital instability, to the loss of jobs, and to invasions of privacy.

This statute provides that a collector must, within five days of contacting a debtor, send the debtor a written notice containing the amount of the debt, the name of the creditor to whom the debt is owed, and a statement that if the debtor disputes the debt (in writing), the collector will cease all collection efforts until it has sent evidence of the debt.

Under the FDCPA, collectors may *not*:

- Call or write a debtor who has notified the collector in writing that he wishes no further contact;

- Call or write a debtor who is represented by an attorney;

- Call a debtor before 8 a.m. or after 9 p.m.;

- Threaten a debtor or use obscene or abusive language;

- Call or visit the debtor at work if the consumer's employer prohibits such contact;

- Threaten to arrest consumers who do not pay their debts;

- Make other false or deceptive threats; that is, threats that would be illegal if carried out or which the collector has no intention of doing—such as suing the debtor or seizing property;

- Contact acquaintances of the debtor for any reason other than to locate the debtor (and then only once); or

- Tell acquaintances that the consumer is in debt.

For example, after Sherri Gradisher bounced a check for $81.30 at Doug Born's Smokehouse, she received three notices on the letterhead of the local sheriff's department threatening to arrest her. It turns out that the notices were sent by a private company, not by the sheriff's department (although the sheriff's department had given its permission to use its letterhead). These letters violated the FDCPA.[6]

Equal Credit Opportunity Act

The Equal Credit Opportunity Act (ECOA) prohibits any creditor from discriminating against a borrower because of race, color, religion, national origin, sex, marital status, age, or because the borrower is receiving welfare. A lender must respond to a credit application within 30 days. If a lender rejects an application, it must either tell the applicant why or notify him that he has the right to a written explanation of the reasons for this adverse action.

As the following case illustrates, the ECOA protects against a broad range of wrongdoing.

---

[6]*Gradisher v. Check Enforcement Unit, Inc.,* 2002 U.S. Dist. LEXIS 6003.

TREADWAY v. GATEWAY CHEVROLET OLDSMOBILE INC.

362 F.3d 971; 2004 U.S. App. LEXIS 6325
United States Court of Appeals for the Seventh Circuit, 2004

CASE SUMMARY

Facts: Gateway Chevrolet Oldsmobile, a car dealership, sent an unsolicited letter to Tonja Treadway notifying her that she was "pre-approved" for the financing to purchase a car. Gateway did not provide financing itself; instead, it arranged loans through banks or finance companies.

Treadway called the dealer to say that she was interested in purchasing a used car. With her permission, Gateway obtained her credit report. Based on this report, the dealer determined that Treadway was not eligible for financing. This was not surprising, given that Gateway had purchased Treadway's name from a list of people who had recently filed for bankruptcy.

Instead of applying for a loan on behalf of Treadway, Gateway told her that it had found a bank that would finance her transaction, but only if she purchased a new car and provided a co-signer. Treadway agreed to purchase a new car and came up with Pearlie Smith, her godmother, to serve as a co-signer.

Concerned as it was with customer convenience, Gateway had an agent deliver papers directly to Smith's house to be signed immediately. If Smith had read the papers before she signed them, she might have realized that she had committed herself to be the sole purchaser and owner of the car. But she had no idea that she was the owner until she began receiving bills on the car loan. After Treadway made the first payment on behalf of Smith, both women refused to pay more—Smith because she did not want a new car; Treadway because the car was

not hers. The car was repossessed, but the financing company continued to demand payment.

It turned out that Gateway was running a scam. The dealership would lure desperate prospects off the bankruptcy rolls and into the showroom with promises of financing for a used car, and then sell a new car to their "co-signer" (who was, in fact, the sole signer). Instead of selling a used car to Tonja Treadway, Gateway sold a new car to Pearlie Smith.

Treadway filed suit against Gateway, alleging that it had violated the ECOA by not notifying her that it had taken an adverse action against her.

Issue: *Did Gateway violate the ECOA?*

Decision: Yes, Gateway's action was an adverse action under the ECOA.

Reasoning: The ECOA requires any lender who rejects a loan application to tell the applicant the reason or notify her that she has the right to a written explanation.

By deciding not to send Treadway's application to *any* lender, Gateway effectively rejected it. But because Gateway did not tell customers that it had done the rejecting, they would naturally assume that a bank or other lender had turned them down. If the dealership's role was secret, it would have no accountability—it could discriminate against any and all without getting caught. Gateway could simply throw the credit report of every minority applicant in the "circular file" and none would be the wiser.

EXAM Strategy

Question: Clyde goes into a Tesla dealership to investigate buying an electric sports car. He does not look as if he can afford a six-figure purchase, so the sales staff order a credit report on him. After all, no point in wasting their time. Do they have the right to order a report on Clyde? Which consumer statute applies?

Strategy: The Fair Credit Reporting Act regulates the issuance of consumer reports. These reports can be used only for a legitimate business need.

> **Result:** Generally, a car dealership cannot obtain a consumer report on someone who simply asks general questions about prices and financing or who wants to test-drive a car. Nor can the dealer order a report to use in negotiations. So the Tesla dealership does not have the right to order a report on Clyde. However, a dealer does have the right to a report if it is needed to arrange financing requested by the consumer or to verify a buyer's creditworthiness when he presents a personal check to pay for the vehicle.

Consumer Leasing Act

The Consumer Leasing Act (CLA) applies to any lease up to $50,000, except for leases on real property (that is, on houses or apartments). The CLA is applied most often to car leases. **Before a lease is signed, a lessor must disclose the following in writing:**

- The number and amount of all required payments,

- The total amount the consumer will have paid by the end of the lease,

- Annual mileage allowance,

- Maintenance requirements and a description of the lessor's wear and use standards,

- The consumer's right to purchase the leased property and at what price, and

- The consumer's right to terminate a lease early.

MAGNUSON-MOSS WARRANTY ACT

The Magnuson-Moss Warranty Act does not require manufacturers or sellers to provide a warranty on their products. **The Act does require any supplier that offers a written warranty on a consumer product that costs more than $15 to disclose the terms of the warranty in simple, understandable language before the sale.** This statute only applies to written warranties on goods (not services) sold to consumers. It does cover sales by catalog or on the Internet. Required disclosure includes the following:

- The name and address of the person the consumer should contact to obtain warranty service.

- The parts that are covered and those that are not.

- What services the warrantor will provide, at whose expense, and for what period of time.

- A statement of what the consumer must do and what expenses he must pay.

Although suppliers are not required to offer a warranty, if they do offer one, they must indicate whether it is *full* or *limited*. Under a **full warranty,** the warrantor must promise to fix a defective product for a reasonable time without charge. If, after a reasonable number of efforts to fix the defective product, it still does not work, the consumer must have the right to a refund or a replacement without charge; but the warrantor is not required to cover damage caused by the consumer's unreasonable use.

CONSUMER PRODUCT SAFETY

In 1969, the federal government estimated that consumer products caused 30,000 deaths, 110,000 disabling injuries, and 20 million trips to the doctor. Toys were among the worst offenders, injuring 700,000 children a year. Children were cut by Etch-a-Sketch glass panels, choked by Zulu gun darts, and burned by Little Lady toy ovens. Although injured consumers had the right to seek damages under tort law, the goal of the Consumer Product Safety Act (CPSA) was to prevent injuries in the first place. This act created the Consumer Product Safety Commission (CPSC) to evaluate consumer products and develop safety standards. Manufacturers must report all potentially hazardous product defects to the CPSC within 24 hours of discovery. The Commission can impose civil and criminal penalties on those who violate its standards. Individuals have the right to sue under the CPSA for damages, including attorney's fees, from anyone who knowingly violates a consumer product safety rule. You can find out about product recalls or file a report on an unsafe product at the Commission's website or at **saferproducts.gov.**

Ethics Defective toys are an obvious source of concern because their victims are so helpless. Mattel's Jeep Wrangler Power Wheels toys were used by children as young as two years old. Thousands of these toys had defective wiring, and over 150 of them caught on fire. Mattel ended up paying a fine of $1.1 million for failing to report this fire hazard. It also recalled millions of the cars.

Legally, Mattel was required to report defects in the toy within 24 hours. Instead, the company delayed its reports for months or years. According to Mattel chairman and CEO Robert Eckert, Mattel failed to comply because the law was unreasonable and the company was better than the CPSC at evaluating when a hazard should be reported and how it should be handled.[7]

Is Mattel's stance ethical? What Life Principle is he applying?

Chapter Conclusion

Virtually no one will go through life without reading an advertisement, ordering online, borrowing money, acquiring a credit report, or using a consumer product. It is important to know your rights.

EXAM REVIEW

1. **UNFAIR PRACTICES** The Federal Trade Commission (FTC) prohibits unfair and deceptive acts or practices. (p. 450)

2. **DECEPTIVE ADVERTISEMENTS** The FTC considers an advertisement to be deceptive if it contains an important misrepresentation or omission that is likely to mislead a reasonable consumer. (pp. 449–450)

---

[7]Based on an article by Nicholas Casey and Andy Pasztor, "Safety Agency, Mattel Clash Over Disclosures," *The Wall Street Journal,* September 4, 2007, p. A1.

3. **BAIT AND SWITCH**   FTC rules prohibit bait and switch advertisements. A merchant may not advertise a product and then then disparage it to consumers in an effort to sell **a** different (more expensive) item. (p. 450)

4. **MERCHANDISE BOUGHT BY MAIL, TELEPHONE, OR ONLINE**   Under FTC rules for this type of merchandise, sellers must ship an item within the time stated or, if no time is given, within 30 days after receipt of the order. (pp. 450–451)

5. **DO-NOT-CALL REGISTRY**   The FTC prohibits telemarketers from calling telephone numbers listed on its do-not-call registry. (p. 451)

6. **UNORDERED MERCHANDISE**   Consumers may keep as a gift any unordered merchandise that they receive in the mail. (p. 451)

7. **DOOR-TO-DOOR SALES**   Under the FTC door-to-door rules, a salesperson is required to notify the buyer that she has the right to cancel the transaction prior to midnight of the third business day thereafter. (p. 451)

8. **TILA DISCLOSURE**   In all loans regulated by the Truth in Lending Act, the disclosure must be clear and in a sensible order. The lender must disclose the finance charge and the annual percentage rate. (pp. 452, 454)

9. **MORTGAGES**   Lenders must make a good faith effort to determine whether a borrower can afford to repay the loan. They may not coerce or bribe an appraiser into misstating a home's value. Nor may they charge prepayment penalties. (pp. 452–453)

10. **SUBPRIME LOANS**   For subprime loans, a lender:
    - May not make loans with balloon payments, and
    - Is limited in the late fees it may charge. (p. 453)

11. **CREDIT V. DEBIT CARDS**   Under TILA, a *credit* card holder is liable only for the first $50 in unauthorized charges made before the credit card company is notified that the card was stolen. If, however, you wait more than two days to report the loss of a *debit* card, your bank will only reimburse you for losses in excess of $500. If you fail to report the lost debit card within 60 days of receipt of your bank statement, the bank is not liable at all. (pp. 453–455)

12. **CREDIT CARD BILL PAYMENT**   Credit card companies cannot increase the interest rate, fees or charges on balances unless the consumer is more than 60 days late in making the minimum payment nor can they charge interest or fees on a bill that is paid on time or during the grace period. Credit card companies must give 45 days' notice before increasing a card's APR. (p. 453)

13. **CREDIT CARD DISPUTES: MERCHANTS**   In the event of a dispute between a customer and a merchant, the credit card company cannot bill the customer if:
    - She makes a good faith effort to resolve the dispute
    - The dispute is for more than $50, and
    - The merchant is in the same state where she lives or is within 100 miles of her house. (p. 454)

14. **DISPUTES WITH CREDIT CARD COMPANY**   Under the Fair Credit Billing Act (FCBA), a credit card company must promptly investigate and respond to any consumer complaints about a credit card bill. (p. 454)

15. **DEBIT CARD FEES**   Banks may not overdraw an account and charge an overdraft fee on a debit card unless the consumer signs up for an overdraft plan. (p. 455)

16. **CREDIT REPORTS**   Under the Fair Credit Reporting Act (FCRA):

   • A consumer report can be used only for a legitimate business need,

   • A consumer reporting agency cannot report information that is more than seven years old (ten for bankruptcies),

   • An employer cannot request a consumer report on any current or potential employee without the employee's permission, and

   • Anyone who penalizes a consumer because of a credit report must reveal the name and address of the reporting agency that supplied the negative information. (pp. 455–456)

17. **ACCESS TO CREDIT REPORTS AND CREDIT SCORES**   The Fair and Accurate Credit Transactions Act (FACTA) permits consumers to obtain one free credit report every year from each of the three major reporting agencies. Also, anyone who penalizes a consumer because of her credit score, must give it to her at no charge. (p. 455)

18. **DEBT COLLECTION**   Under the Fair Debt Collection Practices Act (FDCPA), a debt collector may not harass or abuse debtors. (p. 456)

19. **ECOA**   The Equal Credit Opportunity Act prohibits any creditor from discriminating against a borrower on the basis of race, color, religion, national origin, sex, marital status, age, or because the borrower is receiving welfare. (pp. 456–457)

EXAM Strategy

Question: Kathleen, a single woman, applied for an Exxon credit card. Exxon rejected her application without giving any specific reason and without providing the name of the credit bureau it had used. When Kathleen asked for a reason for the rejection, she was told that the credit bureau did not have enough information about her to establish creditworthiness. In fact, Exxon had denied her credit application because she did not have a major credit card or a savings account, she had been employed for only one year, and she had no dependents. Did Exxon violate the law?

Strategy: Exxon violated two laws. Review the statutes in the consumer credit section of the chapter. (See the "Result" at the end of this section.)

20. **CONSUMER LEASING ACT**   This statute applies to any lease up to $50,000 (except for leases on real property). The lessor is required to make certain disclosures before the lease is signed. (p. 458)

21. **WARRANTIES**   The Magnuson-Moss Warranty Act requires any supplier that offers a written warranty on a consumer product costing more than $15 to disclose the terms of the warranty in simple, understandable language before the sale. (p. 458)

22. **CPSC**   The Consumer Product Safety Commission evaluates consumer products and develops safety standards. Manufacturers must report all potentially hazardous product defects to the CPSC within 24 hours of discovery. (p. 459)

EXAM Strategy

Question: Joel was two years old and his brother, Joshua, was three when their father left both children asleep in the rear seat of his automobile while visiting a friend. A cigarette lighter was on the dashboard of the car. After awaking, Joshua began playing with the lighter and set fire to Joel's diaper. Do the parents have a claim against the manufacturer of the lighter under the Consumer Product Safety Act?

Strategy: The CPSA regulates unsafe products. Was the cigarette lighter unsafe? (See the "Result" at the end of this section.)

19. Result: The court held that Exxon violated both the FCRA and the ECOA. The FCRA requires Exxon to tell Kathleen the name of the credit bureau that it used. Under the ECOA, Exxon was required to tell Kathleen the real reasons for the credit denial.

22. Result: The court held that the defendant did not have a claim because there was no evidence that the manufacturer had knowingly violated a consumer product safety rule.

MATCHING QUESTIONS

Match the following terms with their definitions:

_____ A. FCBA   1. Requires lenders to disclose the terms of a loan

_____ B. FDCPA   2. Regulates credit reports

_____ C. FCRA   3. Regulates debt collectors

_____ D. ECOA   4. Prohibits lenders from discriminating based on race, religion, and sex

_____ E. TILA   5. Regulates disputes between consumers and their credit card companies

TRUE/FALSE QUESTIONS

Circle true or false:

1. T F If a store advertises a product, it must have enough stock on hand to fill every order.

2. T F The FTC has established a national do-not-call registry.

3. T F Under usury laws, lenders are limited in the amount of interest they may charge.

4. T F Under the Truth in Lending Act, it does not matter how the information is disclosed, so long as it is disclosed someplace on the first page of the loan document.

5. T F A consumer reporting agency has the right to keep information in its files secret.

MULTIPLE-CHOICE QUESTIONS

1. Which of the following statements is *false?*
   (a) Mail-order companies must ship a product within the time stated.
   (b) If no time is stated, the mail-order company must ship within 30 days.
   (c) If a company cannot ship a product when promised, the company must cancel the order unless the customer indicates he wants the item.
   (d) If a company cannot ship the product within 30 days of the original shipping date, the company must cancel the order unless the customer indicates he still wants the item.
   (e) Each time the shipping date changes, the company must notify the customer.

2. If you receive a product in the mail that you did not order:
   (a) You must pay for it or return it.
   (b) You must pay for it only if you use it.
   (c) You must throw it away.
   (d) It is a gift to you.
   (e) You must return it, but the company must reimburse you for postage.

3. Zach sells Cutco Knives door to door. Which of the following statements is *false?*
   (a) The buyer has three days to cancel the order.
   (b) Zach must tell the buyer of her rights.
   (c) Zach must give the buyer a written notice of her rights.
   (d) The seller can cancel orally or in writing.
   (e) If the seller cancels, Zach must return her money within 10 days.

4. Depending on state law, if a lender violates the usury laws, the borrower could possibly be allowed to keep:
   I. The interest that exceeds the usury limit
   II. All the interest
   III. All of the loan and the interest
   (a) I, II, and III
   (b) Only I
   (c) Only II
   (d) Only III
   (e) Neither I, II, nor III

5. Jodie is upset because her credit card bill shows a charge of $39 to a pornographic website that she never visited. Under the FCBA:
   (a) She should call the credit card company to tell them that this charge is wrong.
   (b) She should call her parents to let them handle the problem.
   (c) The credit card company has 90 days to acknowledge her complaint.
   (d) The credit card company has the right to close out her account until the dispute is resolved.
   (e) The credit card company must investigate a complaint and respond within 90 days.

ESSAY QUESTIONS

1. Process cheese food slices must contain at least 51 percent natural cheese. Imitation cheese slices, by contrast, contain little or no natural cheese and consist primarily of water and vegetable oil. Kraft, Inc. makes Kraft Singles, which are individually wrapped process cheese food slices. When Kraft began losing market share to imitation slices that were advertised as both less expensive and equally nutritious as Singles, Kraft responded with a series of advertisements informing consumers that Kraft Singles cost more than imitation slices because they are made from 5 ounces of milk. Kraft does use 5 ounces of milk in making each Kraft Single, but 30 percent of the calcium contained in the milk is lost during processing. Imitation slices contain the same amount of calcium as Kraft Singles. Are the Kraft advertisements deceptive?

2. Josephine was a 60-year-old widow who suffered from high blood pressure and epilepsy. A bill collector from Collections Accounts Terminal, Inc., called her and demanded that she pay $56 she owed to Cabrini Hospital. She told him that Medicare was supposed to pay the bill. Shortly thereafter, Josephine received a letter from Collections that stated:

   You have shown that you are unwilling to work out a friendly settlement with us to clear the above debt. Our field investigator has now been instructed to make an investigation in your neighborhood and to personally call on your employer. The immediate payment of the full amount, or a personal visit to this office, will spare you this embarrassment.

   Has Collections violated the law?

3.
   > **GET ENOUGH BROADLOOM TO CARPET ANY AREA OF YOUR HOME OR APARTMENT**
   > **UP TO 150 SQUARE FEET CUT, MEASURED, AND READY FOR INSTALLATION FOR ONLY $77.**
   > **GET 100% DUPONT CONTINUOUS FILAMENT NYLON PILE BROADLOOM. CALL COLLECT**

   When customers called the number provided, New Rapids Carpet Center, Inc. sent salespeople to visit them at home to sell them carpet that was not as advertised—it was not continuous filament nylon pile broadloom, and the price was not $77. Has New Rapids violated a consumer law?

4. **ETHICS:** After TNT Motor Express hired Joseph Bruce Drury as a truck driver, it ordered a background check from Robert Arden & Associates. TNT provided Drury's social security number and date of birth, but not his middle name. Arden discovered that a Joseph Thomas Drury, who coincidentally had the same birthdate as Joseph Bruce Drury, had served a prison sentence for drunk driving. Not knowing that it had the wrong Drury, Arden reported this information to TNT, which promptly fired Drury. When he asked why, the TNT executive refused to tell him. Did TNT violate the law? Whether or not TNT was in violation, did its executives behave ethically? Who would have been harmed or helped if TNT managers had informed Drury of the Arden report?

5. Thomas worked at a Sherwin-Williams paint store that James managed. Thomas and James had a falling out when, according to Thomas, "a relationship began to bloom between Thomas and one of the young female employees, the one James was

obsessed with." After Thomas quit, James claimed that Thomas owed the store $121. Sherwin-Williams reported this information to the Chilton credit reporting agency. Thomas sent a letter to Chilton disputing the accuracy of the Sherwin-Williams charges. Chilton contacted James, who confirmed that Thomas still owed the money. Chilton failed to note in Thomas's file that a dispute was pending. Thereafter, two of Thomas's requests for credit cards were denied. Have James and Chilton violated the Fair Credit Reporting Act?

DISCUSSION QUESTIONS

1. Should employers use credit checks as part of the hiring process? On the one hand, each year, employers suffer losses of $55 million because of workplace violence while retailers lose $30 *billion* a year from employee theft. Those who commit fraud are often living above their means. On the other hand, there is no evidence that workers with poor credit reports are more likely to be violent, steal from their employers, or quit their jobs. And refusing to hire someone with a low credit score may simply be kicking him when he is down. What would you do if you were an employer?

2. The fee on a debit card overdraft can be as high or higher than the amount drawn out. Instead of overdrawing their accounts, consumers would be much better off either not spending the money, using a credit card, or paying cash. Typically, the people most likely to sign up for the right to overdraw their accounts are those who can least afford it—they have maxed out their credit cards and used up any home equity. Is it ethical for a bank to offer an overdraft plan?

3. Look at the section entitled "Credit Cards Bill Payment" on p. 453. All of these activities used to be legal. Which ones were unethical?

4. Go to **youtube.com** and search for "free credit reports." Watch advertisements for **freecreditreport .com.** Although the characters repeat the word "free" over and over, in fact, the reports are not free unless the consumer signs up for a paid credit monitoring service. At the end of the ad, a voice quickly says, "Offer applies with enrollment in Triple Advantage." Are these ads deceptive under FTC rules? Are they ethical under your Life Principles?

5. Advertisements for Listerine mouthwash claimed that it was as effective as flossing in preventing tooth plaque and gum disease. This statement was true, but only if the flossing was done incorrectly. In fact, many consumers do floss incorrectly. However, if flossing is done right, it is more effective against plaque and gum disease than Listerine. Is this advertisement deceptive? Does it violate §5 of the FTC Act?

CHAPTER 26

ENVIRONMENTAL LAW

Michelle has owned a building on Main Street for more than 20 years. At the beginning, one of the businesses in the building was a drycleaning shop. The operators of the shop disposed of the cleaning fluids legally. Recent testing of the groundwater in a nearby park revealed that it was contaminated by dry-cleaning chemicals from that shop. Michelle must pay the cost of cleaning up the chemicals, even though they were disposed of legally years ago. The cost of the cleanup will far exceed the value of the building she owns.

© Steve Allen/Jupiterimages

The cost of the cleanup will far exceed the value of the building she owns.

INTRODUCTION

This scenario is based on a true story. The environment is a complex issue. It is not enough simply to say, "We are against pollution." The question is: Who will pay? Who will pay for past damage inflicted before anyone understood the harm that pollutants cause? Who will pay for current changes necessary to prevent damage now and in the future? Are car owners willing to spend $100 or $1,000 more per car to prevent air pollution? Are easterners ready to ban oil drilling in the Arctic National Wildlife Refuge in Alaska if that means higher prices for heating oil? Will loggers in the West give up their jobs to protect endangered species?

The cost-benefit trade-off is particularly complex in environmental issues because those who pay the cost often do not receive the benefit. If a company dumps toxic wastes into a stream, its shareholders benefit by avoiding the expense of safe disposal. Those who fish or drink the waters pay the real costs, without receiving any of the benefit. Economists use the term **externality** to describe the situation in which people do not bear the full cost of their decisions. Externalities prevent the market system from achieving a clean environment on its own. Most commonly, government involvement is required to realign costs and benefits.

As we begin our discussion of environmental law, please note that violations are a serious matter. Those who break environmental laws are liable not only for civil damages, but also for *criminal* penalties under some statutes such as the Clean Water Act, the Resource Conservation and Recovery Act, and the Endangered Species Act.

Externality

When people do not bear the full cost of their decisions.

AIR POLLUTION

October 26, 1948, was the day on which many Americans first became aware of the real dangers of air pollution. Almost half of the 10,000 people in Donora, Pennsylvania, fell ill when a weather inversion trapped industrial pollutants in the air, creating a lethal smog. Twenty residents ultimately died. Although air pollution rarely causes this type of acute illness, it can cause diseases that are annoying, chronic, or even fatal—such as pneumonia, bronchitis, emphysema, cancer, and heart disease. Exposure before birth is linked to lower IQ scores in children.

There are three major sources of air pollution: coal-burning utility plants, factories, and motor vehicles. Local regulation is ineffective in controlling air pollution. For instance, when cities limited pollution from factory smokestacks, plants simply built taller stacks that sent the pollution hundreds, or even thousands, of miles away. Recognizing the national nature of the problem, Congress passed the Clean Air Act of 1963.

The Clean Air Act

The Clean Air Act of 1963 requires the Environmental Protection Agency (EPA) to establish national air quality standards. These standards must protect public health *without regard to cost*. Once the EPA has established standards, states must develop so-called State Implementation Plans (**SIPs**) to meet them. The Clean Air Act is, however, a work in progress. More than 100 million Americans still live in areas that do not meet the EPA's national air quality standards.

In the following case, a power plant argued that the EPA had imposed a solution whose cost far outweighed its benefit. There is only one Grand Canyon. Should visibility there be preserved at any cost?

SIPs

The Clean Air Act requires states to develop State Implementation Plans (SIPs) for meeting air quality standards set by the EPA.

You be the Judge

Facts: The Navaho Generating Station (NGS) is a power plant 12 miles from the Grand Canyon. To protect the views of this national treasure, the EPA ordered NGS to reduce its sulfur dioxide emissions by 90 percent. To do so would cost NGS $430 million in capital expenditures initially, and then $89.6 million annually. Average winter visibility in the Grand Canyon would be improved by at most 7 percent, but perhaps less. NGS sued to prevent implementation of the EPA's order. A court may nullify an EPA order if it determines that the Agency's action was arbitrary and capricious.

You Be the Judge: *Did the EPA act arbitrarily and capriciously in requiring NGS to spend half a billion dollars to improve winter visibility at the Grand Canyon by at most 7 percent?*

CENTRAL ARIZONA WATER CONSERVATION DISTRICT v. EPA

990 F.2d 1531, 1993 U.S. App. LEXIS 5881
United States Court of Appeals for the Ninth Circuit, 1993

Argument for NGS: This case is a perfect example of environmentalism run amok. Half a billion dollars for the chance of increasing winter visibility at the Grand Canyon by 7 percent? Winter visitors to the Grand Canyon would undoubtedly prefer that NGS provide them with a free lunch rather than a 7 percent improvement in visibility. The EPA order is simply a waste of money.

Argument for the EPA: How can NGS, or anyone else, measure the benefit of protecting a national treasure like the Grand Canyon? Even people who never have and never will visit it during the winter sleep better at night knowing that the canyon is protected. NGS has been causing harm to the Grand Canyon, and now it should remedy the damage.

NEW SOURCES OF POLLUTION

Some states had air so clean that they could have allowed air quality to decline and still have met EPA standards. However, the Clean Air Act declared that one of its purposes was to "protect and enhance" air quality. Using this phrase, the Sierra Club sued the EPA to prevent it from approving any SIPs that met EPA standards but nonetheless permitted a decline in air quality. As a result of this suit, the EPA developed a **prevention of significant deterioration (PSD) program**. **No one may undertake a building project that will cause a major increase in pollution without first obtaining a permit from the EPA.** The agency will grant permits only if an applicant can demonstrate that (1) its emissions will not cause an overall decline in air quality, and (2) it has installed the **best available control technology** for every pollutant.

> **Prevention of significant deterioration (PSD) program**
>
> No one may undertake a building project that will cause a major increase in pollution without first obtaining a permit from the EPA.

The PSD program prohibits any deterioration in current air quality, *regardless of health impact*. In essence, national policy values a clean environment for its own sake, apart from any health benefits.

Greenhouse Gases and Global Warming

During the last century, the average temperature worldwide has increased between 0.5° and 1.1°F. If current trends continue, the world's average temperature during the next 100 years will rise another 2° to 6°F, producing the warmest climate in the history of humankind. (By comparison, the planet is only 5° to 9°F warmer than during the last Ice Age.) The impact of this climate change is potentially catastrophic: a rise in sea level that would engulf coastal areas, a devastating decline in fishing stocks, the death of major forests, and a loss of farmland worldwide.

The scientific evidence underlying the theory of global warming has been debated for a long time, but most reasonable scientists today accept that the burning of fossil fuels produces gases that create a greenhouse effect by trapping heat in the Earth's atmosphere. These emissions are referred to as **greenhouse gases** (GHG).

Identifying the problem, however, does not illuminate the solution. Global warming is the most complex environmental problem of the new millennium because any solution requires international political cooperation coupled with major behavioral changes.

INTERNATIONAL TREATIES

The United States plays a particularly important role in finding a solution because, with 5 percent of the world's population, it consumes 25 percent of the world's energy. However, it is the only leading industrialized nation that has refused to ratify the Kyoto Protocol, which set a limit on emissions for each developed country. From the perspective of the United States, there were two problems with the treaty: (1) developing countries such as China and India, which are important economic competitors of the United States, were not bound by the treaty, and (2) economists had estimated the cost of compliance at $5 trillion, with little benefit to the United States.

In any event, the Kyoto treaty has had little impact on GHG because many countries have been well over their treaty quotas. The same impasse continues over the second phase of the Kyoto treaty (beginning in 2013)—the United States will not be bound by a treaty that excludes China and India, while those countries will not enter into an agreement when America has no real plan to cut its emissions. In short, while countries continue to meet and discuss solutions to climate change, they have been unable to reach an effective, binding agreement.

DOMESTIC REGULATION

In 2007, the Supreme Court ruled that the EPA must regulate GHG if they were found to endanger health or welfare.[1] Beginning in 2011, the EPA has required plants that produce at least 100,000 tons of GHG a year (or that increase their production by 75,000 tons) to obtain a permit from the EPA. Under the permitting process, plants must show that they use the best available technology to reduce emissions.

WATER POLLUTION

One day in 1993, thousands of Milwaukeeans began to suffer nausea, cramps, and diarrhea. The suspected culprit? Cryptosporidium, a tiny protozoan that usually resides in the intestines of cattle and other animals. Ironically, the parasite may have entered Milwaukee's water supply at a purification plant on Lake Michigan. Officials suspect that infected runoff from dairy farms spilled into Lake Michigan near the plant's intake pipe. Doctors advised those with a damaged immune system (such as AIDS patients) to avoid drinking municipal water. Most Milwaukeeans were taking no chances—more than 800,000 switched to boiled or bottled water.

Polluted water can cause a number of loathsome diseases, such as typhus and dysentery. But by 1930, most American cities had dramatically reduced outbreaks of waterborne diseases by chlorinating their water. (The parasite that caused the Milwaukee outbreak is relatively immune to chlorine.) However, industrial discharges into the water supply have increased rapidly, with a significant impact on water quality. These industrial wastes may not

> Polluted water can cause a number of loathsome diseases.

---

[1]*Massachusetts v. Environmental Protection Agency*, 549 U.S. 497; 2007 U.S. LEXIS 3785.

induce acute illnesses like typhus, but they can cause serious diseases, such as cancer. There is more at stake than health alone; clean water is valued for esthetics, recreation, and fishing.

The Clean Water Act

In 1972, Congress passed a statute, now called the Clean Water Act (CWA), with two ambitious goals: (1) to make all navigable water suitable for swimming and fishing; and (2) to eliminate the discharge of pollutants into navigable water. **In support of its goals, the CWA prohibits anyone from discharging pollution into water without a permit from the EPA.** However, like the Clean Air Act, the CWA's goals have not been met.

Traditionally, the courts had interpreted the term *navigable water* very broadly to include wetlands, intermittent streams (those that do not flow all the time), and ponds that might affect other bodies of water. This definition gave the EPA the right to regulate virtually all water polluters. But the Supreme Court changed the interpretation of navigable water to *exclude* (1) intermittent streams or wetlands, (2) ponds or lakes that are not connected to open bodies of water, and (3) waterways that are all within one state, even though pollutants can leak from them into drinking water.[2] The EPA estimates that almost one-third of the nation's population drinks water that is fed by waterways no longer covered by the CWA.

In the Grand Canyon case you read earlier, the Supreme Court dealt with the issue of cost-benefit analysis under the Clean Air Act. In the following case, this court takes up the same issue under the CWA. Until this case, the CWA had been interpreted to prevent the EPA from using cost-benefit analysis. The EPA was required to prevent pollution at any cost. The Supreme Court has now changed that interpretation of the CWA.

ENTERGY CORPORATION v. RIVERKEEPER, INC.

129 S. Ct. 1498; 2009 U.S. Lexis 2498
Supreme Court of the United States, 2009

CASE SUMMARY

Facts: A power plant generates lots of heat. To cool it down, the operator flushes vast amounts of water through its system. In this process, fish, shellfish, and plants that live in the water get squashed against the screens ("impingement") or in the cooling system itself ("entrainment"). Under the CWA, power plants must use the "best technology available for minimizing adverse environmental impact."

It took the EPA three decades to issue regulations for cooling systems. In the end, these rules required *new* power plants to use the best technology available, which reduced fish mortality by 98 percent. But the EPA permitted *existing* plants to use cheaper technology that was between 60 and 95 percent effective in protecting fish. The agency made this choice because the cost of convert-

ing existing plants to the better system would be $3.5 billion per year, which was nine times the cost of the cheaper version.

Riverkeeper, Inc., an environmental organization, challenged the regulations, arguing that the EPA should require both new and existing plants to use the best technology. The appeals court ruled that the EPA could only consider costs in two circumstances: (1) determining if they could be "reasonably borne" by the industry, or (2) if there were two ways to achieve the exact same goal, the EPA could mandate the cheaper option. Otherwise, the EPA could not compare the costs and benefits of various methods and then choose the technology with the best net benefits. The Supreme Court decided to hear the case.

---

[2]*Solid Waste Agency v. United States Army Corps of Eng'Rs*, 531 U.S. 159 (S.Ct. 2001); *Rapanos v. United States*, 547 U.S. 715 (S.Ct. 2006).

Issue: *Is the EPA permitted to use cost-benefit analysis when issuing regulations?*

Decision: Yes, the EPA does have the right to use cost-benefit analysis.

Reasoning: The phrase "the best technology available for minimizing adverse environmental impact" could be interpreted to mean either the technology that achieves the best absolute result at any cost or the option that achieves the *most efficient* result. Riverkeeper argued that

minimizing means reducing harm to the smallest amount possible. But *minimizing* can also mean the greatest relative reduction, given the cost.

The EPA was perfectly reasonable in deciding to use cost-benefit analysis. It was simply avoiding an extreme difference between costs and benefits. As it was, the EPA estimated the cost of its rules at $389 million per year, while the benefits are only $83 million. This trade-off is highly protective of the environment and well within the EPA's legitimate exercise of its discretion.

INDUSTRIAL DISCHARGES

The CWA prohibits any single producer from discharging pollution into water without a permit from the EPA. Before granting a permit, the EPA must set limits, by industry, on the amount of each type of pollution any single producer (called a **point source**) can discharge. These limits must be based on the **best available technology.** The EPA faces a gargantuan task in determining the best available technology that each industry can use to reduce pollution. Furthermore, standards become obsolete quickly as technology changes.

Point source
A single producer of pollution.

WATER QUALITY STANDARDS

The CWA requires states to set EPA-approved water quality standards and develop plans to achieve them. The first step in developing a plan is to determine how each body of water is used. Standards may vary depending upon the designated use—higher for recreational lakes than for a river used to irrigate farmland. No matter what the water's designated use, standards may not be set at a level lower than its current condition. Congress is not in the business of permitting more pollution.

WETLANDS

Wetlands are the transition areas between land and open water. They may look like swamps—they may even *be* swamps—but their unattractive appearance should not disguise their vital role in the aquatic world. They are natural habitats for many fish and wildlife. They also serve as a filter for neighboring bodies of water, trapping chemicals and sediments. Moreover, they are an important aid in flood control because they can absorb a high level of water and then release it slowly after the emergency has passed.

The CWA prohibits any discharge of dredge and fill material into wetlands without a permit. Although filling in wetlands requires a permit, many other activities that harm wetlands, such as draining them, originally did not. (However, many states require permits for draining wetlands.) After some particularly egregious abuses, the EPA issued regulations to limit the destruction of wetlands. These new regulations, however, were successfully challenged in the courts.[3] The EPA then rewrote the regulations to accomplish the same goal within the parameters set out by the courts.

Although, in theory, the government's official policy is no net loss of wetlands, the reality has been different. Since the country was settled, about half of the original 230 million acres of wetlands in the continental United States has been destroyed. In 2002, the Bush administration amended the "no net loss" rule so that it could issue waivers in some cases.

---

[3]*National Mining Ass'n v. U.S. Army Corps of Engineers*, 145 F.3d 1399 (D.C. Cir. 1998).

SEWAGE

Plumbing drains must be attached to either a septic system or a sewer line. A septic system is, in effect, a freestanding waste treatment plant. A sewer line, on the other hand, feeds into a publicly owned wastewater treatment plant, also known as a *municipal sewage plant.* **Under the CWA, a municipality must obtain a permit for any discharge from a wastewater treatment plant.** To obtain a permit, the municipality must first treat the waste to reduce its toxicity. However, taxpayers have resisted the large increases in taxes or fees necessary to fund required treatments. Since the fines imposed by the EPA are almost always less than the cost of treatment, some cities have been slow to comply.

Between 2006 and 2009, more than a third of the sewage systems in this country admitted to violating the law by dumping incompletely treated human waste and harmful chemicals into waterways. Fewer than 20 percent of those were penalized. There have, however, been some notable successes. For instance, the Charles River in Boston, which was the inspiration for the pop song, "Dirty Water," recently received a grade of B+ by the EPA—an impressive improvement over the D it received in 1995. The river is now almost always safe for boating and is swimmable 62 percent of the time.

EXAM Strategy

Question: Edward lives on a ranch near Wind River. He uses water from the river for irrigation. To divert more water to his ranch, he builds a dike in the river using scrap metal, cottonwood trees, car bodies, and a washing machine. This material does not harm downstream water. Has Edward violated the CWA?

Strategy: The CWA prohibits the discharge of pollution. Was this pollution?

Result: Yes, the court ruled that the material Edward placed in the water was pollution. It was irrelevant that the material did not flow downstream.

WASTE DISPOSAL

Do not be fooled by the name. Love Canal, in Niagara Falls, New York, was decidedly an unlovely place after 1945, when Hooker Chemical Co. dumped 21,800 tons of chemicals into the canal and on nearby land. Hooker then sold the land to the local school board to build an elementary school. Children swam in the canal. They played with hot balls of chemical residue—what they called "fire stones"—that popped up through the ground. Cancer, epilepsy, respiratory problems, and skin diseases were common in the neighborhood. Finally, a national health emergency was declared, and 800 families were relocated.

In its time, what Hooker did was not unusual. Companies historically dumped waste in waterways, landfills, or open dumps. Out of sight was out of mind. Waste disposal continues to be a major problem in the United States. It has been estimated that the cost of cleaning up existing waste products will exceed $1 *trillion.* At the same time, the country continues to produce more than 6 billion tons of agricultural, commercial, industrial, and domestic waste each year.

Two major statutes regulate wastes. The Resource Conservation and Recovery Act (RCRA) focuses on preventing future Love Canals by regulating the production, transportation, and disposal of solid wastes, both toxic and otherwise. It also regulates spills at RCRA-regulated facilities. The Comprehensive Environmental Response, Compensation, and Liability Act (CERCLA), also referred to as "Superfund," focuses on cleaning up inactive or abandoned hazardous waste sites.

Resource Conservation and Recovery Act

The RCRA establishes rules for treating both hazardous wastes and other forms of solid waste (such as ordinary garbage). The disposal of nonhazardous solid waste has generally been left to the states, but they must follow guidelines set by the RCRA. The RCRA:

- Bans new open garbage dumps;

- Requires that garbage be sent to sanitary landfills;

- Sets minimum standards for landfills;

- Requires landfills to monitor nearby groundwater;

- Requires states to develop a permit program for landfills; and

- Provides some financial assistance to aid states in waste management.

The RCRA also regulates hazardous wastes. **It provides that anyone who creates, transports, stores, treats, or disposes of more than a certain quantity of hazardous wastes must apply for an EPA permit.** All hazardous wastes must be tracked from creation to final disposal. They must be disposed of at a certified facility.

Superfund

The official name of **Superfund** is the Comprehensive Environmental Response, Compensation, and Liability Act (CERCLA). Its goal is to clean up hazardous wastes that have been improperly dumped in the past.

The philosophy of Superfund is that "the polluter pays." **Therefore, anyone who has *ever* owned or operated a site on which hazardous wastes are found, or who has transported wastes to the site, or who has arranged for the disposal of wastes that were released at the site, is liable for (1) the cost of cleaning up the site; (2) any damage done to natural resources; and (3) any required health assessments.**

In a "shovels first, lawyers later" approach, Congress established a revolving trust fund for the EPA to use in cleaning up sites even before obtaining reimbursement from those responsible for the damage. The trust fund was initially financed by a tax on the oil and chemical industries, which produce the bulk of hazardous waste. In 1995, however, the taxes expired, and Congress refused to renew them. Since then, the EPA has had to rely on reimbursements from polluters and congressional appropriations of about $1.2 billion a year. That sounds like a lot of money but, according to the EPA, there could be as many as 355,000 hazardous waste sites that would require up to $250 billion to restore. Currently, the EPA has a list of about 1,300 sites that represent a "significant risk to human health or the environment."

EXAM Strategy

Question: In 1963, FMC Corp. purchased a manufacturing plant in Virginia from American Viscose Corp., the owner of the plant since 1937. During World War II, the government's War Production Board had commissioned American Viscose to make rayon for airplanes and truck tires. In 1982, inspections revealed carbon disulfide, a chemical used to manufacture this rayon, in groundwater near the plant. American Viscose was out of business by then. Who is responsible for cleaning up the carbon disulfide? Under what statute?

Strategy: Look at the statutes that govern waste disposal.

Result: Both FMC and the U.S. government are liable for cleanup under CERCLA.

CHEMICALS

Under the Toxic Substances Control Act (TSCA), manufacturers must register any new chemicals (or any old chemicals used for a new purpose) with the EPA. However, *registering* a chemical under the TSCA does not require *testing* it. The EPA can require the testing of a chemical only if there already is evidence that it is dangerous. Since this statute was passed in 1976, the EPA has required testing of only 200 of the more than 80,000 chemicals currently sold in the United States. Thus, for example, many manufacturers have elected to remove BPA from their products because of concern that it is dangerous, particularly for children. But they have replaced BPA with untested chemicals, such as PES plastic, which have some of the same characteristics as BPA. Not a reassuring choice for parents trying to buy a safe bottle for their child.

NATURAL RESOURCES

Thus far, this chapter has focused on the regulation of pollution. Congress has also passed statutes whose purpose is to preserve the country's natural resources.

National Environmental Policy Act

The National Environmental Policy Act of 1969 (NEPA) requires all federal agencies to prepare an environmental impact statement (EIS) for every major federal action significantly affecting the quality of the human environment. An EIS is a major undertaking—often hundreds, if not thousands, of pages long. It must discuss:

- Environmental consequences of the proposed action,

- Available alternatives,

- Direct and indirect effects,

- Energy requirements,

- Impact on urban quality and historic and cultural resources, and

- Means to mitigate adverse environmental impacts.

Once a draft report is ready, the federal agency must hold a hearing to allow for outside comments.

The EIS requirement applies not only to actions *undertaken* by the federal government, but also to activities *regulated* or *approved* by the government. For instance, the following projects required an EIS:

- Expanding the Snowmass ski area in Aspen, Colorado—because approval was required by the Forest Service

- Killing a herd of wild goats that was causing damage at the Olympic National Park, outside Seattle

- Creating a golf course outside Los Angeles—because the project required a government permit to build in wetlands.

The EIS process is controversial. If a project is likely to have an important impact, environmentalists almost always litigate the adequacy of the EIS. Industry advocates argue that environmentalists are simply using the EIS process to delay—or halt—any projects they oppose. In 1976, seven years after NEPA was passed, a dam on the Teton River in Idaho burst, killing 17 people and causing $1 billion in property damage. The Department of the Interior had built the dam in the face of allegations that its EIS was incomplete; it did not, for example, confirm that a large earth-filled dam resting on a riverbed was safe. To environmentalists, this tragedy graphically illustrated the need for a thorough EIS.

Researchers have found that the EIS process generally has a beneficial impact on the environment. The mere prospect of preparing an EIS tends to eliminate the worst projects. Litigation over the EIS eliminates the next weakest group. If an agency does a good-faith EIS, honestly looking at the available alternatives, projects tend to be kinder to the environment, at little extra cost.

Endangered Species Act

Worldwide, 25 percent of mammals, 22 percent of reptiles, and 13 percent of birds are threatened with extinction. This threat is largely caused by humans. **The Endangered Species Act (ESA):**

- Requires the Department of the Interior's Fish and Wildlife Service (FWS) to prepare a list of species that are in danger of becoming extinct;

- Requires the government to develop plans to revive these species;

- Requires all federal agencies to ensure that their actions will not jeopardize an endangered species;

- Prohibits any sale or transport of these species;

- Makes any taking of an endangered animal species unlawful—with *taking* defined as harassing, harming, killing, or capturing any endangered species or modifying its habitat in such a way that its population is likely to decline; and

- Prohibits the taking of any endangered plant species on federal property.

No environmental statute has been more controversial than the ESA. In theory, everyone is in favor of saving endangered species. In practice, however, the cost of saving a species can be astronomical. One of the earliest ESA battles involved the snail darter—a three-inch fish that lived in the Little Tennessee River. The Supreme Court upheld a decision under the ESA to halt work on a dam that would have blocked the river, flooding 16,500 acres of farmland and destroying the snail darter's habitat. To the dam's supporters, this decision was ludicrous: stopping a dam (on which $100 million in taxpayer money had already been spent) to save a little fish that no one had ever even thought of before the dam (or damn) controversy. The real agenda, they argued, was simply to halt development. Environmental advocates argued, however, that the wanton destruction of whole species will ultimately and inevitably lead to disaster for humankind. In the end, Congress overruled the Supreme Court and authorized completion of the dam. It turned out that the snail darter has survived in other rivers.

The snail darter was the first in a long line of ESA controversies that have included charismatic animals such as bald eagles, grizzly bears, bighorn sheep, and rockhopper penguins, but also more obscure fauna such as the Banbury Springs limpet and the triple-ribbed milkvetch. In 2007, a federal court moved to protect the delta smelt by ordering officials to shut down temporarily pumps that supplied as much as a third of southern California's water.[4] Opponents argue that too much time and money have been spent on litigation to save too few species of too little importance.

---

[4]*Natural Resources Defense Council v. Kempthorne*, 2007 U.S. Dist. LEXIS 91968.

Environmentalists also complain about (and file suit over) the slowness with which the EPA lists endangered species. In the four decades since Congress passed the ESA, species have been listed at a rate of about 35 a year. Nearly 100 species have become extinct while on the list or waiting to be listed. Over the past few years, environmental groups have asked that 1,200 species be listed as endangered. The EPA is trying to work out a compromise so that it can use its resources to list species rather than responding to lawsuits over its speed of action.

The following case discusses the advantages of protecting endangered species.

GIBBS V. BABBITT

214 F.3d 483, 2000 U.S. App. LEXIS 12280
United States Court of Appeals for the Fourth Circuit, 2000

CASE SUMMARY

Facts: The red wolf used to roam throughout the southeastern United States. Owing to wetlands drainage, dam construction, and hunting, this wolf is now on the endangered species list. The Fish and Wildlife Service (FWS) trapped the remaining red wolves, placed them in a captive breeding program, and then reintroduced them into the wild in national wildlife refuges in North Carolina and Tennessee.

After reintroduction, about 41 red wolves wandered from federal refuges onto private property. Richard Mann shot a red wolf that he feared might attack his cattle. Mann pled guilty to violating a provision of the ESA that prohibits the taking of any endangered species without a permit.

Under the commerce clause of the Constitution, Congress may only regulate commercial activity if it has an impact on interstate commerce. Plaintiffs filed suit against the U.S. government, alleging that the ESA was unconstitutional because it did not affect interstate commerce.

Issue: *Is the anti-taking provision of the ESA constitutional?*

Decision: The ESA is constitutional.

Reasoning: The red wolf has great impact on interstate commerce, to wit:

- Red wolves are part of the $29 billion national tourism industry. Many tourists travel each year to take part in "howling events"—evenings spent studying wolves and listening to their howls. It has been predicted that the wolves could contribute somewhere between $40 and $180 million per year to the economy of northeastern North Carolina.

- The red wolf is a subject of scientific research, which is an important industry in its own right. And this research benefits us all—approximately 50 percent of all modern medicines are derived from wild plants or animals.

- It is also possible that if the red wolf thrives, it could be hunted for its pelt. The American alligator is a case in point. In 1975, the American alligator was nearing extinction and listed as endangered, but by 1987, conservation efforts restored the species. Now, there is a vigorous trade in alligator hides.

- Mann shot a wolf that was threatening his livestock. Killing livestock also has an impact on interstate commerce. Under the Commerce Clause, any impact counts even if negative. It is also possible that red wolves help farms by preying on animals like raccoons, deer, and rabbits that destroy their crops.

Congress has the right to decide that protecting red wolves will one day produce a substantial commercial benefit to this country and that failure to preserve it may result in permanent, though unascertainable, loss. If a species becomes extinct, we are left to speculate forever on what we might have learned or what we may have realized. If we conserve the species, it will be available for study by and the benefit of future generations.

Chapter Conclusion

Environmental laws have a pervasive impact on our lives. The cost has been great—whether it is higher prices for fuel-efficient cars or the time spent filling out environmental impact statements. Some argue that cost is irrelevant, that a clean environment has incalculable value for its own sake. Others insist on a more pragmatic approach and want to know if the benefits outweigh the costs. They worry that environmental regulations hurt employment.

Because there is so little consensus, when the time comes to allocate funds, change lifestyles, and make tough choices, resources are too often spent on litigation rather than protection of the environment.

EXAM REVIEW

1. **AIR** The Clean Air Act of 1970 requires the Environmental Protection Agency (EPA) to establish national air quality standards. The EPA must also regulate greenhouse gases (GHG). (pp. 467–469)

2. **WATER** The Clean Water Act prohibits anyone from discharging pollution into navigable water without a permit from the EPA. (pp. 469–472)

EXAM Strategy

Question: In theory, Astro Circuit Corp. in Lowell, Massachusetts, pretreated its industrial waste to remove toxic metals, but in practice, the factory was producing twice as much wastewater as the treatment facility could handle and, therefore, was dumping the surplus directly into the city sewer. It was David Boldt's job to keep the production line moving. Has Boldt violated the law by dumping polluted water into the city sewer? What penalties might he face?

Strategy: Whenever water is involved, look at the provisions of the Clean Water Act. (See the "Result" at the end of this section.)

3. **INDUSTRIAL DISCHARGES** The CWA prohibits any single producer (a point source) from discharging pollution into water without a permit from the EPA. (p. 471)

4. **WATER QUALITY STANDARDS** The CWA requires states to set EPA-approved water quality standards and develop plans to achieve them. (p. 471)

5. **WETLANDS** The Clean Water Act prohibits any discharge of dredge and fill material into wetlands without a permit. (p. 471)

6. **SEWAGE** Under the Clean Water Act, a municipality must obtain a permit for any discharge from a wastewater treatment plant. (p. 472)

7. **RCRA**   The Resource Conservation and Recovery Act establishes rules for treating hazardous wastes and other forms of solid waste. (p. 473)

8. **SUPERFUND**   Under Superfund (also known as CERCLA), anyone who has *ever* owned or operated a site on which hazardous wastes are found, or who has transported wastes to the site, or who has arranged for the disposal of wastes that were released at the site, is liable for (1) the cost of cleaning up the site, (2) any damage done to natural resources, and (3) any required health assessments. (p. 473)

9. **NEPA**   The National Environmental Policy Act requires all federal agencies to prepare an environmental impact statement (EIS) for every major federal action significantly affecting the quality of the environment. (pp. 474–475)

EXAM Strategy

Question: The U.S. Forest Service planned to build a road in the Nez Perce National Forest in Idaho to provide access to loggers. The road was very narrow. Is the Forest Service required to prepare an EIS before building it?

Strategy: Does a road significantly affect the quality of the environment? Is an EIS required? (See the "Result" at the end of this section.)

10. **ESA**   The Endangered Species Act requires the FWS to list endangered species and then prohibits activities that harm them. (pp. 475–476)

2. Result: Although Boldt was in an unfortunate situation—he could have lost his job if he had not been willing to dump the industrial waste—he was found guilty of a criminal violation of the Clean Water Act. There are worse things than being fired—like being fired *and* sent to prison.

9. Result: Although the road itself may not be significant enough to require an impact statement, its purpose was to provide access for logging, which did require an EIS.

MATCHING QUESTIONS

___ A. EPA

___ B. ESA

___ C. NEPA

___ D. CERCLA

___ E. RCRA

1. Regulates the cleanup of hazardous wastes improperly dumped in the past

2. Establishes rules for treating newly created wastes

3. Protects red wolves

4. The agency that regulates environmental policy in the United States

5. Requires all federal agencies to prepare an environmental impact statement

TRUE/FALSE QUESTIONS

1. T F In establishing national standards under the Clean Air Act, the EPA need not consider the cost of compliance.
2. T F The Clean Water Act requires anyone discharging pollution into navigable water to obtain a permit from the EPA.
3. T F Any individual, business, or federal agency that significantly affects the quality of the environment must file an EIS.
4. T F Since the United States was founded, about half of its existing wetlands have been destroyed.
5. T F Violating the environmental laws can be a criminal offense, punishable by a prison term.

MULTIPLE-CHOICE QUESTIONS

1. Which of the following statements are true of Superfund?

   I.   Anyone who has ever owned a site is liable for cleanup costs.
   II. Anyone who has ever transported waste to a site is liable for cleanup costs.
   III. Anyone who has ever disposed of waste at a site is liable for cleanup costs.

   (a) Neither I, II, nor III
   (b) I, II, and III
   (c) I and II
   (d) II and III
   (e) I and III

2. Which of the following statements are true?

   I.   The EPA sets national air quality standards.
   II. The EPA develops plans to meet air quality standards.
   III. States set their own air quality standards.
   IV. The states develop plans to meet air quality standards.

   (a) II and III
   (b) III and IV
   (c) I and IV
   (d) I, III, and IV
   (e) I and II

3. Which of the following statements are true about the *Central Arizona* case? (There can be more than one correct answer.)

   (a) Emissions from the Navajo Generating Station (NGS) were greatly degrading the view of the Grand Canyon.

   (b) The cost of reducing emissions from the NGS was trivial.

   (c) The EPA performed a cost-benefit analysis before ordering the NGS to reduce its emissions.

   (d) Under the Clean Air Act, the cost of reducing the emissions was irrelevant.

   (e) A court may overturn an EPA order if it believes that the preponderance of the evidence is on the plaintiff's side.

4. The RCRA does *not:*

   (a) Ban new open garbage dumps

   (b) Require garbage to be treated before it is taken to an existing dump

   (c) Require landfills to monitor groundwater

   (d) Provide financial assistance to states

   (e) Require states to develop a permit program for landfills

5. An environmental impact statement (EIS) is *not* required to include a discussion of:

   (a) The commercial value of any threatened species

   (b) Available alternatives to the proposed actions

   (c) Direct impacts

   (d) Indirect impacts

   (e) Impact on cultural resources

Essay Questions

1. Tariq Ahmad decided to dispose of some of his laboratory's hazardous chemicals by shipping them to his home in Pakistan. He sent the chemicals to Castelazo (in the United States) to prepare the materials for shipment. Ahmad did not tell the driver who picked up the chemicals that they were hazardous, nor did he give the driver any written documentation. Has Ahmad violated U.S. law? What penalties might he face?

2. The marbled murrelet is a seabird on the list of endangered species. Pacific Lumber Co. received permission to harvest trees from land on which the murrelet nested, on the condition that it would cooperate with regulators to protect the murrelet. But the company went in one weekend and cut down trees before it had done anything for the murrelet. Caught in the act, it promised no more logging until it had a plan to protect the birds. It waited until the long weekend over Thanksgiving to take down some more trees. A federal court then ordered a permanent halt to any further logging. There was no evidence that the company had harmed the murrelet. Had it violated the law?

3. **YOU BE THE JUDGE WRITING PROBLEM:** The Lordship Point Gun Club operated a trap and skeet shooting club in Stratford, Connecticut, for 70 years. During this time, customers deposited millions of pounds of lead shot and clay target fragments on land around the club and in the Long Island Sound. A total of 45 percent of sediment samples taken from the Sound exceeded the established limits for lead. Was the Gun Club in violation of the RCRA? **Argument for the Gun Club:** The Gun Club does not dispose of hazardous wastes, within the meaning of the RCRA. Congress meant the statute to apply only to companies in the business of manufacturing articles that produce hazardous waste. If the Gun Club happens to produce wastes, that is only incidental to the normal use of a product. **Argument for the Plaintiff:** Under the RCRA, lead shot is hazardous waste. The law applies to anyone who produces hazardous waste, no matter how.

4. Shell Oil sold pesticides to B&B, which allowed these chemicals to leak into the ground. Shell was aware that the leaks were occurring. B&B ultimately went bankrupt. Is Shell liable for the costs of cleaning up this site? If so, under what law?

5. Suppose that you are the manager of General Motors plant that is about to start producing Hummers. The Hummer requires special protective paint that, as it turns out, reacts with other chemicals during the application process to create a pollutant. What does the Clean Air Act require of you?

DISCUSSION QUESTIONS

1. Life is about choices—never more so than with the environment. Being completely honest, which of the following are you willing to do:

   • Drive a smaller, lighter, more fuel-efficient car?

   • Take public transportation or ride your bike to work?

   • Vote for political candidates who are willing to impose higher taxes on pollutants?

   • Insulate your home?

   • Unplug appliances when not in use?

   • Recycle your wastes?

   • Pay higher taxes to clean up Superfund sites?

   • Buy (more expensive) pesticide-free produce?

2. Externalities pose an enormous problem for the environment. Often, the people making decisions do not bear the full cost of their choices. Thus, the owners of a power plant that emits tons of greenhouse gases are shifting some of these costs to the rest of the world, and even to future generations. Businesses tend to fight efforts to make them pay these externalities. For example, CropLife America lobbied against a bill that would support research on the effects of chemicals on children. On the other hand, Nike recently announced that it had resigned its seat on the board of the United States Chamber of Commerce in response to the Chamber's active lobbying against legislation that would regulate greenhouse gases. But Nike will remain a member of this group. What ethical obligation do American companies have to support environmental legislation that may impose higher costs? Do they have an obligation to look out for the greater good, or should they focus on maximizing their shareholder returns? What Life Principles would you apply?

3. Is cost-benefit analysis an effective tool in environmental disputes? How do we measure the costs and benefits? How do we know what benefits we might gain from saving endangered species? Or improving visibility at the Grand Canyon? In the *Entergy* case, how does the EPA calculate the benefits of not squashing fish? Should you survey people to ask them how much it is worth? Or just think in terms of lives saved or sick days avoided? Or should we protect the environment regardless of cost?

4. Many of the environmental statutes permit ordinary citizens to file suit to enforce the law. As a result, environmental groups bring many lawsuits against both the EPA and polluters, alleging violations of these statutes. Are these suits a good idea? The Fish and Wildlife Service says that it spends so much of its resources responding to litigation over why it has not listed endangered species that it has no resources left to actually do the listing. Businesses argue that it is unfair for every citizen to be a cop on the beat. On the other hand, environmental groups often supplement the limited resources of the EPA.

5. Greenhouse gases pose a potentially devastating threat to this planet. But harm may not occur for a while, maybe not even in your lifetime. What costs should we bear to protect future generations? Some people argue that instead of incurring the huge costs of preventing global warming, we should instead learn to adapt to the effects. Is this a reasonable approach? Is it ethical?

CHAPTER 27

CYBERLAW

© Steve Allen/Jupiterimages

Garrett always said that his computer was his best friend. He was online all the time, g-chatting with his friends, listening to music, doing research for his courses, and, okay, maybe playing a few games now and again. Occasionally, the computer could be annoying. It would crash once in a while, trashing part of a paper he had forgotten to save. And there was the time that a copy of an email he sent Lizzie complaining about Caroline somehow ended up in Caroline's mailbox. He was tired of all the spam advertising pornographic websites. But these things happen, and despite the petty annoyances, his computer was an important part of his life. Then one day, Garrett received a panicked text message from a teammate on the college wrestling squad telling him to click on a certain website pronto to see someone they knew. Garrett eagerly clicked on the website and discovered, to his horror, that *he* was featured—in the nude. The website was selling DVDs showing him and other members of the wrestling team in the locker room in various states of undress. Other DVDs, from other locker and shower rooms, were for sale, too, showing football players and wrestlers from dozens of universities. No longer trusting technology, Garrett pulled on his running shoes and dashed over to the office of his business law professor.

> Garrett eagerly clicked on the website and discovered, to his horror, that *he* was featured—in the nude.

While the Internet has opened up enormous opportunities in both our business and personal lives, it has also created the need for new laws, both to pave the way for these opportunities and to limit their dangers. This chapter deals with issues that are unique to the cyberworld, such as online privacy, spam, and cybercrimes.

Before beginning the chapter in earnest, let's return briefly to Garrett, the wrestler. What recourse does Garrett have for his Internet injuries? The nude video incident happened at Illinois State University and seven other colleges. Approximately 30 athletes filed suit against GTE and PSINet for selling the DVDs online, but the two web hosts were found not liable under the Communications Decency Act because they had not produced the DVDs themselves; they had simply permitted the sale of someone else's content. What about Garrett's other computer injuries? Lizzie was not being a good friend, but it was perfectly legal for her to forward Garrett's email to Caroline. The federal CAN-SPAM Act regulates spam—unsolicited commercial email—but a lawsuit is a slow and awkward tool for killing such a flourishing weed. Thus far, the available legal tools have been relatively ineffectual (as you can tell from your email inbox).

Privacy

The Internet has vastly increased our ability to communicate quickly and widely. But as wonderful as cyber communication can be, it is not without its dangers.

Tracking Tools

Consumers enter the most personal data—credit card numbers, bank accounts, lists of friends, medical information, product preferences—on the Internet. Yet, even as they do so, most people are unaware of who has access to what personal information, how it is being used, and with what consequences.

It used to be that marketers geared their ads to specific websites, but now they target individual consumers. Websites install thousands of tracking tools on the computers of people who visit them, a tactic called *behavioral targeting.* The tools not only collect data on *all* the websites someone visits, they also record keystrokes to keep track of whatever information the consumer has entered online. These tools are placed on computers without notice or warning to the consumer. In a recent report, Dictionary.com was the worst offender, placing over 200 tools on to the computer of the unaware visitor. Wikipedia.org is one highly popular site that installs none.[1]

Once the trackers have gathered financial, health, and other personal information, they sell it to data-gathering companies who build profiles which, while technically anonymous, can include so much personal information that it is possible to identify individuals. Just three pieces of information—ZIP code, birthdate and gender—are usually enough to identify an individual's name and address. The profiles are then sold to advertisers. Now that cell phones have GPS tracking devices and readers use electronic books, where you have been and what you are reading is also available.

---

[1]Julia Angwin and Tom McGinty, "Sites Feed Personal Details to New Tracking Industry," *The Wall Street Journal,* July 30, 2010.

One company markets a databank with the names of 150 million registered voters. Anyone can buy a list of voters that is sliced and diced however they want, say, Republicans between the ages of 45 and 60 with Hispanic surnames and incomes greater than $50,000 who live in Kansas City. If marketers can put together a databank of Hispanic Republican voters, they can also find out who has visited a website for recovering alcoholics or unrecovered gamblers or Nazi sympathizers. Or who uses antidepressants or reads socialist writings. Do you want all this information available to anyone who is willing to pay for it? What if employers buy information about job candidates so that they can refuse to hire someone with health issues?

Many commentators argue that, without significant changes in the law, our privacy will be obliterated. But, so far, consumers have been relatively unconcerned. They tend to be unaware of the dangers and they appreciate the benefits—for example, this tracking software can be used to store passwords so that when you log onto Amazon.com, the site recognizes you and lets you in without your having to enter your email address and password. Consumers can also benefit from targeted advertisements—long-distance runners may like seeing ads for running shoes, not cigarettes. Industry representatives argue that, without the revenue from ads, many Internet sites would not be free to consumers. As a result, privacy on the Internet is very much like the weather—everyone talks about it, but (so far) no one has done much about it. But this you should believe: highly personal information about *you* has been collected without your knowledge or approval.

Regulation of Online Privacy

There is a wide range of possible sources of laws and regulations to protect online privacy, but they are in an early, and relatively ineffective, stage of development.

SELF-REGULATION

In an effort to forestall government regulation, several marketing trade groups issued their own report "Self-Regulatory Principles for Online Behavioral Advertising." These principles require websites that use tracking tools to provide notice of data collection that is "clear, prominent, and conveniently located." In addition, the websites must permit consumers to opt out of tracking, with only a few clicks. However, we have been unable to find a single website that complies with these principles, even among companies that sponsored the report.

Members of Congress have filed many bills to regulate online privacy. So intense, however, is the debate between industry and consumer advocates that no consensus—and little law—has emerged. There is, however, some applicable government regulation.

THE FIRST AMENDMENT

How would you like to be called a cockroach, mega scumbag, and crook in front of thousands of people? What would you think if your ex-wife told 55,000 people that your insensitivity made her so sick she was throwing up every day? **The First Amendment to the Constitution protects free speech,** and that includes these postings and worse, which have appeared on Internet message boards and blogs. As upsetting as they may be, they are protected as free speech under the First Amendment so long as the poster is not violating some other law. In these particular cases, the plaintiffs argued that the statements were defamatory but the courts disagreed, ruling that they were simply opinions.

In the following case, a teacher received hostile emails. Should the First Amendment protect the anonymous person who sent them?

You be the Judge

Facts: Juzwiak was a teacher at Hightstown High School in New Jersey. He received three emails from someone who signed himself "Josh," with the address, "Josh Hartnett jharthat@ yahoo.com." The teacher did not know anyone of that name. These emails said:

Juzwiak v. John/Jane Doe

415 N.J. Super. 442; 2 A.3d 428; 2010 N.J. Super. LEXIS 154
Superior Court of New Jersey, Appellate Division, 2010

1. Subject line: "Hopefully you will be gone permanently"
   Text: "We are all praying for that. Josh"

2. Subject line: "I hear Friday is 'D' day for you"
   Text: "I certainly hope so. You don't deserve to be allowed to teach anymore. Not just in Hightstown but anywhere. If Hightstown bids you farewell I will make it my lifes (sic) work to ensure that wherever you look for work, they know what you have done."

3. Subject line: "Mr. Juzwiak in the Hightstown/East Windsor School System."
   Text: It has been brought to my attention and I am sure many of you know that Mr. J is reapplying for his position as a teacher in this town. It has further been pointed out that certain people are soliciting supporters for him. This is tantamount to supporting the devil himself. I am not asking anyone to speak out against Mr. J but I urge you to then be silent as we can not continue to allow the children of this school system nor the parents to be subjected to his evil ways. Thank you. Josh

It seems that this third email was sent to other people, but it was not clear to whom.

Because Juzwiak did not know who "Josh" was, he filed a complaint against John/Jane Doe, seeking damages for intentional infliction of emotional distress. As part of the lawsuit, he served a subpoena on Yahoo!, asking it to reveal "Josh's" identity. When Yahoo! notified "Josh" of the lawsuit, he asked the court to quash the subpoena.

In a court hearing, Juzwiak testified that the threatening emails had severely disrupted his life, causing deep anger, depression, insomnia, back problems, and weight loss.

When the trial court refused to issue the subpoena against Yahoo!, Juzwiak appealed.

You Be the Judge: *Should the trial court have issued the subpoena?*

Argument for Juzwiak: These emails are not entitled to the protection of the First Amendment. First of all, they contained death threats: "Hopefully you will be gone permanently" and "I hear Friday is 'D' day for you." Juzwiak was frightened enough to go to the police. He suffered serious physical and emotional harm.

Furthermore, the emails constituted intentional infliction of emotional distress. They were extreme and outrageous conduct designed to cause harm. They achieved their goal.

In balancing the rights in this case, why would the court protect "Josh," who has set out to cause harm, over the innocent teacher?

Argument for "Josh": These emails were protected free speech under the Constitution. Nothing in them was a realistic threat to the teacher's safety. "Hopefully you will be gone permanently" could easily mean "Hope you will move out of town." Juzwiak reported these emails to the police, but they took no action. Presumably they would have done so if there had been any real threat.

Nor did these emails constitute an intentional infliction of emotional distress. They were not so extreme and outrageous as to be utterly intolerable in a civilized community. "Josh" did not accuse Juzwiak of vile or criminal acts. The language was not obscene or profane. In short, if Juzwiak is going to teach high school, he needs to develop a thicker skin and a better sense of humor.

THE FOURTH AMENDMENT

The Fourth Amendment to the Constitution prohibits unreasonable searches and seizures by the government. In enforcing this provision of the Constitution, the courts ask: did the person being searched have a legitimate expectation of privacy in the place searched or the item seized? If yes, then the government must obtain a warrant from a court before conducting the search. The Fourth Amendment applies to computers.

The architecture professor in the following case would have benefited from a course in business law—and perhaps in computer science, too.

UNITED STATES OF AMERICA
v. ANGEVINE

281 F.3d 1130, 2002 U.S. App. LEXIS 2746
United States Court of Appeals for the Tenth Circuit, 2002

CASE SUMMARY

Facts: Professor Eric Angevine taught architecture at Oklahoma State University. The university provided him with a computer that was linked to the university network, and through it to the Internet. Professor Angevine used this computer to download more than 3,000 pornographic images of young boys. After viewing the images and printing some of them, he deleted the files. Tipped off by Professor Angevine's wife, police officers seized the computer and turned it over to a police computer expert, who retrieved the pornographic files that the professor had deleted. The police had not obtained a search warrant.

The Oklahoma State University computer policy states that:

- The contents of all storage media owned or stored on university computing facilities are the property of the university.

- Employees cannot use university computers to access obscene material.

- The university reserves the right to view or scan any file or software stored on a computer or passing through the network, and will do so periodically to audit the use of university resources. The university cannot guarantee confidentiality of stored data.

- System administrators keep logs of file names that may indicate why a particular data file is being

erased, when it was erased, and what user identification has erased it.

The trial court held that federal agents did not need a warrant to search Professor Angevine's office computer because he had no expectation of privacy. He was sentenced to 51 months in prison for "knowing possession of child pornography." The professor appealed.

Issue: *Did Professor Angevine have a reasonable expectation of privacy for his office computer?*

Decision: Professor Angevine did not have a reasonable expectation of privacy.

Reasoning: The university's computer-use policy reserves the right to monitor Internet use by employees. The policy explicitly cautions computer users that information flowing through the university network is not confidential, either in transit or in storage on a computer. As a result, employees cannot have a reasonable expectation of privacy for downloaded data.

Professor Angevine made a careless effort to protect his privacy. Although he did attempt to erase the pornography, the university computer policy warned that system administrators kept logs recording when and by whom files were deleted. In any event, having transmitted pornographic data through a monitored university network, Professor Angevine could not create a reasonable expectation of privacy merely by deleting the files.

This case involved someone who transmitted information through an electronic system owned by his employer. What happens if a suspect in a crime sends emails through a system that he personally pays for? Does he have a reasonable expectation of privacy? The following case answers these questions.

UNITED STATES OF AMERICA V. WARSHAK

631 F.3d 266; 2010 U.S. App. LEXIS 25415
United States Court of Appeals for the Sixth Circuit, 2010

CASE SUMMARY

Facts: Steven Warshak sold Enzyte, a supplement that promised to increase masculine endowment. As is the case with all such products, Enzyte was a fraud. Advertisements quoted surveys that had never been conducted and doctors who did not exist. As a result, customers typically did not buy the product a second time. Warshak had a solution to this problem—an auto-ship program. A man would order a free sample, providing his credit card to pay for the shipping. Warshak's company would then automatically send him more product, and, of course, charge his credit card.

Without obtaining a search warrant first, a federal prosecutor asked Warshak's Internet service provider (ISP) for copies of his emails. Based on the evidence contained in these 25,000 emails, Warshak was convicted of mail, wire, and bank fraud and sentenced to 25 years in prison. He appealed on the grounds that the government had violated the Fourth Amendment by obtaining his emails without a search warrant. He argued that he had had a reasonable expectation of privacy for these emails.

Issue: *Did Warshak have a reasonable expectation of privacy for his emails?*

Decision: Yes, his expectation of privacy was reasonable.

Reasoning: Clearly, Warshak thought his emails were private, or he would not have made so many incriminating statements in them. Most people would not unfurl so much dirty laundry in plain view.

However, the defendant has to show not only that he had an expectation of privacy, but also that it was reasonable. Given how significant email is to most of us, this question is very important. People are always sending sensitive and intimate information to friends, family, and colleagues around the world. Sweet nothings, business plans, online purchases, and medical information are transferred with the click of a mouse. *Account* is an apt word to use for email because it does provide an account of its owner's life.

The Fourth Amendment must keep pace with the inexorable march of technological progress, or its guarantees will wither and perish. The law requires the police to obtain a warrant before they read a letter at the post office or listen to a private telephone call. An ISP is the functional equivalent of a post office or a telephone company. It only stands to reason that the government may not compel a commercial ISP to turn over the contents of a subscriber's emails without first obtaining a warrant. Warshak's expectation of privacy was reasonable.

The courts are feeling their way in this new electronic territory, but at this writing, for criminal cases:

1. If your employer has a reasonably articulated policy notifying you that it has the right to access and read electronic communications on a system that it provides, then you do not have a reasonable expectation of privacy when using that system. The police need not obtain a search warrant before reading your messages.

2. You do have a reasonable right to privacy on a system that you provide for yourself, so the police must obtain a search warrant before accessing these messages.

THE FTC

Section 5 of the FTC Act prohibits unfair and deceptive acts or practices. The FTC applies this statute to online privacy policies—it does not require websites to have a privacy policy, but if they do have one, they must comply with it, and it cannot be deceptive. For example, the FTC brought action against Twitter.com after hackers gained access through its administrative system to Twitter accounts. Twitter had allowed all employees access to the administrative system, which was protected by a easy-to-guess password. The hackers reset passwords and sent fake tweets. Some unauthorized person sent a tweet from

President-elect Barack Obama's Twitter account offering free gasoline to users who took an Internet poll (which seems benign compared with what the hacker could have said, but still, not a good situation). The FTC found that Twitter had engaged in deceptive acts because its (lack of) security practices had violated the company's promise to users that it would protect their information from unauthorized access. As part of the settlement, Twitter agreed to strengthen its security practices.

Also, under FTC rules, bloggers face fines as high as $1,000 if they do not disclose all compensation they receive (either in cash or free products) for writing product reviews. Moreover, celebrities must disclose their relationships with advertisers when making endorsements outside of traditional ads, such as on talk shows or in social media.

ELECTRONIC COMMUNICATIONS PRIVACY ACT OF 1986

The Electronic Communications Privacy Act of 1986 (ECPA) is a federal statute that prohibits unauthorized interception of, access to, or disclosure of wire and electronic communications. The definition of electronic communication includes email and transmissions from pagers and cell phones. Violators are subject to both criminal and civil penalties. An action does not violate the ECPA if it is unintentional or if either party consents. Also, the USA Patriot Act, passed after the September 11 attacks, has broadened the *government's* right to monitor electronic communications.

Under the ECPA:

1. **Any intended recipient of an electronic communication has the right to disclose it.** Thus, if you sound off in an email to a friend about your boss, the (erstwhile) friend may legally forward that email to the boss or anyone else.

2. **ISPs are generally prohibited from disclosing electronic messages to anyone other than the addressee,** unless this disclosure is necessary for the performance of their service or for the protection of their own rights or property.

3. **An employer has the right to monitor workers' electronic communications if (1) the employee consents, (2) the monitoring occurs in the ordinary course of business, or (3) the employer provides the computer system (in the case of email).**[2] Note that an employer has the right to monitor electronic communication even if it does not relate to work activities.

One lesson from the ECPA: email is not private, and it is dangerous. Although the *Warshak* court ruled that defendants have an expectation of privacy in emails they have sent over a system that they provide for themselves, that simply means the police must first obtain a search warrant before accessing emails, which is not that difficult. To get a search warrant, the police just need probable cause that they will find evidence of a crime in the place to be searched.

The majority of employers monitor their employees' email. In the event of litigation, the opposing party can access email, even messages that have in theory been deleted. Many people who should have known better have been caught in the email trap. Merrill Lynch stock analyst Henry Blodget praised stocks to the public even as he was referring to them in emails as a "piece of s***." He has been banned for life from the securities industry. Then there was Harry Stonecipher, the CEO of Boeing, who sent explicit emails to the employee with whom he was having an extramarital affair. When copies of the emails were sent to the board of directors, he was fired.

CHILDREN'S ONLINE PRIVACY PROTECTION ACT OF 1998

The Children's Online Privacy Protection Act of 1998 (COPPA) prohibits Internet operators from collecting information from children under 13 without parental permission. It also requires sites to disclose how they will use any information they acquire. The FTC is charged with enforcing COPPA. The website for Mrs. Fields cookies offered birthday

---

[2]The ECPA provides that under certain circumstances, the police can access email without a warrant, but the *Warshak* court declared that provision unconstitutional.

coupons for free cookies to children under 13. Although the company did not share information with outsiders, it did collect personal information without parental consent from 84,000 children. This information included name, home address, and birthdate. Mrs. Fields paid a penalty of $100,000 and agreed not to violate the law again.

STATE REGULATION

An exhaustive list of state laws is beyond the scope of this book, but be aware that some states have passed their own online privacy laws. To take some examples, the California Online Privacy Act of 2003 requires any website that collects personal information from California residents to post a privacy policy conspicuously and then abide by its terms. Connecticut, Nebraska, and Pennsylvania also regulate online privacy policies.

Two states, Minnesota and Nevada, require ISPs to obtain their customers' consent before providing information about them. Connecticut and Delaware require employers to notify their workers before monitoring emails or Internet usage.

SPAM

Spam is officially known as *unsolicited commercial email (UCE)* or *unsolicited bulk email (UBE).* As much as 90 percent of all email is spam. **The Controlling the Assault of Non-Solicited Pornography and Marketing Act (CAN-SPAM) is a federal statute that does not prohibit spam but instead regulates it.** Under this statute, commercial email:

> As much as 90 percent of all email is spam.

- May not have deceptive headings (From, To, Reply To, Subject)
- Must offer an opt-out system permitting the recipient to unsubscribe (and must honor those requests promptly)
- Must provide a valid physical return address (not a post office box)

CAN-SPAM seems to have had little impact on the quantity of spam (although it has made opt-out provisions more common in legitimate commercial emails). And spammers have found other outlets. They post messages in the comment section of websites and on social media sites such as Facebook and Twitter. Their goal is to entice you to click on a link that may take you to a website that sells foolproof "investments" or that simply steals bank information from your computer. If that link seems to come from a Facebook friend or someone whom you follow on Twitter, it seems more reliable. A recent study found that 8 percent of links sent via Twitter are fraudulent, but they are 20 times more likely to be clicked than those in spam email.[3]

EXAM Strategy

Question: Cruise.com operated a website selling cruise vacations. It sent unsolicited email advertisements—dubbed "E-deals"—to prospective customers, and 11 of these "E-deals" went to **inbox@webguy.net**. Each message offered the recipient an opportunity to be removed from the mailing list by clicking on a line of text or by writing to a specific postal address. Has Cruise.com violated the CAN-SPAM Act?

---

[3]"Long life spam," *The Economist*, November 20, 2010, p. 67.

> **Strategy:** Remember that this Act does not prohibit all unsolicited emails.
>
> **Result:** Cruise.com was not in violation because it offered the recipients a way to unsubscribe.

INTERNET SERVICE PROVIDERS AND WEB HOSTS: COMMUNICATIONS DECENCY ACT OF 1996

ISPs are companies, such as Earthlink, that provide connection to the Internet. Web hosts post web pages on the Internet.

The Internet is an enormously powerful tool for disseminating information. But what if some of this information happens to be false or in violation of our privacy rights? Is an ISP liable for transmitting it to the world? In 1995, a trial judge in New York held that an ISP, Prodigy Services Company, was potentially liable for defamatory statements that an unidentified person posted on one of its bulletin boards.[4] The message alleged that the president of an investment bank had committed "criminal and fraudulent acts." It was not only a false statement, it was posted on the most widely read financial computer bulletin board in the country. Although one can only feel sympathy for the target of this slur, the decision nonetheless alarmed many observers, who argued that there was no way ISPs could review every piece of information that hurtles through their portals. The next year, Congress overruled the *Prodigy* case by passing the Communications Decency Act of 1996 (CDA).[5] **Under the CDA, ISPs and web hosts are not liable for information that is provided by someone else. Only content providers are liable.** The following case lays out the arguments in favor of the CDA, but it also illustrates some of the costs of the statute (and of the Internet).

CARAFANO V. METROSPLASH.COM, INC.

339 F.3d 1119, 2003 U.S. App. LEXIS 16548
United States Court of Appeals for the Ninth Circuit, 2003

CASE SUMMARY

Facts: Matchmaker.com is an Internet dating service that permits members to post profiles of themselves and to view the profiles of other members. Matchmaker reviews photos for impropriety before posting them but does not examine the profiles themselves.

Christianne Carafano is an actor who uses the stage name Chase Masterson. She has appeared in numerous films and television shows, such as *Star Trek: Deep Space Nine* and *General*

Hospital. Without her knowledge or consent, someone in Berlin posted a profile of her in the Los Angeles section of Matchmaker. In answer to the question "Main source of current events?" the person posting the profile put "*Playboy Playgirl*" and for "Why did you call?" responded "Looking for a one-night stand." In addition, the essays indicated that she was looking for a "hard and dominant" man with "a strong sexual appetite" and that she "liked sort of being controlled

---

[4]*Stratton Oakmont, Inc. v. Prodigy Services Company*, 1995 N.Y. Misc. LEXIS 229.
[5]47 U.S.C. 230.

by a man, in and out of bed." Pictures of the actor, taken off the Internet, were included with the profile. The profile also provided her home address and an email address, which, when contacted, produced an automatic email reply stating, "You think you are the right one? Proof it !!" [sic], and providing Carafano's home address and telephone number.

Unaware of the improper posting, Carafano began receiving sexually explicit messages on her home voice mail, as well as a sexually explicit fax that threatened her and her son. She received numerous phone calls, letters, and email from male fans expressing concern that she had given out her address and phone number (but simultaneously indicating an interest in meeting her). Feeling unsafe, Carafano and her son stayed in hotels or away from Los Angeles for several months.

One Saturday a week or two after the profile was first posted, Carafano's assistant, Siouxzan Perry, learned of the false profile through a message from "Jeff." Acting on Carafano's instructions, Perry contacted Matchmaker, demanding that the profile be removed immediately. The Matchmaker employee did not remove it then because Perry herself had not posted it, but on Monday morning, the company blocked the profile from public view, and then deleted it the following day.

Carafano filed suit against Matchmaker alleging invasion of privacy, misappropriation of the right of publicity, defamation, and negligence. The district court rejected Matchmaker's argument for immunity under the CDA on the grounds that the company provided part of the profile content.

Issue: *Does the CDA protect Matchmaker from liability?*

Decision: Matchmaker is not liable.

Reasoning: Under the CDA, Internet publishers are not liable for false or defamatory material if someone else provided the information. In this way, Internet publishers are different from print, television, and radio publishers.

Interactive computer services have millions of users. It would be impossible for these services to screen each of their millions of postings. If they were liable for content, they might choose to severely limit the number and type of messages. To avoid any restriction on free speech, Congress chose to protect computer services from liability if someone else provided the content.

The fact that some of the content in Carafano's fake profile was provided in response to Matchmaker's questionnaire does not make the company liable. The answers to the questions were provided exclusively by the user. No profile has any content until a user actively creates it. In this case, Carafano's home address and the email address that revealed her phone number were transmitted unaltered to profile viewers. Thus, Matchmaker did not play a significant role in creating, developing, or transforming the relevant information.

Despite the serious and utterly deplorable consequences in this case, Matchmaker cannot be sued under the CDA.

Note that the CDA does not protect web hosts and ISPs from contract liability. For example, after Cynthia Barnes broke up with her boyfriend, he created a profile of her on a Yahoo! website. He then spitefully posted nude photos of the two of them, taken without her knowledge, together with her addresses and phone numbers at home and at work. He also suggested that she was interested in sex with random strangers. Many men were willing to oblige. For months, Yahoo! did not even respond to Barnes's request to remove the profile. Not until a TV show prepared to run a story about the incident did the company's director of communications contact Barnes to promise that the profile would be removed immediately. Still, Yahoo! took no action until Barnes sued two months later. The appeals court ruled that Barnes could bring a contract claim against Yahoo! under a theory of promissory estoppel—that she had relied on the company's promise.[6]

EXAM Strategy

Question: Someone posted an anonymous review on TripAdvisor.com alleging that the owner of a restaurant had entertained a prostitute there. The allegation was false. TripAdvisor refused to investigate or remove the review. Does the restaurant owner have a valid claim against the website?

---

[6]*Barnes v. Yahoo!, Inc.*, 570 F.3d 1096 (9th Cir., 2008). Promissory estoppel is discussed at greater length in Chapter 9.

Strategy: Remember that web hosts are liable only if they have engaged in wrongdoing.

Result: As a web host, TripAdvisor is not liable for content. It would only be liable if it promised to take down the review and then did not.

CRIME ON THE INTERNET

Although the Internet provides many benefits, it has also opened new frontiers in crime.

Hacking

During the 2008 presidential campaign, college student David Kernell guessed Sarah Palin's email password, accessed her personal Yahoo! account and published the content of some of her emails. To many, his actions seemed like an amusing prank. The joke turned out not to be so funny when Kernell was sentenced to one year in prison.

Gaining unauthorized access to a computer system is called **hacking.** The goal of hackers is varied; some do it for little more than the thrill of the challenge. The objective for other hackers may be industrial espionage, extortion, theft of credit card information, or revenge for perceived slights. Kernell hoped to prevent Palin from being elected vice president.

Hacking is a crime under the federal Computer Fraud and Abuse Act of 1986 (CFAA). This statute applies to any computer, cell phone, iPod, or other gadget attached to the Internet. **The CFAA prohibits:**

- Accessing a computer without authorization and obtaining information from it

- Theft of information from the U.S. government

- Computer fraud

- Intentional, reckless, and negligent damage to a computer

- Computer extortion

Hacking
Gaining unauthorized access to a computer system.

Fraud

Fraud is the deception of another person for the purpose of obtaining money or property from him. Common scams include advance fee scams,[7] the sale of merchandise that is either defective or nonexistent; the so-called Nigerian letter scam;[8] billing for services that are touted as "free;" fraudulent stock offers; fake scholarship search services; romance fraud (you meet someone online who wants to visit you but needs money for "travel expenses"); and credit card scams (for a fee, you can get a credit card, even with a poor credit rating). One new scam involves *over* payment. You are renting out a house or selling something and

---

[7]As in, "If you are willing to pay a fee in advance, then you will have access to (take your pick) favorable financing, lottery winnings from overseas, or attractive investment opportunities that will make you rich."

[8]Victims receive an email from someone alleging to be a Nigerian government official who has stolen money from the government. He needs someplace safe to park the money for a short time. The official promises that, if the victim will permit her account to be used for this purpose, she will be allowed to keep a percentage of the stolen money. Instead, of course, once the "official" has the victim's bank information, he cleans out the account.

"by accident" are sent too much money. You wire the excess back, only to find out that the initial check or fund transfer was no good. You have lost whatever money you wired.

Fraud can be prosecuted under state law or the CFAA. In addition, federal mail and wire fraud statutes prohibit the use of mail or wire communication in furtherance of a fraudulent scheme. The FTC can bring civil cases under §5 of the FTC Act.

IDENTITY THEFT

Identity theft is one of the scariest crimes against property. Thieves steal the victim's social security number and other personal information such as bank account numbers and mother's maiden name, which they use to obtain loans and credit cards. The money owed is never repaid, leaving victims to prove that they were not responsible for the debts. The thieves may even commit (additional) crimes under their new identities. Meanwhile, the victim may find himself unable to obtain a credit card, loan, or job. One victim spent several nights in jail after he was arrested for a crime that his alter ego had committed.

Although identity fraud existed before computers, the Internet has made it much easier. For example, consumer activists were able to purchase the social security numbers of the director of the CIA, the Attorney General of the United States, and other top administration officials. The cost? Only $26 each. No surprise then that 8 million Americans are victims of this crime each year.

A number of federal statutes deal with identity theft or its consequences. **The Identity Theft and Assumption Deterrence Act of 1998 prohibits the use of false identification to commit fraud or other crime, and it also permits the victim to seek restitution in court.**[9] The Truth in Lending Act limits liability on a stolen credit card to $50. The Social Security Protection Act of 2010 prohibits government agencies from printing social security numbers on checks.

A number of states have also passed identity theft statutes. Almost every state now requires companies to notify consumers when their personal information has been stolen.

What can you do to prevent the theft of your identity?

1. Check your credit reports at least once a year. (Consumers are entitled by law to one free credit report every year from each of the three major reporting agencies. You can order these reports at **https://www.annualcreditreport.com.**)

2. Place a freeze on your credit report so that anyone who is about to issue a loan or credit card will double-check with you first.

3. If you suspect that your identity has been stolen, contact the FTC at 877-IDTHEFT, 877-438-4338, or **http://www.consumer.gov/idtheft**. Also, file a police report immediately and keep a copy to show creditors. Notify the three credit agencies.

PHISHING

Have you ever received an instant message from a Facebook friend saying, "Hey, what's up?" with a link to an IQ test? This instant message is not from a friend, but rather from a fraudster hoping to lure the recipient into revealing her personal information. In this case, people who clicked on the link were told that they had to provide their cell phone number to get the test results. Next thing they knew, they had been signed up for some expensive cell phone service. This scam is part of one of the most rapidly growing areas of Internet fraud: **phishing. In this crime, a fraudster sends an email directing the recipient to enter personal information on a website that is an illegal imitation of a legitimate site.**

In a traditional phishing scam, large numbers of generic emails are sprayed over the Internet asking millions of people to log in to, say, a fake bank site. But the latest development—called **spear phishing**—involves personalized messages sent from someone

Phishing
When a fraudster sends an email directing the recipient to enter personal information on a website that is an illegal imitation of a legitimate site.

---

[9] 18 U.S. Section 1028.

the victim knows. For example, your sister asks for your social security number so she can add you as a beneficiary to her life insurance policy. In reality, this email has come from a fraudster who hacked into her Facebook account to gain access to her lists of friends and family.[10] Even "like" buttons can be "clickjacked" to take unwary users to bogus sites.

Prosecutors can bring criminal charges against phishers for fraud. The companies whose websites have been copied can sue these criminals for fraud, trademark infringement, false advertising, and cybersquatting.

No reputable company will ask customers to respond to an email with personal information. When in doubt, close the suspicious email, relaunch your web browser, and then go to the company's main website. If the legitimate company needs information from you, it will so indicate on the site.

Chapter Conclusion

The Internet has changed our lives in ways that were inconceivable a generation ago. Like a racer coming off a delayed start, the law is rushing to catch up. Not only will laws change as legislators and courts learn from experience, but new laws will inevitably be needed.

EXAM REVIEW

1. **THE FIRST AMENDMENT**   The First Amendment to the Constitution protects speech on the Internet so long as the speech does not violate some other law. (p. 486)

2. **THE FOURTH AMENDMENT**   The Fourth Amendment to the Constitution prohibits unreasonable searches and seizures by government agents. This provision applies to computers. (pp. 486–487)

3. **REASONABLE EXPECTATION OF PRIVACY**   If your employer has a reasonably articulated policy notifying you that it has the right to access and read electronic communications on a system that it provides, then you do not have a reasonable expectation of privacy when using that system. You do have a reasonable right to privacy on a system that you provide for yourself. (pp. 487–488)

Question: Three travel agents use fictitious accounts to steal millions of frequent flyer miles. Must the police obtain a warrant before searching their email accounts?

Strategy: The answer depends on what type of email account is involved. (See the "Result" at the end of this section.)

EXAM Strategy

---

[10]To prevent your Facebook account from being hijacked, be careful when accessing it over a public network (such as in a hotel or airport), where fraudsters might be able to capture your password. If you text "otp" to 32665, you will receive a password that can only be used once (a "one-time password"). Fraudsters cannot use this password to access your account.

4. **THE FTC ACT**   Section 5 of the FTC Act prohibits unfair and deceptive practices. The FTC does not require websites to have a privacy policy, but if they do have one, it cannot be deceptive and they must comply with it. (pp. 488–489)

5. **THE ECPA**   The Electronic Communications Privacy Act of 1986 is a federal statute that prohibits unauthorized interception or disclosure of wire and electronic communications. However, it permits an employer to monitor workers' electronic communications if (1) the employee consents, (2) the monitoring occurs in the ordinary course of business, or (3) the employer provides the computer system (in the case of email). (p. 489)

6. **COPPA**   The Children's Online Privacy Protection Act of 1998 prohibits Internet operators from collecting information from children under 13 without parental permission. It also requires sites to disclose how they will use any information they acquire. (pp. 489–490)

7. **CAN-SPAM**   Under the Controlling the Assault of Non-Solicited Pornography and Marketing Act, spam email cannot contain deceptive headings. It must include a valid physical return address and must also offer recipients an unsubscribe option. (p. 490)

8. **THE CDA**   Under the Communications Decency Act of 1996, ISPs and web hosts are not liable for information that is provided by someone else. (pp. 491–492)

EXAM Strategy

Question: Ton Cremers was the director of security at Amsterdam's famous Rijksmuseum and the operator of the Museum Security Network (the Network) website. Robert Smith, a handyman working for Ellen Batzel in North Carolina, sent an email to the Network alleging that Batzel was the granddaughter of Heinrich Himmler (one of Hitler's henchmen) and that she had art that Himmler had stolen. These allegations were completely untrue. Cremers posted Smith's email on the Network's website and sent it to the Network's subscribers. Cremers exercised some editorial discretion in choosing which emails to send to subscribers, generally omitting any that were unrelated to stolen art. Is Cremers liable to Batzel for the harm that this inaccurate information caused?

Strategy: Cremers is only liable if he is a content provider. (See the "Result" at the end of this section.)

9. **THE CFAA**   Hacking is illegal under the federal Computer Fraud and Abuse Act of 1986. The CFAA prohibits:

- Accessing a computer without authorization and obtaining information from it
- Theft of information from the U.S. government
- Computer fraud
- Intentional, reckless, and negligent damage to a computer
- Computer extortion (p. 493)

10. **FRAUD**   Fraud is the deception of another person for the purpose of obtaining money or property from him. (pp. 493–494)

11. **IDENTITY THEFT**   The Identity Theft and Assumption Deterrence Act of 1998 prohibits the use of false identification to commit fraud or other crime. (p. 494)

---

3. Result: If their employer owns the email system, the agents have no expectation of privacy and the police do not need a search warrant. If, however, they are sending emails over a personal system they are paying for themselves, then the police do need a warrant.

8. Result: The court found that Cremers was not liable.

MATCHING QUESTIONS

Match the following terms with their definitions:

_____	A. ECPA	1. Regulates access to email
_____	B. Fourth Amendment to the Constitution	2. Regulates Internet service providers
		3. Regulates collection of information from children
_____	C. CFAA	4. Prohibits unreasonable searches and seizures of computers
_____	D. COPPA	
_____	E. CDA	5. Regulates computer hacking

TRUE/FALSE QUESTIONS

Circle true or false:

1. T F The First Amendment to the Constitution protects bloggers who post insults about other people.
2. T F The FTC requires bloggers to disclose any free products they receive for writing product reviews.
3. T F The FTC requires websites to establish a privacy policy and then abide by it.
4. T F Any intended recipient of an email may forward it to whomever she wishes.
5. T F The police can read anyone's email as long as they have probable cause to believe that the email will reveal evidence of a crime.

MULTIPLE-CHOICE QUESTIONS

1. Rory is concerned that the employees in her division are wasting too much time on personal matters. She would like to monitor them. Which of the following activities is she *not* allowed to do?

   (a) Ask key employees to forward to her any emails they receive from their colleagues that contain jokes or other silly content

   (b) Read all messages sent to employee pagers

(c)   Read all employee emails sent through the office system

(d)   Read employees' private email accounts

(e)   Read all emails sent in the ordinary course of business

2. Three terrorists are plotting to blow up a high-rise office building, which could lead to thousands of deaths. The police capture their computers and read the files before obtaining a warrant. Which of the following searches would be *illegal*?

 I.   Marshall has written elaborate plans, which are stored on the hard drive of his laptop.

 II. Winston has violated school policies by downloading plans for bombs from the Internet through the school's network.

 III. Montgomery has made rental car reservations over the Internet in a cybercafe.

(a)   I, II, and III

(b)   Neither I, II, nor III

(c)   Just I

(d)   Just II

(e)   Just III

3. The Computer Fraud and Abuse Act prohibits all of the following activities except:

(a)   Accessing a computer without authorization and obtaining information from it

(b)   Illegal file sharing over the Internet

(c)   Theft of information from the U.S. government

(d)   Negligent damage to a computer

(e)   Computer extortion

4. Under the CAN-SPAM Act, it is legal to:

(a)   Send out advertisements for sexually explicit websites

(b)   Send emails with false return addresses

(c)   Send emails with fake headers

(d)   Refuse to unsubscribe recipients

(e)   Use a post office box as a return address

5. Your novel has just been published and is now for sale on Amazon.com. You access Amazon via Earthlink one day and are horrified to see that a reader (or alleged reader) has posted a bad review that is not only totally unfair but also totally inaccurate. (You did not plagiarize portions of the book!) Which of the following would be liable to you:

 I.   Amazon.com

 II. Earthlink

 III. The person who wrote the review

(a)   I, II, and III

(b)   Neither I, II, nor III

(c)   I and III

(d)   Just I

(e)   Just III

ESSAY QUESTIONS

1. To demonstrate the inadequacies of existing computer security systems, Cornell student Robert Morris created a computer virus. His plan, however, went awry, as plans sometimes do. He thought his virus would be relatively harmless, but it ran amok, crashing scores of computers at universities, military sites, and medical research sites. Under what statute might Morris be charged? Does it matter that he did not intend to cause damage?

2. Nancy Garrity and Joanne Clark worked for John Hancock Mutual Life Insurance Company. On their office computers, they regularly received sexually explicit emails from friends and from Internet joke sites, which they then sent to coworkers. When a fellow employee complained, Hancock searched their email folders and, finding inappropriate emails, fired the two women. The Hancock email policy states: "Messages that are defamatory, abusive, obscene, profane, sexually oriented, threatening, or racially offensive are prohibited. Company management reserves the right to access all email files." The two employees filed suit against Hancock, alleging that the company had invaded their privacy. How would you rule as judge?

3. Over the course of 10 months, Joseph Melle sent more than 60 million unsolicited email advertisements to AOL members. What charges could be brought against him? Would you need more information before deciding?

4. What can you do to protect your privacy online? Draw up a concrete list of steps that you might reasonably consider. Are there some actions that you would not be willing to take because they are not worth it to you?

5. Craig Hare offered computers and related equipment for sale on various Internet auction websites. He accepted payment but not responsibility—he never shipped the goods. Which government agencies might bring charges against him?

DISCUSSION QUESTIONS

1. **ETHICS** Chitika, Inc. provided online tracking tools on websites. When consumers clicked the "opt-out" button, indicating that they did not want to be tracked, they were not—for ten days. After that, the software would resume tracking. Is there a legal problem with Chitika's system? An ethical problem? What Life Principles were operating here?

2. **ETHICS:** Matt Drudge published a report on his website that White House aide Sidney Blumenthal "has a spousal abuse past that has been effectively covered up…. There are court records of Blumenthal's violence against his wife." The Drudge Report is an electronic publication focusing on Hollywood and Washington gossip. AOL paid Drudge $3,000 a month to make the Drudge Report available to AOL subscribers. Drudge emailed his reports to AOL, which then posted them. Before posting, however, AOL had the right to edit content. Drudge ultimately retracted his allegations against Blumenthal, who sued AOL. He alleged that under the Communications Decency Act of 1996, AOL was a "content provider" because it paid Drudge and edited what he wrote. Do you agree? Putting liability aside, what moral obligation did AOL have to its members? To Blumenthal? Should AOL be liable for content it bought and provided to its members?

3. Roommate.com operated a website designed to match people renting out spare rooms with those looking for a place to live. Before subscribers could search listings or post housing opportunities on Roommate's website, they had to create profiles, a process that required them to answer a series of questions that included the subscriber's sex, sexual orientation, and whether he would bring children to a household. The site also encouraged subscribers to provide "Additional Comments," describing themselves and their desired roommates in an open-ended essay. Here are some typical ads:

- "I am not looking for Muslims"

- "Not acceptable: freaks, geeks, prostitutes (male or female), druggies, pet cobras, drama queens, or mortgage brokers"

- "Must be a black gay male!"

- "We are 3 Christian females who Love our Lord Jesus Christ.... We have weekly bible studies and bi-weekly times of fellowship"

Many of the ads violated the Fair Housing Act. Is roommates.com liable?

4. Jerome Schneider wrote several books on how to avoid taxes. These books were sold on Amazon.com. Amazon permits visitors to post comments about items for sale. Amazon's policy suggests that these comments should be civil (e.g., no profanity or spiteful remarks). The comments about Schneider's books were not very kind. One person alleged that Schneider was a felon. When Schneider complained, an Amazon representative agreed that some of the postings violated its guidelines and promised that they would be removed within one to two business days. Two days later, the posting had not been removed. Schneider filed suit. Is Amazon liable?

5. Tracking tools provide benefits to consumers, but they also carry risks. Should Congress regulate them? If so, what should the law provide?

CHAPTER 28

INTELLECTUAL PROPERTY

© Steve Allen/Jupiterimages

Cooper is a producer at a small indie film company in Los Angeles. He puts together packages that have a script, a director, and actors. He then finds investors who pay to make the movie and distributors who purchase the right to release it in cinemas, on TV, and on DVD. (Although most people think that box office results are what count, the reality is that, historically, over half of most movies' revenue came from home entertainment options such as DVD rentals and sales.)

Cooper is pretty excited about two packages he has put together: one stars established actor Robert de Niro, and the other features an up-and-coming director working with movie star Clive Owen. But his excitement has turned to disappointment—shockingly, he cannot find anyone willing to invest in either movie. Cooper hears the same thing from everyone: "DVD sales are way down, so we know we won't get the payback we used to. We can't afford to invest in as many movies."

On a flight to New York in search of investors, Cooper finds himself sitting next to a man who is watching a movie on his computer. Cooper knows this movie has not even been released to DVD yet. Clearly, the man has downloaded it from an illegal website. Cooper slowly crushes the plastic cup in his hand. What's wrong with that guy? Doesn't he know that movies cost money to make? Doesn't he realize people like him are killing an industry?

> On a flight to New York in search of investors, Cooper finds himself sitting next to a man who is watching a movie on his computer.... Clearly, the man has downloaded it from an illegal website.

INTRODUCTION

For much of history, land was the most valuable form of property. It was the primary source of wealth and social status. Today, intellectual property is a major source of wealth. New ideas—for manufacturing processes, computer programs, medicines, books—bring both affluence and influence.

Although both can be valuable assets, land and intellectual property are fundamentally different. The value of land lies in the owner's right to exclude, to prevent others from entering it. Intellectual property, however, has little economic value unless others use it. This ability to share intellectual property is both good news and bad. On the one hand, the owner can produce and sell unlimited copies of, say, a software program; but on the other hand, the owner has no easy way to determine if someone is using the program for free. The high cost of developing intellectual property, combined with the low cost of reproducing it, makes it particularly vulnerable to theft.

Because intellectual property is nonexclusive, many people see no problem in using it for free. But when consumers take intellectual property—movies, songs, and books—without paying for it, they ensure that fewer of these items will be produced.

Some commentators suggest that the United States has been a technological leader partly because its laws have always provided strong protection for intellectual property. The Constitution provided for patent protection early in the country's history.

PATENTS

Patent

A grant by the government permitting the inventor exclusive use of an invention for a specified period.

A patent is a grant by the government permitting the inventor exclusive use of an invention for 20 years from the date of filing. During this period, no one may make, use, or sell the invention without permission. In return, the inventor publicly discloses information about the invention that anyone can use upon expiration of the patent.

A patent is not available solely for an idea, but only for its tangible application. Thus, patents are available for:

Type of Invention	Example
Mechanical invention	A hydraulic jack used to lift heavy aircraft
Electrical invention	A prewired, portable wall panel for use in large, open-plan offices
Chemical invention	The chemical 2-chloroethylphosphonic acid used as a plant growth regulator
Process	A method for applying a chemical to a plant—such as a process for applying a weed killer to rice

Patents are not available for laws of nature, scientific principles, mathematical algorithms, or formulas such as $a^2 + b^2 = c^2$.

Business Method Patents

In recent years, so-called business method patents have been controversial. These patents involve a particular way of doing business that often includes data processing or mathematical calculations. Business method patents have been particularly common in e-commerce.

For example, Amazon.com patented its One-Click method of instant ordering. The company then obtained an injunction to prevent barnesandnoble.com from using its Express Lane service, which was similar to One-Click. The judge directed barnesandnoble.com to add another step to its ordering process. The Patent and Trademark Office (PTO) affirmed the Amazon patent, which will expire in 2017.

Facebook has been granted a patent on a process that "dynamically provides a news feed about a user of a social network." Most social media sites, such as LinkedIn, Twitter, and Flickr, use some version of this technology. At this writing, two important issues are unknown: the exact scope of the patent and how aggressive Facebook will be in enforcing it.

It would be very helpful if the courts provided more clarity—and certainty—about the scope and enforceability of business method patents. In a recent case, *Bilski v. Kappos*, the Supreme Court ruled that business methods are *generally* patentable, even as it held that the *particular* patent in the case (a method for hedging risk in commodities trading) was too abstract to be acceptable.[1] In the same case, the Supreme Court encouraged lower courts to narrow the scope of business method patents, but did not offer guidance as to what these limits should be. For the time being, it seems that inventors will continue to apply for business method patents while waiting for lower courts to develop standards that meet the approval of the Supreme Court.

However, in 2011 Congress passed a new patent statute entitled "America Invents Act." Under this statute, anyone who has been charged with infringement of certain financial service business method patents will have the right (from 2012 to 2020) to challenge the validity of that patent.

Requirements for a Patent

To receive a patent, an invention must be:

- **Novel.** An invention is not patentable if it (1) is known or has already been used in this country; (2) has been described in a publication here or overseas or (3) is otherwise available to the public. For example, an inventor discovered a new use for existing chemical compounds but was not permitted to patent it because the chemicals had already been described in prior publications, though the new use had not.[2]

- **Nonobvious.** An invention is not patentable if it is obvious to a person with ordinary skill in that particular area. An inventor was not allowed to patent a waterflush system designed to remove cow manure from the floor of a barn because it was obvious.[3]

- **Useful.** To be patented, an invention must be useful. It need not necessarily be commercially valuable, but it must have some current use. Being merely of scientific interest is not enough. Thus, a company was denied a patent for a novel process for making steroids because they had no therapeutic value.[4]

EXAM Strategy

Question: In 1572, during the reign of Queen Elizabeth I of England, a patent application was filed for a knife with a bone rather than a wooden handle. Would this patent be granted under current U.S. law?

---

[1] 2010 U.S. LEXIS 5521 (S.Ct. 2010).
[2] *In re Schoenwald*, 964 F.2d 1122, 1992 U.S. App. LEXIS 10181 (Fed. Cir. 1992).
[3] *Sakraida v. Ag Pro, Inc.*, 425 U.S. 273, 96 S. Ct. 1532, 1976 U.S. LEXIS 146 (1976).
[4] *Brenner v. Manson*, 383 U.S. 519, 86 S. Ct. 1033, 1966 U.S. LEXIS 2907 (1966).

Strategy: Was a bone handle novel, nonobvious, and useful?

Result: It was useful—no splinters from a bone handle. It was novel—no one had ever done it before. But the patent was denied because it was obvious.

Patent Application and Issuance

To obtain a patent, the inventor must file a complex application with the PTO. If a patent examiner determines that the application meets all legal requirements, the PTO will issue the patent. If an examiner denies a patent application for any reason, the inventor can appeal that decision to the Patent Trial and Appeal Board in the PTO and from there to the Court of Appeals for the Federal Circuit in Washington.

As of 2012, third parties have the right to submit evidence that an invention is not novel. Even after a patent has been granted, third parties have limited rights to challenge its validity.

PRIORITY BETWEEN TWO INVENTORS

When two people invent the same product, who is entitled to the patent—the first to invent or the first to file an application? Until 2013, the person who invents and puts the invention into practice has priority over the first filer. But in 2013 the law changes so that the first person to *file* a patent application has priority. This change brings the United States into conformity with the patent systems in most of the rest of the world.

PRIOR SALE

An inventor must apply for a patent within one year of selling the product commercially. The purpose of this rule is to encourage prompt disclosure of inventions. It prevents someone from inventing a product, selling it for years, and then obtaining a 20-year monopoly with a patent.

PROVISIONAL PATENT APPLICATION

Inventors who are unable to assess the market value of their ideas sometimes hesitate to file a patent application because the process is expensive and cumbersome. To solve this problem, the PTO now permits inventors to file a **provisional patent application (PPA).** The PPA is a simpler, shorter, cheaper application that gives inventors the opportunity to show their ideas to potential investors without incurring the full expense of a patent application. **PPA protection lasts only one year.** To maintain protection after that time, the inventor must file a regular patent application.

PATENT TROLLS

Patent applicants are not required to *demonstrate* that their invention is novel, and often the examiner neither understands nor has the time to research the issue. Thus, patents are sometimes issued for inventions that are not really new.

Traditionally, this issue was not that important because companies with overlapping patents did not litigate who the real inventor was. But then came **patent trolls**. They do not make or market products—they simply buy portfolios of patents for the purpose of bringing patent infringement claims against companies already using the technology. Typically, patent trolls request an injunction to prevent the use of the technology during litigation, potentially harming a multimillion-dollar product over a patent that is worth much less. Often, patent trolls are simply hoping that even legitimate users of a patent will pay them to go away.

Some hedge funds have entered the patent troll business. In addition, a company owned by Paul Allen, who was one of Microsoft's founders, recently began filing suit against

Patent troll

Someone who buys a portfolio of patents for the purpose of making patent infringement claims.

companies that are using technology that his research lab allegedly invented prior to 2005. These suits have been filed against most of the major players in Silicon Valley—Apple, eBay, Facebook, Google, and Netflix—for their use of technology that improves the users' online experience. The technology at issue is key to these companies. In response to criticism, patent trolls argue that they are encouraging innovation by making patents more valuable.

Ethics Is the patent troll business ethical? Under what circumstances would you be willing to engage in this practice? Paul Allen is wealthy beyond most people's dreams. Why would he be involved in such litigation? What is your Life Principle in this case?

INTERNATIONAL PATENT TREATIES

Suppose you have a great idea that you want to protect around the world. **The Paris Convention for the Protection of Industrial Property requires each member country to grant to citizens of other member countries the same rights under patent law as its own citizens enjoy.** Thus, the patent office in each member country must accept and recognize all patent and trademark applications filed with it by anyone who lives in any member country. For example, the French patent office cannot refuse to accept an application from an American, as long as the American has complied with French law.

The **Patent Cooperation Treaty** (PCT) is a step toward providing more coordinated patent review across many countries. Inventors who pay a fee and file a so-called PCT patent application are granted patent protection in the 143 PCT countries for up to 30 months. During this time, they can decide how many countries they actually want to file in.

The United States PTO has bilateral agreements with 16 other patent offices under a so-called **Patent Prosecution Highway**. Under this system, once a patent is approved by one country, it goes to the head of the line for patent examination in the other country.

COPYRIGHTS

The holder of a copyright owns the *particular expression* of an idea, but not the underlying idea or method of operation. Abner Doubleday could have copyrighted a book setting out his particular version of the rules of baseball, but he could not have copyrighted the rules themselves, nor could he have required players to pay him a royalty.

Unlike patents, the ideas underlying copyrighted material need not be novel. For example, three movies—*Like Father Like Son*, *Vice Versa*, and *Freaky Friday*—are about a parent and child who switch bodies. The movies all have the same plot, but there is no copyright violation because their *expressions* of the basic idea are different.

A work is copyrighted *automatically* once it is in tangible form. For example, when a songwriter puts notes on paper, the work is copyrighted without further ado. But if she whistles a happy tune without writing it down, the song is not copyrighted, and anyone else can use it without permission. Registration with the Copyright Office of the Library of Congress is necessary only if the holder wishes to bring suit to enforce the copyright. Although authors still routinely place the copyright symbol (©) on their works, such a precaution is not necessary in the United States. However, some lawyers still recommend using the copyright symbol because other countries recognize it. Also, the penalties for intentional copyright infringement are heavier than for unintentional violations, and the presence of a copyright notice is evidence that the infringer's actions were intentional.

In the following case, you can imagine the author's frustration when a celebrity stole her thunder and her sales by writing a book on the very same topic. But did the celebrity violate copyright law?

LAPINE V. SEINFELD

375 Fed. Appx. 81; 2010 U.S. App. LEXIS 8778
United States Court of Appeals for the Second Circuit, 2010

CASE SUMMARY

Facts: Missy Chase Lapine wrote a book called *The Sneaky Chef: Simple Strategies for Hiding Healthy Foods in Kids' Favorite Meals,* which was about how to disguise vegetables so that children would eat them. Her strategy was to add pureed vegetables to food that children like, such as macaroni and cheese. (We are not making this up.) Four months later, Jessica Seinfeld, the wife of comedian Jerry Seinfeld, published a book entitled *Deceptively Delicious: Simple Secrets to Get Your Kids Eating Good Food,* which featured recipes involving pureed vegetables in (guess what?) macaroni and cheese and other kid-friendly foods.

Lapine filed suit against Seinfeld, alleging violation of her copyright in *The Sneaky Chef.*

Issue: *Did Seinfeld violate Lapine's copyright in* **The Sneaky Chef?**

Decision: No, Seinfeld did not violate Lapine's copyright.

Reasoning: While it is true that the two books have a similar subject matter, no one can copyright the *idea* of

stockpiling vegetable purees for secret use in children's food. It is a fundamental principle of our copyright doctrine that ideas, concepts, and processes are not protected from copying.

As for the *expression* of the ideas in Lapine's work, it is true that the two books take a vaguely similar approach, including their titles, illustrations, health advice, recipes, and language about children's healthy eating. But any book with this subject matter would be likely to do the same. These features follow naturally from the work's theme rather than from the author's creativity.

In any event, the total concept and feel of the two books is different. *Deceptively Delicious* lacks an extensive discussion of child behavior, food philosophy, and parenting. Its recipes are simpler. And it uses brighter colors and more photographs than *The Sneaky Chef.*

In short, Lapine cannot copyright the *idea* of the book. And because the books look so different, it is clear that Seinfeld has not stolen the *expression* of Lapine's idea.

Copyright Term

More than 300 years ago, on April 10, 1710, Queen Anne of England approved the first copyright statute. Called the Statute of Anne, it provided copyright protection for 14 years, which could be extended by another 14 years if the copyright owner was still alive when the first term expired. Many credit the Statute of Anne with greatly expanding the burst of intellectual activity that we now refer to as the Enlightenment.

American law adopted these same time limits, which stayed in effect until the 20th century. Since then, copyright holders have fought aggressively to lengthen the copyright period. These efforts have been led by the Walt Disney Company, which wants to protect its rights in Mickey Mouse. Today, a copyright is valid until 70 years after the death of the work's last living author or, in the case of works owned by a corporation, the copyright lasts 95 years from publication or 120 years from creation, whichever is shorter. Once a copyright expires, anyone may use the material. Mark Twain died in 1910, so anyone may now publish *Tom Sawyer* without permission and without paying a copyright fee.

Infringement

Anyone who uses copyrighted material without permission is violating the Copyright Act. **To prove a violation, the plaintiff must present evidence that the work was original and that either:**

- The infringer actually copied the work; or

- The infringer had access to the original and the two works are substantially similar.

Damages can be substantial. In a recent case, a jury ordered SAP to pay Oracle $1.3 billion for copyright infringement of Oracle's software.

First Sale Doctrine

Suppose you buy a CD that, in the end, you do not like. Under the **first sale doctrine,** you have the legal right to sell that CD. **The first sale doctrine permits a person who owns a lawfully made copy of a copyrighted work to sell or otherwise dispose of that copy.** Note, however, that the first sale doctrine does not permit the owner to *make a copy* and sell it or give it away. If you listen to a CD and then decide to sell or give it away that is legal. But it is not legal to copy the CD onto your iPod and then sell or give away the original or any copy of it.

Fair Use

Because the period of copyright protection is so long, it has become even more important to uphold the exceptions to the law. Bear in mind that the point of copyright laws is to encourage creative work. A writer who can control, and profit from, artistic work will be inclined to produce more. If enforced oppressively, however, the copyright laws could stifle creativity by denying access to copyrighted work. **The doctrine of fair use permits limited use of copyrighted material without permission of the author for purposes such as criticism, news reporting, scholarship, or research.** Courts generally do not permit a use that will decrease revenues from the original work by, say, competing with it. A reviewer is permitted, for example, to quote from a book without the author's permission, but could not reproduce so much that the review was competing with the book itself.

Fair use doctrine
Permits limited use of copyrighted material without permission of the author.

Also under the fair use doctrine, faculty members are permitted to photocopy and distribute copyrighted materials to students, so long as the materials are brief and the teacher's action is spontaneous. If, over his breakfast coffee one morning, Professor Learned spots a terrific article in *Mad Magazine* that perfectly illustrates a point he intends to make in class that day, the fair use doctrine permits him to photocopy the page and distribute it to his class. However, when professors put together course packets, they (or the copy shop) must obtain permission and pay a royalty for the use of copyrighted material. Likewise, it is illegal for students to make photocopies of a classmate's course packet or textbook.

Digital Music and Movies

One of the major challenges for legal institutions in regulating copyrights is simply that modern intellectual property is so easy to copy. Many consumers are in the habit of violating the law by downloading copyrighted material—music, movies and books—for free. They seem to believe that if it is easy to steal something, then the theft is somehow acceptable. In one survey of adolescents aged 12 to 17, 75 percent agreed with the statement, "file sharing is so easy to do, it's unrealistic to expect people not to do it."[5]

---

[5] *http://pewinternet.org/Reports/2009/9-The-State-of-Music-Online-Ten-Years-After-Napster/The-State-of-Music-Online-Ten-Years-After-Napster.aspx?view=all#footnote25*, or google "pew 10 years after napster."

The entertainment world used to turn a blind eye, but illegal downloading is threatening the viability of recording companies, movie studios, and publishers. The statistics are compelling: in 2008, 40 *billion* songs were downloaded illegally, which is as much as 95 percent of all downloaded music! In the first decade of this century, music sales at American record labels declined by 58 percent. Without profitable record labels, who will find and promote new stars? As we saw in the opening scenario, which is a true story, this type of theft is having a profound effect on entertainment and publishing. But it is not just "big companies" that suffer—it is also the artists, musicians, actors, and writers, most of whom are not wealthy rock stars.

Industry is striking back. The Recording Industry Association of America (RIAA) developed a strategy of aggressively suing those who download large amounts of music illegally. In addition, a coalition of entertainment businesses sued Grokster, Ltd., and StreamCast Networks, Inc., two companies in the business of distributing free peer-to-peer software that allowed computer users to share electronic files. Although this software can be used for legal purposes (such as sharing the very briefs in that case), nearly 90 percent of the files available for download through Grokster or StreamCast were copyrighted. Even worse, the two companies encouraged the illegal uses of their software. For example, the chief technology officer of StreamCast said that "the goal is to get in trouble with the law and get sued. It's the best way to get in the news." The Supreme Court ruled that anyone who distributes a product or software and then promotes its use for the purpose of infringing copyrights is liable for the resulting acts of infringement by third parties.[6]

THE DIGITAL MILLENNIUM COPYRIGHT ACT

Tom Tomorrow drew a cartoon that was syndicated to 100 newspapers, but by the time the last papers received it, the cartoon had already gone zapping around cyberspace. Because his name had been deleted, some editors thought he had plagiarized it.

In response to incidents such as this, Congress passed the **Digital Millennium Copyright Act (DMCA),** which provides that:

- **It is illegal to delete copyright information, such as the name of the author or the title of the article.** It is also illegal to distribute false copyright information. Thus, anyone who emailed Tom Tomorrow's cartoon without his name on it, or who claimed it was his own work, would be violating the law.

- **It is illegal to circumvent encryption or scrambling devices that protect copyrighted works.** For example, some software programs are designed so that they can only be copied once. Anyone who overrides this protective device to make another copy is violating the law.

- **It is illegal to distribute tools and technologies used to circumvent encryption devices.** If you help others to copy that software program, you have violated the statute.

- **Online service providers (OSPs) are not liable for posting copyrighted material so long as they are unaware that the material is illegal and they remove it promptly after receiving notice that it violates copyright law.** Thus, when Viacom sued YouTube for allowing copyrighted material to be posted online, the court ruled for YouTube. General awareness that many postings infringed copyright law did not impose a duty on YouTube to monitor its videos. Its only requirement was to respond when notified of infringement. YouTube had done just that, removing Viacom's property within one day of receiving its "takedown notice."[7]

---

[6]*Metro-Goldwyn-Mayer Studios Inc. v. Grokster, Ltd.,*125 S. Ct. 2764, 2005 U.S. LEXIS 5212, (S. Ct., 2005).
[7]*Viacom Int'l, Inc. v. YouTube, Inc.,* 718 F. Supp. 2d 514 (S.D.N.Y., 2010).

International Copyright Treaties

The Berne Convention requires member countries to provide automatic copyright protection to any works created in another member country. The protection expires 50 years after the death of the author.

TRADEMARKS

A trademark is any combination of words and symbols that a business uses to identify its products or services and distinguish them from others. Trademarks are important to both consumers and businesses. Consumers use trademarks to distinguish between competing products. People who feel that Nike shoes fit their feet best can rely on the Nike trademark to know they are buying the shoes they want. A business with a high-quality product can use a trademark to develop a loyal base of customers who are able to distinguish its product from another.

Trademark
Any combination of words and symbols that a business uses to identify its products or services and distinguish them from others.

Ownership and Registration

Under common law, the first person to use a mark in trade owns it. Registration under the federal Lanham Act is not necessary. However, registration has several advantages:

- Even if a mark has been used in only one or two states, registration makes it valid nationally.

- Registration notifies the public that a mark is in use, which is helpful because anyone who applies for registration first searches the Public Register to ensure that no one else has rights to the mark.

- The holder of a registered trademark generally has the right to use it as an Internet domain name.

Under the Lanham Act, the owner files an application with the PTO in Washington, D.C. The PTO will accept an application only if the owner has already used the mark attached to a product in interstate commerce or promises to use the mark within six months after the filing. In addition, the applicant must be the *first* to use the mark in interstate commerce. Initially, the trademark is valid for 10 years, but the owner can renew it for an unlimited number of 10-year terms long as the mark is still in use.

Valid Trademarks

Words (Reebok); symbols (Microsoft's flying window logo); phrases (Nike's "Just do it"); shapes (Apple's iPod); sounds (NBC's three chimes); colors (Owens Corning's pink insulation); and even scents (plumeria blossoms on sewing thread) can be trademarked. To be valid, a trademark must be distinctive—that is, the mark must clearly distinguish one product from another.

The following categories are not distinctive and *cannot* be trademarked:

- **Similar to an existing mark.** To avoid confusion, the PTO will not grant a trademark that is similar to one already in existence on a similar product. Once the PTO had granted a trademark for "Pledge" furniture polish, it refused to trademark "Promise" for the same type of product.

- **Generic trademarks.** No one is permitted to trademark an item's ordinary name—"shoe" or "book," for example. Sometimes, however, a word begins as a trademark and later becomes a generic name. *Zipper, escalator, aspirin, linoleum, thermos, yo-yo,* *band-aid*, *ping-pong*, and *nylon* all started out as trademarks, but eventually became generic. Once a name is generic, the owner loses the trademark because the name can no longer be used to distinguish one product from another—all products are called the same thing. That is why Xerox Corp. encourages people to say, "I'll photocopy this document," rather than "I'll xerox it." Jeep, Rollerblade, and TiVo are names that began as trademarks and may now be generic. What about "app store"? Microsoft has sued Apple, disputing its right to trademark this term. Meanwhile, Facebook has trademarked "face," "book," "like," "wall," and "poke." The goal is not to prevent consumers from using these terms, but rather to warn off other companies.

- **Descriptive marks.** Words cannot be trademarked if they simply describe the product—such as "low-fat," "green," or "crunchy." Descriptive words can be trademarked, however, if they do not describe that particular product because they then become distinctive rather than descriptive. "Blue Diamond" is an acceptable trademark for nuts so long as the nuts are neither blue nor diamond-shaped.

- **Names.** The PTO generally will not grant a trademark in a surname because other people are already using it and have the right to continue. No one could register "Jefferson" as a trademark.

- **Scandalous or immoral trademarks.** The PTO refused to register a mark that featured a nude man and woman embracing.[8] This author once had a client who wanted to apply for a trademark for marijuana: "Sweet Mary Jane, she never lets you down." However, the client was unwilling to admit to affixing the name to his product and shipping it in interstate commerce. Medical marijuana is legal in 16 states today, but the PTO refuses to register marijuana trademarks.

The following case raises an issue of confusion in cyberspace. Once again, the Internet is challenging intellectual property laws that were not conceived with this technology in mind.

---

[8]*In re McGinley*, 660 F.2d 481, 211 U.S.P.Q. (BNA) 668, 1981 CCPA LEXIS 177 (C.C.P.A. 1981).

You be the Judge

Facts: Network Automation and Advanced Systems Concepts sold competing software that they both advertised on the Internet. Systems sold its product under the trademarked name ActiveBatch. Customers paid between $995 and $10,995 for these software programs.

Google AdWords is a program that sells "keywords," which are search terms that trigger the display of a sponsor's advertisement. Although ActiveBatch was Systems's

NETWORK AUTOMATION, INC. v. ADVANCED SYSTEMS CONCEPTS, INC.

2011 U.S. App. Lexis 4488
United States Court of Appeals for the Ninth Circuit, 2011

trademark, Network purchased it as a keyword. This purchase meant that anyone who googled "ActiveBatch" would see a web page where the top results were links to Systems's own website and various articles about the product. But in the "Sponsored Sites" section of the page, users saw Network's ad. This ad did not use the word "ActiveBatch."

You Be the Judge: *Has Network violated Systems's trademark by purchasing ActiveBatch as a Google keyword?*

Argument for Systems: By purchasing ActiveBatch as a Google keyword, Network is deliberately confusing customers about whose product it really is. When consumers use the Internet, they tend not to read carefully—they just click away. Few customers analyze the web address of an ad to make sure they are going to the right website. Indeed, customers may not even be aware of who owns Active-Batch. The Network ad does not reveal that Systems owns this software. Customers could easily assume that whatever web address comes up belongs to the rightful owner.

When customers search for a generic term, they know that they will encounter links from a variety of sources, but when they look for a trade name, their expectation is that they will be linked only to that specific product. For this reason, the use of another company's trade name can create tremendous confusion.

Argument for Network: Today, most consumers are sophisticated about the Internet. They skip from site to site, ready to hit the Back button whenever they are not satisfied with a site's contents. They fully expect to find some sites that are not what they imagine based on a glance at the domain name or search engine summary. Consumers do not form any firm expectations about the sponsorship of a website until they have seen the landing page—if then.

Even if Systems's arguments were true for consumer purchases, the typical customer for this software is a sophisticated businessperson buying an expensive product. These purchasers are likely to be very careful and will not be confused by Google ads. Also, they will probably understand the mechanics of Internet search engines and the nature of sponsored links.

In the end, Network's intent was not to confuse consumers but rather to allow them to compare its product to ActiveBatch. That goal is a completely appropriate use of a trademark.

Domain Names

Internet addresses, known as domain names, can be immensely valuable. Suppose you want to buy a new pair of jeans. Without thinking twice, you type in **http://www.jcrew.com** and there you are, ready to order. What if that address took you to a different site altogether, say, the personal site of one Jackie Crew? The store might lose out on a sale. Companies not only want to own their own domain name, they want to prevent complaint sites such as **http://www.untied.com** (about United Airlines) or **http://www.ihatestarbucks.com**. Generic domain names can be valuable, too. Shopping.com paid $750,000 to acquire its domain name from the previous (lucky) owner.

The **Anticybersquatting Consumer Protection Act permits both trademark owners and famous people to sue anyone who registers their name as a domain name in "bad faith."** The rightful owner of a trademark is entitled to damages of up to $100,000. For example, Jay Leno won a cybersquatting case against someone who was using thejaylenoshow.com to attract viewers to his own real estate website.

International Trademark Treaties

Under the **Paris Convention,** if someone registers a trademark in one country, then he has a grace period of six months during which he can file in any other country using the same original filing date. Under the **Madrid Agreement,** any trademark registered with the international registry is valid in all signatory countries. (The United States is a signatory.) The **Trademark Law Treaty** simplifies and harmonizes the process of applying for trademarks around the world. Now, a U.S. firm seeking international trademark protection need file only one application, in English, with the PTO, which sends the application to the World Intellectual Property Organization (WIPO), which transmits it to each country in which the applicant would like trademark protection.

EXAM Strategy

Question: Jerry Falwell was a nationally known Baptist minister. You can read about him on falwell.com. You can also read about him at fallwell.com—a site critical of his views on homosexuality. This site has a disclaimer indicating that it is not affiliated with Reverend Falwell. The minister sued fallwell.com, alleging a violation of trademark law and the anticybersquatting statute. Is there a violation?

Strategy: To win a trademark claim, the reverend must show that there was some confusion between the two sites. To win the cybersquatting claim, he must show bad faith on the part of fallwell.com.

Result: The reverend lost on both counts. The court ruled that there was no confusion—fallwell.com had a clear disclaimer. Also, there was no indication of bad faith. The court was reluctant to censor political commentary.

TRADE SECRETS

Trade secrets—such as the formula for Coca-Cola—can be a company's most valuable asset. It has been estimated that the theft of trade secrets costs U.S. businesses $100 billion a year. Under the Uniform Trade Secrets Act (UTSA), **a trade secret is a formula, device, process, method, or compilation of information that, when used in business, gives the owner an advantage over competitors who do not know it.** In determining if information is a trade secret, courts consider:

Trade secret
A formula, device, process, method, or compilation of information that, when used in business, gives the owner an advantage over competitors.

- How difficult (and expensive) was the information to obtain? Was it readily available from other sources?

- Does the information create an important competitive advantage?

- Did the company make a reasonable effort to protect it?

Although a company can patent some types of trade secrets, it may be reluctant to do so because patent registration requires that the formula be disclosed publicly. In addition, patent protection expires after 20 years. Some types of trade secrets cannot be patented—customer lists, business plans, and marketing strategies.

The following case deals with a typical issue: how much information can employees take with them when they start their own, competing business?

POLLACK V. SKINSMART DERMATOLOGY AND AESTHETIC CENTER P.C.

2004 Pa. Dist. & Cnty. Dec. LEXIS 214
Common Pleas Court of Philadelphia County, Pennsylvania, 2004

CASE SUMMARY

Facts: Dr. Andrew Pollack owned the Philadelphia Institute of Dermatology (PID), a dermatology practice. Drs. Toby Shawe and Samy Badawy worked for PID as independent contractors, receiving a certain percentage of the revenues from each patient they treated. Natalie Wilson was Dr. Pollack's medical assistant.

Pollack tentatively agreed to sell the practice to Shawe and Badawy. But instead of buying his practice, the two doctors decided to start their own, which they called Skinsmart. They executed a lease for the Skinsmart office space, offered Wilson a job, and instructed PID staff members to make copies of their appointment books and printouts of the patient list. Then they abruptly resigned from PID. Wilson called PID patients to reschedule procedures at Skinsmart. The two doctors also called patients and sent out a mailing to patients and referring physicians to tell them about Skinsmart.

Pollack filed suit, alleging that the two doctors had misappropriated trade secrets.

Issue: *Did Shawe and Badawy misappropriate trade secrets from PID?*

Decision: The two doctors did misappropriate trade secrets.

Reasoning: The right to protect trade secrets must be balanced against the right of individuals to pursue whatever occupation they choose. For this reason, secrets will only be protected if they are the particular information of the employer, not general secrets of the trade. Pollack must also demonstrate that the trade secrets had value and importance to his business and that he either discovered or owned the secrets.

Against this backdrop, it is clear the patient list is a trade secret, worthy of protection. Patient information is confidential and is not known to anyone outside the practice. Pollack relied upon the patient list as the core component of his practice. For this reason, it is valuable. He made substantial effort to compile the list over a number of years. It contained 20,000 names with related information. He spent money on computers, software, and employees to keep and maintain the list. He also sought to protect the secrecy of the information. Within PID's offices, the information was not universally known or accessible. Not every staff member, including the practicing physicians, could pull the records. Wilson did not have access to them, and the doctors relied on other PID employees to access the patient list.

Chapter Conclusion

For many individuals and companies, intellectual property is the most valuable asset they will ever own. As its economic value increases, so does the need to understand the rules of intellectual property law.

EXAM REVIEW

	Patent	Copyright	Trademark	Trade Secrets
Protects:	An invention that is the tangible application of an idea	The tangible expression of an idea, but not the idea itself	Words and symbols that a business uses to identify its products or services	Information that, when used in business, gives its owner an advantage over competitors
Requirements for protections:	Application approved by the PTO	Automatic once it is in tangible form	Must be used on the product in interstate commerce	Must be kept confidential
Duration:	20 years	70 years after death of the author or, for a corporation, 95 years from publication or 120 years from creation, whichever is shorter	10 years, but can be renewed an unlimited number of times	As long as it is kept confidential

MATCHING QUESTIONS

Match the following terms with their definitions:

___A. Patent

___B. Copyright

___C. Trade secrets

___D. Trademark

___E. Paris Convention

1. Protects the particular expression of an idea

2. A word that a business uses to identify a product

3. Extends patent protection overseas

4. Grants the inventor exclusive use of an invention

5. Compilation of information that would give its owner an advantage in business

TRUE/FALSE QUESTIONS

Circle true or false:

1. T F Once you have purchased a CD and copied it onto your iPod, it is legal to give the CD to a friend.

2. T F A provisional patent lasts until the product is used in interstate commerce.

3. T F In the case of corporations, copyright protection lasts 120 years from the product's creation.

4. T F Under the fair use doctrine, you have the right to make a photocopy of a chapter of this textbook for a classmate.

5. T F The first person to file the application is entitled to a patent over someone else who invented the product first.

MULTIPLE-CHOICE QUESTIONS

1. To receive a patent, an invention must meet all of the following tests, except:

   (a) It has not ever been used anyplace in the world.

   (b) It is a new idea.

   (c) It has never been described in a publication.

   (d) It is nonobvious.

   (e) It is useful.

2. After the death of Babe Ruth, one of the most famous baseball players of all time, his daughters registered the name "Babe Ruth" as a trademark. Which of the following uses would be legal without the daughters' permission?

   I.   Publication of a baseball calendar with photos of Ruth

   II. Sales of a "Babe Ruth" bat

   III. Sales of Babe Ruth autographs

(a) Neither I, II, nor III

(b) Just I

(c) Just II

(d) Just III

(e) I and III

3. To prove a violation of copyright law, the plaintiff does not need to prove that the infringer actually copied the work, but she does need to prove:

I. The item has a © symbol on it.

II. The infringer had access to the original.

III. The two works are similar.

(a) I, II, and III

(b) II and III

(c) I and II

(d) I and III

(e) Neither I, II, nor III

4. Eric is a clever fellow who knows all about computers. He:

I. Removed the author's name from an article he found on the Internet and sent it via email to his lacrosse team, telling them he wrote it

II. Figured out how to unscramble his roommate's cable signal so they could watch cable on a second TV

III. Taught the rest of his lacrosse team how to unscramble cable signals

Which of these activities is legal under the Digital Millennium Copyright Act?

(a) I, II, and III

(b) Neither I, II, nor III

(c) II and III

(d) Just III

(e) Just I

5. Which of the following items *cannot* be trademarked?

(a) A color

(b) A symbol

(c) A phrase

(d) A surname

(e) A shape

Essay Questions

1. Rebecca Reyher wrote (and copyrighted) a children's book entitled *My Mother Is the Most Beautiful Woman in the World*. The story was based on a Russian folktale told to her by her own mother. Years later, the children's TV show *Sesame Street* televised a

skit entitled "The Most Beautiful Woman in the World." The *Sesame Street* version took place in a different locale and had fewer frills, but the sequence of events in both stories was identical. Has *Sesame Street* infringed Reyher's copyright?

2. **ETHICS:** After Edward Miller left his job as a salesperson at the New England Insurance Agency, Inc., he took some of his New England customers to his new employer. At New England, the customer lists had been kept in file cabinets. Although the company did not restrict access to these files, it said there was an understanding to the effect that "you do not peruse my files and I do not peruse yours." The lists were not marked "confidential" or "not to be disclosed." Did Miller steal New England's trade secrets? Whether or not he violated the law, was it ethical for him to use this information at his new job? What is your Life Principle?

3. In the documentary movie *Expelled: No Intelligence Allowed,* there was a 15-second clip of "Imagine," a song by John Lennon. The purpose of the scene was to criticize the song's message. His wife and sons, who held the copyright, sued to block this use of the song. Under what theory did the movie makers argue that they had the right to use this music? Did they win?

4. Roger Schlafly applied for a patent for two prime numbers. (A prime number cannot be evenly divided by any number other than itself and 1. Examples of primes are 2, 3, 5, 7, 11, 13.) Schlafly's numbers are a bit longer—one is 150 digits, the other is 300. His numbers, when used together, can help perform the type of mathematical operation necessary for exchanging coded messages by computer. Should the PTO issue this patent?

5. The Susan G. Komen breast cancer charity trademarked the term "for the cure." It has brought suit against other charities that use the term, as in "run for the cure" or "kites for the cure." It also sues charities that use the same shade of pink that it has long used on its ribbons. Should Komen be able to trademark "for the cure" and the color pink?

EXAM Strategy

6. **Question:** A man asked a question of the advice columnist at his local newspaper. His wife had thought of a clever name for an automobile. He wanted to know if there was any way they could own or register the name so that no one else could use it. If you were the columnist, how would you respond?

Strategy: The couple want to trademark this name. Can they do so? (See the "Result" at the end of this section.)

EXAM Strategy

7. **Question:** Frank B. McMahon wrote one of the first psychology textbooks to feature a light and easily readable style. He also included slang and examples that appealed to a youthful student market. Charles G. Morris wrote a psychology textbook that copied McMahon's style. Has Morris infringed McMahon's copyright?

Strategy: McMahon cannot copyright an idea—only the *expression* of an idea. (See the "Result" at the end of this section.)

6. Result: The couple could not trademark the name unless they had already or were intending to attach it to a product used in interstate commerce. So unless they had plans to manufacture a car, they could not trademark the name.

7. Result: The style of a textbook is an idea and not copyrightable. Thus, Morris could write a book with funny stories, just not the same stories told in the same way as in McMahon's book. Morris did not infringe McMahon's copyright.

DISCUSSION QUESTIONS

1. **ETHICS** Virtually any TV show, movie, or song can be downloaded for free on the Internet. Most of this material is copyrighted and was very expensive to produce. Most of it is also available for a fee through such legitimate sites as iTunes. What is your ethical obligation? Should you pay $1.99 to download an episode of *American Idol* from iTunes or take it for free from an illegal site? What is your Life Principle?

2. For much of history, the copyright term was limited to 28 years. Now it is as long as 120 years. What is a fair copyright term? Some commentators argue that because so much intellectual property is stolen, owners need longer protection. Do you agree with this argument?

3. Should Amazon be able to patent the One-Click method of ordering? What about Facebook's patent on a process that "dynamically provides a news feed about a user of a social network"? Were these inventions novel and nonobvious? What should the standard be for business method patents?

4. Fredrik Colting wrote a book entitled *60 Years Later: Coming Through the Rye*, a riff on J. D. Salinger's famous *Catcher in the Rye*. Colting's book imagined how Salinger's protagonist, Holden Caulfield, would view life as a 76-year-old. Alice Randall wrote a novel entitled *The Wind Done Gone*, which retells the Civil War novel *Gone with the Wind* from the perspective of Scarlett O'Hara's (imagined) black half-sister. Both Colting and Randall were sued and both alleged fair use. Should they win?

5. Should a wildflower garden be eligible for intellectual property protection?

CHAPTER 29

REAL PROPERTY AND LANDLORD-TENANT LAW

© Steve Allen/Jupiterimages

Some men have staked claims to land for its oil, others for its gold. But Paul Termarco and Gene Murdoch are staking their claim to an island using ... hot dogs. Their quest to market frankfurters in the New Jersey wilderness has made their children blush with embarrassment, their wives shrug in bewilderment, and strangers burst into laughter. But for three years, the two friends from West Milford have sold chili dogs, cheese dogs, and the ever-traditional, hold-everything-but-the-mustard hot dogs from a tiny island in Greenwood Lake. Now it seems as though everyone knows about "Hot Dog Island."

> Paul Termarco and Gene Murdoch are staking their claim to an island using ... hot dogs.

"People love it," said Termarco. "They say, 'Thank you for being here.' I always say, 'No. Thank you.'" The personalized service and the inexpensive prices (hot dogs cost $1.75, chili dogs, cheese dogs, and sauerkraut $2) have cultivated a base of regulars. "I think it's great. It's better than going to a restaurant for two hours and spending a lot of money," said Joan Vaillant, who frequently jet-skis to the island for hot dogs slathered in mustard.

At two-eighths of an acre, the island's pile of craggy rocks, scrubby bushes, and a few ash trees are difficult to spot. Termarco doesn't mind. "Not everyone can say they own an island," he boasted. Termarco and Murdoch decided to claim the slip of land after chatting with a local restaurateur a few years ago. Termarco had just finished suggesting that the man expand his lakeside business to the island when Murdoch kicked his friend under the table.

"We left thinking, 'We can do this ourselves,'" said Murdoch, who rushed to the township offices the following day to see who owned the island. Property records showed that the state owned the lake and lake floor, but nobody owned the island. An attorney told them about the law of adverse possession written in the 1820s. If Murdoch and Termarco could show that they used the island for five years, it would be theirs. As crazy as the scheme sounded, Murdoch figured it was worth trying.[1]

Can two friends acquire an island simply by pretending they own it? Possibly. The law of adverse possession permits people to obtain title to land by using it if they meet certain criteria, which we examine later in the chapter. Real property law can provide surprises.

NATURE OF REAL PROPERTY

Property falls into three categories: real, personal, and intellectual. Real property, which is the focus of this chapter, usually consists of the following:

- **Land.** Land is the most common and important form of real property. In England, land was historically the greatest source of wealth and social status, far more important than industrial or commercial enterprises. As a result, the law of real property has been of paramount importance for nearly 1,000 years, developing very gradually to reflect changing conditions. Some real property terms sound medieval for the simple reason that they *are* medieval. By contrast, the common law of torts and contracts is comparatively new.

  Real property usually also includes anything underground ("subsurface rights"), and some amount of airspace above land ("air rights").

- **Buildings.** Buildings are real property. Houses, office buildings, apartment complexes, and factories all fall in this category.

- **Plant life.** Plant life growing on land is real property whether the plants are naturally occurring, such as trees, or cultivated crops. When a landowner sells his property, plant life is automatically included in the sale, unless the parties agree otherwise. A landowner may also sell the plant life separately if he wishes. A sale of the plant life alone, without the land, is a sale of goods. (Goods, as you may recall, are movable things.)

- **Fixtures.** Fixtures are goods that have become attached to real property. A house (which is real property) contains many fixtures. The furnace and heating ducts were goods when they were manufactured and when they were sold to the builder because they were movable. But when the builder attached them to the house, the items became fixtures. By contrast, neither the refrigerator nor the grand piano is a fixture.

When an owner sells real property, the buyer normally obtains the fixtures unless the parties specify otherwise. Sometimes it is difficult to determine whether something is a fixture. The general rule is this: **an object is a fixture if a reasonable person would consider the item to be a permanent part of the property,** taking into account attachment, adaptation, and other objective manifestations of permanence:

- *Attachment.* If an object is attached to property in such a way that removing it would damage the property, it is probably a fixture. Heating ducts could be removed from a house, but only by ripping open walls and floors, so they are fixtures.

---

[1]Leslie Haggin, "Pair Stake Their Claim to Hot Dog Island," *Record* (Bergen, NJ), September 5, 1994, p. A12. Excerpted with permission of the *Record*, Hackensack, NJ.

- *Adaptation.* Something that is made or adapted *especially for attachment* to the particular property is probably a fixture, such as custom-made bookshelves fitted in a library.

- *Other manifestations of permanence.* If the owner of the property clearly intends the item to remain permanently, it is probably a fixture. Suppose a homeowner constructs a large concrete platform in his backyard, then buys a heavy metal shed and bolts it to the platform. His preparatory work indicates that he expects the shed to remain permanently, and a court would likely declare it a fixture.

CONCURRENT ESTATES

Concurrent estate
Two or more people owning property at the same time.

When two or more people own real property at the same time, they have **concurrent estates**. The most common forms of concurrent estates are tenancy in common, joint tenancy, and tenancy by the entirety.

Tenancy in Common

Tenancy in common
Two or more people holding equal interest in a property, but with no right of survivorship.

The most common form of concurrent estate is **tenancy in common**. Suppose Patricia owns a house. Patricia agrees to sell her house to Quincy and Rebecca. When she **conveys** the deed (that is, transfers the deed) "to Quincy and Rebecca," those two now have a tenancy in common. This kind of estate can also be created in a will. If Patricia had died still owning the house, and left it in her will to "Sam and Tracy," then Sam and Tracy would have a tenancy in common. Tenancy in common is the "default setting" when multiple people acquire property. Co-owners are automatically considered tenants in common unless another type of interest (joint tenancy, tenancy by the entirety) is specified.

A tenancy in common might have 2 owners, or 22, or any number. The tenants in common do not own a particular section of the property; they own an equal interest in the entire property. Quincy and Rebecca each own a 50 percent interest in the entire house.

Any co-tenant may convey her interest in the property to another person. Thus, if Rebecca moves 1,000 miles away, she may sell her 50 percent interest in the house to Sidney.

PARTITION

Since any tenant in common has the power to convey her interest, some people may find themselves sharing ownership with others they do not know or, worse, dislike. What to do? Partition, or division of the property among the co-tenants. Any co-tenant is entitled to demand partition of the property. If the various co-tenants cannot agree on a fair division, a co-tenant may request a court to do it. **All co-tenants have an absolute right to partition.**

A court will normally attempt a **partition by kind,** meaning that it actually divides the land equally among the co-tenants. If three co-tenants own a 300-acre farm and the court can divide the land so that the three sections are of roughly equal value, it will perform a partition in kind, even if one or two of the co-tenants oppose partition. If partition by kind is impossible because there is no fair way to divide the property, the court will order the real estate sold and the proceeds divided equally.

Joint Tenancy

Joint tenancy
Two or more people holding equal interest in a property, with the right of survivorship.

Joint tenancy is similar to tenancy in common but is used less frequently. The parties, called *joint tenants,* again own a percentage of the entire property and also have the absolute right of partition. The primary difference is that a **joint tenancy** includes the right of survivorship.

Recall that a tenant in common, by contrast, has the power to leave his interest in the real estate to his heirs. Because a joint tenant cannot leave the property to his heirs, courts do not favor this form of ownership. The law presumes that a concurrent estate is a tenancy in common; a court will interpret an estate as a joint tenancy only if the parties creating it clearly intended that result.

Joint tenancy has one other curious feature. Although joint tenants may not convey their interest by will, they may do so during their lifetime. If Frank and George own vacation property as joint tenants, Frank has the power to sell his interest to Harry. But as soon as he does so, the joint tenancy is **severed,** that is, broken. Harry and George are now tenants in common, and the right of survivorship is destroyed.

EXAM Strategy

Question: Thomas, aged 80, has spent a lifetime accumulating unspoiled land in Oregon. He owns 16,000 acres, which he plans to leave to his five children. He is not so crazy about his grandchildren. Thomas cringes at the problems the grandchildren would cause if some of them inherited an interest in the land and became part-owners along with Thomas's own children. Should Thomas leave his land to his children as tenants in common or joint tenants?

Strategy: When a co-tenant dies, her interest in property passes to her heirs. When a joint tenant dies, his interest in the property passes to the surviving joint tenants.

Result: Thomas is better off leaving the land to his children as joint tenants. That way, when one of his children dies, that child's interest in the land will go to Thomas's surviving children, not to his grandchildren.

ADVERSE POSSESSION

Recall Paul Termarco and Gene Murdoch, who opened this chapter by trying to sell us a hot dog from the middle of a New Jersey lake. The pair had their sights set on more than mustard and relish: they hoped that by using the island as if they owned it, they *would* own it. They were relying on the doctrine of adverse possession. **Adverse possession allows someone to take title to land if she demonstrates possession that is (1) exclusive; (2) notorious; (3) adverse to all others; and (4) continuous.**

Adverse possession
Allows someone to take title to land without paying for it, if she meets four specific standards.

Entry and Exclusive Possession

The user must take physical possession of the land and must be the only one to do so. If the owner is still occupying the land, or if other members of the public share its use, there can be no adverse possession.

Open and Notorious Possession

The user's presence must be visible and generally known in the area, so that the owner is on notice that his title is contested. This ensures that the owner can protect his property by ejecting the user. Someone making secret use of the land gives the owner no opportunity to do this, and hence acquires no rights in the land.

A Claim Adverse to the Owner

The user must clearly assert that the land is his. He does not need to register a deed or take other legal steps, but he must act as though he is the sole owner. If the user occupies the land with the owner's permission, there is no adverse claim and the user acquires no rights in the property.

Continuous Possession for the Statutory Period

State statutes on adverse possession prescribe a period of years for continuous use of the land. Originally, most states required about 20 years to gain adverse possession, but the trend has been to shorten this period. Many states now demand 10 years, and a few require only 5 years of use. The reason for shortening the period is to reward those who make use of land.

Regardless of the length required, the use must be continuous. In a residential area, the user would have to occupy the land year round for the prescribed period. In a wilderness area generally used only in the summer, a user could gain ownership by seasonal use.

How did Murdoch and Termarco fare? They certainly entered on the land and established themselves as the exclusive occupants. Their use has been open and notorious, allowing anyone who claimed ownership to take steps to eject them from the property. Their actions have been adverse to anyone else's claim. If the two hot dog entrepreneurs have grilled those dogs for the full statutory period, they should take title to the island.

In the following case, the couple claiming adverse possession have taken up residence in a ghost town.

RAY V. BEACON HUDSON MOUNTAIN CORP.

88 N.Y.2d 154, 666 N.E.2d 532, 1996 N.Y. LEXIS 676
Court of Appeals of New York, 1996

CASE SUMMARY

Facts: In 1931, Rose Ray purchased a cottage in a mountaintop resort town in the Adirondacks, at the same time agreeing to rent the land on which the structure stood. The long-term lease required her to pay the real estate taxes and provided that when the tenancy ended, the landlord would buy back the cottage at fair market value. In 1960, the landlord terminated the lease of everyone in the town, so Ray and all other residents packed up and left. She died in 1962, without ever getting a penny for the cottage. The next year, Mt. Beacon Incline Lands, Inc., bought all rights to the abandoned 156-acre resort.

Robert and Margaret Ray, the son and daughter-in-law of Rose Ray, reentered the cottage and began to use it one month per year, every summer from 1963 to 1988. They paid taxes, insured the property, installed utilities, and posted "No Trespassing" signs.

In 1978, Beacon Hudson bought the resort in a tax foreclosure sale. Finally, in 1988, the Rays filed suit, claiming title to the cottage by adverse possession. Beacon Hudson counterclaimed, seeking to eject the Rays. The

trial court ruled for the couple. The appellate court reversed, stating that the Rays had been absent too frequently to achieve adverse possession. The Rays appealed to New York's highest court.

Issue: *Did the Rays acquire title by adverse possession?*

Decision: The Rays acquired title by adverse possession. Reversed.

Reasoning: To obtain property by adverse possession, the claiming party must prove continuous possession, among other elements. However, the actual occupancy need not be constant. The claimant must simply use the land as ordinary owners would.

Beacon Hudson argues that the Rays cannot demonstrate continuous possession because they only occupied the property one month per year. However, that argument fails to consider the Rays' other acts of control over the premises. The couple maintained and improved the cottage and installed utilities. They also repelled trespassers, posted the land, and padlocked the cottage. These acts demonstrated continuous control of the property.

The Rays' seasonal use of the cottage, along with the improvements described, put the owner on notice of the couple's hostile and exclusive claim of ownership, especially considering that all neighboring structures had collapsed due to vandalism and neglect. The Rays have obtained title by adverse possession.

LAND USE REGULATION

Zoning

Zoning statutes are state laws that permit local communities to regulate building and land use. The local communities, whether cities, towns, or counties, then pass zoning ordinances that control many aspects of land development. For example, a town's zoning ordinance may divide the community into an industrial zone where factories may be built, a commercial zone in which stores of a certain size are allowed, and several residential zones in which only houses may be constructed. Within the residential zones, there may be further divisions—for example, permitting two-family houses in certain areas and requiring larger lots in others.

Zoning statutes

State laws that permit local communities to regulate land use.

Ethics   Many people abhor "adult" businesses, such as strip clubs and pornography shops. Urban experts agree that having a large number of these concerns in a neighborhood often causes crime to increase and property values to drop. Nonetheless, many people patronize such businesses, which can earn a good profit. Should a city have the right to restrict adult businesses? Some cities have passed zoning ordinances that prohibit adult businesses from all residential neighborhoods, from some commercial districts, or from being within 500 feet of schools, houses of worship, daycare centers, or other sex shops (to avoid clustering). Owners and patrons of these shops have protested, claiming the restrictions unfairly deny access to a form of entertainment that the public obviously desires. Who are the stakeholders? What are the consequences of these restrictions?

Eminent Domain

Eminent domain is the power of the government to take private property for public use. A government may need land to construct a highway, an airport, a university, or public housing. All levels of government—federal, state, and local—have this power. But the Fifth Amendment to the United States Constitution states: "… nor shall private property be taken for public use, without just compensation." The Supreme Court has held that this clause, the Takings Clause, applies not only to the federal government but also to state and local governments. So, although all levels of government have the power to take property, they must pay the owner a fair price.

A "fair price" generally means the reasonable market value of the land. Generally, if the property owner refuses the government's offer, the government will file suit seeking **condemnation** of the land; that is, a court order specifying what compensation is just and awarding title to the government.

A related issue arose in the following case. A city used eminent domain to take property on behalf of *private developers*. Was this a valid public use? The *Kelo* decision was controversial, and in response, some states passed statutes prohibiting eminent domain for private development.

Eminent domain

The power of the government to take private property for public use.

KELO V. CITY OF NEW LONDON, CONNECTICUT

545 U.S. 469, 125 S.Ct. 2655
United States Supreme Court, 2005

CASE SUMMARY

Facts: New London, Connecticut, was declining economically. The city's unemployment rate was double that of the state generally, and the population at its lowest point in 75 years. In response, state and local officials targeted a section of the city called Fort Trumbull for revitalization. Located on the Thames River, Fort Trumbull comprised 115 privately owned properties and 32 additional acres of an abandoned naval facility. The development plan included one section for a waterfront conference hotel and stores; a second one for 80 private residences; and one for research facilities.

The state bought most of the properties from willing sellers. However, nine owners of 15 properties refused to sell, and they filed suit. The owners claimed that the city was trying to take land for *private* use, not public, in violation of the Takings Clause. The case reached the United States Supreme Court.

Issue: *Did the city's plan violate the Takings Clause?*

Decision: No, the plan was constitutional. Affirmed.

Reasoning: The Takings Clause allows for some transfers of real property from one private party to another, so long as the land will be used by the public. For example, land may be taken to allow for the construction of a railroad even if private railroad companies will be the primary beneficiaries of the transfer.

New London's economic development plan aimed to create jobs and increase the city's tax receipts. The Supreme Court had not previously considered this type of public use, but it now determined that economic development is a legitimate public purpose. New London did not violate the Takings Clause.

Dissent by Justice O'Connor: Any public benefit in this case would be incidental and secondary. Under the majority's opinion, the government can now take private property for *any* purpose. This case will most likely benefit those with inside access to government officials at the expense of small property owners.

LANDLORD-TENANT LAW

Landlord-tenant law is is really a combination of three areas of law: property, contract, and negligence. We begin our examination of landlord-tenant law with an analysis of the different types of tenancy.

When an owner allows another person temporary, exclusive possession of the property, the parties have created a landlord-tenant relationship. The owner is the **landlord**, and the person allowed to possess the property is the **tenant**. The landlord has conveyed a **leasehold** interest to the tenant, meaning the right to temporary possession. Courts also use the word *tenancy* to describe the tenant's right to possession. A leasehold may be commercial or residential.

Three Legal Areas Combined

Property law influences landlord-tenant cases because the landlord is conveying rights in real property to the tenant. She is also keeping a reversionary interest in the property, meaning the right to possess the property when the lease ends. Contract law plays a role because the basic agreement between the landlord and tenant is a contract. **A lease is a contract that creates a landlord-tenant relationship.** And negligence law increasingly determines the liability of landlord and tenant when there is an injury to a person or property.

Lease

The statute of frauds generally requires that a lease be in writing. Some states will enforce an oral lease if it is for a short term, such as one year or less, but even when an oral lease is permitted, it is wiser for the parties to put their agreement in writing because a written lease helps to avoid many misunderstandings. At a minimum, a lease must state the names of the parties, the premises being leased, the duration of the agreement, and the rent. But a well-drafted lease generally includes many provisions, called *covenants* and *conditions*. A **covenant** is simply a promise by either the landlord or the tenant to do something or refrain from doing something. For example, most leases include a covenant concerning the tenant's payment of a security deposit and the landlord's return of the deposit, a covenant describing how the tenant may use the premises, and several covenants about who must maintain and repair the property, who is liable for damage, and so forth. Generally, tenants may be fined but not evicted for violating lease covenants. A **condition** is similar to a covenant, but it allows for a landlord to evict a tenant if there is a violation. In many states, conditions in leases must be clearly labeled as "conditions" or "evictable offenses."

TYPES OF TENANCY

There are four types of tenancy: a tenancy for years, a periodic tenancy, a tenancy at will, and a tenancy at sufferance. The most important feature distinguishing one from the other is how each tenancy terminates. In some cases, a tenancy terminates automatically, while in others, one party must take certain steps to end the agreement.

Tenancy for Years

Any lease for a stated, fixed period is a tenancy for years. If a landlord rents a summer apartment for the months of June, July, and August of next year, that is a tenancy for years. A company that rents retail space in a mall beginning January 1, 2012, and ending December 31, 2015, also has a tenancy for years. A tenancy for years terminates automatically when the agreed period ends.

Periodic Tenancy

A periodic tenancy is created for a fixed period and then automatically continues for additional periods until either party notifies the other of termination. This is probably the most common variety of tenancy, and the parties may create one in either of two ways. Suppose a landlord agrees to rent you an apartment "from month to month, rent payable on the first." That is a periodic tenancy. The tenancy automatically renews itself every month unless either party gives adequate notice to the other that she wishes to terminate. A periodic tenancy could also be for one-year periods—in which case it automatically renews for an additional year if neither party terminates—or for any other period.

Tenancy at Will

A tenancy at will has no fixed duration and may be terminated by either party at any time.[2] Typically, a tenancy at will is vague, with no specified rental period and with payment, perhaps, to be made in kind. The parties might agree, for example, that a tenant farmer

---

[2]The courts of some states, annoyingly, use the term *tenancy at will* for what are, in reality, periodic tenancies. They do this to bewilder law students and even lawyers, a goal at which they are quite successful. This text uses *tenancy at will* in its more widely known sense, meaning a tenancy terminable at any time.

could use a portion of his crop as rent. Since either party can end the agreement at any time, it provides no security for either landlord or tenant.

Tenancy at Sufferance

A tenancy at sufferance occurs when a tenant remains on the premises, against the wishes of the landlord, after the expiration of a true tenancy. Thus, a tenancy at sufferance is not a true tenancy because the tenant is staying without the landlord's agreement. The landlord has the option of seeking to evict the tenant or of forcing the tenant to pay rent for a new rental period.

LANDLORD'S DUTIES

Duty to Deliver Possession

The landlord's first important duty is to **deliver possession** of the premises at the beginning of the tenancy; that is, to make the rented space available to the tenant. In most cases, this presents no problems, and the new tenant moves in. But what happens if the previous tenant has refused to leave when the new tenancy begins? In most states, the landlord is legally required to remove the previous tenant. In some states, it is up to the new tenant either to evict the existing occupant or begin charging him rent.

Quiet Enjoyment

All tenants are entitled to quiet enjoyment of the premises, meaning the right to use the property without the interference of the landlord. Most leases expressly state this covenant of quiet enjoyment. And if a lease includes no such covenant, the law implies the right of quiet enjoyment anyway, so all tenants are protected. If a landlord interferes with the tenant's quiet enjoyment, he has breached the lease, entitling the tenant to damages.

The most common interference with quiet enjoyment is an eviction, meaning some act that forces the tenant to abandon the premises. Of course, some evictions are legal, as when a tenant fails to pay the rent. But some evictions are illegal. There are two types of eviction: actual and constructive.

Actual Eviction

If a landlord prevents the tenant from possessing the premises, he has actually evicted her. Suppose a landlord decides that a group of students are "troublemakers." Without going through lawful eviction procedures in court, the landlord simply waits until the students are out of the apartment and changes the locks. By denying the students access to the premises, the landlord has actually evicted them and has breached their right of quiet enjoyment.

Constructive Eviction

If a landlord substantially interferes with the tenant's use and enjoyment of the premises, he has constructively evicted her. Courts construe certain behavior as the equivalent of an eviction. In these cases, the landlord has not actually prevented the tenant from possessing the premises, but has instead interfered so greatly with her use and enjoyment that the law regards the landlord's actions as equivalent to an eviction. Suppose the heating system in an apartment house in Juneau, Alaska, fails during January. The landlord, an avid sled-dog racer, tells the tenants he is too busy to fix the problem. If the tenants move out, the landlord has constructively evicted them and is liable for all expenses they suffer.

To claim a constructive eviction, the tenant must vacate the premises. The tenant must also prove that the interference was sufficiently serious and lasted long enough that she was forced to move out. A lack of hot water for two days is not fatal, but lack of any water for two weeks creates a constructive eviction.

Duty to Maintain Premises

In most states, a landlord has a **duty to deliver the premises in a habitable condition** and a continuing duty to maintain the habitable condition. This duty overlaps with the quiet enjoyment obligation, but it is not identical. The tenant's right to quiet enjoyment focuses primarily on the tenant's ability to use the rented property. The landlord's duty to maintain the property focuses on whether the property meets a particular legal standard. The required standard may be stated in the lease, created by a state statute, or implied by law.

LEASE

The lease itself generally obligates the landlord to maintain the exterior of any buildings and the common areas. If a lease does not do so, state law may imply the obligation.

BUILDING CODES

Many state and local governments have passed building codes, which mandate minimum standards for commercial property, residential property, or both. The codes are likely to be stricter for residential property and may demand such things as minimum room size, sufficient hot water, secure locks, proper working kitchens and bathrooms, absence of insects and rodents, and other basics of decent housing. Generally, all rental property must comply with the building code whether the lease mentions the code or not.

IMPLIED WARRANTY OF HABITABILITY

Students Maria Ivanow, Thomas Tecza, and Kenneth Gearin rented a house from Les and Martha Vanlandingham. The monthly rent was $900. But the roommates failed to pay any rent for the final five months of the tenancy. After they moved out, the Vanlandinghams sued. How much did the landlords recover? Nothing. The landlords had breached the implied warranty of habitability.

 The implied warranty of habitability requires that a landlord meet all standards set by the local building code, or that the premises be fit for human habitation. Most states, though not all, imply this warranty of habitability, meaning that the landlord must meet this standard whether the lease includes it or not.

 The Vanlandinghams breached the implied warranty. The students had complained repeatedly about a variety of problems. The washer and dryer, which were included in the lease, frequently failed. A severe roof leak caused water damage in one of the bedrooms. Defective pipes flooded the bathroom. The refrigerator frequently malfunctioned, and the roommates repaired it several times. The basement often flooded, and when it was dry, rats and opossums lived in it. The heat sometimes failed.

 In warranty of habitability cases, a court normally considers the severity of the problems and their duration. In the case of Maria Ivanow and friends, the court abated (reduced) the rent 50 percent. The students had already paid more than the abated rent to the landlord, so they owed nothing for the last five months.[3]

---

[3]*Vanlandingham v. Ivanow*, 246 Ill. App. 3d 348, 615 N.E.2d 1361, 1993 Ill. App. LEXIS 985 (Ill. Ct. App. 1993).

> ## One tenant slept with blankets over her head, to keep heat in and bugs out.

DUTY TO RETURN SECURITY DEPOSIT

Most landlords require tenants to pay a security deposit, to be used to finance repairs in case the tenant damages the premises. In many states, a landlord must either return the security deposit soon after the tenant has moved out or notify the tenant of the damage and the cost of the repairs. A landlord who fails to do so may owe the tenant damages of two or even three times the deposit.

Your authors are always grateful when plaintiffs volunteer to illustrate half a dozen legal issues in one lawsuit. The landlord in the following case demonstrates problems of security deposit, quiet enjoyment, constructive eviction, and, well, see how many you can count.

HARRIS V. SOLEY

2000 Me. 150, 756 A.2d 499,
Supreme Judicial Court of Maine, 2000

CASE SUMMARY

Facts: Near Labor Day, Andrea Harris, Kimberly Nightingale, Karen Simard, and Michelle Dussault moved into a large apartment in the Old Port section of Portland, Maine. The apartment had been condemned by the city of Portland, but Joseph Soley, the landlord, assured the tenants that all problems would be repaired before they moved in. Not quite. When the women arrived, they found the condemnation notice still on the door, and the apartment an uninhabitable mess. Soley's agent told the tenants that if they cleaned the unit themselves, they would receive a $750 credit on their first month's rent of $1,000. So the four rented a steam cleaner, bought supplies, and cleaned the entire apartment. Unfortunately, their problems had only begun.

The tenants suffered a continuous problem with mice and cockroaches, along with a persistent odor of cat urine. They ultimately discovered a dead cat beneath the floorboards. During October, the apartment had no heat. One tenant slept with blankets over her head, to keep heat in and bugs out. In November, the women submitted a list of complaints to Soley, including a broken toilet, an inoperable garbage disposal, and a shattered skylight, as well as a leaking roof and cockroach infestation. Snow began to fall into the living room through the skylight.

Soley made no repairs, and the women stopped paying the rent. He phoned them several times, aggressively demanding payments. The tenants found another place to live, but before they had moved, Soley's agents broke into the apartment and took many of their belongings. The tenants located Soley at the restaurant he owned and asked for their possessions back, but he refused to return the belongings unless they paid him $3,000. He threatened them by saying that he knew where their families lived.

The tenants sued, claiming breach of contract, conversion [wrongful taking of property], intentional infliction of emotional distress, wrongful eviction, and wrongful retention of a security deposit. Soley refused to respond to discovery requests, and eventually the trial court gave a default judgment for the plaintiffs. The judge instructed the jury that all allegations were deemed true, and their job was to award damages. The jury awarded damages for each of the claims, including $15,000 to each tenant for emotional distress and a total of *$1 million* in punitive damages. Soley appealed.

Issue: *Are the tenants entitled to such large damages?*

Decision: The tenants are entitled to all damages. Affirmed.

Reasoning: Soley argues that the identical awards to all four tenants indicates the verdict is a result of irrational thinking, passion, and prejudice. However, the jury could reasonably have found that the emotional distress suffered by each tenant deserved comparable compensation, even if the harm was not identical to each. Among the factual findings from the trial court was this statement:

The plaintiffs were shaken up, infuriated, violated, intimidated, and in fear for their physical safety. The conduct of

[Soley] was so extreme and outrageous as to exceed all possible bounds of decency. Defendant acted intentionally, knowingly, willfully, wantonly, and with malice.

The jury was entirely justified in awarding substantial punitive damages. The tenants had to endure insect and rodent infestation, dead animals, and falling snow. Soley refused to repair conditions that made the apartment unfit for human habitation, violently removed the tenants' property, destroyed some of their belongings, and threatened the young women. His conduct was utterly intolerable, and the verdict is reasonable.

TENANT'S DUTIES

Duty to Pay Rent

Rent is the compensation the tenant pays the landlord for use of the premises, and paying the rent is the tenant's foremost obligation. The lease normally specifies the amount of rent and when it must be paid. Typically, the landlord requires that rent be paid at the beginning of each rental period, whether that is monthly, annually, or otherwise.

If the tenant fails to pay rent on time, the landlord has several remedies. She is entitled to apply the security deposit to the unpaid rent. She may also sue the tenant for nonpayment of rent, demanding the unpaid sums, cost of collection, and interest. Finally, the landlord may evict a tenant who has failed to pay rent.

State statutes prescribe the steps a landlord must take to evict a tenant for nonpayment. Typically, the landlord must serve a termination notice on the tenant and wait for a court hearing. At the hearing, the landlord must prove that the tenant has failed to pay rent on time. If the tenant has no excuse for the nonpayment, the court grants an order evicting him. The order authorizes a sheriff to remove the tenant's goods and place them in storage, at the tenant's expense. However, if the tenant was withholding rent because of unlivable conditions, the court may refuse to evict.

EXAM Strategy

Question: Leo rents an apartment from Donna for $900 per month, both parties signing a lease. After six months, Leo complains about defects, including bugs, inadequate heat, and window leaks. He asks Donna to fix the problems, but she responds that the heat is fine and that Leo caused the insects and leaks. Leo begins to send in only $700 for the monthly rent. Donna repeatedly phones Leo, asking for the remaining rent. When he refuses to pay, she waits until he leaves for the day, then has a moving company place his belongings in storage. She changes the locks, making it impossible for him to reenter. Leo sues. What is the likely outcome?

Strategy: A landlord is entitled to begin proper eviction proceedings against a tenant who has not paid rent. However, the landlord must follow specified steps, including a termination notice and a court hearing. Review the consequences for actual eviction, described in the section "Quiet Enjoyment."

Result: Donna has ignored the legal procedures for evicting a tenant. Instead, she engaged in *actual eviction*, which is quick and, in the short term, effective. However, by breaking the law, Donna has ensured that Leo will win his lawsuit. He is entitled to possession of the apartment, as well as damages for rent he may have been forced to pay elsewhere, injury to his possessions, and the cost of retrieving them. He may receive punitive damages as well. Bad strategy, Donna.

Duty to Mitigate

Pickwick & Perkins, Ltd., was a store in the Burlington Square Mall in Burlington, Vermont. Pickwick had a five-year lease but abandoned the space almost two years early and ceased paying rent. The landlord waited eight months before renting the space to a new tenant and then sued, seeking the unpaid rent. Pickwick defended on the grounds that Burlington had failed to **mitigate damages,** that is, to keep its losses to a minimum by promptly seeking another tenant. The winner? Pickwick, the tenant. Today, most (but not all) courts rule that **when a tenant breaches the lease, the landlord must make a reasonable effort to mitigate damages.** Burlington failed to mitigate, so it also failed to recover its losses.

Duty to Use Premises Properly

A lease normally lists what a tenant may do in the premises and prohibits other activities. For example, a residential lease allows the tenant to use the property for normal living purposes, but not for any retail, commercial, or industrial purpose. A tenant may never use the premises for an illegal activity, such as gambling or selling drugs, whether or not the lease mentions the issue. A tenant may not disturb other tenants, and a landlord has the right to evict anyone who unreasonably disturbs neighbors.

A tenant is liable to the landlord for any significant damage he causes to the property. The tenant is not liable for normal wear and tear. If, however, he knocks a hole in a wall or damages the plumbing, the landlord may collect the cost of repairs, either by using the security deposit or, if necessary, by suing.

CHANGE IN THE PARTIES

Sometimes the parties to a lease change. This can happen when the landlord sells the property or when a tenant wants to turn the leased property over to another tenant.

Sale of the Property

Generally, the sale of leased property does not affect the lease but merely substitutes one landlord, the purchaser, for another, the seller. The lease remains valid, and the tenant enjoys all rights and obligations until the end of the term. The new landlord may not raise the rent during the period of the existing lease or make any other changes in the tenant's rights.

EXAM Strategy

Question: Julie, an MBA student, rents an apartment from Marshall for $1,500 a month. The written lease will last for two years, until Julie graduates. Julie moves in and enjoys the apartment. However, after 10 months, Marshall sells the building to Alexia, who notifies Julie that the new rent will be $1,750, effective immediately. If Julie objects, Alexia will give her one month to leave the apartment. Julie comes to you for advice. What are her options?

Strategy: What effect does the sale of leased property have on existing leases?

Result: Generally, the sale of leased property does not affect the lease but merely substitutes one landlord, the purchaser, for another, the seller. Alexia has no right to raise the rent during Julie's tenancy. Julie is entitled to the apartment, for $1,500 per month, until the lease expires.

Assignment and Sublease

A tenant who wishes to turn the property over to another tenant will attempt to assign the lease or to sublet it. In an **assignment**, the tenant transfers all of his legal interest to the other party. If a tenant validly assigns a lease, the new tenant obtains all rights and liabilities under the lease. The new tenant is permitted to use and enjoy the property and must pay the rent. **However, the original tenant remains liable to the landlord unless the landlord explicitly releases him, which the landlord is unlikely to do.** This means that if the new tenant fails to pay the rent on time, the landlord can sue *both* parties, old and new, seeking to evict both and to recover the unpaid rent from both.

A landlord generally insists on a covenant in the lease prohibiting the tenant from assigning without the landlord's written permission. Some states permit a landlord to deny permission for any reason at all, but a growing number of courts insist that a landlord act reasonably and grant permission to sublease unless he has a valid objection to the new tenant.

INJURIES

Tenant's Liability

A tenant is generally liable for injuries occurring within the premises she is leasing, whether that is an apartment, a store, or something else. If a tenant fails to clean up a spill on the kitchen floor, and a guest slips and falls, the tenant is liable. If a merchant negligently installs display shelving that tips onto a customer, the merchant pays for the harm. Generally, a tenant is not liable for injuries occurring in common areas over which she has no control, such as exterior walkways. If a tenant's dinner guest falls because the building's common stairway has loose steps, the landlord is probably liable.

Landlord's Liability

Historically, the common law held a landlord responsible only for injuries that occurred in the common areas, or those due to the landlord's negligent maintenance of the property. Increasingly, though, the law holds landlords liable under the normal rules of negligence law. In many states, a landlord must use reasonable care to maintain safe premises and is liable for foreseeable harm. For example, most states now have building codes that require a landlord to maintain structural elements in safe condition. States further imply a warranty of habitability, which mandates reasonably safe living conditions.

Crime

Landlords may be liable in negligence to tenants or their guests for criminal attacks that occur on the premises. Courts have struggled with this issue and have reached opposing results in similar cases. The very prevalence of crime sharpens the debate. What must a landlord do to protect a tenant? Courts typically answer the question by looking at four factors:

- *Nature of the crime.* How did the crime occur? Could the landlord have prevented it?

- *Reasonable person standard.* What would a reasonable landlord have done to prevent this type of crime? What did the landlord actually do?

- *Foreseeability.* Was it reasonably foreseeable that such a crime might occur? Were there earlier incidents or warnings?

- *Prevalence of crime in the area.* If the general area, or the particular premises, has a high crime rate, courts are more likely to hold that the crime was foreseeable and the landlord responsible.

The following case highlights one issue that courts face as they apply changing mores to a tragic loss. Should the landlord be responsible?

You be the Judge

DICKINSON ARMS-REO, L.P. v. CAMPBELL
4 S.W.3d 333 Texas Court of Appeals, 1999

Facts: About midnight, Joe Campbell and his girlfriend, Jenny Cady, left a club in separate cars, agreeing to meet at her apartment. Campbell parked his pickup truck in a space at the Dickinson Arms Apartments, where Cady lived.

Meanwhile, two 16-year-olds, Jeremy Gartrell and Donald Nichols, members of the Assassins, were visiting a fellow gang member who lived at the apartments. Gartrell approached Campbell, demanded the truck, and shot Campbell, killing him. Gartrell was convicted of murder and sentenced to 50 years.

Campbell's parents sued the Dickinson Arms, claiming that the landlord's neglect of security had permitted the killing. Testimony indicated as follows: over a three-year period at the Dickinson Arms, there had been 184 reported criminal offenses at the apartments, including 20 burglaries, 13 auto thefts, 11 assaults, and 8 thefts.

Gartrell had wanted to do a carjacking throughout much of the day. But at a nearby Taco Bell, and then at a different apartment complex, the security and bright lighting deterred him.

The plaintiffs' expert witness stated that because of the high crime rates, the Dickinson Arms should have been protected with a perimeter fence, gates, and a security guard. With such precautions, the crime would likely not have occurred.

The Dickinson Arms' expert witness testified that a security guard, perimeter fencing, and limited access gates would not have stopped an offender like Gartrell, who was an impulsive, explosive individual—a ticking time bomb. Teachers and peers testified that Gartrell was violent and could not be deterred.

A resident stated that the lighting in the parking lot was good enough for her to see Campbell's body and truck from her apartment window. But Nichols testified it was dark in the parking lot, with no working lights.

The jury found that the landlord failed to provide adequate security and awarded $341,000 to the plaintiffs. The Dickinson Arms appealed.

You Be the Judge: *Was the landlord liable for the death?*

Argument for the Dickinson Arms: This family tragedy has nothing to do with the landlord. Yes, an apartment complex is an easy target for liability, but this court should not hold the Dickinson Arms responsible for a murder it did not commit and did not want.

What good would a fence have done? Gartrell would have been free to enter through the main gate. He was a lawful visitor to the apartments. If there had been a security guard, he would have—should have—admitted Gartrell. The lower court decision imposes an unfair punishment on an inexpensive apartment complex. The result will be greater expense to the owner, higher rents for tenants—and no more security for anyone. Those who commit terrible crimes should pay the price—but injured plaintiffs should not be allowed to go where they think the money is.

Argument for the Campbells: The 184 crimes at the complex had all been dangerous, and many violent. The owner could not only *foresee* a more serious crime, it could confidently *predict* such a tragedy. The Dickinson Arms was a land mine, waiting to destroy innocent life.

Yes, Gartrell was an impulsive young man, but despite his eagerness for violence, he refused to commit a carjacking at two locations earlier in the day because they had proper security and lighting. If a Taco Bell can light its parking lot and deter crime, then the Dickinson Arms can do so as well—and should have.

The defendant's argument about higher costs is a phony one. In fact, the Dickinson Arms has increased its profits at the expense of law-abiding tenants and guests, one of whom has paid the ultimate price. The landlord should pay for its terrible negligence in this case—and then make improvements so this does not happen again.

Chapter Conclusion

Real property law is ancient but forceful. Although real property today is not the dominant source of wealth that it was in medieval England, it is still the greatest asset that most people will ever possess—and therefore, it is worth understanding the law that applies to it. Landlord-tenant law places many special obligations on both parties. The current trend is clearly for expanded landlord liability, but how far that will continue is impossible to divine.

EXAM REVIEW

1. **REAL PROPERTY**   Real property includes land, buildings, air and subsurface rights, plant life, and fixtures. A fixture is any good that has become attached to other real property. (pp. 519–520)

EXAM Strategy

Question: Paul and Shelly Higgins had two wood stoves in their home. Each rested on, but was not attached to, a built-in brick platform. The downstairs wood stove was connected to the chimney flue and was used as part of the main heating system for the house. The upstairs stove, in the master bedroom, was purely decorative. It had no stovepipe connecting it to the chimney. The Higginses sold their house to Jack Everitt, and neither party said anything about the two stoves. Is Everitt entitled to either stove? Both stoves?

Strategy: An object is a fixture if a reasonable person would consider the item to be a permanent part of the property, taking into account attachment, adaptation, and other objective manifestations of permanence. (See the "Result" at the end of this section.)

2. **CONCURRENT ESTATES**   When two or more people own real property at the same time, they have a concurrent estate. (pp. 520–521)

3. **ADVERSE POSSESSION**   Adverse possession permits the user of land to gain title if he can prove entry and exclusive possession, open and notorious possession, a claim adverse to the owner, and continuous possession for the required statutory period. (pp. 521–523)

EXAM Strategy

Question: In 1966, Arketex Ceramic Corp. sold land in rural Indiana to Malcolm Aukerman. The deed described the southern boundary as the section line between sections 11 and 14 of the land. Farther south of this section line stood a dilapidated fence running east to west. Aukerman and Arketex both believed that this fence was the actual southern boundary of his new land, though in fact it lay on Arketex's property.

Aukerman installed a new electrified fence, cleared the land on "his" side of the new fence, and began to graze cattle there. In 1974, Harold Clark bought the land that bordered Aukerman's fence, assuming that the fence was the correct boundary. In 1989, Clark had his land surveyed and discovered that the true property line lay north of the electric fence. Aukerman filed suit, seeking a court order that he had acquired the disputed land by adverse possession. The statutory period in Indiana is 20 years. Who wins?

Strategy: There are four elements to adverse possession. Has Aukerman proved them? (See the "Result" at the end of this section.)

4. **REGULATION**   Nuisance law, zoning ordinances, and eminent domain all permit a government to regulate property and, in some cases, to take it for public use. (pp. 523–524)

5. **LANDLORD-TENANT RELATIONSHIP**   When an owner of a freehold estate allows another person temporary, exclusive possession of the property, the parties have created a landlord-tenant relationship. (pp. 524–525)

6. **TENANCIES**   Any lease for a stated, fixed period is a tenancy for years. A periodic tenancy is created for a fixed period and then automatically continues for additional periods until either party notifies the other of termination. A tenancy at will has no fixed duration and may be terminated by either party at any time. A tenancy at sufferance occurs when a tenant remains, against the wishes of the landlord, after the expiration of a true tenancy. (pp. 525–526)

7. **QUIET ENJOYMENT**   All tenants are entitled to the quiet enjoyment of the premises, without the interference of the landlord. (p. 526)

8. **CONSTRUCTIVE EVICTION**   A landlord may be liable for constructive eviction if he substantially interferes with the tenant's use and enjoyment of the premises. (pp. 526–527)

9. **IMPLIED WARRANTY OF HABITABILITY**   The implied warranty of habitability requires that a landlord meet all standards set by the local building code and/or that the premises be fit for human habitation. (p. 527)

10. **RENT**   The tenant is obligated to pay the rent, and the landlord may evict for nonpayment. The modern trend is to require a landlord to mitigate damages caused by a tenant who abandons the premises before the lease expires. (p. 529)

EXAM Strategy

Question: Loren Andreo leased retail space in his shopping plaza to Tropical Isle Pet Shop for five years, at a monthly rent of $2,100. Tropical Isle vacated the premises 18 months early, turned in the key to Andreo, and acknowledged liability for the unpaid rent. Andreo placed a "for rent" sign in the store window and spoke to a commercial real estate broker about the space. But he did not enter into a formal listing agreement with the broker, or take any other steps to rent the space, for about nine months. With approximately nine months remaining on the unused part of Tropical's lease, Andreo hired a commercial broker to rent the space. He also sued Tropical for 18 months' rent. Comment.

Strategy: When a tenant abandons leased property early, the landlord is obligated to mitigate damages. Did Andreo? (See the "Result" at the end of this section.)

11. **DAMAGES TO PROPERTY**   A tenant is liable to the landlord for any significant damage that he causes to the property. (p. 530)

12. **ASSIGNMENT**   A tenant typically may assign a lease or sublet the premises only with the landlord's permission, but the current trend is to prohibit a landlord from unreasonably withholding permission. (p. 531)

Question: Doris Rowley rented space from the city of Mobile, Alabama, to run the Back Porch Restaurant. Her lease prohibited assignment or subletting without the landlord's permission. Rowley's business became unprofitable, and she asked the city's real estate officer for permission to assign her lease. She told the officer that she had "someone who would accept if the lease was assigned." Rowley provided no other information about the assignee. The city refused permission. Rowley repeated her requests several times without success, and finally she sued. Rowley alleged that the city had unreasonably withheld permission to assign and had caused her serious financial losses as a result. Comment.

Strategy: A landlord may not unreasonably refuse permission to assign a lease. Was the city's refusal unreasonable? (See the "Result" at the end of this section.)

13. **MAINTENANCE OF THE PROPERTY**   Many courts require a landlord to use reasonable care in maintaining the premises, and hold her liable for injuries that were foreseeable. (p. 531)

14. **CRIME**   Landlords may be liable in negligence to tenants or their guests for criminal attacks on the premises. Courts determine liability by looking at factors such as the nature of the crime, what a reasonable landlord would have done to prevent it, and the foreseeability of the attack. (pp. 531–532)

1. Result: A buyer normally takes all fixtures. The downstairs stove was permanently attached to the house and used as part of the heating system. The owner who installed it *intended* that it remain, and it was a fixture; Everitt got it. The upstairs stove was not permanently attached and was not a fixture; the sellers could take it with them.

3. Result: Aukerman wins. He considered himself to be the owner, as had Arketex for 8 years and Clark for 15. All the owners had maintained the land and kept everyone else off for more than 20 years.

EXAM Strategy

> **10. Result:** For about nine months, Andreo made no serious effort to lease the store. The court rejected his rent claim for that period, permitting him to recover unpaid money only for the period that he made a genuine effort to lease the space.
>
> **12. Result:** A landlord is allowed to evaluate a prospective assignee, including its financial stability and intended use of the property. Mobile could not do that because Rowley provided no information about the proposed assignee. Mobile wins.

MATCHING QUESTIONS

Match the following terms with their definitions:

___A. Constructive eviction

___B. Adverse possession

___C. Fixture

___D. Tenancy at will

___E. Tenancy at sufferance

1. A landlord's substantial interference with a tenant's use and enjoyment of the premises

2. Goods that have become attached to real property

3. A tenancy without fixed duration, which either party may terminate at any time

4. A method of acquiring ownership of land without ever paying for it

5. A tenant remains on the premises after expiration of true tenancy

TRUE/FALSE QUESTIONS

Circle true or false:

1. T F If one joint tenant dies, his interest in the property passes to surviving joint tenants, not to his heirs.

2. T F The federal government has the power to take private property for public use, but local governments have no such power.

3. T F A landlord could be liable for a constructive eviction even if he never asked the tenant to leave.

4. T F A nonrenewable lease of a store, for six months, establishes a tenancy for years.

5. T F A landlord may charge a tenant for normal wear and tear on an apartment, but the charges must be reasonable.

MULTIPLE-CHOICE QUESTIONS

1. **CPA QUESTION:** On July 1, 2010, Quick, Onyx, and Nash were deeded a piece of land as tenants in common. The deed provided that Quick owned one-half the property and Onyx and Nash owned one-quarter each. If Nash dies, the property will be owned as follows:

   (a) Quick $\frac{1}{2}$, Onyx $\frac{1}{2}$
   (b) Quick $\frac{5}{8}$, Onyx $\frac{3}{8}$
   (c) Quick $\frac{1}{3}$, Onyx $\frac{1}{3}$, Nash's heirs $\frac{1}{3}$
   (d) Quick $\frac{1}{2}$, Onyx $\frac{1}{4}$, Nash's heirs $\frac{1}{4}$

2. Marta places a large, prefabricated plastic greenhouse in her backyard, with the steel frame bolted into concrete that she poured specially for that purpose. She attaches gas heating ducts and builds a brick walkway around the greenhouse. Now, the town wants to raise her real property taxes, claiming that her property has been improved. Marta argues that the greenhouse is not part of the real property. Is it?

   (a) The greenhouse is not part of the real property because it was prefabricated.
   (b) The greenhouse is not part of the real property because it could be removed.
   (c) The greenhouse cannot be part of the real property if Marta owns a fee simple absolute.
   (d) The greenhouse is a fixture and is part of the real property.

3. **CPA QUESTION:** Which of the following forms of tenancy will be created if a tenant stays in possession of the leased premises without the landlord's consent, after the tenant's one-year written lease expires?

   (a) Tenancy at will
   (b) Tenancy for years
   (c) Tenancy from period to period
   (d) Tenancy at sufferance

4. **CPA QUESTION:** A tenant renting an apartment under a three-year written lease that does not contain any specific restrictions may be evicted for:

   (a) Counterfeiting money in the apartment
   (b) Keeping a dog in the apartment
   (c) Failing to maintain a liability insurance policy on the apartment
   (d) Making structural repairs to the apartment

5. Michael signs a lease for an apartment. The lease establishes a periodic tenancy for one year, starting September 1 and ending the following August 31. Rent is $800 per month. As August 31 approaches, Michael decides he would like to stay another year. He phones the landlord to tell him this, but the landlord is on vacation and Michael leaves a message. Michael sends in the September rent, but on September 15, the landlord tells him the rent is going up to $900 per month. He gives Michael the choice of paying the higher rent or leaving. Michael refuses to leave and continues to send checks for $800. The landlord sues. Landlord will

(a) Win possession of the apartment because the lease expired

(b) Win possession of the apartment because Michael did not renew it in writing

(c) Win possession of the apartment because he has the right to evict Michael at any time, for any reason

(d) Win $1,200 (12 months times $100)

(e) Lose

ESSAY QUESTIONS

1. **ETHICS:** Lisa Preece rented an apartment from Turman Realty, paying a $300 security deposit. Georgia law states: "Any landlord who fails to return any part of a security deposit which is required to be returned to a tenant pursuant to this article shall be liable to the tenant in the amount of three times the sum improperly withheld plus reasonable attorney's fees." When Preece moved out, Turman did not return her security deposit, and she sued for triple damages plus attorney's fees, totaling $1,800. Turman offered evidence that its failure to return the deposit was inadvertent and that it had procedures reasonably designed to avoid such errors. Is Preece entitled to triple damages? Attorney's fees? What is the rationale behind a statute that requires triple damages? Is it ethical to force a landlord to pay $1,800 for a $300 debt?

2. Philip Schwachman owned a commercial building and leased space to Davis Radio Corp. for use as a retail store. In the same building, Schwachman leased other retail space to Pampered Pet, a dog grooming shop. Davis Radio complained repeatedly to Schwachman that foul odors from Pampered Pet entered its store and drove away customers and workers. Davis abandoned the premises, leaving many months' rent unpaid. Schwachman sued for unpaid rent and moved for summary judgment. What ruling would you make on the summary judgment motion?

3. Nome 2000, a partnership, owned a large tract of wilderness land in Alaska. The Fagerstrom family had used the property for camping and vacationing since about 1944. In 1966, Charles and Peggy Fagerstrom marked off an area for a cabin and brought material to build the cabin, but they never did so. In about 1970, they built a picnic area on the land, and in about 1974, they placed a camper trailer on the land, where it remained until the lawsuit. In 1987, Nome 2000 sued to eject the Fagerstroms from the land. The Fagerstroms had used the land only during the summer months. No one lived in the area during the winter months, when it was virtually uninhabitable. Has the family adversely possessed the land from Nome 2000?

4. **YOU BE THE JUDGE WRITING PROBLEM** Frank Deluca and his son David owned the Sportsman's Pub on Fountain Street in Providence, Rhode Island. The Delucas applied to the city for a license to employ topless dancers in the pub. Did the city have the power to deny the Delucas' request? **Argument for the Delucas:** Our pub is perfectly legal. Further, no law in Rhode Island prohibits topless dancing. We are morally and legally entitled to present this entertainment. The city should not use some phony moralizing to deny customers what they want. **Argument for Providence:** This section of Providence is zoned to prohibit

topless dancing, just as it is zoned to bar manufacturing. There are other parts of town where the Delucas can open one of their sleazy clubs if they want to, but we are entitled to deny a permit in this area.

5. Kenmart Realty sued to evict Mr. and Ms. Alghalabio for nonpayment of rent and sought the unpaid monies, totaling several thousand dollars. In defense, the Alghalabios claimed that their apartment was infested with rats. They testified that there were numerous rat holes in the walls of the living room, bedroom, and kitchen, that there were rat droppings all over the apartment, and that on one occasion, they saw their toddler holding a live rat. They testified that the landlord had refused numerous requests to exterminate. Please rule on the landlord's suit.

DISCUSSION QUESTIONS

1. Is the doctrine of adverse possession sensible? Should a squatter be able to "steal" land? Why or why not?

2. Leslie buys a house from Jamal. Consider the following items in the house.

– A ceiling fan	– A bathtub
– The carpeting	– A floor lamp
– A dishwasher	– A television

   Which of the above are Jamal's personal property? Which are real property? Which will Jamal get to take when he moves, and which will Leslie own?

3. Donny Delt and Sammy Sigma are students and roommates. They lease a house in a neighborhood near campus. Few students live on the block.

   The students do not have large parties, but they often have friends over at night. The friends sometimes play loud music in their cars, and they sometimes talk loudly when going to and from their cars. Also, beer cans and fast food wrappers are often left in the street by departing late-night guests.

   Neighbors complain about being awakened in the wee hour in the morning. They are considering filing a nuisance lawsuit against Donny and Sammy. Would such an action be reasonable? Do you think Donny and Sammy are creating a nuisance? If so, why? If not, where is the line—what amount of late-night noise does amount to a nuisance?

4. Imagine that you sign a lease and that you are to move into your new apartment on August 15. When you arrive, the previous tenant has not moved out. In fact, he has no intention of moving out. Compare the English and the American rules. Should the landlord be in charge of getting rid of the old tenant, or should you have the obligation to evict him?

5. When landlords wrongfully withhold security deposits, they can often be sued for three times the amount of the security deposit. Is this reasonable? Should a landlord have to pay $3,000 for a $1,000 debt? What if you fail to pay a rent on time? Should you have to pay three times the amount of your normal rent? If your answers to the two situations presented here are different, why are they different?

CHAPTER 30

PERSONAL PROPERTY AND BAILMENT

"My only child is a no-good thief," Riley murmurs sadly to his visitors. "He has always treated me contemptuously. Now he's been sentenced to five years for stealing from a children's charity. He is my only heir, but why should I leave him everything?" Riley continues talking to his three guests: a bishop, a rabbi, and Earnest, a Boy Scout leader. "I have $500,000 in stocks in my bank deposit box. Tomorrow morning, I'm going to the bank and hand the shares to the Boy Scouts so that other kids won't turn out so bad." Everyone applauds. But the following morning, on his way to the bank, Riley is struck by an ambulance and killed. A dispute arises over the money. The three witnesses assure the court that Riley was on his way to give the money to the Boy Scouts. From prison, the ne'er-do-well son demands the money as Riley's sole heir. Who wins? Personal property law holds the answer.

> My only child is a no-good thief. He is my only heir, but why should I leave him everything?

Personal property means all tangible property other than real property. In Chapter 29, we saw that real property is land and things firmly attached to it, such as buildings, crops, and minerals. All other physical objects are personal property—a bus, a toothbrush, a share of stock.

In this chapter, we look at several ways in which personal property can be acquired. In the section on gifts, we learn that Riley's no-good son gets the money. Riley intended to give the stocks and bonds to the Boy Scouts the following day, but he never completed a valid gift because he failed to *deliver* the papers. We will then turn to disputes over found property. And finally, we examine bailments, which occur when the owner of personal property permits another to possess it.

Personal property
All tangible property other than real property.

GIFTS

A gift is a voluntary transfer of property from one person to another without any consideration. Recall from Chapter 9 that, for consideration to exist, parties must normally make an exchange. But a gift is a one-way transaction, without anything given in return. The person who gives property away is the **donor,** and the one who receives it is the **donee.**

A gift involves three elements:

- The donor intends to transfer ownership of the property to the donee immediately.

- The donor delivers the property to the donee.

- The donee accepts the property.

If all three elements are met, the donee becomes the legal owner of the property. If the donor later says, "I've changed my mind, give that back!" the donee is free to refuse.

Gift
A voluntary transfer of property from one person to another, without consideration.

Donor
A person who gives property away.

Donee
A person who receives a gift of property.

Intention to Transfer Ownership

The donor must intend to transfer ownership to the property right away, immediately giving up all control of the item. Notice that the donor's intention must be to give title to the donee. Merely proving that the owner handed you property does not guarantee that you have received a gift; if the owner only intended that you use the item, there is no gift, and she can demand it back.

The donor must also intend the property to transfer immediately. A promise to make a gift in the future is unenforceable. Promises about future behavior are governed by contract law, and a contract is unenforceable without consideration. That is why the Boy Scouts will never touch the promised stocks. If Riley had handed Earnest the shares as he spoke, the gift would have been complete. However, the promise to make a gift the next day is legally worthless. Nor does Earnest have an enforceable contract since there was no consideration for Riley's promise.

A *revocable gift* is governed by a special rule, and it is actually not a gift at all. Suppose Harold tells his daughter Faith, "The mule is yours from now on, but if you start acting stupid again, I'm taking her back." Harold has retained some control over the animal, which means he has not intended to transfer ownership. There is no gift, and no transfer of ownership. Harold still owns the mule.

Delivery
PHYSICAL DELIVERY

The donor must deliver the property to the donee. Generally, this involves physical delivery. If Anna hands Eddie a Rembrandt drawing, saying, "I want you to have this forever," she has satisfied the delivery requirement.

CONSTRUCTIVE DELIVERY

Physical delivery is the most common and the surest way to make a gift, but it is not always necessary. **A donor makes constructive delivery by transferring ownership without a physical delivery.** Most courts permit constructive delivery only when physical delivery is impossible or extremely inconvenient. Suppose Anna wants to give her niece Jen a blimp, which is parked in a hangar at the airport. The blimp will not fit through the doorway of Jen's dorm. Anna may simply deliver to Jen the certificate of title and the keys to the blimp.

Inter Vivos Gifts and Gifts *Causa Mortis*

Inter vivos gift

A gift made during the donor's life, with no fear of impending death.

Gift *causa mortis*

A gift made in contemplation of approaching death.

A gift can be either *inter vivos* or *causa mortis*. An ***inter vivos* gift** means a gift made "during life," that is, when the donor is not under any fear of impending death. The vast majority of gifts are *inter vivos*, involving a healthy donor and donee. Shirley, age 30 and in good health, gives Terry an eraser for his birthday. This is an *inter vivos* gift, which is absolute. The gift becomes final upon delivery, and the donor may not revoke it. If Shirley and Terry have a fight the next day, Shirley has no power to erase her gift.

A **gift *causa mortis*** is one made in contemplation of approaching death. The gift is valid if the donor dies as expected, but it is revoked if he recovers. Suppose Lenny's doctors have told him he will probably die of a liver ailment within a month. Lenny calls Jane to his bedside and hands her a fistful of cash, saying, "I'm dying; these are yours." Jane sheds a tear and then sprints to the bank. If Lenny dies of the liver ailment within a few weeks, Jane gets to keep the money. But note that this gift is revocable. Since a gift *causa mortis* is conditional (upon the donor's death), the donor has the right to revoke it at any time before he dies. If Lenny telephones Jane the next day and says that he has changed his mind, he gets the money back. Further, if the donor recovers and does not die as expected, the gift is automatically revoked.

EXAM Strategy

Question: Julie does good deeds for countless people, and many are deeply grateful. On Monday, Wilson tells Julie, "You are a wonderful person, and I have a present for you. I am giving you this baseball, which was the 500th home run hit by one of the greatest players of all time." He hands her the ball, which is worth nearly half a million dollars.

Julie's good fortune continues on Tuesday, when another friend, Cassandra, tells Julie, "I only have a few weeks to live. I want you to have this signed first edition of *Ulysses*. It is priceless, and it is yours." The book is worth about $200,000. On Wednesday, Wilson and Cassandra decide they have been foolhardy, and both demand that Julie return the items. Must she do so?

Strategy: Both of these donors are attempting to revoke their gifts. An *inter vivos* gift cannot be revoked, but a gift *causa mortis* can be. To answer the question, you must know what kind of gifts these were.

Result: A gift *causa mortis* is one made in fear of approaching death, and this rule applies to Cassandra. Such a gift is revocable any time before the donor dies, so Cassandra gets her book back. A gift *inter vivos* is one made without any such fear of death. Most gifts fall in this category, and they are irrevocable. Wilson was not anticipating his demise, so his was a gift *inter vivos*. Julie keeps the baseball.

Acceptance

The donee must accept the gift. This rarely leads to disputes, but if a donee should refuse a gift and then change her mind, she is out of luck. Her repudiation of the donor's offer means there is no gift, and she has no rights in the property.

The following case offers a combination of love, alcohol, and diamonds—always a volatile mix.

You be the Judge

ALBINGER V. HARRIS

2002 Mont. 118, 2002 WL 1226858
Montana Supreme Court, 2002

Facts: Michelle Harris and Michael Albinger lived together, on and off, for three years. Their roller-coaster relationship was marred by alcohol abuse and violence. When they announced their engagement, Albinger gave Harris a $29,000 diamond ring, but the couple broke off their wedding plans because of emotional and physical turmoil. Harris returned the ring. Later, they reconciled and resumed their marriage plans, and Albinger gave his fiancee the ring again. This cycle repeated several times over the three years. Each time they broke off their relationship, Harris returned the ring to Albinger, and each time they made up, he gave it back to her.

On one occasion, Albinger held a knife over Harris as she lay in bed, threatening to chop off her finger if she didn't remove the ring. He beat her and forcibly removed the ring. Criminal charges were brought but then dropped when, inevitably, the couple reconciled. Another time, Albinger told her to "take the car, the horse, the dog, and the ring and get the hell out." Finally, mercifully, they ended their stormy affair, and Harris moved to Kentucky—keeping the ring.

Albinger sued for the value of the ring. The trial court found that the ring was a conditional gift, made in contemplation of marriage, and ordered Harris to pay its full value. She appealed. The Montana Supreme Court had to decide, in a case of first impression, whether an engagement ring was given in contemplation of marriage. (In Montana and in many states, neither party to a broken engagement may sue for breach of contract.)

You Be the Judge: *Who owns the ring?*

Argument for Harris: The problem with calling the ring a "conditional gift" is that there is no such thing. The elements of a gift are intent, delivery, and acceptance, and Harris has proven all three. Once a gift has been accepted, the donor has no more rights in the property and may not demand its return. Hundreds of years of litigation have resulted in only one exception to this rule—a gift *causa mortis*—and despite some cynical claims to the contrary, marriage is not death. What is more, to create a special rule for engagement rings would be blatant gender bias because the exception would only benefit men. This court should stick to settled law and permit the recipient of a gift to keep it.

Argument for Albinger: The symbolism of an engagement ring is not exactly news. For decades, Americans have given rings—frequently diamond—in contemplation of marriage. All parties understand why the gift is made and what is expected if the engagement is called off: the ring must be returned. Albinger's intent, to focus on one element, was conditional—and Michelle Harris understood that. Each time the couple separated, she gave the ring back. She knew that she could wear this beautiful ring in anticipation of their marriage, but that custom and decency required its return if the wedding was off. We are not asking for new law, but for confirmation of what everyone has known for generations: there is no wedding ring when there is no wedding.

The following chart distinguishes between a contract and a gift.

A Contract and a Gift Distinguished

A Contract:

| Lou: I will pay you $2,000 to paint the house, if you promise to finish by July 3. | Abby: I agree to paint the house by July 3, for $2,000. |

Lou and Abby have a contract. Each promise is consideration in support of the other promise. Lou and Abby can each enforce the other's promise.

A Gift:

| Lou hands Phil two opera tickets, while saying: I want you to have these two tickets to *Rigoletto*. | Phil: Hey, thanks. |

This is a valid *inter vivos* gift. Lou intended to transfer ownership immediately and delivered the property to Phil, who now owns the tickets.

Neither Contract nor Gift:

| Lou: You're a great guy. Next week, I'm going to give you two tickets to *Rigoletto*. | Jason: Hey, thanks. |

There is no gift because Lou did not intend to transfer ownership immediately, and he did not deliver the tickets. There is no contract because Jason has given no consideration to support Lou's promise.

FOUND PROPERTY

As you stagger to your 8 a.m. class, there is a gleam of light, not in your mind (which is vacant), but right there on the sidewalk. A ring! You stop in at the local jewelry shop, where you learn the ruby marvel is worth just over $70,000. Is it yours to keep?

The primary goal of the common law has been to get found property back to its proper owner. The finder must make a good-faith effort to locate the owner. In some states, the finder is obligated to notify the police of what she has found and entrust the property to them until the owner can be located or a stated period has passed. A second policy has been to reward the finder if no owner can be located. But courts are loath to encourage trespassing, so finders who discover personal property on someone else's land generally cannot keep it. Those basic policies yield various outcomes, depending on the nature of the property. The common-law principles follow, although some states have modified them by statute.

Abandoned property
Property that the owner has knowingly discarded because she no longer wants it.

- **Abandoned property** is something that the owner has knowingly discarded because she no longer wants it. A vase thrown into a garbage can is abandoned. Generally, a finder is permitted to keep abandoned property, provided he can prove that the owner intended to relinquish all rights.

Lost property
Property accidentally given up.

- **Lost property** is something accidentally given up. A ring that falls off a finger into the street is lost property. Usually, the finder of lost property has rights superior to all the world except the true owner. If the true owner comes forward, he gets his property back; otherwise, the finder may keep it. However, if the finder has discovered the item on land belonging to another, the landowner is probably entitled to keep it.

- **Mislaid property** is something the owner has intentionally placed somewhere and then forgotten. A book deliberately placed on a bus seat by an owner who forgets to take it with her is mislaid property. Generally, the finder gets no rights in property that has simply been mislaid. If the true owner cannot be located, the mislaid item belongs to the owner of the premises where the item was found.

Mislaid property
Property the owner has intentionally placed somewhere and then forgotten.

The following case has contributed significantly to modern legal ideas on found property. It may seem to come from a Charles Dickens novel, but it actually happened. A villainous goldsmith sought to take advantage of a poor chimney sweep's boy. Would he get away with it? Read on.

Landmark Case

ARMORIE V. DELAMIRIE
93 ER 664
Middlesex, 1722

CASE SUMMARY

Facts: Before Parliament banned the practice in 1840, many English chimney sweeps forced young children to climb the narrow flues and do the cleaning. Armorie was one such boy. But fortune smiled on him, and he found a jeweled ring. To discover its value, he carried the ring to a local goldsmith.

Armorie handed the ring to the goldsmith's apprentice, who removed the jewels from the ring and pretended to weigh it. He called out to the goldsmith that the ring was worth three halfpence. The goldsmith then offered that amount to Armorie.

Not being a fool, Armorie refused the offer and demanded that the ring be returned. The apprentice gave him the ring, but without the jewels.

Issue: *Did the chimney sweep boy have a legal right to retain possession of the found jewels?*

Decision: Yes, he had a right to the jewels.

Reasoning: Someone who finds property has a right to keep it unless the true owner claims it. In this case, the chimney sweep found the jewels, so they belonged to him. The goldsmith wrongfully withheld the stones from Armorie. The judge instructed the jury to award damages and to assume that the missing stones had been of the highest quality.

BAILMENT

A bailment is the rightful possession of goods by someone who is not the owner. The one who delivers the goods is the **bailor,** and the one in possession is the **bailee.** Bailments are common. Suppose you are going out of town for the weekend and lend your motorcycle to Stan. You are the bailor, and your friend is the bailee. When you check your suitcase with the airline, you are again the bailor, and the airline is the bailee. If you rent a car at your destination, you become the bailee, while the rental agency is the bailor. In each case, someone other than the true owner has rightful, temporary possession of personal property. **Parties generally create a bailment by agreement.** In each of the examples above, the parties agreed to the bailment. In two cases, the agreement included payment, which is common but not essential. When you buy your airline ticket, you pay for your ticket, and the price includes the airline's agreement, as bailee, to transport your suitcase. When you rent a car,

Bailment
The rightful possession of goods by one who is not the owner, usually by mutual agreement between the bailor and bailee.

Bailor
The one who delivers the goods.

Bailee
The one who possesses the goods.

you pay the bailor for the privilege of using it. By loaning your motorcycle, you engage in a bailment without either party paying compensation.

A bailment without any agreement is called a constructive, or involuntary, bailment. Suppose you find a wristwatch in your house that you know belongs to a friend. You are obligated to return the watch to the true owner, and until you do so, you are the bailee, liable for harm to the property. This is called a constructive bailment because, with no agreement between the parties, the law is construing a bailment.

Involuntary bailment

A bailment that occurs without an agreement between the bailor and bailee.

Control

To create a bailment, the bailee must assume physical control of an item with intent to possess. A bailee may be liable for loss or damage to the property, and so it is not fair to hold him liable unless he has taken physical control of the goods, intending to possess them.

Disputes about whether someone has taken control often arise in parking lot cases. When a car is damaged or stolen, the lot's owner may try to avoid liability by claiming it lacked control of the parked auto and therefore was not a bailee. If the lot is a "park and lock" facility, where the car's owner retains the key and the lot owner exercises *no control at all*, there is probably no bailment and no liability for damage.

By contrast, when a driver leaves her keys with a parking attendant, the lot clearly is exercising control of the auto, and the parties have created a bailment. The lot is probably liable for loss or damage in that case.

EXAM Strategy

Question: Jack arrives at Airport Hotel's valet parking area in a Ferrari, just as Kim drives up in her rustbucket car. A valet drives Kim's car away, but the supervisor asks Jack to park the Ferrari himself, in the hotel's lot across the street. Jack parks as instructed, locking the Ferarri and keeping the keys. During the night, both vehicles are stolen. The owners sue for the value of their vehicles—about $2,000 for Kim's clunker and $350,000 for Jack's Ferrari. Each owner will win if there was a bailment but lose if there was not. Can either or both prove a bailment?

Strategy: To create a bailment, the bailee must assume physical control with intent to possess.

Result: When the valet drove Kim's car away, the hotel assumed control with intent to possess. The parties created a bailment, and the hotel is liable. But Jack loses. The hotel never had physical control of the Ferarri. Employees did not park the vehicle, and Jack kept the keys. Jack's Ferarri was a "park and lock" case, with no bailment.

Ethics Many companies post their parking policies on the Internet, often including a disclaimer stating that use of their facility creates no bailment or liability. Find such a statement and analyze it. Why does the owner claim (or hope) that no bailment exists? If a parked car is damaged, will a court honor the disclaimer? Does the facility operator have any control of the cars as they enter, or while parked, or as they leave? Do you consider the facility's policy fair, or is it an unjust effort to escape responsibility?

Rights of the Bailee

The bailee's primary right is possession of the property. **Anyone who interferes with the bailee's rightful possession is liable to her.** The bailee is typically, though not always, permitted to use the property. When a farmer loans his tractor to a neighbor, the bailee is entitled to use the machine for normal farm purposes. But some bailees have no authority to use the goods. If you store your furniture in a warehouse, the storage company is your bailee, but it has no right to curl up in your bed.

A bailee may or may not be entitled to compensation, depending on the parties' agreement. A warehouse will not store your furniture for free, but a friend might.

> If you store your furniture in a warehouse, the storage company is your bailee, but it has no right to curl up in your bed.

Duties of the Bailee

The bailee is strictly liable to redeliver the goods on time to the bailor or to whomever the bailor designates. Strict liability means there are virtually no exceptions. Rudy stores his $6,000 drum set with Melissa's Warehouse while he is on vacation. Blake arrives at the warehouse and shows a forged letter, supposedly from Rudy, granting Blake permission to remove the drums. If Melissa permits Blake to take the drums, she will owe Rudy $6,000, even if the forgery was a high-quality job.

DUE CARE

The bailee is obligated to exercise due care. **The level of care required depends upon who receives the benefit of the bailment.** There are three possibilities:

- *Sole benefit of bailee.* If the bailment is for the sole benefit of the bailee, the bailee is required to use **extraordinary care** with the property. Generally, in these cases, the bailor loans something for free to the bailee. Since the bailee is paying nothing for the use of the goods, most courts consider her the only one to benefit from the bailment. If your neighbor loans you a power lawn mower, the bailment is probably for your sole benefit. You are liable if you are even slightly inattentive in handling the lawn mower, and you can expect to pay for virtually any harm done.

- *Mutual benefit.* When the bailment is for the mutual benefit of bailor and bailee, the bailee must use **ordinary care** with the property. Ordinary care is what a reasonably prudent person would use under the circumstances. When you rent a car, you benefit from the use of the car, and the agency profits from the fee you pay. When the airline hauls your suitcase to your destination, both parties benefit. Most bailments benefit both parties, and courts decide the majority of bailment disputes under this standard.

- *Sole benefit of bailor.* When the bailment benefits only the bailor, the bailee must use only **slight care.** This kind of bailment is called a *gratuitous bailment,* and the bailee is liable only for gross negligence. Sheila enters a pie-eating contest and asks you to hold her $14,000 diamond engagement ring while she competes. You put the ring in your pocket. Sheila wins the $20 first prize, but the ring has disappeared. This was a gratuitous bailment, and you are not liable to Sheila unless she can prove gross negligence on your part. If the ring dropped from your pocket or was stolen, you are not liable. If you used the ring to play catch with friends, you are liable.

BURDEN OF PROOF

In an ordinary negligence case, the plaintiff has the burden of proof to demonstrate that the defendant was negligent and caused the harm alleged. In bailment cases, the burden of proof is reversed. **Once the bailor has proven the existence of a bailment and loss or harm to the goods, a presumption of negligence arises,** and the burden shifts to the bailee to prove adequate care. This is a major change from ordinary negligence cases. Georgina rents Sam her sailboat for a month. At the end of the month, Sam announces that the boat is at the bottom of Lake Michigan. If Georgina sues Sam, she only needs to demonstrate that the parties had a bailment and that he failed to return the boat. The burden then shifts to Sam to prove that the boat was lost through no fault of his own. If he cannot meet that burden, Georgina recovers the full value of the boat.

The following case raises many of the issues in this section. Long before his time as president, Abraham Lincoln was a lawyer who argued more than 150 cases before the Supreme Court of Illinois. The case for Weedman is modeled after the arguments that a young Lincoln actually made.

You be the Judge

JOHNSON V. WEEDMAN

5 Ill. 495
Supreme Court of Illinois, 1843

Facts: Johnson left his horse with Weedman, paying him to board and feed the animal. Johnson did not grant Weedman permission to ride the horse. Nonetheless, Weedman took the horse for a 15-mile ride.

Later that day, the horse died. However, the trial court found that Weedman had not abused the animal and that the ride had not caused the horse's death. The court did not grant damages to Johnson, and Johnson appealed.

You Be the Judge: *Should Weedman pay for Johnson's dead horse?*

Argument for Johnson: Your honor, Weedman was in possession of my client's horse only to feed him and see to his basic needs. My client did not give him permission to take the horse out of the pasture. Weedman made personal use of my client's property when he took a 15-mile ride that was in no way necessary. The trial court's finding that Weedman did not abuse the horse during the ride is irrelevant. My client must be compensated for the loss of his animal.

Argument for Weedman: My client had a legal right to possession of the horse. Riding the horse was not a substantial abuse of his rights as bailee. The horse was returned to the pasture in good condition. It was not abandoned and was not devalued in any way by the ride. The plaintiff is therefore not entitled to any compensation. The coincidental death of the horse does not change that fact.

Rights and Duties of the Bailor

The bailor's rights and duties are the reverse of the bailee's. The bailor is entitled to the return of his property on the agreed-upon date. He is also entitled to receive the property in good condition and to recover damages for harm to the property if the bailee failed to use adequate care.

Liability for Defects

Depending upon the type of bailment, the bailor is potentially liable for known or even unknown defects in the property. **If the bailment is for the sole benefit of the bailee, the bailor must notify the bailee of any known defects.** Suppose Megan lends her stepladder to

Dave. The top rung is loose and Megan knows it, but she forgets to tell Dave. The top rung crumbles, and Dave falls onto his girlfriend's iguana. Megan is liable to Dave and the girlfriend unless the defect in the ladder was obvious. Notice that Megan's liability is not only to the bailee, but also to any others injured by the defects. Megan would not be liable if she had notified Dave of the defective rung.

In a mutual-benefit bailment, the bailor is liable not only for known defects, but also for unknown defects that the bailor could have discovered with reasonable diligence. Suppose RentaLot rents a power sander to Dan. RentaLot does not realize that the sander has faulty wiring, but a reasonable inspection would have revealed the problem. When Dan suffers a serious shock from the defect, RentaLot is liable to him, even though it was unaware of the problem.

Common Carriers and Contract Carriers

A carrier is a company that transports goods for others. It is a bailee of every shipment entrusted to it. There are two kinds of carriers: common carriers and contract carriers. The distinction is important because each type of company has a different level of liability.

A **common carrier** makes its services available on a regular basis to the general public. For example, a trucking company located in St. Louis that is willing to haul freight for anyone, to any destination in the country, is a common carrier. **Generally, a common carrier is strictly liable for harm to the bailor's goods.** A bailor needs only establish that it delivered property to the carrier in good condition and that the cargo arrived damaged. The carrier is then liable unless it can show that it was not negligent *and* that the loss was caused by an act of God (such as a hurricane) or some other extraordinary event, such as war. These defenses are difficult to prove, and in most cases, a common carrier is liable for harm to the property.

A common carrier, however, is allowed to limit its liability by contract. For example, a common carrier might offer the bailor the choice of two shipping rates: a low rate, with a maximum liability, say, of $10,000, or a higher shipping rate, with full liability for any harm to the goods. In that case, if the bailor chooses the lower rate, the limitation on liability is enforceable. Even if the bailor proves a loss of $300,000, the carrier owes merely $10,000.

A **contract carrier** does not make its services available to the general public, but engages in continuing agreements with particular customers. Assume that Steel Curtain Shipping is a trucking company in Pittsburgh that hauls cargo to California for two or three steel producers and carries manufactured goods from California to Pennsylvania and New York for a few West Coast companies. Steel Curtain is a contract carrier. **A contract carrier does not incur strict liability.** The normal bailment rules apply, and a contract carrier can escape liability by demonstrating that it exercised due care of the property.

Common carrier
A company that transports goods and makes its services regularly available to the general public.

Contract carrier
A company that transports goods for particular customers.

Innkeepers

Hotels, motels, and inns frequently act as bailees of their guests' property. Most states have special innkeeper statutes that regulate liability.

Hotel patrons often assume that anything they bring to a hotel is safe. But some state innkeeper statutes impose an absolute limit on a hotel's liability. Other statutes require guests to leave valuables in the inn's safe deposit box. And even that may not be enough to protect them fully. For example, a state statute might require the guest to register the nature and value of the goods with the hotel. If a guest fails to follow the statutory requirements, he receives no compensation for any losses suffered.

Chapter Conclusion

Personal property law plays an almost daily role in all of our lives. The manager of a parking lot, the finder of lost property, and the operator of an airport security system must all realize that they may incur substantial liability for personal property, whether they intend to accept that obligation or not. Understanding personal property can be worth a lot of chips—but do not leave them lying around your hotel room.

EXAM REVIEW

1. **GIFTS**   A gift is a voluntary transfer of property from one person to another without consideration. The elements of a gift are intention to transfer ownership immediately, delivery, and acceptance. (pp. 541–544)

2. **FOUND PROPERTY**   The finder of property must attempt to locate the true owner unless the property was abandoned. The following principles generally govern:

   - Abandoned property—the finder may keep it.

   - Lost property—the finder generally has rights superior to everyone but the true owner, except that if she found it on land belonging to another, the property owner generally is entitled to it.

   - Mislaid property—generally, the finder has no rights in the property. (pp. 544–545)

EXAM Strategy

Question: The government accused Carlo Francia and another person of stealing a purse belonging to Frances Bainlardi. A policeman saw Francia sorting through the contents of the purse, which included a photo identification of Bainlardi. Francia kept some items, such as cash, while discarding others. At trial, Francia claimed that he had thought the purse was lost or abandoned. Besides the fact that Francia's accomplice was holding burglary tools, what is the weakness in Francia's defense?

Strategy: The finder of property must attempt to locate the true owner unless the property was abandoned. Is there any likelihood that the purse was abandoned? If it was not abandoned, did Francia attempt to locate the owner? (See the "Result" at the end of this section.)

3. **BAILMENT**   A bailment is the rightful possession of goods by one who is not the owner. The one who delivers the goods is the bailor and the one in possession is the bailee. To create a bailment, the bailee must assume physical control with intent to possess. (pp. 545–546)

4. **BAILEE'S RIGHTS**   The bailee is always entitled to possess the property, is frequently allowed to use it, and may be entitled to compensation. (p. 547)

5. **REDELIVERY**   The bailee is strictly liable to redeliver the goods to the bailor. (p. 547)

6. **DUE CARE**   The bailee is obligated to exercise due care. The level of care required depends upon who receives the benefit of the bailment: if the bailee is the sole beneficiary, she must use extraordinary care; if the parties mutually benefit, the bailee must use ordinary care; and if the bailor is the sole beneficiary of the bailment, the bailee must use only slight care. (p. 547)

7. **PRESUMPTION OF NEGLIGENCE**   Once the bailor has proven the existence of a bailment and loss, a presumption of negligence arises, and the burden shifts to the bailee to prove adequate care. (p. 548)

EXAM Strategy

Question: Lonny Joe owned two rare 1955 Ford Thunderbird automobiles, one red and one green, both in mint condition. He stored the cars in his garage. His friend Stephanie wanted to use the red car in a music video, so Lonny Joe rented it to her for two days, for $300 per day. When she returned the red car, Lonny Joe discovered a long scratch along one side. That same day, he noticed a long scratch along the side of the green car. He sued Stephanie for harm to the red car. Lonny Joe sued an electrician for damage to the green car, claiming that the scratch occurred while the electrician was fixing a heater in the garage. Explain the different burdens of proof in the two cases.

Strategy: In an ordinary negligence case, the plaintiff must prove all elements by a preponderance of the evidence. However, in a bailment, a *presumption* of negligence arises. To answer this question, you need to know whether Lonny Joe established a bailment with either or both defendants. (See the "Result" at the end of this section.)

8. **BAILOR'S RESPONSIBILITY**   The bailor must keep the property in suitable repair, free of any hidden defects. If the bailor is in the business of renting property, the bailment is probably subject to implied warranties. (pp. 548–549)

9. **COMMON CARRIERS**   Generally, a common carrier is strictly liable for harm to the bailor's goods. A contract carrier incurs only normal bailment liability. (p. 549)

10. **INNKEEPER LIABILITY**   The liability of an innkeeper is regulated by state statute. A guest intending to store valuables with an innkeeper must follow the statute to the letter. (p. 549)

2. Result: Abandoned property is something that the owner has knowingly discarded because she no longer wants it. The burden is on the finder to prove that the property was abandoned, which will be impossible in this case since no one would throw away cash and credit cards. Because the purse contained photo identification, Francia could easily have located its owner. He made no attempt to do so and his defense is unpersuasive.

7. Result: Lonny Joe had no bailment with the electrician because the electrician never assumed control of the car. To win that case, Lonny Joe must prove that the electrician behaved unreasonably and caused the scratch. However, when Lonny Joe rented Stephanie the red car, the parties created a bailment, and the law *presumes* Stephanie caused the damage unless she can prove otherwise. That is a hard burden, and Stephanie will likely lose.

MATCHING QUESTIONS

Match the following terms with their definitions:

___A. Extraordinary care

___B. *Inter vivos* gift

___C. Ordinary care

___D. Gift *causa mortis*

___E. Slight care

1. A gift made with no fear of death, cannot be revoked

2. Required level of care in a bailment made for the sole benefit of the bailee

3. A gift made in contemplation of approaching death, can be revoked

4. Required level of care in a bailment made for the mutual benefit of bailor and bailee

5. Required level of care in a bailment made for the sole benefit of the bailor

TRUE/FALSE QUESTIONS

Circle true or false:

1. T F A gift is unenforceable unless both parties give consideration.

2. T F A gift *causa mortis* is automatically revoked if the donor dies shortly after making it.

3. T F A bailee always has the right to possess the property.

4. T F A finder of lost property generally may keep the property unless the true owner comes forward.

5. T F A common carrier is strictly liable for harm to the bailor's goods.

MULTIPLE-CHOICE QUESTIONS

1. **CPA QUESTION:** Which of the following requirements must be met to create a bailment?

   I.   Delivery of personal property to the intended bailee

   II. Possession by the intended bailee

   III. An absolute duty on the intended bailee to return or dispose of the property according to the bailor's directions

      (a) I and II only

      (b) I and III only

      (c) II and III only

      (d) I, II, and III

2. Martin is a rich businessman in perfect health. On Monday morning, he tells his niece, Stephanie, "Tomorrow I'm going to give you my brand new Ferrari." Stephanie is ecstatic. That afternoon, Martin is killed in a car accident. Does Stephanie get the car?

(a) Stephanie gets the car because this is a valid *inter vivos* gift.

(b) Stephanie gets the car because this is a valid gift *causa mortis.*

(c) Stephanie gets the car because there is no reason to dispute that Martin made the promise.

(d) Stephanie gets the car unless Martin left a wife or children.

(e) Stephanie does not get the car.

3. Margie has dinner at Bill's house. While helping with the dishes, she takes off her Rolex watch and forgets to put it back on when she leaves for the night. Bill finds the watch in the morning and decides to keep it.

(a) This is abandoned property, and Bill is entitled to it.

(b) This is lost property, and Bill is entitled to it.

(c) This is lost property, and Margie is entitled to it.

(d) This is mislaid property, and Bill is entitled to it.

(e) This is mislaid property, and Margie is entitled to it.

4. Arriving at a restaurant, Max gives his car keys to the valet. When the valet returns the car three hours later, it has a large, new dent. The valet says he did not cause it. Max sues the valet service.

(a) The burden is on the valet service to prove it did not cause the dent.

(b) The burden is on Max to prove that the valet service caused the dent.

(c) The valet service is strictly liable for harm to Max's car.

(d) The valet service has no liability to Max, regardless of how the dent was caused.

(e) The valet service is only liable for gross negligence.

5. Car Moves hauls autos anywhere in the country. Valerie hires Car Moves to take her Porsche from Chicago to Los Angeles. The Porsche arrives badly damaged because the Car Moves truck was hit by a bus. The accident was caused by the bus driver's negligence. If Valerie sues Car Moves for the cost of repairs, what will happen?

(a) Valerie will win.

(b) Valerie will win only if she can prove Car Moves was partly negligent.

(c) Valerie will win only if she can prove that Car Moves agreed to strict liability.

(d) Valerie will lose because Car Moves did not cause the accident.

(e) Valerie will lose because this was a bailment for mutual benefit.

ESSAY QUESTIONS

1. While in her second year at the Juilliard School of Music in New York City, Ann Rylands had a chance to borrow for one month a rare Guadagnini violin, made in 1768. She returned the violin to the owner in Philadelphia, but then she telephoned her father to ask if he would buy it for her. He borrowed money from his pension fund and paid the owner. Ann traveled to Philadelphia to pick up the violin. She had exclusive possession of the violin for the next 20 years, using it in her professional career. Unfortunately, she became an alcoholic, and during one period when she was in a treatment center, she entrusted the violin to her mother for safekeeping. At about that time, her father died. When Ann was released from the center, she requested return of the violin, but her mother refused. Who owns the violin?

2. Ronald Armstead worked for First American Bank as a courier. His duties included making deliveries between the bank's branches in Washington, D.C. Armstead parked the bank's station wagon near the entrance of one branch in violation of a sign saying: "No Parking—Rush Hour Zone." In the rear luggage section of the station wagon were four locked bank dispatch bags containing checks and other valuable documents. Armstead had received tickets for illegal parking at this spot on five occasions. Shortly after Armstead entered the bank, a tow truck arrived, and its operator prepared to tow the station wagon. Transportation Management, Inc., operated the towing service on behalf of the District of Columbia. Armstead ran out to the vehicle and told the tow truck operator that he was prepared to drive the vehicle away immediately. But the operator drove away with the station wagon in tow. One-and-a-half hours later, a bank employee paid for the car's release, but one dispatch bag, containing documents worth $107,000, was missing. First American sued Transportation Management and the District of Columbia. The defendants sought summary judgment, claiming they could not be liable. Were they correct?

3. Eileen Murphy often cared for her elderly neighbor, Thomas Kenney. He paid her $25 per day for her help and once gave her a bank certificate of deposit worth $25,000. She spent the money. Murphy alleged that shortly before his death, Kenney gave her a large block of shares in three corporations. He called his broker, intending to instruct him to transfer the shares to Murphy's name, but the broker was ill and unavailable. So Kenney told Murphy to write her name on the shares and keep them, which she did. Two weeks later, Kenney died. When Murphy presented the shares to Kenney's broker to transfer ownership to her, the broker refused because Kenney had never endorsed the shares as the law requires—that is, signed them over to Murphy. Was Murphy entitled to the $25,000? To the shares?

4. Artist James Daugherty painted six murals on the walls of the public high school in Stamford, Connecticut. Many years later, the city began to restore its high school. The architect and school officials agreed that the Daugherty murals should be preserved. They arranged for the construction workers to remove the murals to prevent harm. By accident, the workers rolled them up and placed them near the trash dumpsters for disposal. A student found the murals and took them home, and he later notified the federal government's General Services Administration (GSA) of his find. The GSA arranged to transport the murals to an art restorer named Hiram Hoelzer for storage and eventual restoration when funds could be arranged. Over *19 years* went by before anyone notified the Stamford School system where the murals were. In the meantime, neither the GSA nor anyone else paid Hoelzer for the storage or restoration. By 1989,

the murals were valued at $1.25 million by Sotheby's, an art auction house. Hoelzer filed suit, seeking a declaration that the murals had been abandoned. Were they abandoned? What difference would that make when determining ownership?

5. Marjan International Corp. sells handmade Oriental rugs. V. K. Putman, Inc., is a Montana trucking company. Marjan delivered valuable rugs to Putman for shipment from New York City to Tacoma, Washington. Unfortunately, there were several delays in transit. The truck driver encountered snowstorms and closed roads. His truck also overheated and required repairs in a garage. Before the driver resumed the trip, he stopped to pick up and load other goods. When the truck finally arrived in Tacoma, two bales of rugs were missing. Marjan sued on the grounds that Putman was a common carrier, but Putman claimed it was a contract carrier. What difference does it make whether Putman was a common carrier or a contract carrier, and how is that determined?

DISCUSSION QUESTIONS

1. Ann is Becky's best friend. Tomorrow, Ann will move across the country to start a new job. Feeling sentimental on a night of goodbyes, Becky gives Ann a necklace that has been in Becky's family for 50 years. "You've always liked this, and I want you to have it," she says. Ann accepts the necklace. Early the next morning, Becky reconsiders. She finds Ann at the airport and sees her wearing the necklace. "Ann, my grandmother gave me that necklace. I'm sorry, but I want it back," she pleads. "You know," Ann replies with a smile, "I think I'm going to keep it." Is Ann legally required to return the necklace? Is she ethically required to return the necklace?

2. Consider revocable gifts. The example early in the chapter was, "The mule is yours from now on, but if you ever start acting stupid again, I'm taking her back." In such a case, the giver still owns the mule, and can take it back at any time. Is this reasonable? Should stating a condition "cancel" a gift, or should the gift recipient in this example own the mule?

3. Is it sensible to distinguish between *inter vivos* gifts and gifts *causa mortis*? Should someone "on his deathbed" be able to change his mind so easily?

4. After a baseball game, Randy cannot find his car in the stadium parking lot. For the life of him, he cannot remember where he parked. He wanders down row after row for an hour, and then another hour. Eventually, he gives up and calls a cab. Is Randy's car lost, abandoned, or mislaid? If Randy never returns to reclaim the car, who owns it?

5. Dan checks into a nice beachfront hotel. He does not want to expose his $10,000 Patek Phillipe wristwatch to salt water, and so he leaves it in the dresser in the room. When he returns from the beach, the watch is gone. He is shocked to learn that the hotel is not legally responsible for the value of his watch. Is the law reasonable in such cases? Should the hotel be liable? Why or why not?

ESTATE PLANNING

Pablo Picasso, the renowned artist, created hundreds of paintings and sculptures as well as thousands of drawings and sketches. His personal life was unconventional, featuring a series of wives, mistresses, and children, both legitimate and illegitimate. Despite this large group of feuding heirs, he died in France without a will.

After four years of litigation, the French court decided that his estate would be shared by his widow, Jacqueline (who later committed suicide); two grandchildren by his legitimate child, Paulo (who died of cirrhosis of the liver); and his three illegitimate children, Maya, Claude, and Paloma. But by the time the decision was reached, legal fees had swallowed up all the cash in the estate.[1]

> Despite having a large group of feuding heirs, Picasso died without a will.

---

[1]Adapted from Lynn Barber, "A Perfectly Packaged Picasso," *The Independent*, December 9, 1990, p. 8.

INTRODUCTION

There is one immutable law of the universe: "You can't take it with you." But you can control where your assets go after your death. Or you can decide not to bother with an estate plan and leave all in chaos behind you.

Definitions

Like many areas of the law, estate planning uses its own terminology:

- **Estate Planning.** The process of giving away property after (or in anticipation of) death.

- **Estate.** The legal entity that holds title to assets after the owner dies and before the property is distributed.

- **Decedent.** The person who has died.

- **Testator or Testatrix.** Someone who has signed a valid will. *Testatrix* is the female version of this word (from the Latin).

- **Intestate.** To die without a will.

- **Heir.** Technically, the term *heir* refers to someone who inherits from a decedent who died intestate. **Devisee** means someone who inherits under a will. However, many courts use *heir* to refer to anyone who inherits property, and we follow that usage in this chapter.

- **Probate.** The process of carrying out the terms of a will.

- **Executor or Executrix.** A personal representative *chosen by the decedent* to carry out the terms of the will. An *executrix* is a female executor.

- **Administrator or Administratrix.** A personal representative *appointed by the probate court* to oversee the probate process for someone who has died intestate (or without appointing an executor). As you can guess, an *administratrix* is a female administrator.

- **Grantor or Settlor.** Someone who creates a trust.

- **Donor.** Someone who makes a gift or creates a trust.

Purpose

Estate planning has two primary goals: to ensure that property is distributed as the owner desires and to minimize estate taxes. Although tax issues are beyond the scope of this chapter, they are an important element of estate planning, often affecting not only how people transfer their property but, in some cases, to whom. For instance, wealthy people may give money to charity, at least in part, to minimize the taxes on the rest of their estate. In the *Paradee* case later in this chapter, grandparents set up a trust as a means of passing tax-free money to their grandchild.

Probate Law

The federal government and many states levy estate taxes (although traditionally, state taxes have been much lower). But only the states, and not the federal government, have probate codes to regulate the creation and implementation of wills and trusts. These codes vary from state to state. This chapter, therefore, speaks only of general trends among the states. Certainly, anyone who is preparing a will must consult the laws of the relevant state. To make probate law more consistent, the National Conference of Commissioners on Uniform State Laws issued a Uniform Probate Code (UPC). However, fewer than half of the states have adopted it.

WILLS

Will
A legal document that disposes of the testator's property after death.

A will is a legal document that disposes of the testator's property after death. It can be revoked or altered at any time until death. Virtually every adult, even those with only modest assets, should have a will to:

- Ensure that their assets (modest though they may be) are distributed in accordance with their wishes.

- Select a personal representative to oversee the estate. If the decedent does not name an executor in a will, the court will appoint an administrator. Generally, people prefer to have a friend, rather than a court, in charge of their property.

- Avoid unnecessary expenses. Those who die intestate often leave behind issues for lawyers to resolve. A properly drafted will can also reduce the estate tax bill.

- Provide guardians for minor children. If parents do not appoint a guardian before they die, a court will. Presumably, the parents are best able to make this choice.

Requirements for a Valid Will

Generally speaking, a person may leave his assets to whomever he wants. However, the testatrix must be:

- Of **legal age** (which is 18).

- Of **sound mind.** That is, she must be able to understand what a will is, more or less what she owns, who her relatives are, and how she is disposing of her property.

- Acting without **undue influence.** Undue influence means that one person has enough power over another to force him to do something against his free will.

Legal Technicalities

A testator must comply with the legal requirements for executing a will: It must be in writing, and the testator must sign it or, if he is too weak, direct someone else to sign it for him. Generally, two witnesses must also sign the will. Under the 2008 amendment to the UPC, a notarized will does not require any witnesses, but only four states have passed this amendment. No one named in a will should also serve as a witness because, in many states, a witness may not inherit under a will. The importance of abiding by these legal technicalities cannot be overstated. No matter what the testator's intent, courts will not enforce a will unless each requirement of the law has been fully met. As we have observed before, close counts only in horseshoes and hand grenades.

HOLOGRAPHIC WILL

Holographic will
A will that is handwritten and signed by the testator, but not witnessed.

Sometimes courts will accept a **holographic will: a will that is handwritten and signed by the testatrix, but not witnessed.** Note that a holographic will *must* be written in a testator's own handwriting—it cannot be typed. Suppose Rowena is on a plane that suffers engine trouble. For 15 minutes, the pilot struggles to control the plane. Despite his efforts, it crashes, killing everyone aboard. During those 15 minutes, Rowena writes on a Post-it note, "This is my last will and testament. I leave all my assets to the National Gallery of Art in Washington, D.C." She signs her name, but her fellow passengers are too frantic to witness it. This note is found in the wreckage of the plane. Her previous will, signed and witnessed in a lawyer's office, left everything to her friend, Ivan. If Rowena resides in one of the majority of states that accepts a holographic will, then Ivan is out of luck and the National Gallery will inherit all. Indeed, one court has accepted as a will a handwritten Post-it note that had not been witnessed.

NUNCUPATIVE WILL

Some states will also accept a **nuncupative will**. This is the formal term for an oral will. For a nuncupative will to be valid, the testatrix must know she is dying, there must be three witnesses, and these witnesses must know that they are listening to her will. Suppose that Rowena survives the airplane crash for a few hours. Instead of writing a will on the plane, she whispers to a nurse in the hospital, "I'd like all my property to go to the Angell Memorial Cat Hospital." This oral will is valid if there are two other witnesses and Rowena also says, "I'm dying. Please witness my oral will."

Nuncupative will
An oral will.

Spouse's Share

A spouse is entitled to a **forced share** of the decedent's estate (unless she waives that right by written contract). In community property states, a spouse can override the will and claim one-half of all marital property acquired during the marriage, except property that the testator inherited or received as a gift.[2] Although this rule sounds easy and fair, implementation can be troublesome. If a couple has been married for many years and has substantial assets, it can be very difficult to sort out what is and is not community property. Suppose that the testatrix inherited $1 million 20 years before her death. She and her husband both earned sizable incomes during their careers. How can a court tell what money bought which asset? Anyone in a situation such as this should keep detailed records.

In most non-community property states, a spouse can override the will and claim some percentage of the decedent's probate estate (again, unless he has waived that right by written contract). The UPC provides a complex formula that depends on how long the couple was married and what percentage of marital assets each held.

Children's Share

Parents are not required to leave assets to their children. They may disinherit their children for any reason.[3] However, the law presumes that a **pretermitted child** (that is, a child left nothing in the parent's will) was omitted by accident unless the parent clearly indicates in the will that he has omitted the child on purpose. To do so, he must either leave her some nominal amount, such as $1, or specifically write in the will that the omission was intentional: "I am making no bequest to my daughter because she has chosen a religion of which I disapprove."

Pretermitted child
A child who is left nothing in the parent's will.

If a pretermitted child is left out by accident, she is generally entitled to the same share she would have received if her parent had died intestate; that is, without a will. Does this rule make sense? How likely is it that a parent with sufficient mental capacity to make a valid will would *forget* a child? Do you think the father in the following case simply forgot?

---

[2]Arizona, California, Idaho, Louisiana, Nevada, New Mexico, Texas, and Washington all have community property laws; Wisconsin's system is a variation of the same principle.
[3]Except in Louisiana, whose laws are based on the French model.

In Re Estate of Josiah James Treloar, Jr.

151 N.H. 460; 859 A.2d 1162; 2004 N.H. LEXIS 177
Supreme Court of New Hampshire, 2004

CASE SUMMARY

Facts: Josiah James Treloar, Jr.'s first will left his estate to his wife unless she died before he did, in which case one piece of land was to go to his daughter Evelyn, another to his son, Rodney, and the rest of his estate was to be divided equally among Evelyn, Rodney, and another daughter, Beverly.

After his daughter Evelyn died, Josiah executed a new will. To help his lawyer in preparing this document, Josiah gave him a copy of the old will with handwritten changes, including Evelyn's name crossed out. The new will left the estate to Rodney and Beverly equally. Evelyn's children and her husband, Leon, got nothing, although Leon was named as executor. Josiah referred to Leon as "my son-in-law."

Under New Hampshire law, all *issue* (including children and grandchildren) can qualify as pretermitted heirs. The law assumes that if the testator does not leave anything to his issue or does not refer to them in his will, it is because he has forgotten them. They are therefore entitled to a share of his estate. If Josiah had mentioned Evelyn, then the assumption would be that he had not forgotten her or her children. Evelyn's children argued that they were entitled to a share of Josiah's estate because he had not left her or them out on purpose. Josiah's attorney was serving as executor (not Leon). When he refused to pay the children, they sued.

Issue: *Are Evelyn's children entitled to a share of Josiah's estate?*

Decision: Yes, Evelyn's children are entitled to a share of the estate.

Reasoning: Most people leave their money to their children and grandchildren. Therefore, when a parent omits one or more of these heirs from his will, the law in New Hampshire assumes that it was a mistake unless he clearly specifies *in the will* that he had left them out on purpose. In this case, it seemed from circumstantial evidence that Josiah had not forgotten Evelyn or her children. After all, he had crossed her name out of the old will he had given his lawyer to use as a basis for the new document. He also listed her husband, Leon, as executor. Presumably, he remembered that Leon was married to Evelyn.

Nonetheless, it is not the court's job to try to figure out what Josiah did or did not remember. The law is clear—indirectly alluding to the children or grandchildren is not sufficient. Because Josiah did not specifically refer to Evelyn or her children within the four corners of the will, it is presumed he forgot them, and therefore they are entitled to a share of his estate.

As we have observed before, the laws regarding wills are very precise. It seems highly unlikely that Josiah remembered his son-in-law but forgot the daughter to whom the son-in-law had been married. No matter—the will did not meet the requirements of the statute, so Evelyn's children were in luck.

In drafting a will, lawyers almost always use the term *issue* instead of *children*. *Issue* means all descendants such as children, grandchildren, and so on. If a will left property just to "my children" and one child died before the testator, that child's children would not inherit their parent's share. But if the will says "to my issue" and one child dies first, her children will inherit her share.

The will must also indicate whether issue are to inherit *per stirpes* or *per capita*. **Per stirpes** means that each *branch* of the family receives an equal share. Each child of the deceased receives the same amount, and, if a child has already died, her heirs inherit her share. **Per capita** means that each *heir* receives the same amount. If the children have died, then each grandchild inherits the same amount.

Suppose that Gwendolyn has two children, Lance and Arthur. Lance has one child; Arthur has four. Both sons predecease their mother. If Gwendolyn's will says *"per stirpes,"* Lance's child will inherit her father's entire share, which is half of Gwendolyn's estate. Arthur's four children will share their father's portion, so each will receive one-eighth ($\frac{1}{4} \times \frac{1}{2}$).

Issue
A person's direct descendants, such as children and grandchildren.

Per stirpes
Each branch of the family receives an equal share.

Per capita
Each heir receives the same amount.

If Gwendolyn's will says *"per capita,"* each of her grandchildren will inherit one-fifth of her estate. Although it might sound fairer to give all grandchildren the same inheritance, most people choose a *per stirpes* distribution on the theory that they are treating their children equally. The following chart illustrates the difference between *per stirpes* and *per capita*.

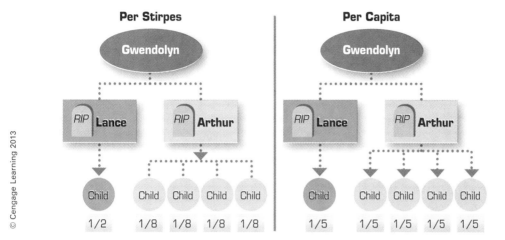

Amending a Will

A testator can generally revoke or alter a will at any time prior to death. In most states, he can revoke a will by destroying it, putting an *X* through it, writing "revoked" (or some synonym) on it, or signing a new will. He can also execute an amendment—called a **codicil**—to change specific terms of the will, while keeping the rest of it intact. A codicil must meet all the requirements of a will, such as two witnesses. Suppose that Uncle Herman, who has a long and elaborate will, now wants his sterling silver Swiss Army knife to go to Cousin Larry rather than Niece Shannon. Instead of redoing his whole will, he can ask his lawyer to draw up a codicil changing only that one provision.

Codicil
An amendment to a will.

Intestacy

When singer John Denver died unexpectedly in a plane accident, he had had several marriages, children, and platinum albums. His estate was worth $20 million. What he did not have was a will, as is the case with 60 percent of Americans. When someone dies intestate, the law steps in and determines how to distribute the decedent's property. Although, in theory, intestacy laws are supposed to be based on what most people would prefer, in practice, they are not. The vast majority of married people, for instance, leave all their assets to their surviving spouse. Most intestacy laws do not. In some states, if a married person dies intestate, some portion of her property (one-half or two-thirds) goes to her spouse, and the remainder to her issue (including grandchildren). Few people would actually want grandchildren to take a share of their estate in preference to their spouse.

Power of Attorney

A **durable power of attorney** is a document that permits the attorney-in-fact to act for the principal. (An attorney-in-fact need not be a lawyer.) Typically, a power of attorney expires if the principal revokes it, becomes incapacitated, or dies. But a *durable* power is valid even

Durable power of attorney
Grants someone the authority to act for another person. Valid even if the principal can no longer make decisions.

if the principal can no longer make decisions for herself. The power of attorney is effective until the principal dies or revokes it.

Lawyers generally recommend that their clients execute a durable power of attorney, particularly if they are elderly or in poor health. The power of attorney permits the client not only to choose the person who will act for him, but also to give advance instructions, such as "lend money to my son, Billy, if ever he needs it." If a client becomes incompetent and has no power of attorney, a court will appoint a guardian. As a general rule, it is better to make choices yourself rather than leave them to a court.

Probate

The testatrix cannot implement the terms of the will from beyond the grave, so she appoints an executor for this task. Typically, the executor is a family member, lawyer, or close friend. If the decedent does not select an executor, the probate court appoints an administrator to fulfill the same functions. Both the executor and the administrator are entitled to reasonable compensation—typically between 1 percent and 5 percent of the estate's value, although family members and friends often waive the fee.

Anatomical Gifts

Doctors have become increasingly successful at transplanting human organs such as hearts, corneas, kidneys, pituitary glands, and skin. The demand for these organs is much greater than the supply. **The Uniform Anatomical Gift Act (UAGA) allows an individual to indicate her desire to be a donor either by putting a provision in her will or by signing an organ donation card in the presence of two witnesses.** Alternatively, DonateLives is an iPhone app that allows users to register as organ donors. The UAGA also provides that, unless a decedent has affirmatively indicated her desire not to be a donor, family members have the right to make a gift of her organs after death.

Living Wills

Living will

In the event that a person is unable to make medical decisions, this document indicates her preferences and may also appoint someone else to makes these decisions for her. Also known as an *advance directive*.

Health care proxy

Someone who is authorized to make health care decisions for a person who is incompetent.

At the age of 32, Nancy Cruzan was in a devastating car accident. Lying face down in a ditch, she stopped breathing for 14 minutes. Medics revived her, but she remained in a deep coma, unable to interact with her surroundings, although she did seem to feel pain. For seven years, she lay in a fetal position in a hospital bed. Her hands were so twisted that her nails cut her wrists. No one in her situation had ever recovered, but if she were fed, she could live 25 years. Cruzan's parents believed that their daughter would not have wanted to live this way, so they asked a court for permission to stop feeding her.

Ultimately, the Supreme Court upheld a Missouri law that family members cannot choose to discontinue treatment for an incompetent person unless there is clear and convincing evidence the patient would have made that choice herself.[4] After the Supreme Court decision, the probate court in Missouri heard new witnesses testify that Cruzan had said she would not want to live "like a vegetable." The lower court considered this clear and convincing evidence of Cruzan's wishes and granted the family permission to withhold feeding.

Spurred by the Cruzan case, many people executed so-called **living wills** or **advance directives.** Living wills permit adults to refuse extreme medical treatment that would unreasonably prolong their lives, such as artificial feeding or cardiac resuscitation. In addition, a living will can be used to appoint a **health care proxy** to make decisions for

---

[4]*Cruzan v. Director, Missouri Department of Health*, 497 U.S. 261, 110 S. Ct. 2841, 1990 U.S. LEXIS 3301 (1990).

a person who has become incompetent. Concerned that living wills are not detailed enough, the Center for Ethics in Health Care developed Physician Orders for Life-Sustaining Treatment (POLST). These forms provide more detailed instructions on specific interventions.

Experts estimate that more than 75 percent of the population will not be capable of making their own medical decisions at the end of their lives. What happens if their family members disagree about what to do? A living will can resolve those disputes. Terri Schiavo was only 26 years old when her heart stopped beating one evening, causing brain damage that put her in a persistent vegetative state. Her husband said she would not have wanted to live that way, and asked to have her feeding tube removed; her parents disagreed and fought him through the courts. Even Congress intervened to try to keep the tube in place. Her husband ultimately prevailed and the tube was removed, but only after 15 years of litigation and public uproar. If Schiavo had had a living will, her family would have had more privacy, fewer legal bills, and, perhaps, greater peace.

> If Schiavo had had a living will, her family would have had more privacy, fewer legal bills, and, perhaps, greater peace.

Doctors are permitted to shorten a patient's life by withholding medical treatment. Can they go the next step and prescribe medication to end the life of a terminal patient who is suffering intolerably? Montana, Oregon, and Washington are the only states that specifically allow doctors to prescribe a fatal dose of drugs to a dying patient. In Oregon and Washington, about 50 terminally ill people die from **assisted suicide** each year.

Assisted suicide
The process of hastening death for a terminally ill patient at the request of the patient.

EXAM Strategy

Question: Tim's will leaves all of his money to his cat, Princess Ida. After he dies, his widow and children claim that they are entitled to a share of his estate. Is this true? Will Princess Ida be living like royalty?

Strategy: The answer is different for his wife and children.

Result: Tim's wife is entitled to a share of his assets unless she signed a contract waiving that right. His children are entitled to a share of his assets unless he clearly indicated in his will that he intended to leave them out.

Trusts

Trusts are an increasingly popular method for managing assets, both during life and after death. In the United States, over $1 trillion is held in personal trusts. **A trust is an entity that separates legal and beneficial ownership.** It involves three people: the **grantor** (also called the **settlor** or **donor**), who creates and funds it; the **trustee**, who manages the assets; and the **beneficiary,** who receives the financial proceeds. A grantor can create a trust during her lifetime or after her death through her will.

Trust
An entity that separates the legal and beneficial ownership of assets.

Grantor
Someone who creates and funds a trust. Also called a *settler* or *donor*.

Trustee
Someone who manages the assets of a trust.

Beneficiary
Someone who receives the financial proceeds of a trust.

Advantages and Disadvantages

Why do people use trusts? These are among the advantages:

- **Control.** The grantor can control her assets after her death. In the trust document, she can direct the trustees to follow a specific investment strategy, and she can determine how much income the beneficiaries receive. As an example, suppose the grantor has a husband and children. She wants to provide her husband with adequate income after her death, but she does not want him to spend so lavishly that nothing is left for the children. Nor does she want him to spend all her money on his second wife. The grantor could create a trust in her will that allows her husband to spend the income and, upon his death, gives the principal to their children.

- **Caring for children.** Minor children cannot legally manage property on their own, so parents or grandparents often establish trusts to take care of these assets until the children grow up.

- **Tax savings.** Although tax issues are beyond the scope of this chapter, it is worth noting that trusts can reduce estate taxes. For example, many married couples use a **marital trust** and parents or grandparents can establish **generation-skipping trusts** to reduce their estate tax bill.

- **Privacy.** A will is filed in probate court and becomes a matter of public record. Anyone can obtain a copy of it. Some companies are even in the business of providing copies to celebrity hounds. Jacqueline Kennedy Onassis's will is particularly popular. Trusts, however, are private documents and are not available to the public.

- **Probate.** Because a will must go through the often-lengthy probate process, the heirs may not receive assets for some time. Assets that are put into a trust *before the grantor dies* do not go through probate; the beneficiaries have immediate access to them.

- **Protecting against creditors.** A minority of states now permit so-called asset protection trusts. These trusts permit someone to place all his assets in a trust. He can spend the trust funds himself, but his creditors have no right to the assets. For example, Hartwell has an unfortunate alcohol and drug problem, but he is no fool. When he inherited millions on his 21st birthday, he placed them all in an asset protection trust. Later, he married, and then got divorced. He also was in a car accident that caused the death of a young investment banker. Both his wife and the banker's husband sued him, looking for financial support. But they are both out of luck. His assets are protected from all creditors.

Marital trust
A legal entity created for the purpose of reducing a married couple's estate taxes.

Ethics   Is an asset protection trust fair? Why would states permit their citizens to hide money from legitimate creditors? The short answer: to attract trust business from out of state. Trusts generate billions of dollars in fees each year. If you were a state legislator, how would you vote when this legislation came up for approval? If you had substantial assets, would you put them in such a trust? What Life Principles apply here?

The major *disadvantage* of a trust is expense. Although it is always possible for the grantor to establish a trust himself with the aid of software or form books, trusts are complex instruments with many potential pitfalls. Do-it-yourself trusts are a recipe for disaster. In addition to the legal fees required to establish a trust, the trustees may have to be paid. Professional trustees typically charge an annual fee of about 1 percent of the trust's assets. Family members usually do not expect payment.

Types of Trusts

Depending upon the goal in establishing a trust, a grantor has two choices.

LIVING TRUST

Also known as an *inter vivos* trust, a living trust is established while the grantor is still alive. In the typical living trust, the grantor serves as trustee during his lifetime. He maintains total control over the assets and avoids a trustee's fee. If the grantor becomes disabled or dies, the successor trustee, who is named in the trust instrument, takes over automatically. All of the assets stay in the trust and avoid probate. Most (but not all) living trusts are **revocable**, meaning that the grantor can terminate or change the trust at any time.

TESTAMENTARY TRUST

A testamentary trust is created by a will. It goes into effect when the grantor dies. Naturally, it is **irrevocable** because the grantor is dead. The grantor's property must go through probate on its way to the trust.

Living trusts are particularly popular with older people because they want to ensure that their assets will be managed properly if they become disabled. Younger people typically opt for a testamentary trust because the probability they will become disabled anytime soon is remote. Also, they want to avoid the effort of transferring their assets to the trust while they are still alive.

Trust Administration

The primary obligation of trustees is to carry out the terms of the trust. They may exercise any powers expressly granted to them in the trust instrument and any implied powers reasonably necessary to implement the terms of the trust. In carrying out the terms of the trust, the trustees have a fiduciary duty to the beneficiary. This fiduciary duty includes:

- **A duty of loyalty.** In managing the trust, the trustees must put the interests of the beneficiaries first. They must disclose any relevant information to the beneficiaries. They may not mix their own assets with those of the trust, do business with the trust (unless expressly permitted by the terms of the trust), or favor one beneficiary over another.

- **A duty of care.** The trustee must act as a reasonable person would when managing the assets of another. The trustee must make careful investments, keep accurate records, and collect debts owed the trust.

A trustee is liable to the beneficiaries of the trust if she breaches her duty. The following case provides an excellent example of a trustee who violated her fiduciary duty. The bad trustee was not only liable for violating *her* duty, but also for aiding *someone else's* misbehavior.

Living trust

A trust established while the grantor is still alive.

Revocable trust

A trust that the grantor can terminate or change at any time.

Testamentary trust

A trust that goes into effect when a grantor dies.

PARADEE V. PARADEE

2010 Del. Ch. LEXIS 212
Court of Chancery of Delaware, 2010

CASE SUMMARY

Facts: Charles Paradee, Sr. (Senior) had a grandson, Charles III (who was called Trey). After Senior's first wife died, he married Eleanor. He was 71; she was 54. To provide for Trey, Senior created an irrevocable trust, which bought an insurance policy on the lives of Senior and Eleanor. Once both of them died, Trey would receive $1.7 million. Eugene Sterling, the life insurance agent who sold the policy to the Trust, was the initial trustee, but Trey had the right to become trustee when he turned 30.

When Senior began to slip mentally, Eleanor took over the management of his finances. She was desperate to terminate the Trust because she detested Senior's family. First, she told Sterling to revoke the Trust, but it turns out that irrevocable trusts are, well, irrevocable. So Eleanor instructed Sterling to borrow money, using the insurance policy as security. If the Trust did not pay back the loan, the policy would lapse and Trey would get nothing. Acting against the advice of the family lawyer, Sterling did what Eleanor had asked.

You will not be surprised to learn that when Trey turned 30, Sterling further tarnished his own reputation by neglecting to tell Trey that he was entitled to be trustee. After Sterling died, Eleanor appointed herself as trustee. She allowed the insurance policy to lapse, so the Trust became worthless.

When Trey finally found out about the Trust, he sought full recovery from Eleanor on the grounds that she had violated her fiduciary duties and had also aided and abetted Sterling in the violation of his.

Issue: *Did Eleanor violate her fiduciary duty? Is she liable for aiding and abetting Sterling?*

Decision: Eleanor was liable for violating her own fiduciary duty *and* for aiding and abetting Sterling in the violation of his.

Reasoning: Eleanor's motive was simple and straightforward: she hated the idea that Trey would profit from her death. So she took revenge on him by allowing the policy to lapse.

Eleanor herself admitted that, as trustee, she had an obligation to maintain the insurance policy and to tell Trey of his right to be trustee. That she did neither is sufficient evidence that she violated her duty and is liable. Sterling was also to blame because he acted in Eleanor's best interest rather than Trey's. But, by the time Trey brought this case, Sterling was dead, so he was no longer able to pay back the Trust.

Because Eleanor induced Sterling to breach his fiduciary duties, she must also assume his liability to the Trust. She must pay (1) what the policy would have been worth if it had not lapsed and (2) Trey's legal fees and expenses.

Termination

A trust ends upon the occurrence of any of these events:

- On the date indicated by the grantor.

- If the trust is revocable, when revoked by the grantor. Even if the trust is irrevocable, the grantor and all the beneficiaries can agree to revoke it.

- When the purpose of the trust has been fulfilled. If the grantor established the trust to pay college tuition for his grandchildren, the trust ends when the last grandchild graduates.

EXAM Strategy

Question: Maddie set up a trust for her children, with Field as trustee. Field decided to sell a piece of trust real estate to his wife without obtaining an appraisal, attempting to market the property, or consulting a real estate agent. Maddie was furious and ordered him not to make the sale. Can she stop him? Would she have to go to court?

Strategy: The answer depends upon what type of trust she has established.

Result: If the trust is revocable, Maddie can simply terminate it and take the property back. If it is irrevocable, she could still prevent the sale by going to court because Field has violated the duties he owes to the beneficiaries. He has violated the duty of loyalty by selling trust property to his wife, and he has violated the duty of care by failing to act as a reasonable seller would.

Chapter Conclusion

Most people do not like to think about death, especially their own. And they particularly do not want to spend time and money thinking about it in a lawyer's office. However, responsible adults understand how important it is not to leave their financial affairs in chaos when they do eventually die.

EXAM REVIEW

1. **WILL**   A will is a legal document that disposes of the testator's property after death. (p. 558)

2. **HOLOGRAPHIC WILL**   A will that is handwritten by the testator but not witnessed. (pp. 558–559)

3. **NUNCUPATIVE WILL**   The formal term for an oral will. For a nuncupative will to be valid, the testatrix must know she is dying, there must be three witnesses, and these witnesses must know that they are listening to her will. (p. 559)

EXAM Strategy

Question: If you were in an emergency situation and desperately wanted to prepare a new will, under what circumstances would a holographic will be preferable to the nuncupative option?

Strategy: The two types of wills have different requirements for witnesses. (See the "Result" at the end of this section.)

4. **SURVIVING SPOUSE AND CHILDREN**   A spouse is entitled to a certain share of the decedent's estate, but children have no automatic right to share in a parent's estate so long as the parent indicates in his will that the pretermitted child has been left out on purpose. (pp. 559–560)

EXAM Strategy

Question: Josh was a crotchety fellow, often at outs with his family. In his will, he left his son an autographed copy of his book, *A Guide to Federal Prisons.* He completely omitted his daughter, instead leaving the rest of his substantial estate to the Society for the Assistance of Convicted Felons. Which child fared better?

Strategy: Pretermitted children fare differently from those named in the will. (See the "Result" at the end of this section.)

5. **PER STIRPES V. PER CAPITA**   In a will, a *per stirpes* distribution means that each branch of the family receives an equal share. *Per capita* means that each heir receives the same amount. (pp. 560–561)

EXAM Strategy

CPA Question   A decedent's will provided that the estate was to be divided among the decedent's issue, *per capita* and not *per stirpes.* If there are two surviving children and three grandchildren who are children of a predeceased child at the time the will is probated, how will the estate be divided?

(a)   1/2 to each surviving child

(b)   1/3 to each surviving child and 1/9 to each grandchild

(c)   1/4 to each surviving child and 1/6 to each grandchild

(d)   1/5 to each surviving child and grandchild

Strategy: Remember that *per stirpes* divides equally among the children, while *per capita* divides equally among the issue.

6. **REVOCATION OF A WILL**   A testator may generally revoke or alter a will at any time prior to death. (p. 561)

7. **INTESTACY**   Dying without a will. In this event, the law determines how the decedent's property will be distributed. (p. 561)

8. **DURABLE POWER OF ATTORNEY**   A durable power of attorney is a document that permits the attorney-in-fact to act for the principal. A durable power remains in force even if the principal becomes incapacitated. (pp. 561–562)

9. **ANATOMICAL GIFTS**   The Uniform Anatomical Gift Act (UAGA) allows an individual to indicate her desire to be an organ donor either by putting a provision in her will or by signing an organ donation card in the presence of two witnesses. (p. 562)

10. **LIVING WILL**   A living will permits an adult to refuse medical treatment that would prolong life. (pp. 562–563)

11. **TRUST**   A trust is an entity that separates legal and beneficial ownership. (pp. 563–564)

12. **LIVING TRUST**   Also known as an *inter vivos* trust, a living trust is established while the grantor is still alive. (p. 564)

13. **TESTAMENTARY TRUST**   A testamentary trust is created by a will. (p. 564)

14. **TRUSTEE'S DUTY**   In carrying out the terms of a trust, a trustee has a fiduciary duty to the beneficiary, which includes a duty of loyalty and a duty of care. (p. 565)

> **3. Result:**   A holographic will does not require witnesses; a nuncupative will requires three.
>
> **4. Result:**   Because the son was not totally omitted from the will, he is entitled to nothing more than the book, while the daughter who received nothing under the will actually gets more than her brother—she receives whatever share she would be entitled to if Josh had died intestate.
>
> **5. Result:**   There are five surviving issue (two children and three grandchildren), so they each get one-fifth of the estate. D is the correct answer.

MATCHING QUESTIONS

Match the following terms with their definitions:

___A. Executor

___B. Intestate

___C. Testator

___D. Administrator

___E. Testatrix

1. A woman who has signed a valid will
2. A man who has signed a valid will
3. A personal representative chosen by the decedent to carry out the terms of a will
4. Dying without a will
5. A personal representative appointed by the probate court to oversee the probate process

TRUE/FALSE QUESTIONS

Circle true or false:

1. T F Under the Uniform Probate Code, one spouse is not required to leave any money to the other spouse.
2. T F A holographic will does not need to be witnessed.

3. T F A nuncupative will does not need to be witnessed.

4. T F A principal may not revoke a durable power of attorney.

5. T F A grantor may not be the trustee of a trust.

MULTIPLE-CHOICE QUESTIONS

1. **CPA QUESTION:** A personal representative of an estate would breach her fiduciary duties if she:

   (a) Combined personal funds with funds of the estate so that both could purchase Treasury bills

   (b) Represented the estate in a lawsuit brought against it by a disgruntled relative of the decedent

   (c) Distributed property to satisfy the decedent's debts

   (d) Engaged a non-CPA to prepare the records for the estate's final accounting

2. Hallie is telling her cousin Anne about the will she has just executed. "Because of my broken arm, I couldn't sign my name, so I just told Bertrand, the lawyer, to sign it for me. Bertrand also witnessed the will." Anne said, "You made a big mistake:

   I. You should have made at least some sort of mark on the paper."

   II. The lawyer is not permitted to witness the will."

   III. You did not have enough witnesses."

   Which of Anne's statements is true?

   (a) I, II, and III

   (b) Neither I, II, nor III

   (c) Just I

   (d) Just II

   (e) Just III

3. Owen does not want to leave any money to his son, Kevin. What must he do to achieve this goal?

   I. Nothing. If he dies without a will, Kevin will inherit nothing.

   II. Make a will that omits Kevin entirely.

   III. Leave Kevin $1 in his will.

   (a) I, II, or III

   (b) II or III

   (c) Just I

   (d) Just II

   (e) Just III

4. Lauren, a resident of Kansas, appointed her husband to be her health care proxy. Now that she is dying of cancer and suffering terribly, she is begging her husband and her doctors to give her an overdose of drugs. Which of the following statements is true?

    I. If she goes into a coma, her husband has the right to direct her doctors to withhold treatment.

    II. Her doctor has the right to give her an overdose of pills that will kill her.

    III. Her husband has the right to give her an overdose of pills that will kill her.

    (a) I, II, and III

    (b) Neither I, II, nor III

    (c) Just I

    (d) Just II

    (e) Just III

5. Blake tells his client that there are five good reasons to set up a trust. Which of the following is *not* a good reason?

    (a) To pay his grandchildren's college tuition if they go to the same college he attended

    (b) To save money, since a trust is cheaper than a will

    (c) To make sure the money is invested properly

    (d) To avoid probate

    (e) To safeguard his privacy

Essay Questions

1. William Cook was a very successful undertaker. When he died, his will left all of his property to his brother Eugene. There were two other pieces of paper in the safe with the will. One said that that his stamp collection should go to his housekeeper, Bertha. This document was signed by two witnesses—the gardener and the cook. There was also a piece of paper stating that he would like all of his assets to go to his sister's daughter, Evangeline. Who will get what?

2. Kevin Fitzgerald represented the down-and-out Mission Hill and Roxbury districts in the Massachusetts House of Representatives. A priest alerted him that Mary Guzelian, a street person who roamed his district, had trash bags in her ghetto apartment stuffed with cash, bonds, and bankbooks. Fitzgerald visited the apartment with his top aide, Patricia McDermott. Two weeks later, Guzelian signed a will, drafted by one of Fitzgerald's acquaintances, that left Guzelian's $400,000 estate to Fitzgerald and McDermott. Fitzgerald claimed not to know about the will until Guzelian's death four years later. Guzelian, 64, suffered from chronic paranoid schizophrenia and severe health problems. Would Guzelian's sister have a claim on Guzelian's estate?

3. When Bill died, he left all of his property in a trust to take care of his wife, Doris, for the rest of her life. On her death, the money would go to their son, Rob. The Bank of

Tulsa was the trustee. Fifty years later, Rob needed money, so he began writing checks out of Doris's checking account. She knew about the checks, but she could never say no to him. At the rate at which Rob was spending her money, the trust funds would all be gone within a couple of years. What was the bank's responsibility? Was it obligated to let Doris have as much money as she wanted?

4. After nearly 40 years of marriage, Frank Honigman executed a new will that left his wife only the minimum required by law. The balance went to his brothers and sisters (the couple had no children). For some time before his death, Honigman had repeatedly told both friends and strangers, using obscene and abusive language, that his wife was unfaithful. Honigman was normal and rational in other respects, but by all evidence, his suspicions of his wife were untrue. They were based on such evidence as the fact that, when he left the house, his wife would ask him when he planned to return. Also, whenever the telephone rang, Mrs. Honigman answered it. For the last two years of his life, he positively forbade her to answer the telephone. Is Mr. Honigman's will valid?

5. When Gregg died, his will left his money equally to his two children, Max and Alison. Max had died a few years earlier, leaving behind a widow and four children. Who will get Gregg's money?

DISCUSSION QUESTIONS

1. In the *Paradee* case, the trustees behaved very badly. Often, wrongdoers are able to convince themselves that they have not behaved badly because they rationalize what they have done. It is important in your own life to beware the easy rationalization. Imagine how Eleanor and Sterling might have rationalized their actions.

2. Is an asset protection trust fair? Should wealthy people be able to avoid paying their liabilities? What about perpetual trusts that avoid estate taxes forever? If you were a state legislator, how would you vote when this legislation came up for approval? If you had substantial assets, would you put them in such a trust? What Life Principles apply here?

3. Should you have a will? *Do* you have one?

4. Billionaire Warren Buffett said that children should inherit enough money so that they can do anything, but not so much that they can do nothing. Is it good for people to inherit money?

How much? At what age? How much would you like to leave your children?

5. The rules on wills are very exact. If the testator does not comply precisely, then the will is invalid. Suppose a man discovers that his daughter has broken virtually every law in this book—she has engaged in insider trading, price-fixing, and fraud, to name just a few. At his birthday party, the man says to the videographer, in front of 100 witnesses, "I have an appointment with my lawyer tomorrow. but in the meantime, you should know that I want all of my assets to go to the Home for Little Wanderers, the orphanage that raised me." On his way home that night, he dies in a car accident. Under his will, his daughter inherits all, and a court would undoubtedly enforce that will, despite all the evidence about the man's real wishes. Is that right? Courts are often called upon to make difficult decisions about facts. In the case of disputed wills, why not let the courts decide what the decedent really wanted?

INSURANCE

What insurance policies are right for Jamie? When he bought a 3-D television at Shopping World for $1,000, the salesperson offered him a two-year service plan for $80. Should he buy it? What about renter's insurance for his apartment? And then his mother suggested he get a term life insurance policy while he is young and the rates are low. Is that a good idea? When he applies for health insurance, should he admit to being a smoker? And what about the travel insurance available at the airport in case his flight home crashes?

He applied for health insurance. Should he admit to being a smoker?

How should Jamie evaluate his options? To answer these questions, it is important to understand the economics of the insurance industry. Suppose that you have recently purchased a $500,000 house. The probability your house will burn down in the next year is 1 in 1,000. That is a low risk, but the consequences would be devastating, especially since you could not afford to rebuild. Instead of bearing that risk yourself, you take out a fire insurance policy. You pay an insurance company $1,200 in return for a promise that, if your house burns down in the next 12 months, the company will pay you $500,000. The insurance company sells the same policy to 1,000 similar homeowners, expecting that on average, one of these houses will burn down. If all 1,000 policyholders pay $1,200, the insurance company takes in $1.2 million each year but expects to pay out only $500,000. It will put some money aside in case two houses burn down, or even worse, a major forest fire guts a whole tract of houses. It must also pay overhead expenses, such as marketing and administration. And, of course, shareholders expect profits.

When purchasing insurance, it is important to remember that insurance companies have a lot of data on people like you so they can predict accurately the probability that a calamity will befall you. They then price their premiums so that they will make a profit. For that reason, most people who buy insurance pay more in premiums than they take in from the policy. If that were not the case, insurance companies would go out of business. So why do people buy insurance? To protect themselves from disasters—no matter how improbable—that they simply cannot afford.

To review Jamie's situation: televisions are reliable and unlikely to need repairs in the first two years. These service plans are remarkably profitable—for the seller. Stores often make a larger profit from the insurance than from the product itself. Does Jamie need rental insurance? Not to replace the $10 couch he bought off craigslist, but he should consider buying a policy that would protect him from liability if someone is injured in his apartment. If he buys life insurance, term is the cheapest form—but does he need it? Whom is he protecting? He has no spouse or children. He is not supporting his mother. It seems that he does not need life insurance now. When applying for health insurance, he must admit that he is a smoker—otherwise, the health insurance company can cancel his policy if he becomes ill. There is no point in lying on *any* insurance application because then the policy is voidable. As for travel insurance, those last-minute policies are almost always a bad deal. And if Jamie needs to protect someone, he should have life insurance that covers him all the time, not just on his trip home.

INTRODUCTION

Insurance has its own terminology, so it is important to understand key terms:

- **Person.** An individual, corporation, partnership, or any other legal entity
- **Insurance.** A contract in which one person, in return for a fee, agrees to guarantee another against loss caused by a specific type of danger
- **Insurer.** The person who issues the insurance policy and serves as guarantor
- **Insured.** The person whose loss is the subject of the insurance policy
- **Owner.** The person who enters into the insurance contract and pays the premiums
- **Premium.** The consideration that the owner pays under the policy
- **Beneficiary.** The person who receives the proceeds from the insurance policy

The beneficiary, the insured, and the owner can be, but are not necessarily, the same person. If a homeowner buys fire insurance for her house, she is the insured, the owner, and the beneficiary because she bought the policy and receives the proceeds if her house burns down. If a mother buys a life insurance policy on her son that is payable to his children in the event of his death, then the mother is the owner, the son is the insured, and the grandchildren are the beneficiaries.

INSURANCE CONTRACT

An insurance policy must meet all the common law requirements for a contract. There must be an offer, acceptance, and consideration. The owner must have legal capacity, that is, he must be an adult of sound mind. Fraud, duress, and undue influence invalidate a policy. In theory, insurance contracts need not be in writing because the Statute of Frauds does not apply to any contract that can be performed within one year, and it is possible that the house may burn down or the car may crash within a year. Some states, however, specifically require insurance contracts to be in writing.

Offer and Acceptance

The purchaser of a policy makes an offer by delivering an application and a premium to the insurer. The insurance company then has the option of either accepting or rejecting the offer. **It can accept by oral notice, by written notice, or by delivery of the policy. It also has a fourth option—a written binder.** A *binder* is a short document acknowledging receipt of the application and premium. It indicates that a policy is *temporarily* in effect but does not constitute *final* acceptance. The insurer still has the right to reject the offer once it has examined the application carefully. Kyle buys a house on April 1 and wants insurance right away. The insurance company issues a binder to him the same day. If Kyle's house burns down on April 2, the insurer must pay, even though it has not yet issued the final policy. If, however, there is no fire, but the company decides on April 2 that Kyle is a bad risk, it has the right to reject his application at that time because it has not yet issued the policy.

Limiting Claims by the Insured

Insurance policies can sometimes look like a quick way to make easy money. More than one person suffering from overwhelming financial pressure has insured a building to the hilt and then burned it down for the insurance money. Unbelievably, more than one parent has killed a child to collect the proceeds of a life insurance policy. Therefore, the law has created a number of rules to protect insurance companies from fraud and bad faith on the part of insureds.

INSURABLE INTEREST

An insurance contract is not valid unless the owner has an *insurable interest* in the subject matter of the policy. To understand why an insurable interest is important, read this tragic story. To celebrate their engagement, Deana Wild and James Coates took a sightseeing trip along the California coast with Coates's mother, Virginia Rearden. They seemed to be just one big happy family. Tragically, Wild slipped while walking along the edge of a cliff at Big Sur and fell to her death. That would have been the end of the story, except that the day before, Rearden had taken out a $35,000 life insurance policy on Wild, naming Coates and Rearden as beneficiaries. When the insurance company investigated, it learned that Coates was married to someone else. Therefore, he could not be Wild's fiance, and neither he nor Rearden had an insurable interest in Wild. It also turned out that Rearden had taken out the policy without Wild's knowledge. Rearden was convicted of first-degree murder and sentenced to life in prison without parole.

Insurable interest
Means that someone would suffer a loss if the insured event occurs.

These are the rules on insurable interest:

- **Definition.** A person has an insurable interest if she would be harmed by the danger that she has insured against. If Jessica takes out a fire insurance policy on her own barn, she will presumably be reluctant to burn it down. However, if she buys a policy on Nathan's barn, she will not mind (she may even be delighted) when fire sweeps through the building. It is a small step to saying that she might even burn the barn down herself.

- **Amount of loss.** The insurable interest can be no greater than the actual amount of loss suffered. If the barn is worth $50,000, but Jessica insures it (and pays premiums) for $100,000, she will recover only $50,000 when it burns down. Nor is she entitled to a refund of the excess premiums she has paid. The goal is to make sure that Jessica does not profit from the policy.

- **Life insurance.** A person always has an insurable interest in his own life and the life of his spouse or fiancee. Parents and minor children also have an insurable interest in each other. Creditors have a legitimate interest in someone who owes them money. For some states, the standard is that you have an insurable interest in someone if the person is worth more to you alive than dead.

- **Work relationships.** Business partners, employers, and employees have an insurable interest in each other if they would suffer some financial harm from the death of the insured. For example, companies sometimes buy **key person life insurance** on their officers to compensate if they were to die.

Life insurance
Provides for payments to a beneficiary upon the death of the insured.

Misrepresentation

Insurers have the right to void a policy if, during the application process, the insured makes a material misstatement or conceals a material fact. The policy is voidable whether the misstatement was oral or in writing, and in many states, intentional or unintentional. **Material** means that the misstatement or omission would affect the insurer's decision to issue the policy or set a premium amount. Note that a lie can void a policy even if it does not relate to the actual loss.

Material
Important to the insurer's decision to issue a policy or set a premium amount.

Brian Hopkins submitted an application to Golden Rule Insurance Co. for medical and life insurance. In filling out the application, he answered "no" to questions asking whether he had had any of the following conditions: heart murmur, growths, skin disorders, immune deficiencies, sexually transmitted diseases, or any disorders of the glands. In fact, he had had all of the above. Two years later, Hopkins died of AIDS. Golden Rule rescinded Hopkins's policies because his application contained material misrepresentations.[1]

EXAM Strategy

Question: During a visit to a hospital emergency room for treatment of a gunshot wound to his chest, John Cummings tested positive for cocaine. Six months later, he applied for a life insurance policy, which was to benefit his mother. The application asked if he had, within the prior five years, used any controlled drugs without a prescription by a physician. Cummings answered, "No." A year after the policy was issued, Cummings died of a gunshot wound. Was the policy valid?

---

[1]*Golden Rule Insurance Co. v. Hopkins*, 788 F. Supp. 295, 1991 U.S. Dist. LEXIS 19970.

Strategy: If the insured makes a material misstatement during the application process, the insurer has the right to void a policy, whether or not the misstatement relates to the cause of death.

Result: Cummings's mother argued that the policy was valid because her son had not died from taking drugs. The gunshot wound was unrelated to his cocaine use. However, an insurer has a right to void a policy if the insured makes *any* material misstatement. Here, the misstatement was material because the insurance company would not have issued the policy if it had known about the cocaine. As a result, the policy is voidable.

Bad Faith by the Insurer

Insurance policies often contain a covenant of *good faith and fair dealing.* Even if the policy itself does not *explicitly* include such a provision, an increasing number of courts (but not all) *imply* this covenant. An insurance company can violate the covenant of good faith and fair dealing by (1) fraudulently inducing someone to buy a policy; (2) unreasonably refusing to pay a valid claim; or (3) refusing to accept a reasonable settlement offer that has been made to an insured. When an insurance company violates the covenant of good faith and fair dealing, it becomes liable for both compensatory and punitive damages.

FRAUD

In recent years, a number of insurance companies have paid substantial damages to settle fraud charges involving the sale of life insurance. The companies trained their salespeople to tell elderly customers that a new policy was better when, in fact, it was much worse. State Farm Insurance agreed to pay its customers $200 million to settle such a suit. Officials in Florida ordered Prudential Insurance Company of America to pay as much as $2 billion in damages after they determined that, for more than a decade, the company had deliberately cheated its customers. Prudential also trained agents to target the elderly. In short, both insurance companies had trained their agents to commit fraud.

> In short, both insurance companies had trained their agents to commit fraud.

 **Ethics** Presumably the agents knew that defrauding elderly people was wrong. Why did they do it? How could you protect yourself from being involved in such a fraud?

REFUSING TO PAY A VALID CLAIM

Perhaps because juries feel sympathy for those who must deal with an immovable bureaucracy, damage awards are often sizeable when an insurance company unreasonably refuses to pay a legitimate claim. For example, a jury in Ohio entered a $13 million verdict against Buckeye Union Insurance Co. for its bad faith refusal to pay a claim. An Ohio sheriff stopped the automobile of 19-year-old Eugene Leber. As the sheriff approached Leber's car, he slipped on ice and his gun discharged. By incredible bad luck, the bullet struck Leber, permanently paralyzing him from the rib cage down. The insurance company recognized that it was liable under the policy, but it nonetheless fought the case for *16 years*.

Consumers complain that insurance companies often "lowball"—that is, they make an unreasonably low offer to settle a claim. Some insurance companies even set claims quotas that limit how much their adjusters can pay out each year, regardless of the merits of each individual claim. If juries continue to award multimillion-dollar verdicts, however, insurance companies may decide simply to pay the claims.

In the following case, the insurance company ultimately paid the claim, but not fast enough to satisfy the jury.

GOODSON V. AMERICAN STANDARD INSURANCE COMPANY OF WISCONSIN

89 P.3d 409, 2004 Colo. LEXIS 388
Supreme Court of Colorado, 2004

CASE SUMMARY

Facts: Dawn Goodson and her two children were in an automobile accident while driving a car owned by Chet Weber. He was insured by American Standard Insurance Company of Wisconsin.

To treat injuries that she and her children suffered in the accident, Goodson sought care from a chiropractor. She submitted these bills, totaling about $8,000, to American Standard. The insurance company offered a number of erroneous reasons why it should not pay the claims: that the chiropractor was not a member of American Standard's preferred provider organization; that Weber's policy was not in effect at the time of the accident; and that Goodson and her children needed to undergo an independent medical evaluation to determine whether their injuries were related to the accident and whether their medical treatment was reasonable and necessary. In the end, American Standard did pay Goodson's bills, but it took 18 months to do so.

Goodson filed suit against American Standard, alleging that it had engaged in a bad faith breach of the insurance contract. Although the company's delay in payment had not actually cost Goodson any money, it had caused her substantial emotional distress. The jury awarded Goodson and her children $75,000 in actual damages and an additional $75,000 in punitive damages. The appeals court overturned the verdict. Goodson appealed to the state Supreme Court.

Issue: *Can Goodson recover damages for the emotional distress caused by American Standard's delay in paying her claim?*

Decision: Yes, Goodson can recover for her emotional distress.

Reasoning: An insurer that violates its duties of good faith and fair dealing is liable for both compensatory and punitive damages. Compensatory damages include emotional distress, pain and suffering, inconvenience, fear and anxiety, and impairment of the quality of life. The goal of punitive damages is to punish the insurer and deter wrongful conduct by other companies. To recover punitive damages, the insured must show that the insurer acted with fraud, malice, or willful and wanton conduct.

Goodson suffered emotional distress as a result of the company's delay. Her worries about the medical bills left her anxious, fearful, stressed, and concerned about whether she would have to pay the bills herself.

The whole point of buying insurance is to enjoy peace of mind. The fact that the company finally paid the bill, after 18 months of unreasonable delays, does not undo the distress caused by the bad faith conduct.

REFUSING TO ACCEPT A SETTLEMENT OFFER

An insurer also violates the covenant of good faith and fair dealing when it *wrongfully* refuses to settle a claim. An insurance company is supposed to negotiate a settlement as if the policy had no limits. Suppose that Dmitri has a $1 million liability policy on his house. When

Tanya slips on his icy front walk, she breaks her back and ends up paralyzed. She sues him for $5 million. As provided in the policy, Dmitri's insurance company defends him against Tanya's claim. She offers to settle for $1 million, but the insurance company refuses because it only has $1 million at risk anyway. It may get lucky with the jury. Instead, a jury comes in with a $3 million verdict. The insurance company is liable for only $1 million, but Dmitri must pay $2 million. In this instance, a court might well find that the insurance company had violated its covenant of good faith and fair dealing and is liable for the full $3 million.

EXAM Strategy

Question: Geoff takes out renter's insurance with Fastball Insurance Co. On the application, where it asks if he has any pets, he fills in "poodle." Although he does not know it, his "poodle" is really a Portuguese water dog. The two breeds look a lot alike. A month later, his apartment is robbed. Fastball investigates and discovers that Geoff does not have a poodle, after all. It denies his claim. Geoff files suit. What result?

Strategy: There are two issues here: Was Geoff's answer on the application a material misstatement? Was Fastball's denial in bad faith?

Result: Geoff's misrepresentation was not material—the difference between these two breeds of dog would not have affected liability on the renter's policy. If he had said he had an attack dog such as a Doberman, perhaps the premium would have been lower because the dog would scare off intruders (or higher because the dog would also attack friends and neighbors), but poodles and Portuguese water dogs are equally friendly. Fastball would have to pay the claim and it might also be liable for punitive damages if a court determined that its refusal was in bad faith.

TYPES OF INSURANCE

Insurance is available for virtually any risk. Bruce Springsteen insured his voice and Jamie Lee Curtis her legs. When Kerry Wallace shaved her head to promote the *Star Trek* films, she bought insurance in case her hair failed to grow back. Food critic Egon Ronay insured his taste buds. And an amateur dramatics group took out insurance to protect against the risk that a member of the audience might die laughing. Most people, however, get by with six different types of insurance: property, life, health, disability, liability, and automobile.

Property Insurance

Property insurance (also known as **casualty insurance**) covers physical damage to real estate, personal property (boats, furnishings), or inventory, from causes such as fire, smoke, lightning, wind, riot, vandalism, or theft.

Life Insurance

Life insurance is really death insurance—it provides for payments to a beneficiary upon the death of the insured. The purpose is to replace at least some of the insured's income so that her family will not be financially devastated.

Property insurance
Covers physical damage to real estate, personal property, or inventory from causes such as fire, smoke, lightning, wind, riot, vandalism, or theft.

TERM INSURANCE

Term insurance is the simplest, cheapest life insurance option. It is purchased for a specific period, such as 1, 5, or 20 years. If the insured dies during the period of the policy, the insurance company pays the policy amount to the beneficiary. If the owner stops paying premiums, the policy terminates, and the beneficiary receives nothing. As the probability of death rises with age, so do the premiums. A $200,000 policy on a 25-year-old nonsmoking woman costs as little as $95 annually; at age 60, the same policy costs about $400. Term insurance is the best choice for a person who simply wants to protect his family by replacing his income if he dies young.

WHOLE LIFE INSURANCE

Whole life or **straight life** insurance is designed to cover the insured for his entire life. A portion of the premiums pays for insurance, and the remainder goes into savings. This savings portion is called the *cash value* of the policy. The company pays dividends on this cash value, and typically, after some years, the dividends are large enough to cover the premium so that the owner does not have to pay any more. The cash value accrues without being taxed until the policy is cashed in. The owner can borrow against the cash value, in many cases at a below-market rate. In addition, if the owner cancels the policy, the insurance company will pay her the policy's cash value. When the owner purchases the policy, the company typically sets a premium that stays constant over the life of the policy. A healthy 25-year-old nonsmoking woman pays annual premiums of roughly $1,900 per year on a $200,000 policy.

The advantage of a whole life policy is that it forces people to save. However, it also has some significant disadvantages:

- The investment returns from the savings portion of whole life insurance have traditionally been mediocre. Mutual funds may offer better investment opportunities.

- A significant portion of the premium for the first year goes to pay overhead and commissions. Agents have a great incentive to sell whole life policies, rather than term, because their commissions are much higher.

- Unless the customer holds a policy for about 20 years, it will typically generate little cash value. Half of all whole life policyholders drop their policies in the first seven or eight years. At that point, the policy has generated little more than commissions for the agent.

- Whole life insurance provides the same amount of insurance throughout the insured's life. In contrast, most people need more insurance when they have young children and less as they approach retirement age.

UNIVERSAL LIFE

Universal life insurance is a flexible combination of whole life and term. The owner can adjust the premiums over the life of the policy and also adjust the allocation of the premiums between insurance and savings. The options are complex and often difficult for the customer to understand.

ANNUITIES

Annuity
Provides payment to a beneficiary during his lifetime.

As life expectancy has increased, people have begun to worry as much about supporting themselves in their old age as they do about dying young. **Annuities are the reverse of life insurance—they make payments *until* death, whereas life insurance pays *after* death.** In the basic annuity contract, the owner makes a lump-sum payment to an insurance company in return for a fixed annual income for the rest of her life, no matter how long she lives. If she dies tomorrow, the insurance company makes a huge profit. If she lives to be 95, the company loses money. But whatever happens, she knows she will have an income until the day she dies.

In a **deferred annuity contract,** the owner makes a lump-sum payment but receives no income until some later date, say, in 10 or 20 years when he retires. From that date forward, he will receive payments for the rest of his life.

Health Insurance

Traditional health insurance plans are **pay for service.** The insurer pays for virtually any treatment that any doctor orders. The good news under this system is that policyholders have the largest possible choice of doctor and treatment. The bad news is that doctors and patients have an incentive to overspend on health care because the insurance company picks up the tab. It has been estimated that as many as one-third of the medical procedures performed in pay for service plans have little medical justification, which in the end is not good for the patient.

Instead of, or in addition to, pay for service plans, many insurers offer **managed care plans.** There are many variations on this theme, but they all work to limit treatment choices. In some plans, the patient has a primary care physician who must approve all visits to specialists. In **health maintenance organizations,** known as **HMOs,** the patient can be treated only by doctors in the organization unless there is some extraordinary need for an outside specialist.

Neither type of plan is perfect. In pay for service plans, doctors have an incentive to overtreat. In managed care plans, they may have an incentive to undertreat. For example, a recent study revealed that managed care plans tend to treat mental illness primarily with drugs. A combination of drugs and therapy tends to be more successful, but also more expensive.

Disability Insurance

Disability insurance replaces the insured's income if he becomes unable to work because of illness or injury. Perhaps you are thinking, "That will never happen to me." In fact, the average person is seven times more likely to be disabled for at least 90 days than she is to die before age 65. A significant percentage of all mortgage foreclosures are caused by an owner's disability. Everyone should have disability insurance to replace between 60 percent and 75 percent of their income. (There is no need for 100 percent replacement because expenses while unemployed are lower.) Many employers provide some disability protection.

Disability insurance

Replaces the insured's income if he becomes unable to work because of illness or injury.

Liability Insurance

Most insurance—property, life, health, disability—is designed to reimburse the insured (or her family) for any harm she suffers. **Liability insurance** is different. **Its purpose is to reimburse the insured for any liability she incurs by (*accidentally*) harming someone else.** (Note that this insurance does not cover any *intentional* torts the insured commits.) This type of insurance covers tort claims by:

Liability insurance

Reimburses the insured for any liability she incurs by accidentally harming someone else.

- Those injured on property owned by the insured—the mail carrier who slips and falls on the front sidewalk, or the parents of the child who drowns in the pool;

- Those injured by the insured away from his home or business—the jogger crushed by an insured who loses control of his rollerblades; and

- Those whose property is damaged by the insured—the owner whose stone wall is pulverized by the insured's swerving car.

These are the types of claims covered in a *personal* liability policy. *Business* liability policies may also protect against other sorts of claims:

- Professional malpractice on the part of an accountant, architect, doctor, engineer, or lawyer.

- Product liability for any injuries caused by the company's products.

- Employment practices liability insurance to protect employers against claims of sexual harassment, discrimination, and wrongful termination on the part of an employee. Note that this insurance typically does not protect the person who actually commits the wrongdoing—the sexual harasser, for instance—but it does protect the innocent insureds, such as the company itself.

The following case explores the boundaries of liability policies.

You be the Judge

METROPOLITAN PROPERTY AND CASUALTY INSURANCE COMPANY V. MARSHALL

2010 NY Slip Op 51149U; 2010 N.Y. Misc. LEXIS 2824
Supreme Court of New York, 2010

Facts: Jacqueline Marshall's son, Evan, lived in a psychiatric facility. The hospital gave him a weekend pass to visit his mother. While at his mother's house, he murdered Denise Fox, decapitating and dismembering her and depositing her body in his mother's garbage cans. He pleaded guilty and was sentenced to 30 years to life.

Fox's family sued Jacqueline Marshall, alleging that she was negligent in not notifying the neighbors that her son was out on a weekend pass—and not telling them that he had a basement room in which he liked to dismember mannequins and watch violent pornography. Marshall said that she did not even know the hospital had issued a pass to her son.

Marshall had a homeowners liability policy with Metropolitan Property. Ordinarily, if an insured is sued, the insurance company represents her at trial. But instead, Metropolitan asked a court to rule that Marshall's policy did not cover this murder and the company did not have to represent her in the case brought by Fox's family.

Marshall's policy:

- Covered damages caused by an accident;

- Defined an accident as an event that is "unexpected, unusual, and unforeseeable;" and

- Excluded coverage for an intentional act committed by an insured or at the direction of the insured.

Metropolitan refused coverage on the grounds that Evan's acts were intentional, not accidental. **You Be the Judge:** *Was Fox's murder an accident for purposes of the policy? Is Marshall covered by her insurance policy?*

Argument for Metropolitan: Newspapers described this murder as "one of the most gruesome murders in Long Island history." This crime was the opposite of an accident; it was cold-blooded and deliberate.

Insurance policies are not intended to protect against this type of behavior. Indeed, it would be bad public policy if they did. As a society, we want people to be held responsible for murders and not have insurance companies pay their liabilities. Besides, the policy clearly states that it does not apply to any intentional act.

Argument for Marshall: Jacqueline Marshall did not murder Denise Fox; her son did. The intentional act was his, not hers. If he had been the insured, the policy would not apply, but such was not the case.

Clearly, this murder was unexpected—the psychiatric hospital would never have released Evan if the doctors had known how dangerous he was. From Jacqueline Marshall's perspective, it was an accident. Nothing could have been more "unexpected, unusual and unforeseeable."

Automobile Insurance

An automobile insurance policy is a combination of several different types of coverage that, depending on state law, are either mandatory or optional. These are the basic types of coverage:

- **Collision** covers the cost of repairing or replacing a car that is damaged in an accident.

- **Comprehensive** covers fire, theft, and vandalism—but not collision.

- **Liability** covers harm the owner causes to other people or their property—their body, car, or stone wall. Most states require drivers to carry liability insurance.

- **Uninsured motorist** covers the owner and anyone else in the car who is injured by an uninsured motorist.

Most Americans spend a considerable percentage of their disposable income on insurance. What can you do to reduce this expense?

- **Do not insure against every risk.** If you can afford the loss yourself, it is better not to purchase insurance. For example, Jamie in the opening scenario did not need to buy an insurance plan on his 3-D television.

- **Do not buy "special occasion" insurance.** After a major plane crash, sales of flight accident insurance jump. If you need life insurance, you should have it, no matter how you die. Your family does not need more money because you die in a plane crash rather than a car accident. The same rule holds true for other special occasion policies, such as cancer insurance. You need health insurance to cover all serious illnesses.

- **Select as high a deductible as you can afford.** The higher the deductible, the lower the premium. Over the lifetime of your house or car, you can save thousands of dollars by self-insuring the small losses and buying insurance to protect only against major catastrophes.

- **Shop for the best price.** The lowest-cost company may charge as little as two-thirds as much as its highest-price competitor. The Internet offers a great opportunity to compare prices for different types of insurance.

- **Shop for quality.** An insurance company can fail as easily as any other business. What a disaster to pay premiums, only to discover later that you are not in safe hands after all.

Chapter Conclusion

Life is a risky business. Cars crash, people die, houses burn. So what can we do? Buy insurance and get on with our lives, knowing that we have prepared as best we can.

EXAM REVIEW

1. **CONTRACT**   An insurance policy must meet all the common law requirements for a contract—offer, acceptance, and consideration. (p. 575)

2. **INSURABLE INTEREST**   A person has an insurable interest if she would be harmed by the danger that she has insured against. (pp. 575–576)

3. **MATERIAL MISREPRESENTATION**   Insurers have the right to void a policy if the insured makes a material misstatement or conceals a material fact. (pp. 576–577)

EXAM Strategy

Question: When Mark applied for life insurance with Farmstead, he indicated on the application that he had not received any traffic tickets in the preceding five years. In fact, he had received several such citations for driving while intoxicated. Two years later, Mark was shot to death. When Farmstead discovered the traffic tickets, it denied coverage to his beneficiary. Was Farmstead in the right?

Strategy: A misrepresentation is material if it affects the insurer's decision to issue a policy or set a premium amount. (See the "Result" at the end of this section.)

4. **BAD FAITH BY INSURER**   Many courts have held that insurance policies contain a covenant of good faith and fair dealing and have found insurance companies liable for compensatory and punitive damages if they commit fraud, refuse to pay legitimate claims in a timely manner, or wrongfully refuse to settle a claim. (pp. 577–579)

EXAM Strategy

Question: Pamela Stone was in a car accident. Her policy did not cover any damages she suffered if she was more than 50 percent to blame. The insurance company investigated and determined that the accident was at least 60 percent her fault, so it refused to pay her claim. When Stone sued the company, the jury determined she was only 45 percent at fault. Did the insurance company violate its covenant of good faith and fair dealing?

Strategy: The insurance company violated its covenant of good faith and fair dealing if it was unreasonable when it failed to pay Stone's claim. Was it unreasonable? (See the "Result" at the end of this section.)

5. **PROPERTY INSURANCE**   Property insurance covers physical damage to real estate, personal property (boats, furnishings), or inventory from causes such as fire, smoke, lightning, wind, riot, vandalism, or theft. (p. 579)

6. **LIFE INSURANCE**   Life insurance is really death insurance—it provides for payments to a beneficiary upon the death of the insured. (pp. 579–580)

7. **ANNUITIES** Annuities are the reverse of life insurance policies; they make payments until death. (pp. 580–581)

8. **HEALTH INSURANCE** Health insurance is available in pay for service plans, managed care plans, or HMOs. (p. 581)

9. **DISABILITY INSURANCE** Disability insurance replaces the insured's income if he becomes unable to work because of illness or injury. (p. 581)

10. **LIABILITY INSURANCE** Liability insurance reimburses the insured for any liability she incurs by accidentally harming someone else. (pp. 581–582)

3. Result: If Mark had told the truth, Farmstead still would have issued the policy, but the premium would have been higher. Therefore, it can deny coverage even though his lie was not about something that was a factor in his death.

4. Result: No, it was not unreasonable. The two parties had a good faith disagreement about the validity of the claim. The insurance company had to pay the claim, but not any penalty for violating the covenant of good faith and fair dealing.

MATCHING QUESTIONS

Match the following terms with their definitions:

___A. Insured

___B. Insurer

___C. Owner

___D. Beneficiary

___E. Insurable interest

1. The person who issues the insurance policy

2. The person who receives the proceeds from the insurance policy

3. The person who takes out the policy would be harmed by the danger that she has insured against

4. The person who enters into the policy and pays the premiums

5. The person whose loss is the subject of an insurance policy

TRUE/FALSE QUESTIONS

Circle true or false:

1. T F If the insured makes any false statement in the application process, the insurance policy is voidable.

2. T F Once an insurance company issues a binder, the policy is irrevocable.

3. T F Although whole life insurance is more expensive than term, it is the best choice because it forces the customer to save money.

4. T F You are more likely to die before 65 than to become disabled before 65.

5. T F An annuity is simply a type of life insurance.

MULTIPLE-CHOICE QUESTIONS

1. Lucas has bought the following insurance this week:

    I. A life insurance policy on his brother

    II. A life insurance policy on the partner in his accounting practice

    III. A fire insurance policy on the fitness club he belongs to, so that if it burns down, he will receive a large enough payment to enable him to join a different club

    In which of these policies does he have an insurable interest?

    (a) I, II, and III

    (b) Neither I, II, nor III

    (c) I and II

    (d) I and III

    (e) II and III

2. An insurance company does *not* violate its covenant of good faith and fair dealing if it:

    (a) Charges elderly customers higher premiums than it charges younger customers

    (b) Tells potential customers that their premiums will decline when that is not true

    (c) Tells potential customers that their returns on a whole life policy are certain to be higher than an equivalent amount invested in the stock market

    (d) Refuses to pay a valid claim until after four years of litigation

    (e) Refuses to accept a settlement offer on behalf of an insured that was reasonable, but not in the company's best interest

3. If you are a smart consumer, you will:

    I. Insure against as many different kinds of risks as you can so that no matter what happens, you will be protected

    II. Select as low a deductible as possible so that no matter what happens, you will not have to pay large sums out of pocket

    III. Buy flight insurance when you take long airplane flights so that your family will be protected if your plane crashes

    (a) I, II, and III

    (b) Neither I, II, nor III

    (c) I and II

    (d) Just I

    (e) Just II

4. Hamish owned an office building with a fair market value of $250,000. He insured it for $300,000. When it burned down, he was entitled to:

    (a) Nothing

    (b) $250,000 and a return of the excess premiums he paid on the $300,000 policy

    (c) $250,000

    (d) $300,000

5. Which of the following policies are you likely to need in your lifetime?

  I. Service plan on an appliance

  II. Whole life insurance

  III. Disability insurance

  IV. Health insurance

  (a) All of the above

  (b) None of the above

  (c) II, III, and IV

  (d) III and IV

  (e) IV

Essay Questions

1. Linda and Eddie had two children before they were divorced. Under the terms of their divorce, Eddie became the owner of their house. When he died suddenly, their children inherited the property. Linda moved into the house with the children and began paying the mortgage, which was in Eddie's name alone. She also took out fire insurance. When the house burned down, the insurance company refused to pay the policy because she did not have an insurable interest. Do you agree?

2. Armeen ran a stop sign and hit the Smiths' car, killing their child. He had $1.5 million in insurance. The Smiths offered to settle the case for that amount, but Liberty State, Armeen's insurance company, refused and proposed $300,000 instead. At trial, the jury awarded the Smith's $1.9 million, which meant that Armeen was liable for $400,000 rather than the zero dollars he would have had to pay if Liberty had accepted the Smiths' offer. What is Liberty's liability? Under what theory?

3. Dannie Harvey sued her employer, O. R. Whitaker, for sexual harassment, discrimination, and defamation. Whitaker counterclaimed for libel and slander, requesting $1 million in punitive damages. Both Whitaker and Harvey were insured by Allstate, under identical homeowner's policies. This policy explicitly promised to defend Harvey against the exact claim Whitaker had made against her. Harvey's Allstate agent, however, told her that she was not covered. Because the agent kept all copies of Harvey's insurance policies in his office, she took him at his word. She had no choice but to defend against the claim on her own. Whitaker mounted an exceedingly hostile litigation attack, taking 80 depositions. After a year, Allstate agreed to defend Harvey. However, instead of hiring the lawyer who had been representing her, it chose another lawyer who had no expertise in this type of case and was a close friend of Whitaker's attorney. Harvey's new lawyer refused to meet her or to attend any depositions. Harvey and Whitaker finally settled. Whitaker had spent $1 million in legal fees, Harvey $169,000, and Allstate $2,513. Does Harvey have a claim against Allstate?

4. Clyde received a letter from his automobile insurance company notifying him that it would not renew his policy that was set to expire on February 28. Clyde did not obtain another policy, and in a burst of astonishing bad luck, at 2:30 a.m.on March 1, he struck another vehicle, killing two men. Later that day, Clyde applied for insurance coverage. As part of this application, he indicated that he had not been involved in any accident in the last three years. The new policy was effective as of 12:01 a.m. on March 1. Will the estates of the two dead men be able to recover under this policy?

5. Jason lived in an apartment with Miri, to whom he was not married. When he applied for homeowners insurance, the form asked their marital status. He checked the box that said "married." Later, the apartment was robbed, and Jason filed a claim with his insurance company. When the company discovered that Jason and Miri were not married, it refused to pay the claim on the grounds that he had made a material misrepresentation. Jason argued that the misrepresentation was not material because the insurance company would have issued the policy no matter how he answered that question. Is Jason's policy valid?

DISCUSSION QUESTIONS

1. Suzy Tomlinson, 74, met a tragic end—she drowned, fully clothed, in her bathtub after a night out partying with 36-year-old JB Carlson. He had taken her home at 1 a.m. and was the last person to see her alive. The two were not only party buddies—Suzy was on the board of directors of a company JB had started. Her family was stunned to find out that she had a $15 million life insurance policy, with the proceeds payable to a company JB controlled. He said it was a key person policy. He wanted to protect the company if Suzy died because she had frequently introduced him to potential investors. Is the life insurance policy valid?

2. Tomlinson's family sued the insurance company, claiming that the policy was valid, but that they were the beneficiaries, not JB. Is the family entitled to the proceeds of the policy? Should they be?

3. **ETHICS** Most people who rent cars do not need to buy the extra coverage that the rental agencies offer because credit cards already provide this type of insurance. However, this coverage is very profitable for the rental companies. If you were the manager of a car rental agency, how aggressive would you be in encouraging your agents to sell these policies? Would you pay them a commission or base their salaries on the number of policies they sold? Train them to remind customers that their credit card company might provide coverage?

4. **ETHICS** After your car was injured in an accident, your insurance agency told you to get a repair estimate. Would it be ethical for you to obtain an estimate from the most expensive body shop in town, knowing that you plan to have the car fixed at a much cheaper place? What if you do not plan to have the car repaired at all—is it ethical to take money from the insurance company?

5. Jason applied for a homeowners policy through CPM Insurance Services, Inc. An employee of CPM filled out the application form using information provided by Jason's housemate, Tricia. The two-page form asked: "Does applicant or any tenant have any animals or exotic pets?" The CPM employee checked an adjacent box stating that the answer was "No." At the time, Jason owned two dogs, a Doberman and a German shepherd. Although Jason had not read this part of the form, he nonetheless signed the application attesting that he had read it and that the answers were true. When Jason was sued by someone who claimed to have been bitten by one of his dogs, CPM rescinded his policy for material misrepresentation. In his defense, Jason said that the question about pets was confusing. He thought it applied only to exotic animals, not dogs. Also, he had not filled out the form, a CPM employee had. Is Jason's policy with CPM valid?

THE CONSTITUTION OF THE UNITED STATES

Preamble

We the People of the United States, in Order to form a more perfect Union, establish Justice, insure domestic Tranquility, provide for the common defense, promote the general Welfare, and secure the Blessings of Liberty to ourselves and our Posterity, do ordain and establish this Constitution for the United States of America.

ARTICLE I

Section 1.

All legislative Powers herein granted shall be vested in a Congress of the United States, which shall consist of a Senate and House of Representatives.

Section 2.

The House of Representatives shall be composed of Members chosen every second Year by the People of the several States, and the Electors in each State shall have the Qualifications requisite for Electors of the most numerous Branch of the State Legislature.

No Person shall be a Representative who shall not have attained to the Age of twenty five Years, and been seven Years a Citizen of the United States, and who shall not, when elected, be an Inhabitant of that State in which he shall be chosen.

Representatives and direct Taxes shall be apportioned among the several States which may be included within this Union, according to their respective Numbers, which shall be determined by adding to the whole Number of free Persons, including those bound to Service for a Term of Years, and excluding Indians not taxed, three fifths of all other Persons. The actual Enumeration shall be made within three Years after the first Meeting of the Congress of the United States, and within every subsequent Term of ten Years, in such Manner as they shall by Law direct. The number of Representatives shall not exceed one for every thirty Thousand, but each State shall have at Least one Representative; and until such enumeration shall be made, the State of New Hampshire shall be entitled to chuse three, Massachusetts eight, Rhode Island and Providence Plantations one, Connecticut five, New-York six, New Jersey four, Pennsylvania eight, Delaware one, Maryland six, Virginia ten, North Carolina five, South Carolina five, and Georgia three.

When vacancies happen in the Representation from any State, the Executive Authority thereof shall issue Writs of Election to fill such vacancies.

The House of Representatives shall chuse their Speaker and other Officers; and shall have the sole Power of Impeachment.

Section 3.

The Senate of the United States shall be composed of two Senators from each State, chosen by the Legislature thereof, for six Years; and each Senator shall have one Vote.

Immediately after they shall be assembled in Consequence of the first Election, they shall be divided as equally as may be into three Classes. The Seats of the Senators of the first Class shall be vacated at the Expiration of the second Year, of the second Class at the Expiration of the fourth Year, and of the third Class at the Expiration of the sixth Year, so that one third may be chosen every second Year; and if Vacancies happen by Resignation or otherwise, during the Recess of the Legislature of any State, the Executive thereof may make temporary Appointments until the next Meeting of the Legislature, which shall then fill such Vacancies.

No Person shall be a Senator who shall not have attained to the Age of thirty Years, and been nine Years a Citizen of the United States, and who shall not, when elected, be an Inhabitant of that State for which he shall be chosen.

The Vice President of the United States shall be President of the Senate, but shall have no Vote, unless they be equally divided.

The Senate shall chuse their other Officers, and also a President pro tempore, in the Absence of the Vice President, or when he shall exercise the Office of President of the United States.

The Senate shall have the sole power to try all Impeachments. When sitting for that Purpose, they shall be on Oath or Affirmation. When the President of the United States is tried, the Chief Justice shall preside: And no Person shall be convicted without the Concurrence of two thirds of the Members present.

Judgment in Cases of Impeachment shall not extend further than to removal from Office, and disqualification to hold and enjoy any Office of honor, Trust or Profit under the United States: but the Party convicted shall nevertheless be liable and subject to Indictment, Trial, Judgment and Punishment, according to Law.

Section 4.

The Times, Places and Manner of holding Elections for Senators and Representatives, shall be prescribed in each State by the Legislature thereof: but the Congress may at any time by Law make or alter such Regulations, except as to the Places of chusing Senators.

The Congress shall assemble at least once in every Year, and such Meeting shall be on the first Monday in December, unless they shall by Law appoint a different Day.

Section 5.

Each House shall be the Judge of the Elections, Returns and Qualifications of its own Members, and a Majority of each shall constitute a Quorum to do Business; but a smaller Number may adjourn from day to day, and may be authorized to compel the Attendance of absent Members, in such Manner, and under such Penalties as each House may provide.

Each House may determine the Rules of its Proceedings, punish its Members for disorderly Behaviour, and, with the Concurrence of two thirds, expel a Member.

Each House shall keep a Journal of its Proceedings, and from time to time publish the same, excepting such Parts as may in their Judgment require Secrecy; and the Yeas and Nays of the Members of either House on any question shall, at the Desire of one fifth of those Present, be entered on the Journal.

Neither House, during the Session of Congress, shall, without the Consent of the other, adjourn for more than three days, nor to any other Place than that in which the two Houses shall be sitting.

Section 6.

The Senators and Representatives shall receive a Compensation for their Services, to be ascertained by Law, and paid out of the Treasury of the United States. They shall in all Cases, except Treason, Felony and Breach of the Peace, be privileged from Arrest during their Attendance at the Session of their respective Houses, and in going to and returning from the same; and for any Speech or Debate in either House, they shall not be questioned in any other Place.

No Senator or Representative shall, during the Time for which he was elected, be appointed to any civil Office under the Authority of the United States, which shall have been created, or the Emoluments whereof shall have been encreased during such time; and no Person holding any Office under the United States, shall be a Member of either House during his Continuance in Office.

Section 7.

All Bills for raising Revenue shall originate in the House of Representatives; but the Senate may propose or concur with Amendments as on other Bills.

Every Bill which shall have passed the House of Representatives and the Senate, shall, before it become a Law, be presented to the President of the United States; If he approve he shall sign it, but if not he shall return it, with his Objections to that House in which it shall have originated, who shall enter the Objections at large on their Journal, and proceed to reconsider it. If after such Reconsideration two thirds of that House shall agree to pass the Bill, it shall be sent, together with the Objections, to the other House, by which it shall likewise be reconsidered, and if approved by two thirds of that House, it shall become a Law. But in all such Cases the Votes of both Houses shall be determined by Yeas and Nays, and the Names of the Persons voting for and against the Bill shall be entered on the Journal of each House respectively. If any Bill shall not be returned by the President within ten Days (Sundays excepted) after it shall have been presented to him, the Same shall be a Law, in like Manner as if he had signed it, unless the Congress by their Adjournment prevent its Return, in which Case it shall not be a Law.

Every Order, Resolution, or Vote to which the Concurrence of the Senate and House of Representatives may be necessary (except on a question of Adjournment) shall be presented to the President of the United States; and before the Same shall take Effect, shall be approved by him, or being disapproved by him, shall be repassed by two thirds of the Senate and House of Representatives, according to the Rules and Limitations prescribed in the Case of a Bill.

Section 8.

The Congress shall have Power to lay and collect Taxes, Duties, Imposts and Excises, to pay the Debts and provide for the common Defence and general Welfare of the United States; but all Duties, Imposts and Excises shall be uniform throughout the United States;

To borrow Money on the credit of the United States;

To regulate Commerce with foreign Nations, and among the several States, and with the Indian Tribes;

To establish an uniform Rule of Naturalization, and uniform Laws on the subject of Bankruptcies throughout the United States;

To coin Money, regulate the Value thereof, and of foreign Coin, and fix the Standard of Weights and Measures;

To provide for the Punishment of counterfeiting the Securities and current Coin of the United States;

To establish Post Offices and post Roads;

To promote the Progress of Science and useful Arts, by securing for limited Times to Authors and Inventors the exclusive Right to their respective Writings and Discoveries;

To constitute Tribunals inferior to the supreme Court;

To define and punish Piracies and Felonies committed on the high Seas, and Offenses against the Law of Nations;

To declare War, grant Letters of Marque and Reprisal, and make Rules concerning Captures on Land and Water;

To raise and support Armies, but no Appropriation of Money to that Use shall be for a longer Term than two Years;

To provide and maintain a Navy;

To make Rules for the Government and Regulation of the land and naval Forces;

To provide for calling forth the Militia to execute the Laws of the Union, suppress Insurrections and repel Invasions;

To provide for organizing, arming, and disciplining, the Militia, and for governing such Part of them as may be employed in the Service of the United States, reserving to the States respectively, the Appointment of the Officers, and the Authority of training the Militia according to the discipline described by Congress;

To exercise exclusive Legislation in all Cases whatsoever, over such District (not exceeding ten Miles square) as may, by Cession of particular States, and the Acceptance of Congress, become the Seat of the Government of the United States, and to exercise like Authority over all Places purchased by the Consent of the Legislature of the State in which the Same shall be, for the Erection of Forts, Magazines, Arsenals, dock-Yards, and other needful Buildings;—And

To make all Laws which shall be necessary and proper for carrying into Execution the foregoing Powers, and all other Powers vested by this Constitution in the Government of the United States, or in any Department or Officer thereof.

Section 9.

The Migration or Importation of such Persons as any of the States now existing shall think proper to admit, shall not be prohibited by the Congress prior to the Year one thousand eight hundred and eight, but a Tax or Duty may be imposed on such Importation, not exceeding ten dollars for each Person.

The Privilege of the Writ of Habeas Corpus shall not be suspended, unless when in Cases of Rebellion or Invasion the public Safety may require it.

No Bill of Attainder or ex post facto Law shall be passed.

No Capitation, or other direct, Tax shall be laid, unless in Proportion to the Census or Enumeration herein before directed to be taken.

No Tax or Duty shall be laid on Articles exported from any State.

No Preference shall be given by any Regulation of Commerce or Revenue to the Ports of one State over those of another; nor shall Vessels bound to, or from, one State, be obliged to enter, clear, or pay Duties in another.

No Money shall be drawn from the Treasury, but in Consequence of Appropriations made by Laws; and a regular Statement and Account of the Receipts and Expenditures of all public Money shall be published from time to time.

No Title of Nobility shall be granted by the United States: And no Person holding any Office of Profit or Trust under them, shall, without the Consent of the Congress, accept of any present, Emolument, Office, or Title, of any kind whatever, from any King, Prince, or foreign State.

Section 10.

No State shall enter into any Treaty, Alliance, or Confederation; grant Letters of Marque and Reprisal; coin Money; emit Bills of Credit; make any Thing but gold and silver Coin a Tender in Payment of Debts; pass any Bill of Attainder, ex post facto Law, or Law impairing the Obligation of Contracts, or grant any Title of Nobility.

No State shall, without the Consent of the Congress, lay any Imposts or Duties on Imports or Exports, except what may be absolutely necessary for executing its inspection Laws: and the net Produce of all Duties and Imposts, laid by any State on Imports or Exports, shall be for the Use of the Treasury of the United States; and all such Laws shall be subject to the Revision and Controul of the Congress.

No State shall, without the Consent of Congress, lay any Duty of Tonnage, keep Troops, or Ships of War in time of Peace, enter into any Agreement or Compact with another State, or with a foreign Power, or engage in War, unless actually invaded, or in such imminent Danger as will not admit of delay.

ARTICLE II

Section 1.

The executive Power shall be vested in a President of the United States of America. He shall hold his Office during the Term of four Years, and, together with the Vice President, chosen for the same Term, be elected, as follows:

Each State shall appoint, in such Manner as the Legislature thereof may direct, a Number of Electors, equal to the whole Number of Senators and Representatives to which the State may be entitled in the Congress: but no Senator or Representative, or Person holding an Office of Trust or Profit under the United States, shall be appointed an Elector.

The Electors shall meet in their respective States, and vote by Ballot for two Persons, of whom one at least shall not be an Inhabitant of the same State with themselves. And they shall make a list of all the Persons voted for, and of the Number of Votes for each; which List they shall sign and certify, and transmit sealed to the Seat of the Government of the United States, directed to the President of the Senate. The President of the Senate shall, in the presence of the Senate and House of Representatives, open all the Certificates, and the Votes shall be counted. The Person having the greatest Number of Votes shall be the President, if such Number be a Majority of the whole Number of Electors appointed; and if there be more than one who have such Majority, and have an equal Number of Votes, then the House of Representatives shall immediately chuse by Ballot one of them for President; and if no Person have a Majority, then from the five highest on the List the said House shall in like Manner chuse the President. But in chusing the President, the Votes shall be taken by States, the Representation from each State having one Vote; A quorum for this Purpose shall consist of a Member or Members from two thirds of the States, and a Majority of all the States shall be necessary to a Choice. In every Case, after the Choice of the President, the Person having the greatest Number of Votes of the Electors shall be the Vice President. But if there should remain two or more who have equal Votes, the Senate shall chuse from them by Ballot the Vice President.

The Congress may determine the Time of Chusing the Electors, and the Day on which they shall give their Votes; which Day shall be the same throughout the United States.

No Person except a natural born Citizen, or a Citizen of the United States, at the time of the Adoption of this Constitution, shall be eligible to the Office of President; neither shall any Person be eligible to that Office who shall not have attained to the Age of thirty five Years, and been fourteen Years a Resident within the United States.

In Case of the Removal of the President from Office, or of his Death, Resignation, or Inability to discharge the Powers and Duties of the said Office, the Same shall devolve on the Vice President, and the Congress may by Law provide for the Case of Removal, Death, Resignation or Inability, both of the President and Vice President, declaring what Officer shall then act as President, and such Officer shall act accordingly, until the Disability be removed, or a President shall be elected.

The President shall, at stated Times, receive for his Services, a Compensation, which shall neither be encreased nor diminished during the Period for which he shall have been elected, and he shall not receive within that Period any other Emolument from the United States, or any of them.

Before he enter on the Execution of his Office, he shall take the following Oath or Affirmation:—"I do solemnly swear (or affirm) that I will faithfully execute the Office of President of the United States, and will to the best of my Ability, preserve, protect and defend the Constitution of the United States."

Section 2.

The President shall be Commander in Chief of the Army and Navy of the United States, and of the Militia of the several States, when called into the actual Service of the United States; he may require the Opinion, in writing, of the principal Officer in each of the executive Departments, upon any Subject relating to the Duties of their respective Offices, and he shall have Power to grant Reprieves and Pardons for Offenses against the United States, except in Cases of Impeachment.

He shall have Power, by and with the Advice and Consent of the Senate, to make Treaties, providing two thirds of the Senators present concur; and he shall nominate, and by and with the Advice and Consent of the Senate, shall appoint Ambassadors, other public Ministers and Consuls, Judges of the supreme Court, and all other Officers of the United States, whose Appointments are not herein otherwise provided for, and which shall be established by Law: but the Congress may by Law vest the Appointment of such inferior Officers, as they think proper, in the President alone, in the Courts of Law, or in the Heads of Departments.

The President shall have Power to fill up all Vacancies that may happen during the Recess of the Senate, by granting Commissions which shall expire at the End of their next Session.

Section 3.

He shall from time to time give to the Congress Information of the State of the Union, and recommend to their Consideration such Measures as he shall judge necessary and expedient; he may, on extraordinary Occasions, convene both Houses, or either of them, and in Case of Disagreement between them, with Respect to the Time of Adjournment, he may adjourn them to such Time as he shall think proper, he shall receive Ambassadors and other public Ministers; he shall take Care that the Laws be faithfully executed, and shall Commission all the Officers of the United States.

Section 4.

The President, Vice President and all civil Officers of the United States, shall be removed from Office on Impeachment for, and Conviction of, Treason, Bribery, or other high Crimes and Misdemeanors.

ARTICLE III

Section 1.

The judicial Power of the United States, shall be vested in one supreme Court, and in such inferior Courts as the Congress may from time to time ordain and establish. The Judges, both of the supreme and inferior Courts, shall hold their Offices during good Behaviour, and shall, at Times, receive for their Services, a Compensation, which shall not be diminished during their Continuance in Office.

Section 2.

The judicial Power shall extend to all Cases, in Law and Equity, arising under this Constitution, the Laws of the United States, and Treaties made, or which shall be made, under their Authority;—to all Cases affecting Ambassadors, other public Ministers and Consuls;—to all Cases of admiralty and maritime Jurisdiction;—to Controversies to which the United States shall be a Party;—to controversies between two or more States;—between a State and Citizens of another State;—between Citizens of different States;—between Citizens of the same State claiming Lands under Grants of different States; and between a State, or the Citizens thereof, and foreign States, Citizens or Subjects.

In all Cases affecting Ambassadors, other public Ministers and Consuls, and those in which a State shall be Party, the supreme Court shall have original Jurisdiction. In all the other Cases before mentioned, the supreme Court shall have appellate Jurisdiction, both as to Law and Fact, with such Exceptions, and under such Regulations as the Congress shall make.

The Trial of all Crimes, except in Cases of Impeachment, shall be by Jury; and such Trial shall be held in the State where the said Crimes shall have been committed; but when not committed within any State, the Trial shall be at such Place or Places as the Congress may by Law have directed.

Section 3.

Treason against the United States, shall consist only in levying War against them, or in adhering to their Enemies, giving them Aid and Comfort. No Person shall be convicted of Treason unless on the Testimony of two Witnesses to the same overt Act, or on Confession in open Court.

The Congress shall have Power to declare the Punishment of Treason, but no Attainder of Treason shall work Corruption of Blood, or Forfeiture except during the Life of the Person attainted.

ARTICLE IV

Section 1.

Full Faith and Credit shall be given in each State to the public Acts, Records, and judicial Proceedings of every other State. And the Congress may by general Laws prescribe the Manner in which such Acts, Records and Proceedings shall be proved, and the Effect thereof.

Section 2.

The Citizens of each State shall be entitled to all Privileges and Immunities of Citizens in the several States.

A Person charged in any State with Treason, Felony, or other Crime, who shall flee from Justice, and be found in another State, shall on Demand of the executive Authority of the State from which he fled, be delivered up, to be removed to the State having Jurisdiction of the Crime.

No Person held to Service or Labour in one State, under the Laws thereof, escaping into another, shall, in Consequence of any Law or Regulation therein, be discharged from such Service or Labour, but shall be delivered up on Claim of the Party to whom such Service or Labour may be due.

Section 3.

New States may be admitted by the Congress into this Union; but no new State shall be formed or erected within the Jurisdiction of any other State; nor any State be formed by the Junction of two or more States, or Parts of States, without the Consent of the Legislatures of the States concerned as well as the Congress.

The Congress shall have Power to dispose of and make all needful Rules and Regulations respecting the Territory or other Property belonging to the United States; and nothing in this Constitution shall be so construed as to Prejudice any Claims of the United States, or of any particular State.

Section 4.

The United States shall guarantee to every State in this Union a Republican Form of Government, and shall protect each of them against Invasion; and on Application of the Legislature, or of the Executive (when the Legislature cannot be convened) against domestic Violence.

ARTICLE V

The Congress, whenever two thirds of both Houses shall deem it necessary, shall propose Amendments to this Constitution, or, on the Application of the Legislatures of two thirds of the several States, shall call a Convention for proposing Amendments, which, in either Case, shall be valid to all Intents and Purposes, as Part of this Constitution, when ratified by the Legislatures of three fourths of the several States, or by Conventions in three fourths thereof, as the one or the other Mode of Ratification may be proposed by the Congress; Provided that no Amendment which may be made prior to the Year One thousand eight hundred and eight shall in any Manner affect the first and fourth Clauses in the Ninth Section of the first Article; and that no State, without its Consent, shall be deprived of its equal Suffrage in the Senate.

ARTICLE VI

All Debts contracted and Engagements entered into, before the Adoption of this Constitution, shall be as valid against the United States under this Constitution, as under the Confederation.

This Constitution, and the Laws of the United States which shall be made in Pursuance thereof; and all Treaties made, or which shall be made, under the Authority of the United States, shall be the supreme Law of the Land; and the Judges in every State shall be bound thereby, any Thing in the Constitution or Laws of any State to the Contrary notwithstanding.

The Senators and Representatives before mentioned, and the Members of the several State Legislatures, and all executive and judicial Officers, both of the United States and of the Several States, shall be bound by Oath or Affirmation, to support this Constitution; but no religious Test shall ever be required as a Qualification to any Office or public Trust under the United States.

ARTICLE VII

The Ratification of the Conventions of nine States, shall be sufficient for the Establishment of this Constitution between the States so ratifying the Same.

Amendment I [1791].

Congress shall make no law respecting an establishment of religion, or prohibiting the free exercise thereof; or abridging the freedom of speech, or the press; or the right of the people peaceably to assemble, and to petition the Government for a redress of grievances.

Amendment II [1791].

A well regulated Militia, being necessary to the security for a free State, the right of the people to keep and bear Arms, shall not be infringed.

Amendment III [1791].

No Soldier shall, in time of peace be quartered in any house, without the consent of the Owner, nor in time of war, but in a manner to be prescribed by law.

Amendment IV [1791].

The right of the people to be secure in their persons, houses, papers, and effects, against unreasonable searches and seizures, shall not be violated, and no Warrants shall issue, but upon probable cause, supported by Oath or Affirmation, and particularly describing the place to be searched, and the persons or things to be seized.

Amendment V [1791].

No person shall be held to answer for a capital, or otherwise infamous crime, unless on a presentment or indictment of a Grand Jury, except in cases arising in the land or naval forces, or in the Militia, when in actual service in time of War or public danger; nor shall any person be subject for the same offense to be twice put in jeopardy of life or limb; nor shall be compelled in any criminal case to be a witness against himself, nor be deprived of life, liberty, or property, without due process of law; nor shall private property be taken for public use, without just compensation.

Amendment VI [1791].

In all criminal prosecutions, the accused shall enjoy the right to a speedy and public trial, by an impartial jury of the State and district wherein the crime shall have been committed, which district shall have been previously ascertained by law, and to be informed of the nature and cause of the accusation; to be confronted with the Witnesses against him; to have compulsory process for obtaining witnesses in his favor, and to have the Assistance of counsel for his defence.

Amendment VII [1791].

In suits at common law, where the value in controversy shall exceed twenty dollars, the right of trial by jury shall be preserved, and no fact tried by a jury, shall be otherwise re-examined in any Court of the United States, than according to the rules of the common law.

Amendment VIII [1791].

Excessive bail shall not be required, no excessive fines imposed, nor cruel and unusual punishments inflicted.

Amendment IX [1791].

The enumeration in the Constitution, of certain rights, shall not be construed to deny or disparage others retained by the people.

Amendment X [1791].

The powers not delegated to the United States by the Constitution, nor prohibited by it to the States, are reserved to the States respectively, or to the people.

Amendment XI [1798].

The judicial power of the United States shall not be construed to extend to any suit in law or equity, commenced or prosecuted against one of the United States by Citizens of another State, or by Citizens or Subjects of any Foreign State.

Amendment XII [1804].

The Electors shall meet in their respective states and vote by ballot for President and Vice-President, one of whom, at least, shall not be an inhabitant of the same state with themselves; they shall name in their ballots the person voted for as President, and in distinct ballots the person voted for as Vice-President, and they shall make distinct lists of all persons voted for as President, and of all persons voted for as Vice-President, and of the number of votes for each, which lists they shall sign and certify, and transmit sealed to the seat of the government of the United States, directed to the President of the Senate;—The President of the Senate shall, in the presence of the Senate and House of Representatives, open all the certificates and the votes shall then be counted;—The person having the greatest number of votes for President, shall be the President, if such number be a majority of the whole number of Electors appointed; and if no person have such majority, then from the persons having the highest numbers not exceeding three on the list of those voted for as President, the

House of Representatives shall choose immediately, by ballot, the President. But in choosing the President, the votes shall be taken by states, the representation from each state having one vote; a quorum for this purpose shall consist of a member or members from two-thirds of the states, and a majority of all the states shall be necessary to a choice. And if the House of Representatives shall not choose a President whenever the right of choice shall devolve upon them, before the fourth day of March next following, then the Vice-President shall act as President, as in the case of the death or other constitutional disability of the President. The person having the greatest number of votes as Vice-President, shall be the Vice-President, if such number be a majority of the whole number of Electors appointed, and if no person have a majority, then from the two highest numbers on the list, the Senate shall choose the Vice-President; a quorum for the purpose shall consist of two-thirds of the whole number of Senators, and a majority of the whole number shall be necessary to a choice. But no person constitutionally ineligible to the office of President shall be eligible to that of the Vice-President of the United States.

Amendment XIII [1865].

Section 1. Neither slavery nor involuntary servitude, except as a punishment for crime whereof the party shall have been duly convicted, shall exist within the United States, or any place subject to their jurisdiction.

Section 2. Congress shall have power to enforce this article by appropriate legislation.

Amendment XIV [1868].

Section 1. All persons born or naturalized in the United States, and subject to the jurisdiction thereof, are citizens of the United States and of the State wherein they reside. No State shall make or enforce any law which shall abridge the privileges or immunities of citizens of the United States; nor shall any State deprive any person of life, liberty, or property, without due process of law; nor deny to any person within its jurisdiction the equal protection of the laws.

Section 2. Representatives shall be apportioned among the several States according to their respective numbers, counting the whole number of persons in each State, excluding Indians not taxed. But when the right to vote at any election for the choice of electors for President and Vice President of the United States, Representatives in Congress, the Executive and Judicial officers of a State, or the members of the Legislature thereof, is denied to any of the male inhabitants of such State, being twenty-one years of age, and citizens of the United States, or in any way abridged, except for participation in rebellion, or other crime, the basis of representation therein shall be reduced in the proportion which the number of such male citizens shall bear the whole number of male citizens twenty-one years of age in such State.

Section 3. No person shall be a Senator or Representative in Congress, or elector of President and Vice President, or hold any office, civil or military, under the United States, or under any State, who, having previously taken an oath, as a member of Congress, or as an officer of the United States, or as a member of any State legislature, or as an executive or judicial officer of any State, to support the Constitution of the United States, shall have engaged in insurrection or rebellion against the same, or given aid or comfort to the enemies thereof. But Congress may by a vote of two-thirds of each House, remove such disability.

Section 4. The validity of the public debt of the United States, authorized by law, including debts incurred for payment of pensions and bounties for services in suppressing insurrection or rebellion, shall not be questioned. But neither the

United States nor any State shall assume or pay any debt or obligation incurred in aid of insurrection or rebellion against the United States, or any claim for the loss or emancipation of any slave; but all such debts, obligations and claims shall be held illegal and void.

Section 5.   The Congress shall have power to enforce, by appropriate legislation, the provisions of this article.

Amendment XV [1870].

Section 1.   The right of citizens of the United States to vote shall not be denied or abridged by the United States or by any State on account of race, color, or previous condition of servitude.

Section 2.   The Congress shall have power to enforce this article by appropriate legislation.

Amendment XVI [1913].

The Congress shall have power to lay and collect taxes on incomes, from whatever source derived, without apportionment among the several States, and without regard to any census or enumeration.

Amendment XVII [1913].

The Senate of the United States shall be composed of two Senators from each State, elected by the people thereof, for six years; and each Senator shall have one vote. The electors in each State shall have the qualifications requisite for electors of the most numerous branch of the State legislatures.

When vacancies happen in the representation of any State in the Senate, the executive authority of each State shall issue writs of election to fill such vacancies; *Provided,* That the legislature of any State may empower the executive thereof to make temporary appointments until the people fill the vacancies by election as the legislature may direct.

This amendment shall not be construed as to affect the election or term of any Senator chosen before it becomes valid as part of the Constitution.

Amendment XVIII [1919].

Section 1.   After one year from the ratification of this article the manufacture, sale, or transportation of intoxicating liquors within, the importation thereof into, or the exportation thereof from the United States and all territory subject to the jurisdiction thereof for beverage purposes is hereby prohibited.

Section 2.   The Congress and the several States shall have concurrent power to enforce this article by appropriate legislation.

Section 3.   This article shall be inoperative unless it shall have been ratified as an amendment to the Constitution by the legislatures of the several States, as provided in the Constitution, within seven years from the date of the submission hereof to the States by the Congress.

Amendment XIX [1920].

The right of citizens of the United States to vote shall not be denied or abridged by the United States or by any State on account of sex.

Congress shall have power to enforce this article by appropriate legislation.

Amendment XX [1933].

Section 1. The terms of the President and Vice President shall end at noon on the 20th day of January, and the terms of Senators and Representatives at noon on the 3d day of January, of the years in which such terms would have ended if this article had not been ratified; and the terms of their successors shall then begin.

Section 2. The Congress shall assemble at least once in every year, and such meeting shall begin at noon on the 3d day of January, unless they shall by law appoint a different day.

Section 3. If, at the time fixed for the beginning of the term of the President, the President elect shall have died, the Vice President elect shall become President. If a President shall not have been chosen before the time fixed for the beginning of his term, or if the President elect shall have failed to qualify, then the Vice President elect shall act as President until a President shall have qualified; and the Congress may by law provide for the case wherein neither a President elect nor a Vice President elect shall have qualified, declaring who shall then act as President, or the manner in which one who is to act shall be selected, and such person shall act accordingly until a President or Vice President shall have qualified.

Section 4. The Congress may by law provide for the case of the death of any of the persons from whom the House of Representatives may choose a President whenever the right of choice shall have devolved upon them, and for the case of the death of any of the persons from whom the Senate may choose a Vice President whenever the right of choice shall have devolved upon them.

Section 5. Sections 1 and 2 shall take effect on the 15th day of October following the ratification of this article.

Section 6. This article shall be inoperative unless it shall have been ratified as an amendment to the Constitution by the legislatures of three-fourths of the several States within seven years from the date of its submission.

Amendment XXI [1933].

Section 1. The eighteenth article of amendment to the Constitution of the United States is hereby repealed.

Section 2. The transportation or importation into any State, Territory, or possession of the United States for delivery or use therein of intoxicating liquors, in violation of the laws thereof, is hereby prohibited.

Section 3. This article shall be inoperative unless it shall have been ratified as an amendment to the Constitution by conventions in the several States, as provided in the Constitution, within seven years from the date of the submission hereof to the States by the Congress.

Amendment XXII [1951].

Section 1. No person shall be elected to the office of the President more than twice, and no person who has held the office of President, or acted as President, for more than two years of a term to which some other person was elected President shall be elected to the office of the President more than once. But this Article shall not apply to any person holding the office of President when this Article was proposed by the Congress, and shall not prevent any person who may be holding the office of President, or acting as President, during the term within which this Article becomes operative from holding the office of President, or acting as President during the remainder of such term.

Section 2. This article shall be inoperative unless it shall have been ratified as an amendment to the Constitution by the legislatures of three-fourths of the several States within seven years from the date of its submission to the States by the Congress.

Amendment XXIII [1961].

Section 1. The District constituting the seat of Government of the United States shall appoint in such manner as the Congress may direct:

A number of electors of President and Vice President equal to the whole number of Senators and Representatives in Congress to which the District would be entitled if it were a State, but in no event more than the least populous State; they shall be in addition to those appointed by the States, but they shall be considered, for the purposes of the election of President and Vice President, to be electors appointed by a State; and they shall meet in the District and perform such duties as provided by the twelfth article of amendment.

Section 2. The Congress shall have power to enforce this article by appropriate legislation.

Amendment XXIV [1964].

Section 1. The right of citizens of the United States to vote in any primary or other election for President or Vice President, for electors for President or Vice President, or for Senator or Representative in Congress, shall not be denied or abridged by the United States or any State by reason of failure to pay any poll tax or other tax.

Section 2. The Congress shall have power to enforce this article by appropriate legislation.

Amendment XXV [1967].

Section 1. In case of the removal of the President from office or of his death or resignation, the Vice President shall become President.

Section 2. Whenever there is a vacancy in the office of the Vice President, the President shall nominate a Vice President who shall take office upon confirmation by a majority vote of both Houses of Congress.

Section 3. Whenever the President transmits to the President pro tempore of the Senate and the Speaker of the House of Representatives his written declaration that he is unable to discharge the powers and duties of his office, and until he transmits to them a written declaration to the contrary, such powers and duties shall be discharged by the Vice President as Acting President.

Section 4. Whenever the Vice President and a majority of either the principal officers of the executive departments or of such other body as Congress may by law provide, transmit to the President pro tempore of the Senate and the Speaker of the House of Representatives their written declaration that the President is unable to discharge the powers and duties of his office, the Vice President shall immediately assume the powers and duties of the office as Acting President.

Thereafter, when the President transmits to the President pro tempore of the Senate and the Speaker of the House of Representatives his written declaration that no inability exists, he shall resume the powers and duties of his office unless the Vice President and a majority of either the principal officers of the executive department or of such other body as Congress may by law provide, transmit within four days to the President pro tempore of the Senate and the Speaker of the House of Representatives their written declaration that the President is unable to discharge the powers and duties of his office. Thereupon Congress shall decide the issue, assembling within forty-eight hours for that purpose if not in session. If the Congress, within twenty-one days after receipt of the latter written declaration, or, if Congress is not in session, within twenty-one days after Congress is required to assemble, determines by two-thirds vote of both Houses that the President is unable to discharge the powers and duties of his office, the Vice President shall continue to discharge the same as Acting President; otherwise, the President shall resume the powers and duties of his office.

Amendment XXVI [1971].

Section 1. The right of citizens of the United States, who are eighteen years of age or older, to vote shall not be denied or abridged by the United States or by any State on account of age.

Section 2. The Congress shall have power to enforce this article by appropriate legislation.

Amendment XXVII [1992].

No law, varying the compensation for the services of the Senators and Representatives, shall take effect, until an election of Representatives shall have intervened.

The Uniform Commercial Code can be found at:

http://www.law.cornell.edu/ucc/ucc.table.html or http://www.law.cornell.edu

A

Abandoned property Something that the owner has knowingly discarded because she no longer wants it. (Chapter 30)

Accounts Any right to receive payment for goods sold or leased, other than rights covered by chattel paper or instruments. (Chapter 15)

Accredited investor Under the Securities Act of 1933, an accredited investor is an institution (such as a bank or insurance company) or any individual with a net worth of more than $1 million or an annual income of more than $200,000. (Chapter 23)

Acquit To find the defendant not guilty of the crime for which he was tried. (Chapter 7)

Actual malice The defendant in a defamation suit knew that his or her statement was false or acted with reckless disregard of the truth. (Chapter 5)

Actus reus The guilty act. The prosecution must show that a criminal defendant committed some proscribed act. In a murder prosecution, taking another person's life is the *actus reus*. (Chapter 7)

Additional terms Raise issues not covered in an offer. (Chapter 13)

Adjudicate To hold a formal hearing in a disputed matter and issue an official decision. (Chapter 4)

Administrative law Concerns all agencies, boards, commissions, and other entities created by a federal or state legislature and charged with investigating, regulating, and adjudicating a particular industry or issue. (Chapter 1)

Administrative law judge An agency employee who acts as an impartial decision maker. (Chapter 4)

Administrator A person appointed by the court to oversee the probate process for someone who has died intestate (that is, without a will). (Chapter 31)

Administratrix A female administrator. (Chapter 31)

Adversary system A system based on the assumption that if two sides present their best case before a neutral party, the truth will be established. (Chapter 3)

Adverse possession A means of gaining ownership of land belonging to another by entering upon the property, openly and notoriously, and claiming exclusive use of it for a period of years. (Chapter 29)

Affidavit A written statement signed under oath. (Chapter 7)

Affirm A decision by an appellate court to uphold the judgment of a lower court. (Chapters 1, 3)

Affirmative action A plan introduced in a workplace for the purpose of either remedying the effects of past discrimination or achieving equitable representation of minorities and women. (Chapter 19)

After-acquired property Items that a debtor obtains after making a security agreement with the secured party. (Chapter 15)

Agent A person who acts for a principal. (Chapter 17)

Alternative dispute resolution Any method of resolving a legal conflict other than litigation, such as negotiation, arbitration, mediation, mini-trials, and summary jury trials. (Chapter 3)

Amendment Any addition to a legal document. The constitutional amendments, the first ten of which are known collectively as the Bill of Rights, secure numerous liberties and protections directly for the people. (Chapter 1)

Annual report Each year, public companies must send their shareholders an annual report that contains detailed financial data. (Chapter 22)

Annuity A policy that makes payments to a beneficiary during his lifetime. (Chapter 32)

Answer The pleading, filed by the defendant in court and served on the plaintiff, which responds to each allegation in the plaintiff's complaint. (Chapter 3)

Apparent authority A situation in which conduct of a principal causes a third party to believe that the principal consents to have an act done on his behalf by a person purporting to act for him when, in fact, that person is not acting for the principal. (Chapter 17)

Appellant The party who appeals a lower court decision to a higher court. (Chapter 3)

Appellate court Any court in a state or federal system that reviews cases that have already been tried. (Chapter 3)

Appellee The party opposing an appeal from a lower court to a higher court. (Chapter 3)

Arbitration A form of alternative dispute resolution in which the parties hire a neutral third party to hear their respective arguments, receive evidence, and then make a binding decision. (Chapters 3, 20)

Arms Export Control Act Prohibits the export of specific weapons. (Chapter 8)

Arson Malicious use of fire or explosives to damage or destroy real estate or personal property. (Chapter 7)

Assault An intentional act that causes the plaintiff to fear an imminent battery. (Chapter 5)

Assignee The party who receives an assignment of contract rights from a party to the contract. (Chapter 11)

Assignment A tenant's transfer of all legal interest in a property to another party. (Chapter 29)

Assignment of rights A contracting party transfers his rights under a contract to someone else. (Chapters 11, 12)

Assignor The party who assigns contract rights to a third person. (Chapter 11)

Assisted suicide The process of hastening death for a terminally ill patient at the request of the patient. (Chapter 31)

Assumption of the risk The principle that a person who voluntarily enters a situation of obvious danger cannot complain if she is injured. (Chapter 6)

Attachment A court order seizing property of a party to a civil action, so that there will be sufficient assets available to pay the judgment. (Chapter 15)

Authenticate To sign a document or use any symbol or encryption method that identifies the person and clearly indicates she is adopting the record as her own. (Chapter 15)

Authorized and issued stock Stock that has been approved by the corporation's charter and subsequently sold. (Chapter 22)

Authorized and unissued stock Stock that has been approved by the corporation's charter but has not yet been sold. (Chapter 22)

Automatic stay Prohibits creditors from collecting debts that the bankrupt incurred before the petition was filed. (Chapter 16)

B

Bailee A person who rightfully possesses goods belonging to another. (Chapter 30)

Bailment Giving possession and control of personal property to another person. (Chapter 30)

Bailor One who creates a bailment by delivering goods to another. (Chapter 30)

Bait and switch A practice where sellers advertise products that are not generally available but are being used to draw interested parties in so that they will buy other items. (Chapter 25)

Bank fraud Using deceit to obtain money, assets, securities, or other property under the control of any financial institution. (Chapter 7)

Bankrupt Someone who files for protection under the bankruptcy code. Another term for *debtor*. (Chapter 16)

Bankruptcy estate The new legal entity created when a debtor files a bankruptcy petition. All the debtor's existing assets pass into the estate. (Chapter 16)

Battery The intentional touching of another person in a way that is unwanted or offensive. (Chapter 5)

Bearer paper An instrument payable "to bearer." Any holder in due course can demand payment from the issuer. (Chapter 13)

Beneficiary Someone who receives the financial proceeds of a trust. (Chapter 31)

Beyond a reasonable doubt The government's burden in a criminal prosecution; the case against the defendant must be proved to such an extent that no reasonable person would doubt it. (Chapters 3, 7)

BFOQ See *Bona fide occupational qualification (BFOQ).*

Bilateral contract A binding agreement in which each party has made a promise to the other. (Chapter 9)

Bilateral mistake Occurs when both parties negotiate based on the same factual error. (Chapter 10)

Bill A proposed statute that has been submitted for consideration to Congress or a state legislature. (Chapter 4)

Bill of lading A receipt for goods, given by a carrier such as a ship, that minutely describes the merchandise being shipped. A negotiable bill of lading may be transferred to other parties and entitles any holder to collect the goods. (Chapter 8)

Bill of Rights The first ten amendments to the Constitution. (Chapter 4)

BIOC See *Buyer in ordinary course of business (BIOC).*

Blue sky laws State securities laws. (Chapter 22)

Bona fide occupational qualification (BFOQ) A job requirement that would otherwise be discriminatory is permitted in situations in which it is *essential* to the position in question. (Chapter 19)

Breach of duty A defendant breaches his duty of due care by failing to behave the way a reasonable person would under similar circumstances. (Chapter 6)

Brief The written legal argument that an attorney files with an appeal court. (Chapter 3)

Bulk sale A transfer of most or all of a merchant's assets. (Chapter 13)

Burden of proof The allocation of which party must prove its case. In a civil case, the plaintiff has the burden of proof to persuade the fact finder of every element of her case. In a criminal case, the government has the burden of proof. (Chapter 3)

Business judgment rule A common law rule that protects managers from liability if they are acting without a conflict of interest and make informed decisions that have a rational business purpose. (Chapter 22)

Buyer in ordinary course of business (BIOC) Someone who buys goods in good faith from a seller who routinely deals in such goods. (Chapter 15)

Bylaws A document that specifies the organizational rules of a corporation or other organization, such as the date of the annual meeting and the required number of directors. (Chapter 22)

C

Capacity The legal ability to enter into a contract. (Chapter 10)

Chattel paper Any writing that indicates two things: (1) a debtor owes money; and (2) a secured party has a security interest in specific goods. The most common chattel paper is a document indicating a consumer sale on credit. (Chapter 15)

Check An instrument in which the drawer orders the drawee bank to pay money to the payee. (Chapter 14)

Choice of forum provisions Determines the state in which any litigation would take place. (Chapter 12)

Choice of law provisions Determine which state's laws will be used to interpret the contract. (Chapter 12)

Civil law The large body of law concerning the rights and duties between parties. It is distinguished from criminal law, which concerns behavior outlawed by a government. (Chapter 1)

Class action A method of litigating a civil lawsuit in which one or more plaintiffs (or occasionally defendants) seek to represent an entire group of people with similar claims against a common opponent. (Chapter 3)

Classification The process by which the Customs Service decides what label to attach to imported merchandise, and therefore what level of tariff to impose. (Chapter 8)

Close corporation A company whose stock is not publicly traded. Also known as a *closely held corporation*. (Chapter 21)

Codicil An amendment to a will. (Chapter 31)

Collateral The property subject to a security interest. (Chapter 15)

Collateral promises A promise to pay the debt of another person, as a favor to the debtor. (Chapter 15)

Collective bargaining Contract negotiations between an employer and a union. (Chapter 20)

Collective bargaining agreement A contract between a union and management. (Chapter 20)

Collective bargaining unit The precisely defined group of employees who are represented by a particular union. (Chapter 20)

Commerce Clause One of the powers granted by Article I, section 8 of the U.S. Constitution, it gives Congress exclusive power to regulate international commerce and concurrent power with the states to regulate domestic commerce. (Chapter 4)

Commercial exploitation Prohibits the unauthorized use of another person's likeness or voice for business purposes. (Chapter 5)

Commercial impracticability When, after the creation of a contract, an entirely unforeseen event occurs that makes enforcement of the contract extraordinarily unfair. (Chapter 11)

Commercial paper Instruments such as checks and promissory notes that contain a promise to pay money. Commercial paper includes both negotiable and non-negotiable instruments. (Chapter 14)

Common carrier A transportation company that makes its services available on a regular basis to the general public. (Chapter 30)

Common law Judge-made law, that is, the body of all decisions made by appellate courts over the years. (Chapters 1, 4)

Common stock Certificates that reflect ownership in a corporation. Owners of this equity security are last in line for corporate payouts such as dividends and liquidation proceeds. (Chapter 22)

Comparative negligence A rule of tort law that permits a plaintiff to recover even when the defendant can show that the plaintiff's own conduct contributed in some way to her harm. (Chapter 6)

Compensatory damages Damages that flow directly from the contract. (Chapters 5, 11)

Complaint A pleading, filed by the plaintiff, providing a short statement of the claim. (Chapter 3)

Compliance program A plan to prevent and detect criminal conduct at all levels of a company. (Chapter 7)

Concerted action Tactics, such as a strike, used by a union to gain a bargaining advantage. (Chapter 20)

Concurrent estate Two or more people owning property at the same time. (Chapter 29)

Condition An event that must occur in order for a party to be obligated under a contract. (Chapter 11)

Conditional promises Promises that a party agrees to perform only if the other side has first done what it promised. (Chapter 12)

Condition precedent A condition that must occur before a particular contract duty arises. (Chapter 11)

Condition subsequent A condition that must occur after a particular contract duty arises, or the duty will be discharged. (Chapter 11)

Confirmed irrevocable line of credit A promise made by the seller's bank to pay for goods, and then guaranteed by the buyer's bank. (Chapter 8)

Confiscation Expropriation without adequate compensation of property owned by foreigners. (Chapter 8)

Conforming goods Items that satisfy the contract terms. If a contract calls for blue sailboats, then green sailboats are non-conforming. (Chapter 13)

Consequential damages Damages resulting from the unique circumstances of *this injured party*. (Chapters 11, 13)

Consideration In contract law, something of legal value that has been bargained for and given in exchange by the parties. (Chapter 9)

Constitutional rights Protect against government acts. (Chapter 4)

Constructive eviction When a landlord substantively interferes with the tenant's use and enjoyment of his property. (Chapter 29)

Consumer credit contract A contract in which a consumer borrows money from a lender to purchase goods and services from a seller who is affiliated with the lender. (Chapter 14)

Contract A legally enforceable promise or set of promises. (Chapter 9)

Contract carrier A transportation company that does not make its services available to the general public but engages in continuing agreements with particular customers. (Chapter 30)

Contributory negligence A rule of tort law that permits a negligent defendant to escape liability if she can demonstrate that the plaintiff's own conduct contributed in any way to the plaintiff's harm. (Chapter 6)

Conversion A tort committed by taking or using someone else's personal property without his permission. (Chapter 5)

Copyright Under federal law, the holder of a copyright owns a particular expression of an idea, but not the idea itself. This ownership right applies to creative activities such as literature, music, drama, and software. (Chapter 28)

Counterclaim A claim made by the defendant against the plaintiff. (Chapter 3)

Covenant A promise in a contract. (Chapter 12)

Cover The buyer's right to obtain substitute goods when a seller has breached a contract. (Chapter 13)

Criminal law Rules that permit a government to punish certain behavior by fine or imprisonment. (Chapter 1)

Criminal procedure The process of investigating, interrogating, and trying a criminal defendant. (Chapter 7)

Cross-examination When a lawyer questions an opposing witness during a hearing. (Chapter 3)

Cure The seller's right to respond to a buyer's rejection of non-conforming goods; the seller accomplishes this by delivering conforming goods before the contract deadline. (Chapter 13)

D

Damages (1) The harm that a plaintiff complains of at trial, such as an injury to her person, or money lost because of a contract breach. (2) Money awarded by a trial court for injury suffered. (Chapter 5)

Debtor (1) A person who owes money or some other obligation to another party. (2) Someone who files for protection under the bankruptcy code. (Chapters 15, 16)

Decedent A person who has died. (Chapter 31)

Deed A document that proves ownership of property. (Chapter 29)

Defamation The act of injuring someone's reputation by stating something false about her to a third person. *Libel* is defamation done either in writing or by broadcast. *Slander* is defamation done orally. (Chapter 5)

Default The failure to perform an obligation, such as the failure to pay money when due. (Chapter 15)

Default judgment A court order awarding one party everything it requested because the opposing party failed to respond in time. (Chapter 3)

Defective products Generally lead to strict liability. (Chapter 6)

Defendant The person being sued. (Chapter 1)

Delegatee A person who receives an obligation under a contract to someone else. (Chapter 11)

Delegation of duties A contracting party transfers her duties pursuant to a contract to someone else. (Chapters 11, 12)

Delegator A person who gives his obligation under a contract to someone else. (Chapter 11)

Deponent The person being questioned in a deposition. (Chapter 3)

Deposition A form of discovery in which a party's attorney has the right to ask oral questions of the other party or of a witness. Answers are given under oath. (Chapter 3)

Devisee Someone who inherits under a will. (Chapter 31)

Different terms Contradict the terms of an offer. (Chapter 13)

Direct examination During a hearing, for a lawyer to question his own witness. (Chapter 3)

Directed verdict The decision by a court to instruct a jury that it must find in favor of a particular party because, in the judge's opinion, no reasonable person could disagree on the outcome. (Chapter 3)

Disabled person Someone with a physical or mental impairment that substantially limits a major life activity, or someone who is regarded as having such an impairment. (Chapter 19)

Disability insurance Replaces the insured's income if she becomes unable to work because of illness or injury. (Chapter 32)

Disaffirm To give notice of refusal to be bound by an agreement. (Chapter 10)

Discharge (1) A party to a contract has no more duties. (2) A party to an instrument is released from liability. (Chapter 16)

Disclaimer A statement that a particular warranty does not apply. (Chapter 13)

Discovery A stage in litigation, after all pleadings have been served, in which each party seeks as much relevant information as possible about the opposing party's case. (Chapter 3)

Dismiss To terminate a lawsuit, often on procedural grounds, without reaching the merits of the case. (Chapter 3)

Dissociation A dissociation occurs when a partner leaves a partnership. (Chapter 21)

Diversity case A lawsuit in which the plaintiff and defendant are citizens of different states *and* the amount in dispute exceeds $75,000. (Chapter 3)

Domestic corporation A corporation is considered a domestic corporation in the state in which it was formed. (Chapter 22)

Donee A person who receives a gift. (Chapter 30)

Donee beneficiary When one party to a contract intends to make a gift to a third party, that third party is referred to as a *donee beneficiary*. (Chapter 11)

Donor A person who makes a gift to another or creates a trust. (Chapters 30, 31)

Double jeopardy A criminal defendant may be prosecuted only once for a particular criminal offense. (Chapter 7)

Draft The drawer of this instrument orders someone else to pay money. Checks are the most common form of draft. The drawer of a check orders a bank to pay money. (Chapter 14)

Drawee The person who pays a draft. In the case of a check, the bank is the drawee. (Chapter 14)

Drawer The person who issues a draft. (Chapter 14)

Due diligence An investigation of the registration statement by someone who signs it. (Chapter 24)

Due Process Clause Part of the Fifth Amendment. *Procedural due process* ensures that before depriving anyone of liberty or property, the government must go through procedures that ensure that the deprivation is fair. *Substantive due process* holds that certain rights, such as privacy, are so fundamental that the government may not eliminate them. (Chapter 4)

Dumping Selling merchandise at one price in the domestic market and at a cheaper, unfair price in an international market. (Chapter 8)

Durable power of attorney An instrument that permits an attorney-in-fact to act for a principal. A durable power is effective until the principal revokes it or dies. It continues in effect even if the principal becomes incapacitated. (Chapter 31)

Duress (1) A criminal defense in which the defendant shows that she committed the wrongful act because a third person threatened her with imminent physical harm. (2) An improper threat made to force another party to enter into a contract. (Chapter 7)

Duty (1) If a defendant can foresee injury to a particular person, she has a duty to him. (Chapter 6) (2) A tax imposed on imported items. (Chapter 8)

Duty of care The requirement under the business judgment rule that a manager act with care and in the best interests of the corporation. (Chapter 22)

Duty of loyalty The obligation of a manager under the business judgment rule to act without a conflict of interest. (Chapter 22)

E

Economic loss doctrine A common law rule holding that when an injury is purely economic and arises from a contract made between two businesses, the injured party may sue only under the Uniform Commercial Code. (Chapter 13)

Element A fact that a plaintiff to a lawsuit must prove in order to prevail. (Chapter 5)

Embezzlement Fraudulent conversion of property already in the defendant's possession. (Chapter 7)

Eminent domain The power of the government to take private property for public use. (Chapter 29)

Engagement letter A written contract by which a client hires an accountant. (Chapter 24)

Equal Protection Clause Part of the Fourteenth Amendment, it generally requires the government to treat equally situated people the same. (Chapter 4)

Error of law A mistake made by a trial judge that concerns a legal issue as opposed to a factual matter. Permitting too many leading questions is a legal error; choosing to believe one witness rather than another is a factual matter. (Chapter 3)

Estate The legal entity that holds title to assets after the owner dies and before the property is distributed. (Chapter 31)

Ethics The study of how people ought to act. (Chapter 2)

European Union An association of 27 European countries joined together for the purpose of facilitating trade, free movement between nations, and setting economic and foreign policy. (Chapter 8)

Eviction When a landlord prevents a tenant from possessing the premises. (Chapter 29)

Evidence, rules of Law governing the proof offered during a trial or formal hearing. These rules limit the questions that may be asked of witnesses and the introduction of physical objects. (Chapter 3)

Exclusionary rule In a criminal trial, a ban on the use of evidence obtained in violation of the U.S. Constitution. (Chapter 7)

Exculpatory clause A contract provision that attempts to release one party from liability in the event the other party is injured. (Chapter 10)

Executed contract A binding agreement in which all parties have fulfilled all obligations. (Chapter 9)

Executive agency An administrative agency within the executive branch of government. (Chapter 4)

Executor A person chosen by the decedent to oversee the probate process. (Chapter 31)

Executory contract A binding agreement in which one or more of the parties has not fulfilled its obligations. (Chapter 9)

Executrix A female executor. (Chapter 31)

Exhaustion of remedies A principle of administrative law that no party may appeal an agency action to a court until she has utilized all available appeals within the agency itself. (Chapter 4)

Expectation interest A remedy in a contract case that puts the injured party in the position he would have been in had both sides fully performed. (Chapter 11)

Expert witness A witness in a court case who has special training or qualifications to discuss a specific issue, and who is generally permitted to state an opinion. (Chapter 3)

Export To transport goods or services out of a country. (Chapter 8)

Express authority Words or conduct of a principal that, reasonably interpreted, cause the agent to believe that the principal desires him to do a specific act. (Chapter 17)

Express contract A binding agreement in which the parties explicitly state all important terms. (Chapter 9)

Express warranty A guarantee, created by the words or actions of the seller, that goods will meet certain standards. (Chapter 13)

Externality When people do not bear the full cost of their decisions. (Chapter 26)

Extraterritoriality The power of one nation to impose its laws in other countries. (Chapter 8)

F

Fact finder The one responsible, during a trial, for deciding what occurred, that is, who did what to whom, when, how, and why. It is either the jury or, in a jury-waived case, the judge. (Chapter 4)

Factual cause The defendant's breach led to the ultimate harm. (Chapter 6)

Fair representation, duty of The union's obligation to act on behalf of all members impartially and in good faith. (Chapter 19)

Fair use doctrine Permits limited use of copyrighted material without permission from the author. (Chapter 28)

False imprisonment The intentional restraint of another person without reasonable cause and without her consent. (Chapter 5)

Federalism A double-layered system of government, with the national and state governments each exercising important but limited powers. (Chapter 1)

Federal question case A claim based on the U.S. Constitution, a federal statute, or a federal treaty. (Chapter 3)

Federal sentencing guidelines The detailed rules that judges follow when sentencing defendants in federal court. (Chapter 7)

Fee simple absolute The greatest possible ownership right in real property, including the right to possess, use, and dispose of the property in any lawful manner. (Chapter 29)

Fee simple defeasible Ownership interest in real property that may terminate upon the occurrence of some limiting event. (Chapter 29)

Felony The most serious crimes, typically those for which the defendant could be imprisoned for more than a year. (Chapter 7)

Fiduciary duty An obligation to behave in a trustworthy and confidential fashion toward the object of that duty. (Chapter 17)

Fifth Amendment The amendment to the U.S. Constitution that prohibits self-incrimination. (Chapter 7)

Financing statement A document that a secured party files to give the general public notice that the secured party has a secured interest in the collateral. (Chapter 15)

First Amendment The amendment to the U.S. Constitution that protects freedom of speech. (Chapter 4)

Fixtures Goods that are attached to real estate. (Chapter 15)

Force majeure event A disruptive, unexpected occurrence for which neither party is to blame that prevents one or both parties from complying with a contract. (Chapter 12)

Foreign corporation A corporation formed in another state. (Chapter 22)

Foreign Corrupt Practices Act A federal statute that prohibits an American businessperson from giving anything of value to a foreign official to influence an official decision. (Chapter 8)

Foreseeable type of harm Refers to injury that a reasonable person could anticipate. (Chapter 6)

Founding Fathers The authors of the U.S. Constitution, who participated in the Constitutional Convention in Philadelphia in 1787. (Chapter 1)

Fourth Amendment The amendment to the U.S. Constitution that prohibits the government from making illegal searches and seizures. (Chapter 7)

Framers See *Founding Fathers.*

Fraud Deception of another person to obtain money or property from her. (Chapters 5, 7, 10)

Freehold estate The present right to possess property and to use it in any lawful manner. (Chapter 29)

Fresh start After the termination of a bankruptcy case, creditors cannot make a claim against a debtor for money owed before the initial bankruptcy petition was filed. (Chapter 16)

Fundamental rights In constitutional law, those rights that are so basic that any governmental interference with them is suspect and likely to be unconstitutional. (Chapter 4)

G

GAAP See *Generally accepted accounting principles (GAAP).*

GAAS See *Generally accepted auditing standards (GAAS).*

Gap fillers Rules set by the Uniform Commercial Code for supplying missing terms. (Chapter 13)

GATT See *General Agreement on Tariffs and Trade (GATT).*

General Agreement on Tariffs and Trade (GATT) An international treaty designed to eliminate trade barriers and bolster international commerce, negotiated in stages between the 1940s and 1994 and signed by over 130 nations. (Chapter 8)

General intangibles Potential sources of income such as copyrights, patents, trademarks, goodwill and certain other rights to payment. (Chapter 15)

Generally accepted accounting principles (GAAP) Rules set by the Financial Accounting Standards Board to be used in preparing financial statements. (Chapter 24)

Generally accepted auditing standards (GAAS) Rules set by the American Institute of Certified Public Accountants (AICPA) to be used in conducting audits. (Chapter 24)

Gift A voluntary transfer of property from one person to another without consideration. (Chapter 30)

Gift *causa mortis* A gift made in contemplation of approaching death. (Chapter 30)

Good faith An honest effort to meet both the spirit and letter of a contract. (Chapter 12)

Goods Anything movable, except for money, securities, and certain legal rights. (Chapter 9)

Grand jury A group of ordinary citizens that decides whether there is probable cause the defendant committed the crime with which she is charged. (Chapter 7)

Grantee The person who receives property, or some interest in it, from the owner. (Chapter 29)

Grantor (1) An owner who conveys property, or some interest in it. (2) Someone who creates a trust. (Chapter 31)

Grievance A formal complaint alleging a contract violation. (Chapter 20)

Guilty A judge or jury's finding that a defendant has committed a crime. (Chapter 7)

H

Hacking Gaining unauthorized access to a computer system. (Chapter 27)

Health care proxy Someone who is authorized to make health care decisions for a person who is incompetent. (Chapter 31)

Heir Technically, someone who inherits from a decedent who died intestate (that is, without a will). However, this term is often used more broadly to indicate anyone who inherits, even under a will. (Chapter 31)

Holder For order paper, anyone in possession of the instrument if it is payable to or indorsed to her. For bearer paper, anyone in possession. (Chapter 14)

Holder in due course Someone who has given value for an instrument, in good faith, without notice of outstanding claims or other defenses. (Chapter 14)

Holding A court's decision. (Chapter 1)

Holographic will A handwritten and signed will that has not been witnessed. (Chapter 31)

I

Identify In sales law, to designate the specific goods that are the subject of a contract. (Chapter 13)

IFRS See *International financial reporting standards (IFRS).*

Illegal contract An agreement that is void because it violates a statute or public policy. (Chapter 10)

Implied authority When a principal directs an agent to undertake a transaction, the agent has the right to do acts that are incidental to it, usually accompany it, or are reasonably necessary to accomplish it. (Chapter 17)

Implied contract A binding agreement created not by explicit language but by the informal words and conduct of the parties. (Chapter 9)

Implied warranty Guarantees created by the Uniform Commercial Code and imposed on the seller of goods. (Chapter 13)

Implied warranty of fitness for a particular purpose If the seller knows that the buyer plans to use goods for a particular purpose, the seller generally is held to warrant that the goods are in fact fit for that purpose. Also known as *warranty of fitness*. (Chapter 13)

Implied warranty of habitability A landlord must meet all standards set by the local building code or otherwise ensure that the premises are fit for human habitation. (Chapter 30)

Implied warranty of merchantability Goods must be of at least average, passable quality in the trade. (Chapter 13)

Import To transport goods or services into a country. (Chapter 8)

Incidental damages The relatively minor costs, such as storage and advertising, that the injured party suffered when responding to a contract breach. (Chapter 11)

Incorporator The person who signs a corporate charter. (Chapter 22)

Independent contractor Someone who undertakes tasks for others but whose work is not closely controlled. (Chapter 17)

Indictment The government's formal charge that a defendant has committed a crime and must stand trial. (Chapter 7)

Indorsement The signature of the payee. (Chapter 14)

Infliction of emotional distress A tort. It can be the *intentional infliction of emotional distress*, meaning that the defendant behaved outrageously and deliberately caused the plaintiff severe psychological injury, or it can be the *negligent infliction of emotional distress*, meaning that the defendant's conduct violated the rules of negligence. (Chapter 5)

Initial public offering (IPO) A company's first public sale of securities. (Chapter 23)

Injunction A court order that a person either do or stop doing something. (Chapter 11)

Injury Must be genuine, not speculative. (Chapter 6)

Instructions or charge The explanation given by a judge to a jury, outlining the jury's task in deciding a lawsuit and the underlying rules of law the jury should use in reaching its decision. (Chapter 3)

Instruments Drafts, checks and notes. (Chapter 14)

Insurable interest A person has an insurable interest if she would be harmed by the danger that she has insured against. (Chapter 32)

Insured A person whose loss is the subject of an insurance policy. (Chapter 32)

Insurer The person who issues an insurance policy. (Chapter 32)

Intentional infliction of emotional distress Extreme and outrageous conduct that causes serious emotional harm. (Chapter 5)

Intentional tort An act deliberately performed that violates a legally imposed duty and injures someone. (Chapter 5)

International financial reporting standards (IFRS) A set of rules for preparing financial statements that international companies follow. The Securities and Exchange Commission is proposing that U.S. companies follow these rules as well. (Chapter 24)

Interest A legal right in something, such as ownership or a mortgage or a tenancy. (Chapter 11)

Interference with a contract See *Tortious interference with a contract*.

Interpretive rules A formal statement by an administrative agency expressing its view of what existing statutes or regulations mean. (Chapter 4)

Interrogatory A form of discovery in which one party sends to an opposing party written questions that must be answered under oath. (Chapter 3)

Inter vivos gift A gift made "during life," that is, when the donor is not under any fear of impending death. (Chapter 30)

Inter vivos trust A trust established while the grantor is still living. (Chapter 31)

Intestate To die without a will. (Chapter 31)

Intrusion Interfering in someone's life in a way that a reasonable person would find offensive. (Chapter 5)

Inventory Goods that the seller is holding for sale or lease in the ordinary course of its business. (Chapter 15)

Invitee Someone who has the right to be on property, such as a customer in a shop. (Chapter 6)

Involuntary bailment A bailment that occurs without an agreement between the bailor and bailee. (Chapter 30)

IPO See *Initial public offering (IPO)*.

Issue All direct descendants such as children and grandchildren. (Chapter 31)

Issuer (1) The maker of a promissory note or the drawer of a draft. (2) A company that issues stock. (Chapters 14, 23)

J

Joint and several liability All members of a group are liable. They can be sued as a group, or any one of them can be sued individually for the full amount owing. (Chapters 17, 21, 24)

Joint tenancy Two or more people holding equal interest in a property, with the right of survivorship. (Chapter 29)

Judicial activism The willingness shown by certain courts (and not by others) to decide issues of public policy, such as constitutional questions (free speech, equal protection, etc.) and matters of contract fairness (promissory estoppel, unconscionability, etc.). (Chapter 4)

Judicial restraint A court's preference to abstain from adjudicating major social issues and to leave such matters to legislatures. (Chapter 4)

Judicial review The power of the judicial system to examine, interpret, and even nullify actions taken by another branch of government. (Chapter 4)

Jurisdiction The power of a court to hear a particular dispute, civil or criminal, and to make a binding decision. (Chapter 3)

Jurisprudence The study of the purposes and philosophies of the law, as opposed to particular provisions of the law. (Chapter 1)

L

Labor-Management Relations Act Designed to curb union abuses. (Chapter 20)

Landlord The owner of a freehold estate who allows another person to live on his property temporarily. (Chapter 29)

Larceny Taking personal property with the intention of preventing the owner from ever using it. (Chapter 7)

Law case The decision a court has made in a civil lawsuit or criminal prosecution. (Chapter 1)

Lease A contract creating a landlord-tenant relationship. (Chapter 29)

Legal positivism The legal philosophy holding that law is what the sovereign says it is, regardless of its moral content. (Chapter 1)

Legal realism The legal philosophy holding that what really influences law is who makes and enforces it, not what is put in writing. (Chapter 1)

Legal remedy Generally, money damages. It is distinguished from equitable remedy, which includes injunctions and other non-monetary relief. (Chapter 11)

Legislative history Used by courts to interpret the meaning of a statute, this is the record of hearings, speeches, and explanations that accompanied a statute as it made its way from newly proposed bill to final law. (Chapter 4)

Legislative rules Regulations issued by an administrative agency. (Chapter 4)

Letter of credit A commercial device used to guarantee payment in international trade, usually between parties that have not previously worked together. (Chapter 8)

Liability insurance Reimburses the insured for any liability she incurs by accidentally harming someone else. (Chapter 32)

Libel See *Defamation*.

License To grant permission to another person (1) to make or sell something or (2) to enter on property. (Chapter 29)

Licensee A person who is on the property of another for her own purposes but with the owner's permission. A social guest is a typical licensee. (Chapter 6)

Lien A security interest created by rule of law, often based on labor that the secured party has expended on the collateral. (Chapter 15)

Life estate An ownership interest in real property entitling the holder to use the property during his lifetime, but which terminates upon his death. (Chapter 29)

Life insurance Provides for payments to a beneficiary upon the death of the insured. (Chapter 32)

Life tenant A person who has the use of a property during his lifetime only. (Chapter 29)

Limited liability company An organization that has the limited liability of a corporation but is not a taxable entity. (Chapter 21)

Limited liability limited partnership In a limited liability limited partnership, the general partner is not personally liable for the debts of the partnership. (Chapter 22)

Limited partnership A partnership with two types of partners: (1) limited partners, who have no personal liability for the debts of the enterprise nor any right to manage the business; and (2) general partners, who are responsible for management and personally liable for all debts. (Chapter 22)

Litigation The process of resolving disputes through formal court proceedings. (Chapter 3)

Living trust A trust established while the grantor is alive. See also inter vivos *trust*. (Chapter 31)

Living will An instrument that permits adults to refuse medical treatment. It can also appoint a health care proxy to make medical decisions for a person who has become incompetent. Also called an *advance directive*. (Chapter 31)

Lockout A management tactic, designed to gain a bargaining advantage, in which the company refuses to allow union members to work (and hence deprives them of their pay). (Chapter 20)

Lost property Something that is given up accidentally. (Chapter 30)

M

Maker The issuer of a promissory note. (Chapter 14)

Marital trust A legal entity created for the purpose of reducing a married couple's estate taxes. (Chapter 31)

Material (1) Meaning that the maker of an agreement expected the other party to rely on her words. (2) Important enough to affect the decision of an investor or a life insurance company. (Chapters 23, 32)

Material breach A violation of a contract that defeats an essential purpose of the agreement. (Chapter 12)

Mediation The process of using a neutral person to aid in the settlement of a legal dispute. A mediator's decision is non-binding. (Chapter 3)

Medicare fraud Using false statements, bribes, or kickbacks to obtain Medicare payments from the federal or state government. (Chapter 7)

Merchant Someone who routinely deals in a particular good. (Chapter 13)

Merger An acquisition of one company by another. (Chapter 23)

Minor A person under the age of 18. (Chapter 10)

Minute book Records of shareholder meetings and directors' meetings are kept in the corporation's minute book. (Chapter 22)

Mirror image rule A contract doctrine that requires acceptance to be on exactly the same terms as the offer. (Chapter 9)

Misdemeanor A less serious crime, typically one for which the maximum penalty is incarceration for less than a year, often in a jail, as opposed to a prison. (Chapter 7)

Mislaid property Something that the owner intentionally placed somewhere and then forgot about. (Chapter 30)

Misrepresentation A factually incorrect statement made during contract negotiations. (Chapter 10)

Mitigation One party acts to minimize its losses when the other party breaches a contract. (Chapter 11)

Modify An appellate court order changing a lower court ruling. (Chapter 3)

Money laundering Taking the profits of criminal acts and either (1) using the money to promote more crime or (2) attempting to conceal the money's source. (Chapter 7)

Monopolization When a company acquires or maintains a monopoly through the commission of unacceptably aggressive acts. A violation of §2 of the Sherman Act. (Chapter 23)

Mortgage A security interest in real property. (Chapter 29)

Mortgagee A creditor who obtains a security interest in real property, typically in exchange for money given to the mortgagor to buy the property. (Chapter 29)

Mortgagor A debtor who gives a mortgage (security interest) in real property to a creditor, typically in exchange for money used to buy the property. (Chapter 29)

Motion A formal request that a court take some specified step during litigation. For example, a motion to compel discovery is a request that a trial judge order the other party to respond to discovery. (Chapter 3)

Motion to suppress A request that the court exclude evidence because it was obtained in violation of the U.S. Constitution. (Chapter 7)

N

NAFTA See *North American Free Trade Agreement (NAFTA)*.

National Labor Relations Act (NLRA) A law that ensures the right of workers to form unions and encourages management and unions to bargain collectively. (Chapter 20)

National Labor Relations Board (NLRB) The administrative agency charged with overseeing labor law. (Chapter 20)

Nationalization A government's seizure of property or companies. (Chapter 8)

Natural law The theory that an unjust law is no law at all, and that a rule is legitimate only if based on an immutable morality. (Chapter 1)

Negligence *per se* Violation of a standard of care set by statute. Driving while intoxicated is illegal; thus, if a drunk driver injures a pedestrian, he has committed negligence *per se*. (Chapter 6)

Negotiable instrument A type of commercial paper that is freely transferable. (Chapter 14)

Negotiation The transfer of an instrument by someone other than the issuer. To be negotiated, order paper must be indorsed and then delivered to the transferee. For bearer paper, no indorsement is required—it must simply be delivered to the transferee. (Chapter 14)

NLRA See *National Labor Relations Act (NLRA)*.

NLRB See *National Labor Relations Board (NLRB)*.

Nominal damages A token sum, such as $1, given to an injured plaintiff who cannot prove damages. (Chapter 11)

Noncompetition agreement A contract in which one party agrees not to compete with another in a stated type of business. (Chapter 10)

Norris-LaGuardia Act Prohibits federal court injunctions in peaceful labor disputes. (Chapter 20)

North American Free Trade Agreement (NAFTA) A commercial association among Canada, the United States, and Mexico designed to eliminate almost all trade barriers. (Chapter 8)

Note An unconditional, written promise that the maker of the instrument will pay a specific amount of money on demand or at a definite time. (Chapter 14)

Novation If there is an existing contract between *A* and *B*, a novation occurs when *A* agrees to release *B* from all liability on the contract in return for *C*'s willingness to accept *B*'s liability. (Chapter 22)

Nuncupative will An oral will. (Chapter 31)

O

Obligee The party to a contract who is entitled to receive performance from the other party. (Chapter 11)

Obligor The party to a contract who is required to do something for the benefit of the other party. (Chapter 11)

Offer In contract law, an act or statement that proposes definite terms and permits the other party to create a contract by accepting those terms. (Chapter 9)

Offeree The party in contract negotiations who receives the first offer. (Chapter 9)

Offeror The party in contract negotiations who makes the first offer. (Chapter 9)

Order for relief An official acknowledgment that a debtor is under the jurisdiction of the bankruptcy court. (Chapter 16)

Order paper An instrument that includes the words "pay to the order of" or their equivalent. (Chapter 14)

Output contract An agreement that obligates the seller of goods to sell everything he produces during a stated period to a particular buyer. (Chapter 10)

Override The power of Congress or a state legislature to pass legislation despite a veto by a president or governor. A congressional override requires a two-thirds vote in each house. (Chapter 4)

P

Partnership An unincorporated association of two or more persons to carry on as co-owners of a business for profit. (Chapter 21)

Partnership at will A partnership that has no fixed duration. Any partner has the right to resign from the partnership at any time and for any reason. (Chapter 21)

Patent A grant by the government permitting the inventor the exclusive use of an invention. (Chapter 28)

Patent troll Someone who buys a portfolio of patents for the purpose of making patent infringement claims. (Chapter 28)

Payable on demand The holder of an instrument is entitled to be paid whenever she asks. (Chapter 14)

Payee Someone who is owed money under the terms of an instrument. (Chapter 14)

Per capita distribution Under a will, each heir receives the same amount. (Chapter 31)

Peremptory challenge During *voir dire*, a request by one attorney that a prospective juror be excused for an unstated reason. (Chapter 3)

Perfection A series of steps a secured party must take to protect its rights in collateral against people other than the debtor. (Chapter 15)

Periodic tenancy A lease for a fixed period, automatically renewable unless terminated. (Chapter 29)

Per se violation of an antitrust law An automatic breach. Courts will generally not consider mitigating factors. (Chapter 23)

Personal property All property other than real property. (Chapter 30)

Per stirpes distribution Under a will, each branch of a family receives an equal share. (Chapter 31)

Phishing When a fraudster sends an email directing the recipient to enter personal information on a website that is an illegal imitation of a legitimate site. (Chapter 27)

Pierce the corporate veil A court holds shareholders personally liable for the debts of the corporation. (Chapter 22)

Plaintiff The person who is suing. (Chapter 1)

Plea bargain An agreement between prosecution and defense that the defendant will plead guilty to a reduced charge in exchange for a reduced sentence. (Chapter 7)

Pleadings The documents that begin a lawsuit: the complaint, the answer, the counterclaim, and the reply. (Chapter 3)

Plurality voting To be elected, a candidate only needs to receive more votes than her opponent, not a majority of the votes cast. (Chapter 22)

PMSI See *Purchase money security interest (PMSI)*.

Point source A single producer of pollution. (Chapter 26)

Precedent An earlier case that decided the same legal issue as that presently in dispute and which therefore will control the outcome of the current case. (Chapters 1, 3)

Predatory pricing A violation of §2 of the Sherman Act, in which a company lowers its prices below cost to drive competitors out of business. (Chapter 22)

Preemption The doctrine, based on the Supremacy Clause, by which any federal statute takes priority whenever (1) a state statute conflicts or (2) there is no conflict, but Congress indicated an intention to control the issue involved. (Chapter 4)

Preferred stock Owners of preferred stock have a right to receive dividends and liquidation proceeds of the company before common shareholders. (Chapter 22)

Preference When a debtor unfairly pays creditors immediately before filing a bankruptcy petition. (Chapter 16)

Preponderance of the evidence The level of proof that a plaintiff must meet to prevail in a civil lawsuit, it means that the plaintiff must offer evidence that, in sum, is slightly more persuasive than the defendant's evidence. (Chapter 3)

Pretermitted child A child omitted from a parent's will. (Chapter 31)

Prevention of significant deterioration (PSD) program Stipulates that no one may undertake a building project that will cause a major increase in pollution without first obtaining a permit from the Environmental Protection Agency. (Chapter 26)

Prima facie "At first sight," a fact or conclusion that is presumed to be true unless someone presents evidence to disprove it. (Chapter 19)

Principal In an agency relationship, the principal is the person for whom the agent is acting. (Chapter 17)

Privity The relationship that exists between two parties who make a contract, as opposed to a third party who, though affected by the contract, is not a party to it. (Chapter 13)

Probable cause In a search and seizure case, it means that the information available indicates that it is more likely than not that a search will uncover particular criminal evidence. (Chapter 7)

Probate The process of carrying out the terms of a will. (Chapter 31)

Procedural due process See *Due Process Clause*.

Procedural law The rules establishing how the legal system itself is to operate in a particular kind of case. (Chapter 1)

Proceeds Anything that a debtor obtains from the sale or disposition of collateral. Normally, the term *proceeds* refers to cash obtained from the sale of the secured property. (Chapter 15)

Production of documents and things A form of discovery in which one party demands that the other furnish original documents or physical things, relating to the suit, for inspection and copying. (Chapter 3)

Product liability The potential responsibility that a manufacturer or seller has for injuries caused by defective goods. (Chapter 12)

Professional corporation A form of organization that permits professionals (such as doctors, lawyers, and accountants) to incorporate. Shareholders are not personally liable for the torts of other shareholders or for the contract debts of the organization. (Chapter 21)

Profit The right to enter land belonging to another and take something away, such as minerals or timber. (Chapter 29)

Promisee The person to whom a promise is made. (Chapter 11)

Promisor The person who makes the promise that a third party beneficiary benefits from. (Chapter 11)

Promissory estoppel A doctrine in which a court may enforce a promise made by the defendant even when there is no contract, if the defendant knew that the plaintiff was likely to rely on the promise, the plaintiff did in fact rely, and enforcement of it is the only way to avoid injustice. (Chapter 9)

Promissory note The maker of the instrument promises to pay a specific amount of money. (Chapter 14)

Promoter The person who organizes a corporation. (Chapter 22)

Promulgate To issue a new rule. (Chapter 4)

Proof of claim A form stating the name of an unsecured creditor and the amount of the claim against the debtor. (Chapter 16)

Property insurance Covers physical damage to real estate, personal property, or inventory from causes such as fire, smoke, lightning, wind, riot, vandalism, or theft. (Chapter 32)

Prosecution The government's attempt to convict a defendant of a crime by charging him, trying the case, and forcing him to defend himself. (Chapter 7)

Prospectus Under the Securities Act of 1933, an issuer must provide this document to anyone who purchases a security in a public transaction. The prospectus contains detailed information about the issuer and its business, a description of the stock, and audited financial statements. (Chapter 23)

Protective order A court order limiting one party's discovery. (Chapter 3)

Proximate cause Refers to a party who contributes to a loss in a way that a reasonable person could anticipate. (Chapter 6)

Proxy (1) A person whom the shareholder designates to vote in his place. (2) The written form (typically a card) that the shareholder uses to appoint a designated voter. (Chapter 22)

Proxy statement When a public company seeks proxy votes from its shareholders, it must include a proxy statement. This statement contains information about the company, such as a detailed description of management compensation. (Chapter 22)

Publicly traded corporation A company that (1) has completed a public offering under the Securities Act of 1933, (2) has securities traded on a national exchange, or (3) has 500 shareholders and $10 million in assets. (Chapter 22)

Punitive damages Money awarded at trial not to compensate the plaintiff for harm but to punish the defendant for conduct that the fact finder considers extreme and outrageous. (Chapter 5)

Purchase money security interest (PMSI) A security interest taken by the person who sells the collateral to the debtor or by a person who advances money so that the debtor may buy the collateral. (Chapter 15)

Q

Qualified privilege The principle that employers are liable only for false statements that they know to be false or that are primarily motivated by ill will. (Chapter 18)

Quantum meruit "As much as she deserves," the damages awarded in a quasi-contract case. (Chapter 9)

Quasi-contract A legal fiction in which, to avoid injustice, the court awards damages as if a contract had existed, although one did not. (Chapter 9)

Quid pro quo A Latin phrase meaning "one thing in return for another," it refers to a form of sexual harassment in which some aspect of a job is made contingent upon sexual activity. (Chapter 19)

Quiet enjoyment A tenant's right to use property without the interference of the landlord. (Chapter 29)

Quorum The number of voters that must be present for a meeting to count. (Chapter 22)

Quota A limit on the quantity of a particular good that may enter a nation. (Chapter 8)

R

Racketeer Influenced and Corrupt Organizations Act (RICO) Prohibits using two or more racketeering acts to accomplish certain specified goals connected to criminal activity. (Chapter 7)

Racketeering acts Any of a long list of specified crimes, such as embezzlement, arson, mail fraud, and wire fraud. (Chapter 7)

Reaffirm To promise to pay a debt even after it is discharged. (Chapter 16)

Real property Land, together with certain things associated with it, such as buildings, subsurface rights, air rights, plant life, and fixtures. (Chapter 29)

Reasonable Ordinary or usual under the circumstances. (Chapter 12)

Reasonable doubt The level of proof that the government must meet to convict the defendant in a criminal case. The fact finder must be persuaded to a very high degree of certainty that the defendant did what the government alleges. (Chapter 3)

Reciprocal dealing agreement An agreement under which Company *A* will purchase from Company *B* only if Company *B* also buys from Company *A*. These agreements are rule of reason violations of the Sherman Act. (Chapter 23)

Reciprocal promises Promises that are each enforceable independently. (Chapter 12)

Record Information written on paper or stored in an electronic or other medium. (Chapter 15)

Registration statement A document filed with the Securities and Exchange Commission under the Securities Act of 1933 by an issuer seeking to sell securities in a public transaction. (Chapter 23)

Reliance interest A remedy in a contract case that puts the injured party in the position he would have been in had the parties never entered into a contract. (Chapter 11)

Remand The power of an appellate court to return a case to a lower court for additional action. (Chapter 1)

Rent Compensation paid by a tenant to a landlord. (Chapter 29)

Reply A pleading filed by the plaintiff in response to a defendant's counterclaim. (Chapter 3)

Representations and warranties Statements of fact about the past or present. (Chapter 12)

Request for admission A form of discovery in which one party demands that the opposing party either admit or deny particular factual or legal allegations. (Chapter 3)

Resale price maintenance A rule of reason violation of the Sherman Act, in which a manufacturer enters into an agreement with retailers setting the minimum prices they may charge. (Chapter 23)

Rescind To cancel a contract by mutual agreement. (Chapters 10, 11)

Rescission The undoing of a contract, which puts both parties in the positions they were in when they made the agreement. (Chapter 11)

Res ipsa loquitur A doctrine of tort law holding that the facts may imply negligence when the defendant had exclusive control of the thing that caused the harm, the accident would not normally have occurred without negligence, and the plaintiff played no role in causing the injury. (Chapter 6)

Respondeat superior A rule of agency law holding that an employer is liable for a tort committed by his employee acting within the scope of employment or acting with apparent authority. (Chapter 17)

Restitution Restoring an injured party to its original position. (Chapters 7, 10)

Restitution interest A remedy in a contract case that returns to the injured party a benefit that he has conferred on the other party, which it would be unjust to leave with that person. (Chapter 11)

Reverse The power of an appellate court to overrule a lower court and grant judgment for the party that had lost in the lower court. (Chapters 1, 3)

Reverse and remand To nullify a lower court's decision and return a case to trial. (Chapter 3)

Revocable trust A trust that can be undone or changed at any time. (Chapter 31)

Revocation The act of disavowing a contract offer so that the offeree no longer has the power to accept it. (Chapter 10)

RICO See *Racketeer Influenced and Corrupt Organizations Act (RICO).*

Rulemaking The power of an administrative agency to issue regulations. (Chapter 4)

Rule of reason violation An action that breaches the antitrust laws only if it has an anticompetitive impact. (Chapter 23)

S

Sale on approval A transfer in which a buyer takes goods, intending to use them herself, but has the right to return the goods to the seller. (Chapter 13)

S corporation An organization that provides both the limited liability of a corporation and the tax status of a partnership. (Chapter 21)

Scrivener's error A typo. (Chapter 12)

Search warrant Written permission to conduct a search, given by a neutral official. (Chapter 7)

Secondary boycott Picketing, directed by a union against a company, designed to force that company to stop doing business with the union's employer. (Chapter 20)

Secondary offering Any public sale of securities by a company after the initial public offering. (Chapter 23)

Secured party A person or company that holds a security interest. (Chapter 15)

Security Any purchase in which the buyer invests money in a common enterprise and expects to earn a profit predominantly from the efforts of others. (Chapter 23)

Security agreement A contract in which the debtor gives a security interest to the secured party. (Chapter 15)

Security interest An interest in personal property or fixtures that secures the performance of some obligation. (Chapter 15)

Separation of powers The principle, established by the first three articles of the U.S. Constitution, that authority should be divided among the legislative, executive, and judicial branches. (Chapter 4)

Settlor Someone who creates a trust. Also called a *grantor* or *donor.* (Chapter 31)

Sexual harassment Unwelcome sexual advances, requests for sexual favors, and other verbal or physical conduct of a sexual nature that violates Title VII of the 1964 Civil Rights Act. (Chapter 19)

Signatory A person, company, or nation that has signed a legal document, such as a contract, agreement, or treaty. (Chapter 8)

Single recovery principle A rule of tort litigation that requires a plaintiff to claim all damages, present and future, at the time of trial, not afterwards. (Chapter 5)

SIP See *State Implementation Plan (SIP).*

Slander See *Defamation.*

Sole discretion A party to a contract has the absolute right to make a decision on that issue. (Chapter 12)

Sole proprietorship An unincorporated business owned by a single person. (Chapter 20)

Spam Unsolicited commercial or bulk e-mail. ("To spam" is to send such e-mail.) (Chapter 27)

Specific performance A contract remedy requiring the breaching party to perform the contract by conveying land or some unique asset, rather than by paying money damages. (Chapter 11)

Stakeholders Anyone who is affected by the activities of a corporation, such as employees, customers, creditors, suppliers, shareholders, and neighbors. (Chapter 22)

Stale check A check presented more than six months after its due date. (Chapter 26)

Stare decisis "Let the decision stand," a basic principle of the common law that precedent is usually binding. (Chapters 1, 4)

State Implementation Plan (SIP) Under the Clean Air Act, states must establish a plan for meeting the air quality standards set by the Environmental Protection Agency. (Chapter 26)

Statute A law passed by a legislative body, such as Congress. (Chapters 1, 4)

Statute of frauds This law provides that certain contracts are not enforceable unless in writing. (Chapter 10)

Statute of limitations A statute that determines the period within which a lawsuit must be filed. (Chapter 11)

Statutory interpretation A court's power to give meaning to new legislation by clarifying ambiguities, providing limits, and ultimately applying it to a specific fact pattern in litigation. (Chapter 4)

Straight bankruptcy Also known as "liquidation," this form of bankruptcy mandates that the bankrupt's assets be sold to pay creditors but the bankrupt has no obligation to share future earnings. (Chapter 15)

Strict liability A tort doctrine holding to a very high standard all those who engage in ultrahazardous activity (e.g., using explosives) or who manufacture certain products. (Chapter 6)

Strike The ultimate weapon of a labor union, it occurs when all or most employees of a particular plant or employer walk off the job and refuse to work. (Chapter 20)

Strike suit A lawsuit without merit that defendants sometimes settle simply to avoid the nuisance of litigation. (Chapter 20)

Subpoena An order to appear, issued by a court or government body. (Chapter 4)

Subpoena *duces tecum* An order to produce certain documents or items before a court or government body. (Chapter 4)

Subprime loan A loan that has an above-market interest rate because the borrower is high-risk. (Chapter 25)

Subsidiary A company controlled by a foreign company. (Chapter 8)

Substantial performance The promisor performs contract duties well enough to be entitled to his full contract price, minus the value of any defects. (Chapter 11)

Substantive due process See *Due Process Clause*. (Chapter 4)

Substantive law Rules that establish the rights of parties. For example, the prohibition against slander is substantive law, as opposed to procedural law. (Chapter 1)

Summary judgment The power of a trial court to terminate a lawsuit before a trial has begun, on the grounds that no essential facts are in dispute. (Chapter 3)

Superseding cause An event that interrupts the chain of causation and relieves a defendant from liability based on her own act. (Chapter 6)

Supremacy Clause From Article VI of the U.S. Constitution, it declares that federal statutes and treaties take priority over any state law if there is a conflict between the two or, even absent a conflict, if Congress manifests an intent to preempt the field. (Chapter 4)

T

Takings Clause Part of the Fifth Amendment, it ensures that when any governmental unit takes private property for public use, it must compensate the owner. (Chapter 4)

Tariff A duty imposed on imported goods by the government of the importing nation. (Chapter 8)

Tenancy at sufferance A tenancy that exists without the permission of the landlord, after the expiration of a true tenancy. (Chapter 29)

Tenancy at will A tenancy of no fixed duration, which may be terminated by either party at any time. (Chapter 29)

Tenancy by the entirety A form of joint ownership available only to married couples. If one member of the couple dies, the property goes automatically to the survivor. Creditors cannot attach the property, nor can one owner sell the property without the other's permission. (Chapter 28)

Tenancy for years A lease for a stated, fixed period. (Chapter 29)

Tenancy in common Two or more people holding equal interest in a property, but with no right of survivorship. (Chapter 29)

Tenant A person given temporary possession of a landlord's property. (Chapter 29)

Term partnership When the partners agree in advance on the duration of a partnership. (Chapter 21)

Testamentary trust A trust created by the grantor's will that goes into effect when the grantor dies. (Chapter 31)

Testator Someone who dies having executed a will. (Chapter 31)

Testatrix A female testator. (Chapter 31)

Third party beneficiary Someone who stands to benefit from a contract to which she is not a party. An *intended* beneficiary may enforce such a contract; an *incidental* beneficiary may not. (Chapter 11)

Tied product In a tying arrangement, the product that a buyer must purchase as the condition for being allowed to buy another product. (Chapter 23)

Tort A civil wrong, committed in violation of a duty that the law imposes. (Chapter 5)

Tortious interference with a contract A tort in which the defendant deliberately impedes an existing contract between the plaintiff and another. (Chapter 5)

Tracing When an auditor takes an item of original data and tracks it forward to ensure that it has been properly recorded throughout the bookkeeping process. (Chapter 24)

Trademark Any combination of words and symbols that a business uses to identify and distinguish its products or services and that federal law will protect. (Chapter 28)

Trade secret A formula, device, process, method, or compilation of information that, when used in business, gives the owner an advantage over competitors who do not know it. (Chapter 28)

Treasury stock Stock that has been bought back by its issuing corporation. (Chapter 22)

Trespass A tort committed by intentionally entering land that belongs to someone else, or remaining on the land after being asked to leave. (Chapter 6)

Trespasser A person on someone else's property without consent. (Chapter 6)

Trial court Any court in a state or federal system that holds formal hearings to determine the facts in a civil or criminal case. (Chapter 3)

Trust An entity that separates legal and beneficial ownership of assets. (Chapter 31)

Trustee Someone who manages the assets of a trust. (Chapter 31)

Tying arrangement An agreement to sell a product on the condition that the buyer also purchases a different (or tied) product. This arrangement is illegal under the Clayton Act if the seller uses significant power in the market for the tying product to shut out a substantial part of the market for the tied product. (Chapter 23)

Tying product In a tying arrangement, the product offered for sale on the condition that another product be purchased as well. (Chapter 23)

U

Ultrahazardous activity Conduct that is lawful yet unusual and much more likely to cause injury than normal commercial activity. (Chapter 6)

Unconscionable contract An agreement that a court refuses to enforce because it is fundamentally unfair as a result of unequal bargaining power by one party. (Chapter 10)

Unenforceable agreement A contract where the parties intend to form a valid bargain but a court declares that some rule of law prevents enforcing it. (Chapter 9)

Unfair labor practice An act, committed by either a union or an employer, that violates the National Labor Relations Act, such as failing to bargain in good faith. (Chapter 20)

Unilateral contract A binding agreement in which one party has made an offer that the other can accept only by action, not words. (Chapter 9)

Unilateral mistake Occurs when only one party negotiates based on a factual error. (Chapter 10)

United Nations Convention on Contracts for the International Sale of Goods A uniform, international law on trade that has been adopted by the United States and most of its principal trading partners. (Chapter 8)

U.S. Constitution The supreme law of the United States. (Chapter 1)

U.S. Trustee Oversees the administration of bankruptcy law in a region. (Chapter 16)

V

Valid contract A contract that satisfies all the law's requirements. (Chapter 9)

Valuation A process by which the Customs Service determines the fair value of goods being imported, for purposes of imposing a duty. (Chapter 8)

Value When a holder has already done something in exchange for an instrument. (Chapter 14)

Verdict The decision of the fact finder in a case. (Chapter 3)

Veto The power of the president to reject legislation passed by Congress, terminating the bill unless Congress votes by a majority to override. (Chapter 4)

Void agreement An agreement that neither party may legally enforce, usually because the purpose of the bargain was illegal or because one of the parties lacked capacity to make it. (Chapter 9)

Voidable contract An agreement that, because of some defect, may be terminated by one party, such as a minor, but not by both parties. (Chapter 9)

Voir dire The process of selecting a jury. Attorneys for the parties and the judge may inquire of prospective jurors whether they are biased or incapable of rendering a fair and impartial verdict. (Chapter 3)

Vouching When an auditor chooses a transaction listed in the company's books and checks backwards for original data to support it. (Chapter 24)

W

Warranty A guarantee that goods will meet certain standards. (Chapter 13)

Warranty of fitness for a particular purpose An assurance under the Uniform Commercial Code that the goods are fit for the special purpose for which the buyer intends them and of which the seller is aware. (Chapter 13)

Warranty of merchantability An assurance under the Uniform Commercial Code that the goods are fit for their ordinary purpose. (Chapter 13)

Whistleblower Someone who discloses illegal behavior. (Chapter 18)

Will A legal document that disposes of a testator's property after death. (Chapter 31)

Winding up The process whereby the debts of a partnership are paid and the remaining assets are distributed to the partners. (Chapter 21)

Wire fraud and mail fraud Involve the use of mail, telegram, telephone, radio, or television to obtain property by deceit. (Chapter 7)

World Trade Organization A group created by the General Agreement on Tariffs and Trade to resolve trade disputes. (Chapter 8)

Wrongful discharge The principle that an employer may not fire a worker for any reason that violates basic social rights, duties, or responsibilities. (Chapter 18)

Z

Zoning statutes State laws that permit local communities to regulate land use. (Chapter 29)